THE LANAHAN INTRODUCTION TO

# Law and Legal Reasoning

Other books on law available from LANAHAN

*The Supreme Court and Constitutional Law: Rulings on American Government and Society*
THIRD EDITION
A LANAHAN Casebook
Jack Fruchtman

*The Lanahan Readings in Civil Rights and Civil Liberties*
THIRD EDITION
*edited by* David M. O'Brien

THE LANAHAN INTRODUCTION TO

# Law and Legal Reasoning

Rick A. Swanson, J.D, Ph.D

UNIVERSITY OF LOUSIANA at Lafayette

LANAHAN PUBLISHERS, INC.

*Baltimore*

Printed in the United States of America

The text of this book was composed
in Baskerville with display type set in
Adobe Caslon Pro and Monotype Corsiva.
Composition by SHERYL ROWE
Manufacturing by GASCH PRINTING

ISBN-10 1-930398-23-9
ISBN-13 978-1-930398-23-8

LANAHAN PUBLISHERS, INC.
324 Hawthorne Road
Baltimore, MD 21210-2303
1 866 345 1949 [Toll Free]
LANAHAN@AOL.COM
WWW.LANAHANPUBLISHERS.COM

*1 2 3 4 5 6 7 8 9 0*

CONTENTS

# PREFACE

Over the years, I have had the opportunity to teach the introduction to law course at my university. Historically, the course centered primarily on the foundations of law, jurisprudence, court systems, and a detailed study of the substance of law from contracts, torts, and criminal law to family, business, and property law. But in continuing to develop my course over the semesters, I have become more and more focused on another component: legal reasoning. And the rationale for this? First, I think we all realize that many students who take our introduction to law courses and other pre-law courses often have their sights on law school. I ask myself, "am I helping to prepare them for their possible goal?" "Does my course offer any semblance of what law school or lawyering is like?" Second, in light of that, I have become very disenchanted with the available textbooks for the course. These texts are typically lengthy, very expensive, but more so, they are really encyclopedias of the categories of law and their many terms and definitions. In effect, students are asked to learn a huge laundry list of facts about specific areas of the law—but very little about what it is like to be a lawyer, to think like a lawyer, to work like a lawyer. To that end, the course at my university is now entitled "introduction to law and legal reasoning."

Concerning pre-law programs in general, the American Bar Association (ABA) offers an inconsistent message in their statement, "Preparing for Law School." The ABA's official policy is that "The ABA does not recommend any undergraduate majors or group of courses to prepare for a legal education."[1] Yet at the same time the ABA recommends the pre-law student develop certain "Core Skills, Values, Knowledge, and Experience" among them, critical reading, writing, oral communication, and "exposure to the law." The ABA justifies this list by explaining:

1. American Bar Association (ABA), "Preparing for Law School." http://www.americanbar.org/groups/legal_education/resources/pre_law.html (retrieved July 11, 2018)

> If you wish to prepare adequately for a legal education, and for a career in law . . . you should seek educational, extra-curricular, and life experiences that will assist you in developing those attributes. *The student who comes to law school lacking this foundation will face a difficult challenge*[2] (emphasis added).

In sum, the ABA provides inconsistent suggestions regarding pre-law education. On the one hand, "The ABA does not recommend any undergraduate majors or group of courses to prepare for a legal education." Yet, on the other hand, "if you begin law school having already acquired the foundation suggested in this Statement, you will have a significant advantage." Indeed, law schools increasingly want entering students to already possess some legal skills, and students lacking such skills often need to be given remedial training. It is in the spirit of this latter point that I include in this introduction to law some of the *exact same legal skills* that law schools teach, that is, abstract critical thinking skills with concrete, specific applications to law. Put differently, I would like to offer to law-school aspiring students a practice-oriented law-school approach that would teach them *actual legal skills.*

## A Tour of the Book

While introducing abstract critical thinking skills and practice-oriented materials in this textbook, I have not abandoned what we traditionally teach in our introduction to law courses. Part One, The Foundations of Law, includes four chapters: Jurisprudence, U.S. Courts, Statutes, and Interpreting the U.S. Constitution. Here, students will discover among other topics, what is law and its development, the difference between natural law and positive law, the social contract; the structure of the U.S. federal and state court systems, basic civil and appellate procedure, and judicial review; statutes, the challenges to writing them clearly and unambiguously, and case examples of statutory interpretation; and finally, what are constitutions, how are they interpreted, judicial philosophy and political ideology, and originalism and pragmatism.

In Part Two, The Substance of Law, I have chosen to offer three of the most basic and most studied areas of law: contracts, torts, and criminal law, rather than provide that laundry list of areas of law found in larger more expensive texts. Chapters on contracts, torts, and criminal law, as well as criminal procedure, offer students the depth and breadth of major areas of law most likely to be encountered in law school or simply out in the world.

2. Id.

It is in the six chapters in Part Three, The Skills of Legal Reasoning, where I turn to the critical learning skills and concrete applications so central to the study and practice of law. Chapter 9, Legal Reasoning, introduces students to the importance of syllogism, polysyllogisms, and deductive logic so basic to legal thinking. Chapter 10, Case Law Elements, takes up case law, case briefs, and exercises on writing case briefs. Chapter 11, Argument from Precedent, and later, Chapter 14, Legal Briefs, not only provide students with a firm background in precedent, but the chapters also engage students with numerous examples of and exercises in applying precedent. Similarly, Chapter 12, IRAC, and Chapter 13, Issue Spotting, bring students further into the world of lawyering with extensive examples and exercises on Issue-Rule-Application-Conclusion and issue spotting.

The practical mind of a lawyer yields somewhat to the philosopher of law in Chapter 15, Advanced Jurisprudence, the sole chapter in Part Four, Philosophy of Law. There are students whose interest in law extend beyond working at a law firm. For them, this chapter expands on Chapter 1, Jurisprudence, to delve further into positive law, natural law, legal realism, and critical legal studies. This chapter could well follow on Chapter 1, or be read here as a capstone to your course.

I should note, too, that each chapter begins with a set of *Chapter Objectives.* These objectives orient students to what is to come, and they serve as a review section for students once they have finished the chapter. Each chapter ends with a set of *Questions for Review and Discussion.* These questions focus students' attention on some of the essential material in the chapter. There is also a set of *Suggested Readings.* These readings are drawn largely from Court rulings on topics taken up throughout the chapter. Completing the end-of-chapter material is a list of *Advanced Readings* which takes students further into selected areas of the chapter. I have also prepared an *Instructor's Manual* which I hope lends some support to those organizing their course around this text.

Finally, this text is designed for the introduction to law course and other pre-law courses. I presume no prerequisites as I hope I have been able to introduce each topic clearly with examples, cases, and exercises. In the end, I hope I have been able to achieve the goal of laying out the fundamentals of law and introducing the skills, thought processes, and practical approach of the field.

## Acknowledgments

I would like to thank several individuals for their important assistance throughout this project. A great deal of appreciation goes to the following people for offering comments, criticisms, and ideas during the writing of this book: Jack Fruchtman and Jonathan Hensley, both of Towson University, Helen Knowles of SUNY-Oswego, and Genevieve Allard of Bergen County Tech High School. Much thanks likewise goes to the owner, president, and editor of LANAHAN PUBLISHERS, INC., Don Fusting, who provided extensive and extremely helpful commentary that took every chapter of the manuscript to an enhanced level.

As I altered the scope of the pre-law program in the Political Science Department at the University of Louisiana at Lafayette to focus on teaching the practical skills needed for law school and the legal profession, several UL-Lafayette administrators and faculty were strongly supportive of this endeavor, including the writing of this manuscript. Particular thanks in this regard go to prior Political Science Department Heads Pearson Cross and Ryan Teten, as well as to the current Dean of the College of Liberal Arts, Jordan Kellman. More recently, UL-Lafayette Political Science Department faculty member and pre-law advisor Kinzie Hall has, with her introduction of an already highly successful intercollegiate competitive moot court team on our campus, supported these efforts as well. Kinzie has significantly enhanced the skills-based orientation of our pre-law program in the process.

Moreover, ever since I switched the focus of my teaching in my pre-law courses from political and philosophical analysis of law to a skills-based approach to learning law, numerous pre-law students over the past decade have graciously given me endless comments on improving the practice-based lessons, exercises, activities and assignments that are now contained in this textbook. My students' feedback allowed the manuscript for this textbook to go through several iterations. Each subsequent draft was significantly expanded and improved upon thanks to their help.

Finally, I would be remiss if I did not express collective appreciation to all my family and friends who supported me throughout the process of writing and rewriting the many drafts of this manuscript as it transformed into a published textbook. The highest thanks in this regard must particularly go to my amazing wife, Anne Swanson. She not only provided all-important moral support, she also used her professional writing expertise to give me advice on earlier drafts of the manuscript. For these and countless other reasons, I could not have achieved all I have achieved without her.

Rick Swanson
Lafayette, May 2020

Part One

# THE FOUNDATIONS OF LAW

CHAPTER 1

# JURISPRUDENCE

---

*Chapter Objectives*
*After reading this chapter, you should be able to:*

- Define law and jurisprudence
- Compare and contrast natural law and positive law
- Describe and identify the difference between law and morality
- Describe arguments for and against obedience to law
- Describe social contract theory and its flaws, and identify examples of social contracts
- Describe the origins of the U.S. legal system

---

In today's world, law affects everything about our daily lives, from birth to death, and even before and after that. Law tells us how our homes must be built, and the qualifications we must have for us to engage in many occupations. Every time we drive on the road, buy or sell a product or service, or have guests in our home, law governs those activities. Getting married or having children usually results in legal commitments for many years, if not a lifetime. Even what happens to us in the womb and to our bodies after we die is governed by legal rules.

## What is Law?

Yet what is "law"? Unfortunately, there is nothing even close to a fixed, universally agreed-upon definition of "law." Many scholars and legal thinkers have tried to come up with competing definitions, however. Here are just a few. In 1832, one of the most famous legal philosophers in history, John Austin, created what became known as the "command theory" of law. In Austin's view, "a law, in the most general and comprehensive [meaning] . . . [is] a rule laid down for the guidance of an intelligent being by an intelligent being having power over him."[1] Writing in more modern times, legal thinker Lon Fuller defines law as "the enterprise of subjecting human conduct to the governance of rules,"[2] Legal philosopher John Finnis offers a more detailed definition:

> [T]he term 'law' . . . refer[s] primarily to rules made, in accordance with regulative legal rules, by a determinate and effective authority (itself identified and, standardly, constituted as an institution by legal rules) for a 'complete' community, and buttressed by sanctions in accordance with the rule-guided stipulations of adjudicative institutions, this ensemble of rules and institutions being directed to reasonably resolving any of the community's co-ordination problems (and to ratifying, tolerating, regulating, or overriding co-ordination solutions from any other institutions or sources of norms) for the common good of that community."[3]

Other 20th-century legal thinkers such as H.L.A. Hart[4] and Ronald Dworkin[5] have offered even more elaborate definitions and explanations of "law." In contrast to these elaborate philosophical definitions, the eighth edition of the most widely used legal dictionary, *Black's Law Dictionary*, defines "law" as:

> 1. The regime that orders human activities and relations through systematic application of the force of politically organized society. . . . 2. The aggregate of legislation, judicial precedents, and accepted legal principles; the body of authoritative grounds of judicial and administrative action; esp., the body of rules, standards, and principles that the courts of a particular jurisdiction apply in deciding controversies brought before them.[6]

Despite all these widely different wordings and conceptions, however, one can see that at its core "law" is essentially rules enforced by government.

In some sense, any and all "rules" might be considered law. Imagine, for example, a parent tells their child "If you don't eat your carrots, you can't have any ice cream," or "No hitting your little sister," or "Bed-

1. Austin, John. *The Province of Jurisprudence Determined.* W. E. Rumble, ed., Cambridge University Press, 1995, p. 18.
2. Fuller, Lon L. *The Morality of Law.* New Haven: Yale University Press, 1964, p. 106.
3. Finnis, John. *Natural Law and Natural Rights.* Oxford: Clarendon Press, 1980, p. 276.
4. Hart, H.L.A. *The Concept of Law, 2nd Ed.* Oxford: Oxford University Press, 1997.
5. Dworkin, Ronald. *Law's Empire.* Harvard: Harvard University Press, 1987.
6. Gardner, Bryan A. *Black's Law Dictionary, 8th ed.* West Publishing, 1999, p. 900.

time is at 9 o'clock." A parent might say to the child "These are the laws of this household." However, in ordinary use of the word "law," we typically mean a more formal policy, usually in writing, issued and enforced by the acting government of a territory.

In the United States, probably the most commonly quoted definition of "law" is worded quite differently than the more abstract definitions just considered. Supreme Court Justice Oliver Wendell Holmes argued that law is nothing more than "the prophecies of what the courts will do." In a lecture he gave in Boston that was published in the *Harvard Law Review* in 1897 titled *The Path of the Law*, Holmes explained what he meant by "law":

> A [bad] man who cares nothing for an ethical rule which is believed and practiced by his neighbors is likely nevertheless to care a good deal to avoid being made to pay money, and will want to keep out of jail if he can. . . . Take the fundamental question, What constitutes the law? You will find some text writers telling you that it is something different from what is decided by the courts of Massachusetts or England, that it is a system of reason, that it is a deduction from principles of ethics or admitted axioms or what not, which may or may not coincide with the decisions. But if we take the view of our friend the bad man we shall find that he does not care two straws for the axioms or deductions, but that he does want to know what the Massachusetts or English courts are likely to do in fact. I am much of this mind. The prophecies of what the courts will do in fact, and nothing more pretentious, are what I mean by the law.[7]

Holmes' definition has some powerful logic behind it. People guide their decisions not based on the *text* of rules, but on how people believe those rules will *actually be enforced.* Take the highway speed limit, for example. The speed limit sign might say "55 m.p.h." However, if the police and courts will ticket and fine you only if you are going 10 miles or more over the listed limit, then the actual speed limit—the *actual* law that is enforced—is 65 m.p.h, not 55 m.p.h. People will alter their behavior to conform to the 65 m.p.h. limit, and not to the otherwise posted "55 m.p.h." limit. Thus, Holmes' concept of "law" has common everyday experience to back up his definition.

The study of law itself and of theories (philosophies) of law, such as the meaning of laws or what the laws should be, is called *jurisprudence.* This term comes from the Latin "*juris prudentia*": *Juris*, meaning "law,"

7. Holmes, Oliver Wendell. "The Path of the Law," *Harvard Law Review* 10: 457, 1897.

and *prudentia*, meaning "study, knowledge, or science." In short, jurisprudence is the study of law. Broadly defined, jurisprudence includes studying what the law is, as well as the evaluation and the critique of law and legal institutions. Thus, the study of jurisprudence can and does include the fields of law, sociology, political science, and economics, as well as other academic fields. There are numerous different philosophical questions involving law. These questions include what is law; what are the actual laws; who should make the laws; what should the laws be; how should the laws be interpreted and applied, and so on. In this textbook, we will consider all these questions at least briefly, and we will look at some of these questions in depth.

## Natural Law versus Positive Law

For at least a thousand years, there has been a philosophical distinction between *natural law* and *positive law*. Positive law is human-made law. It is usually written, though expressed differently in early pre-literate cultures. The term "positive" in this context does *not* mean "good," nor is it the opposite of "negative." Instead, in the legal context, "positive law" comes from the root verb "to posit," meaning "to assert, declare, put forth, or announce." That is, positive law is simply any law declared by humans as "law."

Natural law, on the other hand, is the collection of fundamental moral laws that do not arise from human thought, but rather, human discovery. The concept of "natural" moral law is analogous to the concept of physical laws of nature like gravity. Natural law is often also called natural justice. This term goes back to ancient Rome: the word "justice" comes from the Latin "*jus*" meaning "law" or "right" (in the legal but abstract sense). The Latin term "*jus naturale*" thus translates as "law of nature," meaning the moral laws inherent in the universe. Proponents of natural law theory believe the natural law (natural justice) is discoverable by rational intelligence and reason, and by observing nature. According to *Black's Law Dictionary*, "justice" is "The fair and proper administration of laws."[8] But what is "fair" and "proper"? *Black's Law Dictionary* has numerous sub-definitions for different types of "justice." "Natural justice" is "justice as defined in a moral, as opposed to a legal, sense."[9] But what is "moral"? In other words, what is the natural law? Here too, there is no consensus.

*Black's Law Dictionary* also defines "positive justice" as "justice as it is conceived, recognized, and incompletely expressed by the civil law or

8. Gardner, Bryan A. *Black's Law Dictionary, 8th ed.* West Publishing, 1999, p. 881.
9. *Ibid.*

some other form of human law."[10] Thus, the term "justice" has two different meanings: one in the legal sense and one in the moral sense. In the moral case, justice is the natural law. By this definition, the term "natural justice" is redundant; it is like saying "wet water." Instead, all you need to say is "water" or "justice. Readers must always be carefully aware, then, of which meaning a writer is indicating when they use the term "justice." In short, the word "justice" can have both a legal meaning and a moral meaning—that is, both a positive law meaning and a natural law meaning. An extremely influential modern thinker on the concept of justice in the positive law sense is John Rawls, who argues for a highly egalitarian definition of "justice."[11]

Natural law usually, but not always, is grounded on religiously-based conceptions. That is, the natural moral laws of the universe are typically justified by reference to a god or gods that have created such moral laws. In the field of religious philosophy, this is called *divine command theory*, meaning a behavior is morally good if the deity says so. This deity could be, for example, a single god (monotheism), a group of gods (polytheism) or simply an impersonal moral force in nature if everything is god (pantheism). The concept of karma is one example of such an impersonal force that nonetheless many believe governs the moral aspects of the universe.

Regardless the particular religious source of morality, in natural law theory, positive (that is, human-made) laws derive their moral "authority" from their correspondence with an objective moral reality. This "objective" moral reality comprises the laws that exist in the universe as a result of being ordered by divine command. Under this conception of the moral foundations of positive law, any positive law that conflicts with natural law is an "unjust law," which means it is really not a law at all. This is akin to saying "counterfeit money" is *not* really money, but is merely falsely posing as money. Thomas Aquinas, for example, argued in his *Summa Theologica* that immoral law cannot be "law."[12]

For thousands of years, natural law theory—even if not stated in such express terms—has been the philosophical justification for the moral correctness of human law. The ancient Greek philosopher Aristotle, although not referring to God, believed there were objective notions of justice that humans could discover through proper reasoning about human life.[13] The ancient Catholic theologian Saint Augustine[14] and the medieval Catholic theologian Thomas Aquinas[15] both grounded their

10. *Ibid.*
11. Rawls, John. *A Theory of Justice, Revised Edition.* Belknap Press, 1999.
12. Aquinas, Thomas. *Summa Theologica.* Christian Classics, 1981.
13. Aristotle. *Nicomachean Ethics.* Joe Sachs, Translator, Focus, 2002.
14. Augustine, Saint. *The City of God.* Penguin Classics, 1961.
15. Aquinas, Thomas. *Summa Theologica.* Christian Classics, 1981.

notions of human law in natural law created by God. The English legal analyst William Blackstone, who wrote his *Commentaries on the Laws of England* in 1765, believed in religiously-grounded natural law as well. Blackstone was the pre-eminent legal scholar of his day. His *Commentaries* were the authoritative legal treatise of his time, and remained so for the next hundred years. Even modern scholars, including U.S. Supreme Court Justices, sometimes still quote Blackstone when discussing important basic legal concepts, especially in a historical context. In Blackstone's *Commentaries,* he states:

> This law of nature, being co-equal with mankind and dictated by God himself, is of course superior in obligation to any other. It is binding over all the globe, in all countries, and at all times: no human laws are of any validity, if contrary to this; and such of them as are valid derive all their force, and all their authority, mediately, or immediately, from this original[16]

More modern thinkers, especially those who opposed certain aspects of the positive law, have grounded their disobedience to the positive law on the fact that they were following a higher, natural law. These thinkers include the American writer Henry David Thoreau, who in his 1849 essay *Civil Disobedience* argued that people should go to jail rather than pay taxes which support war and slavery.[17] A century later, Mohandas Gandhi led the nation of India to independence from the British Empire in the 1930's and 1940's, and Martin Luther King, Jr. led the African-American Civil Rights Movement in the United States in the late 1950's and 1960's. Both engaged in *civil disobedience*—the peaceful (nonviolent) breaking of laws they deemed unjust, as a means of achieving political change of those laws. Both Gandhi[18] and King[19] publicly explained they were basing their behavior on the belief that natural law overrides positive law.

Other modern moral/legal/political philosophers such as Lon Fuller[20] and John Finnis[21] are also proponents of natural law theory. Although all these thinkers vary in the particulars of their beliefs, the commonality in their beliefs is that positive law is legitimate or valid

16. Blackstone, William. *Commentaries on the Laws of England.* Oxford University Press, 2016, Vol 1: 41.
17. Thoreau, Henry David. Civ*il Disobedience and Other Essays.* Dover Publications, 1993.
18. Gandhi, Mohandas. *Autobiography.* Dover Publications, 1983.
19. King, Martin Luther. *I Have a Dream, also Letter from Birmingham Jail.* Perfection Learning, 1990.
20. Fuller, Lon. *The Morality of Law.* Yale University Press, 1969.
21. Finnis, John. *Natural Law and Natural Rights.* Oxford University Press, 1971.

only if it conforms to "natural law." Just as humans cannot repeal the physical law of gravity, human law may not repeal the moral laws of the universe. Again, although this belief is typically justified by reference to religious concepts, some atheists or other thinkers have argued that there are "necessary moral truths" whether any deity exists or not. John Stuart Mill, for example, one of the leading early proponents of the theory of *utilitarianism*, argued that an action is "good" if it maximizes utility—that is, if the action brings the greatest happiness to the greatest number of people, independent of any concept of a religious reality.[22] Under this "Greatest Happiness Principle" definition of morality, there are objectively correct statements of what is "right" and "wrong" independent of any location, time, or (mistaken) human beliefs about what is right or wrong.

Another philosophical-ethical term for this concept in objective moral truths is *universalism*: the idea that there are universal moral truths that are true always, everywhere, for all people. The opposite belief to the existence of universal natural law is called *moral relativism*. This concept has variants in that morality could be relative to each individual or to each group. This later version is called *cultural relativism*. Under the concept of moral relativism, there is no objective, universal moral "truth." Each individual, or each society/culture, determines what is right or wrong for oneself or for one's culture.[23] Taken to its extreme, this means that no action, however seemingly barbaric to most people, could be called "morally wrong": not slavery, cannibalism, human sacrifice, female genital mutilation, child rape, genocide, and so on. None of these atrocities could be called "wrong" or "bad" or "evil" because the individual or culture that decides to practice them has deemed the behavior "right" or "good" in that person or culture's eyes. Die-hard cultural relativists, for example, assert that one can not judge that a practice in another culture is morally wrong. Instead, all one may say is "that's just part of the subjective values of that culture/community/nation."

As one might imagine, staunch moral relativists are rare. For example, the Taliban in Afghanistan have murdered young girls simply for going to school based on the Taliban's belief that the natural law says women should not be educated. When pressed on this issue, even most legal thinkers who reject the concept of moral universalism and who instead embrace cultural relativism will still argue that murdering young girls for going to school is "immoral." This example simply demonstrates that few people take the concept of moral relativism to its log-

22. Mill, John Stuart. *Utilitarianism*. Hackett Publishing Company, 2002.
23. Harman, Gilbert. *Explaining Value and Other Essays in Moral Philosophy*. Clarendon Press, 2000.

ically consistent conclusion. In other words, almost everyone at heart believes in some objective moral truths—that some things are objectively "right" and "wrong."

Obviously the most substantial problem with the concept of natural law is that one person's or culture's moral good is another person's or culture's moral evil. So how does one figure out what the moral truth is? Natural law theorists usually argue that if there is natural law, one should be able to discover it either through divine revelation or human reason. This is because, the argument goes, the natural law should be just like gravity. Just as one can explore, study, and understand the physical laws, so too should one be able to explore, study, and understand the natural moral laws of the universe. The problem with this notion is that humans have never been able to agree on the content of the natural law. If the natural law is religiously grounded, humans have never agreed on the nature of this religious reality. Is there a supernatural being or beings, and/or a force or forces? If so, does this supernatural entity make any rules for us to follow? If so, how can we know what those rules are? Are there any consequences for following or not following any such rules? If so, what are those consequences, and how can we be certain what those consequences are?

Whether the natural law is grounded in a religious reality or is merely part of a purely materialistic universe, human reason has not been able to agree on what is "right" or "wrong." Even in a very homogenous (relatively uniform) culture or group, moral beliefs differ. For example, we might all agree in the abstract that "murder" is wrong. But what constitutes "murder"? What about killing committed in self defense? And self defense under what conditions? What about in defense of others? Again under what conditions? What if the other people definitely could have been saved without killing? What if it is unclear whether killing would save others? What if there is only a small chance killing could save others? And then, what about capital punishment? If capital punishment is sometimes morally good, then for what crimes? And what methods of capital punishment are moral? Or what about euthanasia? Is killing someone to help them ever morally good? If so, who gets to decide, and how? What if the person is unconscious? What if they are depressed? What if they have a terminal illness? What if the person is a young child? Or what about mass killing in war? Or are only certain types of war morally good, such as wars in defense of your nation? Or only wars for particular causes, such as for preventing genocide? And is abortion murder? Or only under some circumstances but not others, such as rape, incest of young girls, or when the life of the woman is in serious danger due to major medical complications from the pregnancy? And so on.

As can be seen, there is nowhere near a consensus—and not even within any one culture—on even the most common moral belief that "one should not kill." So, if there is no demonstrable universal conception of natural law, then any enforcement of so-called "natural law" becomes seemingly arbitrary. But let's say we can all agree on a few points of natural law. Let's assume that everyone can agree that "rape and torturing babies are always wrong." We then agree to outlaw those actions in the positive law. But if those are the only two actions we can agree violate the natural law, the natural law seems not very helpful in guiding positive law. The concept of natural law thus proves to be a problematic concept in general, and one of questionable use.

## Law and Morality

Even natural law theorists themselves agree that not all human made law (positive law) corresponds to the "natural law." Thus, "law" (in the positive law sense) is not equal to "morality." Even if there is a natural law, the positive law overlaps only to a limited degree with the natural law (morality). In the Anglo-Saxon common law tradition, the criminal law expressly recognizes this concept. Acts that are defined as crimes are classified into two types of acts:

First, *malum in se* (Latin for "bad in itself"): an act that is inherently evil, whether or not positive law makes it a crime, such as murder, rape, robbery, and so on. In other words, the act violates the natural law.

Second, *malum prohibitum* (Latin for "bad because it's prohibited"): an act that is wrong only because positive law says it's wrong. A classic example of this is running through a red traffic stoplight. Presumably there is nothing in the natural law that says moving your body while held in a container under a light that is red-colored is an evil act. That notion seems absurd. Indeed, traffic lights are merely a socially agreed-upon convention for convenience sake. Instead of green meaning "go" and red meaning "stop," we could instead all agree that red means "go" and green means "stop" or orange means "go" and blue means "stop," or any other color combination. There is nothing *inherently* evil with passing one's body under a red-colored light, but merely because we have agreed to its meaning by social convention. Similarly, some countries require vehicles be driven on the left-hand side of the road, while other nations mandate that cars be driven on the right-hand side of the road. There is nothing inherently evil about driving on one side of the road versus the other.

When the positive law is viewed in this distinction, we can see that much of the positive law has little to do with "right" or "wrong," and so much of the natural law (assuming there is such a thing) is not codified in the positive law. There is only some overlap where the positive law corresponds with what we conceive the natural law might contain.

On the one hand, there are morally good things the positive law does not require. For example, we should be grateful and express appreciation when someone does us a favor. We should hold a door open for a person coming out of grocery store whose arms are full of groceries or for someone pushing a baby stroller. What about rescuing a person trapped in a burning building? It would be morally good to do this, yet we don't place such a moral or legal obligation on people because of the risk of sacrifice it might ask of us. But what about seeing a two-year-old child playing on a train track with a train coming in the distance? It would take little or no effort, and with little or no risk, simply to yell to the child to move, or to grab the child off the track. Yet under most circumstances (the laws in a handful of U.S. states excepted), the positive law does not require us to perform even this simple action. The positive law doesn't even generally require us to phone for an ambulance if we see a person lying shot in the street or severely injured in a car accident.

On the flipside of morally good things the law does not require, there are also morally bad things the law does not prohibit. This includes two-timing your boyfriend or girlfriend, teaching your children to hate others because of their race or religion, emotionally abusing your spouse, or quickly pulling into a parking space when you see another person is already waiting for it, or just being an all-around generally obnoxious jerk. That is, even though these actions are *malum in se,* they still are not made illegal.

There are also morally neutral things the law requires (e.g. registering before one can vote, responding to the census), and morally neutral things the law prohibits (driving through a red light, driving on the wrong side of the road). These laws are purely *malum prohibitum* since in many countries people by convention drive on the left side of the road, where in other countries, people by convention drive on the right side of the road. Some legal writers would also add "victimless" crimes such as drugs or prostitution to this category as well.

At the far end of the spectrum are morally bad things the law sometimes requires (or used to require), such as slavery and racial segregation. Nazi Germany required the killing of Jews, homosexuals, communists, Roma, the disabled, and other "undesirables." Some thinkers, typically on the political left (i.e. liberal), would add the death penalty to this category, whereas some thinkers on the political right (i.e. conservative) would add abortion. Other thinkers on the far left politically would add the military draft to this category on the grounds that the military supports war and murder. On the other hand, some thinkers on the far right believe the forced payment of taxes is morally outrageous on the grounds that it is the equivalent to armed robbery.

Then finally, there are some things that people have argued are morally good, but the law prohibits. For example, many have argued that prohibiting euthanasia or doctor-assisted suicide causes unnecessarily prolonged human suffering in the case of terminal, incurable illnesses. Similarly, prohibiting the medical use of marijuana causes needless suffering by preventing the reduction of pain, nausea, or other torment. Also, until the U.S. Supreme Court ruled that there is a constitutional right to same-sex marriage, many people argued that the law was prohibiting what would be a morally good thing: for two loving people to marry and create a family, especially if they already have children. Or, take a more mundane example. Out of liability fears, many public school employment policies now forbid teachers, coaches, counselors, bus drivers, and others to hug children. This prohibition applies even if the children are hurt, crying, want a hug, or try to hug the adult out of mere affection. Yet numerous child development studies have clearly established that a lack of physical affection severely injures a child's psychological growth and well-being. In short, all these examples show that "good" and "legal" are not the same thing, nor are "bad" and "illegal."

A simple yet famous example of the conflict between law and morality—between positive law and natural law—occurred in an 1889 case in the state of New York, *Riggs v. Palmer*.[24] In *Riggs*, the judges on the high court of New York divided over whether a young man who murdered his grandfather could inherit most of his grandfather's estate as his grandfather's will directed. The statutory language was clear that wills must be strictly followed unless one of the narrow exceptions applied. There was no exception for the murder of the deceased by someone who stands to inherit from the deceased's will. The majority believed that this unjust outcome could not possibly have been intended by the legislature to be a consequence of the statute regulating wills:

> It was the intention of the law-makers that the donees of a will should have the property given them. But it never could have been their intention that a donee who murdered the testator to make the will operative should have any benefit under it. If such a case had been present to their minds, and it had been supposed necessary to make some provision of law to meet it, it cannot be doubted that they would have provided for it. . . . What could be more unreasonable than to suppose that it was the legislative intention in the general laws passed for the orderly, peaceable and just devolu-

24. *Riggs v. Palmer*, 22 N.E. 188 (N.Y. 1889)

> tion of property, that they should have operation in favor of one who murdered his ancestor that he might speedily come into the possession of his estate? Such an intention is inconceivable. We need not, therefore, be much troubled by the general language contained in the laws. . . . Under such circumstances, what law, human or divine, will allow him to take the estate and enjoy the fruits of his crime?[25]

Applying common law rules of statutory interpretation allowing for judges to create exceptions to statutes, the judges in the majority denied the inheritance to the grandson. The majority basically applied natural law rather than the clear language of the positive law. The dissent, on the other hand, believed the positive law should be followed rather than natural law:

> I concede that rules of law, which annul testamentary provision made for the benefit of those who have become unworthy of them, may be based on principles of equity and of natural justice. . . . But these principles only suggest sufficient reasons for the enactment of laws to meet such cases. The words of the section of the statute are: "No will in writing, except in the cases hereinafter mentioned, nor any part thereof, shall be revoked or altered otherwise," etc. Where, therefore, none of the cases mentioned are met by the facts, and the revocation is not in the way described in the section, the will of the testator is unalterable. I think that a valid will must continue as a will always, unless revoked in the manner provided by the statutes.[26]

As can be seen, both the majority and dissent admitted that there was a direct conflict in the case between natural law and positive law. The judges simply disagreed over which type of law should supersede the other in the case.

## Legal Realism

Whether one believes one is following or applying positive law or natural law, legal thinkers throughout most of human history have applied the concept of *legal formalism.* This view says that judges use logic to apply abstract laws to concrete situations. Law, whether natural law or positive law, can be objectively determined. This means that there is a

25. *Riggs v. Palmer*, 22 N.E. 188, 189-190 (N.Y. 1889)
26. *Riggs v. Palmer*, 22 N.E. 188, 192 (N.Y. 1889)

"legally correct" answer to every possible legal question. Every legal problem has an objectively true solution: one solution is "correct" and the others are "wrong." There is such a thing as "the" law, whether it comes from innate human concepts of justice or from positive law written in the statutes. Legal formalism thus treats law like math. In math, all mathematicians will agree that 1 + 2 = 3. Likewise, under the theory of legal formalism, all neutral, objective judges will agree to the same solution. Law X + Facts Y = objectively correct legal outcome Z. This is how laws schools still teach law for the most part: students must apply the correct law to the facts, and there are "correct" legal analyses—or at least, some legal analyses and conclusions are "better" or more correct than others.

Before we can consider a new idea that challenged both legal formalism and the positive law/natural law distinction, we need to provide some background regarding competing views of human nature. Although there are numerous varying conceptions of human nature, they all generally fall along a spectrum. At one end of the spectrum is a highly optimistic view of nature, either called *idealism* or *utopianism*. This view assumes most or all people are inherently good, or at least are not dangerous, or at least have the potential to be non-dangerous if properly educated. Thus, if we all try hard enough, we can eventually live in peaceful harmony and co-existence. Both Marxism and anarchism often express this view as do many thinkers as well. For example, the 17th century German mathematician and philosopher Gottfried Leibniz, trying to harmonize the existence of evil in the world with the goodness of God, argued that the Earth is "the best of all possible worlds."[27] (But see the French philosopher Voltaire's satire of Leibniz's optimism, in the character of Dr. Pangloss in Voltaire's 1759 work *Candide.*[28])

One famous expression of idealism comes from the *Diary of Anne Frank* (1944). Despite hiding with her family in an attic to avoid being murdered by the Nazis because they were Jewish, she wrote:

> It's difficult in times like these: ideals, dreams and cherished hopes rise within us, only to be crushed by grim reality. It's a wonder I haven't abandoned all my ideals, they seem so absurd and impractical. Yet I cling to them because I still believe, in spite of everything, that people are truly good at heart. I simply can't build my hopes on a foundation of confusion, misery, and death. I hear the approaching thunder that, one day, will destroy us too, I feel

27. Leibniz, Gottfried. *Theodicy: Essays on the Goodness of God, the Freedom of Man, and the Origin of Evil.* Open Court, 1998.
28. Voltaire. *Candide.* Dover Publications, 1991.

> the suffering of millions. And yet, when I look up at the sky, I somehow feel that this cruelty too shall end, and that peace & tranquility will return once again.[29]

In contrast to idealism is the concept of *political realism.* This is a political and/or ethical belief that humans are *not* inherently good; they instead generally act in their own self-interest. People are selfish, greedy, jealous, power-hungry, untrustworthy, violent, and generally dangerous. This means what society deems as "right" will simply be whatever the dominant majority says is right. In other words, might *is* right—that is, "might makes right." Most ideologies that favor the existence of government have adopted the view of realism to some degree. Political realists believe government is needed to impose order because people are largely irrational, driven by petty instincts and emotions, easily manipulated, and so on. This is typically called a "realistic" view of human nature. Not only will individuals do only what they think is best for themselves, nations will act in their own self-interest, and go to war if needed to further that self-interest.

The concept of realism goes at least as far back as the ancient Greek historian and thinker Thucydides in his *Peloponnesian War.*[30] In that work, Thucydides portrays the Athenians as repeatedly making selfish and foolishly short-sighted decisions. The Athenians believe these choices will bring Athens greater glory, yet they end up bringing nothing but utter ruin to Athens. Later prominent political philosophers such as Niccolo Machiavelli,[31] Thomas Hobbes,[32] and to a somewhat lesser extent, John Locke[33] were all political realists. So too were most of the Founding Fathers of the United States. James Madison, for example, wrote in *Federalist Paper #51*: "What is government itself, but the greatest of all reflections on human nature? If men were angels, no government would be necessary."[34] A famous literary portrayal of political realism is the novel *Lord of the Flies* by William Golding[35] (see also the film adaptations of his novel). In *Lord of the Flies*, a group of schoolboys become stranded on a deserted island. They quickly become increasingly violent and warlike.

Beginning in the 1920's, some legal thinkers began to apply the concept of realism to the law. Thus modern *legal realism* was born. One example is the legal scholar H.L.A. Hart, who described what he called

29. Frank, Anne. *Diary of a Young Girl.* Bantam, 1993, entry dated July 15, 1944.
30. Thucydides. *History of the Peloponnesian War.* Penguin Classics, 1972.
31. Machiavelli, Niccolo. *The Prince.* Dover Publications, 1992.
32. Hobbes, Thomas. *Leviathan.* Penguin Classics, 1982.
33. Locke, John. *Second Treatise on Government.* Dover Publications, 2002.
34. Hamilton, Alexander, et al. *The Federalist Papers.* Dover Publications, 2014.
35. Golding, William. *Lord of the Flies.* Penguin Books, 2003.

the *command theory* of the law: law is simply the commands of whoever has political power.[36] Basically, legal realism argues that legal formalism ignores or denies reality. Realistically, there is no such thing as objectively determinable "law," whether it be natural law *or* positive law. There are no "correct" legal answers to legal questions. Because judges have the power to interpret laws, "law" is simply whatever judges say it is. Put differently, law is simply the application of politics—that is, *power*—by judges to decide legal disputes in whichever way the judges want those disputes decided.

Recall the most commonly quoted definition of law in the United States, created by Justice Oliver Wendell Holmes: "The prophecies of what the courts will do in fact." (i.e., a prediction how courts will decide cases). Holmes was a leading legal realist. According to Holmes, in his work *The Path of the Law,*[37] judges' rulings do not reflect any objectively determinable truths about law because there are no such truths. Judges' written opinions instead merely reflect the judges' own personal desires, which the judge is free to impose given the power the judge has as a judge. Judges *first* decide how they want the case to be decided. Then the judges *claim* to be applying law and facts, but are merely using that reasoning to justify their pre-determined political outcome. In short, judging equals sheer naked power politics.

For instance, under the view of legal realism, if I tell you my words are law because the police will throw you in jail if you disobey me, that's the essence of law. It's like the joke about the accountant for an organized crime syndicate. One of the syndicate bosses asks the accountant "What's two plus two?" The accountant replies, "What do you want it to be?" and then "cooks the books" to make the answer come out as the boss wants. Legal realists argue it is the same with judges. When deciding a case, judges first ask themselves "what do I want the law to be?" Their answer is often based on their political ideology. Then the judges "cook the books" in their written opinions, claiming the law and facts have clearly determined the outcome. In this way, judges are free to use positive law, natural law, or any combination—whatever works to achieve the judge's desired goal.

There is also a hybrid view between legal formalism and legal realism. Many legal thinkers believe the law allows for flexibility in interpretation, but nonetheless provides limits on the possible interpretations. For example, a pet bird can move within its cage, but is still limited by the cage. Similarly, the law is a box within which judges can move, but only so far. Thus, there are some limits to how judges may feasibly rule, but within those limits judges have a certain degree of leeway. The dis-

36. Hart, H.L.A. *The Concept of Law,* 2nd Ed. Oxford: Oxford University Press, 1997
37. Holmes, Oliver Wendell. *The Path of the Law.* Martino Fine Books, 2012

agreement between legal formalists and legal realists is simply how small or big those limits are. Legal formalists believe the box is very small, whereas legal realists believe the box is very large—or perhaps even nonexistent at times. A moderate in-between view says the box is medium-sized.

Regardless of the degree of constraint judges have in their ability to rule, recall one of the main problems with positivism: how can one philosophically justify a *moral* obligation to obey the positive law? This problem dissolves under legal realism. It is not that there is an explanation for why there is moral obligation to obey law, but rather the question itself disappears. If law is simply whatever those in power want it to be, then it is neither natural law nor positive law: it is simply power. That is, might makes right. There is no question of any moral duty to obey the law; you simply must obey the law because the government has a gun to your head. That's naked politics, and that's all law is. This is not to say *literally* that might makes right, but simply an acknowledgement of the reality that whoever can exert the most power makes the law. Whether we like it or not, that is just the way the world is. As a practical matter, then, we must obey the law for our own self-interest: to avoid fines, imprisonment, or perhaps even death.

Most lawyers today are still trained in law school to be legal formalists. Almost all political scientists and other social scientists, however, are trained to be legal realists. Thus, the legal education one receives in law school is very different from the law-related education one receives in an undergraduate or graduate program in the social sciences. For example, even an outspoken legal realist judge like Holmes would not admit that *his* decisions were arbitrary. Ironically, Holmes still claimed to be neutrally following objective law rather than imposing his own views. One scholar provides this interesting story about Justice Holmes:

> After having lunch with Judge Learned Hand, Holmes entered his carriage to be driven away. As he left, Judge Hand's parting salute was: "Do justice, sir, do justice." Holmes ordered the carriage stopped. "That is not my job," Holmes said to Judge Hand. "It is my job to apply the law."[38]

Regardless of Holmes' consistency or inconsistency in his statements, all of the disagreements and debates in the previous sections of this chapter over positive law, natural law, and how to reconcile the two are no problem for legal realism. Legislatures, judges, and juries simply do what they want, and then justify those decisions by reference to ei-

38. Sowell, Thomas. *The Quest for Cosmic Justice.* The Free Press, 1999, p. 169.

ther the positive law or natural law depending on what works best at the moment. Law and legal rulings simply reflect those desires. As far as obedience to law goes, we should obey law simply out of the practical necessity to avoid punishment by legal decision-makers. There is no necessarily moral ground for obedience to law. If might makes right, then we obey because of the "might" enforcing the law, not because the law is "right." It is merely in our best practical interest to "do what we're told to do."[39]

In the late 1960's and early 1970's, a new variant of legal realism was created which came to be known as *critical legal studies*, or CLS for short. These thinkers are legal realists, but they go further. They argue that not only is the use of law politically *arbitrary*, but it is almost always, or perhaps always, arbitrary *in the same direction*. That is, the law is biased in favor of the *powerful* against the *powerless*. In other words, the law does not *randomly* favor those who happen to have political power at any one given moment. Instead, there is a consistent, systematic pattern of bias. Law is whatever the most powerful cultural group in society makes it. Since that group tends to be stable over time, the law is consistently an instrument of social, economic, and political domination. The law merely reflects the political ideology of the ruling class and protects their interests. The wealthy and the powerful use the law to maintain their privileged place in the social hierarchy. In short, law and legal institutions are abused as tools of oppression over the weak in society. As such, in the United States this means the law favors employers over employees, creditors over debtors, businesses over consumers, government over citizens, landlords over tenants, educators over students, insurance companies over the injured, whites over racial minorities, men over women, Christians over religious minorities, and so on. The goal, then, should be to make law, legal institutions and society as a whole more egalitarian.[40]

Although CLS formally began in the 1970's, its roots go back much farther, not just to the legal realists of the 1920's, but to the 19th century thinker Karl Marx.[41] CLS today has strong Marxist or neo-Marxist leanings. A number of social scientists believe that as an empirical matter, law is generally used by the powerful against the weak, and that this inequity should be corrected, but not all would necessarily adopt Marxist solutions. CLS also includes many sub-theories focused on how the law oppresses various particular sub-groups within the larger population. The two largest, most influential and most discussed CLS theories are

39. For an excellent representation of the tension between positive law, natural law, and legal realism in an imaginary court opinion, see Fuller, Lon. "The Case of the Speluncean Explorers," *Harvard Law Review* 62: 616–645 (1949).

40. Unger, Roberto. *What Should Legal Analysis Become?* Verso, 1996.

41. Karl Marx, *Das Kapital*, Createspace Independent Publishing Platform, 2012.

*feminist legal theory*,[42] which examines the role of sexuality, gender, and the law, and *critical race theory*,[43] which examines the role of race in the law. Other CLS theorists examine the concept of *intersectionality*, or how different types of discrimination and oppression interact to uniquely impact people who have overlapping sub-group membership, such as Asian women or gay Black men.[44] There are many other sub-theories within the many variants of CLS, some even contradictory to one another. All variants of CLS, however, share a common claim that law is generally made by the powerful against the powerless. For example, the argument has been made that no wealthy people could exist without other people necessarily being poor. That is, wealthy individuals could not be wealthy without poor people who are willing to do the work commanded by the money (and hence power) of the wealthy (see John Ruskin's essay *Unto this Last.*)[45] We will look more closely at CLS in a later chapter on advanced jurisprudence.

## Why Obey Law?

The previous discussions should make clear that whether one is a proponent of natural law or positive law, almost no thinkers believe the positive law and natural law perfectly correspond. Indeed, as we just saw, many thinkers are highly critical when the positive law does not follow their own particular conceptions of natural law. The fact that law is not the same as morality, however, raises a serious philosophical issue. If the law is not "morally good" then why obey it? It is easy to say we should obey the law if the law is a moral commandment from the gods, but if the gods are taken out of the picture, then an alternative moral justification must be offered.

There is an enormous philosophical problem with the argument that we should obey law simply because it is law. If law (that is, the positive law) does not correspond to morality (that is, the natural law) then why should we obey it? What moral obligation do we have to obey a law if the action prohibited is not *malum in se*, but merely *malum prohibitum*? Legal positivists need to argue why, and they began to do so in the 1600's. They said human-made law is self-legitimizing if it is created within the legal system. This argument says that something inherent in

42. MacKinnon, Catherine. *Toward a Feminist Theory of the State*. Harvard University Press, 1991.

43. Bell, Derrick. *Faces at the Bottom of the Well: The Permanency of Racism*. Basic Books, 1993.

44. Crenshaw, Kimberle. *On Intersectionality: Essential Writings*. The New Press, forthcoming 2022.

45. Ruskin, John. *Unto this Last and Other Writings*. Penguin Classics, 1986.

the law itself—either the source, origin, or procedure of the law itself—properly commands obedience from us. Whatever law is "posited" ("put forward") by the state must therefore be obeyed. It is important to understand that this goes beyond arguing that the law was made by the legitimate sovereign (ruler) with the power to threaten and use coercion. Positivists argue we have a moral duty to obey the law simply because it is law, period.

This argument simply begs the question: *why* do we have a moral duty to obey a command simply because it comes from the government? What right does the government have to tell us what to do? Why should we blindly do what we're told apart from the practical concern of keeping out of prison? Put differently, what right does any other human being or group of human beings have to tell us (adults of competent mind) what to do or not to do under threat of violent force? How is this different from what is called slavery? For example, what difference is there between a gunman who says "your money or your life" and a government that says "pay your taxes by April 15 or else"? Why is it wrong for a robber to threaten us with being shot, but it is okay for the government to threaten us with fines or imprisonment ? In both situations, our money is taken against our will. What difference does it make that it is the government telling us what to do, or that this rule is written down, or that this rule is made through some regular procedure, as opposed to a stranger just walking up to me and giving me a random spontaneous order? Where is my moral duty to obey the law if it is not *natural* law?

Of course there are the practical arguments that we need government to keep order, and since government will use violent force if necessary to keep that order, you should obey the law out of practicality. Obey the law, and avoid trouble. But again, that is not the argument that positivists make: they argue that we have a *moral* duty to obey the law, so it is morally wrong to disobey the law. So apart from the practical argument that one might want to avoid fines or keep out of prison, positivists have argued that there are moral-philosophic justifications why we should obey the positive law.

To understand the modern positivist argument we must first go back many hundreds of years to the old view that we should obey the positive law because it came from the gods. Prior to just a few hundred years ago and across all human cultures, lawmakers claimed they were either gods themselves, or children of gods, or prophets of god, or otherwise inspired by the gods, when they made the laws. This meant that the positive law was essentially the codification of natural law. Thus, there was a moral duty to obey the positive law not because it was positive law, but because the positive law was a direct embodiment of the natural law. In Europe of a few hundred years ago, this was known as the theory of "divine right of kings" and was based on the Bible, most importantly the Christian New Testament. In the New Testament, the book of Romans, chapter 13, verses 1–2 state "Everyone must submit himself to the governing authorities, for there is no authority except that which God has established. The authorities that exist have been established by God."[46] In England, this theory stated that god granted not just the king, but the king's *family* the authority to rule. Thus, political leadership stayed in the hands of the same family from generation to generation, with no "right" to question this one-family monopoly on power.

Indeed, under the theory of divine right, one could not disagree with the king's authority or declared laws because to disagree with the king would be to disagree with god's decision to let the king rule. Such disobedience would be heresy, and could result in fines, imprisonment, torture, or execution. In short, under divine right theory, one had a moral obligation to obey the law because the law comes directly or indirectly from god. Just as there is no such thing as a "right" to disagree with the physical laws of the universe such as gravity, there is no such thing as a "right" to disagree with the moral laws of the universe put there by the same god who created the physical laws. As a result, under the theory of divine right of kings, there was no such thing as the "freedom of speech" or a "right" to speak freely—nor any right of religious liberty, either. The most famous work defending the divine right of kings was written by the English scholar Robert Filmer, in his work titled *Patriarcha* (roughly meaning "rule by fathers") published in 1680.[47]

## The Social Contract

By the time Filmer wrote *Patriarcha*, ideas of Enlightenment were rapidly taking shape and becoming the basis of humanist intellectual thought. Enlightenment thinkers rejected many of the ideas of the past, and increasingly favored the concepts of liberty, equality, and democracy. It followed that they would reject the divine right of kings. But this brought back the question: why obey the law if not because it was proclaimed by the divine right? This set the stage for an alternative explanation: positive law derives its moral authority merely by the fact that humans say it is law. This idea actually has its origins in the 1600's. In 1651, The English philosopher Thomas Hobbes, wrote a work of political philosophy titled *Leviathan*.[48] Hobbes was the first thinker to argue that we owe obedience to the law due simply to our permanent agreement to obey the law once we turn authority over to a political ruler who will enforce

46. *The Bible*. New International Version, Zondervan, 2017.
47. Filmer, Robert. *Patriarcha and Other Writings*, Cambridge University Press, 1991.
48. Hobbes, Thomas. *Leviathan*. Penguin Classics, 1982.

social order so as to prevent violent lawless anarchy. Writers across the centuries since then have continued to argue that the law has moral force simply by the fact that it is law. Such thinkers include the founder of utilitarianism, Jeremy Bentham, writing in 1780,[49] as well as John Austin writing in 1820,[50] and H.L.A. Hart writing in 1961.[51]

By far the most influential thinker in this regard was the English philosopher John Locke. Among his other writings, he published a work of political thought that arguably changed the course of human history. Locke greatly disliked the theory of divine right of kings because obviously it offered a convenient excuse for any tyrant to have absolute rule without question. In 1690, Locke published *Two Treatises on Government*.[52] A "treatise" is a detailed scholarly work. It is not necessarily the case that Locke was the first one to think of all the concepts he presented in his *Two Treatises*, but he developed the ideas more fully, and expanded on some of them, and presented them in a more clear, coherent, and forceful way than anyone had done before. Thus, his work became the most influential political writing in arguing against the theory of divine right by offering an alternative theory to justify the existence of government and obedience to the law.

In Locke's *First Treatise on Government*, he systematically, point-by-point, attacked the theory of divine right of kings as defended by Filmer in *Patriarcha*. Locke argued in detail that nothing in the Bible could be used to justify absolute rule by any particular king, queen, or family bloodline. After pulling the rug out from under the authority of every government on the planet at the time, however, Locke realized he needed to replace the theory of divine right kings so that government would have some justification for its existence. Thus, Locke's *Second Treatise on Government* provided such an alternative theory. Although Locke didn't give his theory a name, it has since come to be called his *social contract theory*.

Locke begins by having the reader imagine going back in time before there was any human civilization. Humans were living just as other animals do: without any laws or government. This was, as Locke called it, living in the *state of nature*. Yet he declared that even without any human-made laws, there are moral laws of nature, just as there are physical laws of nature like gravity, all created by the supreme deity. These *natural rights* are comprised of a right to life, a right to liberty, and a right to "estate," meaning property—and by "property" he also includes even

49. Bentham, Jeremy. "An Introduction to the Principles of Morals and Legislation," in *The Collected Works of Jeremy Bentham*. Clarendon Press, 1996.

50. Austin, John. *The Province of Jurisprudence Determined*. W. E. Rumble, ed., Cambridge University Press, 1995.

51. Hart, H.L.A. *The Concept of Law, 2nd Ed.* Oxford: Oxford University Press, 1997.

52. Locke, John. *Two Treatises of Government*. Cambridge University Press, 1998.

one's family and one's reputation. Even though these natural rights are inherent in the universe as provided by a god, they are unprotected rights. That is, in a state of nature, any person can easily interfere with our natural rights at any time. People do not like feeling so insecure about their basic natural rights, and so the solution is to join together in groups for mutual protection. In such groups, everyone agrees to live by common rules in which everyone's rights are protected. Once a group forms laws to live by for each other's benefit, the group advances from a state of nature to a *civil society*. The mutual agreement to create, obey, and enforce common rules can be verbal or written, but either way, this agreement is called a *social contract*.

A government of laws is thus formed for the people's own mutual advantage and protection. According to Locke, this is the *only* reason government exists: to protect each other's natural rights. Government power is based on the fact that the people have agreed to give the government the power of enforcing the social contract. The source of government authority is not the divine, but rather the consent of the people themselves. Thus, consent of the governed is necessary for any government to claim it has legitimate moral authority to rule. That legitimacy remains subject to the consent of the people. Since the people have created the government, and not the other way around, the people remain supreme over the government. This concept is called *popular sovereignty*. Locke's ideas of popular sovereignty, the consent of the governed, and government formed the basis of what Locke believed was the only morally legitimate form of government, *democracy*—rule by the people.

Just as each of the parties in a legal contract have both rights and responsibilities, in a social contract people have rights protected by law but also corresponding duties to obey the laws. Also, in a legal contract, if one party to the contract violates the terms of the contract, the other party is free to break the contract as well. Similarly, if one party to the social contract violates its side of the bargain, the other party is free to ignore its side of the agreement. Thus, if the government begins to violate its obligations under the social contract to protect the people's natural rights—such as would happen if the government begins to abuse the people's rights—then the people are no longer bound by their agreement to obey the government. Since the people are supreme, they are now free to withdraw their consent to be ruled by that government. In other words, the people are free to abolish an abusive government and replace it with it new one. This includes using violence against government if necessary when the rulers in power refuse to give up their now-illegitimate power. Thus, according to Locke, the people always have a right to revolution if the government infringes on the natural rights of the people. Put simply, the democratic masses may always rebel if the government becomes undemocratic.

Under social contract theory, people have either expressly or implied promised obedience to the positive law—that is, they have promised to obey the government they have created—in exchange for the government's protection of the people's natural law rights. In other words, the people promise to obey the positive law that is supposed to protect them. Yet even Locke was careful to explain that the positive law must conform to the natural law. In Chapter 11 (Of the Extent of the Legislative Power) of his "Second Treatise on Civil Government," Locke wrote:

> The law of Nature stands as an eternal rule to all men, legislators as well as others. The rules that they make for other men's actions must, as well as their own and other men's actions, be conformable to the law of Nature- i.e., to the will of God, of which that is a declaration, and the fundamental law of Nature being the preservation of mankind, no human sanction can be good or valid against it.[53]

We can look to a famous example that illustrates some of Locke's basic concepts. Although the document was written before Locke published his *Two Treatises*, the Mayflower Compact, written in 1620, is a simple example of a written social contract. It is comprised of merely a few short paragraphs written by a group of religious Puritans while still on their ship the *Mayflower.* They were traveling across the Atlantic Ocean coming from Europe and on route to what would become their new home, eventually named Plymouth, Massachusetts. In the agreement, the adult men on board the ship all sign their names in agreement that they will live together in a society for each other's mutual benefit and protection.

> THE MAYFLOWER COMPACT:
>
> In the name of God, Amen. We, whose names are underwritten, the Loyal Subjects of our dread Sovereign Lord, King James, by the Grace of God, of England, France and Ireland, King, Defender of the Faith, e&.
>
> Having undertaken for the Glory of God, and Advancement of the Christian Faith, and the Honour of our King and Country, a voyage to plant the first colony in the northern parts of Virginia; do by these presents, solemnly and mutually in the Presence of God and one of another, covenant and combine ourselves together into a civil Body Politick, for our better Ordering and Preservation, and Furtherance of the Ends aforesaid; And by Virtue hereof to enact,

53. *Id.* Chapter 11, Section 135.

> constitute, and frame, such just and equal Laws, Ordinances, Acts, Constitutions and Offices, from time to time, as shall be thought most meet and convenient for the General good of the Colony; unto which we promise all due submission and obedience.
>
> In Witness whereof we have hereunto subscribed our names at Cape Cod the eleventh of November, in the Reign of our Sovereign Lord, King James of England, France and Ireland, the eighteenth, and of Scotland the fifty-fourth. Anno Domini, 1620.[54]
>
> [There followed the signatures of 41 of the 102 passengers—that is, only the adult men.]

In theory, it would only take one short sentence to create a social contract, such as a declaration that: "We the undersigned agree to form a common society, government, and laws for our common good." Of course, most social contracts are much more detailed, setting out the structure, functions, powers, and limitations of government. More detailed social contracts are typically called *constitutions* because those documents "constitute"—that is, they create, form, establish, make up, comprise, compose—the social contract that forms the essence of that society. Regardless of the terms used, the key point here is that according to social contract theory, we have consented to be governed through a *promise* made in a social contract. Because promises are morally binding, we've now become ethically/morally bound to obey the law. At least, that is the argument by proponents of social contract theory.

## Obedience to the Social Contract

Even assuming laws are made via a social contract, there are a variety of views as to when obedience to law is morally obligated under such a social contract. These views vary along a spectrum from the idea that obedience to law is always required to the view that obedience to laws is never morally obligated. A staunch, die-hard positivist would argue that under the social contract, we have agreed to obey *all* laws. Just as one rarely finds a perfectly consistent moral relativist, one also rarely finds a completely consistent legal positivist. If die-hard positivism were taken to its logical extreme conclusion, a democratic majority could do anything to a minority group, including exterminate the minority. For example, in Nazi Germany it was against the law to hide Jews, but not too many positivists would say that this law should have been followed.

Most positivists, then, are what one might call weak positivists. This

54. Pilgrim Fathers. *Mayflower Compact.* Amazon Digital Services, 2011

means that most positivists believe the law should be generally obeyed, but it is permissible to disobey the law in certain rare circumstances. Disobedience would be permitted when either the law in general, or the application of the law in a particular circumstance, would result in a morally bad outcome. This would allow one to disobey the Nazi law in the example just given. Also, exceptions to laws would be allowed, such as running a red traffic light in order to take a seriously ill or injured person to the hospital to prevent their death. Notice, though, that if a positivist says the law should be disobeyed because of some "higher principle" or "higher law" or because the application of law in that instance would be "unethical" or "bad," then the positivist is actually applying *natural* law, not positive law, to this exception. Thus, when pressed on the issue, even most positivists seem to believe in at least some limited conception of natural law.

If one believes that unjust, that is, immoral positive laws should be peacefully disobeyed because they violate the natural law, then one is engaging in *civil disobedience.* As mentioned earlier, Henry David Thoreau,[55] Mohandas Gandhi,[56] and Martin Luther King, Jr.,[57] are probably the three most well-known proponents of civil disobedience, and their writings on the subject have been very influential. The U.S. Civil Rights Movement of the 1950's and 1960's incorporated civil disobedience, and began with a single act of civil disobedience: a Black woman named Rosa Parks refused to yield her seat on a bus to a white person as the law required. She peacefully submitted to arrest by police officers at the next bus stop, and her arrest sparked the modern Civil Rights Movement for racial equality in the United States.

If, on the other hand, one believes that unjust (immoral) laws should be *violently* disobeyed, then this meets the modern definition of *terrorism*—the use of violence as a means of achieving political change. There is a saying, though, that "one person's terrorist is another person's freedom fighter." In other words, if the cause is just, then might violence be morally justified? Put simply, do the ends justify the means? For example, in 1859 abolitionist John Brown used deadly violence to try to inspire a slave revolt in Harper's Ferry, Virginia, in the hope of freeing slaves. Brown's plan failed, he was caught, and he was hanged for his crimes. Was he acting morally or immorally? Ultimately, of course, only the passage of time determines whether history records a person who uses political violence as a "freedom fighter" or a "terrorist." People in 1859 were deeply divided on whether John Brown was a

55. Thoreau, Henry David. *Civil Disobedience and Other Essays.* Dover Publications, 1993.
56. Gandhi, Mohandas. *Autobiography.* Dover Publications, 1983.
57. King, Martin Luther. *I Have a Dream, also Letter from Birmingham Jail.* Perfection Learning, 1990.

criminal or a martyr, and historians and ethical philosophers are still divided today on whether John Brown should be praised or condemned.

Toward the other end of the obedience-disobedience spectrum, many *libertarians* believe that most laws are unjust. According to libertarians, the government's only role is to protect people from violence against their body or their property. Other than laws prohibiting murder, kidnapping, rape, robbery, theft, vandalism, and other similar crimes, all other so-called "laws" are themselves an unjust interference with human liberty. This means there is no moral duty to obey most laws, as laws that restrict non-harmful human choices are themselves unjust/immoral. Tax laws and building codes, for example, interfere with the freedom to control one's money and property. One might choose to obey these laws merely due to the practical necessity of avoiding criminal prosecution, but there is no *moral* duty to obey these laws. One of the most prominent modern libertarian writers is philosopher Robert Nozick.[58]

At the final extreme end-point is the view that *all* laws are unjust. This is the theory of *anarchy*, from the Greek *an-archia*, meaning "no-ruler." Disobedience to law is thus always morally permissible if it goes against one's moral beliefs. This outlook is based on the theory that no one, including the government, has the "right" to rule over another person. We have a natural law right to life, liberty, and property. Our natural law right to personal autonomy means we have a right to *self-rule* over all that we own, which includes our minds (speech, religion), our bodies (food, drugs, sex, medicine, travel) and our property (housing, land, business, labor). Attempted state control over any of these things violates an anarchist's natural law right to choose how we ourselves decide what to do with our life, liberty, and property. Any and all forms of government or laws therefore violate the natural law, so disobedience to law is always morally justified. Put differently, all forms of government are illegitimate so the phrase "legitimate government" is an oxymoron. The only obligation anarchists have is to obey laws that are "good" or "just" or "moral" as they deem.[59]

## Social Contract Theory Problems

For the legal positivist, the reason we have a moral obligation to obey the law is because we have agreed to obey the law as part of our consent-

58. Nozick, Robert. *Anarchy, State and Utopia.* Basic Books, 2013.
59. Godwin, William. *An Enquiry Concerning Political Justice.* Oxford University Press, 2013; Bakunin, Michael. *God and the State.* Dover Publications, 1970.

ing to a social contract. However, as many political philosophers—especially anarchist thinkers—have pointed out, there are serious problems with this theory. To begin with, other than a small percent of the population—perhaps naturalized citizens, military members, or politicians who have taken an oath of office—the vast majority of people have never given any express consent to be governed or to obey any laws. Social contractarians respond to this obvious point by arguing that our consent to be governed is not expressed, but *implied*. There are several paths this argument takes. One argument is that all of us accept the protections and benefits of the state, such as police and fire protection, public schools, roads, and social welfare benefit programs like Social Security or Medicare. By accepting these benefits, we take on a reciprocal obligation to obey the law. Put differently, by letting government do us a favor, we owe a favor in return, and that favor is to do what the government tells us to do. The flaw in this particular argument is that we are forced to accept government benefits whether we want them or not. There is no way to opt-out of paying taxes for police, fire, schools, roads, Social Security, Medicare, or any other government program. If we don't pay for them, we can be charged with the crime of tax evasion. Under generally accepted ethical standards, we do not have a reciprocal obligation if we have no choice in the agreement. This would be like salespeople leaving all sorts of things on our doorstep and then charging us for those items. Then the local courts make us pay for the items even though we never ordered any of them on the theory that we are now benefitting from the items so we should pay.

Another common argument by social contract proponents is that by remaining in a location where a particular social contract is in operation (that is, by choosing to stay within the government of a certain locality), one has consented to be governed by that particular system of laws. The counter-argument to this, especially by anarchist thinkers, is that there is no feasible alternative. Since every habitable geographic territory on Earth is governed by a social contract, there is no law-free territory that anarchists can move to if they wish to express non-consent to any social contract. An analogy that has been given is if you were born on a ship that travels forever in the middle of the ocean and is ruled by a tyrannical captain. Upon reaching adulthood, you object to the captain's rules. The captain tells you "if you don't like my rules, you're free to leave!" Obviously there is no viable alternative to remaining on the ship so "leaving" is not a legitimate option. Choosing to stay, then, does not indicate consent to being governed, but is simply a reflection that there is no realistic alternative.

Another possible argument by the social contractarian (a.k.a. the legal positivist) is that by voting—taking part in the political system—you have impliedly consented to be ruled by the laws produced by the outcome of the election system. Anarchists may once again, however, respond that there is no real alternative. The situation has been compared to a slave who is given a choice between two masters: one will beat you six days a week versus the other who will beat you all seven days of the week. You don't want either choice, but if forced to choose you'll pick the "lesser of two evils." In other words, being forced to choose between Satan and Beelzebub does not imply you want to suffer in hell. If you are forced to choose between *only* those two options, it is not a "legitimate" choice and thus your act of choosing does not imply consent to the outcome of your choice.

Another argument on behalf of implied consent is that the act of *not* voting implies you have waived your right to object to laws produced by the outcome of the election. As ordinary people sometimes say, "if you don't vote, you have no right to object." The problem with this argument, though, as anarchists point out, is the fact that there is no real alternative. Election ballots do not have "none of the above" or "no government" as a choice. In these circumstances, the only way to indicate a lack of consent is to *not* participate in the procedure to select a government. In short, whether one chooses to vote or chooses to abstain from voting, neither choice can be deemed as consent to be governed by the laws made by the government that results from the outcome of the election.[60]

The endpoint of the entire philosophical discussion between a staunch positivist and an anarchist thus establishes that the positivist has a difficult time logically demonstrating why there is a *moral* obligation to obey laws. This leaves the weak positivist, libertarian, and anarchist all on relatively firm ground that the only positive laws that must be *morally* obeyed are those that conform to the natural law.

## Origins of U.S. Postive Law

As we discussed earlier in this chapter, the United States Constitution created an agreement, a "social contract," among its citizens as well as between its citizens and their government. Regardless of any philosophical problems that might exist with the concept of the social contract, it is the nonetheless the philosophical foundation of the United States as a democratic nation. Yet the origins of the U.S. legal system go back much further in time.

60. For general critiques of social contract theory, see Spooner, Lysander. *No Treason: the Constitution of No Authority*. Createspace Independent Publishing Platform, 2018; Wolff, Jonathan. *An Introduction to Political Philosophy, 3rd Edition*. Oxford University Press, 2016.

Western law originates in part from two ancient Middle-East cultures. The first are the legal codes issued by King Hammurabi of Babylonia. He issued his law around 1780 B.C., and it became known as the "Code of Hammurabi."[61] Hammurabi claimed that the Babylonian gods called upon him to establish law in the land. Later, roughly around 1200 B.C., the Hebrew Torah, which later became part of the Old Testament, listed extensive legal codes in the books of Leviticus and Deuteronomy.[62] The Prophet Moses claimed to have received these rules directly from the Hebrew god, and they became known as the "Ten Commandments." These Ten Commandments include such laws as "Thou shalt not kill," "Thou shalt not commit adultery," and "Thou shalt not steal."

Much later, the Roman Empire peaked around the year 100 A.D. It had an extensive, well-developed legal code. Roman law heavily influenced the law in Southern and Western Europe, including what later became Spain and France. The Germanic tribes, however, were largely independent of the influence of Roman law because most had successfully fought off attempted invasions by the Romans. After the fall of the Roman Empire, two Germanic tribes, the Angles and the Saxons, emigrated from what is now Germany to the Southeast part of the British Isles or what is now England. Although the tribe of Britons already lived on the British Isles, the Angles named their land Angleland, whose spelling later became England. (Hence "England" is not the same thing as "Britain" because England is only one part of Great Britain). The foundations of the new *Anglo-Saxon* legal system developed between 500 and 1000 A.D.

In the 11th century, the Normans lived in Normandy or what is now northern France. In the year 1066 the Normans invaded and conquered England. The Normans brought with them their French-language legal code that had been heavily influenced by Roman law. This Roman-influenced Norman law mixed with the Anglo-Saxon English legal system to form a new hybrid legal system. A century after the Norman invasion and conquest of England, a new "common" system of law was created to unify and stabilize law over time and across the different regions of England. Hence this unified legal system became known as the *common law.* The key to this commonality was that judges were expected to rely on, and rule consistently with, the rulings of other judges in prior similar cases.

Eventually England joined with two other kingdoms on the Isle of Britain, Scotland and Wales. Together, England, Scotland, and Wales formed the nation of Great Britain. As Great Britain achieved a world

61. Hammurabi. *The Code of Hammurabi.* Createspace Independent Publishing Platform, 2016.
62. Moses. *The Torah.* The Jewish Publication Society, 2000.

empire in the 1600's and 1700's, the English/British common-law system spread to all the British Colonies. These colonies included what is now the United States of America, as well as what is now Canada, Australia, New Zealand, India, and Hong Kong. As these colonies achieved independence, they typically adopted some, if not most, of their common law British heritage. Because a key part of the common law system is uniformity of case law, courts in these several countries still frequently cited and relied on cases from the other common law nations well into the 1800's and early 1900's. This cross-national reliance on the common law made by courts in other common law nations still occurs today, though rarely.

Outside of Great Britain, Roman law eventually influenced the rest of Europe to adopt what is called *civil law*. Unlike the common law that is primarily judge-made, the civil law is based on an extensive legislative-made statutory code. This tradition began with the *Code of Justinian*, named after the Roman Emperor Justinian. Justinian issued his extensive legal code around the year 530 A.D.[63] As France and Spain and to a lesser extent Portugal became world powers in the 1600's and 1700's, their colonies spread civil law systems to the Western Hemisphere. Spain's colonies included Mexico and Cuba, along with most of Central and South America. France's colonies included Louisiana and what is now Quebec, and Portugal's colonies included Brazil. As all these colonies eventually achieved independence or admission to other nations, they largely kept their civil law systems. Thus, most of the nations of Central and South America have civil law systems due to their Spanish heritage. Brazil is a civil law country because of its Portuguese origins. Quebec has a civil code thanks to its French origins, as does the U.S. state of Louisiana. When Louisiana became part of the United States, however, its civil code became influenced by the common law tradition in the rest of the United States. Thus, today, Louisiana has a modified hybrid civil law/common law system, with elements of both types of systems. On the one hand, Louisiana has a detailed and extensive statutory code that still contains many concepts from French civil law, and this code officially has higher legal authority than caselaw. On the other hand, courts in Louisiana borrow heavily from case law precedents in Louisiana and sometimes from other jurisdictions in the United States. This results in a style of legal argument in Louisiana that might often appear indistinguishable from the common law, depending on the particular legal issues involved.

As the United States became an independent nation, Thomas Jefferson led the early founders of the United States in basing the existence of the United States on social contract theory in the 1776 Declara-

63. Fried, Bruce W., Editor. *The Codex of Justinian*. Cambridge University Press, 2016.

tion of Independence.[64] This was a wholesale rejection of the prior theory of divine right of kings. Yet for the most part, the legal system which governed the daily operation of the United States continued using the common law and civil code concepts that had developed over many centuries. Still today in the United States, the positive law of 49 states uses a common-law legal system and one state (Louisiana) uses a hybrid common law/civil law system. This distinction, however, along with the other aspects of jurisprudence discussed in this chapter, together comprise only a small part of the broad field of jurisprudence.

---

*Questions for Review and Discussion*

1. Define "law" and explain the definition, with examples.
2. Explain the difference between natural law and positive law and give examples
3. Explain the difference between legal formalism and legal realism and give examples.
4. Have your class list all the natural law rules of morality everyone in the class can agree on. How many did you come up with? Could a system of morality be based on *only* those rules?
5. Is there a moral duty to obey the law? Why or why not?

---

*Suggested Readings*

*Riggs v. Palmer,* 2 N.E. 188 (N.Y. 1889) (enforcement of will)
*In Re Pavlinko Will,* 148 A.2d 528 (Pa. 1959) (enforcement of will)
*Strunk v. Strunk,* 445 S.W.2d 145 (Ky. Ct. App. 1969) (forced kidney transplant)
John Locke, *Second Treatise on Government* (1690)
Lysander Spooner, *No Treason* (1867)
Henry David Thoreau, *On the Duty of Civil Disobedience* (1849)
John Austin, *The Province of Jurisprudence Determined* (1832)
Lon Fuller. "The Case of the Speluncean Explorers," *Harvard Law Review* 62: 616–645 (1949).

---

*Advanced Readings*

H.L.A. Hart, *The Concept of Law* (1961)
Lon L. Fuller, *The Morality of Law* (1964)
Jonathan Wolff, *An Introduction to Political Philosophy* (2016)

64. Thomas Jefferson, *The Declaration of Independence,* Applewood Books, 1997

# CHAPTER 2

# U.S. COURTS

---

*Chapter Objectives*
*After reading this chapter, you should be able to:*

- Describe the organization, function, and basic procedures of the federal courts
- Describe the basic elements of Supreme Court opinions
- Explain and apply the concept of justiciability
- Explain judicial review and identify examples
- Describe founding-era debates over judicial review and the subsequent history of judicial review

---

James Obergefell and John Arthur met in 1992. They fell in love and lived together as a committed couple for more than 20 years in Cincinnati, Ohio. Throughout all that period, Ohio law did not recognize same-sex marriages as legally valid. By 2013, however, several other states had legalized same-sex marriage. At this time, John was now suffering from a terminal illness called ALS, also known as Lou Gehrig's disease. Wanting to be married before John died, the couple flew to Maryland in July 2013. Maryland had by then legalized same-sex marriage. Because John was too ill to leave the medical transport plane, he and James were married on the plane while the plane was still on the airport tarmac. They then flew back to their home in Ohio. Three months later, in October 2013, John died. Because Ohio law would not recognize same-sex marriages, James could not have himself listed as the surviving spouse on John's death certificate.

In December 2013, James filed a lawsuit in a Federal District Court in Ohio requesting that the District Court order his name be placed on John's death certificate as John's spouse. The District Court granted the order describing how denying same-sex couples death certificates indicating marriage places such couples at a serious legal disadvantage. The court ruled that death certificates "are important not only for the dignity of the surviving spouse and his or her family, but also have evidentiary value for rights such as receiving life insurance payouts, claiming social security survivors benefits, administering wills, and title transfers for automobiles, real estate, and other property."

Officials for the State of Ohio then appealed the decision of the Federal District Court to the federal Sixth Circuit Court of Appeals which reviews appeals from all federal district courts in four states: Michigan, Ohio, Kentucky, and Tennessee. The Sixth Circuit reversed the District Court decision declaring that the Constitution did not provide a right to same-sex marriage.

James Obergefell then appealed the Sixth Circuit decision to the U.S. Supreme Court. In an opinion issued in June 2015, the U.S. Supreme Court first explained how the Ohio prohibition on same-sex marriage personally affected James Obergefell and John Arthur: "By statute, they must remain strangers even in death, a state-imposed separation Obergefell deems 'hurtful for the rest of time.'" Then, by a 5-4 majority, the Court declared that the Constitution's Due Process and Equal Protection clauses provide a right for same-sex couples to marry. This allowed Obergefell to have himself listed as Arthur's legal spouse on Arthur's death certificate. More significantly, the Court's decision allowed all same-sex couples within the United States to marry if they so choose, and thereby receive all the same legal protections and benefits as opposite-sex married couples.[1]

This example provides a brief introduction to federal court procedures, specifically how cases can proceed from one court to another higher court. Also importantly, *Obergefell* illustrates how federal court cases can have profound impact on the lives of ordinary people. To understand better how federal courts are involved in such issues, we must first look to the U.S. Constitution and Congress's role in organizing the court system.

## Federal Judicial Organization

Article III of the U.S. Constitution creates the federal judicial branch and empowers it by giving federal courts "the judicial power." Under the U.S. system of separation of powers, the basic function or power of the courts is to interpret laws. In other words, whenever there is a disagreement about the meaning of a law, the courts have the authority to make the final determination.

The Constitution provides only a few details about the federal courts. As part of the system of checks and balances described by the

1. *Obergefell v. Hodges*, 576 U.S. 644 (2015)

Constitution, all federal judges must be nominated by the President and confirmed by the Senate. The Constitution does not list any minimum age or other requirements or qualifications to be a federal judge. The Constitution does not even require that federal judges be attorneys. As a practical matter, though, having a legal background is an unwritten requirement as the Senate would be extremely unlikely to confirm a Presidential nominee for a federal judicial position unless the nominee had a substantial legal background.

Federal judges at all levels of the federal courts serve in office "during good behavior." This means they receive life terms in office until they die, choose to retire, or are removed by the impeachment process for improper behavior. Behavior warranting impeachment would be the commission of serious crimes such as accepting bribes, as well as abuse of power or neglect of duty. The impeachment process for judges is the same process as for the removal of executive officials: a majority of the House must issue articles of impeachment alleging wrongdoing, and then a two-thirds majority of the Senate must vote to find the person guilty of the wrongdoing. If the Senate convicts the federal judge, the individual is removed from office, but if the Senate acquits the judge then the judge continues to serve indefinitely.

Article III creates only the *U.S. Supreme Court,* but no other courts. It is often referred to by the acronym "SCOTUS" (meaning Supreme Court of the United States). The Constitution then gives Congress the power to organize a system of federal courts other than the Supreme Court. For this reason, federal courts other than the Supreme Court are called *Article III courts.* Congress currently has divided the United States into 94 geographic districts. Each state has one or more U.S. District Courts. Louisiana, for example, has three: The Eastern District of Louisiana, the Middle District of Louisiana, and the Western District of Louisiana. The District Courts are the trial courts in the federal court system. If you want to file a lawsuit in federal court, or are sued in federal court, or are charged with a federal crime, your case will first be heard in a U.S. District Court.

If you lose at the trial court level, you can appeal your case to the next higher level of court, a system of intermediate appellate courts called the U.S. Circuit Courts of Appeal. Congress has divided the U.S. into 12 geographic districts, each of which comprises one of the circuits within the U.S. Circuit Courts of Appeal. Eleven of these Circuits are numbered: First Circuit, Second Circuit, and so on. A twelfth circuit is called the D.C. Circuit. In addition, there is a "Federal Circuit," also located in Washington, D.C., which has exclusive jurisdiction to hear patent case appeals. This makes a total of 13 Circuit Courts. Each Circuit Court hears appeals from the District Courts from multiple states or the District of Columbia. The 5th Circuit Court of Appeals, for example, based in New Orleans, hears the appeals from all the U.S. District Courts in Texas, Louisiana, and Mississippi. Also, separate from the main federal court system of District Courts and Circuit Courts, Congress has also created several specialized trial and appellate courts. Each of these specialized federal courts hears trials or appeals involving a particular area of law, such as bankruptcy, tax, trade, or military court martials.

The size of each Circuit Court of appeals—as measured by the number of judges working on that Circuit Court—varies depending on the population contained within the territorial jurisdiction of the court. The smallest circuit is the First Circuit, which hears appeals from all federal District Courts in the upper New England states of Maine, New Hampshire, Massachusetts, and Rhode Island, as well as the territory of Puerto Rico. The largest circuit is the Ninth Circuit, which hears appeals from all federal District Courts in the Western and West Coast states of Washington, Idaho, Montana, Oregon, California, and Nevada, as well as Alaska and Hawaii, and the territories of Guam and the Mariana Islands.

At the federal level, the losing litigant at the intermediate appellate level Circuit Court can then file an appeal to the highest court in the U.S., the U.S. Supreme Court. The Constitution does not specify how many judges should be on the Supreme Court, thus leaving it to Congress to decide. Under current congressional law, there are nine judges called *justices* on the Supreme Court. We will return to focus on the Supreme Court in more detail later in this chapter.

## Federal Jurisdiction

All courts, including federal courts, must have *jurisdiction* to hear a case. This means the court has authority to hear the case, either because of the type of case, where the case comes from, or both. There are several types of jurisdiction. *Geographic jurisdiction* means the court may hear cases that arise within the territory overseen by the court. Another important type of jurisdiction is *subject matter jurisdiction*, meaning the types of legal issues the court can hear. In this regard, most courts have *general jurisdiction*, meaning they can hear any type of legal issue. Some specialized courts, however, have *special jurisdiction*, meaning they can hear only certain types of cases. At the local levels, some examples might be traffic court or juvenile court. Some examples of federal courts with special jurisdiction are the U.S. Bankruptcy Courts or U.S. Tax Court.

The U.S. Constitution gives federal courts jurisdiction over all disputes involving the U.S. Constitution, Congressional statutes, treaties made by the United States, rules and regulations issued by the federal bureaucracy, and all other federal law. Section 2 of Article III of the Constitution also lists type of litigants that give federal courts jurisdiction:

> The judicial power shall extend to all cases, in law and equity, arising under this Constitution, the laws of the United States, and treaties made, or which shall be made, under their authority;—to all cases affecting ambassadors, other public ministers and consuls;—to all cases of admiralty and maritime jurisdiction;—to controversies to which the United States shall be a party;—to controversies between two or more states;—between a state and citizens of another state;—between citizens of different states;—between citizens of the same state claiming lands under grants of different states, and between a state, or the citizens thereof, and foreign states, citizens or subjects

Criminal cases are common in federal district courts, especially violations of federal law covering drugs, immigration, and firearms. Other common areas of federal law include bankruptcy, federal taxation, intellectual property, copyrights, and patents, and enforcement of federal employment, health, safety, and environmental regulations. Some examples of these latter federal matters include employment discrimination, pharmaceutical prescriptions, chemical plant safety guidelines, and auto emission limits.

Section 2 of Article III of the Constitution also gives the U.S. Supreme Court *original jurisdiction*: "In all cases affecting ambassadors, other public ministers and consuls, and those in which a state shall be party, the Supreme Court shall have original jurisdiction." This means that the Supreme Court has authority to conduct the trial in the case rather than wait for an appeal of the case from other federal courts. For example, many U.S. states use rivers as their state boundaries, yet the course of rivers continually changes as rivers meander, causing state borders to come into question. If, for example, Illinois and Missouri disagree about which state owns a new or altered piece of land along the Mississippi River, those states would have their case heard for the first time by the U.S. Supreme Court, and not by a U.S. District Court.

Other than the handful of cases involving original jurisdiction, Section 2 of Article III of the Constitution provides: "In all the other cases before mentioned, the Supreme Court shall have appellate jurisdiction, both as to law and fact, with such exceptions, and under such regulations as the Congress shall make." Put simply, Congress is free to define almost all of the *appellate* jurisdiction of the U.S. Supreme Court along with all the jurisdiction of other federal courts. One example of jurisdiction Congress has defined for federal courts is called *diversity jurisdiction.* As we just saw, Article III gives federal courts appellate jurisdiction over lawsuits between citizens (which includes businesses and corporations) of different states. Congress has decided, however, that diversity jurisdiction is allowed only if a minimum amount of money is as stake. This amount is currently set by Congress as $70,000 minimum.

The U.S. Supreme Court has appellate jurisdiction over all cases from the Circuit Courts of Appeal, any specialized federal courts such as bankruptcy courts, and all high courts within the 50 state court systems if a federal legal issue is involved. For example, if a case involves the freedom of speech or religion, the equal protection of the laws, or the rights of criminal defendants, all these issues involve rights protected by the U.S. Constitution. Therefore, if a state court issues a ruling in these areas, that ruling is subject to eventual appeal to, and decision by, the U.S. Supreme Court. Once the Supreme Court decides a case, however, there is no higher court and no further appeals. For all cases within the United States legal system, the Supreme Court gets the final say on the outcome of the case.

## State Courts

The U.S. Constitution says nothing about state court systems. This leaves it up to each state to design its own state court system, whether through the state constitution, state statutes, or both. States differ, for example, in the number of levels in their court system, the number of judges on their supreme courts, the method of selecting state judges, and how long state judges serve. Because there is so much variation in state judicial systems, we will use the highest courts in the states to illustrate merely some of the key differences. For example, the number of justices on states supreme courts is either five, seven, or nine justices depending on the state. Indeed, states differ even in what they call the highest court of appeals in their state, but we will refer to these courts by the general term most commonly used, *state supreme courts.*

*Selecting State Court Judges* One important institutional difference between state and federal court systems is judicial tenure in office. Federal judges are nominated by the president and upon confirmation by the Senate, they then serve for life. Most state supreme court justices, by contrast, are selected in other ways. At one end of the spectrum, in just over a half-dozen states (Alabama, Arkansas, Illinois, Louisiana, New Mexico, Pennsylvania, and Texas), state supreme court judicial candidates face opponents in partisan elections where party affiliation is expressly indicated during the campaign and on election ballots. Such partisan elections are more susceptible to being politicized than other methods of judicial selection and retention. In over a dozen other states, including Michigan, Ohio, Oregon, Washington and Wisconsin, judicial candidates face opponents in elections, but in non-partisan elections. That is, no party identification is provided by the candidates during the campaign nor is party affiliation listed on the ballots.

In almost two dozen states, including California, Colorado, Iowa, Michigan, and Utah, justices do not face an opponent, but instead are appointed by what is known as a "merit plan." Since Missouri was the first state to adopt such a system, this method of selecting and retaining judges is also commonly referred to as the "Missouri Plan." Under this system, when a state supreme court seat becomes available, an expert panel or commission submits a list of names of recommended judicial appointees to the governor, who then selects one. After a designated term in office, the appointed justice then runs on their record and, depending on the state, they must get the approval of a majority or supermajority of voters to retain their office. Voters choose either "yes" or "no" to continue the justice in office. These elections are also appropriately called "retention" elections. If the justice does not win a high enough percent of votes to retain them in office, then their judicial seat becomes open and the appointment process starts over.

Other states use still other judicial selection methods. Almost a dozen states, including Hawaii, Maryland, Massachusetts, New Jersey, and New York use an appointment system somewhat like the federal system. The governor nominates a state supreme court justice, but that nominee is subject to confirmation by one or both chambers of the state legislature. In Virginia, however, the state legislature acting on its own selects states supreme justices. Moreover, at the opposite end of the spectrum from partisan judicial elections, supreme court justices in four states (Massachusetts, New Hampshire, New Jersey, and Rhode Island) have the opportunity to serve terms to age 70 or life. These latter states thus more closely match the federal system which attempts to make judges relatively insulated from political influences and pressures.

*Terms of Judicial Service* Another institutional difference between the federal government and the states is judicial term length. Judicial term lengths vary not only across states as well but can also vary across the different trial court and appellate court levels within a state. To illustrate merely some of this variety, we can look at how terms of state supreme court justices differ across states. State supreme court justices in over a dozen states, including Arizona, Nevada, Ohio, Texas, and Washington, serve 6-year terms. Florida and Maine justices serve 7-year terms. State high court justices in about a dozen states, including Connecticut,

Iowa, Mississippi, North Carolina, and Tennessee, serve 8-year terms. Justices in about another dozen states, including Colorado, Illinois, Indiana, Pennsylvania, and South Carolina, serve 10-year terms. In a handful of states, including California, Missouri, and Virginia, high court justices serve 12-year terms. New York justices serve the longest fixed-length term in office, fourteen years. In a few other states, supreme court justices have the opportunity to serve potentially much longer terms in office. In Massachusetts, supreme court justices serve until age 70. In New Jersey, supreme court justices serve an initial 7-year term followed by tenure to age 70 if they are re-appointed by the governor. Justices in New Hampshire get to serve a single term lasting until the age of 70. Finally, in Rhode Island, justices serve for life, mirroring the federal system.

*Levels of State Courts* Another organizational difference across states is the number of court levels. Most states parallel the federal system by having an intermediate appellate court, but nine states do not have an intermediate appellate court: Delaware, Maine, Montana, New Hampshire, Rhode Island, South Dakota, Vermont, West Virginia, and Wyoming. One can see that these states tend to be states with smaller populations where the supreme courts of these states are able to handle the entire load of cases being appealed from the state trial courts. In states with larger populations, the large number of appeals from the state trial courts requires an intermediate appellate court to help handle the workload. It would logistically be impossible, for example, for the state supreme court of California to single-handedly address every legal appeal from every trial court within the state.

Yet another, although minor, variation across states is the number of supreme courts a state has. Two states, Texas and Oklahoma, have divided their appellate jurisdiction between two supreme courts that go by different names. In both these states, one supreme court has jurisdiction over civil case appeals and the other supreme court has jurisdiction over criminal case appeals.

State courts have geographic jurisdiction only over legal issues arising within the territorial boundaries of their states. This could occur for example, when one of the litigants is located within the state, or when a transaction was completed within the state even though the parties to the transaction all reside out-of-state. For example, the Louisiana Supreme Court has jurisdiction to hear cases arising in Louisiana, but not (with exceptions just noted) legal issues arising in other states. The subject-matter jurisdiction of state courts covers all areas of state law, both civil and criminal. This especially includes areas of state law that are not usually addressed by federal law, and so under principles of federalism, are mostly left to state legislatures to decide. This includes legal areas such as torts, contracts, property, business and occupational licensing, wills, trusts and estates, as well as family law issues such as marriage, divorce, and child custody.

Appeals by losing litigants in state trial courts are brought to the appellate court within that state, with the state supreme court being the "court of last resort" on questions of interpretation of state law. If, however, a case involves a "federal question,"—that is, a question of federal law—then a litigant that has lost in a state supreme court is allowed to appeal that state supreme court decision to the U.S. Supreme Court.

*State Court to U.S. Supreme Court—the 2000 Election* One famous example of the U.S. Supreme Court reviewing a state supreme court decision due to a federal legal question being involved was the case of *Bush v. Gore* (2000). In that case, the U.S. Supreme Court reviewed Florida election procedures during the 2000 presidential election between Democratic candidate Al Gore and Republican candidate George Bush. Florida had used paper ballots where the voter used a small stylus to push a "chad"—a small perforated square—out of the ballot, leaving a hole in the ballot next to the selected candidate. The voting machine counted the hole as a vote. Among other flaws in this voting system, if the voter had not pushed the stylus far enough, the chad either was indented, or left hanging by one, two, or three corners. In such cases, the machine typically did not count that vote because it could not determine the existence of a hole in the ballot.

Bush won the Florida vote by less than one-half of one percent. This triggered an automatic machine recount, after which Bush's margin of victory was a few hundred votes out of almost three million votes cast, with several thousand ballots not recorded as votes. Gore then requested, as state law allowed, a manual vote recount, but he requested the recount only in four large, heavily democratic counties. Each individual punch-card ballot was to be reviewed by a team of people who would determine if that vote had been correctly recorded. Gore also filed a lawsuit in Florida state trial court requesting the recount continue past the Florida election law deadline for reporting presidential election results to Congress. The Florida trial court denied this request. Gore appealed the Florida trial court decision to the Florida intermediate appellate court, which passed the case on to the Florida Supreme Court without a ruling given the exceptional importance and pressing need for an immediate, final ruling. The Florida Supreme Court reversed the Florida trial court ruling and ordered the manual recount to continue with results to be submitted past the normal statutory deadline.

There were several issues with this recount procedure. Most importantly, there was no uniform state rule for how disputed punch-card ballots should be counted. That is, there was no statewide standard how indented or "dimpled" chads, nor how "hanging" chads, were to be counted. This left each Florida county recounting team to create, on the spot, its own spontaneous vote count guidelines. Also, not all counties were necessarily to be recounted, and there was no standard regarding the number or qualifications of members of these manual vote-count teams. Bush therefore filed a lawsuit in federal court arguing that voters in different Florida counties would have a different likelihood of having their votes accurately recorded depending on whether and how each county manually determined the intent of the voter based on visual inspection of each ballot. According to Bush, this lack of uniform standards in the Florida Supreme Court's ruling violated the Equal Protection Clause of the Fourteenth Amendment to the U.S. Constitution. Since a federal question was involved, the U.S. Supreme Court agreed to hear the case.

A majority [5-4] of the U.S. Supreme Court agreed with Bush. The Court ruled the inconsistent ad-hoc recount procedures violated the U.S. Constitution's Equal Protection Clause. A majority of the Court also ruled that there was not sufficient time to remedy the problem given the Congressional deadline for the submission of electoral votes was the same day as the U.S. Supreme Court's ruling. The U.S. Supreme Court thus reversed the Florida Supreme Court ruling, ordering Florida to end its manual recount. This effectively meant Florida would cast its electoral votes for the candidate who won Florida based on votes already counted, George W. Bush. As a result of winning Florida's electoral votes, Bush became President. In short, this example illustrates how the U.S. Supreme Court's appellate jurisdiction over state court cases involving federal law can have profoundly important consequences.

## Justiciability

Besides needing jurisdiction, for federal courts to hear a case, the case must be *justiciable.* Using the noun form of this term, a case must have *justiciability.* This concept comes from the U.S. Constitution, Article III, sec. 2: "The judicial power shall extend to all cases . . . ; to controversies . . . " Based on this requirement, courts will not hear a case unless it is a "case or controversy." The Supreme Court has defined "case or controversy" to mean a "a justiciable dispute," which is generally defined as *a dispute that is appropriate for resolution in court.* There are infinite disputes that are not appropriate for resolution in a court. The Supreme Court has clarified several requirements that must be met for a case to be justiciable, otherwise the case is said to be nonjusticiable. Because states are free to create their own rules for the types of disputes state courts will hear, they need not follow the federal rules of justiciability, but most generally do. There are many different factors that might cause a case to be nonjusticiable. Here are the most common:

*No Advisory Opinions* Federal courts will not give advice in hypothetical cases, such as "What if law X were passed?" Or "Would law Y outlaw action Q?" There are several reasons for not giving advisory opinions. First, these court opinions would be pointless if these cases never came up in the future. If these cases never occur, how can a ruling on them be useful as precedent? There are several more practical reasons, however, for the rule against advisory opinions. Without litigants that have an actual stake in the outcome of a real dispute, mere advisory cases are not likely to be fully or strenuously argued on both sides. Yet courts need these types of arguments to make well-informed decisions. Also, courts are already involved in controversial issues. Giving advisory opinions would put courts in the position of making unnecessary and complex constitutional decisions in an even greater number of controversial areas. As a practical matter, the federal court system already has a backlog of actual cases. Every possible legal issue can be hypothetical, even if hypothetical analyses were limited only to Congressional and Presidential requests. Thus, regardless of how few entities are allowed to request the additional caseload of infinite "what if's", these cases could (and probably would) easily overwhelm the federal courts.

*No Collusive Suits* A collusive suit is a "friendly" suit where the litigants have colluded together to try to get the same outcome. There is no real dispute if both sides want the same outcome. Disallowing collusion ensures sincere efforts that all the litigants will present both opposing sides fully so courts can make well-informed decisions. For example, imagine your mother slips on the sidewalk entrance to your house. Her attorney advises her to file a friendly lawsuit against you (and thus against your insurance company). You take the stand and testify "Yes! it was entirely my defective sidewalk that caused my poor mama to fall!" Why would you admit this? So that your homeowner's insurance will have to pay poor mother's medical bills which she could not otherwise afford. This would be collusion.

*The Case Must be Ripe* You can not bring a case too early. Just as a fruit can be picked before it is ripe, if you file a lawsuit too soon, the case might not be ripe. If the party who is filing the lawsuit (that is, the plaintiff) has not had any rights violated yet, the case is unripe, and the court will not decide the issue. This most often occurs when a law has been enacted but does not take effect for some time. Only when the plaintiff is suffering an actual injury, or is about to, will the case be ripe for resolution. The policy against unripe cases exists for the same reason as the policies against collusion and advisory opinions: to minimize the court's caseload and to ensure vigorous advocacy by all the parties involved.

*The Case Must not be Moot* The concept of *mootness* is the opposite of ripeness. Mootness occurs when you have filed a lawsuit too late. This can occur if there's a settlement in the case before the court has issued its opinion. The case is then moot so the court will not bother to decide the case since it basically doesn't exist anymore. Mootness occurs also when there's no longer a need for the decision. This can happen, for example, if a criminal defendant has died; if a child has turned 18 in a child custody case, or in a lawsuit seeking an injunction against tearing down a building that has already been destroyed prior to the hearing on the injunction. Once again, the policy against mootness exists for the same reasons as the policy against advisory opinions, collusive suits, and unripe cases.

There is an exception to the rule against moot cases being justiciable: if the legal issue involved is an issue that is "capable of repetition yet evading review." This means that the type of legal question involved is one such that the nature of facts will usually cause the cases to become moot before courts can ever fully rule on the legal question. If so, then courts can hear the case even though the case is moot. Examples of these types of issues are short criminal sentences, laws regulating pregnancy and abortions, school admissions, elections, and exercise of the right to die. As a particular example, imagine a law that imposes a sentence of one day in jail for a crime that is defined in a way that violates the Constitution. By the time any appeal is decided, the defendant has already served the sentence, so the case is moot. But then, appeals would always be moot for people convicted of this crime, so the constitutional issue would never be decided by an appellate court. Thus, an appellate court will likely decide to hear the appeal because that issue is "capable of repetition yet evading review."

*The Party Bringing the Lawsuit Must Have Standing* The party filing the lawsuit—that is, the plaintiff—must have an *actual* stake in the outcome of the case, and not merely a wish that the universe be a certain way. Having a real, tangible interest in a lawsuit is called *standing*. Otherwise, without the requirement of standing, everyone would be able to sue everyone for everything. As one simple example, imagine you see your next-door-neighbor to your north throw a brick at the car of your next-door-neighbor to your south. You can't sue your neighbor to the north just because you don't like what your neighbor did to your neighbor on the south. Since it wasn't *your* car that was involved, you lack standing.

As one can imagine, the policy reasons behind requiring a direct stake in the outcome of case are the same as the requirements already discussed for justiciability. Without this requirement, the courts would be overwhelmed. Also, generalized desires or grievances between people, groups, and government—such as whether government should provide free universal health care—are best settled through the political process. The U.S. Supreme Court now has strict requirements for standing. See *Lujan v. Defenders of Wildlife* (1992)[2] for an explanation and application of the current standing rules. Basically, the plaintiff must have suffered an actual, concrete injury that is ongoing or immediately about to occur, and the defendant's actions directly caused that injury.

## Civil Procedure

We have just looked at a large-scale overview of the organization of the U.S. legal system. Now let's turn to the procedure that occurs within the judicial branch. We'll begin with procedure in the trial courts. The two (or more) entities who are involved in a lawsuit are called the *parties* to the lawsuit. The parties to a lawsuit could be individuals, businesses, organizations, or government agencies. The parties are also called *litigants* because they are *litigating* (suing each other) in a lawsuit. In a civil case, the *plaintiff* is the party which is bringing the lawsuit against the other litigant. The party defending against the legal claim is appropriately called the *defendant*. In a criminal case, the government that is charging someone with a crime is called the *prosecution*, and the accused person is called the *defendant*. With rare exceptions, lawsuits are first filed in the trial court, which at the federal level is the Federal District Court.

Some nations have what is called an *inquisitorial* system. This means that the goal of the court system is to discover the truth. If truth is the highest goal, for example, jurors themselves might be able to ask about or investigate possible evidence, call witnesses to testify, and ask questions of witnesses. The U.S. legal system, however, is an *adversarial* system. The highest goal is to give each party its best chance to defend itself, even if this means the truth is not achieved in the case. Each party can attack and undermine even accurate evidence on the opposite side. Defendants can refuse to cooperate. The judge and jury are merely passive evaluators of whatever limited evidence and arguments the two sides present. The hope is that truth prevails, but the top priority is allowing the two parties to present their best attacks and defenses. U.S. trial procedure is designed with this goal in mind.

2. 504, U.S. 555

When one party to a lawsuit sues another party, this is a *civil* lawsuit, as opposed to a *criminal* lawsuit where someone is charged by the state with a crime. There are standard legal procedures for both civil lawsuits and criminal prosecutions. These procedures are appropriately called *civil procedure* and *criminal procedure.* Here are some basic terms and elements of *civil* procedure. (Criminal procedure has many similarities, but also many important differences.)

*Pre-Trial Procedure* Pre-trial procedure is the formal legal procedure that occurs from the start of a lawsuit, but before any trial begins. Here are some of the most important concepts that involve pre-trial civil procedure.

1. *Plaintiff:* the party/litigant (individual person, business, organization, government agency, etc.) alleging a legal injury.

2. *Defendant:* the party/litigant alleged to have committed the legal injury against the plaintiff.

3. *Complaint/Pleading:* formal filing in court of a lawsuit by a plaintiff, which states a legal claim against a defendant.

4. *Statute of limitations*; the legal time limit for a plaintiff to file a complaint (e.g. typically 2 years for breach of contract, 5 years for a tort).

5. *Class Action:* A consolidation of complaints by many plaintiffs against the same defendant into a single case (e.g. a bad consumer product).

6. *Service of Process:* Formal notification to the defendant by the court of the lawsuit by the plaintiff against the defendant.

7. *Answer:* the formal filing with the court by the defendant responding to the plaintiff's complaint.

8. *Counter-complaint/cross-claim:* a complaint filed by the defendant against the original plaintiff.

9. *Discovery:* formal investigation by each party involved in the lawsuit of the other parties' alleged claims and facts.

10. *Affidavits:* formal, written, notarized statements of testimony by the parties and any witnesses for each side.

11. *Interrogatories:* formal written questions given by each party for the other party to formally provide written answers.

12. *Depositions:* Formal interviews of the parties by the lawyers for the opposing party about matter material to the case.

13. *Subpoenas:* a formal court order that a party provide testimony/evidence.

14. *Contempt of Court:* violation by a party of a court order which can result in fines or jail time.

15. *Pre-trial conference:* a meeting between the parties and their attorneys to narrow the factual or legal issues in the case.

16. *Stipulations:* Facts and laws the parties agree to at the pre-trial conference.

17. *Settlement:* a private agreement by the parties for them to dismiss the lawsuit (this often occurs at a pre-trial conference).

18. *Motion:* a formal request by a party to the court for a legal ruling; in asking you "move" that the court take the requested action.

19. *Motion to reconsider:* a formal request by a party that the court reconsider its denial of that party's motion.

20. *Summary judgment:* A formal ruling by a court in a lawsuit that no further trial is needed because the law or facts are so one-sided.

*Trial Procedure* If a case goes to trial, trial procedure is the formal legal procedure that governs what happens during the trial. There are numerous rules of evidence which dictate what type of evidence is allowed and disallowed, how it must be authenticated, and how objections must be made and responded to. The rules of evidence differ somewhat between civil and criminal trials. Aside from the rules of evidence, however, there are many other general concepts that comprise trial procedure. Here are a few of the most important trial concepts.

- *Bench trial:* a judge hears the case and decides the ruling.

- *Jury trial:* a judge presides over the court, but a jury (a group of citizens) hears the case and decides the ruling.

- *Venue:* the location of the court where the trial will be held.

- *Voir dire:* in a jury trial, the formal selection by the opposing parties in court to achieve an unbiased jury. This includes interviewing, choosing, and possibly dismissing potential jurors.
  - *For-cause challenge:* each party has an unlimited number of for-cause challenges during *voire dire* where the party can have a potential juror dismissed if the potential juror admits bias.
  - *Peremptory challenge:* each party has a very limited number of peremptory challenges where the party can have a potential juror dismissed without reason. The number of peremptory challenges allowed differs depending on the jurisdiction.

- *Dismissal:* a formal ruling by the court that the plaintiff's complaint is invalid and so the case is "thrown out of court."

- *Default judgment:* a formal ruling by the court for the plaintiff against defendant if the defendant does not defend against the lawsuit.

- *Burden of proof:* how much evidence the plaintiff must show to demonstrate the legal injury was committed by the defendant. The required burden of proof differs depending on the type of case.
  - *Preponderance of evidence:* the plaintiff's version of the facts is more likely true than not (greater than 50%). This standard applies in most civil cases.
  - *Clear and convincing evidence:* Roughly 67–75% evidence is on the plaintiff's side. This standard applies in a few types of civil cases, such as termination of parental rights and involuntary commitment to a mental health facility.
  - *Beyond a reasonable doubt:* Greater than 95% of the evidence is on the prosecution side indicating the defendant is guilty. This is the standard in criminal cases, not civil cases, but is listed here for comparison.

- *Opening statement/argument:* the initial statement made by each party's attorney at the start of the trial.

- *Case-in-chief:* each party's presentation of the facts in support of their side. First the plaintiff will present the plaintiff's case-in-chief; then the defendant will present the defendant's case-in-chief. During each case-in-chief, the following elements will occur:

- o *Direct examination:* questioning in court by an attorney of that attorney's party or a witness for that party.
- o *Cross examination:* an optional questioning in court by an attorney of the opposing party or a witness for that opposing party.
- o *Redirect examination:* an optional secondary direct examination after a cross-examination has occurred.
- o *Recross examination:* an optional secondary cross examination after a re-direct examination has occurred.

- *Closing statement/argument:* the final statement made by each party's attorney at the close of the trial.

- *Judgment:* in a bench trial, the judge's decision which party won the lawsuit

- *Verdict:* in a jury trial, the jury's decision on which party won the lawsuit.

- *Directed verdict:* in a jury trial, a formal ruling by a judge that the law or facts are so one-sided, no jury decision is needed.

The period immediately after the verdict is reached in a trial, but before any appeal is filed, involves *post-trial procedure.* One common motion that the losing parties often request is a *judgment notwithstanding the verdict.* This is a formal ruling by the judge that the jury's verdict is overturned and reversed. This can occur only if the evidence is so one-sided, no rational jury could have reached the decision it did. The shorthand term for a judgment notwithstanding the verdict is *judgment n.o.v.* or simply *j.n.o.v.* The initials "n.o.v." come from the Latin *non obstante verdicto,* meaning "notwithstanding the verdict." In a civil trial, the judge can issue a j.n.o.v for either party. In jurisdictions that allow a j.n.o.v. in criminal trials, however, the judge can issue a j.n.o.v. only in favor of the defendant and never against the defendant. In other words, a judge can acquit a defendant whom the jury has convicted, but a judge can never convict a defendant whom the jury has acquitted.

## Appellate Procedure

Whichever litigant—the plaintiff or the defendant—loses at trial, the losing litigant can file an *appeal* at the next higher court, the *intermediate appellate* court, by arguing that the trial court made a legal mistake. The intermediate appellate courts at the federal level are called the *U.S. Circuit Courts of Appeal.* Depending on the court, the party bringing the appeal is called either the *appellant* or the *petitioner* because the losing litigant is petitioning (asking) the appellate court to reverse the lower court ruling. The party responding to the appeal is called either the *appellee* or the *respondent* because the winning litigant is merely responding to the request (the petition) by the losing litigant that the appellate court reverse the ruling of the trial court. Here are some of the most common and important concepts involving post-trial procedure.

- *Appeal:* the formal request by the party that lost the trial for a higher court to review and overturn the outcome of the trial.
- *Appellate court:* the higher court that is hearing and deciding the appeal.
- *Appellant/petitioner:* The party who lost in the court below and is now filing the appeal—that is, the party who is petitioning the higher court to review the lower court decision.
- *Appellee/respondent:* the party that won in the court below is now responding to the appeal by the appellant/petitioner.
- *Reversible error:* a serious mistake that occurred during the trial, such that the appellate court should overturn the trial decision.
- *Harmless error:* a minor mistake that occurred during the trial such that the appellate court will uphold the trial decision.
- *Disposition:* How the appellate court "disposes of" (handles) the lower court decision. There are many possible dispositions, but here are the three most common dispositions:
  - *Affirmed:* the appellate court upholds the decision of the lower court so that the same party wins.
  - *Reversed:* the appellate court reverses the decision of the lower court so that the opposite party wins.
  - *Remanded:* the appellate court sends the case back to the lower court for a reconsideration (re-do) of the case.

Although the designations of the parties as plaintiff and defendant will never change throughout the lawsuit, the designations of the parties as appellant/petitioner versus appellee/respondent can and often do change as the parties go through the appeals process. Also, depending on what the law is in each particular legal area, the legal *burden of proof* regarding the evidence the parties need to show to win the lawsuit may be placed either on the plaintiff or defendant, or switch back and forth. Thus, do not confuse the separate legal issues of (a) which party filed the lawsuit to begin with, (b) which party lost and so is appealing the lower court decision, and (c) which party has the burden of proof. All three of these might be different, and might change back and forth depending on who decides to sue whom, when (what level of court), and how (what is the basic legal claim).

Let's look at an example. Assume that the Social Security Administration Office in Lafayette, Louisiana denies an application for disability benefits by Jane Doe on the alleged basis that she did not provide enough medical evidence of her disability to prove she was disabled. If Jane still is unable to obtain benefits after going through the administrative appeals process within the Social Security Administration itself, she can file a lawsuit in the Western District of Louisiana. If Jane loses her case in the federal District Court, she can file an appeal in the 5th Circuit Court of Appeals in New Orleans. Under Congressional law, the U.S. District Court must hear any lawsuit filed, and the Court of Appeals must hear your appeal once. Thus, both the District Court and the Court of Appeals have what is called *mandatory jurisdiction.* If Jane loses her appeal, then she can ask the U.S. Supreme Court to hear her case. She would continue to be the appellant/petitioner and the U.S. government would be the appellee/respondent. If, however, Jane wins at the Circuit Court of Appeals and the U.S. government decides to appeal its loss to the Supreme Court, now the U.S. government would become the appellant/petitioner, and Jane would become the appellee/respondent.

Unlike the District Courts and Circuit Courts, however, most of the Supreme Court's jurisdiction is *discretionary appellate jurisdiction.* This means the Supreme Court can itself decide whether to hear a case, but these cases are only appeals that have already been ruled on by lower courts. Typically, each year there are over 7,000 cases appealed to the Supreme Court, but the justices usually agree to hear only about 150 cases at most.

In the remaining small percent of cases before the Supreme Court, according to the Constitution, the Supreme Court has *mandatory original jurisdiction.* This means the Supreme Court acts as the trial court and must hear the case for the first time, rather than on appeal. Such cases involve disputes between states, between a state and the U.S. government, or disputes between a citizens or state and a foreign government.

In cases where the Supreme Court has discretionary jurisdiction, the party asking the court to hear its case will technically file a petition for a *writ of certiorari*. That is, the party that lost in the decision by the court below will ask (petition) the Court to grant a writ (order) that the lower court send all of its information about the case to the Supreme Court so that the Supreme Court can hear and decide the appeal. By the current rule decided by the Supreme Court itself, at least four of the nine justices must agree that the case is important enough to hear the appeal. Thus, if four or more justices vote to listen to the appeal, the Supreme Court will hear the case. To be technically precise, this means four out of the nine justices voted to grant the petition for the writ of certiorari. A more common shorthand way of saying this is that the Court "granted certiorari" or even just "granted cert." If only three or fewer of the nine justices vote to hear the appeal, then the court "denied certiorari" or more simply "denied cert."

Because the Supreme Court has discretion whether to grant certiorari, the Court has come up with its own guideline in this regard. Supreme Court Rule 10 states "A petition for a writ of certiorari will be granted only for compelling reasons." Rule 10 then provides a non-exhaustive list of types of cases that will make the granting of certiorari more likely. Such cases include "a United States court of appeals has entered a decision in conflict with the decision of another United States court of appeals on the same important matter" and "a state court or a United States court of appeals has decided an important question of federal law that has not been, but should be, settled by this Court." Both of these situations, for example, were present in *Obergefell v. Hodges* (2015). Not only did it involve an important federal question that had never been directly addressed by the Supreme Court, there was a "circuit split" on the issue. The Sixth Circuit case had declared there was no constitutional right to same-sex marriage, but all the other federal circuits that had ruled on the issue so far had declared the Constitution did protect a right. As a result of this circuit split, there was contradictory federal law regarding the constitutional right to same-sex marriage depending on which state one lived in. The Supreme Court therefore needed to rule on the issue either way to provide uniformity of U.S. constitutional law on such a major constitutional question.

Once the Court agrees to hear a case, both sides in the case have a chance to file written arguments with the Court. These are called *appellate briefs* because they are a relatively short (i.e. 50 pages) summary of the entire area of law and legal arguments that applies to the particular legal question involved in the case. Other interested parties also may file a brief on behalf of either of the parties actually involved in the lawsuit if the interested parties believe they have some possible stake in the outcome of the case. For example, if the Court is going to rule on a question of business law, then different industries, labor unions, or environmental groups might file briefs attempting to persuade the Court how to rule. These briefs are called *amicus curiae* briefs. *Amicus curiae* is Latin for "friend of the court." In major cases, there can be many *amicus curiae* briefs, as occurred in *Obergefell v. Hodges* (2015) where almost 150 *amcius curiae* briefs were filed with the Court. These briefs were provided by religious and civil rights groups, governmental organizations, and legal scholars among others. That number was unusually high, though, due to the landmark nature of the case.

Once all the briefs (and any reply briefs) are filed with the Court, the Court will hear *oral argument* in the case. This is a chance for the lawyers for both sides to personally appear before the entire panel of judges on the Supreme Court and verbally explain and defend their position, as well as answer the often numerous questions the justices have. Oral argument typically occurs in all appellate level courts at both the state and federal level, if requested by one or more of the litigants, or if requested by the panel.

After the written and oral arguments, a majority vote by the Supreme Court decides the outcome of the case. That is, whichever side can convince five or more of the nine justices to agree with its position will win the case. It doesn't matter if the justices in the minority believe the universe will implode due to the majority opinion—however the majority rules is the court's decision. Since there is no higher court in the United States, whatever the Supreme Court decides is the final determination of the legal matter in question. This is why the Supreme Court is also called a "court of last resort." Unless the Court declares that its decision has only a limited application to future cases (a "narrow ruling"), the Court's final ruling becomes legally binding precedent which future courts must generally look to when resolving future cases.

On rare occasions, one or more of the justices will have retired or died but no replacement has been appointed yet. Or, one or more justices might "recuse" themselves from the case (not take part in the decision) if they have a conflict of interest in the case, such as being friends with one of the litigants or having financial involvement with a company involved in the litigation. In any of these situations, there will be less then nine justices who end up voting on the outcome of the case. By the Supreme Court's own rules, a minimum number of justices (called a *quorum*) of at least seven justices must sit in session to hear the case or else the Court will not issue a decision in the case. In that instance, the lower court ruling is the final ruling in the case. Or, if the Supreme Court reaches a tie vote of four-to-four, then by the Court's own rules, the lower decision is the final decision in the case, and the Court's equally divided opinion has no legal significance.

## Appellate Opinions

Most court cases that have extra legal and educational importance come from higher appellate courts. This would be either intermediate appellate courts or supreme courts, be it state supreme courts, or ultimately, the U.S. Supreme Court. In the U.S., all trial court rulings are made by a single judge only. All appellate-level courts in the U.S., however, make their decisions by an odd-numbered team of judges called a *panel.* In the U.S. Circuit Courts of Appeal, panels are typically three judges. A litigant who loses the decision of a three-judge panel, however, can ask the appellate court to re-hear the case with a larger group of judges who work on that circuit. This is called an *en banc hearing,* which is typically comprised of 11 judges at the U.S. Circuit Courts. And, as we've seen, by current Congressional mandate the U.S. Supreme Court has nine judges on its panel. State high courts within the United States typically have 5-, 7-, or 9-judge panels. In all appellate-level courts at either the state or federal level, the court will have a single judge who is administratively in charge of the court, known either as the *chief judge* or *chief justice,* depending on the court. The other judges on the court are referred to as *associate judges* or *associate justices,* again depending on the court.

Regardless of the size of the panel, appellate-level courts rule by majority vote of the panel. The court's decision itself as to who wins the case is variously referred to as the court's *decision* or *ruling* or *judgment* or *holding.* The written statement issued by the court which lists and usually explains the court's decision is called the court's *opinion.* The decision reached by the majority is called the *majority opinion.* Although the term "opinion" is used, this can be misleading, because the majority opinion is not merely an "opinion" as used in layperson's terms, but is instead the official legal ruling in the case, and has the full force of law. That is, the majority opinion becomes the controlling precedent for all future court cases in all lower courts beneath that court in the judicial hierarchy. Because of this legal significance, the written majority opinion is usually published publicly so that the litigants in the case, the rest of the legal profession, and the public can understand the *facts* of the case, the precise legal issues involved (the *issue* or *question*), the court's decision (its *holding*), and (most importantly) the court's explanation (its *reasoning* or *rationale*) as to how the majority reached its decision through applying the relevant law to the facts of the case.

Sometimes a panel will rule *unanimously,* where all the judges agree to the ruling. Sometimes, however, a judge on the panel will agree with the majority's holding but not with the reasoning of the majority. That is, a judge will agree with the majority on which litigant should win, but the judge will disagree as to the legal reason *why* the litigant should win. For example, the judge might believe a different law applies, or the judge might think the litigant should win due to different facts than those the majority has emphasized. This judge is called a *concurring* judge. To legally concur, then, means you agree with the result but disagree with the reason for the result. A concurring judge may choose to write an opinion separate from the majority opinion. This separate opinion is called either a *concurrence* or a *concurring opinion*. If so many judges concur such that no majority of the court exists, then whichever concurring opinion is joined by the largest number of judges is called the *plurality* opinion.

Another judge on the court's panel, however, might disagree with both the holding *and* the reasoning of the court. To disagree with the result, and by necessity, the explanation of the majority opinion is to *dissent* from the majority opinion. This is a *dissenting judge,* and he or she may choose to write a separate *dissenting opinion*, also called simply a *dissent*. Thus, the word "dissent" can be used both as a verb and a noun, as in "Judge Smith dissented and wrote a dissent."

The various judges on a panel have the choice of joining the majority opinion, joining any plurality or other concurring opinions, joining one or more dissenting opinions, or instead writing their own separate concurrences or dissents. This can sometimes result in very *divided* or *fractured* courts. For example, the Court's vote for the winning litigant might be 5-4: five judges in the majority and four dissenting. Or, the court might be divided 4-2-3: four in the plurality, two concurring, and three dissenting. As you can see, there are numerous other possible combinations. At the opposite end of the spectrum, occasionally a panel will unanimously feel that a case is so straightforward that no individual judge should be given credit for the court's written opinion. Instead, the court as a whole simply issues a relatively short opinion authored *per curiam* (Latin for "by the court").

What the appellate-level court ultimately does with the lower-court decision is called the *disposition*. That is, the higher court "disposes" of the lower court decision. There are many different things an appellate-level court can do with the case being appealed to it, but only three possibilities account for the vast majority of all outcomes. When the higher-court majority agrees with the lower court decision, it *affirms* the lower court decision. When the majority disagrees with the lower court decision, it *reverses* the lower court decision. There is another possibility, though. The majority might agree that the trial court did not apply the law correctly, but not know how the trial court would have ruled had the judge applied the law correctly. That is, the trial court judge might have ruled differently had the correct law been applied, but the judge might still have ruled for the same litigant even with the application of different law. In such a situation, the higher court *remands* the case back to the trial court to re-try the case applying the correct law this time. If a case has multiple legal issues, it is common for one part of a lower-court case to be affirmed, reversed, or remanded, while another part of the lower-court case is disposed of differently. It might even be the situation that an appellate-level court will dispose of a lower court case by affirming in part, reversing in part, and remanding in part, all in the same case.

## The Theory of Judicial Review

Recall that under the U.S. system of separation of powers, the courts are to interpret laws. This function and role of the courts is not controversial. What *is* somewhat controversial is the strongest power courts have in fulfilling this role: the power to declare actions by other branches of government to be unconstitutional. This power of *judicial review* essentially means that when the courts review what legislatures or executives do, courts can declare those actions illegal, and hence, null and void.

Although neither the term, judicial review, nor its definition is found in the Constitution, it is clearly a direct implication of what *is* found in the Constitution. All the writers of the Constitution understood this. Even though basic principles of law are not described in the Constitution, all the writers of the Constitution understood that a basic, foundational principle of law is that higher law always overrides lower law. Article VI of the Constitution expressly declares that the Constitution is the "supreme law of the land." Under the separation of powers, the federal courts must interpret the meaning of laws. Thus, when faced with a conflict between what the U.S. Constitution says and what the President, Congress, or the state governments are doing, the courts must say the Constitution overrides any such actions. This can be expressed logically as follows (1 + 2 + 3 + 4 = 5):

1. Higher law overrides contradictory lower law.

2. The Constitution is the highest law in the United States.

3. Therefore, the Constitution overrides any contradictory action by Congress or the President, or the state governments.

4. The courts have the power to interpret laws, including when there is a conflict between laws.

5. Therefore, 1 + 2 + 3 + 4 = 5: *Judicial Review.* The courts not only have the power, but it is their responsibility to evaluate all U.S. law for its constitutionality. When faced with a contradiction

> between what the government is doing and what the Constitution says, the courts must declare that the Constitution overrides the contrary action. In such a situation, the action is unconstitutional—that is, illegal.

In *Federalist Paper #78,* Hamilton explained the logic as follows:

> There is no position which depends on clearer principles than that every act of a delegated authority, contrary to the tenor of the commission under which it is exercised, is void. No legislative act, therefore, contrary to the Constitution, can be valid. . . . The courts were designed to be an intermediate body between the people and the legislature in order, among other things, to keep the latter within the limits assigned to their authority. The interpretation of the laws is the proper and peculiar province of the courts. A constitution is, in fact, and must be regarded by the judges as, a fundamental law. It therefore belongs to them to ascertain its meaning as well as the meaning of any particular act proceeding from the legislative body. If there should happen to be an irreconcilable variance between the two, that which has the superior obligation and validity ought, of course, to be preferred; or, in other words, the Constitution ought to be preferred to the statute, the intention of the people to the intention of their agents.

The U.S. Supreme Court agreed with this logic and expressly described it in the landmark legal decision *Marbury v. Madison* (1803).[3] In that case, outgoing President John Adams made various appointments just prior to leaving office. One of those appointments was making William Marbury a Justice of the Peace. The paperwork for that commission, however, was not delivered prior to incoming President James Madison taking office. One of Madison's first acts as President was to cancel the appointments made by Adams that had not yet been delivered. Marbury filed a lawsuit, asking the U.S. Supreme Court to order the commission be delivered to him. Writing for the Court, Chief Justice Marshall concluded that it was probably illegal for Madison to refuse to deliver a legally valid commission. Yet, Marshall also decided that the Supreme Court did not have jurisdiction to hear the case, and so could not grant any legal relief to Marbury.

Marshall reached this latter conclusion by announcing that the Court has the power of judicial review:

3. 5 U.S. 137

> Certainly all those who have framed written constitutions contemplate them as forming the fundamental and paramount law of the nation, and consequently the theory of every such government must be, that an act of the legislature repugnant to the constitution is void. This theory is essentially attached to a written constitution, and is consequently to be considered by this court as one of the fundamental principles of our society. . . . It is emphatically the province and duty of the judicial department to say what the law is. . . . If two laws conflict with each other, the courts must decide on the operation of each. So if a law be in opposition to the constitution: if both the law and the constitution apply to a particular case, so that the court must either decide that case conformably to the law, disregarding the constitution; or conformably to the constitution, disregarding the law: the court must determine which of these conflicting rules governs the case. This is of the very essence of judicial duty. . . . In declaring what shall be the supreme law of the land, the Constitution itself is first mentioned, and not the laws of the United States generally, but those only which shall be made in pursuance of the Constitution, have that rank. Thus, the particular phraseology of the Constitution of the United States confirms and strengthens the principle, supposed to be essential to all written Constitutions, that a law repugnant to the Constitution is void, and that courts, as well as other departments, are bound by that instrument.

Marshall explained that when Congress gave the Supreme Court jurisdiction over Marbury's type of claim in the Judiciary Act of 1789, Congress had acted inconsistently with the jurisdiction given the Supreme Court in Article III of the Constitution. Marbury's request was therefore denied.

Essentially, the power of judicial review is the ability of the courts to enforce the social contract of the United States. Courts must be able to evaluate—that is, review—actions by the other branches of government to make sure the Constitution is being obeyed. If either of the other two branches of government violate that social contract—the Constitution—then the courts have the power to rule that the other branches are violating that social contract, and so their action is forbidden, null, and void. *Obergefell v. Hodges*, the same-sex marriage case discussed at the start of this chapter, is a prime example of judicial review. Recall that in that case, the Supreme Court reviewed the marriage law restrictions passed by state legislatures and determined those limits on who may marry violated the Constitution.

Today, not only the U.S. Supreme Court, but *all* courts within the

United States at both the federal and state level possess the power of judicial review. The *existence* of this power of judicial review is not very controversial. What *is* controversial is the *how* and *when* this power is used or should be used, especially when it comes to interpreting the U.S. Constitution. This debate goes all the way back to the founding of the United States. Recall from basic American history regarding the founding period that when the new U.S. Constitution was first proposed, it caused much debate. Those favoring the Constitution became known as Federalists, and those opposed became known as Anti-Federalists. Although there were many areas of dispute between the Federalists and Anti-Federalists, the proper use of the constitutionally implied power of judicial review was the key issue of debate between the Federalists and Anti-federalists when it came to the federal courts.

The Anti-federalists argued the power of judicial review was dangerously too much power being given to the federal courts. The Federalists responded to this argument, especially in *Federalist Paper No. 78*, written by Alexander Hamilton. There, Hamilton makes the famous statement that the judicial branch is the "least dangerous branch" of government. But why is this so? Hamilton compares the power of the courts to the powers of the other branches of government. The legislature possesses the "power of the purse." That is, the legislative branch controls money. If it wants to do something, it can raise taxes and spend money to accomplish its goals. The executive branch, on the other hand, possesses the "power of the sword." In other words, the executive branch, especially the President, contains the power of the U.S. military. If the President wants something done, the President is Commander-in-Chief of the entirety of the U.S. armed forces. This is an enormous power to command such a force.

Yet as Hamilton then further explains in *Federalist No. 78*, the courts have neither the power of the purse nor the power of the sword. Courts cannot raise taxes, nor do courts have a large budget from which they can assign money to implement their decisions. Nor do the courts command any police force or military that can go out and enforce judicial rulings. All the courts can do is issue their decisions, and then hope that the other branches of government, along with the public, decide to voluntarily respect and obey those court decisions. If the public and other branches of government were to ignore court decisions, there would be no way for the courts to enforce their decisions. Thus, the judicial branch is entirely impotent on its own, and is entirely dependent on the other branches of government to ensure that its decisions are enforced. In this way, Hamilton argued that the power of judicial review was not something that people should be worried about.

Hamilton further argued in *Federalist Paper No. 81* that even if the Supreme Court abuses its power of judicial review, the impeachment process for federal judges will keep the justices in line. In other words, Hamilton argued that the fear of impeachment and losing their position as federal judges will keep federal judges from abusing their power of judicial review. This will lead federal judges to use judicial review sparingly and carefully, Hamilton argued.

The Anti-federalists did not agree with Hamilton's assessment, however. Perhaps most famously, the Anti-federalist Brutus (whose actual identity remains unknown) argued that judicial review was too powerful a weapon to give to the federal courts. For example, in the checks and balances in the Constitution, the President can veto Congressional laws, but then Congress has a counter-check by overriding that veto by a two thirds vote of both chambers of Congress. Yet judicial review is an unchecked check. The President cannot veto judicial review. Congress cannot vote to override judicial review. Once the Supreme Court exercises judicial review, there is no way to counteract that power except to amend the U.S. Constitution, a politically difficult process. Brutus went on to further argue that impeachment will not be an obstacle to judicial review because using the power given the courts will not be a legal grounds for impeachment. In other words, impeachment would be appropriate in the case of bribery, corruption, or other wrongdoing, but there is nothing wrong with using a power given by the Constitution. Thus, Brutus argued, as long as the Constitution says federal judges serve in office "during good behavior," the possible threat of impeachment will not deter federal judges from using the power of judicial review as frequently as they wish, or in whatever circumstances they wish.

## Judicial Review in Practice

Once the Court has used its power of judicial review, what are the consequences of that decision? The lessons of history have shown us that both Hamilton and Brutus were each partially correct in their prophecies about the power of judicial review. Hamilton was correct that without support from the other branches of government, court decisions would go unenforced. In the early 1830's, the U.S. government wanted to forcibly remove members of the Cherokee Nation from their lands in northern Georgia and eastern South Carolina. The Supreme Court ruled in favor of the treaty rights of the Cherokee, but President Andrew Jackson is recorded as having responded "Chief Justice Marshall has made his decision, now let him enforce it." The forced march of the Cherokee Nation and other eastern Native American tribes to Indian Territory (now Oklahoma) at the gunpoint of the U.S. military during which thousands of Native Americans died from starvation, freezing, and physical exhaustion became known as the *Trail of Tears*.

Another example that shows the U.S. Supreme Court is powerless on its own is its 1954 ruling in *Brown v. Board of Education.*[4] Although the U.S. Supreme Court had ruled that racially segregated public schools violated the 14th Amendment of the U.S. Constitution, southern governors, state legislatures, and local schools boards openly defied the ruling and did everything they could to obstruct the ruling. It was only when the other branches of the U.S. government—both the Congress and the Presidency—took an active role in enforcing the ruling in *Brown v. Board of Education* that public schools in the southern states finally became racially integrated consistent with the Supreme Court's rulings.

Although Hamilton was correct that court rulings have no effect unless enforced by the other branches of government, Brutus was also correct that there is no counter-check to judicial review. Once the Supreme Court has ruled on an interpretation of the U.S. Constitution, there is no counter-check except for amending the Constitution. This is rarely done. As a rare example, the Supreme Court ruled in 1937 that poll taxes—requiring a fee to vote—did not violate the Constitution. Only after the Constitution was amended in 1964 by the ratification of the 24th Amendment were poll taxes prohibited by the Constitution. Indeed, since the original ten amendments contained in the Bill of Rights were ratified in 1791, there have only been seventeen additional amendments added to the U.S. Constitution through the present day. Many amendments have been proposed, but extremely few have been added.

Brutus was further correct that impeachment is not a counter-check to the exercise of judicial review. Although investigations were begun to impeach dozens of federal judges over the course of U.S. history, less than a dozen federal judges have ever been impeached for wrongdoing, and none of those impeachments were initiated because of a justice's exercise of judicial review. Moreover, no justice of the U.S. Supreme Court has ever been removed from their position as judge by the impeachment process, for any reason. Even after some of the most controversial Supreme Court rulings in *Dred Scott v. Sanford* (1856) (allowing slavery everywhere in the U.S.), *Brown v. Board of Education* (1954) (ending racially segregated schools), *Roe v. Wade* (1973) (creating a right to an abortion) and *Bush v. Gore* (2000) (invalidating a Florida Supreme Court ruling and thereby effectively deciding the 2000 Presidential election), there was no serious movement to impeach Supreme Court justices despite widespread public anger at each of these rulings. Thus, justices on the Supreme Court know that regardless how controversial their rulings might be, the justices themselves are essentially immune from impeachment on the grounds of using judicial review.

4. 347 U.S. 483

At the same time, however, public opposition to controversial Supreme Court rulings can continue for decades. For example, in a landmark 1973 case, *Roe v. Wade*,[5] the Court ruled that women have a constitutional right to obtain an abortion. Public opinion on whether abortion should be legal has barely changed since then. Large minorities of the public—especially religious conservatives—still believe abortion is immoral and should be severely restricted or outlawed entirely by the government. Thus, when conservative Republicans gain majorities in state legislatures or Congress, they regularly try to find legislative ways to minimize the right defined in *Roe v. Wade* and subsequent cases. More importantly, whenever possible, Republican Presidents attempt to appoint Supreme Court nominees who will likely vote to overturn *Roe v. Wade*. Likewise, Democratic Presidents typically attempt to appoint Supreme Court nominees who will uphold the core of the *Roe v. Wade* decision. In general, by becoming involved in a controversial social issue, the Court does not always put an end to the politics of an issue, but simply transfers the primary political battleground from the legislative or executive arena to the judicial arena instead. Such legal and constitutional battles over the question of abortion and other controversial issues will continue as long as the public remains deeply divided over such issues.

Sometimes when exercising judicial review the Supreme Court's decision *not* to invalidate congressional or executive action can be just as controversial as when it does invalidate such action. For example, in 2012, by a narrow 5-4 vote, the Court declined to overturn the Congressional mandate for individuals to buy health insurance as part of the Affordable Care Act, more commonly known as "Obamacare." By upholding the mandate as a valid use of the Congressional power to tax, the Court angered those who believed Congress had no constitutional authority to force people to buy a product they did not want. Was the Court abandoning its constitutional responsibility to uphold the Constitution, or was it simply acknowledging a valid constitutional power of Congress? One's perspective on the Court's rulings always depends on one's interpretation of the Constitution. One person's "right" is another person's "injustice," and vice versa. Hence, the Court's interpretation of the Constitution will always be a matter of political controversy no matter how the Court rules.

The only realistic way the public can make it likely that the Court will issue rulings the public likes is for the public to elect Presidents and members of the Senate who will nominate and confirm judges to the Court who will rule in line with the public's wishes. This, however, can sometimes take decades to achieve given that Supreme Court justices serve for life. Thus, vacancies on the Court occur only once every few

5. 410 U.S. 113

years on average. For example, sometimes a president will serve out an entire presidential term of office without having even a single chance to nominate a judge for the Supreme Court. The public must then continue to elect president after president, and Senate after Senate, until there are enough judges on the Court who agree with the public. This explains why change in Supreme Court legal doctrines typically occurs so slowly. Yet the public need not always wait, as sometimes justices end up voting quite differently from how the President and Senate expected them to vote.

The Court's power to interpret the Constitution underlies why presidential nominations for the Supreme Court can result in such prolonged and heated battles in the Senate. Each judge on the Supreme Court will likely shape U.S. law for several decades during his or her time on the Court. Also, their collective decisions can change the meaning of the Constitution for future decades or even centuries. This sometimes radically reshapes U.S. society, as occurred when the Court reinterpreted the Commerce Clause and upheld the New Deal legislation during the Great Depression. These rulings greatly expanded the power of Congress into many new areas of public policy that Congress had never before regulated. For better or for worse (depending on one's point of view), everyone agrees we would live in a very different U.S. today if the Court had not ruled the way it had in the late 1930's. And, unless a future Court were to reverse the New Deal rulings (which seems very unlikely), we will continue to live in a United States with a large, powerful central government for decades or centuries to come.

---

*Questions for Review and Discussion*

1. Describe the basic organizational structure of state and federal courts.
2. Describe the basic appellate procedure of the federal courts.
3. Describe several different situations that make a case nonjusticiable.
4. Describe the concept of judicial review and explain what gives U.S. courts that power.
5. Who was more accurate in their prophecy about the future of the U.S. Supreme Court: Hamilton or Brutus? Give evidence in support.

---

*Suggested Readings*

*Marbury v. Madison*, 5 U.S. 137 (1803)
*Nixon v. U.S.*, 506 U.S. 224 (1993)
*Lujan v. Defenders of Wildlife*, 504 U.S. 555 (1992)

*Federal Rules of Civil Procedure*
*Rules of the Supreme Court of the United States*

---

*Advanced Readings*

Lawrence Baum, *American Courts: Policy and Process* 7th Edition (2013)
Gerald Rosenberg, *The Hollow Hope: Can Courts Bring About Social Change, 2d Edition* (2008)

CHAPTER 3

# STATUTES

*Chapter Objectives*
*After reading this chapter, you should be able to:*

- Describe the concept of statutes and identify examples
- List and explain several reasons why statutes need interpretation
- List and explain many common canons of statutory construction
- Describe legislative purpose and the problem in applying the concept
- Apply principles of statutory interpretation to a factual hypothetical

*Statutes*, also called *codes*, are laws made by legislatures or other collective law-making bodies according to procedures set out by constitutions. In the United States, there are state statutes made by state legislatures acting under authority given to them by their state constitutions, and there are federal statutes made by Congress, acting under authority given to Congress by the U.S. Constitution. Laws made by city councils or other legislative bodies in towns, villages, and cities, collectively called municipalities, are called *ordinances*. Laws made by administrative bodies, such as the federal Environmental Protection Agency, are called *administrative rules* or *administrative regulations*. Statutes, ordinances, and regulations are all interpreted in a very similar manner, and together comprise the most common types of laws. Statutes are the most frequently applied type of laws in the United States. Federal statutes define, among many other things, immigration law, bankruptcy law, environmental law, and labor law, and include education law and tax law as well. Federal statutes also increasingly determine how health care in the U.S. is regulated and funded. State statutes define and significantly regulate torts, contracts, real estate, education, marriage and divorce, child custody, inheritance, business licensing, and crimes, and include state-regulated components of education and taxation. Local city ordinances define, among other things, what type of building you may build and where, how you have to build it, and how tall you can let the grass in your lawn grow. Also, there is often much overlap in what the federal, state, and local governments regulate, such as when it relates to environmental regulations or taxation. The principles of statutory interpretation apply to statutes, ordinances and regulations, although there are a few relatively minor differences as we will see later in this chapter.

Before we look at a list of some specific canons of statutory construction, there are some general background legal principles that are important. First, under basic principles of law, higher law always overrides any inconsistent lower law. As a result, constitutions supersede statutes and regulations, federal statutes and regulations supersede state statutes and local ordinances, and state statutes and regulations supersede local ordinances. For example, the U.S. Constitution supersedes all Congressional statutes and state laws, whereas the New York Constitution supersedes all New York statutes. Also, administrative agencies get their authority from statutes. As a result, any statute enacted by a legislative body overrides any administrative regulation created by a bureaucratic agency that gets its authority from that legislative body. For example, Congressional statutes override federal administrative regulations, and Florida statutes override regulations made by any of Florida's administrative agencies.

Second, under the U.S. system of federalism, all federal law supersedes all state and local law under what is called the *pre-emption doctrine*. That is, federal law pre-empts (overrides) any contrary state and local law. This doctrine comes from the Supremacy Clause in Article VI of the U.S. Constitution:

> This Constitution, and the Laws of the United States which shall be made in pursuance thereof; and all treaties made, or which shall be made, under the authority of the United States, shall be the supreme law of the land; and the judges in every state shall be bound thereby, anything in the constitution or laws of any state to the contrary notwithstanding.

The order of priority of U.S. law thus goes as follows:

U.S. Constitution<br>
↓<br>
Federal statutes<br>
↓<br>
Federal administrative regulations<br>
↓<br>
State constitutions<br>
↓

State statutes
↓
State administrative regulations
↓
Municipal ordinances

If there is any conflict, contradiction, or inconsistency between any lower law and higher law, the higher law always overrides the lower law.

A third basic principle of law is that all laws apply only prospectively (to future conduct), not retroactively (to the past), unless the law expressly declares otherwise. This is true for constitutional provisions, statutes, administrative regulations, municipal ordinances, and so on. In the case of these types of laws, they often include a date upon which the law takes effect. If no such date is listed, then the law takes effect immediately upon enactment. For example, the U.S. Constitution requires that all bills (proposed federal statutes) be passed by both chambers of Congress and then be signed by the President. If Congress passes a bill with no effective date listed in it, then the moment the President signs that bill it not only becomes a federal statute, it also takes effect immediately.

## Why Interpret Statutes?

Human beings are imperfect creatures. Our language and communication is correspondingly imperfect as well. Any written law will therefore be imperfectly written. Although no law is perfectly written, there are degrees of imperfection. The more imperfectly written the law, the more the need for courts to figure out what the statutes means. Here are a few common types of situations where the provisions of a statute especially call for judicial interpretation.

*Clarification of Vague or Ambiguous Terms* Let's look at merely a few of the countless ways statutes can be vague or ambiguous:

- A statute outlaws "defacing public buildings" (plural). What if a defendant defaces only one (singular) public building?

- A statute forbids possessing a gun "in the vicinity of a school." What if a defendant possesses a gun "in" a school?

- A statute imposes an additional sales tax on businesses engaged in "lodging" but not on businesses engaged in "recreation." Is a commercially run tent campground engaged in "lodging" or "recreation"?

- A federal tariff is applied to imported "vegetables" but not "fruit." Is a tomato a fruit or a vegetable under this law? Even such a mundane question as this made it to the U.S. Supreme Court given the financial stakes involved. See *Nix v. Hedden*, 149 U.S. 403 (1893).

- A statute forbids "using" a gun during a crime. What if a robber "uses" a gun as barter for drugs? What if the robber "uses" a non-working antique rifle as a walking cane during the crime? See *Smith v. U.S.*, 508 223 (1993) and Justice Scalia's dissent.

*Resolution of Omissions or Other Mistakes* Legislative drafters often overlook errors or fail to foresee the potential consequences of the language they have chosen to use in the statute. Here are a few examples:

- A person commits robbery if "he uses force or threat of force." What if the defendant is a woman?

- A "not" is accidentally inserted into a bill, thereby radically changing the meaning of the law to something entirely unintended and undesirable. For example:

*Mistake in Arkansas Law Allows Any Age to Marry if Parents Agree*
[Associated Press, August 17, 2007]

A law passed this year allows Arkansans of any age—even infants—to marry if their parents agree, and the governor may have to call a special session to fix the mistake, lawmakers said Friday.

The legislation was intended to establish 18 as the minimum age to marry but also allow pregnant teenagers to marry with parental consent, bill sponsor Rep. Will Bond said. An extraneous "not" in the bill, however, allows anyone who is not pregnant to marry at any age if the parents allow it.

"It's clearly not the intent to allow 10-year-olds or 11-year-olds to get married," Bond said. "The legislation was screwed up."

The bill reads: "In order for a person who is younger than eighteen (18) years of age and who is not pregnant to obtain a marriage license, the person must provide the county clerk with evidence of parental consent to the marriage." . . .

> "We need a special session to fix this," Sen. Sue Madison said. "I am concerned about pedophiles coming to Arkansas to find parents who are willing to sign a very young child's consent." . . .

*Address Unforeseen Developments* Unforeseen developments typically occur with technological advancement. For example, after the invention of the automobile, Congress outlawed the theft of "motor vehicles." Later, the airplane was invented, and its use became widespread. If a defendant steals an airplane, is the defendant guilty of stealing a "motor vehicle?" The U.S. Circuit Court of Appeals said yes; the U.S. Supreme Court said no. [See *McBoyle v. U.S.*, 283 U.S. 25 (1931)]

Another instance of technology outpacing the law is in the area of end-of-life care and decision-making. Statutes regarding living wills, durable power of attorneys, euthanasia, doctor-assisted suicide, guardianship, and other related laws have usually failed to keep up with medical advancements. If machines can keep a physical body alive far past the point where the brain—that is, the *person*—has already died, then when does "death" occur?

Similarly, privacy laws have failed to keep pace with digital technology. People currently have surprisingly little legal protection against the collection, storage, and use of personal information. This data collection is done both by private companies and the government, and is obtained through individuals' e-mail, texts, phone calls, and web surfing on the internet, as well as other electronic communication and electronic transactions.

*Resolve Internal Conflict* Sometimes within a code of laws, one statute will say "x" yet another statute will say "not-x." Sometimes the contradiction can occur even within the same statute. A famous example of statutory contradiction occurred in the U.S. Presidential election in the year 2000. One section of the Florida election law statute stated that votes in the presidential election *must* be turned in by a deadline to be valid and counted. Another section in that same statute, however, declared that votes could be turned in *after* that same deadline. So, must votes be counted prior to the deadline or can they still be counted after that deadline? In light of the direct contradiction in the law, the Florida Supreme Court ruled that the statute must be interpreted in favor of counting votes regardless of the deadline. The U.S. Supreme Court then overruled that decision,[1] ruling that the state law must be interpreted consistent with the *goal* of federal election law, which is to ensure a speedy and final vote count in presidential elections. Thus, once the statutory deadline passed, no more presidential votes could be counted.

1. *Bush v. Gore*, 531 U.S. 98 (2000)

## Plain Meaning and Textualism

Given the never-ending need to clear up confusion in the way statutes are written, courts must offer clarifications of the meaning of statutes. The principles used to interpret statutes are called principles of *statutory interpretation.* Statutory interpretation is also frequently called *statutory construction* from the verb "to construe" meaning "to interpret." Legal scholars have written multi-volume treatises on statutory construction. A basic understanding of a relatively few number of principles, however, will probably address at least ninety-five per cent or more of all questions of statutory construction. These principles generally apply to ordinances and administrative regulations as well.

The first step in interpreting a statute begins with the text of the law—what does the law actually say? The first thing to consider in this regard is whether the words used in the law have a *plain meaning.* Is there an obvious meaning on the face of the law from the language used? For example, a judge could look to dictionary definitions of the words used so as to determine the statutory meaning of the words. That section of the statute would then be interpreted to mean whatever the plain meaning of the words are based on their common definitions.

The problem is that the plain meaning of words is not always clear. Some statutes are very clear. For example, some laws involve what are called *bright-line rules,* also known as *bright-line distinctions.* This means there is an extremely clear division in the law between what is required or not, or prohibited or not, or between classifications, and so on. Bright-line rules commonly involve laws that have numerical components. This can involve age, as in a law that requires people to be 21 years of age to purchase alcohol. It doesn't matter if one's age is 20 years, 364 days, 23 hours, 59 minutes, and 59 seconds: it's still illegal to buy alcohol. Merely one second later, however, that same person may legally buy alcohol. Time can also be a bright-line distinction if defined precisely. For example, a statute might say that a response to a lawsuit must be filed within 30 days. If the business office of the clerk of court closes at exactly 5:00 p.m. the end of that 30th day, and the plaintiff has failed to filed the lawsuit before the business window closed, then the lawsuit is now late. Another example might be construction codes involving the precise measurements of door widths, window heights, and so on. Or, an anti-pollution statute might fix the limit of a pollutant in a public drinking water supply at 5 ppm (parts per million) and no more. There may be non-numerical bright-line distinctions as well, but numerically-based statutes offer the best examples of bright-line rules.

Unfortunately, bright-line distinctions are relatively uncommon in the law. Most statutes use words that are vague or ambiguous. Many statutes also contain gaps and omissions. Some statutes may even contradict other statutes, contain text that is inconsistent with other text within that same statute, or seem contrary to the overall purpose of the statute itself. So how should a statute be interpreted in these instances? If one followed only the "plain meaning" of the words of the statute, that interpretation might not resolve the ambiguity or inconsistency within the statute. This is why some legal scholars prefer a theory of statutory interpretation called *textualism*. Textualism looks at the larger political and social context of a statute and its language.

The most famous proponent of statutory textualism was U.S. Supreme Court Justice Antonin Scalia who died in 2016. Under his theory of textualism, one should not look only at the dictionary definitions or originally intended "plain meaning" of isolated words within a statute. Instead, one must look at the larger context of what those words usually mean within the law or within the larger society. Justice Scalia regularly defended this approach to statutory interpretation. As he explained in one case:

> The statute excludes only merchandise "of foreign manufacture," which the majority says might mean "manufactured by a foreigner" rather than "manufactured in a foreign country." I think not. Words, like syllables, acquire meaning not in isolation but within their context. While looking up the separate word "foreign" in a dictionary might produce the reading the majority suggests, that approach would also interpret the phrase "I have a foreign object in my eye" as referring, perhaps, to something from Italy. The phrase "of foreign manufacture" is a common usage, well understood to mean "manufactured abroad."[2]

A year later, Justice Scalia offered a more refined explanation of his general approach:

> The meaning of terms on the statute books ought to be determined, not on the basis of which meaning can be shown to have been understood by a larger handful of the Members of Congress; but rather on the basis of which meaning is (1) most in accord with context and ordinary usage, and thus most likely to have been understood by the whole Congress which voted on the words of the statute (not to mention the citizens subject to it), and (2) most compatible with the surrounding body of law into which the provision must be integrated—a compatibility which, by a benign fic-

2. *K-Mart v. Cartier, 486 U.S. 281 319* (1988) Scalia, J., concurring in part and dissenting in part.

tion, we assume Congress always has in mind. I would not permit any of the historical and legislative material discussed by the Court, or all of it combined, to lead me to a result different from the one that these factors suggest."[3]

## Canons of Statutory Construction

Besides looking at plain meaning and textual context, there are hundreds of legal principles that can be employed when trying to interpret the meaning of a statute. The principles of statutory interpretation are also collectively called the *canons* of statutory construction. Given that so many statutes are unclear in their meaning, judges use the canons of statutory construction as guidelines in determining the meaning of a statute. Ironically, canons of statutory construction are used to help one to decide the plain meaning of a statute when the statute does *not* have a plain meaning on its face.

If one consults a treatise on statutory construction, one will find hundreds of principles of statutory construction. A few dozen canons, however, comprise the principles of statutory construction referred to in the large majority of all cases of statutory interpretation. These canons are *not* rigid rules, but are merely helpful guidelines. The canons sometimes contradict each other, and are often ignored. Indeed, the so-called rules of statutory interpretation are so flexible that a court can almost always find *some* canon to support nearly any desired interpretation of a statute. Nevertheless, judges frequently cite these principles as legal support when concluding that a statute has a particular meaning.

Below are a few of the more basic and most common canons of statutory construction. The rules below are not numbered because there is no rank ordering of the canons of statutory construction. In other words, one or more of the canons can be applied by a judge in a case depending on how that individual judge believes the rules should be prioritized in that particular case. The rules themselves can roughly be grouped into sets of rules that address interpretation of individuals words, phrases comprised of multiple words, sections of a statute, or the statute as a whole. We will consider a few of the interpretive rules that apply in each these situations.

*Meaning of Individual Words* One group of rules of statutory construction addresses the meaning of individual words. Some of the most common such rules are:

3. *Green v Bock Laundry Mach. Co.*, 490 U.S. 504, 528 (1989) Scalia, J., concurring.

- The legislature intends to use ordinary words in their ordinary senses according to the dictionary and common everyday use. That is, words are intended to be used according to their plain meaning unless indicated otherwise.

- If the law in general or a particular statute defines a word other than how a dictionary would defines that word, then the legal definition becomes a legal "term of art." The legal definition should be used, not the dictionary definition. For example, if a statute defines "vehicle" as "any vehicle that travels on land" then the statutory "vehicle" would not include boats or planes.

- The word "may" means an action is permissible but not required. That is, the word "may" indicates the action is optional. The word "shall," on the other hand, means the action is mandatory. For example, Article II of the U.S. Constitution says the President "shall from time to time give to the Congress information of the state of the union." The President's delivery of the State of the Union address is therefore a legal obligation (although the address could be either written or spoken).

- The word "and" means that the term or condition on both sides of the "and" must occur. The word "or," on the other hand, means that only one term or condition on either side of the "or" must occur. The crime of robbery, for example, is not committed unless a defendant both commits theft *and* does so with the threat or use of force.

- Whether a noun found in a statute is singular or plural, it shall be treated as covering both singular and plural occurrences of the noun. In this way, the crime of "stealing street signs" occurs even if only a single street sign is stolen. Likewise, a prohibition on "defacing a building" is violated when multiple buildings are defaced.

*Statutes with Exceptions, Exemptions* Another set of canons of statutory interpretation deals with the situation when a statute includes a list, exception(s), or exemption(s). What exactly is included and excluded from them? Some of the rules that apply in these circumstances are:

- If a list in a statute does not expressly include an item, that item is not included in the scope of the law. This is known as the principle of *expressio unius est exclusio alterius.* This is Latin for "The expression of one thing is the exclusion of another." For example, let's say a municipal ordinance reads "Residents may keep dogs or cats as household pets." The listing of only dogs and cats implies no other pets may be kept. Thus, a pot-bellied pig would be forbidden.

- If a list in a statute includes a catch-all phrase covering that list, the catch-all coverage is narrowly limited to only items that are similar to the listed items. This is known as the principle of *ejusdem generis*, Latin for "of the same kind." For example, imagine a city ordinance that reads "City residents may keep dogs, cats, or other household pets." The phrase "other household pets" would probably include ferrets or pot-bellied pigs, but it would not include alligators or elephants.

- If a statute expressly contains an exception to a rule, this implies there are no other exceptions to the rule. For example, imagine a statute that imposes a tax on businesses engaged in temporary commercial lodging (that is, a hotel tax). If the statute clearly exempts private tent campgrounds from the tax, but offers no other exceptions, then a private RV (recreational vehicle) park would not be able to claim the exemption.

*Problems of Statutory Inconsistency* Another group of rules of statutory interpretation involves the frequent problem of statutory inconsistency. This occurs when part of a statute contradicts another part of the same statute, or when part or all of one statute contradicts part or all of another statute. Some of the relevant rules that address these situations are:

- All parts of the same statute must be harmonized with the rest of the statute, rather than eliminating any part of the statute. Courts must assume the legislature meant every part of a statute to work together consistently, such that no parts would be internally contradictory.

- A more specific part of a statute overrides a contradictory general part. A general real estate tax on all commercial buildings, for example, would not apply to hotels if a specific tax exemption applies to "temporary commercial lodging."

- A later-enacted statute overrides a prior statute to the degree they are clearly contradictory. Put differently, a law made later in time by a legislative body supersedes a law made by that same legislative body made earlier in time. However, for a potentially contradictory canon of interpretation, see the next canon below.

- A prior statute is not to be deemed fully repealed unless the legislature expressly repeals it. For example, imagine that a 1996 real estate tax law imposes a 2% tax on owned homes and 3% tax on rental apartments. A new 2006 tax law raising rental apartment taxes to 4% would automatically override the prior 3% tax on rental apartments even if the legislature did not expressly say they were repealing the prior tax. Since the new tax rate did not mention anything about the tax rate on home ownership, however, the prior 2% tax on home ownership would remain untouched.

- Contradictory statutes must be harmonized with each other to the degree possible, rather than eliminating parts of either statute. Courts must assume the legislature did not intend to contradict itself, unless the statute expressly said it was superseding other previously enacted statutes that differ. Sometimes this assumption is impossible, though, such as if one statute says specifically "x" but another later statute says specifically "not-x." You can see that this principle somewhat goes against the principle that later statutes override earlier contradictory statutes.

*Apparent Redundancy* In addition to statutes contradicting themselves, the opposite problem sometimes occurs: apparent redundancy. How does one interpret two sections of a statute to mean different things when the language is similar but not identical? The rule that addresses this situation states that all parts of a statute should have a separate meaning and not be redundant with the rest of the statute. That is, the statute should not be interpreted so as to render one of its provisions or sections meaningless, as if that part doesn't exist, or is "mere surplusage." It should be assumed that the legislature meant something different in the two parts of the statute.

*The Statute as a Whole* A different set of rules of statutory interpretation deals with the broader question of how interpretation of a statute should be approached as a whole. Some of these rules include:

- If the language of a statute is clear (that is, if the statutory language has a plain meaning), then the courts should not look beyond the words of the statute for additional evidence of the meaning or legislative purpose of the statute.

- Even if the words of a statute are clear, the plain meaning of a statute should not be interpreted in a manner that directly conflicts with the legislative purpose of the statute. Notice that this rule contradicts the rule just listed that when a statute has a plain meaning, then no other evidence of legislative intent should be considered.

- Similarly, and also contradictory to the first rule listed in this section, courts are to assume legislatures did not intend an absurd or unjust result when they wrote the statute. That is, if the apparently plain language of a statute causes an absurd or grossly unjust result, courts should conclude that such a possible interpretation of the statute's language is incorrect. This may mean a court has to essentially rewrite the statue to add an exception or eliminate an exception. On rare occasion, a court might even declare that where a statute says "x," the statute really means (or was intended to mean) "not-x," or vice versa.

- If the words of a statute are ambiguous, the legislative purpose of the statute can help clarify the meaning of the statute. Legislative purpose can be derived from the surrounding circumstance of the making of the law, such as the problem(s) the legislature was trying to solve. Legislative purpose might also be indicated in quotes by legislators or legislative committee reports during the lawmaking process, or might be stated in the law itself. Even the title of a statute can often provide evidence as to the legislative purpose.

*Severability* In addition to the rules of statutory interpretation listed above, there is one that is somewhat more complex to apply. This is the doctrine of "severability." Under this rule, if one part of a statute is ruled unconstitutional, but the rest of the statute can survive even without the unconstitutional part, then the unconstitutional part is *severable.* That is, the unconstitutional part can be "severed," or cut out of, the rest of the statute. If the unconstitutional part is integral to the overall working of the statute, however, then the statute lacks severability, and the entire statute must be ruled unconstitutional. Severability is generally presumed unless a statute says otherwise. That is, legislatures often expressly declare in a statute whether that statute is severable or nonseverable.

A famous example where the issue of severability came up was in the U.S. Supreme Court case of *NFIB v. Sebelius* in 2012.[4] Congress had

4. *NFIB v. Sebelius*, 567 U.S. 519 (2012)

passed extensive health care legislation called the Patient Protection and Affordable Care Act. Because President Barack Obama was the lead advocate of the legislation, the health care program was more commonly referred to as "Obamacare." The law required all adult individuals to purchase health care insurance; this requirement was called the "individual mandate." The law correspondingly required all health insurance companies to provide insurance for their customers regardless of any pre-existing medical conditions the insured person might have. The U.S. Supreme Court had to decide if requiring individuals to buy health insurance violated Congress's power under the Commerce Clause. However, if the individual mandate were struck down, no one would bother to buy health insurance until they are sick or injured, knowing that insurance companies would be legally required to insure them. This would mean that all health insurance companies would quickly go bankrupt. In oral argument before the Court, it seemed clear that the individual mandate to buy health insurance was not severable from the mandate that insurance companies must cover anyone with a pre-existing condition. That is, if the individual mandate was struck down, then the requirement for coverage of pre-existing conditions had to be struck down also. Even though the question of severability had been heavily briefed by the parties in the case and was extensively argued during oral argument, the Court never decided the question. Since the Court upheld the individual mandate, the Court did not need to decide whether that part of the statute was severable from the rest of the statute.

In addition to the canons of statutory construction discussed so far, there are also additional rules of statutory interpretation that apply when particular types of laws are involved. For example, the U.S. Supreme Court has said that when a statute might possibly violate part of the U.S. Constitution, then a particular rule of statutory interpretation applies. If there is a choice between two interpretations of the statute, one that causes a potential problem of the constitutionality of the statute and one that does not, the interpretation is preferred that does not raise a constitutional concern. This principle is part of a general policy put forth by the U.S. Supreme Court to avoid constitutional issues unless necessary.

The Supreme Court has also announced particular rules of interpretation that apply when the meaning of a federal administrative regulation is in question. In cases involving interpretation of regulations issued by federal bureaucratic agencies, one such rule is that courts are to give significant deference, though not absolute deference, to the agency's interpretation of its own rule if that rule was made through the regular rulemaking process of that agency. This particular interpretive rule is known as the *Chevron* rule since the Supreme Court announced the rule in the 1984 case *Chevron v. Natural Resources Defense Council.*[5]

Moreover, in federal criminal law, the U.S. Supreme Court applies a "rule of lenity." This rule states that a vague or ambiguous criminal statute must be interpreted in favor of the defendant. Thus, if there is doubt about how a statute legally defines a crime, the statute should be given whichever interpretation prohibits the least amount of conduct. This rule is based on notions of due process. One aspect of due process includes the principle that it is unjust to charge people with a crime if the law was not clear enough to give fair warning to people about what the law either required or prohibited. In short, this rule gives accused persons the "benefit of the doubt."

The canons listed and described here are only a few of the most commonly used ones. Again, keep in mind that these are not hard-and-fast rules, nor do they have any ranking. These "rules" of interpretation are merely general guidelines. Moreover, as can be seen, different principles of statutory construction can contradict each another in a given case. For example, when a statutory list is in question, judges often disagree whether the principle of *ejusdem generis* or the principle of *expressio unius est exclusio alterius* applies. If a statute lists "X or Y," then *ejusdem generis* might say Z is impliedly included, but *expressio unius* says Z is impliedly excluded. This gives judges some leeway in interpreting the statute, and judges often disagree with each other about the "correct" meaning of a statute.

## Legislative Purpose

Even though some of the canons of statutory interpretation involve legislative purpose, the concept of legislative purpose needs more detailed discussion. If a statute has a "plain meaning," then the courts do not need to look any further for the meaning of the statute. If the statute lacks a plain meaning, then courts can look to canons of statutory construction. Yet because the canons are merely helpful but not mandatory rules, courts will also often look to the intent of the legislature in passing the statute anyway, even when there is a "plain meaning." This commonly occurs when the literal application of a statute results in an absurd or unjust result. The legislature's goal it had in mind when passing the law is called either *legislative purpose* or *legislative intent*. This purpose

5. *Chevron v. Natural Resources Defense Council*, 467 U.S. 834 (1984)

or intent can be determined by looking at committee reports, statements by committee members during legislative hearings, and records of public debates on the chamber floors when amending or voting on the statute.

This technique sounds simple in theory, but is often difficult if not impossible in practice. The problem in finding "the" legislature's intent is that often there is little or no evidence of the legislature's intent. When some evidence does exist it is often contradictory and can support multiple different interpretations of the evidence. This could happen when two legislators or groups of legislators who are all voting in favor of a law differ in what they believe the law is intended to accomplish. For example, this could be a narrow purpose versus a broad purpose, or even two different opposing purposes. Or, even if there is clear evidence, it might show the legislature as a whole had multiple purposes, some of which are in tension with each other.

A judge seeking to reach a particular interpretation of a statute can usually find *some* piece of legislative history to support the judge's conclusion. This means the majority and dissenting judges in a case interpreting a statute will often engage in what has sometimes been called the "battle of the quotes." Each judge will try to outdo the other in mustering quotes supporting a particular reading of "the" legislative purpose behind the statute. Judges are often able to pick and choose the quotes they like the most in order to interpret the statute however they wish. And, as we have seen, one of the canons of statutory interpretation is that if the "plain meaning" of a statute contradicts the purpose of the legislation, then a court should ignore the plain meaning. In such situations, courts should instead interpret the statute in a manner that is consistent with the purpose of the statute, even if that means completely contradicting the plain meaning.

Ironically, as we have seen under another of the canons of statutory interpretation, if a statute has what appears to be a plain meaning, then courts are not supposed to look at the legislative purpose. Yet the legislative purpose might show that the alleged plain meaning is contrary to the legislative purpose! Indeed, a pair of famous U.S. Supreme Court cases illustrate how judges can choose to follow either the plain meaning of a statute or the legislative purpose when the two are in conflict.

In *Church of the Holy Trinity v. U.S.* (1892),[6] the federal Alien Contract Labor Law prohibited "importation" of "foreigners" to perform "labor or service of any kind." Despite the all-encompassing language of the statute, the Court said that Congress could not have intended the purpose of the statute to prevent the hiring of a Christian minister from overseas. The Court asserted "It is a familiar rule, that a thing may be

6. *Church of the Holy Trinity v. U.S.*, 143 U.S. 457 (1892)

within the letter of the statute and yet not within the statute, because not within its spirit, nor within the intention of its makers."

Yet only a couple decades later, in *Caminetti v. U.S.* (1917)[7], the Supreme Court interpreted the Mann Act, whose clear and express legislative purpose was to target the interstate enslavement of women as prostitutes. The statute criminalized not just enslavement, but the transportation of women across state borders for "any other immoral purpose." Applying the literal "plain meaning" of the catch-all phrase, the Court upheld a conviction of a married man who drove his mistress across a state border where they planned on having an extramarital affair. The Court announced "Where the language is plain and admits of no more than one meaning, the duty of interpretation does not arise, and the rules which are to aid doubtful meanings need no discussion."

The fact that the canons of statutory interpretation provide so much interpretive leeway to judges means that sometimes statutory interpretation simply comes down to the personal moral, political, or policy preferences of the judges. Indeed, we saw in the earlier chapter on jurisprudence how sometimes judges divide over whether to follow the positive law or the natural law. This comes down to the judicial philosophy of the judges deciding the case: is justice more important than following the exact letter of the law. For example, imagine an eighteen-year-old high school senior has consensual sex with his seventeen-year-old high school senior girlfriend on prom night. She becomes pregnant, her parents find out, and they insist that the local prosecutor bring charges against the boy for "statutory rape." In that jurisdiction, statutory rape is clearly defined as any sexual behavior by an adult with a minor regardless of consent or the circumstances. The state law there also says if someone is found guilty of statutory rape, the defendant must be sentenced to 20-years mandatory minimum imprisonment and be publicly labeled as "sex offender" for life. If the parents of the girl convince a prosecutor to bring charges against the boy, how should the trial judge rule? What was the legislature's purpose in criminalizing such behavior? Did the legislature intend it to apply in this instance? Should the judge rule strictly according to the "plain meaning" of the law or according to what the judge believes is "just" in this instance?

A famous historical example of the choice between natural law and positive law being decided by rules of statutory construction is the 1889 case of *Riggs v. Palmer* discussed in the earlier chapter on jurisprudence. Recall that in *Riggs*, the judges on the high court of New York divided over whether a young man who murdered his grandfather could inherit most of his grandfather's estate as his grandfather's will directed. The statutory language was clear that wills must be strictly followed unless

7. *Caminetti v. U.S.*, 242 U.S. 470 (1917)

one of the specific exceptions were met. There was no specific exception for when the deceased is murdered by someone who stands to inherit from the deceased's will. The court majority believed that this unjust outcome could not possibly have been intended by the legislature to be a consequence of the statute governing wills.

> It is quite true that statutes regulating the making, proof and effect of wills, and the devolution of property, if literally construed, and if their force and effect can in no way and under no circumstances be controlled or modified, give this property to the murderer. The purpose of those statutes was to enable testators to dispose of their estates to the objects of their bounty at death, and to carry into effect their final wishes legally expressed; and in considering and giving effect to them this purpose must be kept in view. It was the intention of the law-makers that the donees in a will should have the property given to them. But it never could have been their intention that a donee who murdered the testator to make the will operative should have any benefit under it. If such a case had been present to their minds, and it had been supposed necessary to make some provision of law to meet it, it cannot be doubted that they would have provided for it. It is a familiar canon of construction that a thing which is within the intention of the makers of a statute is as much within the statute as if it were within the letter; and a thing which is within the letter of the statute is not within the statute, unless it be within the intention of the makers.

As can be seen in *Riggs v. Palmer*, the judges in the majority used a canon of statutory interpretation regarding legislative purpose as a justification in applying natural law rather than the statutory positive law. The dissent, on the other hand, believed the plain language of the statute should be followed, thereby validating the will:

> The statutes of this state have prescribed various ways in which a will may be altered or revoked; but the very provision, defining the modes of alteration and revocation, implies a prohibition of alteration or revocation in any other way. The words of the section of the statute are: "No will in writing, except in the cases hereinafter mentioned, nor any part thereof, shall be revoked or altered otherwise," etc. Where, therefore, none of the cases mentioned are met by the facts, and the revocation is not in the way described in the section, the will of the testator is unalterable. I think that a valid will must continue as a will always, unless revoked in the manner provided by the statutes.

A more recent example of flexibility in statutory construction by reference to legislative purpose when interpreting a Congressional statute is the 2015 U.S. Supreme Court case *King v. Burwell.*[8] In *King*, the Court had to interpret the meaning of a small but important part of the Patient Protection and Affordable Care Act, more commonly referred to as "Obamacare." A majority of the Court read the phrase "established by the state" to mean "established by the state *or federal government.*" The majority basically rewrote the statute to add in the clarifying words to make this part of the statute consistent with what the Court majority saw was Congress's legislative purpose: expanding affordable health care to the uninsured and underinsured.

In Justice Antonin Scalia's dissent, however, he believed the statute's plain meaning was "established by the state," and not "established by the state or federal government." He then accused the majority of "interpretive jiggery-pokery." In response to media coverage of Scalia's humorous use of an obscure term, *Time* magazine ran a short article explaining the origin and meaning of the term:

> Jiggery-pokery dates back to at least the late 1800s, a rhythmic English phrase describing dishonest manipulation or nonsense, akin to hocus pocus, humbug, bambosh, baloney, berley (among the Australians), bunkum, hogwash (also known as eyewash), flapdoodle, flim-flam, flumadiddle, rubbish, galbanum (coming from a French word for empty representations), hooey, hot air, motormouthing, poppycock or malarkey.[9]

Indeed, as can be seen from the chapter here and from looking at real-world examples of statutory construction cases, there are numerous and contradictory rules of statutory interpretation. Judges may pick freely from among the rules to reach differing conclusions about the "plain meaning" of a statute. When legislative purpose is examined, judges can often engage in a "battle of the quotes" to reach differing conclusions about legislative purpose. Together these tactics often allow judges to engage in a significant degree of "jiggery-pokery" to conclude the words in statutes mean something other than what the words actually say. Indeed, in 1950 the prominent legal scholar Karl Llewelyn wrote what is now a famous law review article listing a side-by-side chart showing how canons of statutory construction can be used to counteract each other.[10] In short, judges have a great deal of leeway to pick and

8. *King v. Burwell*, 576 U.S. ___ (2015)

9. Katy Steinmetz, "This is what 'jiggery-pokery' means," in *TIME* Magazine online, June 25, 2015

10. Karl Llewelyn, "Remarks on the Theory of Appellate Decision and the Rule or Canons about how Statutes are to be Construed," 3. *Vand. L. Rev.* 395 (1950)

choose canons of interpretation to reach quite different and even opposite interpretations of statutes.

## Statutory Interpretation: "No Vehicles in the Park"

Let's examine statutory interpretation in the following example. Suppose the City of Ricksville enacts the following ordinance:

> Ordinance 42: Park Security Ordinance
>
> Section 1. The City of Ricksville finds that the presence of vehicles in city parks disturbs the peace and enjoyment of such parks and threatens the safety of persons using such parks. Therefore, the Ricksville City Council resolves:
>
> Section 2. No vehicles shall enter, be driven on, into, or through, or parked in, any sidewalks and grassy areas of city parks.
>
> Section 3. Any person violating section 2 shall be fined $500.

Imagine you are a judge and you must decide how the ordinance applies in each of the following cases that comes before you. In announcing each outcome you must explain which principles of statutory interpretation directly support your interpretation, and how those principles support your decision.

1. A large remote-controlled model plane being flown in the park's airspace.
2. A small remote-controlled model boat being used on the park pond.
3. A large motorized fishing boat being used on the park pond.
4. A police car parked on a lawn area to monitor a large music event in that area.
5. An ambulance driving on a lawn to reach a pregnant woman who went into labor.
6. A fire truck called to put out an unattended campfire in a lawn area.
7. A city garbage truck collecting trash from trash barrels in the lawn areas.
8. A city tree-trimming crane trimming large dead limbs off the trees in the lawn areas.

9. A plumbing truck driving on the sidewalk to reach the park restroom to repair it.

10. A sit-in toy car pushed by a child's feet being driven on the park sidewalks.

11. A large motorized electric sit-in kid's car being driven in a playground area.

12. A skateboard being used for trick stunts on fences and railings in the park.

13. A mountain bike being ridden on the tennis and basketball courts.

14. A non-motorized scooter being ridden on the park sidewalks.

15. A motorized scooter being driven on the park's tennis and basketball courts.

16. A baby stroller being pushed on the park sidewalks.

17. A wheelchair being pushed on the park sidewalks.

18. A motorized wheelchair being driven on the park sidewalks.

19. A parked and drivable army tank used as a war memorial in a lawn area.

20. A parked but undrivable army tank used as a war memorial in a lawn area.

## Statutory Interpretation Exercise: *Ricksville v. Konsor*

The previous practice exercise in statutory construction involving vehicles in a park was more simple than most statutory construction cases are in the real world. Let's now engage in a more elaborate practice exercise in statutory construction using an expanded hypothetical situation. In 2015, the City of Ricksville passed Ordinance 66, which states:

> Ordinance 66: *Prevention of Animal-Spread Disease*
>
> Section 1. The City Council finds that the keeping of livestock within residential areas of the city disturbs neighborhood quiet,

> causes unpleasant odors in the area, damages surface vegetation thereby leading to increased erosion and water quality problems, and contains risks to public health and safety through the possible spread of disease.
>
> Section 2. The keeping of live chickens, sheep, goats, cows, and other related livestock animals within city limits is prohibited.
>
> Section 3. Section 2 of this ordinance does not apply to animals used for medical research, as sports team mascots, in not-for-profit charity fundraising, commercial entertainment purposes, or any other similar purposes that do not involve raising animals for food production.
>
> Section 4. Section 2 of this ordinance does not apply to farms or licensed and regulated restaurants or slaughterhouse operations.
>
> Section 5. Violation of section 2 is punishable by $500 dollars fine and is subject to a judicial order requiring removal of the offending animals.

In 2016, the City of Ricksville passed Ordinance 72, which states:

> Ordinance 72: *Promotion of Animal Companions*
>
> Section 1. The City Council finds that animal companions provide therapeutic benefits that improve the physical and mental health of the persons sharing such companionships.
>
> Section 2. The City Council wishes to foster and promote the mental and physical health of its residents.
>
> Section 3. The keeping of cats, dogs, rabbits, ferrets, or other domesticated animals as personal animal companions within city limits is encouraged and is permitted without a license.
>
> Section 4. Definitions.
>
> a. "Domesticated" means tamed, typically by breeding, to live in close association with humans as a pet or work animal and usually making the animal dependent on human care for its survival.
>
> b. "Animal companion" means an animal whose needs can be readily met by living in a human home or through close daily relations with a human.

Greg Konsor, an elderly single homeowner living in Ricksville who suffers from mild depression, purchased a 65-pound pet pot-bellied pig named Mr. Oinkers as a pet. Greg played with Oinkers regularly and walked him around the neighborhood every day. Greg's mood noticeably improved as a result. Greg could have kept Mr. Oinkers in the house, but Greg wanted Mr. Oinkers to get plenty of fresh air and exercise. As a result, Greg kept Mr. Oinkers in his back yard at night and when Greg wasn't at home. Mr. Oinkers tore up the vegetation in the entire back yard, causing soil erosion and increased water drainage onto the neighbor's lots. Mr. Oinkers also made grunting and occasional squealing noise at various intervals throughout the night, sometimes waking the neighbors. After complaints by neighbors, an officer with the city code enforcement came by Greg's residence. The officer told Greg he was in violation of Ordinance 66. When Greg cited Ordinance 72 as a defense, the officer replied that Ordinance 72 did not apply to pigs. Greg refused to get rid of Mr. Oinkers and was ticketed with a fine of $500. The city also filed a motion requesting that the court order Greg to remove Mr. Oinkers from the premises. Greg is now appearing in city court challenging the fine and the motion for a court order that Mr. Oinkers be removed from Greg's home.

1. What canons of statutory construction would Greg Konsor and the City of Ricksville each use to support their interpretations of the two relevant ordinances? What would those specific legal arguments be—that is, how would those canons apply in this instance according to each of the parties? On balance, who do you believe has the better legal arguments, and why?

2. Now take the same hypothetical, except instead of Greg keeping a pot-bellied pig as a pet, he buys a miniature horse named Winnie as a companion pet. What would be the legal arguments on both sides now?

3. Once again, take the same hypothetical, but this time Greg buys a domesticated turkey named Princess Gobbles as a companion pet. As before, what would be the legal arguments on both sides?

4. Yet again, the same hypothetical, but Greg buys a domesticated and retired sleigh-pulling reindeer named Rudolf. What would be the legal arguments on both sides?

5. Now Greg adopts a 150-pound orangutan named Dr. Zaius. Dr. Zaius is calm, peaceful, gentle, and obedient to humans. Greg's depression completely disappears. However, Dr. Zaius moderately tears up the yard simply due to his size and constant pacing around the yard as part of his daily exercise routine. Dr. Zaius is well-groomed and only occasionally makes noise. Yet he sometimes climbs over the neighbor's fences to play in their yards, unintentionally frightening the neighbors and their children. What would be the legal arguments on both sides?

6. Can you see other possible interpretive issues or problems that might come up with these two ordinances?

---

*Questions for Review and Discussion*

1. Why do statutes need interpretation? Give examples.
2. What are the major approaches to interpreting statutes? How do these approaches harmonize with each other or conflict with each other?
3. What are canons of statutory construction? List and describe five of them, with an example of each.
4. Do all the canons of statutory construction make sense? That is, are there any you disagree with such that they should be modified or eliminated?
5. As open-ended or inconsistent as the canons of statutory construction are, is there any other better method to interpreting the meaning of statutes?

---

*Suggested Readings*

*Nix v. Hedden*, 149 U.S. 403 (1893) ("fruit" versus "vegetable")
*Church of the Holy Trinity v. U.S.*, 143 U.S. 457 (1892) ("service of any kind")
*Caminetti v. U.S.*, 242 U.S. 470 (1917) ("or any other immoral purpose")
*Peacock v. Lubbock Compress Company*, 252 F.2d 892 (5th Cir. 1958) ("and")
*People v. Garcia*, 29 A.3d 255(N.Y. 2006) ("companion animal")
*Chevron, USA, Inc. v. Natural Resources Defense Council*, 467 U.S. 834 (1984) (administrative agency deference)
*Smith v. U.S.*, 508 U.S. 223 (1993) ("uses")
*King v. Burwell*, 576 U.S. ___ (2014) ("established by the state")
*U.S. v. McBoyle*, 283 U.S. 25 (1931) ("vehicle")
*State v. Stagno*, 739 P.2d 198 (Alaska 1987) ("motor vehicle")
*State v. Williams*, 449 So. 2d 744 (La. Ct. App. 1984) ("other means of conveyance")
*People ex rel. J.L.*, 800 N.W.2d 720 (S.D. 2011) (statutory rape)
*Riggs v. Palmer*, 2 N.E. 188 (N.Y. 1889) (enforcement of will)
*In Re Pavlinko Will*, 148 A.2d 528 (Pa. 1959) (enforcement of will)

---

*Advanced Readings*

Karl Llewelyn, "Remarks on the Theory of Appellate Decision and the Rule or Canons about how Statutes are to be Construed," 3. *Vand. L. Rev.* 395 (1950)
Antonin Scalia and Bryan A. Garner, *Reading Law: The Interpretation of Legal Texts* (2012)

CHAPTER 4

# INTERPRETING THE U.S. CONSTITUTION

---

*Chapter Objectives*

*After reading this chapter, you should be able to:*

- Describe the concept of a constitution and identify examples of it
- Explain why constitutions need interpretation and who interprets them
- Describe judicial philosophy and explain how it differs from political ideology
- Describe social science findings regarding the basis for judicial decision-making
- Explain originalism and nonoriginalism and identify examples of each
- Describe constitutional pragmatism and identify examples if it

---

A *constitution* is the highest law of an entity, such as a nation or a state, or of an organization such as a business, a not-for-profit group, or a social club. It is called a constitution because the document and the rules contained within it "constitute" the entity involved. That is, the document establishes, creates, founds, comprises, and makes up the entity referred to in the document. Acting in this capacity, the relevant constitution almost always states how the entity's leaders are selected, what the leaders' powers are, and the procedures the leaders must follow when making new rules that govern the entity. Because a constitution is the highest governing law of an entity, it overrules all rules or actions by officials within that entity that contradict the constitution. Although a written constitution could give absolute, unlimited authority to a ruler or rulers, generally constitutions are written specifically to limit the powers of the governing body of the entity, both in what they do and how they do it. In other words, constitutions provide both substantive limits and procedural rules regarding how the entity can function. In the context of this chapter, we'll consider the constitution for the United States as a nation.

## The U.S. Constitution

The United States Constitution puts many direct limits on what the different branches of government can do. The Constitution defines the powers of the Congress, the President, the Supreme Court, and the procedures that these government institutions must necessarily follow in exercising their powers. The U.S. Constitution provides for a government of specifically "enumerated powers" (a list of specific powers) rather than a broad, general, open-ended "police power." The U.S. Constitution creates a system of separation of powers with checks and balances that each branch of the government can apply against each other, rather than a consolidation of government power into any one single person or group of people. Under the Constitution, Congress is a bicameral (two-chamber) legislature rather than a unicameral (one-chamber) legislature. Rather than provide for a single national level of government, the Constitution creates a "federal system" that divides power between a central national government and regional state governments, but with the national government supreme over the state governments.

Under specific rules and procedures contained in the Constitution itself, the Constitution also allows for the possibility of it being added to or amended. Within four years of the signing of the Constitution in 1787, the states ratified the first ten amendments known as the Bill of Rights. These amendments guarantee basic and essential rights to citizens of the United States. Among other things, the Bill of Rights minimizes the involvement of government in religious matters, a principle more commonly known as the "separation of church and state." The Bill of Rights also protects the freedom of speech of individuals and the press, and gives many procedural and substantive protections to people suspected or accused of crimes.

The net effect of the seven articles in the U.S. Constitution and the original ten amendments reveals an overall design philosophy behind the writers of the U.S. Constitution to create *limited government.* A democratic form of government that is defined and limited by a constitution is called a *constitutional democracy.* The U.S. is therefore a constitutional democracy based on the concept of limited government.

## Why Interpret Constitutions?

Constitutions need interpretation for all the same reasons that statutes need interpretation: imperfect humans using imperfect human language will imperfectly write imperfect laws. Let's look at a few examples of how courts are needed to deal with issues in interpreting the meaning of the U.S. Constitution.

*Clarify Broad and Ambiguous Clauses* First, courts are needed to clarify vague and ambiguous provisions found in the Constitution. The U.S. Constitution is notorious for using extremely broad and vague terms. Such undefined terms include "the executive power," "the power to regulate commerce among the states," "the judicial power," "the freedom of speech," "the free exercise of religion," "unreasonable searches and seizures," "cruel and unusual punishment," "due process," "equal protection," and so on. Since the writing of the Constitution, the U.S. Supreme Court has had to create extremely elaborate and complex definitions to explain the meaning of these and other constitutional terms. As merely one example, over a period of a century, the Court has created many different categories of speech under the First Amendment. Each of those categories has different definitions, along with different rules regarding the circumstances under which government may regulate that type of speech. The various kinds of speech, each with its own definition and rules, include threats, fighting words, advocating violence, political dissent, religious expression, defamation, obscenity, and commercial advertising and labeling. Moreover, the Court has created differing rules for speech depending on the factual circumstances in which the speech occurs, such as books or other print media, broadcast media, the internet, public schools and universities, government employment, public spaces, prisons, or other restricted government-managed areas. As a result, there is no single definition of "free speech" but rather a wide array of rules that apply to different types of speech in different contexts.

*Resolve Internal Conflict* Second, courts are also needed to resolve internal conflict within the Constitution. Some of the clauses in the Constitution arguably contradict each other. Again, in the First Amendment, the people have the right to "the free exercise of religion." Yet that same First Amendment also says government "shall make no law respecting an establishment of religion." So, if a majority of public school students vote to have a prayer read over the loudspeaker to start each school day, which rule is followed: the right of the majority of students to practice their religion as they desire or the prohibition on government imposing an establishment of religion on the unwilling minority of students in a public setting?

As another example, the Commerce Clause in Article I, section 8 of the Constitution says Congress may regulate commerce among the several states. Yet the Tenth Amendment says the states have all powers reserved to them that are not given to the federal government. May Congress regulate the licensing of small local businesses on the claim that even such small local businesses have a remote but indirect effect on interstate commerce? Or is such local regulation a power reserved to the states?

As a final example, Article I, Section 8 of the Constitution says Congress has the power to raise armies, whereas the Thirteenth Amendment prohibits involuntary servitude. Is imposing a military draft a valid exercise of Congressional power, or does forcing someone into the military against their will constitute involuntary servitude? (So far the courts have said the military draft is not involuntary servitude.)

*Adjudicate Omissions* Third, constitutions also contain omissions that courts need to address. Nowhere in the U.S. Constitution or any of its amendments is there listed any right to marry, a right to refuse to be forcibly married, a right to decide whom to marry, a right to decide to have children, a right to refuse to be forced to have children, or a right to teach one's children any particular knowledge, skills, or values. There is similarly no listing of any right to decide whether, when, where, or how one's life will end. There is also no right of the individual to travel. There isn't even any right to vote listed in the Constitution! (All it says in the Fifteenth Amendment is that the government may not prohibit someone from voting simply because of that person's race). In the past half-century or more, the U.S. Supreme Court has increasingly expanded the meaning of the Constitution to include most of the above-listed "rights," even though there is no such language found anywhere in the Constitution. We will return to talk about this in more detail later in this chapter.

*Address Unforeseen Developments* Fourth, courts must also address unforeseen developments. As society changes, eventually situations arise that the writers of the Constitution did not consider when they wrote the document. Technological advancement in particular has often necessitated the Supreme Court addressing how the Constitution's principles apply to more modern times. For example, the Fourth Amendment prohibits "unreasonable searches and seizures" by the government of "persons, houses, papers, and effects." To what degree does this limit the government's ability to regulate or monitor electronic communication such as phone calls, e-mail, text messages, and internet web surfing? Or, to what degree does the Second Amendment's right to bear arms in self-defense protect an individual's right to possess advanced weapons technologies such as armor-piercing bullets, exploding shells, automatic assault rifles, or weapons more powerful than guns? For example, is there a right to own a bazooka, a tank, a cruise missile, or a stealth jet fighter, none of which existed at the time the Second Amendment was written? Or, how do the increases in size, population, urbanization, mobility, communication, and education of the people affect Congress's ability to regulate interstate commerce under the Commerce Clause? Because humans cannot foresee the future, no constitution can take into account all possible future scenarios.

## Who Interprets the Constitution?

The four points above—vague language, internal conflict, omissions, and unforeseen developments—clearly suggest that the Constitution needs to be interpreted because of disputes that might arise. What creates controversy are two questions flowing from the need to interpret constitutions: *who* will interpret constitutions, and *how*?

In the United States, as in most if not all other countries, public officials take an oath to follow their relevant constitution. Article II of the U.S. Constitution requires the President to vow to "preserve, protect, and defend the Constitution." Article VI states "The Senators and Representatives before mentioned, and the Members of the several State Legislatures, and all executive and judicial Officers, both of the United States and of the several States, shall be bound by Oath or Affirmation, to support this Constitution." Combined, these oaths are all-encompassing of government officials in the United States. That is, *all* state and federal judges and elected and appointed officials must vow to uphold the Constitution.

One cannot uphold a constitution, however, without understanding what that constitution means. Since the language of the Constitution does not cover every possible interaction between public officials and citizens, disputes naturally arise about whether and how one might be upholding the Constitution. For example, a county clerk might decide not to grant a same-sex couple a marriage license because she believes the First Amendment's Free Exercise Clause allows her to refuse to issue such licenses on religious grounds. Or, in a criminal trial a local prosecutor might use cell phone tower data to prove the location of a defendant based on the belief that obtaining such information without a warrant does not violate the Fourth Amendment's prohibition on "unreasonable searches and seizures." Also, city councils, state legislatures, and Congress pass ordinances and statutes based on their evaluation that such legislation complies with the Constitution.

Despite the fact that officials in all branches and levels of government must make decisions based on their understanding of the Constitution, within the U.S. system of separation of powers, the courts are the final arbiters. This means the judicial branch has the *final, authoritative* say on the meaning of the Constitution. Whatever the courts say about the meaning of the Constitution therefore overrides any interpretation given by the other branches of government, such as in the examples in the paragraph above. As we considered in the earlier chapter describing the U.S. court system, this power is known as the power of *judicial review*. The power of judicial review essentially means that when the courts review what legislatures or executives do, courts can declare those actions illegal, and hence null and void. Although judicial review is not expressly stated in the Constitution, it is directly implied, and this implication was understood by everyone at the time of the writing of the Constitution. Thus, the *existence* of this power of judicial review is not controversial. What is controversial is *how* this power should be used, especially when it comes to interpreting the Constitution. The theory about how judges should use the power of judicial review is an important component of what is called *judicial philosophy*.

## Judicial Philosophy

All workers in any type of job have a philosophy about how best to do their job. For example, teachers have beliefs about how best to help students learn. Police officers have beliefs about how they can best prevent and solve crime. Business owners have ideas about how to best run their business. The same is true of judges. The philosophy a judge adopts about how best to go about doing the job of judging is called one's *judicial philosophy*. There are many different aspects of judicial philosophy. For example, one component of judicial philosophy might be how one should treat criminal litigants. Should one be lenient and merciful towards criminal defendants so as to give them another chance in life, or should one be harsh and punitive so as to hold them accountable and teach them to be responsible for their actions? And should this differ depending on the type of criminal case, such as when fines or imprisonment are involved, as opposed to when the actual life of the defendant is at stake in death penalty cases?

Another aspect of judicial philosophy is the question how a judge should interact with one's fellow judges, such as regarding the effort to obtain consensus on an appellate-level court. That is, should one try to vote with the majority as much as possible so as to create unity on the court and stability in the law? Or, as a matter of conscience, should one always vote to dissent no matter how slight the disagreement one has with one's colleagues even if that results in poor working relations with one's fellow judges? One famous example of the application of a norm of consensus was the landmark Supreme Court decision *Brown v. Board of Education* in 1954 that ruled racial segregation in schools violated the Equal Protection Clause of the Fourteenth Amendment.[1] Chief Justice Earl Warren heavily lobbied his fellow justices who were at first inclined to dissent in the case to instead join the majority opinion. The Chief Justice finally obtained a unanimous 9-0 decision in the case. This gave the court's opinion more political weight and influence than it would have had if the court had issued a divided decision.

1. *Brown v. Board of Education*, 387 U.S. 483 (1954)

*Judicial Review* By far the most publicly discussed aspect of judicial philosophy, however, is how a judge should exercise the power of judicial review. In other words, what is the proper role of judges and courts in exercising their power of judicial review? Although there are numerous variations, combinations, and exceptions regarding judicial philosophy and judicial roles, the main argument is between the judicial philosophies of *judicial activism* and *judicial restraint.* These competing philosophies about the proper role of judges provide different answers regarding how freely judges should use their power of judicial review.

The philosophy of judicial activism argues that judges should be relatively unconstrained in exercising their power of judicial review. The purpose of judicial review is to uphold the social contract of the United States—the U.S. Constitution. Thus, if there is any disagreement between what the Constitution says and what other branches of government are attempting to do, the courts should not hesitate to enforce the legal limits on government action placed in the Constitution. Judicial review makes sure our political leaders, and the public, act within the limits imposed by the Constitution. Thus, as activists argue, judges should actively and without hesitation impose judicial review whenever there is a violation of the Constitution. Moreover, because one of the roles of judges is to achieve justice, if achieving justice in a case means interpreting the Constitution in a way that stretches its meaning, so be it. Activists typically believe the meaning of the Constitution should change with the times. Judicial activists often refer to the Constitution as a "living," or "breathing" or "organic" document, indicating the meaning of the Constitution should "evolve" or "grow" to accommodate new unforeseen social, economic, or technological circumstances.

On the other hand, the philosophy of judicial restraint argues that the exercise of judicial review should be rare. Legislatures and executives are democratically elected by the public. Federal court judges, though, are not elected but are instead appointed. The exercise of judicial review therefore puts an undemocratic branch of government in the place of overriding decisions by the democratically elected branches of government. The exercise of judicial review therefore is not only undemocratic, but *anti-democratic.* That is, judicial review blocks the wishes of the political majority acting through their democratically elected representatives. Indeed, according to the U.S. system of separation of powers, courts are to interpret law, not make law. Blocking law "X," however, essentially results that "not-X" then becomes the de facto law. Judicial restraintists argue that such acts of judicial review therefore comprise *judicial legislation,* with judges inappropriately acting as lawmakers rather than as law interpreters as they are supposed to be. Judicial restraintists therefore argue that judges should be highly restrained in their use of judicial review. It should only be applied in exceptional circumstances—only where there is a clear, direct, blatant violation of the Constitution. That is, unless the Constitution forbids it, a judge should uphold the law even if he or she disagrees with it, or personally believes the law is silly, stupid, or even unjust. Otherwise, if the meaning of the Constitution can change depending on whatever a majority of old men and women wearing black robes happens to think at any one moment, the meaning of the Constitution becomes merely a matter of personal whim. Restraintists therefore believe that judges should follow the law, not their own personal preferences, or else the law—including the Constitution—becomes meaningless and arbitrary.

Wherever one stands on the activist-restraintist debate, judicial review is highly problematic. The reason is that we inevitably encounter what is known as the *counter-majoritarian difficulty*. In other words, antidemocratic power acting within a supposedly democratic system poses a problem: how can a democracy call itself a democracy if it has an antidemocratic component as part of it? Pure democracy would mean majority rule without any protection for minority rights. Yet upholding the rights of any minority means the democratic majority must often be overridden. One can have full democracy or full protection of rights, but not both. This tension is irresolvable. The more one promotes either the value of democracy or the value of rights, the more the other value is compromised. Activists and restraintists simply disagree about which value is more important. Either way, then, there is no uncontroversial way to decide the question. If one wishes to have both democracy and rights at the same time, then some of both must be sacrificed.

*Judicial Activism and Restraint: the Right to Privacy* The debate between judicial activism and judicial restraint is probably most pronounced in debates over the "right of privacy," also called the "right of familial privacy" or the "right of autonomous decision-making." Nowhere in the Constitution or its amendments is there any listed right of individuals to have sexual relationships or a right to choose one's sexual partner, nor a right of marriage or choice of marriage partner. Likewise, there is no express constitutional right to choose whether to have children, or how many children to have, or whether to use birth control to avoid having children, or how to raise one's children. There is similarly no expressly listed constitutional right of what to do with one's body such as refusing medical care, including food and water, if one wants to die. Yet the Supreme Court has declared that all these choices are such intimate personal decisions that the Constitution guarantees individuals the "liberty" to make these choices free of government interference.

The modern foundational case that created a constitutional "right of privacy" was the landmark 1965 Supreme Court case of *Griswold v.*

*Connecticut.*[2] To fully understand the nature of the case, one must go back to the 1800s. In the early 1870's, Anthony Comstock led a nationwide moral crusade based on strict Victorian-era notions of sexuality. He convinced Congress to pass a federal statute prohibiting the sending of "obscene, lewd, lascivious," or "filthy" or "indecent or immoral" material in the U.S. mail.[3] This prohibition expressly included information or materials involving sexual pleasure, abortion, or birth control. That same year Comstock was made a U.S. postal inspector with authorization to implement the law. Within the first six months of enforcement, Comstock claimed he had seized "194,000 obscene pictures and photographs, 134,000 pounds of books, 14,200 stereopticon plates, 60,300 'rubber articles,' 5,500 sets of playing cards and 31,500 boxes of pills and powders, mostly 'aphrodisiacs.'"[4] During the next decade, about half the states enacted similar "Comstock laws," most of which included express prohibitions on birth control. Connecticut was one of those states, enacting its own Comstock law in 1879.[5]

By the 1960s, Congress and almost all state legislatures had repealed their Comstock laws, or at least as far as repealing the ban on contraception. Connecticut had not done so, however, and several legal challenges to the contraceptive part of the Connecticut Comstock Law were defeated in the 1940s and 1950s. In 1961, Estelle Griswold, Executive Director of the Planned Parenthood League of Connecticut, opened a birth control clinic in New Haven. She hired C. Lee Buxton, a medical doctor of obstetrics and gynecology at Yale University in New Haven as the Medical Director of the clinic. During the ten days the clinic was open in November 1961, Griswold and Buxton provided birth control information and contraceptive devices to married women. Rather than prosecute the clients of the clinic, prosecutors targeted Griswold and Buxton who were both convicted of violating the 1879 Connecticut Comstock Law. In their appeal to the Connecticut Supreme court, the lawyers for Griswold and Buxton argued that the court should reach a different outcome than in past challenges to the law due to "current developments in medical, social and religious thought in this area."[6] The Connecticut Supreme Court, however, upheld their convictions, de-

2. *Griswold v. Connecticut*, 381 U.S. 479 (1965)
3. Comstock Act, Section 211 (1873).
4. Edward de Grazia, *Girls Lean Back Everywhere: The Law of Obscenity and the Assault on Genius*, New York: Vintage Books, 1993, p. 4.
5. Much literature has been written about Comstock and how he influenced the law of obscenity in the United States. See, for example, Nicola Beisel, *Imperiled Innocents: Anthony Comstock and Family Reproduction in Victorian America,* Princeton University Press, 1997; Amy Werbel, *Lust on Trial: Censorship and the Rise of American Obscenity in the Age of Anthony Comstock,* Columbia University Press, 2018.
6. *Connecticut v. Griswold*, 200 A.2d 479, 480 (1964).

claring "defendants did aid, abet and counsel married women in the commission of an offense."[7]

Griswold and Buxton then appealed to the U.S. Supreme Court on the grounds that the law infringed their constitutional rights. The question was *which* constitutional rights, if any, did the law infringe? The Constitution expressly includes a Free Speech Clause in the First Amendment that protects a right to *talk* or *write* about contraception, but there is nothing in the Constitution that expressly protects a right to *possess* or *provide* or *use* a physical product or device other than the "right to bear arms" in the Second Amendment. Engaging in judicial review of the Connecticut law, the Court majority ruled by a 7-2 vote that the Constitution contained an unwritten "right of privacy" that allowed married couples a right of access to contraceptive devices and products.

Writing for the majority in the case, Justice William O. Douglas admitted the Constitution did not expressly include a right to use contraception. He concluded, however, that several rights expressly contained in the Constitution such as the freedom of speech and the right against unreasonable searches and seizures combined together to create a "zone of privacy" that includes marital privacy:

> Would we allow the police to search the sacred precincts of marital bedrooms for telltale signs of the use of contraceptives? The very idea is repulsive to the notions of privacy surrounding the marriage relationship. We deal with a right of privacy older than the Bill of Rights—older than our political parties, older than our school system. Marriage is a coming together for better or for worse, hopefully enduring, and intimate to the degree of being sacred. It is an association that promotes a way of life, not causes; a harmony in living, not political faiths; a bilateral loyalty, not commercial or social projects. Yet it is an association for as noble a purpose as any involved in our prior decisions. [8]

The two dissenting justices, on the other hand, agreed that they disliked the law itself on policy grounds, but disagreed with the majority that anything in the Constitution prohibited the law. Dissenting Justice Hugo Black, joined by Justice Potter Stewart, explained not only his disagreement with the outcome in the particular case, but also his broader disagreement with the philosophical approach to constitutional interpretation that the majority used. He rejected the idea the Constitution should be interpreted in an evolving way:

> In order that there may be no room at all to doubt why I vote as I do, I feel constrained to add that the law is every bit as offensive

7. Id.
8. *Griswold*, 485–486.

> to me as it is to my Brethren . . . The Court talks about a constitutional "right of privacy" as though there is some constitutional provision or provisions forbidding any law ever to be passed which might abridge the "privacy" of individuals. But there is not. . . .
>
> I realize that many good and able men have eloquently spoken and written, sometimes in rhapsodical strains, about the duty of this Court to keep the Constitution in tune with the times. The idea is that the Constitution must be changed from time to time and that this Court is charged with a duty to make those changes. For myself, I must with all deference reject that philosophy. The Constitution makers knew the need for change and provided for it. Amendments suggested by the people's elected representatives can be submitted to the people or their selected agents for ratification.[9]

Cases like *Griswold* show the difficult choice judges face when confronted with such moral issues. On the one hand, it seems hard to say that "liberty" exists for married couples if they are legally prohibited from using contraception. On the other hand, the Constitution says nothing about a right to contraception. To reach an answer to this dilemma, the justices in the majority in *Griswold v. Connecticut* chose to use an activist approach, whereas the dissenting justices applied judicial restraint.

## Judicial Philosophy versus Political Ideology

It has not always been the case, but nowadays, Senate confirmations of presidents' supreme court nominations have become very contentious. The source of the highly charged debates, typically between senators of the major political parties, is the nominee's judicial philosophy. The first step in the confirmation process is the senate judicial committee hearings. During the hearings, senators will inquire and debate whether the candidate favors judicial activism or judicial restraint. Senators who favor one judicial philosophy will oppose judicial candidates who they believe favor another philosophy.

While judicial philosophy is one of the key factors in these debates, the concept of *judicial philosophy* should not be confused with the concept of *political ideology*. Many members of the public, and sometimes even members of Congress, presidential candidates, and presidents themselves often confuse the two concepts. Judicial philosophy is not the same thing as political ideology. A nominee to the Court can be politically liberal or conservative, yet still adopt the judicial philosophy of either activism or restraint. There is no logical connection between political

9. Griswold, 507–508, 522 (Justice Black dissenting).

ideology and judicial philosophy. There are even other political ideologies besides liberal and conservative, but the over-simplified table below illustrates that political ideology and judicial philosophy are not the same concepts. In short, there are many different possible combinations of political ideology and judicial philosophy on the part of judges.

If one follows Supreme Court decisions and closely reads the statements judges make in their written opinions, one can see examples of individual judges in particular decisions by the Court that fit into all these four categories. Indeed, even the same judges will act differently across different cases. Sometimes a liberal judge might vote for an activist outcome in one case but for a restraintist outcome in another. So, too, will a conservative judge sometimes vote for an activist outcome in one case but a restraintist outcome in another. The approach a judge will use in a case can also vary depending on the type of case involved. For example, some judges will be activist when people's lives are involved but restraintist when only property or money is at stake. In short, the judicial philosophy of most judges across all levels of courts is dynamic and fluid, not static and rigid.

Four Possible Combinations of Judicial Philosophy and Political Ideology

| Judicial Philosophy | Political Ideology | | |
|---|---|---|---|
| | Liberalism | or | Conservatism |
| Activism | 1. Liberal activist | | 2. Conservative activist |
| or | | | |
| Restraint | 3. Liberal restraintist | | 4. Conservative restraintist |

*Griswold v. Connecticut,* discussed in the previous section of this chapter, illustrates that personal ideological or policy preference is not the same as judicial philosophy. Recall that Justice Black, writing for himself and Justice Stewart in dissent, agreed that he disliked the law, but could not find anything in the Constitution that would prohibit such a law. Justice Stewart also wrote a separate dissent, joined in turn by Justice Black. He first made clear how much he personally disliked the law, but he then argued for judicial restraint and so voted to uphold the law as constitutional:

> Since 1879 Connecticut has had on its books a law which forbids the use of contraceptives by anyone. I think this is an uncommonly silly law. As a practical matter, the law is obviously unenforce-

> able, except in the oblique context of the present case. As a philosophical matter, I believe the use of contraceptives in the relationship of marriage should be left to personal and private choice, based upon each individual's moral, ethical, and religious beliefs. As a matter of social policy, I think professional counsel about methods of birth control should be available to all, so that each individual's choice can be meaningfully made. But we are not asked in this case to say whether we think this law is unwise, or even asinine. We are asked to hold that it violates the United States Constitution. And that I cannot do. . . . What provision of the Constitution, then, does make this state law invalid? The Court says it is the right of privacy "created by several fundamental constitutional guarantees." With all deference, I can find no such general right of privacy in the Bill of Rights, in any other part of the Constitution, or in any case ever before decided by this Court. . . . At the oral argument in this case we were told that the Connecticut law does not "conform to current community standards." But it is not the function of this Court to decide cases on the basis of community standards. We are here to decide cases "agreeably to the Constitution and laws of the United States." It is the essence of judicial duty to subordinate our own personal views, our own ideas of what legislation is wise and what is not. If, as I should surely hope, the law before us does not reflect the standards of the people of Connecticut, the people of Connecticut can freely exercise their true Ninth and Tenth Amendment rights to persuade their elected representatives to repeal it. That is the constitutional way to take this law off the books.[10]

In short, even though dissenting Justices Stewart and Black disagreed with the Connecticut ban on contraceptives on political and policy grounds, they also believed it was not their role as judges to vote based on their personal preferences. That is, although their personal views on this issue seemed to be liberal, their philosophy of judicial restraint led them to vote for a conservative policy outcome. The judges in the majority, on the other hand, seemed to prefer a liberal policy outcome while at the same time exercising judicial activism. Put differently, all the judges on the Court personally disliked the law, but they disagreed on whether the Constitution prohibited such a law.

These distinctions and debates surrounding judicial activism and judicial restraint can also arguably be viewed as disputes between the positive law and the natural law (i.e. *justice*). Liberal and conservative judges differ in their conception of the natural law. Yet among both liberal and conservative judges, they also differ regarding whether the

10. Griswold, p. 527, 530–531 (Justice Stewart Dissenting).

proper role of judges is to follow the positive law or natural law. We can see that there is no necessary logical connection between one's conception of the natural law and one's belief regarding whether that natural law should be imposed on the positive law. Some liberal judges as well as some conservative judges will try to impose their views of the natural law on the positive law. Other liberal and conservative judges, on the other hand, will follow the positive law regardless of their personal conception of the natural law.

## Judicial Voting Behavior

As we just saw, there are competing philosophies about how judges should use their power of judicial review. Yet what factors do judges *actually* use when deciding court cases? In other words, what things influence judges to decide cases as they do? Remember from our earlier chapter on legal philosophy (Chapter 1, Jurisprudence) that legal formalism holds that judges use only the law and the facts when deciding cases. Within the social scientific study of the behavior of judges in deciding which litigant wins, the theory of legal formalism is called the *legal model* of judicial decision making. Because very few social scientists are legal formalists, very few social scientists believe in the legal model of judicial voting behavior. On the other hand, the view that judges are influenced by factors *in addition to* or *other than* the law when deciding cases is called the *extra-legal model.* One might also think of this as the *law plus model,* because the theory argues that judges based their decisions on the law *plus other factors.* Most social scientists believe the extra-legal model is the correct view of how judges decide cases. As a result, social science research on the decisional behavior of judges attempts to determine and measure hypothesized extra-legal factors.

The extra-legal model is consistent with the theory of legal realism, which (also recalling from Chapter 1, Jurisprudence) asserts that judges rule largely however they want in disregard of the law. Indeed, almost all social scientists are legal realists, and most would be embarrassed to be perceived otherwise. There are many different alternative extra-legal models of judicial decision making. Some models look at pressures judges feel as part of small-group decision-making, or whether and how judges respond to public opinion. One of the most well-known model variants, however, is the narrow view that judges' rulings are determined almost exclusively by the political ideology of the judges. This model of judicial behavior is called the *attitudinal model.*[11]

11. Jeffrey Segal and Harold Spaeth, *The Supreme Court and the Attitudinal Model Revisited,* Cambridge University Press, 2002

The empirical study of judicial voting behavior began with the behavioral revolution in the social sciences in the 1940's, 50's, and early 60's. Today the large majority of political science is quantitative, that is, mathematical rather than purely theoretical. The past several decades of political science research on the courts has looked for numerical patterns of influence in judicial decision-making on both state and federal courts. The most researched court in this regard has understandably been the U.S. Supreme Court. Small-scale and large-scale statistical studies have looked at evidence whether Supreme Court judges vote based on extra-legal factors such as influence from Congress, the President, public opinion, political interest groups, or other factors. For the most part, there is unclear, inconsistent, minimal, or disputed evidence in these regards. On the other hand, studies have shown clear and consistent statistical evidence that Supreme Court justices as well as other federal and state court judges vote in significant part based on their political ideology (as liberals or conservatives) and on their judicial philosophy (as activists or restraintists). In other words, and unsurprisingly, liberal judges tend to vote for liberal outcomes and conservative judges tend to vote for conservative outcomes. For example, liberal judges tend to vote to uphold the rights of individual women to obtain abortions, but conservative judges tend to vote to uphold community standards restricting or outlawing abortions.

Political science research studies also show, however, that judges' ideologically based political leanings are moderated by the judges' judicial philosophies. That is, judicial *roles* moderate judicial *attitudes.* For example, imagine a liberal judge who does not like a conservative law passed by a conservative legislature. Yet if that judge also strongly favors the philosophy of judicial restraint, then that judge will vote to uphold the conservative law as constitutional unless the judge believes there is a direct and blatant violation of the Constitution. A conservative judge who strongly believes in judicial restraint will similarly uphold a liberal law as constitutional unless the judge believes the law clearly and directly contradicts the Constitution.

In the previous section of this chapter, we saw the example of *Griswold v. Connecticut* where justices who preferred a liberal policy outcome of allowing legalized contraception nevertheless were moderated by their philosophy of judicial restraint to uphold a conservative law banning contraception. This principle of moderation has also been used to explain the vote of Chief Justice John Roberts—an otherwise consistently conservative justice—in his 2012 ruling upholding the Affordable Care Act (more commonly known as "Obamacare") in *NFIB v. Sebelius.*[12]

The Affordable Care Act was a comprehensive bill designed to

12. *NFIB v. Sebelius,* 567 U.S. 519 (2012)

make healthcare more available and affordable to individuals not otherwise covered by a private health insurance plan or other government plan. It required, though, that those without other health insurance buy into the ACA. If not, they would be subject to a financial penalty on their federal tax forms. This provision was a central issue in *Sebelius*: could congress penalize individuals on their annual income tax return if they did not buy health insurance. Known as the "individual mandate," it was disliked by conservatives who thought government did not have the right to penalize citizens in this way. One would have thought that ideologically conservative Chief Justice Roberts would have taken that opportunity to champion the conservative view. Yet he affirmed the ACA, and its mandate, as constitutional. He explained that his job was not to rule based on whether he agreed with the law. Instead, he declared that his responsibility as a judge was to decide only whether the law was consistent with the Constitution: "We do not consider whether the Act embodies sound policies. That judgment is entrusted to the Nation's elected leaders. We ask only whether Congress has the power under the Constitution to enact the challenged provisions." The Chief Justice then declared that Congress had the power to penalize individuals who do not buy health insurance given that Congress was simply using its express constitutional power to tax.

Yet Chief Justice Robert's judicial philosophy of restraint led him to reach a conservative policy outcome in the 2015 landmark ruling *Obergefell v. Hodges*.[13] In that case, numerous same-sex couples filed suit against various state governments that refused to allow them to get legally married or to recognize marriages that were performed in other states. As one example, April DeBoer and Jayne Rowse, living in Michigan, were raising two special needs children. Michigan, however, allowed adoptions only by individuals or by opposite-sex married couple, so the two were denied adopting the children as a same-sex couple. As the Supreme Court summarized the family's situation: "were tragedy to befall either DeBoer or Rowse, the other would have no legal rights over the children she had not been permitted to adopt."

On appeal to the Supreme Court, a five-to-four majority ruled that there is a constitutional right to same-sex marriage. The majority found this right in a combination of the word "liberty" of the Due Process Clause and the words "equal protection of the law" in the Equal Protection Clause, all contained in the Fourteenth Amendment to the Constitution. The majority led by Justice Anthony Kennedy concluded:

> No union is more profound than marriage, for it embodies the highest ideals of love, fidelity, devotion, sacrifice, and family. In

13. *Obergefell v. Hodges*, 576 U.S.—(2015)

> forming a marital union, two people become something greater than once they were. As some of the petitioners in these cases demonstrate, marriage embodies a love that may endure even past death. It would misunderstand these men and women to say they disrespect the idea of marriage. Their plea is that they do respect it, respect it so deeply that they seek to find its fulfillment for themselves. Their hope is not to be condemned to live in loneliness, excluded from one of civilization's oldest institutions. They ask for equal dignity in the eyes of the law. The Constitution grants them that right.

Chief Justice John Roberts' dissent, on the other hand, vigorously disagreed that the Constitution said anything about same-sex marriage, nor even marriage in general:

> Petitioners make strong arguments rooted in social policy and considerations of fairness. They contend that same-sex couples should be allowed to affirm their love and commitment through marriage, just like opposite-sex couples. That position has undeniable appeal. . . But this Court is not a legislature. Whether same-sex marriage is a good idea should be of no concern to us. Under the Constitution, judges have power to say what the law is, not what it should be. . . . Although the policy arguments for extending marriage to same-sex couples may be compelling, the legal arguments for requiring such an extension are not. . . . In short, our Constitution does not enact any one theory of marriage.

In these different passages on the meaning of the Constitution, we can see illustrated the two different approaches to judicial review. The competing philosophies of the justices on the Court obviously had a major influence on how they voted in *Obergefell*. And, once again, as was the situation in *Griswold v. Connecticut*, we can see the dilemma judges face in such difficult cases. On the one hand, to allow government the power to strip children from a loving parent merely because the parent was never allowed to legally marry seems sadistically cruel. On the other hand, the Constitution says nothing about marriage, adoption, or any other family-related rights. To address this predicament, the activist approach seeks what justices believe to be a just result. In *Obergefell*, the "just" result was granting equal dignity to same-sex families even if that meant stretching the express language of the Constitution. The restraintist approach, on the other hand, would have upheld the law by strictly adhering to the Constitution as it was written even if that meant the result for same-sex families could end up being personally tragic for them.

A full study of all the various factors that influence judges to vote in certain ways and the degree to which those factors do so would take up an entire separate book. As we've just described, however, the two most important factors that affect judicial voting behavior—at least as revealed by the current social science evidence—are political ideology and judicial philosophy.

## Constitutional Interpretation

The question of how the power of judicial review should be used is often closely connected to the issue of how the Constitution should be interpreted. These are not the same thing, however, just as judicial philosophy is not the same thing as political ideology. A view about how judicial review should be used is *not* the same thing as a belief about how the meaning of a constitution should be derived. Put simply, a *power* is not the same thing as an *understanding*. By way of analogy, trying to understand a book on nuclear physics is a different question from whether one should build a nuclear bomb once one understands the book. Clearly the decision whether to make a weapon or not can only happen after the knowledge of physics is achieved, but still these are distinct issues. Similarly, even among judges who have the same philosophy regarding the proper use of judicial review, those judges can have differing approaches to interpreting what the Constitution means. And, even judges who agree on what factors to use when determining the meaning of the Constitution might disagree on what the evidence shows, or how that meaning applies.

The Constitution itself offers no guidelines on how it is to be interpreted. Over the years, judges and scholars have pursued competing philosophies about how to interpret the Constitution. Most if not all of the various approaches can be divided into two categories.

One way to interpret the meaning of a constitution is to study what those who wrote and ratified the constitution originally intended and understood the words in the constitution to mean. The most commonly used term for this philosophy of interpretation is called *originalism*. Another common term sometimes used is *intentionalism*, to indicate the meaning should be based on the intent of the writers. Two other less-used terms are *textualism* and *interpretivism*. For example, the dissents in both *Griswold v. Connecticut* and *Obergefell v. Hodges* basically would have applied the original meaning of the U.S. Constitution. That is, there was no intent or understanding at the time of ratification of the Constitution or its amendments that said anything about family-related choices or rights.

The alternative to looking at the original intent of a constitution is to say the meaning of the text can be derived from something beyond what the writers originally intended. Perhaps this other factor could be current public opinion as to what the Constitution should mean. Perhaps it should be what policy experts say would be the most reasonable, sensible policy. Maybe the judges doing the interpretation believe they should impose their own desires as to what the Constitution should mean. Whatever the other factor or factors, these other approaches are *not* bound to what the writers of the Constitution intended their words to mean. Judges are free, then, to look to any other factor or factors they choose. All these other approaches can collectively and appropriately be referred to by the term *nonoriginalism.* Other terms similarly lacking in cleverness of name are *nonintentionalism, nontextualism,* and *noninterpretevism.* Other scholars may use other terms as well, but the common feature is that the intentions and understandings of the Constitution's writers and ratifiers are *not* binding on future court decisions. For example, the majorities in both *Griswold v. Connecticut* and *Obergefell v. Hodges* applied more modern notions of privacy and equality compared to what most people believed in the 1700s, 1800s, or even early 1900s.

There is another approach to interpreting constitutions that is sometimes confused with originalism even though ironically it is technically a form of nonoriginalism. Some judges believe a constitution's text should be given a literal meaning even if that was not what the constitution's writers or ratifiers intended. This literal interpretation is called a *strict construction* because the words are construed strictly according to their literal definitions without looking at the context or the intent of the words. Relatively few judges believe in the philosophy of strict constructionism, but there have been famous examples in recent decades of justices on the Court who were strict constructionists. Justice Hugo Black, for example, consistently voted against any and all speech regulations that came before the Court. He argued that a literal interpretation should be given to the phrase in the First Amendment that states "Congress shall make *no* [italics added] law abridging the freedom of speech."[14] This would mean that Congress could not even criminalize inciting mass riots or making terroristic threats.

One can see how a strict construction of every constitutional provision would lead to absurd results. The Fourteenth Amendment, for example, states that "no state shall deny to any person within its jurisdiction the equal protection of the laws." Taken literally, this would mean, as merely one example, that ten-year old children should be able to drive, buy alcohol, vote, marry, serve on juries, be tried and sentenced as adults, and register for the draft. Obviously no sane judge would be a

14. See, for example, Justice Black's concurrence in *New York Times v. U.S.*, 403 U.S. 713 (1971)

true strict constructionist. Indeed, even judges who claim they favor strict constructionism do not apply it in a manner that would reach all its logically consistent literal conclusions.

Ironically, as we will consider in more detail shortly, the original writers and ratifiers of the U.S. Constitution stated that future courts should not look to their personal intentions, but should instead look only at the words. Thus, strictly construing the text would *not* follow the original meaning of the text. Strict construction is thus not a form of originalism, but rather a form of nonoriginalism. Despite this fact, politicians and even judges sometimes use the term "strict constructionism" when they want to refer to originalism. What these politicians and judges typically mean to say is that they favor the philosophy of judicial restraint. They believe that following either the original intent of the text or the literal meaning of the text will restrain judges from using judicial review to overturn laws. This result does not logically follow, however. An activist judge could use either original intent or a strict construction of the Constitution to strike down a law the judge disagrees with. Similarly, a restraintist judge could avoid using judicial review by finding that a law is consistent with either the original meaning or a strict construction of the Constitution. In short, judicial philosophy has many components, one of which is how to use judicial review and another of which is how to interpret constitutions. These are interrelated but nevertheless distinct concepts.

## Originalism versus Nonoriginalism

During the 1980's, President Ronald Reagan's Attorney General Ed Meese re-ignited the debate between originalism and nonoriginalism. Meese openly attacked the Supreme Court. He accused what he saw as a liberal, activist Supreme Court improperly ignoring the original intent of the Framers of the U.S. Constitution by instead imposing the Court's own ungrounded, arbitrary, subjective interpretations. In the media and in scholarly journals, many scholars—typically liberal-leaning ones—and even some judges responded to his criticism by rejecting his arguments. Other, more conservative scholars and judges defended Meese's criticisms. Even though there is no logically necessary connection between political ideology and judicial philosophy, the Supreme Court was generally both liberal and activist at the time. This coincidence made it seem as if liberalism was by definition activist, and that conservatism was by definition restraintist. The public mindset therefore adopted this mistakenly conjoined definition as well, even though in more recent years shifting conservative majorities of the Court have also made many activist rulings. Regardless, the current scholarly and political debate over originalism has been raging since Attorney General Meese raised the issue.[15]

All this being said about the differences between judicial review and constitutional interpretation, however, originalism does lend itself more easily to use by restraintists, and restraintists do tend to be more politically conservative. Judicial restraintists usually argue that unless the approach of originalism is used, decisions about the meaning of a constitution will be left to the arbitrary preferences of judges. Put differently, if judges are not bound by the originally intended meaning of a constitution, then there is no *fixed* meaning to the language of that constitution. If there is no fixed meaning, then there is no *objective* interpretation, but rather, only the *subjective* interpretations of the judges. Without such clear guideposts, judges are free to arbitrarily say a constitution means whatever the judges want it to mean, and they will use whatever methods they want to arrive at that answer. Therefore, as commonly argued by judicial restraintists, originalism is the only *principled* method of interpreting the constitution. In their view, all other interpretive methods are unprincipled since they allow any reason (or no reason at all) to be the basis of a constitutional interpretation.

One can see that the approach of originalism would naturally lead to more restrained and conservative outcomes. Political and legal thought overall across the entire political spectrum has moved in a relatively more liberal or progressive direction compared to the past. For example, both liberals and conservatives today take it for granted that government has legitimate authority to do many things that people a century or two ago would have been appalled at. This includes examples such as regulating businesses, the environment, and education, or providing Social Security or Medicare, or requiring people to buy health insurance, or outlawing many types of discrimination. In short, the types and amount of legal regulation in our lives has greatly increased over the centuries. If one were to interpret the Constitution only as it was intended to mean over 200 years ago when it was written, there would be relatively few government powers today compared to what society has come to expect and demand today. The question, then, is what to do about these changed expectations and demands.

As discussed, originalists believe the only principled, objective, non-arbitrary way to interpret a constitution is to follow the original intent of the writers and ratifiers of that constitution. The basic structure, powers, and rights contained in a constitution are what that society has decided should be the basic rules of that society. Whether those rules should change is such an important decision that the political system as

15. For a variety of views, see Jack N. Rakove, Editor, *Interpreting the Constitution: The Debate Over Original Intent*, Northeastern, 1990

a whole should make that decision. The *proper* way to change the meaning of a constitution, then, is for the entire political system to amend the constitution using the procedure provided by that constitution for adding amendments. If a handful of judges can change the meaning of a constitution without following the normal amendment procedure, then those judges are imposing their arbitrary whims on the entire political system. This is not only improper, it threatens the legitimacy of the entire system, or at least the legitimacy of judicial institutions. The desires of society as a whole, and not the desires of a handful of judges, should decide what the constitution should mean. If a constitution means whatever a mere literal handful of people say it means, then the words of the constitution become essentially meaningless. In short, why bother to have a constitution if it has no fixed meaning?

Those opposed to originalism and in favor of nonoriginalism argue that constitutions are evolving documents. Indeed, nonoriginalists use terms like "growing" and "breathing" and "living" to indicate that constitutions are always changing in meaning as society changes. Since the needs, interests, and desires of society change, this means the powers of government and the rights of the people must each change to correspond to that evolution. Judges must be free, then, to adapt the constitution's meaning to changing times. Otherwise, a lack of flexibility on the part of judges to alter a constitution's meaning makes that constitution quickly obsolete. Especially in our modern world, technological, economic, and cultural changes sometimes happen very rapidly. This means that societies can quickly outgrow their constitutions if those constitutions do not keep pace with the fast-changing times. These constitutions would soon be dead, rather than alive, unless their meaning is allowed to breathe and grow. Ironically, then, a lack of ability to change a constitution's meaning would result in it soon becoming meaningless. Why bother to have a constitution if it is unable to be applied as needed?

Notice that both originalists and nonoriginalists believe it is essential for constitutions to remain meaningful to the political system. They differ radically, however, in the method to obtain and/or retain that meaning. Originalists believe the best way to keep a constitution meaningful is to maintain a stable foundation of meaning that changes only after extraordinary deliberation by society as a whole. Nonoriginalists believe constitutions are most meaningful when that meaning can easily evolve as the society itself evolves. When framed in this way, one can see that originalism leans toward a more politically conservative approach: "Keep what works." Nonoriginalism, on the other hand, is a more politically liberal approach: "Change is progress." One can also see that restraintism tends to favor keeping the past and current status quo, whereas activism is more conducive to striking down laws that violate the shifting moral norms of a society.

We saw these connections in *Griswold v. Connecticut* and *Obergefell v. Hodges*. The majorities in those cases applied a nonoriginalist method of interpretation in order to reach an activist result. The dissents would have used an originalist approach to reach a restraintist result. It is important to re-emphasize, though, that these connections are neither absolute nor logically necessary. Whether a court uses originalism or nonoriginalism to strike down a statute, that decision is still by definition an activist ruling. Likewise, a ruling that upholds a statute as constitutional is by definition an example of judicial restraint regardless whether a court applies originalism or nonoriginalism in the ruling. Similarly, whether a liberal judge votes to uphold a liberal statutory policy (such as universal health care), or a conservative judge votes to uphold a conservative statutory policy (such as outlawing marijuana), in either instance it is an example of judicial restraint. However, in these examples just given, whether a conservative judge votes to overturn universal health care (as several dissenting justices did in *NFIB v. Sebelius*) or a liberal judge votes to overturn a ban on marijuana, in both cases these are by definition examples of activism. Again, judicial philosophy is different from political ideology, and both of these are different concepts than the question how to determine constitutional meaning through the approaches of originalism or nonoriginalism.

## Problems with Originalism

Let's return to the main critique against nonoriginalism. Originalists assert that nonoriginalists make decisions arbitrarily based on personal views rather than clear, fixed principles based on the meaning that the writers and ratifiers of a constitution originally intended. But how clear and fixed is originalism really? It turns out there are many difficulties in using—or trying to use—a strict original intent as a means of constitutional interpretation. We will use the U.S. Constitution, written in 1787 and ratified in 1789, as an example.

*Lack of Evidence* Sometimes there is almost a total lack of evidence regarding original intent. The phrase "unreasonable searches and seizures" in the Fourth Amendment and the phrase "cruel and unusual punishment" in the Eighth Amendment both have practically no historical documentation available as to what was intended by those phrases. Exactly what is "unreasonable"? Or "cruel"? Or "unusual"? Searching for the originally intended meaning gives us relatively little help.

*Incomplete Evidence* Even when there is historical evidence as to the meaning of a constitutional provision, that evidence is often woefully incomplete. There were no recording devices in 1787, and often speeches were not transcribed, but merely summarized. James Madison, for example, took notes of the Philadelphia convention during the debating and the writing of the Constitution. Madison recorded only the briefest of condensed summaries of the various delegate's verbally expressed views. By most estimates, he was able to record only about ten percent of the debates at best.[16] So what was in the ninety percent that he left out?

*Biased Evidence* Did the conscious or subconscious biases of Madison or other speech transcribers distort their summaries to make certain positions appear stronger or weaker? Or might the transcribers have even intentionally left out counter-arguments the transcriber opposed? There is some evidence that seems to show Madison intentionally altered his convention notes later to reflect his changed views about the Constitution.[17] And historians know that the Pennsylvania and Maryland debates were recorded by a staunch Federalist who was paid to delete all the Anti-federalist speeches. So what other historical evidence that we have is unbeknownst to us actually highly biased?

*Public v. Private Intent* Sometimes what the writers and ratifiers of the Constitution expressed publicly was different from what they stated privately. Historical evidence seems to show that Madison and Hamilton disagreed with many of the arguments they made in the *Federalist Papers* to get the Constitution approved. For example, both wanted broad powers of the national legislature and thought the Constitution granted broad powers to Congress. Yet publicly, they argued the Constitution did not mean that and such would never happen. So do we go by their compromised public views or by their hidden, secret, but actual views?

*Intent at Which Step* The fact that the ratifiers of the Constitution probably relied on the publicly expressed statements of Madison, Hamilton, and other Federalists raises another problem: At which step of the writing and ratification process should we look for the originally intended meaning? The person who wrote the first draft of a Constitutional provision? The constitutional committee who modified his draft? The entire Constitutional Convention that approved the final version of the text to be sent to the States for ratification? The state convention delegates who ratified the text? Or some or all of the above? And what if the intent at these different stages differs? What Madison or Hamilton intended may be (and sometimes is) quite different than what the rati-

16. Mary Sarah Bilder, *Madison's Hand: Revising the Constitutional Convention*, Cambridge, Massachusetts: Harvard University Press, 2017

17. Id.

fiers intended, yet this latter group would be much larger. Do we simply go by the larger number?

*Ideal v. Compromised Intent* Related to the issue of public versus private intent is the question whether we should go by what the writers and ratifiers *wanted* or by what they *agreed to*? Many constitutional provisions were intentionally left vague and open-ended to achieve majority support. For example, Hamilton wanted the President to have much of the power of a king and Congress to have the power "to make all laws whatsoever." Having lost those battles in the Constitutional Convention, he was willing to settle for the strongest executive and legislative powers he could get. Other Framers wanted a weak presidency with strictly limited powers. They collectively agreed to simply give the President an undefined "executive power" in Article II of the Constitution.[18] Moreover, many delegates fiercely opposed certain elements of the Constitution, but voted in favor of them anyway in order to get other things they wanted passed. That is, many votes for ratification were based on political compromises and bargaining with delegates "holding their noses" and voting for some things they did not want. For example, many northern state delegates strongly opposed slavery, but agreed to leave the question of slavery open-ended in the Constitution to get the support of southern state delegates for the Constitution as a whole. So did Congress's power to regulate "commerce" include slavery? The delegates disagreed, and it took the Civil War to finally settle this question.

*Whose Intent* Even supporters of the same constitutional provision sometimes openly differed in their intent as to the meaning of those provisions. Famously, some supporters of the First Amendment's Establishment Clause thought it would only prohibit a national religion. Others thought it would prohibit favoring one religion over another. Still others thought it would prohibit favoring religion as a whole over nonreligion, whereas some seemed to think it would allow government to favor monotheistic religions collectively. A few others thought it would let government favor Christianity, and a few others even believed it would let government favor Protestant Christianity. Some supporters thought it would allow government financial aid to private religious institutions; others didn't think so and argued against it. Although originalists typically argue we should go by the "majority view" of the Establishment Clause when it was ratified, determining that majority view is extremely difficult.[19] Obviously we can not go back in time and poll the

18. Daniel Farber and Suzanna Sherry, *A History of the American Constitution, 3d Ed.*, West Academic Publishing, 2013
19. Id.

writers and ratifiers. Trying to determine a "majority" view from historical documents provides only an educated guess at best. For example, even if we can calculate that there are more speeches or writings on one side versus the other, this doesn't necessarily mean that position was in the majority. Just as often occurs today in politics, a small but vocal minority can make an opinion seem more popular than it actually is.

*General v. Specific Intent* Should we look at the *general principle* intended by a constitutional provision, or how that constitutional provision was intended to apply in *specific situations*? For example, the Fourteenth Amendment, ratified in 1868, guarantees "the equal protection of the laws." This was intended to establish a general principle of racial equality. Yet at the same time, there were racially segregated schools in Washington D.C., and no one seemed to think that such schools would violate the Fourteenth Amendment. Also, with some constitutional provisions, *none* of the originally intended specific applications would apply today. For example, the Free Speech Clause in the First Amendment was never foreseen to apply to regulations of TV, radio, or the internet. The point is that in many instances of constitutional interpretation, we are faced with a conflict between the general principle intended and how that principle was expected to be applied in specific situations.

*A Lack of Any Intent* In many instances, it is not the case that we lack evidence of what the framers of the Constitution intended, but that the evidence clearly shows they *themselves* did not have any particular intent. In other words, historical evidence shows that many framers and ratifiers simply agreed to sections of the Constitution while not being sure what they meant or not having time to determine their meaning. Instead, these framers or ratifiers made the conscious decision to leave the interpretation and meaning of these parts of the Constitution to be determined in the future. In fact, Federalists often intentionally avoided any specifics during the ratification debates. This was done so that any specifics couldn't then be used to attack the Federalist position and thereby jeopardize the Constitution's ratification. Madison's notes of the 1787 Philadelphia convention, for example, record that Delegate Butler expressed concern that "The vagueness of the terms rendered it impossible for any precise judgment to be formed." In reply, Delegate Ghorum stated: "The vagueness of the terms constitutes the propriety of them. We are now establishing general principles, to be extended hereafter into details which will be precise & explicit."[20]

20. James Madison, *Notes of Debates in the Federal Convention of 1787*, entry dated Monday, July 16, 1787.

*Internal Inconsistency* Ironically, there is a good deal of evidence that the writers and ratifiers of the Constitution originally intended that the meaning of the Constitution would evolve and change with the times! During the 1787 Constitutional Convention in Philadelphia, the Committee on Detail was tasked with drafting the final, exact wording of the Constitution. Edmund Randolph, a member of the Committee on Detail, provided written recommendations to guide the Committee on Detail in their drafting process. The very first goal Randolph listed was: "1. To insert essential principles only, lest the operations of government should be clogged by rendering those provisions permanent and unalterable, which ought to be accommodated to time and events."[21] James Madison, generally known as the "Father of the Constitution," essentially agreed with this assessment. In a letter to Thomas Ritchie, Madison stated: "As a guide in expanding and applying the provisions of the Constitution, the debates and incidental decisions of the Convention can have no authoritative character."[22] In short, following the original intent of the framers ironically requires that one go against the original intent of the framers.

## Constitutional Pragmatism

As we just discussed, there is rarely indisputable evidence of the precise meaning of the original intent of individual provisions of the U.S. Constitution. In fact, the situation is often quite the opposite. There is often enough evidence (or lack thereof) to support *multiple* possible interpretations of constitution provisions. Just as is the case when trying to determine a statute's purpose from the legislative history of that statute, a similar "battle of the quotes" usually results when judges interpret the language of the Constitution based on evidence of original meaning. Thus, a judge or court typically has the leeway to come down on either side—in favor of either litigant in a case—by appealing to "original intent." Given the historical evidence is so divided or unclear, this means judges must resort to some factor or factors *other than* original intent when answering a question about the legal meaning of the Constitution. What they fall back on could be public opinion, the current weight of scholarly opinion, the public policy arguments by the litigants, the personal political preferences of the judges, or some combination of these factors. As a result, even self-proclaimed originalists must sooner-or-later engage in *judicial legislation.* That is, eventually even a die-hard

21. Id, entry dated June 15.

22. Leonard Levy, *Original Intent and the Framers' Constitution*, New York: MacMillan Publishing Co, 1988, p. 1

originalist will necessarily end up resorting to his or her own values in making judicial decisions. Indeed, even the decision that stability is more important than flexibility is a political value. In short, judicial interpretations of the Constitution are always value judgments regardless whether one claims to be following original intent or not.

Because of the problems in finding "the" original intent of constitutions, some scholars have suggested a method of constitutional interpretation that tries to reach a middle ground between originalism and nonoriginalism. This approach is usually called *constitutional pragmatism.*[23] This view argues that since constitutional interpretation is never exact, judges should be free to use whichever method of interpretation works best in each particular case. If an originalist approach works best in a given case, that's fine. If a nonoriginalist approach works best in a different case, that's fine as well. Since there is no indisputably "correct" meaning of any particular constitutional provision, judges may simply use whatever method of interpretation gives the best solution at the moment. In this way, pragmatists can still claim to follow original intent whenever feasible, but it allows them to resort to other factors of interpretation when needed. Technically, though, constitutional pragmatism is still a form of nonoriginalism. That is, even if the default approach for a constitutional pragmatist is the original intent of a constitution, the pragmatist is open to doing whatever works best rather than being strictly bound to the original meaning of the text. Since whatever works best is not the same thing as the originally intended meaning, pragmatism can be categorized as one variant of nonoriginalism. A pragmatic approach that tries to stick closely to original intent as much as possible, though, might also be seen as a "soft" or "weak" form of originalism.

Sophisticated originalists realize all these problems exist, so they have a rebuttal. Originalists counter that despite the difficulties or even paradoxes of originalism, it is still a better, more principled alternative than nonoriginalism. In other words, despite the inherent obstacles in using the approach of originalism, it remains the lesser of two evils. The choice is between total arbitrariness of judicial decision-making versus partial arbitrariness of judicial decision-making. Partial arbitrariness is not ideal, but it is far better than total arbitrariness. Thus, when faced with a difficult choice of interpretative methods, the most principled approach—that is, the least unprincipled approach—is originalism.

As a final consideration, though, recall our discussion of legal realism. Legal realists argue that judges will do what they want, and simply use whatever law and facts they can to justify their decisions. To legal realists, the entire debates between originalism versus nonoriginalism

23. See, e.g., Daniel A. Farber and Suzanna Sherry, *Desparately Seeking Certainty: The MisGuided Quest for Constitutional Foundations*, Chicago: University of Chicago Press, 2002

and activism versus restraint are moot. Judges will simply use whatever judicial philosophy they want, mixing and matching theories of judicial review and of constitutional interpretation, to reach the outcomes those judges desire. Indeed, as we have seen, even originalists admit that the historical evidence or its absence will often support multiple possible constitutional interpretations. Constitutional pragmatism is thus ultimately of necessity the actual default approach of all judges when they interpret the Constitution regardless what approach these judges claim to prefer. If all judges are in reality pragmatists, then the Constitution simply means whatever the Supreme Court thinks is the best meaning for it to have at any moment. What is best, however, is subjective to each individual judge, based on their political, moral, religious, and other views. Stated differently, these facts confirm the legal realist's analysis of constitutional interpretation: the "real" meaning of the Constitution is simply whatever the Supreme Court says it means.

## Constitutional Law

Given that the actual meaning of the Constitution is simply whatever the Supreme Court says it means, and as this chapter explained earlier, Supreme Court decisions are law. The field of *constitutional law* thus is the sum total of the U.S. Constitution and its amendments combined with more than two centuries of Supreme Court (and lower court) interpretation of the specific provisions of the Constitution. The Constitution, however, involves many different topics of law, and there is a huge body of caselaw interpreting the Constitution within each of these areas of law. As a result, law schools and even undergraduate universities typically divide up constitutional law into multiple different courses with different titles. Although sometimes a single course titled "Constitutional Law" is offered by undergraduate institutions, it can only briefly touch on the subfields of constitutional law.

As this chapter described earlier, constitutions list the powers of, and constraints on, the government. These are not airtight categories as these powers and constraints overlap and intertwine. Nevertheless, when only a single course titled "Constitutional Law" is offered by an undergraduate institution, the sub-topic of "Governmental Powers" is the most common constitutional law subfield covered. This is the basic powers of the key federal institutions in the U.S.: The Executive Branch (the President),[24] the Legislative Branch (the Congress),[25] the Judicial

24. See, e.g., *Youngstown Sheet and Tube Co. v. Sawyer*, 343 U.S. 579 (1952); *U.S. v. Curtiss-Wright Export Corp.*, 299 304 (1936); *The Prize Cases*, 67 U.S. 635 (1863); *U.S. v. Nixon*, 418 U.S. 683 (1974)

25. See, e.g., *National Federation of Independent Businesses v. Sebelius*, 567 U.S. 519 (2012) (individual mandate issue)

Branch (the Supreme Court),[26] as well as the checks and balances among them[27] and the division of powers between the federal and state governments (federalism).[28]

Specific constraints on the powers of the federal and state governments are contained primarily in the first ten amendments to the U.S. Constitution, the Bill of Rights. The Bill of Rights includes the most important liberties of citizens and residents of the United States such as the freedom of speech, religious liberty, and the rights of persons suspected or accused of crime. Other key civil rights—especially the rights against arbitrary discrimination by the state and federal governments—are found in the Fourteenth Amendment to the Constitution. A single undergraduate course titled "Civil Liberties" or "Civil Rights and Liberties" might cover all of the Bill of Rights and the Fourteenth Amendment. Once again, however, such a broad subject matter involves a huge amount of cases involving many different areas of law. Thus, in law schools and often in undergraduate institutions as well, multiple courses cover different areas of constitutional constraints on government.

A course titled "Civil Liberties" might cover only the First Amendment; hence it might also be labeled "The First Amendment" or "First Amendment Law." This includes the freedoms of speech and press,[29] the free exercise of religion,[30] and the prohibition on government establishment of religion.[31] In undergraduate and graduate departments of Communication or Journalism, courses in "Communication Law" would typically cover just the First Amendment rights having to do with the freedoms of speech and press. Regardless how this topic is labelled, it includes the degree to which people are free to say what they believe when it comes to religion, politics, and other matters of opinion, as well as the time, place, and manner in which those views are expressed.

An undergraduate course titled "Civil Liberties" might cover the entire Bill of Rights. In this case, the legal subject matter includes not just all of the First Amendment freedoms, but also all of the rights of persons suspected or accused of criminal conduct as found in the Fourth through Eight Amendments to the U.S. Constitution. These rights of the criminally accused, however, are typically covered in both law schools and undergraduate institutions as stand-alone courses titled "Criminal Procedure." This topic is discussed more specifically in a separate chapter in this textbook. Indeed, even the relatively narrow topic

26. See, e.g., *Lujan v. Defenders of Wildlife,* 504 U.S. 555 (1992)
27. See, e.g., *Bowsher v. Synar,* 478 U.S. 714 (1986)
28. See, e.g., *National Federation of Independent Businesses v. Sebelius,* 567 U.S. 519 (2012) (Medicaid funding issue)
29. See, e.g., *Texas v. Johnson,* 491 U.S. 397 (1989); *International Society for Krishna Consciousness v. Lee,* 505 U.S. 672 (1992), *Gertz v. Welch,* 418 U.S. 323 (1974)
30. See, e.g., *Church of the Lukumi Babalu Aye v. City of Hialeah,* 508 U.S. 520 (1993)
31. See, e.g., *Van Orden v. Perry;* 545 U.S. 677 (2005)

of criminal procedure has so much legal detail that law schools usually take multiple courses to cover the subject. In undergraduate institutions, criminal procedure is covered either in Criminal Justice departments and/or in Political Science departments.

The Fourteenth Amendment to the Constitution provides the core civil rights of citizens and residents of the U.S. to be free from arbitrary (unjustified) discrimination. This might happen (among other instances) when differential treatment of individuals by the government on issues of employment, education or marriage occurs because of the individual's race,[32] sex,[33] or sexual orientation.[34] These topics are sometimes included in broad "Civil Liberties" courses, but can also be found both in law school and in undergraduate institutions in stand-alone courses with titles like "Civil Rights Law," "Constitutional Civil Rights," "The Fourteenth Amendment," or "Equal Protection."

As can be seen, the field of "Constitutional Law" is extremely broad and detailed, requiring extensive study for one to gain expertise in the field. At the same time, though, apart from the area of criminal procedure—which is litigated by criminal law attorneys on a daily basis—constitutional law cases are relatively rare for most law firms. Thus, most lawyers are not experts in constitutional law as they have neither sufficient education nor experience. As a result, individual litigants seeking to assert their constitutional rights often turn to interest groups specializing in legal expertise in certain aspects of constitutional law, especially civil rights and liberties. Some of these interest groups include the American Civil Liberties Union (ACLU),[35] the American Center for Law and Justice (ACLJ),[36] and the National Association for the Advancement of Colored People (NAACP).[37] Even though this area of law tends to be highly specialized, however, state bar exams (i.e. attorney license exams) regularly test bar applicants on various aspects of constitutional law. Given this reality, plus the fact that even local governments can sometimes infringe on the constitutional rights of their residents, it is thus important for all lawyers to have a basic understanding of constitutional law.

---

*Questions for Review and Discussion*

1. What are constitutions, why do they need interpretation, and who gets to interpret them?

32. See, e.g., *Grutter v. Bollinger*, 539 U.S. 306 (2003)
33. See, e.g., *U.S. v. Virginia*, 518 U.S. 515 (1996)
34. See, e.g., *Obergefell v. Hodges*, 576 U.S. ___ (2015)
35. http://www.aclu.org
36. http://aclj.org
37. http://www.naacp.org

2. What is judicial philosophy, and what is the difference between judicial activism versus judicial restraint? Which philosophy is best, and why?
3. How are the concepts of judicial philosophy, political ideology, and theories of constitutional interpretation inter-related?
4. What are the strengths and weaknesses of various approaches to constitutional interpretation. Which do you believe is the best approach, and why?
5. What would be the pros and cons of giving the final say over the meaning of the Constitution to the President, the Congress, a vote of the U.S. public, or some combination thereof, as opposed to the Supreme Court? Would any of these other methods be any better?

---

## *Suggested Readings*

*Lochner v. New York* 198 U.S. 45 (1905) (liberty of contract)
*Nebbia v. New York* 291 U.S. 502 (1934) (liberty of contract)
*West Coast Hotel Co. v. Parrish,* 300 U.S. 379 (1937) (liberty of contract)
*Williamson v. Lee Optical,* 348 U.S. 483 (1955) (liberty of contract)
*Ferguson v. Skrupa,* 327 U.S. 726 (1963) (liberty of contract)
*Griswold v. Connecticut,* 381 U.S. 479 (1968) (contraceptives)
*Roe v. Wade,* 410 U.S. 113 (1973) (abortion)
*San Antonio Independent School District v. Rodriguez,* 411 U.S. 1 (1973) (education)
*Bowers v. Hardwick,* 478 U.S. 186 (1986) (same-sex relationships)
*Cruzan v. Director,* 497 U.S. 261 (1990) (right to die)
*Planned Parenthood of Pennsylvania v. Casey,* 505 U.S. 833 (1992) (abortion)
*Washington v. Glucksberg,* 521 U.S. 702 (1997) (assisted suicide)
*Vacco v. Quill,* 521 U.S. 793 (1997) (assisted suicide)
*Lawrence v. Texas,* 539 U.S. 558 (2003) (same-sex relationships)
*Obergefell v. Hodges,* 576 U.S. ___ (2015) (same-sex marriage)
*Jawish v. Morlet,* 86 A.2d 96 (D.C. Ct. App. 1952) (reversal of judicial review)
*Republican Party of Minnesota v. White,* 536 U.S. 765 (2002) (judicial impartiality)
*New York Times v. U.S.,* 403 U.S. 713 (1971) (executive power versus free speech)

---

## *Advanced Readings*

Jeffrey A. Segal and Harold J. Spaeth, *The Supreme Court and the Attitudinal Model Revisited* (2002)
David Strauss, *The Living Constitution* (2010)
Steven Calabresi and Antonin Scalia, Editors, *Originalism: A Quarter-Century of Debate* (2007)
Stephen Breyer, *Active Liberty: Interpreting our Democratic Constitution* (2006)

Part Two

# THE SUBSTANCE OF LAW

# CHAPTER 5

# CONTRACTS

*Chapter Objectives*
*After reading this chapter, you should be able to:*

- List and describe the sources of contract law
- Describe the legal rules for contract offers, revocation, and acceptance
- Define the concept of consideration and identify examples of it
- List and describe the several major limits to contract enforceability
- Describe how contracts are legally interpreted
- Describe the legal rules that define when contracts are breached
- Describe the legal rules that define the damages for breach of contract

We begin our discussion of the substance of law with contracts simply because contracts pervade our lives. Every time you buy gas or groceries, eat at a restaurant, or shop online, you have become a party to a legal contract. Sometimes people make unusual claims that contracts have been created. One famous example happened in 1996. Beginning in 1995, Pepsico, the makers of Pepsi cola, began a marketing campaign targeting a younger audience that Pepsico called the "Pepsi Generation." Pepsico decided that a way to reach younger consumers would be to have them collect "Pepsi Points" by drinking Pepsi. These points could then be turned in for prizes known as "Pepsi Stuff." As part of this marketing campaign, Pepsi introduced a comical television ad during the 1996 National Football League Superbowl game. The ad opened by showing a high-school-age boy wearing a Pepsi t-shirt along with a leather jacket and sunglasses. Large all-caps print at the bottom of the screen accompanied each item: "T-SHIRT 75 PEPSI POINTS. LEATHER JACKET 1450 PEPSI POINTS. SHADES 150 PEPSI POINTS" A voiceover then declared "Introducing the Pepsi Stuff Catalog. Now, the more great Pepsi you drink, the more great stuff you're going to get!" As the voiceover was occurring, the ad showed a military jet landing immediately next to a high school as shocked students looked on and strong wind blew through the classroom windows disturbing their hair and papers. The same high school student shown earlier wearing Pepsi Stuff merchandise was then shown as the pilot of the jet. Sitting in the cockpit holding a Pepsi and looking directly into the camera, he proclaimed "It sure beats the bus!" As the boy dismounted the jet, large-size print at the bottom of the screen displayed the words "HARRIER FIGHTER 7,000,000 PEPSI POINTS." The written words "DRINK PEPSI GET STUFF" closed out the ad.

As an accompanying part of Pepsico's Pepsi Points marketing campaign, the printed Pepsi Stuff Catalog available to consumers allowed people to send in cash if they could not collect enough Pepsi Points. The catalog did not list a Harrier jet. About two months after the Super Bowl ad showed, a 21-year-old business student named John Leonard sent in a Pepsi Stuff order form. John included a check for over $700,000 he had raised from investors that was sufficient to purchase 7,000,000 Pepsi Points. John hand-wrote on the Pepsi Stuff order form that he was purchasing a Harrier jet as shown in their commercial. Pepsi refused to give John a jet so he sued Pepsico in federal court for breach of contract.[1] Had Pepsico made a public offer to give away a Harrier jet? If so, had John Leonard properly accepted this offer? We will learn the outcome of this lawsuit shortly, but the immediate lesson is to be careful about saying or doing things that might be perceived by others as a contractual offer.

## Contracts and Contract Law

So just what are *contracts*? Contracts are voluntary agreements between two or more individuals, businesses, organizations, or institutions. These agreements can be for an exchange of goods, services, money, or other promises, actions, or even forbearance (a lack of action). Contract law governs the legal rights and responsibilities that are created by these voluntary relationships and agreements. Indeed, for each legal right by one party to a contract, there are one or more corresponding legal duties that apply to the other party or parties to a contract. The concept of contracts has existed for as long as human civilization has existed. This is because contracts form one of the basic legal foundations of a functioning society. Imagine, for example, a society where no one could enforce anyone else's promises or agreements to buy or sell food or clothing, or to provide health care, education, or building construction, or to

1. *Leonard v. Pepsico, Inc.*, 88 F. Supp. 2d 116, (S.D.N.Y. 1999), aff'd 210 F.3d 88 (2d Cir. 2000)

provide financial services such as home and car loans, savings and checking accounts in banks, or retirement pensions. That society would have great difficulty functioning. This is why contracts are legally enforceable in courts of law, and an extensive body of contract law exists.

Contract law has many sources. Under the common law, most contract law was originally created by courts. Today much of contract law has been codified by statutes in the various states, and some contract law still evolves from judicial decisions. The most significant and highly influential attempt to provide uniform definitions for contracts and other areas of law has been provided by the American Law Institute (ALI). Since 1923, the ALI has brought together eminent lawyers, judges, and legal scholars to offer updated standard legal principles in many subject areas of the law so as to "clarify, modernize, and otherwise improve the law,"[2] The ALI's mission is "to promote the clarification and simplification of the law and its better adaptation to social needs, to secure the better administration of justice, and to encourage and carry on scholarly and scientific legal work."[3] The primary way the ALI offers its guidance is through the publication of "Restatements" of such legal subject areas as contracts, torts, property, and many others. According to the ALI website:

> Restatements are primarily addressed to courts and aim at clear formulations of common law and its statutory elements and reflect the law as it presently stands or might appropriately be stated by a court.[4]

Over a period of many decades, several areas of law have gone through the second, third, and even fourth editions of ALI "Restatements."

Also, the *Uniform Commercial Code* (UCC) is joint project of the ALI and the Uniform Law Commission (ULC).[5] The UCC is designed to help facilitate business transactions across state borders under a common set of laws. The UCC applies only to contracts involving *goods*, however, and not to contracts for services or land. The principles described in the chapter here are the common law rules that apply between two individuals or between an individual consumer and a business. Not only is there much more to contract law then is shown here, even the principles discussed in this chapter have more detailed rules, variations, and exceptions, often with exceptions to the exceptions. A thorough understanding of contract law takes years of study and practice.

2. https://www.ali.org/about-ali/
3. https://www.ali.org/about-ali/how-institute-works/
4. https://www.ali.org/about-ali/how-institute-works
5. http://uniformlaws.org/home

## Offer and Acceptance

The essence of any contract is a mutual assent called a "bargain," also often called an "agreement." Section 17 of the Restatement (Second) of Contracts states "the formation of a contract requires a bargain in which there is a manifestation of mutual assent to the exchange and a consideration. . . . The element of agreement is sometimes referred to as a "meeting of the minds." This meeting of the minds requires an *offer* and an *acceptance* of that offer. What is called *consideration* will be discussed in the next section.

An offer can be made either expressly or impliedly such that a reasonable person would take it as an offer. Thus, merely joking about agreeing to a contract is still binding if the other party believed it was not a joke. Yet an enforceable contract has not been formed if both parties knew the bargain was a joke. In construction contracts, a "bid," whether competitive or noncompetitive, is considered an offer. Also, a contract can be formed even without any express verbal or written terms. If the parties have been regularly acting a certain way toward each other, this could indicate they have been exercising an agreement by custom. An offer is valid if it is clear and definite, even if the party making the offer later regrets offering the terms after the offer has been accepted. For example, in *Lefkowitz v. Great Minneapolis Supply Store,*[6] the store came up with a plan they believed would get women to visit their store. They intentionally advertised that three fur coats would be sold for $1 each on a "first-come first-served" basis. The store had not planned, however, that a Mr. Lefkowtiz would be the first person to show up to buy one of the coats. The store refused to sell him a coat, telling him that a "house rule" allowed only women to buy the coats. Mr. Lefkowitz took the store to court to order them to sell him one of the coats. The court ruled that the coats must be sold as advertised: "While an advertiser has the right at any time before acceptance to modify his offer, he does not have the right, after acceptance, to impose new or arbitrary conditions not contained in the published offer."[7]

Much bargaining can occur before an offer is formed. The Restatement (Second) of Contracts section 26 says that: "preliminary negotiations" are not offers. That is, if both parties make expressly clear they are only tentatively talking about what they *might* be willing or able to do, no offer has yet been made. Business appointments are generally considered to fall into this exception by implication. For example, doctor or hair stylist appointments, dinner reservations, or agreements by the repair people to visit your home at a certain time are generally *not*

6. *Lefkowitz v. Great Minneapolis Supply Store,* 86 N.W.2d 689 (Del. 1957)
7. *Id.*

enforceable contracts unless otherwise specified in the agreement. For example, a contract with a psychologist might expressly include a term that states cancellation of an appointment is allowed only within 24 hours of the appointment or else the patient will be billed for the appointment. Also, media advertisements that are widely broadcast or published are considered to be merely "invitations." These ads invite consumers to make offers to buy goods or services from merchants, "subject to available supplies," or where the "price is subject to change without notice." If a potential customer shows up, the merchant can then accept or decline the consumer's offer to buy the good at the advertised price. This type of commercial behavior is legal as long as the merchant isn't fraudulently advertising products that don't exist, or that don't exist at the price listed, merely to get the consumer to buy another, more expensive product. This type of illegal practice is called a "bait-and-switch" marketing technique.

Acceptance of an offer can be either expressly stated or implied by performance. Express acceptance by *promising* something in return creates a *bilateral contract.* An open-ended offer that either an individual or the public at-large to take some *action* or *forbearance* (not acting) in response to the offer is called a *unilateral contract.* For example, a lost dog reward posted on a public flyer is a unilateral contract that is accepted when someone shows up with the lost dog to claim the reward. A promise to find the dog would not constitute an acceptance of the offer, only the actual physical return of the dog. This is because the terms of the offer stated the offeror will pay money only if and when the dog is actually returned. Also, the offeree must be aware of the offer to accept it. For example, imagine you find a lost dog and return it just to be nice. If you then later discover that a reward had been offered, you are not contractually entitled to the reward because your return of the dog was not intended as an acceptance of the offer. Similarly, business advertising that provides a "money-back guarantee" or a "lowest price match" is enforceable by following the terms given in the public offer. Acceptance of the offer could be accomplished by bringing in an advertisement from a competitor stating they are selling the item for a lower price.

On the other hand, sometimes business advertisements make intentionally exaggerated promises that are legally unenforceable. For example, imagine Ricardo's Pizzeria publicly advertises that "Ricardo's make the best pizza in the world!" and "You'll absolutely love Ricardo's pizza!" Susan visits Ricardo's and tries their pizza based on the ad, but doesn't like the pizza. May she insist on her money back based on a claim that Ricardo's Pizza committed fraud? In contract law, such obviously exaggerated and unverifiable claims like "Our product is the best!" are called "puffery." Businesses, especially salespeople, "puff" regularly, and "puffing" is an expected part of much bargaining. A legally binding contract would exist only if Susan relied on some additional specific promise on the part of Ricardo, such as "You'll love our pizza or your money back" or "Our pizza uses only 100% Government-Certified Organic and Non-GMO ingredients."

The trouble a party can get into when providing offers containing exaggerated or joking claims was famously demonstrated in a case that received a great deal of media publicity. The start of this chapter introduced the now-famous "Pepsi Points Case." John Leonard sued Pepsico for refusing to give him a Harrier fighter jet after he sent in the money to purchase the 7,000,000 Pepsi Points the commercial advertised. The cost of the Harrier Jet was $23 million dollars, but the Pepsi commercial indicated the jet could be purchased for "7,000,000 Pepsi Points." Since Pepsi Points could be purchased for 10 cents per Pepsi Point, it only cost John $700,000 to buy seven million Pepsi Points. Obviously Pepsico did not intend to lose such enormous sums of money through their Pepsi Points campaign. As the federal District Court noted, at one Pepsi Point per Pepsi soda, earning 7,000,000 Pepsi Points would have required drinking 190 Pepsis a day for 100 years. Such an absurdly unrealistic requirement indicated that the ad was done in jest and was not a serious (i.e. actual) contract offer. As the District Court stated:

> The implication of the commercial is that Pepsi Stuff merchandise will inject drama and moment into hitherto unexceptional lives. The commercial in this case thus makes the exaggerated claims similar to those of many television advertisements: that by consuming the featured clothing, car, beer, or potato chips, one will become attractive, stylish, desirable, and admired by all. A reasonable viewer would understand such advertisements as mere puffery, not as statements of fact. . . . The tongue-in-cheek attitude of the commercial would not cause a reasonable person to conclude that a soft drink company would be giving away fighter planes as part of a promotion.[8]

Even though Pepsico eventually won the case, they altered their "Harrier Jet" commercial twice. Initally they vastly increased the Pepsi Point value for the jet to "HARRIER FIGHTER 700,000,000 PEPSI POINTS." Then later, to be on the extra-safe side, they further modified that statement to "HARRIER FIGHTER 700,000,000 PEPSI POINTS (JUST KIDDING)."

When it comes to written contracts, consumers are often unable to

8. *Leonard v. Pepsico, Inc.*, 88 F. Supp. 2d 116, (S.D.N.Y. 1999), aff'd 210 F.3d 88 (2d Cir. 2000)

read all the fine details of a contract until after they buy a product and then open up the packaging to find the contract details inside. Courts are divided on whether contract details hidden under such "shrink-wrap" are accepted by the performance of buying and opening the packaging. Yet courts agree that "clickwrap" agreements are valid. These are online terms a person must agree to by clicking "accept" in their internet web browser. Since the consumer has the chance to read the terms first, clicking "Yes" or "Accept" or "I agree" constitutes an acceptance to the extensive and detailed terms. This is true even if the buyer reads none of the terms. This is why lawyers always strongly advise "Never sign anything without reading it!" Today's modern internet equivalent is "Never click that you agree to something without reading it!" On the other hand, simply loading a webpage into your web browser does not constitute an acceptance of any terms stated by the website. This is because the person browsing a website does not have a chance to read the terms of the website before visiting the website.

*Revoking an Offer* Generally the offeror may revoke the offer at any time before the offer is accepted even if a time period to accept is stated by the offeror. Revocation of an offer is also often called "rescission" or "termination" of the offer. The communication of the revocation must be made in the same manner that the offer was made. For example, a public offer printed in a newspaper must be revoked by a similar ad in the same newspaper. Revocation is valid upon receipt of the revocation by the offeree unless the revocation is publicly published in which case the revocation is effective upon publication. A deadline to accept an offer means the offer expires at the deadline, but the offeror may also revoke the offer prior to the deadline.

If an offeree pays for the right to have the offer remain irrevocable until a certain time limit, this is called an *option* contract. That is, the offeree has joined in a separate enforceable contract with the offeror in which the offeree has the option to accept the offer at any time until the guaranteed time period expires. In this situation, even if the offeree initially rejects the offer, the offeree can later decide to instead accept the offer, as long as the time period for acceptance of the offer has not expired. A related type of option contract is a "right of first refusal." Let's say you're thinking about selling your house, and I really like your house and its location. I want to be the first person to consider whether to buy your house before anyone else has the chance to buy it. I can pay you for the right to be the first one to receive any offer of sale from you. I will then have the option of either accepting or refusing the offer. If I decline the offer to buy your house, then you as the seller may now legally make the offer to anyone else of your choosing.

An offer lapses after a reasonable time if no time is specified. But what is a "reasonable" time? The Restatement (Second) of Contracts Section 41 states what is "reasonable" varies under the circumstances and includes "the nature of the proposed contract, the purposes of the parties, the course of dealing between them, and any relevant usages of trade." In short, under the Restatement (Second), all the surrounding circumstances of the offer must be considered in determining whether an offer has terminated due to lapse of time. Consider, for example, the differences between the following: an offer of reward for return of a lost cat versus return of a lost child; an offer to buy land versus an offer to buy a toaster at a garage sale; or an offer to pay for your adult child's lunch versus an offer to pay for your adult child's college tuition. These examples reveal how offers can have different expiration deadlines given the vastly different nature of the offers.

A classic example of the expiration of an offer occurred in an 1844 case, *Loring v. City of Boston*.[9] After a rash of arsons within Boston, the mayor took out a newspaper ad offering a $1,000 reward for the apprehension and conviction of any person setting fire to any building within the city limits. The ad ran for only a week or two. Almost four years later, after a particular case of arson, the plaintiff Loring provided information on a suspect who was later caught and convicted for the crime. Loring then tried to claim the $1,000 reward. The court ruled the purpose of the original offer was to put a stop to the rash of arsons, which indeed worked at the time as hoped. Now, though, almost four years later, there was almost no public memory or awareness of the original offer. The city of Boston never renewed the offer nor ran the ad again. Given the changed circumstances, the offer would no longer serve the same purpose as it had four years earlier. In short, it clearly was not the intent of the city of Boston to have the offer remain valid permanently. Thus, the courts ruled that the offer was no longer valid.

*Accepting and Rejecting an Offer* Acceptance of the offer by the offeree must be communicated to the offeror unless the regular practice of the parties is otherwise or unless the parties expressly specify otherwise. The regular practice of how two contract parties have interacted in the past is called their "course of dealing." Acceptance of an offer isn't usually an issue in live face-to-face or telephone conversations. But what if an offer is made via the postal mail, e-mail, fax, or text message? Generally, an offer is valid upon receipt of the offer by the offeree. Yet what if the offeree sends an acceptance in the same manner as the offer, but the offeror has not yet received the acceptance and attempts to revoke the offer in the meantime? Is the contract formed when the acceptance is sent by the offeree, or when the acceptance is received by the offeror? Under the

9. *Loring v. City of Boston*, 48 Mass. 409 (1844).

"mailbox rule," the acceptance is valid (and thus the contract is formed) as soon as the acceptance is sent. This is true even if the acceptance is never received by the offeror unless the offer itself specifies different conditions for a valid acceptance. Also, under the rule in a majority of common law jurisdictions, offers are automatically revoked (also called rescinded) upon the death or incapacity of either party to the contract.

Rejection of an offer by an offeree must be communicated to the offeror. The rejection may be made either expressly or impliedly. Just as the case with offers, the question is whether a reasonable person would understand the offer has been rejected. Once made, a rejection is permanent. An offeree who rejects an offer may not then come back later and try to accept the offer once it has been rejected. In other words, there is no such thing as a "revocation of a rejection of an offer." Rejection of an offer is also implied if the offeree makes any counter-offer whose terms differ in any way from the original offer. If the contract does not involve the sale of goods, then under the "mirror image" rule, the acceptance must completely match the terms of the offer or else the offeree's terms are considered a counter-offer. The original offeror (now the new offeree) can now accept or reject the proposed new offer from the original offeree. Note, however, that if the contract is for the sale of goods between commercial merchants, specific rules apply under the Uniform Commercial Code.[10]

Under the principle of "account stated," if a merchant sends a bill to a consumer or business claiming a purchaser of goods or services owes the merchant money for such goods or services, that statement of the account will be evidence that a contract existed between the seller and buyer. The alleged purchaser must object to the claim that appears on the bill within a reasonable time, often a week to 30 days, depending on the jurisdiction. If the alleged buyer does not object to the bill, the buyer's silence is deemed to indicate agreement with the amount owed as stated on the bill.

In the case of a contract between a promisor (obligor) and a promisee (obligee), a promisee may generally *assign* the rights of the promise to a third party. The promisor would thus render performance of the promise to the third party, not the original promisee. Similarly, the promisor may generally *delegate* the performance of the promise to a third party unless the promisor was hired because the promisor possesses some unique talent—a special "skill, judgment, or taste." For example, assume landscaper Alice contracts with homeowner Betty to provide lawn mowing services to Betty for five years. If Alice decides to retire in the meantime, she may delegate performance of her contractual duties to another landscape company owned by Carry. And, if Betty

10. See, e.g., UCC Sections 2-206 and 2-207.

sells her home, she may assign her rights to having the lawn mowed to the new homeowner Debbie.

In short, rights can be assigned, and duties can be delegated. Both assignment and delegation may occur at the same time, and even multiple times. There is no limit to the number of times assignment or delegation may occur. As a result, the contract might eventually be performed between two parties that had nothing to do with forming the original contract. One other situation might occur if the original promisor and promisee contract for the benefit of a third party. If so, then that third party is called a *beneficiary*. One common example is life insurance. Spouses can contract with an insurance company to provide a cash payout to each other in the event of the death of one of the spouses. Similarly, an employee who pays into a company retirement account will be asked to list a beneficiary as part of the employee's agreement with the investment firm that is managing the employee's retirement fund. If the employee dies before or during retirement, the remainder of the retirement fund goes to the declared beneficiary. In cases where the primary purpose of the contract is to benefit a third party, the third party has the right to sue for breach by the party that fails to provide the benefit.[11]

## Consideration

The difference between a contract and a gratuitous promise is the presence of a mutual exchange of value. If I simply tell you "I'll give you 25 dollars tomorrow" absent any reciprocal promise, action, forbearance, or obligation on your part, then there is no *consideration*. If, on the other hand, I say "I promise to give you 25 dollars tomorrow if you wash my car," then your washing my car would constitute your side of the mutual exchange. The value given in exchange is called *consideration*. According to the Restatement (Second) of Contracts Section 71, consideration can be one of three things: an action (*doing* something), a forbearance (*not* doing something), or a *promise* to either do or not do something. An action, forbearance, or promise can include creating, altering, or ending a legal relationship.

A classic and leading case on the issue of consideration is *Hamer v. Sidway*.[12] In 1869, William Story promised his 16-year-old nephew William Story, II, $5,000 on William's 21st birthday if William went without drinking alcohol, using tobacco, swearing, and playing cards or billiards for money until that time. Nephew William managed to do so, and he

11. See, e.g., *Lawrence v. Fox*, 20 N.Y. 268 (1859)

12. *Hamer v. Sidway*, 27 N.E. 256 (N.Y. 1891)

and his uncle agreed that Uncle William would hold the money for Nephew William for safekeeping. Nephew William assigned the rights to the money to his wife, who then assigned the rights to the money to Louisa Hamer. Some years went by and in 1887 Uncle William died before Nephew William or his legal assignees had collected the money. Louisa then sought to collect the money from Franklin Sidway, the executor of his uncle's estate. The court ruled the Louisa was entitled to the money. The court explained that nephew William had not drunk any alcohol for years or engaged in the other forbidden conduct even though he had a legal right to do. Nephew William's forbearance of these actions was sufficient consideration to make Uncle William's promise become part of an enforceable contract. Since Nephew William had fulfilled his side of the bargain, Uncle William (via his estate) owed Nephew William (or his assignees) the $5,000 that had been promised in exchange.[13]

The amount of consideration can sometimes be undefined. For example, in a *requirement contract* the seller promises to provide whatever quantity of goods the buyer needs. The buyer in turn must buy all their required goods exclusively from the seller. The opposite type of contract is called an *output contract.* In an output contract, the buyer promises to buy whatever quantity of goods the seller produces. In return, the seller must sell all their goods exclusively to the buyer.[14] For example, a grocery store chain might enter into an output contract with a gourmet salsa company by agreeing to buy however much salsa that company produces. In return, that company would agree to sell their salsa only to that particular grocery chain. In short, the amount of consideration need not be specific as long as it has some actual value.

For consideration to exist, there must be an actual exchange of something of concrete value. Otherwise, the agreement has only *sham* or *token* consideration. *Sham* consideration exists where consideration is falsely stated even though there is no actual consideration. *Token* consideration is so small that it's not really giving anything of value in exchange for what was received. That is, nominal token consideration is *not* consideration, but is used merely as a pretense to make a gratuitous promise to give a gift. For example, a promise to give someone money in the future based on an exchange of "one cent" or out of mere "love and affection" is not a legal enforceable contract due to lack of consideration.[15]

An empty, *illusory promise* is not consideration. This can happen, for example, if performance of the promise is subject to a condition occurring that is entirely within the control of the promisor. For example,

13. See also *Feige v. Boehm* 123 A.2d 316 (Md. 1956).
14. See UCC Section 2-306
15. *Schnell v. Nell,* 17 Ind. 29 (1861)

imagine Abby says to Barb "If you pay me $25 dollars right now, I promise to wash your car tomorrow if I feel like doing it then." Even if Barb pays the money to Abby, Abby's promise is illusory. She hasn't really promised to do anything because her choice whether to follow through on the promise is entirely up to her. Or, imagine Angie says to her sister Brie, "If you give me $25 dollars right now, I promise to wash your car tomorrow if our mother tells me in person to do so." Yet Angie knows, and Brie doesn't know, that their mother is in the middle of a three-week backpacking trip through a remote part of the Himalaya Mountains. There is no realistic possibility that their mother will tell Angie "in person" to wash Brie's car tomorrow. Angie's promise to Brie is thus illusory and is not consideration. This means there is no contract.

Moreover, for consideration to exist, neither the offeror nor the offeree need be the person who is providing the things of value exchanged between the offeror and offeree. For example, imagine the following exchange between two neighboring homeowners regarding their two teen-age sons:

*Fred*: "Hello, Bob! My lawn needs mowing and I see your car is looking dirty. I'll have my son wash your car if you have your son mow my lawn."

*Bob*: "That sounds like a great plan, Fred! You got yourself a deal!"

These two fathers have just formed a contract even though neither of them promised that they *themselves* would provide the labor needed to fulfill the contract. Instead, both parties promised that third persons (their sons) would perform the labor to fulfill the contract. This mutual exchange of value by the parties forming the contract constitutes valid consideration.

Under the *pre-existing duty rule*, however, a promise to do something one is already legally obligated to do does not constitute consideration. For example, if I'm already required to do something by the law or by a prior contract, then I'm not exchanging anything of value if I promise to do what I must already do anyway. For example, imagine a merchant has already contracted to provide a service to a customer at a fixed price. Before the merchant's performance, the merchant tells the customer "I want more money to fulfill the contract." Even if the purchaser agrees, there is no consideration. After performance by the merchant, the purchaser would not owe any promised additional money to the merchant. This is because the agreement to pay more money was unenforceable due to lack of consideration.[16] As another example, people who offer public rewards for catching criminals are not obligated to pay the reward to law enforcement personnel because the job of police officers already is to use their best efforts to catch criminals.

16. See, e.g., *Lingenfelder v. Wainwright Brewery*, 103 Mo. 578 (1891)

There is another example of a particular type of application of the pre-existing duty rule. Under a majority of common law jurisdictions, if a creditor agrees to waive the rest of the debt owed by a debtor upon partial payment of the debt, then that debtor has not provided any consideration and the creditor's agreement to waive the rest of the debt is unenforceable. If, however, either the fact of the debt or the amount of the debt is in dispute, then the creditor may waive any additional claims in exchange for a limited payment by the debtor. This type of enforceable agreement is called an *executory accord*. Because the debtor might not have ended up owing anything, or not owing as much, the debtor is providing a *certain, defined* legal claim to the creditor in exchange for having the rest of the *possible* claims waived by the creditor. This process of a *definite partial* payment satisfying a *potential large* claim is called *accord and satisfaction*. If the debtor fails to make the agreed-upon partial payment, however, then the debtor is in material breach of the accord and satisfaction agreement. The creditor may then again come after the debtor for the larger potential claim(s). Also, if a new debtor contracts with a creditor to take on the debt of a prior debtor in exchange for the creditor waiving all claims against that prior debtor, this contract is called a *novation*. This term comes from the Latin *nova* for "new," meaning the old debtor is replaced with a new debtor.

An important exception to the need for consideration is what is most commonly referred to as the concept of *promissory estoppel*. A promise that has no consideration in return can become enforceable in some instances. Under the doctrine of promissory estoppel, a promissor or third party wishing to have a promise enforced must show three elements. First, there must be a promise by the promissor to the promissee. Second, the promissor must reasonably expect that the promissee or other third party might rely on the promise on the part of promissor. That is, the promissee reasonably thought the promise was serious and not joking. Third and finally, the promissee or third party (such as spouse, child, or business partner of the promissee) must rely on the promise to their detriment.[17] Thus, a gratuitous promise on your part to a work colleague such as "I'll treat you to lunch next time" is probably not generally enforceable under promissory estoppel. This is because it is unlikely your work colleague would make important financial decisions based on your promise. On the other hand, a promise by a wealthy local individual that "I'll donate $10,000 to your charity" is probably enforceable under promissory estoppel. This is because charities regularly make important financial decisions based on the funds that have been pledged to them. These spending decisions would cause serious

17. See *Ricketts v. Scothorn*, 77 N.W. 365 (Neb. 1898); Restatement (Second) of Contracts Section 90

financial difficulties for the charity if the promised funds did not come through.

In addition, in rare situations, courts will create a contract even where the parties did not intend to create a contract and where there is no present or future consideration. This is typically called *quasi-contract,* or sometimes called *contract-at-law.* In these relatively rare instances, past consideration will substitute as consideration in the present or future. This most commonly occurs when someone gives voluntary aid to another such that the recipient of the aid acquires a moral and legal duty of some sort of repayment to the giver of the aid. For example, imagine a doctor renders significant medical aid to an unconscious injured victim at the scene of an automobile accident. The doctor may later seek compensation for the services rendered, even though the patient never consented to be treated nor agreed to pay for the services.[18]

## Contract Enforceability

Even though a bargain has been reached through offer and acceptance, and the bargain has consideration, there are many instances where the resulting contract is still not enforceable in court. Here are the most common reasons for this lack of enforceability.

*Statute of Frauds* Some types of contracts must have their terms in writing for them to be enforceable. This rule is called the *Statute of Frauds.* This term originally goes back to an English law in 1677. To help prevent the creation of fraudulent contracts that might result from individuals falsely claiming they are owed money or property, contracts that involve substantial amounts of money or other serious legal interests must be put in writing. The Restatement (Second) of Contracts Section 110 lists contracts that must be in writing. These are contracts for the sale of an interest in land, contracts that are not to be performed within a year of the making of the contract, and any sale of goods over $500. Also, "contracts in consideration of marriage" must be in writing, other than a bare mutual promise to marry. For example, imagine millionaire Monica agrees to marry Gordon only if he'll first consent that he can never sue her for her wealth if they divorce. That prenuptial agreement must be in writing. Or, imagine a single mother contracts with a man that she'll marry him if he agrees to pay child support for her child until the child reaches adulthood. That contract must be in writing as well. If a writing is required by the statute of frauds to enforce the contract against a party, that party must also have signed the contract. "Signature" is broadly in-

18. See, e.g., *Webb v. McGowin,* 168 So. 199 (Ala. 1935).

terpreted, though. It can be handwritten, printed, stamped, initialed only, or be nothing more than letterhead, a business logo, or any other mark by the party indicating agreement to the contract.

The Restatement (Second) of Contracts further notes in subsection 110(5): "In many states other classes of contracts are subject to a requirement of a writing." This is yet another reason why lawyers insistently and consistently say "always get it in writing." If you don't, it could be impossible to prove the existence of either the contract itself or the particular contract terms you're claiming. Or, even if you do prove the contract terms existed, the contract could still be unenforceable because you didn't put it in writing. Thus, one must always be sure to look to state law to determine which specific contracts must be in writing. Indeed, by statute many contracts or other documents require signatures to be officially notarized by a notary public in order for the documents to be legally enforceable. For example, in Louisiana, a valid typed will must not only be signed by the writer and two witnesses, all those signatures must be notarized. If not, the will is invalid.

*Unconscionability* A contract will not be enforced if its terms are extremely harsh or punitive against one party to the contract. This occurs most commonly when a sophisticated seller such as a large company enters into a contract with an unsophisticated buyer (that is, an uneducated consumer). The terms may impose harsh interest rates, excessive penalties for late payments, or other onerous terms. Perhaps the buyer was illiterate, or was literate but didn't understand the terms due to excessive legal language used in the terms. Maybe the buyer understood the terms but overlooked some of the fine print buried in a tiny footnote in the huge, lengthy contract. Or, perhaps the difference in bargaining power between the two parties was so unfairly one-sided that the resulting terms were grossly unfair to the weaker party. In any of these situations, the contract could be unenforceable as a public policy matter if the contract terms are deemed *unconscionable.* According to the Restatement (Second) Section 208, if a contract is unconscionable then the court may refuse to enforce some or all of the contract, depending on what will avoid any unconscionable result. Unconscionability is extremely fact-intensive and so must be determined on a case-by-case basis. Although it is rare that courts rule contracts to be unconscionable, consumer debtors sometimes try to void part or all of their debt using this concept.

*Contrary to Public Policy* Besides unconscionable contracts, there are several other specific types of contracts that are deemed unenforceable as a matter of public policy. Such unenforceable contracts include the sale of body parts or organs. For example, you can not legally sell one of your kidneys to a millionaire medical patient dying of kidney cancer even if you both agree to it. Nor will courts enforce contracts that require racial discrimination. For example, even if your house title has a condition of purchase that you can never in turn sell your house to a non-Caucasian, that restrictive clause is unenforceable. Contracts that involve illegal activity are also unenforceable, such as contracts for illegal drugs, prostitution, bribes, or violent crimes. The contract performance doesn't necessarily have to violate the law, however, to violate public policy. For example, interfering with someone else's family relationships may be unethical or immoral, but is not illegal. Nevertheless, as a matter of public policy, our society doesn't want to aid in the destruction of marriages or the parent-child relationship. As a result, contracts to injure family relationships will not be enforced by the courts.

*Misunderstanding* Occasionally both parties believe they have met all the requirements for a valid contract, but it turns out instead that they have had a serious misunderstanding. This occurred in a classic 1864 common law case from England, *Raffles v. Wichelhaus.*[19] In this case, the seller Raffles agreed to buy cotton from the seller Wichelhaus. The contract specifically stated the cotton would arrive in Liverpool on a ship called *Peerless* coming from Bombay, India. Neither party, however, realized there were *two* ships arriving from Bombay called the *Peerless,* both of which carried cotton, but were scheduled to leave Bombay two months apart. The seller Raffles thought the contract involved the ship named *Peerless* leaving Bombay in December. The buyer Wichelhaus, on the other hand, believed the contract involved the ship named *Peerless* leaving Bombay in October. Neither party knew about the existence of the other ship named *Peerless* that as it turned out the other party had in mind. Since Raffles had nothing to do with the ship named *Peerless* that was leaving Bombay in October, when it arrived in England, Raffles obviously did not sell Wichelhaus any of the cotton from the ship. Wichelhaus therefore believed Raffles had repudiated the contract. When the December *Peerlesss* arrived in England, Raffless expected Wichelhaus to pay for the cotton, but Wichelhaus refused. Wichelaus argued Raffles had already repudiated the contract by not selling him any cotton from the October *Peerless.* Raffles sued Wichelaus for the value of the cotton according to their original contract. The English court ruled that because the parties had not agreed on an essential term to the contract—*which* ship named *Peerless* was involved in the contract—the contract was void. Ever since the *Peerless* case, the common law has held that when both parties have a misunderstanding about the essential nature of the contract, the contract is void.

19. *Raffles v. Wichelhaus,* EWHC Exch J19 (1864).

*Mutual Mistake* What if both parties clearly understand the terms of the contract, but it turns out both of the parties are mistaken about a characteristic of the item they are buying or selling? According to generally accepted common law principles of contract law, in the case of a *mutual mistake of value*, the buyer wins. For example, in *Woods v. Boynton,*[20] the seller Woods sold a pair of jewelers including Boynton a small stone for $1. Both she and the jewelers believed at the time it was probably topaz. Later, however, the jewelers discovered it was actually a rough diamond worth $700. When Woods learned of this, she sought to rescind the contract, but the jewelers refused. Woods then filed a lawsuit insisting that the stone be returned to her. The court held that since there was no evidence of fraud on the part of the jewelers, the parties being mistaken about the value of the item transacted is not grounds for later rescission of the contract.

Yet a later case that is often used as common law precedent arguably contradicts the holding of *Woods v. Boynton.* If both the buyer and seller are mistaken about the *nature of the item,* then the contract is voidable. In *Sherwood v. Walker,*[21] (also known as the "Pregnant Cow Case"), cattle breeders Walker and his partners contracted to sell a cow named "Rose 2d of Aberlone" on their Michigan farm to a farmer named Sherwood. Walker and his partners, along with the buyer Sherwood, all believed that Rose was infertile—that she was not capable of getting pregnant. Before Sherwood took possession of Rose, however, Walker and his partners discovered Rose was pregnant. This made Rose significantly more valuable than if she were infertile. Thus, when Sherwood came to pick up Rose, Walker and his partners refused to hand Rose over to Sherwood. Sherwood filed suit requesting that the court order he be given possession of Rose. The court refused, however, declaring that when both parties are mistaken about the essential nature of the item being transacted, this is grounds for rescission of the contract. Since all the parties were mistaken about Rose's nature (whether she could or could not produce a calf), the contract was rescindable. Note that many legal scholars believe the holding of *Sherwood v. Walker* is hard to reconcile with the holding of *Woods v. Boynton*—that is, why is a mutual mistake about the value of a stone different than a mutual mistake about the value of a cow?

*Unilateral Mistake* If only one party makes a material (serious) mistake when contracting, this is called a *unilateral* mistake. In such an instance, the contract can generally be rescinded by the mistaken party. For example, assume a car dealer sends an e-mail offer to a potential car

20. *Woods v. Boynton,* 25 N.W. 42 (Wisc. 1885).
21. *Sherwood v. Walker,* 33 N.W. 919 (Mich. 1887)

buyer to sell a $20,000 car but accidentally leaves off a zero and offers the car for "$2,000." Or, the car buyer sends an acceptance to buy a $20,000 car but accidentally adds in a zero, and offers to buy the car for "$200,000." In either case, the contract can be rescinded by the party who made the mistake.

*Fraud/Misrepresentation* The older common law followed the principle of *caveat emptor,* meaning "buyer beware." This put the risk of being deceived on the buyer. Today the common law rarely follows the principle of *caveat emptor.* In the case of *fraud* or *misrepresentation,* if one party knowingly deceives the other party about a material (central) matter relating to the contract, the defrauded party may rescind the contract. That is, the fraud must have "induced" the victim to assent to the contract. Misrepresentation about a trivial side matter, though, will not allow the deceived party to void the contract. Today, the common law typically allows the contract to be voided or rescinded by the deceived party if they relied on the material misrepresentation in forming the contract.

One unusual example of this principle occurred in *Stambovsky v. Ackley,*[22] often called the "Ghostbuster's Case." Helen Ackley and her family owned a home in Nyack, New York, a suburb of New York City. Over a nine-year period she claimed the house was haunted by ghosts and poltergeists, who would wake her daughter up by shaking her daughter's bed. Her stories received both local and national news coverage including *Reader's Digest* magazine. Jeffrey Stambovsky, having no knowledge of the alleged haunting, contracted to buy Helen's house. Jeffrey then learned of the home's reputation and filed a lawsuit to rescind the real estate contract. The Court agreed with Jeffrey. There was no duty under New York law to disclose supposed supernatural occurrences associated with a home for sale. Nevertheless, the court announced:

> The impact of the reputation [of the house] thus created goes to the very essence of the bargain between the parties, greatly impairing both the value of the property and its potential for resale. . . . Having undertaken to inform the public-at-large, to whom she has no legal relationship, about the supernatural occurrences on her property, she may be said to owe no less a duty to her contract vendee.

Since Helen had failed to disclose a material fact about the house, Jeffrey was able to legally rescind his agreement to purchase the home.

22. *Stambovsky v. Ackley,* 159 A.2d 264 (N.Y.App.Div. 1991); see also Restatement (Second) of Contracts, Section 161.

*Legal Incapacity* Contracts by minors (individuals under the age of 18) are generally risky to enter into. Most contracts with minors are voidable by the minor at any time prior to a reasonable time after reaching the age of maturity. There are exceptions to this rule, such as contracts for "necessaries" such as food, clothing, medicine, or housing. For example, merchants who sell a teenager an expensive car stereo system are taking a chance that the teenager will not disaffirm the contract and return the system. Also, contracts with a person who is obviously under the influence of alcohol or other illegal substance at the time of the making of the contract are similarly voidable by the intoxicated person. So, too, with persons who have a mental incapacity such as senility, insanity, or extremely low IQ.

*Undue Influence* Regardless whether a victimized party meets the definition of legal incapacity, where one party takes advantage of another party because of unusual weakness or vulnerability, the victimized party can void the contract on the grounds of *undue influence*. For example, imagine an elderly person without family who is physically disabled and has a live-in caretaker. The elderly person might have full mental capacity, but be unable to say no to their caretaker's demand for a huge wage increase, or perhaps to giving the caretaker access to the victim's bank account. In such a case, the employment contract may be rescinded later by the victimized client. Just as with unilateral mistake or legal incapacity, the contract is not necessarily void, but voidable at the option of the party who suffered the unilateral mistake, incapacity, or undue influence.

*Duress* Duress is different from undue influence. In the case of undue influence, one party has a weakness such that they are vulnerable to domination in general. In the case of *duress*, a party might have none of the weaknesses found in cases of undue influence. For example, a victimized party might be a successful, wealthy business owner, yet there is some kind of improper act taken against the party that forces them to make a particular choice against their will. The classic example of duress is putting a gun to someone's head to get them to sign a document. There are other types of physical duress, however, as well as psychological duress. For example, duress could be caused by a threat to commit a criminal act against the coerced party or against the family or property of the coerced party. Duress could also exist by a threat to commit blackmail or extortion against the coerced party.

*Economic duress* can also occur due to a gross inequality of bargaining power under the circumstances. For example, imagine a seller knows a buyer badly needs some goods, and there is no other possible supplier. Even if the seller decides to charge many times more for the goods than originally agreed, the buyer has no choice but to agree to the new price.

This particular agreement can be rescinded later by the buyer both on the grounds of duress and due to the pre-existing duty rule (discussed earlier). A victimized party who enters into a contract due to duress imposed by the other party may later void (rescind) the contract.[23]

*Impossibility and Impracticability* On rare occasions, a contract becomes *impossible* or *impracticable* to perform due to no fault by either party to the contract. Restatement (Second) of Contracts, Section 261, Comment d, defines "impracticable" as "extreme or unreasonable difficulty, expenses, injury or loss." For example, let's assume a fire, flood, or tornado destroys your business. It's basically impossible for you to fulfill your contractual obligations for performances due the next day.[24] In theory, you could still fulfill your contractual obligations if you borrowed one-hundred-million dollars and had your business rebuilt and resupplied overnight. Yet even assuming such were possible, doing so would be an extremely costly and unreasonable solution that would bankrupt you. In such a case, fulfilling your contractual obligation is not technically impossible, but it is *impracticable.* Other reasons for impracticability could be war, embargo, or the death or disability of someone essential to the performance of the contract. In such situations, the contract the party for whom the contract became impracticable may rescind the contract.

*Frustration of Purpose* A situation related to impossibility is called frustration of purpose. It is possible for the contract to be performed, but the purpose for the contract no longer exists. For example, let's say you rent out an apartment balcony along a major Mardi Gras parade route in New Orleans, Louisiana so you can throw a parade-watching party. Unfortunately, though, the parade route is then changed at the last minute. It's neither impossible nor impracticable for you to still rent out the apartment for yourself, but the very reason for you doing so now no longer exists. In this case, you can void the contract because your purpose for entering the contract has been frustrated.[25] Note, however, that even though profit-making is often a financial "purpose" of a contract, the fact that one party to a contract will not make as much money as they originally believed does not count as "frustration of purpose."

## Contract Terms

A contract must have certain key terms, called *material* terms, clearly contained in the understanding between the parties. Otherwise, if the

23. See, e.g., *Odorizzi v. Bloomfield School District,* 246 Cal. App. 2d 123 (Cal. 1964).
24. See, e.g., *Taylor v. Caldwell,* EWHC QB J1 (England 1863)
25. See, e.g. *Krell v. Henry,* 2 K.B. 740 (England 1903).

primary terms of the contract lack reasonable certainty, the contract is too indefinite to be enforceable. The material terms of a contract are generally the subject matter of the contract—the price of the goods or services, payment terms, the quantity and quality of the goods or services, and the duration of the contract. A modern common law trend, though, is that if the parties left out a key term but "agreed to agree" on deciding upon that term in the future, courts will often add in what they believe is a reasonable "gap-filler" term to the contract. The courts will then enforce the contract as including such a term even though that material term was originally lacking. Some key terms such as the price, however, must be specific. Terms such as "fair price," "reasonable price," or "appropriate price" are too vague to be enforceable.

Assuming an agreement has sufficiently clear terms to constitute a contract, questions often arise as to the exclusivity and meaning of those terms. Under the *parol evidence rule,* the terms of a written contract are limited to what is contained within the "four corners" of the written contract itself. This is also called the *four corners rule.* A written contract that contains the exclusive terms of the contract is also called a "completely integrated agreement." That is, no new or additional terms of the contract are allowed based on claims of earlier contracts, prior discussions, or separate verbal agreements.[26] For example, assume you agree in writing to buy a car from a seller for $10,000. You may not then later claim that the seller also verbally agreed to throw in five free car washes or three free oil changes. An important exception to the parol evidence rule, however, is that verbal evidence is allowed to show the *meaning* of the *existing* written terms of the contract. For example, a contract might say "delivery during the day," but it doesn't say *which* day. Or, a contract might say "pick-up in-store," but there are three store locations in the region and the contract doesn't specify which one. In such cases, prior custom or verbal understanding will be allowed to show what the parties meant by the terms of the written contract. It is critical, then, to determine whether one party is trying to *add* an *additional* term to the written contract, or is merely trying to *explain* what the parties meant by an *existing* term. Adding is forbidden, but explaining is allowed.

Another exception to the parol evidence rule is when a party claims the written document in dispute was not the final contract, but was merely an earlier negotiation. If the final integrated contract had different terms than an earlier negotiated contract, then the parol evidence rule would not bar evidence of this fact. Of course, contract parties often try to add new or different terms under the guise of "interpreting" an existing term. Or, one party will try to add new terms by the pretext of claiming the terms were not "final." As a result, these questions are matters for the court to determine. The simple way to avoid these dis-

26. See, e.g., Restatement (Second) of Contracts, Section 213.

putes is to put express language in the contract stating the contract contains the "complete and final terms" of the contract. In the alternative, the written contract could expressly declare that it is the "exclusive" agreement between the parties. This is called a *merger clause* because it merges all verbal and written agreements into a single written document. Merchants will often put this clause into their contract forms as a standard practice.

In the case of the sale of goods, however, the UCC does allow some exceptions to the parol evidence rule. Additional terms of the contract can be shown by "course of performance," "course of dealing," or "usage of trade." The pattern of past behavior of the parties while performing that *particular* contract is called "course of performance" The pattern of past behavior of the parties while performing *prior* contracts with each other is called "course of dealing." The general pattern of that particular industry is called "usage of trade." If the course of performance, course of dealing, or usage of trade creates certain expectations by the parties, then those expectations can constitute additional unwritten terms of the contract. In such situations, the parol evidence rule would not prohibit evidence of such practices.

For example, let's say you're building your own home and you order 500 eight-foot long two-by-four wooden beams from a building supply company. When the shipment comes, the 500 wooden beams measure *exactly* 8 feet long by 2 inches high by 4 inches wide. This is in breach of the contract! The usage of trade in the construction industry is that although the *length* of wooden beams is measured exactly, the height and width are *not.* Two-by-fours are in reality 1.5x3.5 inches in measurement. Similarly, a four-by-six is in reality 3.5x5.5 inches, and so on. Thus, if a construction contract orders "2x4" beams, those beams should not actually be 2x4 inches, but 1.5x3.5 inches. The parol evidence rule would not prevent your introduction of evidence to show what the contract terms meant according to the standard usage of trade in the construction and building supply industry.

There are also some types of contract terms that courts say are implied in the contract, even if the term was never agreed to by the parties either verbally or in writing. For example, sellers under contract to sell goods on commission have an implied contractual requirement that they must exert *reasonable efforts* to sell those goods. This principle was established in the famous 1917 contract law case *Wood v. Lucy, Lady Duff-Gordon.*[27] Lucy was an interesting litigant. Her title "Lady" came from the fact she was marred to Sir Cosmo Duff-Gordon, a Scottish nobleman. She also survived the sinking of the famous ship *Titanic* in 1912. By that time, she had already become a leading, internationally-known

27. *Wood v. Lucy, Lady Duff-Gordon*, 118 N.E. 214 (N.Y. 1917)

British fashion designer. As part of her fashion business, Lucy signed a one-year exclusive contract with New York advertiser Otis Wood to market clothing in the United States under her name. Other designers would design the clothing but Lucy would "endorse" the items to increase their sales. Under the terms of the contract, Otis was required to give Lucy half the revenue earned from sales of any clothing he marketed that she endorsed, but the contract did not require him to actually attempt to market any such clothing. Within the one-year term of the contract, however, Lucy signed an agreement with the Sears-Roebuck department store chain to market lower-cost clothing endorsed by her. Otis then sued Lucy for breach of their contract. Lucy's legal defense was that because Otis was not required to actually market any clothing: the contract lacked consideration and was therefore unenforceable. The court disagreed, ruling that Otis had impliedly agreed to market clothing endorsed by Lucy: "His promise to pay the defendant one-half of the profits and revenues resulting from the exclusive agency and to render accounts monthly, was a promise to use reasonable efforts to bring profits and revenues into existence." Because this agreement to take reasonable efforts constituted consideration on Otis's part, the contract was enforceable against Lucy, so she had breached the contract when she violated the exclusive terms of the contract.

Besides implied terms of reasonable performance, contracts frequently have implied warranties. For example, contracts for the sale of goods generally have an *implied warranty of merchantability*. This means the goods are of reasonable quality appropriate for sale unless the parties expressly specify the goods are sold "*as is*."[28] Similarly, contracts for services typically have an *implied warranty of workmanlike quality*, and sales or leases of residential housing have an *implied warranty of habitability*. Sellers and landlords also are subject to an *implied warranty of title*. This means the seller or landlord guarantees they are the rightful owner who thus has legal authority to sell the item or lease the property. All these various types of warranties can be disclaimed, but generally such disclaimers must be clear and in writing.

Even assuming the expressly written contract terms are agreed upon, how does one interpret the meaning of the written terms? There are many rules of contract interpretation, some of which parallel the rules for interpretation of statutes. Generally the "plain meaning" of the contract words used will be followed unless the words have a technical meaning specific to the industry involved. The terms should be construed consistent with the intent and purpose of the parties, and should be read together to form a consistent, coherent whole. Specific terms override more general terms. Terms that were specifically negotiated

28. See UCC Section 2-314.

will override terms that were placed into the contract as a matter of mere routine formality. Such routine contract language is generally referred to as *boilerplate language* from older-style printing presses that often used the same steel plates from which boilers were made. If the contract was drafted by only one party, however, then generally any ambiguous terms will be interpreted against the party that wrote the contract and in favor of the other non-writing party. This often happens, for example, in the case of contracts between merchants and consumers where there is little or no negotiation of the terms. This type of contract is also called an *adhesion* contract.

## Contract Breach

When is one party to a contract no longer bound to honor the terms of a contract due to the other party's violation of their obligations under the contract? In other words, when may a party void a contract due to nonperformance by the other party? Trivial or minor violations of the terms of the contract by one party do not release the other party from their obligations under the contract. These minor breaches of the contract terms are called *immaterial breaches.* Party A may void the contract with Party B only if Party B has committed a *material breach* of the contract. This means the breach involves a term that is of the essence of the contract or is at the "heart" of the contract. Similarly, even if a party has only partially performed under a contract, they are not in material breach if they have achieved *substantial performance* of their contractual duties. For example, merely using the wrong brand of pipe in the construction of an entire house still constitutes substantial performance of the construction contract and so is not a material breach.[29] Only if one party has committed a *material* breach, or not *substantially* performed their contractual duties, is the other party excused from fulfilling their side of the agreement.

Factors to consider in deciding whether a breach is material are the intent of the breaching party, the hardship on the breaching party, the harm to the non-breaching party, and how easily the breach can be cured. Contracts may themselves also specify what actions will constitute a material breach. For example, very late nonpayment of rent would be a material breach of an apartment lease. On the other hand, putting a single small nail in the wall of your apartment to hang a photo would not be a material breach even if it violated the express terms of the lease. Even many small nails in apartment walls in violation of a lease are also immaterial breaches. Moreover, unless the contract specifies otherwise,

29. *Jacobs & Young v. Kent,* 129 N.E. 889 (N.Y. 1921)

a reasonable delay in performance, such as a week-long construction delay past a completion deadline, is not a material breach. On the other hand, if the nature of the contract focuses on a specific preference or taste of the buyer, then that must be matched or there has not been substantial performance. For example, if I order a hamburger and fries as my meal, but the server brings me pizza and ice cream instead, there has been a material breach. The restaurant has given me a complete meal that will satisfy my *physical* hunger, but there has not been substantial performance under the contract because my *psychological* preference of taste was the basis for the contract.

Usually, a material breach means there has not been substantial performance, and a lack of substantial performance means there has been a material breach. A material breach is not necessarily the same thing as a lack of substantial performance, though. For example, there may yet be no performance at all under a contract, so there has not been substantial performance by either party. Yet neither party has breached because there has been no opportunity to do so.

If during a contract performance one party announces that they are permanently discontinuing performance, this is called *repudiation* of the contract. Whether the breaching party has substantially performed, however, depends on how much of the contract has already been performed by the time of repudiation. If repudiation happens before any performance begins, then there has been a material breach and lack of substantial performance. If one party chooses to let the other party know that they will not honor the contract even before any performance is due, this is referred to as *anticipatory repudiation*. In this case, the non-repudiating party is no longer bound to the contract, and so may cancel the contract, or sue for breach. The repudiation can be retracted, however, unless the aggrieved party has already canceled the contract. Under the common law and UCC Section 2-609, if a seller is concerned a buyer may repudiate or breach the contract, or may be unable to pay, the seller may demand assurance from the buyer that the buyer will perform.

Also, in certain situations, even substantial performance is not enough to prevent a material breach. Under the UCC Section 2-601, in the case of sales of goods, the goods must completely meet the specifications of the contract, or the seller is in material breach. If the goods violate the specifications in any way, the buyer may reject the goods. This is often called the *perfect tender rule.* However, under UCC Section 2-602, the buyer must "seasonably" (within a reasonable time) notify the seller that the goods do not conform to the contract. If such notification is given, then under UCC Section 2-508, the seller has a chance to cure the defect within a reasonable time. For example, let's say you're building your own home and order some ceramic floor tiles from a construction supply company. When the tiles are delivered, they match the material and size of tile you ordered, but the color is one shade slightly darker than the exact tile you ordered. Even though there is very little difference between the tiles you ordered and the tiles you received, you are able to reject the tiles because they are not exactly what you ordered. In this case, you would need to notify the construction supply company, and they would then have a reasonable time to take back the tiles they delivered to you and deliver to you the precisely matching tiles you ordered.

Regardless of the contract's context, however, parties must be careful not to overreact to the failure of the other party not to completely perform all their contractual duties. Unless a breach by one party is material, the other party remains obligated to perform their duties under the contract. A premature repudiation of the contract by the non-breaching party will itself constitute a material breach.[30] If the partially breaching party has substantially performed, the non-breaching party must still fulfill its duties under the contract. However, the non-breaching party may recover damages for the unperformed portion (the immaterial breaches) of the breaching party's duties.

Sometimes a contract will have a clause that allows the buyer to terminate a contract if the buyer is not satisfied with the goods or services. This is called a *satisfaction clause*. One example could be a "money-back guarantee if not satisfied for any reason." Courts impose limits to exercising satisfaction clauses, though. First, the dissatisfied party must be sincerely dissatisfied. In other words, the party claiming dissatisfaction must be acting honestly and in good faith and not merely using the clause as a pretext to avoid paying. Second, the dissatisfaction must be measured on an objective basis: would a *reasonable person* in the same circumstances be dissatisfied. Otherwise, extremely finicky people who are always dissatisfied would never have to pay under such clauses. For example, let's say I hire a pet sitter to feed and groom my dog while I'm on vacation. Our contract has a satisfaction clause. When I return from vacation, my dog is healthy, happy, well-fed, and well-groomed. However, the sitter gave my dog a brand of dog treats I think is unhealthy, so I'm genuinely dissatisfied. It is unlikely a court would allow me to void the contract. Probably no *reasonable* person would be dissatisfied to the point of not paying simply due to such a relatively minor issue. On the other hand, imagine you hire an artist to paint a lifelike portrait of yourself, and the pay is contingent upon your satisfaction with the final portrait. You genuinely hate the end result because it makes you look like you have an enormous nose, even though the rest of your face looks fine. Even though your nose is only one relatively small part of your overall portrait, you can probably void the contract due to dissatisfaction.[31]

30. See, e.g., *Walker v. Harrison*, 81 N.W.2d 352 (Mich. 1957).
31. See, e.g. *Pennington v. Howland*, 41 A. 891 (R.I. 1898).

Often, one party's obligation to perform is dependent on a *condition.* Performance is only required "if," or "if and only if," or "so long as," or "on condition that," or "provided that" some event occurs. Other conditional language might be used as well. If the condition never occurs, then the party is not in breach for failure to perform. More technically, this type of condition is called a *condition precedent.* This means the condition must precede performance or else performance is not required. If the condition precedent occurs and the party fails to perform as required, then that party is in material breach. If so, then the non-breaching party has the same options as with any type of breach: fulfilling their side of the contract anyway, voiding the contract, or suing for damages.

## Contract Damages

Once one party has breached a contract, the non-breaching party can sue the breaching party for the breach. The non-breaching party bringing the lawsuit, however, must also show that they are "ready, willing, and able" to perform their side of the contract. For example, assume I have a right of first refusal to buy your house, but you make the first offer of sale to someone else. I can successfully sue you for breach of contract only if I can show the court that I actually have the money to buy your house.

*Expectation Damages* Generally, with the exceptions noted later, the damages a non-breaching party is entitled to are called *expectation damages.* This is because the non-breaching party is awarded sufficient damages to bring the non-breaching party up to the amount the non-breaching party expected to gain from full performance of the contract. Expectation damages are calculated by the value of the performance promised to the non-breaching party minus the value of the performance delivered to the non-breaching party. In other words, what would the value of the contract have been had the contract been *fully* performed, and what was the value of the contract as it was *actually* performed. The difference between those two values is the amount of damages awarded to the non-breaching party in order to make them "whole" again.

One famous example of expectation damages occurred in the 1929 New Hampshire case *Hawkins v. McGee.*[32] This case became known as the "Hairy Hands Case." It all started when George Hawkins was a young boy and he burned his right hand on an exposed electrical wire in his home. His injured hand was still useable but became severely scarred. Nine years later, in 1922, George's father hired Dr. Edward

32. *Hawkins v. McGee,* 146 A. 641 (N.H. 1929)

McGee to perform an early form of plastic surgery on George's hand. Even though Dr. McGee had little experience in skin grafting, he promised "I will guarantee to make the hand a hundred per cent perfect hand" and "a hundred per cent good hand." Dr. McGee cut out the scar tissue and attached in its place a section of skin taken from George's chest. Unfortunately, the recovery from the operation took three months, and:

> the new tissue grafted upon said hand became matted, unsightly, and so healed and attached to said hand as to practically fill the hand with an unsightly growth, restricting the motion of the plaintiff's hand so that said hand has become useless to the plaintiff.[33]

The main question in the case was the proper amount of damages because of the malpractice. The trial judge instructed the jury to award only the value of the pain and suffering that George suffered. George appealed and the appellate court reversed the trial court decision, concluding:

> The true measure of the plaintiff's damage in the present case is the difference between the value to him of a perfect hand or a good hand, such as the jury found the defendant promised him, and the value of his hand in its present condition, including any incidental consequences fairly within the contemplation of the parties when they made their contract. The extent of the plaintiff's suffering does not measure this difference in value. . . . It represented a part of the price which he was willing to pay for a good hand, but it furnished no test of the value of a good hand or the difference between the value of the hand which the defendant promised and the one which resulted from the operation. The purpose of the law is to put the plaintiff in as good a position as he would have been in had the defendant kept his contract. The measure of recovery is based upon what the defendant should have given the plaintiff, not what the plaintiff has given the defendant or otherwise expended.[34]

In other words, the proper measure of damages in the case was the difference between the value of the hand as expected by George (a 100% good hand as promised by Dr. McGee) versus the value of the hand that Dr. McGee actually gave George (something close to 0%).

33. *McGee v. United States Fidelity and Guaranty Co.*, 53 F. 2d 953 (1st Cir. 1931)

34. *Hawkins v. McGee*, 146 A. 641 (N.H. 1929) (internal quotation marks and citations omitted)

Let's look at some examples to see how expectation damages are calculated. Assume you paid $5,000 for a used car with all-new tires, but the car was delivered with bald tires. If four new tires cost a total of $400 dollars, then the car as it was given to you was worth only $4600. The formula for damages would be expected value of the car ($5,000) minus actual value of the car ($4600). The difference is $400, which is indeed the cost of getting new tires as promised. Similarly, assume you paid contractor Smith $5,000 to fix the leaky roof of your house so that it had no more leaks. But, the roof still leaked in one spot, and you had to pay another contractor Jones $1,000 to fix that remaining leak. This means that the actual the value of the roof after contractor Smith finished was only $4,000 since it cost another $1,000 to get the roof to the condition promised: a non-leaking roof. Thus, the formula for damages is the expected value of the roof Smith gave you ($5,000) minus the actual value of the roof Smith gave you ($4,000). The result is $1,000, the cost to properly repair the roof. As you can see, if a non-breaching party doesn't fully perform, expectation damages are usually the cost to the non-breaching party of paying someone else to complete the rest of the contract as originally contracted.

If there are any indirect expenses incurred by the non-breaching party, these are also included as part of expectation damages. For example, assume an employee is wrongfully terminated by a company. That employee is able to recover lost wages the employee expected to receive had he or she still worked with the company. In addition, the employee would also be able to recover the cost of preparing, mailing, and printing resumes, as well as the cost of interviews, such as gas for travel to the interviews. While employed, the employee did not expect to have to pay for the costs of a job search. Thus, these incidental costs are counted as part of the expectation damages paid to the wrongfully terminated employee.

*Consequential Damages* Generally, breach of contract allows the non-breaching party to recover both direct and indirect damages. However, the non-breaching party may not recover damages for breach of contract unless the possible damages were foreseeable by the other party.[35] Under the common law and UCC Section 2-715, recovery of such *consequential damages* (also sometimes called *special* damages) is allowed by buyers only if the seller was aware or should have been aware of the particular needs of the buyer. For example, let's assume you run your own air conditioning repair business using your personal van. You are also good at fixing your own van, and call up a local automobile parts supply company and order a new transmission. They tell you it will take one week to arrive. You accept the fact that you will lose one week of

35. See, e.g., *Hadley v. Baxendale*, EWHC J70 (England 1854).

business and order the transmission from parts supply company. Unfortunately, the transmission takes three weeks to arrive instead of one. Instead of losing one week of business as you planned, you have now lost three weeks of business. If you didn't tell the parts supply company that you needed your van to conduct your business, then they could not have foreseen that the delay would cost you lost profits. Thus, the parts supplier is not responsible for any consequential damages you suffered. If you had told the parts supply company that you are counting on the transmission arriving in one week for your business to resume operations, then they have been put on notice about your potential to lose profits from any delay. They would then be liable for any of your lost profits due to their delay in delivering the transmission to you. In the case of larger companies, such indirect damages can potentially be enormous—just think of the loss of profits if shipment of a critical replacement part for an oil rig is delayed by the seller for even a few days.

*Restitution and Reliance Damages* What if one party partially performs under a contract but doesn't fully complete performance? For example, assume you hire a contractor to build a house for you with payment to be made upon completion of the house. The contractor lays the foundation, puts up the exterior walls of your house, finishes all the plumbing and wiring, but then doesn't finish the interior. Even though the contractor is in material breach of the contract, you still owe something under the contract. The principle of *quantum meruit* means "the amount earned." You would still be liable to the contractor for the parts and labor they provided thus far. Otherwise you would receive what is called *unjust enrichment.* That is, if you didn't have to pay anything for the materials and labor so far, you would receive most of a house free. That would unjustly enrich you. It would not be fair to the contractor, given the time and money the contractor spent so far on materials and labor. If the contractor sued you, you would owe *restitution damages* to the contractor for the cost of what they have provided so far. Restitution repays what the other person has lost so far.

In addition to restitution damages, sometimes *reliance damages* are paid out in certain instances of breach of contract. Reliance damages are based on the loss a party has suffered in reliance on the words or actions of the other party. Promissory estoppel (discussed earlier) is a common example where reliance damages are awarded to a party. For example, let's say your grandmother promises to pay for your college education. In reliance on her promise, you decide to quit your job and enroll in college full-time. On the first day of class, however, she says she has changed her mind. The wages you lost by quitting your job were caused by your reliance on your grandmother's promise. She would therefore be liable in contract law for those reliance damages.

*Mitigating Damages* Regardless of the type or amount of damages to which a plaintiff is entitled, when a defendant is in breach of contract, the plaintiff always has a duty to *mitigate* damages. This means a plaintiff has a responsibility to reasonably avoid incurring unnecessary damages. For example, let's assume a residential tenant breaches an apartment lease and moves out after only three months which is nine months in advance of the date the year-long lease terminates. The landlord could rent out the apartment to another tenant, and it usually takes around two months to do so. However, the landlord decides not to rent out the apartment to a new tenant for the remaining nine months of the lease. This landlord would *not* be mitigating damages in this instance. As a result, if the landlord sued the tenant for breach of the lease, the landlord would not be able to recover nine month's rent. Instead, the landlord would only be able to recover two months' rent—the time it ordinarily takes to find a replacement tenant. Similarly, an employee who is wrongfully fired has a duty to seek other reasonably similar employment. If the employee makes no such effort, a lawsuit for lost wages will recover only the amount the employee would have lost had the employee made reasonable efforts to seek re-employment. In other words, the unemployed plaintiff has a duty to seek re-employment as soon as reasonably possible and may not simply sit at home collecting endless lost wages.

*Liquidated Damages* Sometimes, though, damages can be difficult or even impossible to quantify. For example, assume an employee works as a lawyer for a law firm under an employment contract that has a *non-competition clause* in it. This means that the lawyer has agreed as a condition of employment that if he or she voluntarily leaves the firm, the lawyer will not compete with the law firm for business. Non-competition clauses must be limited in time and location, however, or they will not be enforced by the courts. Let's assume, then, that if the lawyer leaves employment with the firm, the lawyer is prohibited from representing any of the clients of the law firm within 50 miles for one year. This basically prevents the lawyer from immediately stealing the firm's clients. Now let's assume the lawyer leaves the law firm but starts immediately stealing the firm's clients. What would damages be for breach of the non-competition clause? It's difficult or impossible to predict how much legal representation the firm's clients might need in the future. Courts would find ways to roughly estimate damages in these cases, but because of the difficulty doing so, such contracts often include a provision for *liquidated damages* (sometimes also called *stipulated damages*). Liquidated damages occur when the contract itself specifies in advance the specific amount of damages in case of a breach. So, for example, the lawyer's employment contract might specify "$2,000 liquidated damages per law firm client stolen within one year of leaving employment with the firm."

Liquidated damages are commonly used with non-competition agreements.

Another common use of liquidated damages is in construction contracts. For example, let's say a construction contractor agrees to finish constructing an office building by March. However, the contractor takes until September to finish construction. The business owner who was planning on opening a new start-up business in the office building thus loses six months of profit. But what would have been those six months of profits? The business might have made a lot of money; it might have made only a little money; or it might have lost money. Because the amount of lost profits is completely unknown, a liquidated damages clause might be put in the construction contract. The contract could perhaps specify "$1000 dollars per day liquidated damages for each day past performance due date until performance is completed."

Liquidated damages are allowed by courts, however, only if actual damages are difficult to quantify, and only if the amount of liquidated damages is reasonable. In other words, liquidated damages must roughly provide compensation for *actual* loss only, and *not* be merely a harsh penalty so as to force a party to a contract to perform their contractual duties. Indeed, this is consistent with a general principle of contract law: *punitive damages* are *never* allowed for breach of contract. As a matter of public policy, we want to encourage people to breach contracts if it's economically efficient to do so, as long as the breaching party compensates the other party for any loss.

*Specific Performance* Instead of seeking monetary damages, however, what about asking a court to require the breaching party to actually fulfill their terms of the contract? This remedy is called *specific performance.* Specific performance is not allowed if monetary compensation is sufficient to restore the non-breaching party to the position they would have been in had the contract been fulfilled. Also, legally forcing someone to provide services or labor to another person constitutes either slavery or indentured servitude, both of which are forbidden by the Thirteenth Amendment to the U.S. Constitution. As a result, specific performance is not allowed in the case of social contracts (such as marriage) or contracts for employment or for other services. For example, an opera singer cannot be forced to sing as contracted.[36] As another example, assume a contractor refuses to complete construction of a house. The plaintiff homeowner could sue for monetary damages, but a court would not order that contractor to finish the work. The plaintiff would have to hire a different contractor, paid for with the damages recovered by the plaintiff in a lawsuit against the first contractor.

36. *Lumley v. Wagner*, EWHC Ch J96 (1852)

Although specific performance is not allowed in service or labor contracts, specific performance is sometimes allowed in contracts for the sale of goods, but only if special circumstances apply. The contract must involve the sale of unique goods such that money alone would not be a substitute if the contract had been performed. Specific performance is therefore often allowed in the case of sentimental family heirlooms, such as a photo album, that would be irreplaceable by another object. The same might be true in the case of unique artwork, rare antiques, or one-of-a-kind custom-made items. Specific performance is also often allowed in real estate contracts, on the theory that each piece of land is unique, especially given that every parcel of real estate has a unique location. Indeed, location is so important when it comes to real estate value, it is commonly said that the three rules of real estate are "location, location, location."

---

*Questions for Review and Discussion*

1. What are the necessary elements to make a promise or agreement a legally binding "contract"?
2. In what situations does a contract become legally unenforceable?
3. If the two parties to a contract disagree about the meaning of the terms of the contract, how is the contract to be interpreted?
4. When does a "breach" of contract occur, and what are the damages in such a situation?
5. In each of the following questions, apply contract law to answer the question with a legal explanation.
    a. A few days before Christmas, Noah agreed to pay Lucas $100 if Lucas would bring Noah a Christmas tree "but only if the tree is here by 10 o'clock tomorrow." Lucas showed up with the Christmas tree around dinner the next day. Noah refused to pay, insisting he meant 10 a.m. in the morning, not 10 p.m. at night. Is Noah legally obligated to pay Lucas $100?
    b. Jeff and Larry agreed both on the telephone and then in a follow-up e-mail that Larry would go to Jeff's residence at 8:00 a.m. the next morning to fix Jeff's television. Do Jeff and Larry have a legally binding contract?
    c. While browsing or "surfing" the internet, Olivia chose to visit a news website. A pop-up announcement appeared and said "By visiting our website you have agreed to let us share information we can obtain from your web browser with our advertisers." Is this a legally enforceable agreement?
    d. Emma verbally offered to sell Jacque an office building. He said he would think about it and get back to her soon. Later that day, Jacque

telephoned Emma and left a voicemail message on Emma's voicemail telling her he accepted the offer. Just before Emma checked her voicemail messages, though, she offered to sell the office building to Daniel and he accepted. Who has the contractual right to the office building: Jacque or Daniel?

e. In May, Lucas Movie Studios (LMS) sent a detailed written contract offer to Spielberg Film Productions (SFP) offering to pay SFP $10 million dollars for three new film cameras to be delivered by October. SFP immediately counter-proposed $10 million dollars for three new film cameras delivered by December. Is there a contract? If so, what are the terms?
f. Charlotte Furniture Company (CFC) sent Riley a $1,000 bill for a table, even though Riley had never bought anything from them. When Riley got the bill in the mail, she threw it in the trash. Six months later, CFC sued Riley for the $1,000. Does Riley legally owe CFC the money?
g. Zoe verbally agreed to buy a car from Nora 18 months from now for $400. When the time for performance of the contract arrives, is Nora legally obligated to sell Zoe the car?
h. Abigail is 10 years old. She walked into a grocery store and bought a gallon of milk. A few minutes later she came back inside the grocery store and said "I changed my mind, I want juice instead of milk. Here's the unopened milk back." Is the store legally required to give Abigail a refund?
i. Aubrey agreed to sell Sebastian a package of 10,000 pinto beans for $50. Before Sebastian pays Aubrey, he counts the beans, and comes up with a total of 9, 978. Has Aubrey breached the contract?
j. Isaac hired Ava to build custom kitchen cabinets with a "money-back guarantee if not fully satisfied for any reason." After Ava builds the cabinets, Isaac says he is not fully satisfied because the cabinets are only 23 inches deep as opposed to 24 inches deep as he requested. Is Isaac contractually obligated to pay Ava anything for the cabinets?

---

*Suggested Readings*

*Lucy v. Zehmer,* 84 S.E.2d 516 (Va. 1954) (joke offers)
*Lefkowitz v. Surplus Store,* 86 N.W.2d 689 (Del. 1957) (offer and acceptance)
*Stepp v. Freeman,* 694 N.E.2d 792 (Ohio 1997) (implied contract)
*Day v. Caton,* 119 Mass. 513 (Mass. 1876) (implied acceptance)
*Carlill v. Carbolic Smoke Ball Co.,* 1 Q.B. 256 (England 1893) (acceptance by performance)
*Leonard v. Pepsico,* Inc. 210 F.3d 88 (2000) (acceptance by performance)
*Loring v. City of Boston,* 48 Mass. 409 (Mass. 1884) (offer lapse)
*Schnell v. Nell,* 17 Ind. 29 (Ind. 1861) (token consideration)
*Hamer v. Sidway,* 27 N.E. 256 (N.Y. 1891) (consideration by forbearance)
*Ricketts v. Scothorn,* 77 N.W. 365 (Neb. 1898) (promissory estoppel)
*Wright v. Newman,* 467 S.E.2d 533 (Ga. 1996) (promissory estoppel)
*Webb v. McGowin,* 168 So. 196 (Ala. Ct. App. 1935) (past consideration)

*Wood v. Lucy, Lady Duff Gordon*, 118 N.E. 214 (N.Y. 1917) (implied contract terms)
*Raffles v. Wichelhaus*, EWHC Exch J19 (England 1864) (misunderstanding)
*Sherwood v. Walker*, 33 N.W. 919 (Mich. 1887) (mutual mistake)
*Wood v. Boynton*, 25 N.W. 2d 42 (Wis. 1885) (mutual mistake)
*Krell v. Henry*, 2 KB 740 (England 1903) (frustration of purpose)
*Stambovsky v. Ackley*, 169 A.D.2d 254 (N.Y. 1991) (fraud and rescission)
*Walker and Co. v. Harrison*, 81 N.W.2d 352 (Michigan 1957) (material breach)
*Pennington v. Howland* 41 A. 891 (R.I. 1898) (breach of "satisfaction")
*Hawkins v. McGee*, 146 A. 641 (N.H. 1929) (expectation damages)
*Hadley v. Baxendale*, EWHC Exch J70 (England 1864) (damage foreseeability)
*Lumley v. Wager*, EWHC Ch J96 (England 1852) (specific performance)

---

*Advanced Readings*

Brian Blum, *Contracts: Examples and Explanations*, 6th Ed. (2017)
E. Allen Farnsworth, *Contracts*, 4th Ed. (2004)
John Calamari and Joseph Perillo, *Calamari and Perillo on Contracts*, 6th Ed. (2009)

CHAPTER 6

# TORTS

---

*Chapter Objectives*
*After reading this chapter, you should be able to:*

- Identify and describe the various tort mental states
- Define and identify the legal elements of physical and nonphysical intentional torts and their defenses
- Define negligence and identify examples of it
- Define strict liability and vicarious liability and identify examples of them
- Describe and identify types of joint tortfeasors, including plaintiff fault
- Describe the liability of doctors, attorneys, governments, alcohol providers recreational land owners, and Good Samaritans
- Define and identify compensatory and punitive damages, along with time limits on tort claims

---

While he was driving on a busy street, Glen was reading text messages on his phone. As a result, he did not see that the car in front of him, driven by Vanessa, was stopped for a red light. Because of his inattention, Glen rear-ended Vanessa's car and caused $5,000 worth of damage to the back of the car. Even if texting while driving is not a crime in that state, Glen has committed the *tort* of *negligence.* As a result, Vanessa may choose to sue Glen in civil court if he refuses to pay for the damage to her vehicle. Or imagine that Glen intentionally posted a false accusation on an online website that Vanessa was a drug addict. Lying about other people's behavior is generally not a crime, but falsely harming someone's reputation constitutes the tort of *defamation.* Or imagine Glen was Vanessa's attorney in a criminal trial, but Vanessa was wrongly convicted of the crime because Glen slept through the entire trial. Though he committed no crime by his irresponsible behavior, Glen has committed the tort of *malpractice,* and Vanessa can sue him in civil court if she chooses.

## Torts versus Crimes

To understand what a "tort" is, it helps to distinguish "torts" from "crimes." A crime is a wrong committed against *society*. This is why criminal cases are titled "People v. Smith" or "State v. Smith," and not "Jones v. Smith" (assuming Smith criminally injured Jones.) The injured victim usually has no say in whether criminal charges are filed because the state or federal prosecutor's office is bringing suit for the harm done to society. Sometimes a victim is given a choice whether to "press charges" against their perpetrator, but this just means that the prosecutor has chosen to give the victim some input in the prosecutor's decision. A prosecutor can still decide whether or not to prosecute whether or not the victim wants the alleged perpetrator prosecuted or is willing to cooperate with the prosecution.

A *tort*, on the other hand, is a wrongful harm done to an *individual*. Torts can occur against a person's tangible physical possessions, which includes either one's body or one's property such as a home, business, or automobile. Torts can also occur against a person's intangible, nonphysical possessions like one's reputation, one's emotional state, or one's personal privacy. A person who commits a tort is called a *tortfeasor*. A tortfeasor is an alleged wrongdoer who is subject to civil (not criminal) legal liability for the wrongdoing and who becomes the defendant in a civil legal action brought by the injured plaintiff. The decision whether to file a civil lawsuit for damages is entirely up to the plaintiff that has been harmed by the defendant's conduct.

Often, though not always, wrongful harms constitute *both* a tort and a crime at the same time. Intentional physical harm done to another person, for example, is both a public wrong (a crime) and a private wrong (a tort). In such instances, the public criminal case would occur in criminal court, and the private lawsuit would occur in civil court. In criminal court, government prosecutors decide whether to prosecute alleged perpetrators of crimes for their criminal wrongdoing. In civil court, again, it is entirely up to individual victims to decide whether to seek financial compensation for the *tortious* harms done to them. For example, if Smith injures Jones physically, then the criminal case of "People v. Smith" or "State v. Smith" can occur if a prosecutor decides to prosecute Smith. Separately, either at the same time or typically later, the tort case of "Jones v. Smith" can also occur if Jones chooses to sue Smith in civil court. In short, tort law is the law governing *private* wrongs committed between individuals, businesses, or other organizations and institutions.

## Tort Mental States

Torts can be classified based on the mental state of the wrongdoer. There are four different basic types of mental states along with liability regardless of mental state. These five types of liability range from the most fault to the least fault. Very commonly, and especially depending on the mental state of the person committing the act, torts also constitute crimes. The differentiation of these mental states is therefore the foundation of both tort law and criminal law. Below are the five types of liability in decreasing order of fault.

*Intent* The wrongdoer wanted to cause the harm when the wrongdoer acted; the wrongdoer's purpose or goal was to cause the harm. For example, Anita hates her ex-boyfriend Ben who mistreated her. After he dies of natural causes, Anita shows up at Ben's open casket funeral and in front of Ben's entire extended family begins to spit on his body and yell vulgar insults that he is "rotting in hell like he deserves." She hopes that Ben's family suffers psychologically due to her actions. Her conduct is not criminal, yet she is still acting with the mental state of *intent* for purposes of tort law involving mental harm.

*Knowledge* The wrongdoer didn't necessarily want to cause the harm, but knew the harm would likely happen if the wrongdoer acted. Take the example in the prior paragraph. Imagine Anita wanted to cause psychological harm only to Ben's father by her showing up at Ben's funeral and engaging in the conduct she engaged in. She doesn't care whether Ben's mother, grandparents, siblings, or children are upset by her actions, but she realizes there is a high likelihood that some of them will be traumatized as a result. In such a case, Anita has acted with the mental state of knowledge. She doesn't specifically intend harm to Ben's family other than his father, but she knows the harm to other family members is likely to occur. Usually, both tort law and criminal law treat the mental state of knowledge as equally at fault as the mental state of intent. That is, whenever you see intent required in tort law or criminal law, you can generally presume that knowledge will equally count for purposes of tort liability or criminal responsibility, unless otherwise noted in the law.[1]

*Recklessness* Unfortunately, there is no agreed-upon general term for recklessness. Depending on the jurisdiction, and often even in the same jurisdiction, recklessness might also be called by other terms, most commonly *gross negligence* or *willful and wanton conduct.* Regardless of the

1. See, e.g., *Garratt v. Dailey*, 279 P.2d 1091 (Wash. 1955).

terminology, a person acts recklessly if the person knows there is some significant risk (but not likelihood) of harm to another, but disregards the risk and acts anyway. Note carefully that this is different than the mental state of knowledge. In the mental state of knowledge, the wrongdoer knows that harm is *certain* (or very likely) to occur. In the mental state of recklessness, the wrongdoer knows (is aware) only that there is *some significant risk* of harm. Put differently, awareness of certain or likely harm is *knowledge*, whereas awareness of merely the possibility of harm is *recklessness*. Or, to return to our ongoing example, imagine Anita shows up at Ben's funeral merely to yell at and spit on his body merely for her own personal satisfaction. She lacks much social intelligence, but it does occur to her that there is some possibility that her actions might upset some of Ben's family members. She decides to take that risk and engages in her chosen conduct anyway. Anne has acted with the mental state of recklessness.

Reckless conduct that causes *physical* harm usually constitutes both a tort and a crime, but reckless conduct that causes merely *psychological* harm without any accompanying physical harm is usually neither a tort nor a crime. Also, both civil and criminal law treat reckless actions as less severe than intentional or knowing actions. Criminal law often includes recklessness as part of the definition of crimes, but tort law seldom defines separate torts based on recklessness. You may assume that unless a court or legislature has decided to address the particular mental state of recklessness in that jurisdiction's tort law, a person acting recklessly would only be liable for negligence (discussed below). However, someone found committing a tort with the mental state of intent, knowledge, or recklessness would be subject to punitive damages whereas a person acting only with the mental state of negligence would not be liable for punitive damages. (Tort damages will be addressed later in this chapter).

*Negligence* Negligence occurs when a person does not know their actions pose a risk of harm to others, but a reasonable person *should have known* about the risk. Even if such conduct did not constitute a crime, it constituted the tort of negligence. Notice then that negligence does not require that any and all risks be foreseen, but only risks that *a reasonable person* would foresee.[2] Probably a majority of all tort cases that end up in civil court are examples of negligence, such as injuries caused by cars, trucks, busses, motorcycles, boats, ATV's and other vehicles. Really, there are no such things as vehicle "accidents"—in every case, one or more drivers *should have been* paying better attention or driving more carefully, but they were driving *unreasonably*. Even if such cases do not

2. *Brown v. Kendall*, 60 Mass. 292 (Mass. 1850).

end up in court, every time you hit someone's vehicle or they hit yours, the relevant insurance company pays for the cost of damages to the vehicle(s) and/or injuries to the person(s) because the tort of negligence occurred, thereby creating civil liability.

The difference between negligent conduct and reckless conduct was discussed in the unusual 2005 Massachusetts case *John Doe v. Mary Moe.*[3] Both the plaintiff and defendant used pseudonyms in their court filings because of the embarrassing nature of the case. The court described the incident at issue as follows:

> The plaintiff and the defendant were in a long-term committed relationship. Early in the morning of September 24, 1994, they were engaged in consensual sexual intercourse. The plaintiff was lying on his back while the defendant was on top of him. The defendant's body was secured in this position by the interlocking of her legs and the plaintiff's legs. At some point, the defendant unilaterally decided to unlock her legs and place her feet on either side of the plaintiff's abdomen for the purpose of increasing her stimulation. When the defendant changed her position, she did not think about the possibility of injury to the plaintiff. Shortly after taking this new position, the defendant landed awkwardly on the plaintiff, thereby causing him to suffer a penile fracture. . . . The plaintiff's injuries were serious and required emergency surgery. He has endured a painful and lengthy recovery. He has suffered from sexual dysfunction that neither medication nor counseling have been able to treat effectively.[4]

John sued Mary for both negligence and recklessness. The court rejected the concept of negligent sexual intercourse:

> There are no comprehensive legal rules to regulate consensual sexual behavior, and there are no commonly accepted customs or values that determine parameters for the intensely private and widely diverse forms of such behavior. In the absence of a consensus of community values or customs defining normal consensual sexual conduct, a jury or judge cannot be expected to resolve a claim that certain consensual sexual conduct is undertaken without reasonable care.

On the other hand, the court believed that legal claims for reckless sexual intercourse could be valid:

3. *Doe v. Moe,* 63 Mass. App. Ct. 516 (2005).
4. *Id.*

> While it is inappropriate and unworkable to hold consenting adults to a standard of reasonable care in the conduct of private consensual sexual behavior, we conclude that it is appropriate that they be held to a standard that requires them not to engage in wanton or reckless conduct toward each other during such consensual sexual conduct.[5]

Despite announcing that a claim for reckless sexual intercourse could be valid in some circumstances, however, the court believed this situation was not one of them:

> Here, the undisputed facts demonstrate that the defendant did not think about possible injury to the plaintiff when she changed her position. There is no evidence in this record to suggest that the defendant's conduct created a "high degree of likelihood that substantial harm [would] result to [the plaintiff]," which is required to prove wanton or reckless conduct.[6]

*Strict Liability* Strict liability is often called "liability without fault" or in some jurisdictions "absolute liability." Ordinarily in tort law, if a person does not act negligently then the person is not liable for any tort. That is, if a reasonable person would *not* have foreseen the risk in certain conduct, then even though a tortfeasor caused harm, the tortfeasor was not at legal fault in doing so. For example, imagine you drive your car away from an auto shop that just changed your tires. Suddenly a tire falls off your car and rolls onto the sidewalk hitting a pedestrian. A reasonable person would have presumed the skilled auto mechanic experts at the tire shop made sure the tires were secure. Therefore, even though you were the driver, you were not negligent and so would not be legally at fault. In some situations, however, state legislatures have decided that people should be responsible for the harm caused by their conduct, regardless how carefully they acted. This strict liability is imposed on the theory that there are some types of activities that we want to encourage people to be *extremely* careful about. Indeed, under strict liability, even the most careful person on the planet will still be held legally liable to an injured plaintiff. In the area of tort law, strict liability is imposed for harm caused by defective products, or for engaging in exceptionally dangerous activities such as storage, transportation, or use of explosives or toxic chemicals. (We'll discuss strict liability in more detail later in this chapter).

5. *Id.*
6. *Id.*

## Intentional (Physical) Torts

After harming someone, the perpetrator of the harm rarely admits they wanted to cause harm to another person. A tortfeasor will often say something like "I didn't mean to do it" or "It was only an accident." Obviously we cannot read people's minds, so intent can be and is usually inferred from all the surrounding circumstances. For example, imagine during a heated argument, a tortfeasor punches a victim, but then claims "I meant to stop my fist just before it hit the victim's face. I merely wanted to scare him but hit him on accident." A judge or jury can and will often disregard the testimony of the tortfeasor as not being credible. Instead the judge or jury will find that the factual circumstances provided sufficient circumstantial evidence to infer intent to cause the harm. The same is true of the mental state of knowledge. Whether someone "knows" something can be inferred from all the surrounding facts, even if the person denies knowing something.

Under the tort doctrine of *transferred intent*, an intent to harm one person "transfers" to harm caused to other accidental victims. For example, imagine Albert intends to harm Billy, but mistakenly or accidently harms Cathy. The law automatically declares Albert's intent to harm Billy "transfers" to the harm done to Cathy. Thus, Albert is equally liable in tort law for intentional harm to both Billy and Cathy.

*Battery, Assault, and False Imprisonment* Physical intentional torts include *battery, assault,* and *false imprisonment.* Battery is an unwanted physical touching of either a person's body or an object intimately touching a person's body. Thus, punching someone, spitting on them, pinching someone's butt, knocking a person's hat off their head, or knocking something out of a person's hand all constitute battery. The tort of assault occurs when a person places someone else in apprehension of an imminent battery. For example, imagine a tortfeasor attempts to scare a victim by lunging at a victim and pulling their fist back as if they are about to punch the victim but then the tortfeasor doesn't follow through on the punch. In this case, no battery has occurred, but an assault has occurred. A threat alone is not necessarily an assault, but it can become one depending on the circumstances—such as if the person making the threat is yelling and has a weapon.[7]

A simple example of the tort of battery occurred in *England v. S&M Foods.*[8] Betty England worked at a Dairy Queen Restaurant in Louisiana owned by S&M Foods. The manager Larry Garley became upset after a customer returned several improperly prepared hamburgers. Using vul-

7. See, e.g., *Cullison v. Medley*, 570 N.E.2d 27 (Ind. 1991)
8. *England v. S&M Foods*, 511 So.2d 1313 (La. Ct. App. 1987)

gar language, Larry threw a hamburger at Betty. The burger missed Betty and hit the floor, but some of the mustard and mayonnaise from the burger splattered up onto Betty's leg. Several witnesses testified as to these events. The Louisiana Court of Appeals upheld the trial court finding that a battery had occurred, as well as the award of $1,000 to Betty for humiliation and embarrassment as a result of the battery. This case illustrates that even the slightest intentional unwanted touching upon the clothing of person is sufficient to constitute battery. Also note that although Betty did not additionally sue for assault, she could have. Because Betty saw Larry throw the burger in her direction, this obviously put her in fear of an imminent battery from the burger which was sufficient to constitute the tort of assault.

Another intentional tort is false imprisonment—holding someone against their will. Not only would kidnapping a person constitute this false imprisonment, so would locking a door so as to prevent someone from leaving a room or a residence. Or, depending on the particular circumstances, blocking someone's vehicle in a driveway to prevent the person from leaving the area in their vehicle could constitute false imprisonment.

*Property, Chattel, and Conversion Torts* Intentional torts also include the property torts of *trespass to property*, *trespass to chattels*, and *conversion*. Trespass to property involves land; trespass to chattels and conversion involve things (objects). Traditionally, the common law distinguished between three types of people that come onto your property: *invitees*, *licensees*, and *trespassers*. Invitees are people who you have specifically requested come onto your property. This could include visiting family or friends, or contractors such as plumbers, electricians, or cable repair people that you have requested to fix a problem on your premises. A licensee has not received a request to come onto your property, but has a limited right to come onto your property for a limited time and limited purpose unless you request otherwise. Licensees include public utility workers, delivery persons, or door-to-door solicitors such as political canvassers, religious evangelizers, salespeople, and so on, as well as people who are lost and stop to ask for directions. The moment you ask a licensee to leave your property, however, they must leave immediately or they have become a trespasser. If you post a "no trespassing" or "no soliciting" sign on your premises, then you have revoked any license for people to come on your property. Someone who comes onto your land who you specifically do *not* want to do so is committing trespass to property. Put more formally, trespassers are those who are on your property without your express or implied permission. In common law jurisdictions, the rules vary greatly regarding what type of duty a landowner owes to invitees, licensees, and trespassers. Most commonly, though, a landowner owes the most care to invitees and the least to trespassers. Licensees are sometimes treated more like invitees, sometimes more like trespassers, and sometimes as a middle category.

Instead of trespass to land, someone who borrows or damages an object of yours without your consent is committing a *trespass to chattel.* The word "chattel" simply means "thing" or "object." If the item is lost, damaged beyond repair, so damaged that the cost of repair is at least equal to the cost of replacement, or is never returned, then *conversion* has occurred. That is, the thief or vandal has essentially "converted" ownership of the item to himself without your consent. The difference between trespass to chattel and conversion is simply a question of degree. For example, if your neighbor borrows your lawnmower without your consent, they have committed the tort of trespass to chattel. If your neighbor then breaks the lawnmower beyond repair, or never returns it, your neighbor has committed the tort of conversion.

*Private nuisance* can be either an intentional tort or caused by reckless or negligent conduct. Private nuisance is the unreasonable interference with the right of other property owners to the use and enjoyment of their property. This could include excessive smoke, odors, noise, or light. It could also include excavation or groundwater diversion onto the defendant's property that threatens the function, safety, or value of the plaintiff's land. Whether such activities by a defendant are "unreasonable" takes into consideration several factors such as the type and nature of harm, balanced against the social utility of the defendant's conduct and the suitability of such activity at that location. For example, temporary smoke and odor from a small Sunday barbecue drifting into neighbors' yards would not constitute a private nuisance to the neighbors breathing and smelling the smoke. On the other hand, long-term storage of a large amount of noxious-smelling chemicals in a location that is zoned only for residential use and that causes negative physical symptoms in neighbors such as watery and itchy eyes would probably constitute a private nuisance. The remedy for nuisance can be damages as well as an *injunction*, a court order for the defendant to cease the nuisance activity.

## Nonphysical Torts

Besides intentional physical torts, there are many nonphysical torts, not all of which necessarily require the mental state of intent. We'll examine only a few of them here. One such tort though includes the required mental state in its name: the *intentional infliction of emotional distress* (IIED).[9] This tort, as with all torts, is defined in various specific ways

9. See, e.g. *White v. Monsanto*, 585 So. 2d 1205 (LA. 1991)

depending on the jurisdiction. As we saw in the previous chapter, the most influential attempt to provide uniform tort definitions has been provided by the American Law Institute (ALI) and its recommended "Restatements."

When it comes to the tort of the intentional infliction of emotional distress, the Restatement (Second) of Torts, section 46(1), states:

> One who by extreme and outrageous conduct intentionally or recklessly causes severe emotional distress to another is subject to liability for such emotional distress, and if bodily harm to the other results from it, for such bodily harm.[10]

The ALI also provides additional comments to each section of its recommended laws in its Restatements so as to provide more clarity to its recommended legal principles. Regarding the tort of intentional infliction of emotional distress, the ALI's comments to section 46 state:

> Ordinary insults, harassment, ridicule, and so on do not qualify as 'extreme and outrageous' conduct under this standard. Instead, courts have deemed that the conduct must be something truly 'extreme and outrageous' such that it goes beyond all bounds of decency in a civilized society.[11]

Desecrating a deceased person's body in their gravesite as a means of emotionally hurting someone who loved that deceased person would be an example of an action that "goes beyond all bounds of decency in a civilized society."

Another nonphysical tort is *defamation*, and it has a lengthy legal rule. A layperson's simple definition of defamation is falsely harming someone's reputation. But the legal definition includes many particular elements with many exceptions and important clarifications of these elements and they often vary slightly by state.[12] A full explanation of defamation would require an entire chapter in itself. Briefly, though, defamation requires: (1) a false accusation, (2) the accusation would harm the person's reputation if heard by others, (3) the accusation *is* heard by others, (4) the person's reputation *is* harmed as result of the false accusation, and (5) the maker of the accusation was at fault in making the accusation.[13] As an example, telling one neighbor that another neighbor is a drug dealer is clearly defamation if the person making the accusa-

10. American Law Institute, *Restatement (Second) of Torts,* Section 46
11. American Law Institute, *Restatement (Second) of Torts,* Section 46, Comments.
12. See, e.g. *Hughes v. Hughes,* 122 Cal. App. 4th 931 (Cal. Ct. App. 2004)
13. See Restatement (Second) of Torts, Sections 558 and 559.

tion knows the accusation is false. Notice that although the mental state of intent might be present, it is not necessarily required for someone to be liable for defamation. For example, suppose a person hears a rumor that their neighbor is a drug dealer, but has no other evidence of this. The person hearing the gossip sincerely believes the rumor to be true and so repeats it to another person. Anyone who spreads gossip based on such slim evidence is probably liable for defamation if the rumor turns out to be false. Even though the gossip they repeated was not an *intentional* or *knowing* lie on their part, it was still a *recklessly* or *negligently* told lie that falsely harmed their neighbor's reputation.

The general tort of *invasion of privacy* has several different sub-types.[14] Among these are *intrusion upon seclusion,* which the Restatement (Second) of Torts section 652B defines as:

> One who intentionally intrudes, physically or otherwise, upon the solitude or seclusion of another or his private affairs or concerns, is subject to liability to the other for invasion of privacy, if the intrusion would be highly offensive to a reasonable person.

Another sub-type of invasion of privacy is the tort of *public disclosure of private facts.* The Restatement (Second) of Torts section 652D states:

> One who gives publicity to a matter concerning the private life of another is subject to liability to the other for invasion of his privacy, if the matter publicized is of a kind that (a) would be highly offensive to a reasonable person, and (b) is not of legitimate concern to the public.

For example, imagine a person were to break into your residence, read through your diary, and then post on the internet quotes from your diary where you talk about your sex life or your secret psychological issues. Because the information is factually correct, the tort of defamation does not apply to this situation. This perpetrator, however, has committed both the torts of intrusion upon seclusion and public disclosure of private facts.

## Intentional Tort Defenses

Under the general common law, all the intentional torts can be committed without liability through the use of several possible legal defenses. If one is defending one's self against violence, one can use the

14. See, e.g., *Jaubert v. Crowley Post-Signal,* Inc., 375 So. 2d 1386 (La. 1979)

*defense of self* (commonly called *self-defense*) as a justification for committing battery. To qualify for the defense, however, the force used must be necessary to prevent the harm to oneself, and it must be reasonable, that is, proportional, to the force being used by the attacker. For example, if a person comes up behind you and threatens to flick your earlobe with their finger, you could *not* justify beating up that person. On the other hand, if a person threatens to kill you with a gun they are holding, then even deadly force against the attacker may be justified.

A battery can likewise be used in *defense of others*, but again only if the force used was both necessary to prevent harm to others and proportional to the force used by the attacker. For example, if a five-year-old is committing battery against a two-year-old, you would be excused in committing battery against the five-year-old if you grabbed his arms, but not if you caused severe pain to the child.

A person can also commit battery in *defense of property*, but once again, only if the force is both necessary and reasonable in preventing the harm to one's property. For example, imagine a person comes up to your car and starts spray painting graffiti on it. You would be justified in pushing the person, grabbing the spray paint can, or perhaps even punching the person if he wouldn't stop. On the other hand, even if a person won't get off the porch of your house when you tell him to leave, it is unreasonable to shoot at him, and it is not necessary. If someone trespasses on your property, but is not doing any harm, then you can simply call the police, wait for them to arrive, and let them handle it.

A *defense of private necessity* (often called the *privilege* of private necessity) can be used to commit intentional torts to property, such as trespass, trespass to chattel, or conversion. This means you needed to commit a property tort in order to address an emergency situation. For example, if part of your house is on fire, you can use your neighbor's outside faucet and hose to put out the fire in your house. Under the defense of private necessity, you are not liable for trespass to chattel, but you are still liable for any cost you impose on your neighbor in doing so. Thus, if you damage your neighbor's hose or run up a huge water bill for your neighbor, you are liable for those costs. Similarly, if you see a house on fire with a small child trapped in the house, you may trespass onto the property and break the windows or doors of the house to rescue the child without being liable for either trespass to land or trespass to chattel.

*Consent* is also a defense to a claim of an intentional tort. If the plaintiff agreed that the defendant could engage in otherwise tortious conduct, then the defendant will not be held liable for injury to the plaintiff. This exception is commonly applied, for example, in contact sports such as football, hockey, or boxing. Yet the defense of consent only goes so far as the plaintiff agreed. Even sports like football, hockey, and boxing have rules limiting the types of physical contact allowed. Thus, a football player who makes a tackle by grabbing a facemask, a hockey player who hooks someone's head with a hockey stick, or a boxer who bites an opponent's ear would all be barred from claiming consent as a defense to their intentional torts.

## Negligence

Negligence is a general category of tort that has four necessary legal elements that must be met for negligence to occur: duty, breach, causation, and damages:

- A *duty* to avoid an unreasonable risk of harm to others.
- A *breach* of that duty (that is, you must be at fault).
- *Causation* of harm by that breach of duty.
- *Damages* resulting to the victim.

Let's look at each of these elements.

*Duty* The defendant must have owed the plaintiff a duty of careful conduct. The Restatement (Second) of Torts, Section 282 states negligence is "conduct which falls below the standard established by law for the protection of others against unreasonable risk of harm." Section 283 then explains that "Unless the actor is a child, the standard of conduct to which he must conform to avoid being negligent is that of a reasonable man under like circumstances."[15] The Restatement (Third) of Torts, Section 3 slightly redefines this duty as follows:

> A person acts negligently if the person does not exercise reasonable care under all the circumstances. Primary factors to consider in ascertaining whether the person's conduct lacks reasonable care are the foreseeable likelihood that the person's conduct will result in harm, the foreseeable severity of any harm that may ensue, and the burden of precautions to eliminate or reduce the risk of harm.[16]

15. Restatement (Second) of Torts, Section 283.
16. Restatement (Third) of Torts, Section 3

Notice that one has a duty only to avoid *unreasonable* risk of harm to others, but no duty to avoid *reasonable* risk of harm. Many things we do every day cause what our society deems as a reasonable risk of harm to others. For example, any time you share food with another person, such as at your home at a dinner party, the other person can become sick from food poisoning. However, this risk alone is not unreasonable. The risk becomes unreasonable, for example, if you served uncooked pork or chicken, or never cleaned your pots, pans, or cooking utensils, or used ingredients way past their expiration date. The same thing is true about driving a car. Over 30,000 people die in the United States each year from automobile accidents. Thus, any driving of any car poses a risk of harm to others, but our society deems it reasonable due to the social benefits from having automobiles. The risk becomes *unreasonable* only if you drive while intoxicated, or while you're heavily medicated or sleep deprived, or when you forget to turn your lights on at night, or when you fail to obey traffic signals like stop signs or stop lights, or when you exceed the speed limit, or drive too fast in the rain, snow, or ice, or if you forget to use your turn signals, or you never check if your brake lights are working, or if you're looking at the scenery and not the road, and many other examples you can probably think of.

What society—and hence the legal system—deems *reasonable* risk versus *unreasonable* risk of harm changes over time. Courts in the common law jurisdictions can and do often modify this calculus, for example, as safety features in products become both better and cheaper. Also, state legislatures often decide as a matter of public policy that some risks are reasonable, and so enact statutes that override judicial rulings that would allow liability in some situations. For example, probably due at least in part from the lobbying power of doctors and lawyers, state legislatures often limit liability for medical malpractice or legal malpractice. Among other limits included in these types of laws, such laws can limit the types of behavior where liability will occur, modify the burden of evidence needed by the plaintiff, alter which party has the burden of proof, or cap the amount of damages in certain types of claims.

In the large majority of common law jurisdictions in the United States, there is no duty for bystanders to come to the aid of an injured or imperiled stranger, such as a car accident victim or someone who is drowning. This is true even if the bystander could offer help without posing any risk of harm to herself. The rule that no legal duty exists in such situations is called the *bystander rule*. Yet to encourage such emergency aid, most legislatures have passed laws limiting the liability of individuals who come to the aid of injured or imperiled strangers. These immunity laws are commonly called *Good Samaritan* laws, named after the parable of the "Good Samaritan" in the Christian New Testament. Yet even these laws typically only protect against lawsuits for negligent conduct during the assistance, but not for reckless conduct.

Another important question of duty arises regarding professionals who discover information that could protect others. This was the issue in the foundational 1976 California case *Tarasoff v. Regents of the University of California.*[17] Tatiana Tarasoff and Prosenjit Poddar met at the University of California, Berkeley when they were both students there in 1969. They briefly dated, but Tatiana told Prosenjit she was not interested in a serious relationship with him. Prosenjit then became severely depressed, emotionally disturbed, and began to stalk Tatiana. Eventually Prosenjit sought psychological counseling from a Dr. Moore at UC Berkeley. Prosenjit told Dr. Moore that he planned to kill Tatiana. Dr. Moore asked the campus police to detain Prosenjit and recommended he be committed to a psychiatric hospital due to the danger he posed. Dr. Moore never informed Tatiana nor her parents, however, of Prosenjit's threats. Prosenjit was detained but then released because he appeared rational. Two months later, he killed Tatiana. Her parents then sued Dr. Moore and UC-Berkeley, his employer. The California Supreme Court concluded that because of the nature of being a psychotherapist, Dr. Moore had entered into a "special relationship" with potential victims of his patients:

> When a therapist determines, or pursuant to the standards of his profession should determine, that his patient presents a serious danger of violence to another, he incurs an obligation to use reasonable care to protect the intended victim against such danger. The discharge of this duty may require the therapist to take one or more of various steps, depending upon the nature of the case. Thus it may call for him to warn the intended victim or others likely to apprise the victim of the danger, to notify the police, or to take whatever other steps are reasonably necessary under the circumstances.[18]

The California Supreme Court then remanded the case to the trial court to give Tatiana's parents the chance to make the argument that not only should Dr. Moore have told the police, he should have warned Tatiana herself. A majority of jurisdictions in the United States have adopted a similar "duty to warn" since the *Tarasoff* case.

17. *Tarasoff v. Regents of the University of California*, 551 P.2d 334 (Cal. 1976)
18. *Id.*

*Breach* The defendant must have violated their duty to engage in careful conduct. This is a factual matter for a judge or jury to determine. Even assuming there was a duty to avoid unreasonable harm to others, did the defendant breach that duty? In other words, did the defendant act in a way that a reasonable person should not have acted? This is the "reasonable person" standard. Put differently, the question is "would a reasonable person in the same circumstances have done X?", where "X" is the defendant's behavior that the plaintiff alleges caused the harm in question. Worded even more simply, the question is "Was the defendant's conduct unreasonable?" If the answer is no, then the defendant was not negligent. If the answer is yes, on the other hand, then the defendant breached the general legal duty to avoid an unreasonable risk of harm to others. This doesn't necessary mean the defendant is liable for negligence, however, as the remaining elements of negligence must be met also.

Remember that the mental state in negligence is that the defendant was unaware of the risk of harm to others, but should have been. So, the question is: would a reasonable person have foreseen the risk? If the answer is yes, then the defendant acted unreasonably, thereby breaching the duty to act reasonably. On the other hand, if the risk was unforeseeable to reasonable people, then it was *not* unreasonable for the defendant to fail to foresee the possible risk of harm to others. For example, there are many aggressive car drivers out there who brake hard only at the last minute when they pull up behind a car stopped in front of them at a red light. Imagine that in one of these instances of hard braking, the aggressive driver's car windshield pops out, flies through the air, and hits the car in front of them, causing damage to it. Even though the defendant was driving aggressively, reasonable people probably would not foresee that a car windshield would completely fly out of its frame upon stopping the car fast at a red light. This question, however, as to whether the risk was foreseeable or not would be decided by the judge or jury, depending on who is trying the case. Some judges or juries might think such a risk was foreseeable, some might not.

What is "reasonable" can differ based on the particular defendant. This includes the physical capabilities of the defendant. A blind person, for example, will not be expected to monitor children like a sighted person, nor will a person in a wheelchair be expected to respond in emergency situations like someone who can walk and run. Variations in intelligence of a defendant, however, do not change the reasonableness standard unless the defendant's IQ was exceptionally low, or the individual had a severe mental illness that rendered him or her incapable of reason. As to children, a majority of jurisdictions presume that children under the age of 7 are not capable of acting in a "reasonable" manner.

For children between the ages of 7 and 14, mental incapacity is usually presumed, but can be rebutted by a plaintiff by showing the child was unusually intelligent or mature for their age. Children over the age of 14, however, are generally treated to have the intelligence of adults for the purposes of tort liability. Also, during emergencies, where both information and time to contemplate decisions is lacking, the reasonableness standard takes into account how most reasonable people would behave under such high-stress circumstances.

*Causation* The defendant's conduct caused the harm for which the plaintiff is suing. There are two types of causation required in most jurisdictions: *actual cause* (also called cause in fact) and *legal cause* (also often called proximate cause).

ACTUAL CAUSE/CAUSE IN FACT Actual cause means the plaintiff's harm is directly traceable via a cause-and-effect chain all the way to the defendant's conduct. The chain of actual causation might be quite long, but the question is commonly stated as follows: Would the plaintiff's harm not have occurred, but for the defendant's conduct? This "but for" test determines whether the defendant's actions triggered a chain of events that eventually led to the plaintiff's harm.

To show how far the cause-in-fact chain of events can occur, let's look at an imaginary case, *Jane v. Bob.* Bob is driving and gets a flat tire. Rather than pull over to fix it where cars coming in either direction can see him for some ways, he pulls over to fix it on the side of a blind hill. As he's changing the tire, the spare tire slips out of his hand and rolls across the road into the oncoming lane. A tanker truck carrying a toxic chemical comes over the hill from the opposite direction. The driver of the tanker truck, Fred, does not see Bob or the tire until the last second. Fred swerves to miss both Bob and the tire and drives off the side of the hill. The tanker truck flips over, rolls down the hill, and Fred is injured in the process. The large chemical tank on the truck cracks open, spilling toxic chemical into a small stream at the base of the hill. The toxic chemical (which happens to be clear) flows several miles down river where Jane is fishing for catfish. She catches several catfish, fries them up, and eats them for dinner. Unfortunately for Jane, several of the catfish had absorbed the toxic chemical into their bloodstream before they were caught. Jane becomes severely ill from consuming the toxin and needs hospitalization. When she hears of the tanker truck accident, she sues Bob for negligence. Looking only at cause-in-fact, Bob is the actual cause of Jane's illness. But for Bob's conduct that triggered the bizarre chain of events, Jane would not have become ill. Here is the lengthy chain of causation: Bob pulls over on blind hill and lets spare tire slip from hand→tire rolls into oncoming lane→oncoming truck driver Fred can't see Bob or spare tire until last moment and swerves to miss them→truck flips over and rolls down hill→tank breaks open releasing toxic chemicals into stream→fish in stream absorb toxins→Janes catches fish and eats them→Jane becomes ill.

Sometimes, it's difficult or impossible to show a direct connection between the plaintiff's harm and any particular act by the defendant, even though all the surrounding circumstances indicate the defendant must have done something unreasonable to cause the victim's harm. Yet when it's clear that the defendant must have caused the plaintiff's harm due to circumstantial evidence only, the defendant still can be held liable. This doctrine is called "*res ipsa loquitur*," which is Latin for "the thing speaks for itself." Under the doctrine of *res ipsa loquitur* (often referred to informally simply as "*res ipsa*"), even without any direct evidence of negligence, negligence can be presumed if the harm itself indicates there must have been negligence by the defendant. For example, in the leading common law case that created the doctrine of *res ipsa loquitur*, a flour barrel rolled out of a second-story warehouse window and fell on the plaintiff standing on the ground below. Even though the plaintiff had no evidence of what caused the barrel to roll out the window, it was obvious that the defendant warehouse owner should have done something to prevent barrels from rolling out the window.[19]

Another famous example is *Ybarra v. Spangard*.[20] In 1939 Joseph Ybarra was diagnosed with appendicitis by Dr. Tilley. Joseph was wheeled to the operation room to have his appendix removed by Nurse Gisler. Anesthesiologist Dr. Reser put Joseph to sleep for the operation. Dr. Spangard performed the main operation. Dr. Swift owned and managed the hospital where the surgery was performed. Nurse Thompson was in the room when Joseph woke up from the operation. Although Joseph never had any pain or problem with his neck or right arm, immediately upon awaking from surgery he felt a sharp pain between his neck and right shoulder. Despite attempts at various treatments for the next several months, his right shoulder atrophied and became paralyzed, and his right arm experienced severe pain. Basically his right arm became useless and he had to wear it in a sling. Since Joseph was asleep during the operation he had no ability to testify regarding who was present during the operation or precisely what they did during the operation. Not knowing who was specifically responsible for his injury, he sued all of the above-named medical professionals on a theory of *res ipsa loquitor*. The California Supreme court agreed:

19. *Byrne v. Boadle*, 159 E.R. 299 (England 1863)
20. *Ybarra v. Spangard*, 154 P.2d 687 (Cal. 1944)

> Without the aid of the doctrine [of *res ipsa loquitor*] a patient who received permanent injuries of a serious character, obviously the result of someone's negligence, would be entirely unable to recover unless the doctors and nurses in attendance voluntarily chose to disclose the identity of the negligent person and the facts establishing liability. . . . Plaintiff was rendered unconscious for the purpose of undergoing surgical treatment by the defendants; it is manifestly unreasonable for them to insist that he identify any one of them as the person who did the alleged negligent act.[21]

A common example of *res ipsa loquitor* today is airplane accidents. There might be little or no evidence of what caused a passenger airliner to crash. Yet the deceased victims' families can still sue the passenger airline because we can presume that something went wrong that should not have gone wrong had the plane been properly inspected, maintained, and piloted. The doctrine of *res ipsa loquitur* thus applies.

LEGAL/PROXIMATE CAUSE Even if cause-in-fact can be shown, in most jurisdictions actual cause is not enough to make a defendant liable. There must also be what is called *legal cause,* also commonly referred to as *proximate cause.* This means that even if there was cause-in-fact, there is a second causation question: was the plaintiff's harm so far removed from the defendant's conduct in the causal chain of events, that as a legal matter, courts should deem the plaintiff's particular harm was not foreseeable by a reasonable person in the defendant's situation. If the type of harm the plaintiff suffered was not a foreseeable consequence of the defendant's conduct, then the defendant might have breached a *general* duty to avoid unreasonable risk of harm, but the defendant did not breach a duty to avoid unreasonable risk *to that specific plaintiff* in particular. The doctrine of proximate cause is based on the theory that as a matter of public policy we as a society do not want to hold plaintiffs liable for potentially unlimited harm caused by a stupid though harmful oversight. Thus, if the harm is not "proximate" (close) enough to the defendant's conduct in the causal chain of events, then we won't hold the defendant responsible for the harm.

The leading case that established the doctrine of proximate cause is the landmark 1927 case of *Palsgraf v. Long Island Railroad.*[22] In *Palsgraf,* a passenger carrying a heavy package was hurrying to step from the train platform onto the passenger train as it began pulling away from the station. Two train workers, one on the train and one on the platform, saw the man and tried to help him get on board. The worker on

21. *Id.*

22. *Palsgraf v. Long Island Railroad,* 162 N.E. 99 (N.Y. 1928)

the train pulled the passenger on board while the worker on the platform pushed the passenger on board from behind. In the process, the passenger dropped his package onto the railroad tracks below. The package, containing fireworks, exploded. The explosion shook a weight scale standing on the other end of the train platform. The scale fell over, hitting and injuring Helen Palsgraf in the process. Palsgraf sued the Long Island Railroad for her injuries under a theory of negligence. The Railroad argued that they could not possibly have foreseen—and thus could not have reasonably prevented—such an unusual chain of events. The high court of the state of New York agreed with the Railroad. The court decided that even though the injury would not have occurred but for the actions of the train workers, the injury was so far removed from their actions that the train company should not be held liable. No one could have imagined that by trying to help someone step on board a train, scales would fall down on the other side of the train platform and injure someone. Although potential harm was foreseeable to the passenger stepping on the train, any potential harm to a passenger on the other end of the train platform was not foreseeable. Put differently, the train workers owed a duty not to injure the passenger they were helping get on board the train, yet in doing so did not owe a duty to avoid harm to people on the other end of the train platform. Writing for the court majority, Justice Cardozo stated "Negligence is not actionable unless it involves the invasion of a legally protected interest, the violation of a right. Proof of negligence in the air, so to speak, will not do.[23]

In dissent, Justice Andrew explained that the concept of "proximate" cause was merely an imaginary legal fiction needed for fairness: "What we do mean by the word 'proximate' is, that because of convenience, of public policy, of a rough sense of justice, the law arbitrarily declines to trace a series of events beyond a certain point. This is not logic. It is practical politics."[24]

Although Justice Andrew agreed with the concept of proximate cause, he believed that in this case, Palsgraf's injuries were proximately caused by the Railroad:

> Given such an explosion as here it needed no great foresight to predict that the natural result would be to injure one on the platform at no greater distance from its scene than was the plaintiff. Just how no one might be able to predict. Whether by flying fragments, by broken glass, by wreckage of machines or structures no one could say. But injury in some form was most probable.

23. *Id.*
24. *Id.*, Justice Andrew, dissenting.

> Under these circumstances I cannot say as a matter of law that the plaintiff's injuries were not the proximate result of the negligence.[25]

Let's look at the *Jane v. Bob* example from moments earlier to see how proximate cause would work. A reasonable person in Bob's situation should have foreseen the usual risks of pulling over on a blind hill to change a tire: the tire could roll away, and oncoming drivers wouldn't be able to see the loose tire in time to avoid hitting it. Thus, Bob breached his duty to the truck driver Fred, and Bob's conduct was both the actual (cause-in-fact) and legal (proximate) cause of Fred's injuries. Yet no reasonable person would have imagined that pulling over to change a tire on the side of a blind hill might cause a person to become ill from eating toxic fish. That *particular type* of injury was unforeseeable to reasonable people in the defendant's situation. Thus, in jurisdictions where proximate cause is also required to find the defendant liable for negligence, Jane would lose her lawsuit against Bob. In the lengthy causal chain of events, Jane's injuries were too far removed from Bob's conduct.

We can see that without limits on legal causation, Bob's liability could be potentially unlimited. Imagine the same situation, but with the added fact that Jane is the only surgeon in a small town. She was just about to be called into her hospital to perform emergency surgery on four car accident victims from a separate unrelated accident in the area. All four victims have bad internal bleeding, but Jane is unavailable to perform surgery due to her illness from eating the contaminated fish. The hospital must now transport the four accident victims to the next closest hospital an hour away. All four victims die because the surgery to stop their internal bleeding was administered too late. This chain of causation could be extended to other unforeseeable harm as well. In most jurisdictions, the law says that at some point, we must place a limit on the defendant's liability for what could otherwise be an endless chain of "but-for" causation. Another way to say this is that although Bob was the *actual* cause of harm to Jane and her patients, a judge will rule that Bob was not the *legal* cause of the harm.

*Damages* A plaintiff must have suffered damages for the defendant to be liable. We'll cover damages in a separate section at the end of this chapter since the rules for damages apply to all tort damages, not just damages from negligence. That is, there are no special rules for negligence damages apart from the general rules for damages caused by all torts.

25. *Id.*

## Strict Liability

As a matter of public policy, most state legislatures have deemed that there are some types of activities a person might engage in that the person will be held liable for harm to others caused by the activity no matter how careful the person is to avoid harm. This type of liability is called *strict liability* or sometimes *absolute liability*. The philosophy behind imposing strict liability is that it strongly encourages people who engage in dangerous activities to be extremely careful when they do so.

There are several examples of strict liability in tort law. The most common example is strict product liability. A maker, distributor, or seller of a product that harms an individual due to a defect in the product is liable for harm caused by the defect, regardless how careful the business was to avoid the harm. The defect can be a defect in the product's design, such as a crib that collapses when a baby leans on the railing or a medicine that causes heart attacks. The defect could occur during the manufacturing or construction process, such as the use of poor quality materials, improper assembly of components, or a toxin or hazardous object in food. There might be a defect in the product warning about how to properly and safely use the product, such as failing to warn people not to use a high-voltage device around water due to the risk of electrocution, or failing to warn adults not to let small children play with large plastic shipping bags due to the risk of suffocation. Liability extends not just to the initial purchaser of the product, but any subsequent users of the product.[26]

In most jurisdictions, strict liability doesn't apply to "inherently unsafe" goods, such as alcohol, guns, or fireworks, if they work as intended. That is, if the product has no defect in design or manufacturing or warning, then the consumer is assumed to know about and accept the risk. Yet if such dangerous products do have a design or manufacturing defect, they are subject to lawsuit. Examples might be fireworks with a defectively short fuse that explode prematurely or guns that cause bullets to explode in the chamber. Or, if the public was not properly warned of the risk, then the manufacture can still be liable. One famous example is when tobacco companies told consumers smoking was safe, and many smokers believed those statements even though the tobacco companies knew the evidence showed smoking was unsafe.

In a few jurisdictions, however, a product can be deemed "unreasonably dangerous *per se*." "*Per se*" is Latin for "in itself." This means the product itself is so inherently dangerous, that merely offering the prod-

26. The foundational case for this principle is *MacPherson v. Buick Motor Company*, 111 N.E. 1050 (N.Y. 1916)

uct for sale is deemed negligent. For example, let's assume a manufacturer properly designs, manufactures, and warns about a small practice sword for the carnival act of sword swallowing. The manufacturer then decides to market the product to children. In a jurisdiction that allows strict product liability for products that are "unreasonably dangerous *per se*," the manufacturer might be found liable for any harm caused by the product even though the manufacturer made the product correctly and extensively warned about the risks.

Another example of strict liability is referred to in the First Restatement of Torts as *ultrahazardous* activities and in the Second and Third Restatement of Torts as *abnormally dangerous activities*. This means these types of activities are so dangerous, a person engaging in any of these activities is liable for *any* harm caused by the activity, no matter how careful the person was. The specific list of abnormally dangerous activities varies in each jurisdiction, but typically includes the transportation, storage, or use of explosives, radioactive materials, hazardous chemicals, or wild animals.[27]

## Vicarious Liability

*Vicarious liability* occurs when a person is civilly liable not for his or her own negligent actions, but instead is liable for someone *else's* negligent actions. The most common occurrence of this is when employers are vicariously liable for the actions of their employees. The common law term for this vicarious employer liability is *respondeat superior*. The term *respondeat superior* is Latin for "let the superior person respond" or "let the master answer." This means the person in charge of another person is responsible for the actions of the person he is overseeing. This is also called the *master-servant* rule. This rule applies only to employees, however, and not to independent contractors. This is because employers directly supervise the actions of their employees, but not the actions of any independent contractors whom the employers hire.

Employer vicarious liability applies, however, only when the employee is acting in the *course and scope* of employment.[28] This basically means the employee must be acting in a time and place where he or she is in the process of fulfilling job responsibilities. Commuting to and from work or taking a lunch break at a nearby restaurant do not count as acting in the scope and course of employment. Once the employee arrives at work and begin working, however, he is now acting in the

27. See, e.g. *Toms v. Calvary Assembly of God*, 132 A.3d 866 (Md. 2016)
28. See, e.g. *Timmons v. Silman*, 761 So. 2d 507 (La. 2000)

scope and course of employment. If, for example, an employee at a fast-food restaurant fails to wipe up a spill and a customer slips and falls, the employer is vicariously liable.

Even if an employee is sent on a work errand off the business premise, the employee is still acting in the course and scope of employment while traveling to complete the assigned task. For example, a delivery person is acting in the scope and course of employment while in route to or from a distribution center and the delivery destination. The employer is therefore vicariously liable for any car accidents caused by the delivery driver. A delivery driver may stop briefly to get gas, use the restroom, or grab a bite to eat, but is still deemed to be acting in the course and scope of employment.

On the other hand, employees traveling to perform an employment responsibility must remain on task for employer liability to apply. For example, if while making a delivery the delivery person decides to take a substantial detour off the delivery route to run a personal errand, then the employer is no longer liable if the employee causes a car accident. What constitutes a substantial detour, however, can sometimes be a close call. Examples might be where an employee detours to run a personal errand at the grocery store, their bank, or a post office. In those moments, the employee is not fulfilling any job responsibilities, but is instead engaged in conduct purely of a personal nature. Yet if a company sends an employee on a trip to represent the company as its ambassador during all the employee's interactions, then *all* of the social activities of the employee while traveling might be deemed to be acting in the course and scope of employment.

Employers are not, however, vicariously liable for the *intentional* torts of their employees. This is because no legitimate employer would require, as part of the employee's job responsibilities, that the employee commit intentional torts! Thus, an employee who commits an intentional tort is by definition *not* acting within the course and scope of employment. The employer therefore would not be vicariously liable. In such an instance, however, the employer may be separately liable for the negligent hiring, negligent training, or negligent supervision of its employee.

## Joint Tortfeasors

What happens when more than one person is the cause of a plaintiff's injuries? There are at least three different types of these situations. First, what if the evidence clearly shows *only one* of multiple defendants caused a plaintiff's injuries, but the evidence is unable to determine *which one* of the defendants caused the harm? This interesting situation was addressed in a classic torts case, *Summers v. Tice*.[29] Two bird hunters, Tice and Simonson, were out hunting and simultaneously shot at a low-flying quail. A third person, Summers, was in the direct line of sight of both Tice and Simonson when they fired their guns. Summers was shot in the eye, and obviously the shot from either Tice or Simonson had hit him. Summers could prove all the elements of negligence, except that there was no way for Summers to prove *which* defendant, Tice or Simonson, had actually caused his injury. The California Supreme Court ruled that in this unusual circumstance, it would be unfair to place the burden of proof on Summers. Instead, both Tice and Simonson would be held equally liable unless one of them could prove that they were *not* the person who shot Summers. This type of liability is called *joint and several liability*. Both defendants are individually liable for the harm *and* they are jointly responsible for the full amount of damages. Thus, if one defendant has no money to pay damages, the other defendant is liable for the full amount.

The *Summers v. Tice* situation is relatively unusual. Much more common is a second type of joint tortfeasor. An *intervening cause* happens when a second tortfeasor either causes harm to the plaintiff after an initial tortfeasor, or creates a cause that, when compounded with the cause created by the initial tortfeasor, jointly causes harm to the plaintiff. The action of the second tortfeasor is called an intervening cause. In such cases, the defendants are not jointly liable but are only *severally* liable. That is, each defendant is individually responsible only for their share of the damages or harm caused to the plaintiff.

For example, imagine driver Alex doesn't see that the car ahead of him, driven by Carla, is stopped at a red light. Alex rear ends Carla, pushing her into the middle of the intersection. Ben is driving on the cross street and has the green light, but is going 60 m.p.h. even though it's a 30 m.p.h. zone. Ben crashes into the side of Carla, injuring her. Had Ben been traveling within the speed limit, he could have braked in time to avoid the accident. This means the accident would not have occurred either if Alex hadn't rear ended Carla, or if Ben hadn't been driving too fast. Carla was injured because of the combination of actions by both Alex and Ben. Diagrammed, it would be A + B = C: A's negligence + B's negligence = C's harm. In the case of an intervening cause like this, both the tortfeasors are liable for C's injuries. If many joint tortfeasors have contributed causes, all are liable. For example, if there is one initial tortfeasor but five later ones, all six are liable.

But let's change the facts. Imagine that Carla is stopped at the red light at the intersection as before. Alex doesn't see the red light and rear

29. *Summers v. Tice*, 199 P.2d 1 (Cal. 1948)

ends Carla. But this time, he's traveling so slowly that he only jolts Carla's car forward by a foot or so. This merely gives Carla a sudden but very minor neck pain. And now, Ben is traveling at 60 m.p.h. *behind* Alex and rear ends him. Because Alex's car is touching Carla's car, Carla gets equally rear-ended again. Carla gets severe neck and back injuries as a result. The harm caused by Alex's negligence is overwhelmed by the harm caused by Ben's negligence. As the second tortfeasor, Ben's negligence is said to be a *superseding* cause, also called a *supervening* cause. A superseding cause overrides any prior causes and the tortfeasor who created the superseding cause is solely liable. In rare instances, there might even be one or more superseding causes that override multiple initial and intervening causes. So, in theory, there might be initial cause A, intervening causes B and C, but then superseding causes D and E.

Really, superseding causes are a simply a subset of intervening causes. That is, all superseding causes are intervening causes, but only some intervening causes rise to the level of a superseding cause. A superseding cause basically is an intervening cause that is so major, it far outweighs any other relatively minor cause(s). There is no clear-cut distinction defining whether a cause is "superseding" or merely "intervening." According to Section 442 of the Restatement (Second) of Torts, factors to consider in deciding whether an intervening cause has become superseding are whether the kind of harm is different, whether the cause was completely independent of other intervening causes, and the degree of fault by the intervening tortfeasor. The difference between intervening and superseding causes can often be difficult to decide, but judges and juries often have to make these types of judgments.

## Plaintiff Fault

What if instead of, or in addition to, multiple joint tortfeasors contributing to the plaintiff's harm, the plaintiff has partly caused his or her *own* harm? Under the original 1800's common law doctrine of *contributory negligence*, *any* fault by the plaintiff in contributing to one's own injuries *entirely* barred recovery against any defendant that helped caused the injuries. This meant that if a plaintiff was only 1% at fault and the defendant was 99% at fault, the plaintiff still could not recover for injuries caused by the defendant.

Because of the harshness of this rule, the states, throughout the 1900's, modified their contributory negligence rule. Some continued to call the rule contributory negligence, but other jurisdictions adopted the term *comparative negligence* to differentiate the newer rule. Regardless, under the newer modified contributory negligence rule, a plaintiff is barred from recovery for injuries caused in part by a defendant only if the plaintiff's share of causation is greater than a certain specified amount. In some jurisdictions, the plaintiff's share of causation must be less than the defendant's share of the causation—that is, no more than 49% plaintiff fault compared to 51% or more defendant fault. In some other jurisdictions, the plaintiff's fault must be no more than the defendant's share of causation—that is, no more than 50% plaintiff fault compared to 50% or more of defendant's fault. Thus, there is only a 1% difference between these two variations of the modified contributory negligence rule.

Under either of these two variations of modified contributory negligence, if a plaintiff were only 25% at fault compared to the defendant's 75% fault, then the plaintiff would be able to sue the defendant. If, however, the plaintiff were 60% at fault compared to the defendant's 40% fault, then the plaintiff would be barred from any recovery against the defendant. This doctrine was often called *assumption of the risk* in many jurisdictions. In other words, if a plaintiff knowingly chose to engage in a risky behavior, the plaintiff had "assumed the risk" of harming themselves. Given so, any harm that resulted to the plaintiff would be mostly (if not entirely) his own fault. As a result, the plaintiff would be barred from suing a defendant for the plaintiff's injuries. For jurisdictions that recognize the assumption of the risk doctrine, an example might be waterskiing in a man-made lake or reservoir where the plaintiff knows there are many unmarked tree stumps lurking just below the water's surface. Perhaps the reservoir owner was negligent in not marking where all the stumps are located, but the plaintiff either knows or should know there is a significant risk of injury by waterskiing on such a body of water.

A small minority of states, however, have adopted what is called *pure comparative negligence.* Under this theory, there is no cut-off limit to the percent of a plaintiff's fault that will prevent a negligence lawsuit against a defendant who also caused the plaintiff's injuries in part. So, for example, under pure comparative negligence, even if the plaintiff was 90% at fault and the defendant only 10%, the plaintiff could still potentially recover 10% of the value of plaintiff's injuries from the defendant. Theoretically, a plaintiff could be 99% at fault and the defendant only one percent, but the plaintiff then could still recover one percent of their damages from the defendant. As a practical matter, though, judges and juries rarely assign only one percent fault to a plaintiff. Five or ten percent is typically the lowest amount of fault allocated to a plaintiff who partially caused their own harm.[30]

In all jurisdictions, however, regardless of the tort rules that ad-

30. For a relatively simple example of comparative negligence involving several parties, see *Fontenot v. Patterson Insurance*, 5 So.3d 954 (La. Ct. App. 2009)

dress plaintiff fault, potential plaintiffs may sign a form expressly waiving a defendant's potential liability. This is why school districts often make parents sign a liability waiver so that their children can go on school-sponsored field trips. Another common example involves dangerous recreational activities like skydiving or scuba diving where a recreational business will not provide the service to a customer without a signed liability waiver. Such waivers generally hold up in court unless one of several common situations arises. First, the service provider must fully inform the plaintiff of all of the risks of the activity. Otherwise, the plaintiff did not give the equivalent of informed consent. Second, although such waiver absolves the defendant of liability for negligent conduct, these waivers do not absolve the defendant for intentional or reckless torts, even if the waiver expressly states so. Finally, if there is grossly unequal bargaining power between the plaintiff and the defendant, then the waiver was essentially coerced and so will not be enforced. For example, a liability waiver that an employer makes an employee sign in order to keep their job might be deemed an invalid waiver. Depending on the jurisdiction, there might be other exceptions that can invalidate liability waivers.

## Special Defendant Classes

Due to the lobbying power of certain groups and due to the fact that some categories of defendants are frequently sued, every state legislature has enacted tort laws that deal specifically with certain classes of tort defendants. Among the most common types of defendants that receive special consideration in tort law are product manufacturers and sellers, as well as doctors, lawyers, alcohol providers, recreational land owners, and local and state governments. Liability of these groups is treated differently in every state, but here are some of the most common rules.

*Medical Malpratice* Civil liability for harm caused by negligence by medical professionals is called *medical malpractice*, sometimes referred to as "med mal" for short. There are two major grounds for medical malpractice. First, a medical professional might fail to fully inform the patient of the risks of medical treatment to which the patient is agreeing. Second, a medical professional might negligently cause harm due to the treatment the patient receives.

The first issue is called the question of "informed consent." The patient cannot genuinely consent to medical treatment if they make a choice based on misinformation or inadequate information. For example, as an obvious case, a patient that agrees to chemotherapy as treatment for cancer is not considered by the courts to have given informed consent if the doctor fails to disclose to the patient that a simple surgery would have a 99% chance of curing the cancer. On the other hand, the patient need not be told about risks of death or serious injury that are extremely rare. For example, it is remotely possible that a nearby lightning strike could travel through the electrical wires of a hospital and electrocute a patient hooked up to a vital signs monitor. Such a theoretical possibility would not be required to be revealed, however, for informed consent to be valid.

Besides the question of informed consent, the second type of medical malpractice issue is the standard of care given by the medical provider. In most common law jurisdictions, medical specialists must be as minimally competent as their entire field requires nationwide.[31] Non-specialists, however, need only be as competent as the non-specialists in their local geographic area are required to be. Another way to say this is that specialists are held to a national standard of expertise and care, but generalists are held only to their local standard of expertise and care. This distinction is common in the medical malpractice tort law of most states. The reason for this distinction is that the medical facilities of some geographic areas, such as a small rural community, might not have the resources of other areas, such as a large city with a university research hospital. For example, a state-of-the art laser surgery machine called the LAZER-TECH 3000 might be safer and more effective than traditional knife surgery to remove a wart. Yet if this machine costs several million dollars, few hospitals in small towns will have access to such a machine. Thus, if a patient's standard wart-removal surgery does not go well at a small local hospital, the doctor who performed that surgery will not be faulted for using a traditional scalpel rather than the LAZER-TECH 3000. The doctor might perhaps be liable on other grounds of negligence, but not for failing to use an extremely expensive machine that was not available locally.

*Legal Malpractice* All regulation of attorneys is undertaken by the highest court within each state. Lawyers are generally held to the standard of possessing the "skill of an attorney."[32] In most jurisdictions, the plaintiff has the burden of proving that if the attorney had not been negligent, the plaintiff would have won their case. In some jurisdictions, however, once the plaintiff shows a breach of professional standards, then the burden switches to the attorney to show a defense to attorney liability. The attorney must show that even if the attorney had acted more skillfully, the client still would have lost their case. In short, in

31. See, e.g. *Morrison v. MacNamara*, 407 A.2d. 555 (D.C. 1979)
32. See, e.g. *Smith v. Lewis*, 530 P.2d 589 (Cal. 1975)

some jurisdictions the plaintiff must show they would have won, but in other jurisdictions the attorney must show the defendant would have lost anyway. Plaintiffs are more likely to win a claim of malpractice under the latter standard.

*Alcohol Providers* Liability for providing alcohol to drinkers who then cause harm to others (typically from automobile accidents) is divided into two types of defendants: businesses and social hosts. In the U.S. common law, bars and taverns were originally called "dram shops." This is because alcohol was often originally sold in "drams," a small unit of liquid. Laws regulating liability for the sale of liquor are still called "dram shop" laws or "dram shop" acts today. Dram shop liability depends on state law and varies greatly. In some states, a business that provides alcohol to someone who injures a third person is liable merely if the serving of alcohol contributed in any way to intoxication. In other jurisdictions, businesses that serve or provide alcohol are liable only if the buyer was already "obviously intoxicated." In some other jurisdictions (such as Louisiana), liquor stores and other commercial alcohol providers have no liability on the declared assumption that individuals are solely and fully responsible for their own choices to drink and how they behave after they have been drinking.

The other type of alcohol provider is called a "social host." Here, alcohol is provided in a noncommercial setting. This is most commonly a party in someone's home, but could be a barbecue gathering in a park or a tailgate party outside a sports stadium. In most states, social hosts are not liable for injuries caused by their guests who were served alcohol. In some jurisdictions, however, social hosts are legally responsible if they serve or provide alcohol to guests who are "obviously intoxicated." With both dram shops and social hosts, however, liability exists for injuries caused by minors who were provided alcohol.

*Recreational Land Use* With the explosion in outdoor recreation in recent decades, lawsuits by plaintiffs who used private lands for recreational use became common. Most typically, these were ATV, motorcycle, snowmobile, or motorized boat users who sued the landowner for allegedly unsafe conditions. Other common situations were swimmers who dove into the water and injured themselves, or hikers who became ill after eating wild berries or other plants in recreational areas. To encourage landowners to make their land available to the public, eventually every state passed laws placing significant limits on liability of landowners who make their land *freely* open for outdoor recreational uses. But these statutes limiting the liability of landowners do *not* apply to landowners who are running a commercial recreational business on their land for profit.

*Sovereign Immunity* Traditionally, under old English and French law, the king was "sovereign," meaning the king had supreme political and legal authority. As a result, no one could sue the king. The sovereign was immune to lawsuit. This doctrine of *sovereign immunity* carried over into the period of democratic government when royalty no longer governed. In all jurisdictions within the U.S. today, neither the federal government nor state governments may be sued without their consent. Consent to sue is granted by statutes specifically waiving immunity and authorizing lawsuits against the government. Unless the statute expressly allows the particular type of lawsuit or type of relief (such as damages) sought by the plaintiff against the government, the plaintiff's lawsuit is barred by the doctrine of sovereign immunity. That is, the statute must expressly and specifically allow the particular type of lawsuit the plaintiff seeks to bring, or else the government has not waived its immunity. There are many varieties of what types of lawsuits are allowed against state governments, so one must always consult each individual state's sovereign immunity laws. Also, under U.S. law, local governments are "creatures of the state" governments because state laws define the creation and functioning of local towns and cities. This means that sovereign immunity laws govern lawsuits against local municipalities as well.

## Damages

Assuming a plaintiff has been harmed by a defendant's tort, the question then becomes what amount of damages are owed to the plaintiff by the defendant. There are several different types of damages. We will consider two categories of damages: compensatory damages and punitive damages.

*Compensatory Damages* The most basic and most common type of damages are called *compensatory* damages. These damages are awarded to compensate the plaintiff for the loss suffered. In other words, compensatory damages should be awarded in an amount sufficient to make the plaintiff "whole" again. In theory, compensatory damages are supposed to restore the victim to the position the victim was in before the victim's loss occurred. This is often impossible as a literal matter if a person suffers permanent disability or disfigurement. Yet judges and juries are tasked with the duty to come up with dollar figures in all tort damage situations.

In the case of physical harm, compensatory damages include medical costs to treat the injury, loss of earnings caused by the injury, and the pain and suffering caused by the injury. Such damages include both past and future medical costs, lost earnings, and pain and suffering. Damages for physical pain as well as for mental or emotional suffering are often called "general" damages on the theory that everyone who is injured experiences physical pain and mental suffering. Medical costs and loss of earnings, however, are often called "special damages" because these types of damages will vary more among plaintiffs. One plaintiff might have small medical costs with huge loss of earnings, whereas another plaintiff might have enormous medical costs with little or no loss of earnings. For example, imagine a famous concert pianist who severs her pointer and middle fingers on her right hand due to a defective table saw. The pianist might have only a few thousand dollars in medical bills, but she will have substantial loss of future earning capacity because her career is probably ended. On the other hand, imagine a teacher who becomes a quadriplegic in an auto accident caused by a drunk driver. The teacher might have hundreds of thousands of dollars (or more) in lifetime medical bills. Yet if the teacher is still able to speak, he or she will probably be able to continue with a career. The loss of earnings will only be for the time spent recovering prior to returning to the classroom.

In all jurisdictions there is also a rule of damages that the defendant is liable for physical injuries no matter how physically fragile the plaintiff is at the time of the injury. This is known variously as the "eggshell plaintiff" rule or "eggshell skull" rule or "thin skull rule" or "you take the plaintiff as you find him" rule. For example, imagine Adam punches Bruce hard in the head with Adam's fist simply desiring to cause Bruce pain. Unknown to Adam, however, Bruce has a severe case of brittle bone disease. Bruce's skull is badly broken as a result of Adam's punch, and Bruce dies as a result of the injuries. Adam is guilty of the crime of murder, as well the intentional tort of battery, and is liable to Bruce's heirs for the wrongful death of Bruce. It is no defense for Adam that brittle bone disease is rare or that Adam did not know about Bruce's condition.

Apart from the tort of intentional infliction of emotion distress (covered earlier in this chapter), the common law rule is that mental harm *alone* is generally not sufficient for liability by a defendant. That is, mental pain must accompany a physical injury for the mental pain to be compensable. This was often called the "impact rule." Otherwise, as one can imagine, frivolous (and probably fraudulent) lawsuits for purely mental suffering could run rampant and overrun the civil justice system. In most jurisdictions, however, there are some limited exceptions to the rule prohibiting claims based purely on mental anguish. If the defendant's negligence is of a type likely to cause severe mental distress under the circumstances, courts will often allow recovery for purely mental suffering.[33] Such situations include negligently diagnosing someone with a fatal disease, or negligently mishandling the corpse of a deceased close family member. Also, many jurisdictions have modified the "impact rule" so that a plaintiff can sue for mental suffering if he or she directly witnesses a close family member experience a severe injury or death caused by a tort defendant.[34] This is sometimes called the "zone of danger" rule. This term is used because the victim's relative was in such immediate physical proximity to the victim when the victim's injury or death occurred, the plaintiff could have been physically injured himself. Yet some courts have modified this further so that the plaintiff need merely be in the general presence of the victim, even if observing the victim's injury or death from a distance.

On the other hand, courts have generally been hesitant to expand liability for purely emotional damages due to witnessing a death of a love one beyond the death of immediate family members. This avoidance of liability includes cases in which a plaintiff witnesses the death of a beloved pet which was at issue in the 2012 New Jersey case *McDougall v. Lamm.*[35] Joyce McDougall lived alone with her small nine-year-old dog Angel, a "maltipoo" (a cross between a maltese and poodle). Joyce spent a lot of time with Angel because she did not work outside the home, and Angel slept in a dog bed near Joyce's bed. Joyce described Angel as being friendly and lively, loved children, and was highly trained and could do tricks. In short, Angel was Joyce's companion. One day Joyce was out walking in her neighborhood with Angel. Suddenly a large, loose dog owned by Charlot Lamm came up to Angel, growled and snarled, grabbed Angel by the neck, picked her up and shook her several times, and then dropped her. Joyce screamed as Angel lay dead. Joyce then sued Charlot for significant and continuing emotional distress caused by Joyce witnessing Angel's death. Up to that point New Jersey courts had limited damages for emotional distress to a bystander witnessing the death of someone who possessed "a marital or intimate, familial relationship between plaintiff and the injured person." The question for the New Jersey Supreme Court was whether a pet could count as having a "marital or intimate family relationship" with a bystander plaintiff. Although the court was sympathetic to Joyce's emotional pain, the court declined to extend liability to such situations. The court explained that although increasingly people view pets as "companions," the law treats animals as mere property. It would also be extremely difficult to define *which* pets would specifically qualify as a "companion." Moreover, "creating a cause of action based on observing the death of a pet would result

33. See, e.g. *Falzone v. Busch*, 214 A.2d 12 (N.J. 1965)
34. See, e.g, *Portee v. Jaffee,* 417 A.2d 521 (N.J. 1980)
35. *McDougall v. Lamm*, 48 A.3d 312 (N.J. 2012)

in an ill-defined and amorphous cause of action that would elevate the loss of pets to a status that exceeds the loss of all but a few human beings."[36] In other words, if the argument that a plaintiff felt a close emotional connection to an animal was sufficient for liability for emotional damages, then so too might emotional connections to friends, teachers, coaches, neighbors, babysitters, friends, and neighbors' children, and so on qualify for liability if ended as a result of death. Such potential liability would go too far, according to the court.

Besides damages for physical and emotional suffering, most jurisdictions allow spouses, children, and other survivors to recover loss of consortium, support, service, and society if a loved one is injured or killed. *Consortium* is love and physical affection, including sex in the case of a spouse. *Support* is the financial help provided by the person's work earnings. *Service* is the non-financial help provided by the person, such as house chores, yard work, and errand running. *Society* is the companionship given by the person. This can include stimulating conversation, travel, shared hobbies and pastimes, or athletic recreation together. For example, if a spouse has become severely disabled due to a workplace injury, the other spouse will probably have lost a certain degree of consortium, support, service, and society. In such cases, the spouse, children, or other close family members of a tort victim are allowed to recover damages for their tangible and intangible losses. The judge or jury in each case has the responsibility for assigning dollar values to the various types of losses.

In the case of damage to property instead of harm to people, compensatory damages would be the cost of repair, depreciation in value, or replacement of the item, depending on the situation. Often the cost to repair would be more than replacement, in which case the plaintiff will typically only be awarded the cost of replacement. There is an exception, however, if the damaged item is especially rare, unique, or special to the plaintiff. In such cases, the defendant may owe the cost of repair even if repair is exceptionally expensive. Or, the defendant might have to pay a large sum if the item is irreplaceable. Such items might include, for example, a rare antique, a unique work of art, or an old family photo album.

If a plaintiff lost profits due to the damage or loss of the plaintiff's property, the defendant is liable for those lost profits as well. For example, imagine a negligent driver damages a delivery company's only service vehicle. In that case, the defendant would be liable for the delivery fees the company lost due to the delay in business operations. The financial liability of the defendant in such instances cuts off with the plaintiff's loss. Imagine, for example, that if the delivery vehicle in the ex-

36. *Id.*

ample just mentioned was delivering a key piece of machinery to run an oil well. The well has to shut down. And, all the parts and service suppliers of the well now lose profits as well. All the workers also go temporarily unpaid. If held responsible for all these losses, the defendant could become potentially liable for millions of dollars or more. To prevent this kind of result, the general rule is that a defendant is liable for lost business profits to the plaintiff only, and not for lost business profits to other individuals or merchants connected to the plaintiff in the commercial chain.

In all jurisdictions, the plaintiff has a duty to mitigate tort damages. This means that after a plaintiff suffers a loss caused by a defendant, the plaintiff must take reasonable measures to limit additional losses. These measures do not have to be extraordinary, but they must at least be ordinary. For example, imagine a plaintiff is injured in a car accident caused by a negligent defendant, and is in severe pain. When the ambulance arrives, the plaintiff refuses to go to the hospital or see a doctor. Finally, days later, the plaintiff goes to an emergency room after the pain becomes unbearable. The plaintiff's injuries are now worse because they were left untreated for so long. The plaintiff has failed to mitigate damages, and so the defendant is liable only for those damages that would have resulted had the plaintiff actually been willing to receive medical attention immediately after the accident. Or, imagine a customer negligently damages a soda vending machine at a fast-food restaurant, making the machine inoperable. The business owner may not simply wait for a year to re-order a new vending machine, and then sue the customer for a year's worth of lost soda profits. Instead, the business owner has a duty to order a new vending machine within a "reasonable" time, probably only a few days.

What happens when someone dies as a result of a tort? There are two kinds of tort lawsuits that can occur in this instance. In every jurisdiction, a right of *survivorship* (or *survival*) allows either the closest heirs of the deceased, or a legal representative assigned by the deceased prior to death, to sue in the place of the deceased for the loss that occurred to the deceased. In other words, the legal claims by the injured victim against the defendant "survive" the defendant's death. The closest heirs are usually a spouse or children, but could be parents, siblings, or other close relatives. The closest heirs also may bring a separate *wrongful death* lawsuit seeking compensation for the loss of consortium, support, service, and society they would have received from the deceased victim. In short, a survivorship action allows heirs to collect on behalf of the deceased for the *deceased's* loss, whereas a wrongful death action provides compensation to the heirs for *their own* loss. Commonly, both of these lawsuits are filed by the heirs. Only if a deceased died instantly from a defendant's tort would there be no opportunity for a right of survivorship, since the victim did not experience any pain or suffering before they died. In such a situation, though, the heirs would still have a legitimate wrongful death suit for their own losses.

*Punitive Damages* Besides the many types of compensatory damages just discussed, *punitive damages* are awarded when the defendant had the mental state of either recklessness or intent. Punitive damages go beyond compensatory damages in order to punish the defendant for engaging in such egregious behavior. Punitive damages are often called "exemplary" damages. An "exemplar" is a typical example. Thus, by punishing a tortfeasor, the court is making an example—an "exemplar"—out of the tortfeasor, as a warning to other potential tortfeasors. Punitive or exemplary damages thus serve the dual purpose of punishing the defendant and deterring other possible future defendants from engaging in similar conduct. The U.S. Supreme Court, however, has put constitutional limits on punitive damages. Under the Due Process Clauses of the 5th and 14th Amendments, punitive damages must be limited to ten times the total of compensatory damages except in cases of unusually outrageous conduct by a defendant. This rule has thus placed a general cap on punitive damage awards.

One of the most famous and controversial tort cases of the past several decades involved the issue of punitive damages: *Liebeck v. McDonald's Restaurants,*[37] more commonly known as "The McDonald's Coffee Case" or more simply "the Hot Coffee Case." To keep their coffee hot for a long time after it is poured into a cup, McDonalds keeps their coffee roughly between 180 and 190 degrees Fahrenheit in temperature. That temperature is the industry standard even though coffee at such temperatures can cause severe burns. Because of this risk, McDonald's coffee cups have a "caution" label on it warning consumers the contents are hot. Indeed, in the years 1982 to 1992, McDonalds received over 700 complaints of customers being burned by their hot coffee, many of which McDonald's settled lawsuits over. One such injury occurred in 1992. Stella Liebeck, a 79-year old woman living in Albuquerque, New Mexico, ordered coffee from a McDonald's restaurant. While sitting in a parked car driven by her grandson, she put the coffee between her legs so she could remove the lid to add cream and sugar. As she removed the lid, she spilled the entire cup into her lap. Stella had to be immediately hospitalized for a week because the coffee caused third degree burns in her groin area. She was partially disabled for two years, and where it had been burned, her skin became permanently disfigured.

Stella initially asked McDonalds for $20,000 to cover her current

37. *Liebeck v. McDonald's Restaurants, P.T.S., Inc.,* No. D-202 CV-93-02419, 1995 WL 360309 (Bernalillo County, N.M. Dist. Ct. August 18, 1994).

and future medical expenses on the theory that McDonalds was negligently at fault for having their coffee unnecessarily hot. When McDonald's offered only $800, however, she then sued McDonald's for "gross negligence" (i.e. recklessness) on the theory that McDonalds knew the coffee was likely to cause burns at such excessive temperatures but chose to disregard that risk. At a jury trial, the jury ruled in Stella's favor. Since the mental state of recklessness allows punitive damages, the jury awarded Stella $160,000 in compensatory damages and $2.7 million dollars in punitive damages—roughly two days' worth of McDonald's coffee sales. The judge then reduced the punitive damage award to $480,000—three times the compensatory damages. After McDonald's appealed the decision, Stella settled with McDonald's for a final undisclosed amount less than the total amount the trial judge had awarded. Since then, McDonald's has not changed the temperature of their coffee, but their coffee cups now are made of a more rigid material and have larger caution warnings on them.

Because of the large initial punitive damage award the jury gave Stella, the case sparked enormous media coverage and public discussion about the nature of tort awards and punitive damages. Most of the debate centered around whether there needs to be "tort reform" to reduce "frivolous lawsuits." Much of this debate, however, was based on factually incorrect information about the case, such as that Stella had been driving a car when she tried to remove the lid and that she was simply wanting a large sum of money. Nevertheless, public perceptions about the case still play a large role in general attitudes towards punitive awards in tort cases.[38]

## Time Limits

Regardless of the type of tort or the type of damages involved, however, all tort claims have time limits. One cannot simply be injured by a tort, know about it for thirty years, and then decide to sue the alleged defendant. Obviously, public policy dictates that people should not continually fear endless lawsuits from conduct they committed, or have allegedly committed, many years ago. Thus, in all jurisdictions, there are time limits—deadlines—for when an injured person must file a tort lawsuit. Often jurisdictions provide differing time limits depending on the nature of the tort. For example, civil cases involving murder or child molestation often receive extended time limits or might even have no time limits at all. (The same is true in the criminal law as well).

38. See the HBO documentary "Hot Coffee" for thorough details about the case and its public aftermath.

In common law jurisdictions, the time deadline for filing a lawsuit is called a *statute of limitations*. In the rare situation that there is no applicable statute of limitations, then the common law doctrine of *laches* (sounds like "latches") might apply. The term "laches" is derived from French. It means the plaintiff unreasonably delayed filing the lawsuit. Thus, statute of limitations or no statute of limitations, a plaintiff must file a tort lawsuit in a timely manner. The time limit for filing a tort lawsuit begins to run the moment the plaintiff has suffered the loss in question unless a statute provides otherwise. Across the fifty U.S. states, the most common statutes of limitations for torts provide two- or three-year limits, but some states have one-, four-, five-, or six-year limits. These limits can be delayed, however, either by statutes or by judicial doctrines. One common exception to the statute of limitations deadline is where a plaintiff neither knew nor should have known of their injury. In such a case, the statute of limitations usually begins to run the moment the plaintiff learns of their loss. This might happen, for example, if a plaintiff regularly drinks water from a rural well contaminated by toxins from a nearby chemical plant. The contamination might not be discovered for years, long after internal harm to the victim's body has occurred without the victim's awareness. Here, the time limit set by the statute of limitations does not begin to run until the victim discovers their illness or injury that was caused by the toxins that contaminated the water well.

---

*Questions for Review and Discussion*

1. List, describe, and give an example of each of the four tort mental states.
2. Define and give an example of each of the following torts:
    a. Assault
    b. Battery
    c. False imprisonment
    d. Trespass to land
    e. Trespass to chattel
    f. Conversion
    g. Intentional infliction of emotional distress
    h. Defamation
    i. Intrusion upon seclusion
    j. Public disclosure of private facts
3. List and describe several possible defenses to avoid liability for intentional torts, with examples.
4. List and describe the four elements of negligence, and explain the difference between cause-in-fact and proximate cause, all with examples.
5. Describe the different types of joint tortfeasors as well as the different rules for plaintiff fault. Give an example of each.

6. Explain the special tort liability rules that apply to each of the following classes of defendants, with an example:
   a. Employers
   b. "Good Samaritans"
   c. Manufacturers and sellers of products
   d. People using explosives
   e. Lawyers
   f. Doctors
   g. Alcohol providers
   h. Recreational land wwners
   i. Governmental entities
7. Explain, with examples, the different specific rules regarding compensatory damages for physical harm to people, emotional harm to people, harm to physical property, and lost profits.
8. Are there any rules of tort liability you strongly disagree with? If so, which ones, and why? What do you believe should be the rule of liability instead, and why?

---

*Suggested Readings*

*Garratt v. Dailey*, 279 P.2d 1091 (Wash. 1955) (intent versus knowledge)
*Doe v. Moe*, 827 N.E. 2d 240 (Mass. 2005) (negligence versus recklessness)
*Toms v. Calvary Assembly of God*, 132 A.3d 866 (Md. 2016) (strict liability)
*Cullison v. Medley*, 570 N.E.2d 27 (Ind. 1991) (assault)
*England v. S&M Foods*, 511 So.2d 1313 (La. Ct. App. 1987) (battery)
*McCann v. Wal-Mart Stores, Inc.* 210 F. 3d 51 (1st Cir. 2000) (false imprisonment)
*White v. Monsanto*, 585 So. 2d 1205 (LA. 1991) (intentional infliction of emotional distress)
*Hughes v. Hughes*, 122 Cal. App. 4th 931 (Cal. Ct. App. 2004) (defamation)
*Jaubert v. Crowley Post-Signal*, Inc., 375 So. 2d 1386 (La. 1979) (invasion of privacy)
*Brown v. Kendall*, 60 Mass. 292 (Mass. 1850) (negligence: reasonableness)
*Adams v. Bullock*, 125 N.E. 93 (N.Y. 1919) (negligence: foreseeability)
*U.S. v. Carroll Towing Co.*, 159 F. 2d 169 (2d Cir. 1947) (negligence: balancing test)
*Byrne v. Boadle*, 159 E.R. 299 (England 1863) (res ipsa loquitur)
*Ybarra v. Spangard*, 154 P.2d 687 (Cal.1944) (res ipsa loquitur)
*Linnear v. CenterPoint Energy*, 966 So. 2d 36 (La. 2007) (res ipsa loquitur)
*Tarasoff v. Regents of the University of California*, 551 P.2d 334 (Cal. 1976) (negligence: duty)
*Palsgraf v. Long Island Railroad*, 162 N.E. 99 (N.Y. 1928) (proximate cause)
*Roberts v. Benoit*, 603 So.2d 1032 (La. 1992) (proximate cause)
*Timmons v. Silman*, 761 So. 2d 507 (La. 2000) (employer vicarious liability)
*Summers v. Tice*, 199 P.2d 1 (Cal. 1948) (joint tortfeasors)
*Fontenot v. Patterson Insurance*, 5 So.3d 954 (La. Ct. App. 2009) (comparative negligence)

*MacPherson v. Buick Motor Company*, 111 N.E. 1050 (N.Y. 1916) (product liability)
*Morrison v. MacNamara*, 407 A.2d. 555 (D.C. 1979) (medical malpractice)
*Smith v. Lewis*, 530 P.2d 589 (Cal. 1975) (legal malpractice)
*Falzone v. Busch*, 214 A.2d 12 (N.J. 1965) (bystander emotional harm)
*Portee v. Jaffee*, 417 A.2d 521 (N.J. 1980) (bystander emotional harm)
*Gammon v. Osteopathic Hospital of Maine*, 534 A.2d 1282 (Maine 1987) (bystander emotional harm)
*McDougall v. Lamm*, 48 A.3d 312 (N.J. 2012) (emotional harm to pet owner)

---

*Advanced Readings*

American Law Institute, *Restatement (Second) of Torts*
William Lloyd Prosser and W. Page Keeton, *Prosser and Keeton on Torts, Fifth Edition*
Joseph Glannon, *The Law of Torts: Examples and Explanations, Fifth Edition*

CHAPTER 7

# CRIMINAL LAW

*Chapter Objectives*

*After reading this chapter, you should be able to:*

- List and describe the purpose of the criminal justice system
- Describe the common elements of all crimes, including actus reus and mens rea
- Describe definitions of common crimes against persons and property, as well as inchoate crimes
- Describe the several types of insanity defenses, as well as other common criminal defenses

In 1927, during the early days of airplanes, 25-year-old pilot Charles Lindbergh flew a small plane named the *Spirit of St. Louis* from New York to Paris. In doing so he became the first person to fly a solo non-stop flight over the Atlantic Ocean. Lindbergh instantly became a world-famous celebrity. In the United States, he was practically worshipped. When he returned to America by ship, he was escorted on the last leg of the journey by a fleet of U.S. warships and military aircraft. Later in Washington, D.C., he met with President Coolidge, who gave him the Distinguished Flying Cross; Congress awarded him the Medal of Honor; *Time* magazine gave him their first-ever "Man of the Year" award; and the U.S. Post Office issued a stamp of the *Spirit of St. Louis* rather than of Lindbergh himself since U.S. law and custom prevents displaying a living person on a stamp. Tragedy came, though, five years later, when Lindbergh's infant son Charles Lindbergh Jr. was kidnapped for $50,000 ransom. Although Lindbergh paid the ransom, sadly his son's body was soon found in some woods next to a public road. After some time, suspicion fell onto Richard Hauptman who was eventually found with about $13,000 of the ransom money. He claimed the money was given to him by a deceased friend of his, but other evidence tied him to the crime. He was convicted in a New Jersey court. Despite being offered life-without-parole if he would confess, Hauptman insisted on his innocence even up to his execution in 1936 by the electric chair. From the moment the crime occurred, throughout the investigation and trial, and even after Hauptman's death, the public was intensely fascinated by every detail of news coverage of the case. The media labeled the Lindbergh kidnapping case "the crime of the century."

Decades later, in 1994, Nicole Brown Simpson, ex-wife of National Football League hall-of-fame running back Orenthal James "O.J." Simpson, was found murdered outside her home along with a male friend of hers, Ron Goldman. Simpson soon became the leading suspect. When he tried to avoid police questioning by attempting to flee in a white Ford Bronco, TV stations around the country interrupted their regular broadcasts to show live helicopter camera footage of police cars following his vehicle down a Los Angeles interstate highway in a slow-speed chase. An estimated 95 million people saw the event live. The next year, 1995, O.J. was tried for murder but acquitted. National TV networks provided more airtime to the O.J. Simpson trial than any other news story that year. Cable channel, "Court TV," even provided live "gavel to gavel" coverage of the trial. Judge Lance Ito, who oversaw the case, along with all the prosecution and defense lawyers, became international celebrities. Not only was the public fascinated by O.J.'s celebrity, the case ended up with significant racial components. One of the key police investigators in the case, Lt. Mark Furman, had been found to have made racist statements in the past. Despite DNA evidence and other evidence tying O.J. to the murders, O.J.'s defense lawyers argued to the majority-black jury that Lt. Furman and other white investigators tried to frame O.J. for the murders. They suggested that Furman and other officers manufactured evidence incriminating O.J., such as by planting a blood-stained glove at O.J.'s house. Public opinion surveys showed the U.S. public was deeply divided along racial lines regarding O.J.'s innocence or guilt. As many as 100 million people saw the verdict of "not guilty" announced live on television. Forgetting about earlier "crimes of the century," the media labeled the O.J. Simpson murder case "the crime of the century."

Clearly the public has always been fascinated by crime, and especially crimes involving famous people. But just what is a *crime*? A crime is simply behavior that is prohibited by law and punishable by a fine or imprisonment. It is a decision by the state to forbid certain conduct as so immoral, unhealthy, or dangerous, that society will not leave the wrong to be settled merely between private individuals using tort law. As noted in the chapter on tort law, a crime is a wrong against the peace and good order of society as a whole. This is why the government, acting as the representative of the people, prosecutes the case against *criminal* defendants. To reflect this, criminal lawsuits are titled *State v. Smith* or *People v. Smith* rather than *Victim v. Smith.* Such lawsuits are handled by the criminal justice system. This part of government seeks to detect, prevent, prosecute, and punish crime, as well as provide legal defense for the accused. Reforming and rehabilitating criminals is attempted as well. Police and investigators investigate crime. Prosecuting attorneys, also called state's attorneys or district attorneys, prosecute criminal defendants. Prosecuted criminal defendants are then represented and defended by either their own attorneys or by public defenders and state appellate defenders who are assigned to defendants by the jurisdictions. Judges and juries decide cases and correctional institutions punish defendants. Parole officers, mental health counselors, job trainers, teachers, and social workers attempt to restore criminal defendants to functioning as law-abiding members of society. Altogether, the task of the criminal justice system is a huge and expensive job for government, and it achieves its goals with varying degrees of success.

## Criminal Law Overview

Criminal law is usually divided into two subfields: substantive criminal law and criminal procedure. We'll look first at the substance of crimes and criminal responsibility. Then in the next chapter we'll look at some of the key legal procedures that apply to criminal suspects, the criminally accused, and convicted criminal defendants. As with tort and contract law, the American Law Institute (ALI) has attempted to simplify, clarify, and reform criminal law. After almost 10 years of drafting, in 1962 the ALI published a Model Penal Code (MPC). Variants of the MPC have been adopted by about 35 states, but not by the other 15 nor by the U.S. federal government. Advocates of the MPC, however, continue to push for adoption of the MPC in jurisdictions that have yet to adopt it.

*Crimes Must Be Defined* Under the MPC, as well as in non-MPC jurisdictions, there are many general principles that apply to the criminal law. First, under the Due Process Clause of the Fifth and Fourteenth Amendments to the U.S. Constitution, crimes must be specifically defined. Otherwise, if the definition of the crime is vague, individuals do not have fair notice as to what conduct is prohibited or required. People must be able to know how to avoid breaking the law, or else it gives too much power to police, prosecutors, and judges to arbitrarily apply the law only to individuals or groups they dislike.

*Felony versus Misdemeanor* Second, both MPC and non-MPC jurisdictions organize crime under two categories: felonies and misdemeanors. A *felony* is generally a crime punishable by time in a state prison. Under the MPC Section 1.04, and thus in many states, a felony is defined as any offense punishable by more than one year imprisonment. A *misdemeanor*, on the other hand, is a crime punishable by a fine or by imprisonment not in a state penitentiary, but in a local jail. Or, many states and MPC Section 1.04 define a misdemeanor as any crime receiving less than one year maximum imprisonment in a penitentiary.

*Elements of Crime:* mens rea *and* actus reus Third, regardless of the type of crime, in common law systems such as the United States, all crimes have two necessary legal elements: the *mens rea* ("guilty mind") and the *actus reus* ("guilty act"). The *actus reus* is the simpler element to analyze. "*Actus reus*" is Latin for "the act itself." The *actus reus* can include not just committing the act itself, but encouraging, soliciting, planning, conspiring, or attempting to commit a crime. Leaving aside for the moment the definition of *mens rea*, for a crime to occur, the *actus reus* and *mens rea* must occur simultaneously. For example, imagine Bob breaks into a locked house merely for fun while the owners are away on vacation. Once Bob is inside the house, however, he discovers the owners have a large gold coin collection. Bob then decides to steal the coins. Bob is guilty of both the crimes of "breaking and entering" and "theft." Bob is not guilty, however, of "burglary," because burglary requires an intent to steal at the moment a building is entered. Or, imagine that Bob is drunk driving, and accidentally runs over and kills a person with his car. When Bob gets out of his car to see whom he hit, he realizes it's someone who he was planning to kill the next day. Bob might be guilty of "vehicular homicide," but Bob is not guilty of "murder" because he did not intend to kill the person at the moment he did in fact kill the person. We'll look at the more specific definitions of several of these crimes in more detail later in this chapter.

Under the MPC Section 2.02, the possible mental states a person can have when committing a crime are the same mental states that a person can have in tort law. That is, a criminal defendant can act with the mental states of purpose (intent), knowledge, recklessness, or negligence.

INTENT If Anita shoots Ben purposefully wanting to kill Ben, Anita acts with the mental state of intent. This would be both a tort and a crime. Indeed, every act of intentional violence against a person or property is both a tort and a crime. Intent must be specific to the crime. For example, imagine a man wants to steal some rum hidden in the unlit basement of a business. He lights a match to see his way. He succeeds in stealing some rum, but accidentally lights the basement on fire. In this situation, he has the *mens rea* for theft but not for arson since he did not intend to set the basement on fire.[1]

KNOWLEDGE Anita wants to shoot Bob but Charlotte is standing in the way. Anita doesn't want to shoot Charlotte, but Anita knows that if she shoots directly at Bob, Charlotte will get shot as well. Anita shoots at Bob anyway. For purposes both of tort and criminal law, Anita acted with the mental state of intent with regard to harm to Bob, but with the mental state of knowledge in regard to harm to Charlotte. Usually, both tort law and criminal law treat the mental state of knowledge as equally at fault as the mental state of intent. That is, whenever you see "intent" required in tort law or criminal law, you can generally presume that "knowledge" will equally count for purposes of tort liability or criminal responsibility, unless otherwise noted in the law.

RECKLESSNESS Anita decides to set up a shotgun target on a bench in a wooded urban park knowing there might be other people in the park, but she commences with shotgun practice anyway. Anita knows there is a risk (not certainty) of harm, but chooses to disregard that risk. Anita is acting with the mental state of recklessness. This would also be the case if someone chooses to drive an automobile knowing that they have been drinking, or knowing that they have a medical condition that could cause a blackout or epileptic seizure at any moment.[2] As was the case with the tort mental state of recklessness, this is different than the mental state of knowledge. In the mental state of knowledge, the wrongdoer knows that harm is *certain* (or substantially certain) to occur. In the mental state of recklessness, the wrongdoer knows (is aware) only that there is *some significant risk* of harm. Put differently, awareness of *certain* or *likely* harm is *knowledge*, whereas awareness of the mere *significant possibility* of harm is *recklessness*. Criminal law often includes recklessness as part of the definition of various crimes. Note, though, that some states use the terms "criminal negligence" or "culpable negligence" or other related terms as synonyms for the mental state of recklessness.

NEGLIGENCE Andy sets up a gun range in his backyard in the rural countryside. Andy's neighbor Bryan lives on the property a quarter-mile behind Andy's property. Any has set up a hollow concrete-block backstop behind where Andy hangs his shooting targets. Andy then shoots a powerful, large-caliber gun at the target such that the bullet goes right

1. See, e.g., *Regina v. Faulkner*, 13 Cox CC 550 (1877); *Holloway v. United States*, 526 U.S. 1 (1999)
2. See, e.g., *People v. Decina*, 138 N.E.2d 799 (N.Y.1956)

through the hollow concrete blocks and hits Bryan a quarter-mile away. Even though Andy is unaware that his bullet would go through the concrete block, a *reasonable person* in Andy's situation *should have known* either to build a more solid backstop or use only small-caliber weapons with such a backstop. Andy thus acted with the mental state of negligence. Generally, actions committed with the mental state of "negligence" are not crimes. Be careful, however, to distinguish ordinary negligence from "criminal negligence," which is a legal term referring to the mental state of recklessness.

Most criminal law punishes crimes equally if the defendant acted with either intent or knowledge. Defendants who commit a crime with the mental state of recklessness are often guilty of a lesser offense and thereby receive a lesser sentence, despite the flagrant disregard for human life that is nearly equal to the mental states of knowledge or intent. Most criminal law does not criminalize merely negligent conduct, however. Again note that the terms "criminal negligence" or "negligent homicide" can be confusing, however, because depending on the state, these crimes might require the mental state of recklessness, not negligence.

STRICT LIABILITY There are also some crimes that hold individuals strictly liable for their behavior regardless how innocent or careful the person was to avoid committing the crime. Such *strict liability* crimes are rare in the criminal law. One example is "statutory rape," defined as sexual contact with a minor regardless of whether the minor fully consented. It doesn't matter if the defendant believed that his or her sexual partner was of age. If the defendant's sexual partner turns out to be below the legal age of consent, the defendant is guilty of "statutory rape."[3] Strict liability also applies to a bartender who serves alcohol to a minor even though the minor had a fake identification card showing he or she was 21 years of age or older. The bartender has still violated that jurisdiction's laws forbidding sale of alcohol to a minor. The concept of strict liability for crime is highly criticized on the argument that it unfairly punishes people no matter how careful they are to avoid committing a crime. As a practical matter, though, in the case of strict liability crimes, prosecutors, judges, and juries usually take the defendant's intent and knowledge into consideration in deciding questions of prosecution, conviction, and sentencing.

MOTIVE *Mens rea* must not be confused, however, with *motive.* A motive is the reason *why* a defendant wants to commit a crime. A motive is

3. See, e.g., *Garnett v. State*, 632 A.2d 797 (Md. 1993); See also *Morisette v. U.S.*, 342 U.S. 246 (1952)

not required for conviction unless the definition of the crime itself specifically includes a particular reason or reasons for the conduct. For example, burglary is often simply defined as "breaking and entering with intent to commit a felony or larceny [theft]." Motives are not usually required for conviction for two reasons. First, motive is hard to prove. A person could have any one or more of numerous possible motives for committing a crime or no motive at all. And solid evidence of a motive is rare unless a defendant openly admits it. Second, motive is largely irrelevant. If a person intends to commit a wrongful act and then does so, the harm has been done regardless of the motive. As a society, we want to prevent and punish such harmful behavior regardless of why people do it. A clearly admitted or proven motive might help determine guilt, such as evidence that a defendant stood to gain a million dollars under a life insurance policy if the victim died. Or, a motive might be relevant to sentencing, such as a poor and homeless defendant that shoplifted food only to feed his hungry children. Yet regardless of "good" or "bad" motives, the person has violated the law.

There are a couple exceptions or special principles related to *mens rea.* The intentional tort concept of "transferred intent" also applies to the criminal law. That is, if a defendant intends to victimize one person, but accidentally victimizes one or more other people, the law deems that the defendant's intent "transfers" from the intended victim to the actual victim(s). An intent to commit a lesser offense can also transfer to a greater offense, even if the perpetrator was intending to commit only the lesser offense. For example, if a perpetrator intends to commit only aggravated battery against a victim but the victim then dies as a result of the injuries, the perpetrator can be guilty of intentional murder.[4] The legal doctrine of transferred intent is based on a public policy of wanting to maximize the deterrence against attempts at causing intentional harms.

Similarly, just as tort law recognizes vicarious liability, so too does the criminal law. An "accomplice" is someone who helps a criminal defendant in some way. This assistance could be through soliciting or encouraging the defendant to commit the crime, or by providing information or resources to the defendant to commit the crime (called aiding and abetting). In the criminal law, accomplices are usually held equally guilty for the crimes committed by the defendant whom the accomplice encouraged or aided. A classic example is the lookout or getaway driver for a bank robbery. If the robber inside the bank shoots and kills someone, the lookout and getaway driver are both vicariously guilty of murder. Again, we'll look at these concepts in more detail later in this chapter.

4. See, e.g., *Thompson v. State,* 236 S.W.2d 787 (Tex. Crim. App. 2007)

## Types of Crimes 1: Crimes Against Persons

The MPC not only provides general principles of criminal law, but it also attempts to clarify the definitions of crimes, also called "offenses." Two broad types of crimes are crimes against persons and crimes against property. We'll look at just a few of the crimes defined by the MPC.

*Homicide* Some of the MPC's most nuanced distinctions between crimes involves the several types of mental states with which one person can cause the death of another person. Historically, and as is still the situation with many states, types of murder are defined in various ways as "degrees" of murder, as in first, second and third degree murder. The MPC eliminates the concept of "degrees" of murder by simplifying and standardizing these distinctions through describing sub-categories of "criminal homicide." The types of mental states we learned about in the chapter on torts and again in this chapter are critical in understanding these different alternative types of criminal homicide. If you end up practicing law in a state that has not adopted the MPC, many of the MPC's concepts will still apply, but you will need to learn the particular terms and definitions that apply within the state where you are practicing law.

Under the MPC Section 210.1, a person commits *criminal homicide* if the person "purposely, knowingly, recklessly, or negligently causes the death of another human being." This includes "murder, manslaughter or negligent homicide." The MPC explains that these several types of criminal homicide depend on the *mens rea* of the individual causing the death of another person. According to MPC section 210.2, "murder" is committed when the perpetrator acts either purposefully, knowingly, or recklessly. Such "recklessness and extreme indifference to the value of human life" are presumed if the perpetrator "is engaged or is an accomplice in the commission of, or an attempt to commit, or flight after committing or attempting to commit robbery, rape or deviate sexual intercourse by force or threat of force, arson, burglary, kidnapping or felonious escape." This latter part of the definition is left over from the common law and is often referred to as the "felony murder" rule. That is, if a death is caused by a person committing a major felony, then even if the death was unintended, the death will still be treated as murder.

Through this definition of murder, the MPC attempts to remove vague and confusing terms like "malice aforethought," or "deliberate" or "premeditation" which are used in the definitions of murder in many states. In short, if you either intend to kill someone, or you know that your action will cause death but you don't care either way, then under the MPC (as well as the law of every state, regardless of terminology) you are guilty of murder. In states that have not adopted the MPC, this crime is often labelled *intentional homicide.* Also note that under the common law rule, a victim must die within a year and a day after being injured for the crime to constitute "murder" or "homicide." This is appropriately referred to as the *year and a day rule.* In addition, the MPC exempts suicide and abortion from the definition of "murder."

Section 210.3(1)(a) of the MPC explains that deaths caused by reckless behavior constitutes *manslaughter.* Recall that recklessness means a person is aware of a significant risk of harm, but acts in disregard of that risk. So, for example, imagine a person who drives a car through a residential subdivision at 90 m.p.h. in the afternoon even though he or she is aware of the possibility that children could be playing on the street or adults could be walking their dogs on the street. If that driver kills a pedestrian, the driver would be criminally liable for manslaughter. In jurisdictions that have not adopted the MPC, this crime is often labelled as "reckless homicide."

Section 210.3(1)(b) of the MPC applies its own wording to a principle from the common law known as "provocation." Under the common law concept, if a person kills while acting angrily in a sudden and intense "heat of passion," the charge of murder will be reduced to a lesser charge such as *voluntary manslaughter.* The term "voluntary" means the killer chose to kill. As an example where the concept of "provocation" was historically applied, imagine a husband comes home to find his wife in bed with another man. Acting in a sudden rage, the husband kills either his wife, her lover, or both. Although the common law would not excuse the killing(s), under the rule of provocation any murder charge would be reduced to manslaughter. The MPC says simply that manslaughter includes "a homicide which would otherwise be murder [that] is committed under the influence of extreme mental or emotional disturbance for which there is reasonable explanation or excuse."

Section 210.4 of the MPC defines negligent homicide simply as "homicide when it is committed negligently." Here, the MPC applies its own preferred terminology to what many states label instead as *involuntary manslaughter.* The word, involuntary, in this context means the defendant did not knowingly or intentionally choose to kill, nor was the defendant aware of the risk of death to others. A common example of this is drunk driving resulting in the death of an individual. Presuming the person was too drunk to be aware that he or she should not be driving, states historically would charge the drunk driver with "involuntary manslaughter" or "criminal negligence." With changing social and legal norms, however, drunk drivers are increasingly being charged with "reckless homicide" or "voluntary manslaughter" on the theory that the person knew before they began drinking, and perhaps even while they were driving, that driving while drunk posed a serious risk to others' lives.

*Assault* Moving on to crimes that cause injury other than death, section 211.1 of the MPC differentiates between *simple assault* and *aggravated assault.* The key differences are *mens rea* combined with the seriousness of the inflicted injury. Simple assault occurs when a person causes bodily injury purposefully, knowingly, or recklessly, or when acting negligently while using a deadly weapon, or in attempting by "physical menace to put another in fear of imminent serious bodily injury." Aggravated assault, on the other hand, occurs when a person purposefully, knowingly, or recklessly causes "serious" body injury, or when the person purposefully or knowingly causes bodily injury using a deadly weapon. Depending on the state, the traditional common law terms for assault were "battery," "assault," or "mayhem." These terms can be confusing because in the criminal law—and again depending on the jurisdiction—"assault" can also mean "battery."

Also, many states that have not adopted the MPC create specific statutes that deal with injury or reckless endangerment cause by use of motor vehicles or firearms. The MPC Section 211.2 instead creates a catch-all section that covers all types of "recklessly endangering another person." This misdemeanor occurs if the person "recklessly engages in conduct which places or may place another person in danger of death or serious bodily injury." This is presumed if the person knowingly points a firearm at another person, regrardless whether the perpetrator believed the gun was loaded.

Section 212 of the MPC then moves on to crimes of restraint. Kidnapping has a lengthy definition where the particular motive of the perpetrator is relevant:

> § 212.1. Kidnapping.
>
> A person is guilty of kidnapping if he unlawfully removes another from his place of residence or business, or a substantial distance from the vicinity where he is found, or if he unlawfully confines another for a substantial period in a place of isolation, with any of the following purposes:
>
> (a) to hold for ransom or reward, or as a shield or hostage; or
>
> (b) to facilitate commission of any felony or flight thereafter; or
>
> (c) to inflict bodily injury on or to terrorize the victim or another; or
>
> (d) to interfere with the performance of any governmental or political function.

Section 212.3 of the MPC then simply defines "false imprisonment" as a misdemeanor that occurs when a person "knowingly restrains another unlawfully so as to interfere substantially with his liberty."

Turning to the crime of rape, the question how to precisely define this crime is currently controversial, rapidly evolving, and varies by state. In general, though, the concept of rape can be defined as sexual intercourse by (a) force or (b) threat of force, or (c) without consent. This still leaves many particular questions, though, especially such as how "consent" or lack thereof should be defined. For example, does silence from a person during sexual intercourse indicate consent or non-consent?

Depending on the state, the crime of rape is also commonly labeled "sexual assault," or "sexual battery." Section 213 of the MPC defines "rape," but this part of the MPC has received widespread criticism as offensive and obsolete. Recall that the MPC was written in the 1950's and finally published in 1962. Among the many problems of Section 213, it criminalizes only rape committed by men but not by women, labels rape of a man by a man "deviate," lessens the charge for the situation that today is often called "date rape," and exempts husbands from being held criminally liable for raping their wives. This latter exception was called the "marital rape exception" under the traditional common law, and has been largely—though not entirely—repudiated under the laws of most states. As a result of all these problems, for the most part the MPC is currently disregarded as legal authority when it comes to defining the crime of rape.

*Terrorism* Another type of violent crime is commonly referred to as terrorism. *Terrorism* is simply the use of violence as a means to achieve a political goal, such as by intimidating a civilian population or a government institution into supporting a particular political or legal policy. For example, the federal USA PATRIOT Act, enacted by Congress after the 9/11 terror attacks against the United States in 2001, basically adopts the above definition of terrorism. Thus, any type of violent crime—threats, murder, attempted murder, rape, and so on—can be used to commit acts of terrorism if the violence is committed with a motive of influencing the political system. In addition, the USA PATRIOT Act outlaws and punishes the use of a "weapon of mass destruction" (WMD) regardless of motive. WMDs include large-scale explosive devices (such as a nuclear bomb), toxic chemicals (like nerve gas), deadly biological agents (such as anthrax) or explosives used to distribute lethal radiation (often called "dirty bombs").

## Types of Crimes 2: Crimes Involving Property

Let's turn now to some of the property crimes defined by the MPC. The term *property* can refer to movable physical objects, land and buildings, or financial assets such as stocks, bonds, and bank accounts. Under Section 221.2 of the MPC, a person commits *criminal trespass* if "knowing that he is not licensed or privileged to do so, he enters or surreptitiously remains in any building or occupied structure, or separately secured or occupied portion thereof." Notice that the difference between criminal trespass and burglary is the intent of the perpetrator. For example, if a homeless person seeks merely to sleep on someone's property, it would be criminal trespass. If, however, criminal trespass by an individual includes an intent to commit an additional crime of a felonious nature—theft, robbery, and so on—then the trespass rises to the level of burglary.

Section 223.2 of the MPC defines two types of theft: theft of "movable" property versus theft of "immovable" property. The MPC discusses these two types of theft since the method of the theft differs. In the case of *movable* property, theft occurs if the perpetrator "unlawfully takes, or exercises unlawful control over, movable property of another with purpose to deprive him thereof." Movable property would be things like cars, jewelry, electronic goods, or cash. With these types of items, a thief can take *physical* possession of movable property and change its location. In the case of *immovable* property, theft occurs if the perpetrator "unlawfully transfers immovable property of another or any interest therein with purpose to benefit himself or another not entitled thereto." Immovable property would be things like private residences or commercial real estate. In the case of immovable property, a perpetrator would have to take *legal* ownership, or partial *legal* interest in, the property. This could be done, for example, through creation of fraudulent documents that falsely showed legal ownership of the property. Depending on the state, theft of any type is also sometimes called "larceny."

Section 222.1 of the MPC then defines *robbery* as any kind of theft where the perpetrator either "inflicts serious body injury" or threatens to do so while committing the theft. In other words, robbery involves an attack both on a person themself and their property. Relatedly, Section 221.1 of the MPC states that *burglary* occurs when a person "enters a building or occupied structure, or separately secured or occupied portion thereof, with purpose to commit a crime therein." Notice that both the crimes of burglary and robbery occur when another lesser crime is already involved. In the case of robbery, a theft must be involved. The crime of burglary, however, is committed when a person enters a building intending to commit *any* crime; theft is only one possibility. Thus, like robbery, burglary can involve a crime against a person as well as his or her property.

Certain types of crimes involving property are often referred to as *white collar* crimes. Originally based on the idea of businessmen wearing white dress shirts, the term refers to financial crimes—typically involving large financial amounts—committed by individuals in actual or fraudulent corporations such as banks or investment companies. The term "white collar" distinguishes such criminals from those involved in smaller-scale "blue collar" crimes (ordinary in-person theft or robbery, and so on). White-collar crimes can include:

- Fraud—a misrepresentation of a fact to a person that causes injury to that person due to their reliance on that false fact.

- Bribery—giving something of benefit to a government official to induce them to do something he or she otherwise would not have done.

- Embezzlement—theft of financial assets, such as a bank account.

- Insider trading—using secret information to trade corporate stocks to one's benefit.

- Counterfeiting—creating fake money (currency).

- Money laundering—taking "dirty" (illegally obtained) money and "cleaning" it by hiding its true origins.

- Racketeering—participation in an organized criminal enterprise (such as the "Mafia" or "Mob")

One example of white collar crime is a "Ponzi scheme," named for a man named Charles Ponzi who used the technique in the 1920s. A Ponzi scheme fraudulently promises investors consistently large returns on their financial investment if they invest their money in some (often vague) investment plan. In reality, only a small amount of the moneys are used to pay out the expected interest to a handful of investors, while the criminal(s) simply pocket all the rest of the invested moneys for themselves. This is different than a "pyramid scheme" where investors know that their returns will come only from money invested by new investors.

One of the most famous white collar criminals in U.S. history is Bernard "Bernie" Madoff, responsible for creating the biggest Ponzi scheme—and simultaneously the largest financial fraud—in U.S. history. For several decades until his arrest in 2008, Madoff ran a Wall Street investment firm, Bernard L. Madoff Investment Securities. His clients included businesses, charities, universities, and wealthy individuals, including famous celebrities like Steven Spielberg and Larry King.

Madoff told his clients that he was investing their money in the stock market. In actuality, he was pocketing the money and only paid out enough money to keep investors satisfied that they were earning the consistently high yields Madoff had promised. Despite repeated complaints to, and investigations by, the federal Securities and Exchange Commission (SEC) for over more than a decade, Madoff's fraud went undiscovered. Finally in 2008, the near financial collapse of the stock market caused Madoff to be unable to pay out withdrawals requested by clients. As a result, he confided in his two sons Mark and Andrew, top employees in the company, that the entire business was all just "one big lie." Mark and Andrew then contacted federal authorities and told them about their father's extensive fraud. Madoff was soon charged in federal court with fraud, money laundering, perjury, and other related white-collar crimes. According to various financial figures that came out during Madoff's criminal trial, and depending on the accounting method used, Madoff's fraud totaled somewhere between 10 and 65 billion dollars. Most investors lost everything they had invested. At the close of trial, Madoff was convicted, and the trial judge sentenced him to the maximum sentence allowed by federal law given the charges: 150 years in prison.

## Types of Crimes 3: Inchoate Crimes

Another category of crimes are called *inchoate* crimes. This means a crime is planned, or the beginning of the crime's execution is underway, or the crime was attempted, but the crime is not yet, or was never, completed. For example, a person might smash a window of a home intending to commit burglary, but then be scared off by large guard dogs. Or, a group prepares all the plans to murder someone, but then right at the moment the group is about to enter the victim's home, a member of the group suddenly renounces the entire idea and leaves.

There are several specific terms for particular types of inchoate crimes. A person commits *conspiracy*, when one joins with one or more other people to plan or commit a crime. A classic example would be a plan by a group of thieves to rob a bank. *Solicitation* occurs when a person seeks to receive stolen or illegal goods (such as drugs or a stolen car) or illegal services (such as prostitution). A person commits *incitement* when they encourage someone else to commit a crime. Incitement becomes conspiracy if the two (or more) people agree to work together.

The general term for helping another person commit a crime is "aiding and abetting." Depending on the state, the person doing the aiding and abetting is called an "accessory" or an "accomplice," or both. In some states, though, the term "accomplice" applies to anyone in a group that together commits a crime, such as murder or robbery. Helping to facilitate a crime might consist of creating the plan for the crime, providing needed information (like a security code), giving financial support, or hiding perpetrators or evidence after the crime has been committed.

*Criminal Attempt* The most common type of inchoate crime, and the most complex and difficult to analyze, is *attempt*. MPC Section 5.01 has a lengthy definition regarding what constitutes attempt or lack thereof. Because of the complexity of the analysis, we need to quote much of the definition.

> § 5.01. Criminal Attempt.
>
> (1) Definition of Attempt. A person is guilty of an attempt to commit a crime if, acting with the kind of culpability otherwise required for commission of the crime, he:
>
> (a) purposely engages in conduct that would constitute the crime if the attendant circumstances were as he believes them to be; or
>
> (b) when causing a particular result is an element of the crime, does or omits to do anything with the purpose of causing or with the belief that it will cause such result without further conduct on his part; or
>
> (c) purposely does or omits to do anything that, under the circumstances as he believes them to be, is an act or omission constituting a substantial step in a course of conduct planned to culminate in his commission of the crime.

Under subsections (a) and (b) above, the MPC basically defines attempt as when the person believes he has done all he needs to do for the crime to occur, but the person is mistaken. For example, imagine a computer hacker who believes she has stolen a victim's credit card account password. Unbeknownst to the hacker, though, the stolen "password" is simply the name of the victim's cat and not the credit card password. Under section (a), even though actual theft did not occur, the hacker is guilty of attempted theft (note other computer crimes might have occurred as well). Now, imagine Sally glances over the shoulder of coworker Mia and happens to see Mia enter her credit card account password on her computer. Sally then gives Mia's password to Jeff who agrees to commit credit card fraud using the password. Under section (b), Mia is guilty of attempted theft even if Jeff decides never to go through with the theft.

As to section (c), the term *substantial step* in the last section is an exceptionally vague term open to wide interpretation. Aware of this difficulty, the MPC attempts to offer more detailed clarity on what conduct can, in the right circumstances, constitute a "substantial step":

> § 5.01. Criminal Attempt.
>
> (2) Conduct That May Be Held Substantial Step Under Subsection (1)(c). Conduct shall not be held to constitute a substantial step under Subsection (1)(c) of this Section unless it is strongly corroborative of the actor's criminal purpose. Without negativing the sufficiency of other conduct, the following, if strongly corroborative of the actor's criminal purpose, shall not be held insufficient as a matter of law:
>
> (a) lying in wait, searching for or following the contemplated victim of the crime;
>
> (b) enticing or seeking to entice the contemplated victim of the crime to go to the place contemplated for its commission;
>
> (c) reconnoitering the place contemplated for the commission of the crime;
>
> (d) unlawful entry of a structure, vehicle or enclosure in which it is contemplated that the crime will be committed;
>
> (e) possession of materials to be employed in the commission of the crime, that are specially designed for such unlawful use or that can serve no lawful purpose of the actor under the circumstances;
>
> (f) possession, collection or fabrication of materials to be employed in the commission of the crime, at or near the place contemplated for its commission, if such possession, collection or fabrication serves no lawful purpose of the actor under the circumstances;
>
> (g) soliciting an innocent agent to engage in conduct constituting an element of the crime.

At the end of the main paragraph of section 1 above, the MPC uses a double negative: "shall not be held insufficient as a matter of law." A more clear way to say this would be "may be legally sufficient." That is, the MPC declares that any of the specifically listed types of common criminal conduct *can* constitute a "substantial step" *if* the behavior is strongly consistent with the actor's criminal purpose.[5] Section 2 above also states "without negativing the sufficiency of other conduct." This simply means that none of the listed examples of a "substantial step" is required for an attempt to occur; other substantial steps that are not listed are still enough in themselves to constitute attempt. In other

5. See, e.g., *U.S. v. Jackson*, 560 F.2d 112 (2d Cir. 1977)

words, the list the MPC provides of substantial steps is not a complete or exhaustive list, but merely represents some of the more common examples of types of conduct that comprise a substantial step.

Section 5.01 of the MPC also, however, incorporates the criminal law concept of *abandonment*, taken from the common law. This means that a potential perpetrator is able to avoid being charged with a crime, or the attempt of that crime, if the would-be perpetrator abandons the attempt. Under both the common law and the MPC, however, this abandonment must be unambiguously complete:

> § 5.01. Criminal Attempt.
>
> (4) Renunciation of Criminal Purpose. When the actor's conduct would otherwise constitute an attempt under Subsection (1)(b) or (1)(c) of this Section, it is an affirmative defense that he abandoned his effort to commit the crime or otherwise prevented its commission, under circumstances manifesting a complete and voluntary renunciation of his criminal purpose.

For example, imagine an armed group goes inside a bank during business hours to rob the bank. In the midst of the robbery, one of the robbers then says out loud to his fellow bank-robbing co-conspirators "Gee guys, I'm not sure if we should be doing this." This does *not* constitute abandonment of the attempt. The crime is already underway and it is unclear whether the statement indicates repudiation or mere doubt about the ongoing crime. On the other hand, now imagine that same would-be bank robber, just before entering the bank with his fellow co-conspirators, says out loud to the group "I've changed my mind; I'll have no part of this!" and then immediately leaves and tells the police. Such conduct would legally constitute an abandonment of the attempt. In that situation, even were the rest of the bank robbers to go on and rob the bank and even kill someone in the process, the co-conspirator who completely abandoned the attempt would not be criminally liable for robbery or murder.

The question of abandonment is usually one of sufficient evidence of abandonment to convince the judge or jury. For example, what if a would-be bank robber tells the rest of the group "I'm out!" just before entering the bank. The person immediately leaves, but then never tells the police nor anyone else. If that person is later arrested and charged as an accomplice or accessory to robbery and murder, that person will have a hard time convincing a judge or jury that that defendant abandoned the robbery attempt. The judge or jury is likely to assume based on the evidence—especially if the co-conspirators testify so—that even though the defendant didn't participate in the robbery itself, the defendant was a lookout, or a getaway driver, or provided weapons, or helped in the planning, or had agreed to hide the stolen money, or so on. In short, without strong evidence that demonstrates complete abandonment, it will likely appear to a judge or jury that the defendant is merely trying to evade criminal responsibility by falsely claiming the attempt was abandoned.

## Criminal Defenses

Imagine someone is accused of a crime. That person will likely hire an attorney or be assigned a public defender to offer a defense against the prosecution. Typically that defense will be that the defendant is innocent of the charges, or at least that the prosecution lacks enough evidence to show the defendant is guilty of the alleged crime beyond a reasonable doubt. But what if the evidence clearly shows the defendant *did* commit the act in question, or what if the defendant even admits the alleged conduct? In these circumstances, there are other possible legal defenses a defendant may use to avoid criminal responsibility. Let's look at several of them.

*Consent* Recall that by definition, a crime is a wrong committed against society, not the individual. Yet the common law and MPC Section 2.11 still allows individuals to consent to having harm done to them in limited circumstance, and the harm will not be deemed criminal. Even in these limited situations, though, the harm must not be "substantial" or "serious." For example, consent allows contact sports such as boxing, football, hockey, and soccer to exist. The players know that it's inevitable that they will incur "reasonably foreseeable hazards" (MPC Section 2.11(2)(b)) such as minor injuries from regular play. However, players have *not* consented to having substantial injury inflicted on them. Indeed, the rules of such sports forbid many types of physical contact that could result in serious injury. As a result, intentional harm committed by one player against another in flagrant violations of the rules can be prosecuted. Consent also allows tattooing or body modifications, but again without substantial or serious injury. The limitation on substantial or serious injury occurring is why consent is not a defense against charges of domestic violence, dueling, or assisted suicide. Consent is also allowed as a defense if lack of consent is required as part of the definition of the crime. For example, the crimes of rape and criminal trespass to property require that the victim did not consent to the conduct in question. If the alleged victim consented, then by definition the crime did not occur. On the other hand, consent is not allowed as a defense if the crime specifically forbids such conduct regardless of the victim's consent. Such crimes include statutory rape, prostitution, or murder. Even when consent is allowed as a defense, however, such consent is not valid if the person giving consent is deemed legally incapable of giving consent. This includes cases of mental incapacity due to young age, intoxication, serious mental illness, or other illness such as dementia or Alzheimer's. Consent is also invalid if it is coerced or gained by fraud.

*Defense of Self or Others* Both self-defense and defense of others are recognized as a defense to the use of violent force in all states, as well as the MPC in Sections 3.04 and 3.05. Most jurisdictions, as well as MPC section 3.06, also allow violent force to be used for defense of one's own property in limited circumstances. In all these situations, the person using the force must meet certain conditions. In most states, the person using the violent force must have a reasonable belief that the use of force is both necessary and in reasonable proportion to the need. For example, a homeowner of an unfenced corner lot in a residential neighborhood can not shoot a trespasser cutting diagonally across the front-yard lawn to save a few feet of walking. Violent force in this instance is neither necessary nor proportional to the harm being prevented. The trespasser wasn't harming anything so force wasn't necessary. Also, the homeowner could have simply yelled, or chased the trespasser off the lawn with a stick. Moreover, even if the homeowner believed force was necessary and proportional, the belief itself is not reasonable. That is, no reasonable person in this situation would believe that shooting a trespasser in this instance was either necessary or a proportional response.

The claims of self defense or defense of others are simply more particular applications of a broader defense of "necessity." MPC Section 3.02 declares that generally, violation of law is justifiable if "the harm or evil sought to be avoided by such conduct is greater than that sought to be prevented by the law defining the offense charged." All U.S. jurisdictions allow some variation of the necessity defense, which might include protection of self, others or property. As a simple example, driving over the speed limit may be justified as "necessary" if you are rushing your elderly grandparent to the hospital because he is in the midst of having a heart attack. The necessity defense does not justify all types of crimes, however. For example, some of the most famous criminal law cases covered in law school classes involve claims by person in lifeboats at sea that they needed to kill and eat some of their fellow lifeboat passengers in order to survive. Courts have held in these situations that the necessity defense may not be used to justify murder of innocent people as a means of self-preservation.[6]

6. *U.S. v. Holmes*, 26 F.Cas. 360 (1842); *Queen v. Dudley and Stephens*, 14 QBD 273 DC (1884)

A famous example of the attempted use of self-defense as a legal justification occurred in 1984.[7] Bernard Goetz, a 37-year-old white man, was riding a New York City subway when he was surrounded by four young Black men, one of whom asked him for "five dollars." Goetz, who was carrying a concealed handgun, later testified that he felt threatened. He pulled out the gun and shot at all four of the men. None of them died, and the police charged Goetz with attempted murder. At trial, Goetz argued he had a "reasonable belief" that the four men on a subway were about to attack and rob him when he shot and seriously wounded all of them. During this time he became known as the "subway vigilante," with the public deeply divided over whether his action was a reasonable reaction to justifiable fear or was an excessively aggressive overreaction. The jury concluded Goetz's belief in a need for self-defense was reasonable under the circumstances and so acquitted him of attempted murder, although he was convicted of possession of a firearm. A later civil trial, though, found Goetz liable for $43 million dollars to Darrell Cabey, one of the men Goetz shot and who became paralyzed as a result.

*Mistake* There are two types of mistake in the criminal law: *mistake of law* and *mistake of facts.* Both the common law and MPC Section 2.04 recognize this distinction. Mistake of law is not allowed as a criminal defense except in rare circumstances. As the famous saying goes, "ignorance of the law is no excuse." Citizens and other residents of a legal jurisdiction are expected to know and follow the laws within that jurisdiction. Note, though, that a sincere belief that the law was otherwise might mitigate the sentence.

A *reasonable* mistake of fact, however, can constitute a legal defense under the right conditions. For example, assume you eat at a restaurant on a rainy day and lean your umbrella in a corner near the door with other customers' umbrellas. When you leave the restaurant you take what looks like your umbrella but it's not. In this instance, you would not be guilty of theft as long as you returned the umbrella once you realized it's not yours. If, however, you brought in a small black folding travel umbrella you would be guilty of theft if you leave the restaurant after grabbing a large neon-orange golf umbrella on the way out. In such an instance, you could not reasonably claim that you were mistaken that the umbrella was yours.[8]

*Intoxication* Under the common law, intoxication by alcohol or other drugs is generally not a defense to criminal conviction. As MPC Section

7. *People v. Goetz,* 497 N.E.2d 41, (N.Y. 1986).
8. See, e.g., *Green v. State,* 221 S.W.2d 612, 616 (Tex. Crim. 1949)

2.08(2) states: "When recklessness establishes an element of the offense, if the actor, due to self-induced intoxication, is unaware of a risk of which he would have been aware had he been sober, such unawareness is immaterial." In short, being drunk generally does not excuse criminal drunken behavior. The only exception is if the defendant was so overwhelmingly intoxicated, he was completely unable to know or intend what he was doing at the time. In such an instance, then by definition, the defendant could not have the required *mens rea* to commit a crime of intent or knowledge. However, if the defendant knew she could become intoxicated, then since she knew about the risk but chose to disregard it, she at least acted with the *mens rea* of recklessness. For example, were a victim to die in this kind of situation, a judge or jury could lower the criminal charge from intentional homicide to reckless homicide. Intoxication by alcohol or other drugs might also mitigate the sentence depending on whether the judge or jury is sympathetic to the defendant's situation.

*Incapacity* Depending on the jurisdiction, the common law considers children below a certain age incapable of making the moral choices needed to impose criminal responsibility. Generally, children below the age of seven are conclusively presumed to be unable to realize the gravity of their behavior. Whether termed "incapacity" or "diminished capacity," the concept is that the criminal law will not punish a young child for their actions due to their lower mental capacity. For example, assume two six-year-old children stumble across a gun and one of the children aims at and shoots the other child. The law will presume that the shooter either did not realize it was a real gun or did not realize what "killing" someone is. Generally, however, children between the ages of seven and fourteen are rebuttably presumed to have incapacity. In other words, incapacity is presumed, but a prosecutor may introduce evidence to rebut the presumption by showing the child had awareness of what they were doing. Over the age of 14 (the exact age varies by state), the law generally presumes the defendant possesses full mental capacity. The defendant has a chance to show otherwise, however, such as due to a lower IQ, mental illness, or (typically for older defendants) mental disease such as dementia or Alzheimer's. The MPC does not specifically address diminished capacity due to age, as the proper *mens rea* to meet the elements of the crime must be proven in every case regardless of age. In other words, if either a child or adult lacks the required *mens rea*, then that person is not criminally responsible. On the other hand, if it could be shown that either a child or adult had sufficient understanding to possess the required mens rea, then that person would be criminally responsible.

*Entrapment* Entrapment can occur when police entice a defendant to commit a crime that the defendant was otherwise not planning to commit. The question is whether the idea for the crime was implanted in the defendant by the police. This requires an investigation into the defendant's predisposition to commit the crime. That is, did that defendant have a propensity to commit the crime anyway? Or, was the defendant tempted to do something they otherwise would not have done? This "subjective" test of entrapment that excuses criminal liability has been adopted by the MPC in Section 2.13, as well as by the U.S. Supreme Court in *Jacobson v. U.S.*[9] In that case, for over two years, FBI agents repeatedly mailed numerous advertisements to sell child pornography to Jacobson, a rural farmer in Nebraska. These advertisements also argued that the government was trying to restrict the freedom of speech. When Jacobson finally ordered a single videotape, he was arrested and convicted for child porn. The Supreme Court overturned his conviction on the basis that the evidence showed he did not have a propensity to commit the crime:

> [T]he Government not only excited petitioner's interest in sexually explicit materials banned by law, but also exerted substantial pressure on petitioner to obtain and read such material as part of a fight against censorship and the infringement of individual rights . . . The evidence that petitioner was ready and willing to commit the offense came only after the Government had devoted 2½ years to convincing him that he had or should have the right to engage in the very behavior proscribed by law.

## The Insanity Defense

In addition to the several legal defenses just discussed, another legal defense a criminal defendant can use is the *insanity defense*. Despite the fact that this defense is invoked in only a small fraction of all criminal cases, it elicits serious debate among legal experts and arouses strong emotions in the general public. The term "insanity" is a *legal* definition, and *not* a medical definition. In the fields of medicine and mental health, there is no such diagnosis as "insanity." In fact, the vast majority of individuals who are diagnosed with serious mental illness do not meet the legal definition of "insanity." To understand the insanity defense today, we need to look at the history of the insanity defense.

Prior to 1843, a person could escape criminal responsibility based

9. *Jacobson v. U.S.*, 503 U.S. 540 (1992).

on insanity only if the person was completely unaware of what he or she was doing. In other words, the individual must be acting like a wild animal, such as a rabid dog, and be incapable of rational thought. This test was accordingly known as the "wild beast" test. Then in 1843, an English case changed the common law definition of insanity. The court in *M'Naghten's Case*[10] declared:

> A defendant may be excused from criminal responsibility if at the time of the committing of the act the party accused was labouring under such a defect of reason, from a disease of the mind, as not to know the nature and quality of the act he was doing, or if he did know it, that he did not know that he was doing what was wrong.

This became know as the *M'Naghten Rule*, also called the *Right-Wrong Test*. Notice that under the M'Naghten rule, either the person must be so mentally ill that either he is unaware of what he is doing, or even if he is aware of his actions, he has absolutely no moral concept of "right" and "wrong" that he can apply to his actions.

The Right-Wrong Test soon became the primary test for criminal responsibility in the United States. Defendants could be declared legally "insane" if they were completely unable to distinguish right from wrong. The test was used by almost all U.S. jurisdictions until the 1970's. Even today, the test is still used by half the states and in the federal courts as well, despite there being almost no relationship between the legal test and modern medical science.

Because of the lack of connection between the legal definition and medical science, the test came under increasing criticism during the first half of the 1900s as the fields of psychology, psychiatry, and neuroscience began to make rapid advancements. As a result, in 1957 the D.C. Circuit Court of Appeals, in *Durham v. U.S.*,[11] adopted a new definition of insanity. Under what is often called the *Durham Rule*, an accused is not criminally responsible if the unlawful act was the product of a diagnosable mental disease or defect. Because of the definition, this rule also became known as the *Products Test*. It basically broadened the insanity defense to apply to any action that was caused by serious mental illness. The Products Test was quickly adopted by a few jurisdictions but then just as quickly abandoned. The test was too hard to define: what is a "product"? And what is a "mental disease or defect"?

Also because of criticism of the Right-Wrong Test, another definition of insanity was proposed. Some severely mentally ill persons might know right from wrong, but are still unable to stop themselves from

10. *M'Naghten's Case*, 10 C & F 200 (1843)
11. *Durham v. U.S.*, 214 F.2d 862 (D.C. Cir. 1954)

compulsively hurting others. As a result, several jurisdictions altered their definition of insanity to apply to defendants who were unable to control their own behavior because of an "irresistible impulse." Indeed, this test came to be known as the *irresistible impulse test*, also often called the *policeman at the elbow test.* The theory is that no sane person would commit a crime with a police officer standing behind them. In other words, a sane person would control any desire to commit a crime knowing the certainty of their conviction if a police officer saw them do it. About 15 states use the irresistible impulse test. The test has been criticized, however, for possibly allowing alcoholics, drug abusers, gamblers, or other addicts to use the excuse to absolve them of criminal responsibility on the claim that their addiction "made them do it."

Seeking to provide reform to the definition of insanity, the American Law Institute also offered its own revision. What is known as the *Substantial Capacity Test* is defined in Model Penal Code Sec. 4.01:

> A person is not responsible for criminal conduct if at the time of such conduct as a result of mental disease or defect he lacks substantial capacity either to appreciate his criminality (wrongfulness) of his conduct or to conform his conduct to the requirements of the law.

Basically, the Substantial Capacity Test is a combination of the Right-Wrong Test and the Irresistible Impulse Tests. A defendant can escape criminal responsibility if the defendant can meet either definition of insanity: either not knowing the criminality of the act or being unable to stop oneself from committing the crime.[12] At first, several states and the federal government began using the test. Soon, though, a couple of those states and the federal government returned to the Right-Wrong test. Critics of the Substantial Capacity Test argued that the irresistible impulse part of the test too easily excuses criminal defendants who claim "I just couldn't control myself."

Because of the lack of connection between any of the definitions of legal insanity and modern medical science, the American Medical Association (AMA) has proposed its own standard, called the *Mens Rea Test.* Recall that all crimes require a particular mens rea as part of the definition of a crime. The AMA proposes simply to have medical experts testify as to whether the defendant possessed the necessary mens rea. A defendant would be found "not guilty" if "as a result of mental disease or defect, the defendant lacked the state of mind (mens rea) required as an element of the offense charged." That is, the judge or jury need only determine whether the defendant acted with the relevant

12. *See, e.g., State v. Johnson,* 399 A.2d 469 (R.I. 1979)

mental state of intent, knowledge, or recklessness. If the defendant acted with the required mental state, they are guilty. If the defendant did not act with the required mental state, then by definition, they are not guilty of the crime. The AMA favors the Mens Rea Test because it would allow much more psychiatric testimony. People favoring law and order like the test because it would reduce the number of individuals who would be able to escape conviction. It makes sense as well: a separate insanity test is unnecessary when *mens rea* must already be proven for criminal guilt. Yet the Right-Wrong Test has over 150 years of inertia, and many legislators fear voting to get rid of this legal standard. That is, legislators know that election opponents will portray any votes to change the definition of insanity as being "weak on crime," even if the opposite is true. It is politically safer to simply avoid the issue, rather than risk pressing for criminal justice reform.

Although the use of the insanity defense is rare, it is often controversial high-profile cases that stimulate changes to the insanity defense. One such extremely high-profile case occurred in 1981. That year, John Hinkley, Jr. was an unemployed, mentally disturbed 26-year-old man obsessed with the famous film actress Jodi Foster. He stalked her, and after she rejected his attempts at any kind of relationship, he became convinced that assassinating the President of the United States would get her to notice and admire him. On March 30, 1981, Hinkley fired six gunshots at President Ronald Reagan in Washington, D.C. as Reagan was leaving a hotel conference. The shots wounded a police officer and a secret service agent, severely wounded President Reagan, and permanently disabled Reagan's press secretary, James Brady. Hinkley was tried the next year for multiple crimes including attempted murder. Hinkley pled the insanity defense—that is, he claimed he was "not guilty by reason of insanity." Under the law at the time in all U.S. jurisdictions, if a person was found not guilty by reason of insanity, they were not sent to prison, but to a mental health institution. The defendant would then be released as soon as they were "cured"—no longer posing a threat to themselves or others—even if this meant they might end up being confined in the hospital for only a relatively short time. Since Hinkley was found "not guilty by reason of insanity," this meant he might be released within a short time if he could demonstrate he was over his mental illness.

There was a huge public outcry against the Hinkley verdict. It was seen as unjustly lenient, caused by the fact that judges and juries must choose between the limited options of either "guilty, not guilty, or not guilty by reason of insanity." As a result of this controversy, three states abolished the insanity defense. Several other states added new "guilty but insane" or "guilty but mentally ill" options to the verdicts that judges and juries may impose in criminal cases. Under this new standard, a criminal defendant that is convicted is first required to undergo medical treatment in psychiatric confinement. When and if the defendant is cured, they are then sent to prison to serve the remainder of their term. Moreover, as a result of Hinkley's acquittal based on the insanity defense, Congress amended the federal insanity defense to eliminate the MPC substantial capacity test and instead require that defendants meet the Right-Wrong test to avoid criminal responsibility. This made it more difficult for criminal defendants to assert the insanity defense in federal court.

Eventually President Reagan's press secretary James Brady died in 2014 from complications resulting from the injuries he received from Hinkley 33 years earlier. The coroner ruled Brady's death a homicide on that basis. However, Washington, D.C. follows the rule discussed earlier in this chapter that death must come "a year and a day" within the injury for the crime of murder to occur. As a result, Hinkley was never charged with the murder of Brady. In 2016, Hinkley was released from confinement in a mental health institution, although he remains subject to many court-supervised restrictions on his movements and activities.

Related to the insanity defense is the *diminished capacity* defense. Unlike the insanity defense, this defense does not allow one to escape all criminal responsibility, but instead reduces the degree of criminal responsibility. Several states and the federal government allow a reduction in the charge or sentence if a defendant has a reduced mental capacity. This standard, too, was changed after a controversial high-profile case. California had a "diminished capacity" defense until a murder case in 1978. That year, Dan White was a former member of the San Francisco Board of Supervisors (what they call their city council). After White resigned from the Board, both Mayor George Moscone and Harvey Milk, a member of the Board of Supervisors and one of the first openly gay elected officials in the United States, both opposed White's reappointment. Disgruntled by this opposition, White went to city hall and shot both Moscone and Milk to death. White was charged with their first-degree murders. His legal defense was that he suffered from the mental illness of depression, and thus suffered from a diminished mental capacity which made him unable to premeditate on (plan out) the murders. White's defense attorneys argued that White's depression was evidenced by changes in his behavior, including switching to a diet largely comprised of unhealthy junk foods. The media, however, mistakenly reported that White claimed his junk food diet caused him to kill Moscone and Milk. This led to the media sarcastically calling White's legal argument "the Twinkie Defense." The jury, however, believed White's defense of diminished capacity and convicted him only of the lesser charge of involuntary manslaughter—that is, that he acted suddenly in the heat of emotional passion. As a result, the trial court judge sentenced White to only seven years in prison. The local gay community was so outraged by the trial result that later that evening several thousand people rioted. They smashed windows at San Francisco's city hall and burned over a dozen police cars. Over 100 people ended up hospitalized after violent clashes with police. That evening's events became known as the "White Night Riots." The negative publicity from the trial outcome and the supposed "Twinkie Defense" eventually led to California eliminating the "diminished capacity" defense.

---

*Questions for Review and Discussion*

1. Describe the various possible types of *mens rea* and give examples.
2. Describe how the various types of murder are defined and give examples.
3. Describe the different types of insanity defense and give examples.
4. Other than insanity, describe other possible criminal defense and give examples.
5. Jane Doe, age 30, suffers from hallucinogenic delusions caused by a chemical imbalance in the brain. She believes God has asked her to rid the world of her neighbor, a demon. One day she kills her neighbor believing her neighbor is a demon. At trial, Jane fully admits in testimony that she knows the murder of innocent people is wrong, and she is able to fully control all her actions, but she believes her neighbor is not a person but rather a demon, and she voluntarily chose to follow God's request to kill her demon neighbor. Precisely define M'Naghten's Rule, the Irresistible Impulse Test, the Substantial Capacity test, and the Durham Rule. Explain whether Jane would be declared legally insane under each of those tests, and why.
6. A student, Sally, explains to her college instructor why she is not handing in an assignment that is due that day: "I didn't know the assignment was due today, plus I was celebrating my birthday yesterday, and so I was too drunk to do the assignment, and also you've told the class before to enjoy life to the fullest, and so basically I was following your instructions, and besides I had to work all day on the day before the exam to earn money to pay my rent, so I was too busy to do the assignment." If handing in an assignment late was a crime, specifically what legal defenses did Sally try to assert, and specifically how would each of those defenses apply in this case (i.e. were any of the legal defenses met in this case)?

---

*Suggested Readings*

*Regina v. Faulkner*, 13 Cox CC 550 (1877) (*mens rea* and *actus reus*)
*Thompson v. State*, 236 S.W.2d 787 (Tex. Crim. App. 2007) (transferred intent)
*People v. Decina*, 138 N.E.2d 799 (N.Y.1956) (recklessness)
*Garnett v. State*, 632 A.2d 797 (Md. 1993) (strict liability)
*People v. Goetz*, 497 N.E.2d 41 (N.Y. 1986) (self-defense)

*U.S. v. Holmes*, 26 F.Cas. 360 (1842) (necessity defense)
*Queen v. Dudley and Stephens*, 14 QBD 273 DC (1884) (necessity defense)
*Green v. State*, 221 S.W.2d 612, 616 (Tex. Crim. 1949) (mistake of fact)
*Jacobson v. U.S.*, 503 U.S. 540 (1992) (entrapment)
*Durham v. U.S.*, 214 F.2d 862 (D.C. Cir. 1954) (insanity)
*State v. Johnson*, 399 A.2d 469 (R.I. 1979) (insanity)
*U.S. v. Jackson*, 560 F.2d 112 (2d Cir. 1977) (attempt)

---

*Advanced Readings*

American Law Institute, *Model Penal Code* (1962)
Wayne Lafave, *Criminal Law, 5th Ed.* (2010)

CHAPTER 8

# CRIMINAL PROCEDURE

*Chapter Objectives*

*After reading this chapter, you should be able to:*

- Describe basic law regarding common elements of criminal procedure, including stops, searches, seizures, interrogation, arrests, and charges
- Compare the authority that police officers have to stop and search individuals walking out in public versus individuals driving a vehicle versus individuals in their home
- Describe the exclusionary rule and its exceptions
- Describe the rights of criminal suspects given by the Fifth and Sixth Amendments to the Constitution
- Describe the jury selection and decision process, as well as sentencing options

In the previous chapter we discussed the substance of criminal law: crimes and their defenses. *Criminal procedure*, on the other hand, defines the rights of criminal defendants when they are charged with violating the substantive criminal law. In other words, criminal procedure details the process by which criminal defendants are investigated, detained, questioned, arrested, charged, tried, convicted, and sentenced.

The Fourth, Fifth, Sixth, and Eighth Amendments to the Constitution contain the key rights of criminal defendants. These rights are also referred to as the rights of criminal suspects or the rights of the criminally accused. None of these terms, however, fully captures the meaning and importance of these rights. In a tyrannical government, those who disagree with the government could be subject to immediate arrest, fine, imprisonment, torture, or execution. They will not be told the charges against them; they will not be told what the evidence is against them; they will not be allowed to present their own side in their own defense; they will not be allowed to have a lawyer; and they will be given a biased judge who has already reached a foregone conclusion of guilt.

They might have a confession tortured out of them. It's also often the case that none of their family members will ever know their loved ones have been arrested, and they will never be told what happened. People simply "disappear" one day never to be seen again. This systematic oppression terrorizes the population into submission, and thereby prevents popular uprisings against the totalitarian leadership.

Reacting against such tyranny and in the hope of preventing future such tyranny, James Madison drafted a series of "rights' to be amended to the U.S. Constitution. Congress approved most of his proposal and sent it on to the states for ratification. Eventually, Congress and the state legislatures ratified what became known as the Bill of Rights, ten amendments that prohibit government from actions that tyrannical governments commonly do. It is critical to understand that oppressive governments violate the rights not just of criminals, but quite often those of innocent civilians. The Bill of Rights is therefore intended to protect *all* individuals (both citizens or non-citizen residents) living within the United State against being falsely charged and wrongly convicted of crimes. If the government begins to do any of the actions prohibited by the Bill of Rights, not only would it be unconstitutional, it would serve as a warning to the public that the government is beginning to display the marks of tyranny.

When a criminal case goes to trial, the Fifth and Sixth Amendments provide defendants with the right not to testify against oneself, a right to an attorney, and a right to a speedy and public trial. Defendants also have a right to confront their accuser through cross-examination while the witness is under oath. We'll look at the rights of criminal defendants in much detail later in this chapter.

## Elements of a Criminal Trial

In addition to the basic rights criminal defendants possess, the full rules of criminal procedure, both for the federal government and in each of the separate state governments, are lengthy and complex. The main sources of such rules that apply in federal courts are the *Federal Rules of Criminal Procedure* and the *Federal Rules of Evidence.* Both of these large volumes are updated annually to reflect recent legal developments. Because these rules are so detailed and complex, we will not discuss them further. Here is merely the briefest overview of some of the most important and common trial concepts, some of which we will examine in more detail later in this chapter. You will see that many of the elements are the same or similar to the basic elements of civil procedure we discussed earlier in the chapter on the U.S. court system:

- *Bench trial:* a judge hears the case and decides the ruling.

- *Jury trial:* a judge presides over the court, but a jury (a group of citizens) hears the case and decides the ruling.

- *Venue:* the location of the court where the trial will be held.

- *Voir dire:* in a jury trial, the formal selection by the prosecution and defense to achieve an unbiased jury. This includes interviewing, choosing, and possibly dismissing potential jurors.

- *Dismissal:* a formal ruling by the judge that the criminal charges are invalid or lacking in evidence, so the case is "thrown out of court."

- *Burden of proof:* how much evidence the prosecution must show to demonstrate the crime was committed by the defendant.

- *Opening statement/argument:* the initial statement made by the prosecution and defense at the start of the trial.

- *Case-in-chief:* each party's presentation of the facts in support of their side. First the prosecution will present the prosecution's case-in-chief; then the defendant has the option whether to present the defendant's case-in-chief, or present no defense at all by arguing the prosecution's evidence has not met the required burden of proof (beyond a reasonable doubt). During each case-in-chief, the following elements will occur:
    - *Direct examination:* questioning in court by an attorney of that attorney's party or a witness for that party.
    - *Cross examination:* an optional questioning in court by an attorney of the opposing party or a witness for that opposing party.
    - *Redirect examination:* an optional secondary direct examination after a cross-examination has occurred.
    - *Recross examination:* an optional secondary cross examination after a re-direct examination has occurred.

- *Closing statement/argument:* the final statement made by the prosecution and defense at the close of the trial.

- *Judgment:* in a bench trial, the judge's decision on whether the defendant is guilty.

- *Verdict:* in a jury trial, the jury's decision on whether the defendant is guilty.

- *Directed verdict:* in a jury trial, a formal ruling by a judge that the law or facts are so one-sided, no jury decision is needed. In a criminal trial, a judge can direct a verdict of acquittal (not guilty), but can never direct a verdict of conviction (guilty).

- *Judgment notwithstanding the verdict:* This is a formal ruling by the judge that the jury's verdict finding the defendant guilty is overturned. This can occur only if the evidence is so one-sided, no rational jury could have reached the decision it did.

- *Mistrial:* The judge declares the trial void due to a substantial error in the process that prejudiced the jury in an unfair way against the defendant. For example, maybe a juror later admits that they voted against the defendant due to racial animosity.

Again, criminal procedure is a highly detailed, technical, and complex area of the law. We'll only briefly go into more detail on a few of the more common important issues in the criminal process in the rest of this chapter, looking at the criminal accusation process as it occurs chronologically.

## Investigation: Search and Seizure

Before criminal charges are filed, law enforcement personnel must investigate whether there is evidence that a crime has been committed and who might have committed that crime. After criminal charges are filed, law enforcement personnel need to continue to explore who committed what crimes and why. This is so the prosecutor has the best and most complete evidence available when presenting the prosecution's case during the trial. The Constitution, however, places limitations on criminal investigations by local, state, and federal law enforcement personnel.

*Fourth Amendment Protections* The basic limitations on government investigation of suspected criminal activity are primarily imposed by the Fourth Amendment.

> *The Fourth Amendment:* The right of the people to be secure in their persons, houses, papers, and effects, against unreasonable

> searches and seizures, shall not be violated, and no warrants shall issue, but upon probable cause, supported by oath or affirmation, and particularly describing the place to be searched, and the persons or things to be seized.

Fourth Amendment law is also called the law of *search and seizure.* The right against unreasonable searches and seizures protects the privacy of your body, home, vehicle, and personal information and belongings against unreasonable government intrusion. Let's look briefly at in-person stops, vehicle stops, and searches of one's residence.

IN-PERSON STOPS A police officer is always free ask you a question just like anyone on the street is free to walk up to you and ask anyone anything. In return, you're equally free to ignore whoever asks you a question, including a police officer, unless an exception applies. In the 1968 case *Terry v. Ohio*[1] the U.S. Supreme Court declared that a police officer may require you to stop if the officer has "reasonable, articulable" suspicion that you are possibly engaged in criminal activity. No one particular type of suspicious evidence or activity is needed; instead suspicion is based on the "totality of the circumstances." An officer must have individualized suspicion, and may not simply go around stopping people at random to ask them questions. The practice of an officer stopping someone and asking them questions is called "stop and ask." Because this right of police officers to stop people and ask them questions was affirmed in the Supreme Court case of *Terry v. Ohio,* the practice is often referred to as a "*Terry* Stop."

As noted, suspicion for a *Terry* Stop must be both "reasonable" and "articulable." For example, an officer can not merely say "I had a hunch" or "the person looked suspicious." These statements do not articulate any particular grounds for suspicion. Nor may the officer use the race or religion of the suspect nor some innocuous fact like "the person had long hair" or "the person had a tattoo" or "the person was wearing a t-shirt with a peace symbol on it." All these statements articulate specificity, but none of them by themselves are *reasonable* grounds for suspicion. Examples of reasonable and articulable suspicion might be something like "the person was pacing back and forth looking nervously into a store window while sweating profusely on a cool day" or "the person was sitting alone in a parked car in a dark alley at 3 a.m. with the motor turned off." Running away at the sight of a police officer doesn't create reasonable suspicion on its own, but other facts could give rise to reasonable suspicion. This might include "the person was rapidly running away from a location where a crime had just been reported" or "the

1. *Terry v. Ohio,* 392 U.S. 1 (1968)

person was looking into an open car trunk full of computers and then they ran as soon as they saw me."

When an officer stops a possible suspect and asks him or her questions, the officer may detain the person as long as the officer continues to have "reasonable, articulable suspicion." If the person sets the officer's mind at ease by answering any questions sufficiently, then reasonable articulable suspicion no longer exists, and the officer must allow the person to go. Once stopped in person by a police officer, an individual may invoke the Fifth Amendment right against self-incrimination, meaning he or she has a right not to answer any questions the officer asks. One must, however, at least provide your name.[2] Moreover, if the officer has reasonable, articulable suspicion of danger, such as a knife-shaped or gun-shaped bulge in one's clothing, then the officer may also pat down the outside of the person's clothing to make sure the person is unarmed. If something suspicious is felt, then the office is allowed to remove the item and inspect it. This practice is called "stop-and-frisk."[3]

If a suspect is arrested, then the defendant's clothes may automatically be searched for weapons or illegal items. This latter type of search is called a "search incident to arrest."[4] This practice is supported by two policies. First, police must make sure the suspect is not armed so as to prevent harm to officers or the public and to prevent the suspect from possibly harming himself as well. Second, police must search the suspect to preserve any evidence. Otherwise, the suspect might conceal or destroy evidence, such as stolen goods, drugs, documents, counterfeit bills, or other items the suspect is carrying.

VEHICLE STOPS In U.S. law, driving a vehicle is not a right, but merely a privilege—hence, the driver's license. Nevertheless, the Supreme Court has said that police officers must meet a higher burden of evidence to justify pulling a person over while in their vehicle compared to stopping someone on foot. Stopping a vehicle requires "probable cause" of criminal activity. This roughly means the officer has reasonable grounds for believing criminal activity may be involved. This is more evidence than "reasonable, articulable" suspicion, but less evidence than would be required for conviction or even for winning a civil lawsuit. Probable cause for stopping a vehicle could be a nonfunctioning headlight or taillight, swerving inside or outside lane lines, failure to use a turn signal, failure to come to a complete stop at a stop sign, having an expired license plate or inspection sticker, or driving over the speed limit. One exception to the requirement for probable cause is road-

2. *Hiibel v. 6th Judicial District Crt. of Nevada*, 542 U.S. 177 (2004)
3. *Terry v. Ohio*, 392 U.S. 1 (1968)
4. *U.S. v. Robinson*, 414 U.S. 218 (1973)

blocks used for sobriety checkpoints.[5] These checkpoints, however, must either inspect all drivers or pick drivers to inspect at random. These inspections may not merely pick drivers based on race, or the quality of their car, or the politics displayed on a car's bumper stickers, and so on.

Once a person is stopped in one's vehicle, the police need separate probable cause to search the vehicle.[6] This could occur, for example, if an officer smelled alcohol or marijuana, or if the officer heard noise coming from the trunk. Probable cause might also exist if the officer believes they see something suspicious inside the vehicle, or if the officer believes they saw the driver hide something under the seat while being pulled over. The driver or a passenger might also admit something during questioning such as they have an unlicensed gun in the vehicle. Moreover, police can always ask the driver to give consent to the police for them to search the vehicle. If the driver gives such consent, the resulting search is called a "consent search."[7] If the police lack probable cause to search, the driver is free to refuse to give consent. The Supreme Court has declared, however, that the police need not tell a vehicle driver they have a right to refuse consent. If the driver or a passenger is arrested, police may search the vehicle without consent, but "only if the arrestee is within reaching distance of the passenger compartment at the time of the search or it is reasonable to believe the vehicle contains evidence of the offense of arrest."[8]

HOMES AND BUSINESSES Unlike the situation with in-person stops or vehicle stops, the Fourth Amendment requires a *warrant* to search a person's residence or business and the warrant must describe the places or things to be searched or seized. A warrant is an authorization signed by a judge allowing law enforcement agents to legally search a privately owned building or other items. When it comes to homes, the private area of a residence includes not just the residence itself, but also the outdoor area and nearby related buildings immediately in the vicinity of the residence. This area is called the "curtilage" of the house. So, for example, a fenced in yard enclosing a house, garage, and garden shed all would be considered part of the curtilage of the house. Police may not search the curtilage without a warrant. An "open field" or other land beyond the curtilage, however, may be searched without a warrant even though it is still private property.

The Fourth Amendment requires that the warrant be based on probable cause. Such cause exists, for example, if police surveillance has

5. *Michigan Department of State Police v. Sitz*, 496 U.S. 444 (1990)
6. *California v. Carney*, 471 U.S. 386 (1985)
7. *U.S. v. Robinette*, 519 U.S. 33 (1996)
8. *Arizona v. Gant*, 556 U.S. 332 (2009)

observed known drug dealers repeatedly going in and out of a residence, or if a reliable police informer tells the police that there are drugs located in the residence. The Fourth Amendment also requires that the warrant specify the location to be searched. This means the warrant must specify the exact address with apartment number if applicable. So, for example, a warrant may not say the police may search "anywhere John Doe lives or visits." The warrant also must specify the items to be searched for and seized if found, such as "drugs" or "weapons" or "stolen computers." The warrant may not simply authorize the police to look for "evidence of a crime" or "illegal items" without more specificity.

If a person is arrested in a private building such as one's home, it is unlike the situation regarding in-person arrests and vehicle arrests. After an arrest in a home, there may only be a limited search without a warrant. Police may conduct a "protective sweep" for weapons in the area in the immediate vicinity of a suspect. This could be, for example, under a couch, under seat cushions, on shelves, and in drawers, all in the room where the suspect is currently being held. Any further search of the premises beyond the protective sweep area, however, would need a warrant.

EXCEPTIONS TO A WARRANT The Supreme Court has created several exceptions, however, to the warrant requirement for a search of private premises. First, under the *plain view doctrine*, any evidence of criminal activity that is in plain view of ordinary bodily senses (i.e. sight, sound, smell) may be seized without a warrant.[9] Visual-wise, this includes spotting stolen or illegal goods, as well as personal characteristics such as body size and shape, birthmarks or scars, clothing, jewelry, tattoos, facial hair, or glasses. Hearing-wise, this includes the sound of a firearm being discharged and yells or screams. Smell-wise, it might be the odor of drugs, dangerous chemicals, or something burning. For example, imagine the police knock on your door because a neighbor complained of loud music at your party. When you answer your front door, an officer sees drugs on your living room coffee table. The drugs may be seized and you may be arrested even without a warrant to search your home.

Also under the plain view doctrine, if the police are standing where the public has a right to be, then anything that can be seen from a public street or sidewalk is considered in "plain view." Plain view would thus include criminal activity on your front porch or behind open windows that can be seen from the sidewalk, or in your unfenced backyard that can be seen from the street, or any illegal items that can be seen through your car windows while your car is parked on the street. The Supreme Court has even said that police have a right to look into your backyard

9. *Horton v. California*, 496 U.S. 128 (1990)

from a helicopter, as long as the police are in public airspace.[10] The Court has limited the plain view doctrine, however, to evidence that can be seen using ordinary senses. Thus, this exception does not include evidence that can only be detected by advanced technology not available to the general public. For example, in *Kyllo v. U.S.* (2001), the Court said the police could stand on a sidewalk and use binoculars to look into a suspect's home window, but they could not use infra-red thermal imaging for the same purpose.[11]

The Supreme Court has also said that police do not need a warrant to enter or search a private residence or business if "exigent circumstances" exist. This means there is some emergency situation such that there is an urgent need for the police to conduct a search without taking the time to wait for a warrant.[12] Exigent circumstances might occur where a suspect has fled into a building where evidence is likely to be destroyed or removed, when there is or might be a medical emergency, or if there is a dangerous situation such as burning chemicals are about to explode. Or, imagine a neighborhood resident hears yelling, a gunshot, and then silence coming from their next-door-neighbor's home. If the neighbor calls the police, the police will not need a warrant to enter the home. Any potential victim could need immediate life-saving medical attention so exigent circumstances exist for a search without a warrant.

Another exception to the warrant requirement is a consent search. Just as drivers of vehicles may consent to a search of the vehicle, a resident or business owner may consent to a search of the premises. As in all cases of consent, it must be given freely and without coercion. Anyone with reasonable control over the premises may give consent to search, not only the owner of the premises. In the case of a business, it could be a manager or another employee. In the case of a private residence, it could be a roommate, apartment-mate, or family member at your home, such as a spouse, parent, or older child. Even a friend put in charge of answering the door at a party can give consent to the police to "Come on in!" In such a case, valid consent to enter the premises has been given so no warrant is needed.

THE EXCLUSIONARY RULE In the landmark case of *Mapp v. Ohio* (1961), the Supreme Court ruled that if your Fourth Amendment or other constitutional rights are violated, then any evidence against you gained by the police through violating your rights is "tainted" and there-

10. *Florida v. Riley*, 448 U.S. 445 (1989)
11. *Kyllo v. U.S.*, 533 U.S. 27 (2001)
12. *Welsh v. Wisconsin*, 466 U.S. 470 (1984)

fore inadmissible in court.[13] This legal principle is known as the *exclusionary rule*. Any evidence gained as a result of an illegal search or seizure is likewise inadmissible as such secondary evidence is "fruit of the poisonous tree."[14] For example, let's say the police illegally search a residence, find an address, and then go to that second address and find drugs there. Under the fruit of the poisonous tree doctrine, those drugs are inadmissible as evidence. Similarly, imagine an illegally obtained confession leads to a search of a residence where stolen goods are found. The confession and the stolen goods are all inadmissible. The exclusionary rule also applies to privately-gathered evidence if it was gathered at the direction of law enforcement agents. For example, if the police ask you to go snooping around your neighbor's yard, and you find marijuana growing and tell the police, that information is inadmissible against your neighbor due to the exclusionary rule. On the other hand, if you trespass in your neighbor's yard on your own, discover marijuana and then report it to the police, that evidence is admissible against your neighbor.

The exclusionary rule is not in the text of the Fourth Amendment, but the Court in *Mapp v. Ohio* explained that such a rule is required by principles of the Fourth Amendment. First, the rule deters police from illegal conduct, and the government shouldn't "profit" from illegal activity. Second, it promotes the integrity of the court system since judges and courts will not then be an "accomplice" to illegal government activity. Third, by requiring the government to act legally, the rule promotes public trust in and support for government. As a practical matter, however, the exclusionary rule is rarely applied in criminal cases—only a small fraction of one percent of all criminal cases end up excluding evidence due to the exclusionary rule.

There are also several relatively narrow exceptions to the exclusionary rule in which the Supreme Court has said enforcing the exclusionary rule would not fulfill its purposes. For example, a "good faith" exception applies if officers in good faith believed they were acting legally.[15] For example, maybe police mistakenly believed they had a valid warrant, or valid consent to search, or that they had probable cause to arrest, or believed there were exigent circumstances, or so on. For this exception to apply, the police must be *sincerely* mistaken and not simply claiming a mistake as a pretext.

Under the *inevitable discovery doctrine*, illegally obtained evidence is admissible if it would have been inevitably discovered anyway through

13. *Mapp v. Ohio*, 367 U.S. 643 (1961)
14. *Wong Sun v. U.S.*, 371 U.S. 471 (1963)
15. *U.S. v. Leon*, 468 U.S. 897 (1984)

legal means.[16] For example, imagine police conduct an illegal search of a house without a warrant. But, perhaps a warrant was just issued yet hadn't arrived on the scene yet, or the police already had an interview scheduled with an informer who would have given the police probable cause for a warrant of that residence. If so, then evidence found in the house is admissible according to the inevitable discovery doctrine.

A similar related exception is called the *independent source doctrine.* Under this exception, illegally gathered evidence is admissible if it was discovered simultaneously through both an illegal source and a separate, independent legal (untainted) source.[17] Imagine, for example, that police illegally coerce a suspect to reveal information, but at the same time an informer or witness was giving the police the same information. In this instance, the information obtained illegally is admissible in court because it was also obtained at the same time through a separate, independent legal source.

## Arrest, Charges, and Pleas

As we have seen, the Fourth Amendment requires police to have probable cause to arrest a criminal suspect. A judge-issued warrant is granted upon showing evidence in support of probable cause to arrest the individual on reasonable grounds for believing that criminal activity is involved. There are two common exceptions, however. An arrest warrant is not needed if the crime is a felony. An arrest warrant is also not needed if a police officer directly witnesses a suspect commit a misdemeanor.

*Fifth Amendment Protections* Once a defendant is arrested, the Fifth and Sixth Amendments provide many additional rights to the defendant. The Fifth Amendment states in large part:

> No person shall be held to answer for a capital, or otherwise infamous crime, unless on a presentment or indictment of a Grand Jury . . . nor shall any person be subject for the same offence to be twice put in jeopardy of life or limb; nor shall be compelled in any criminal case to be a witness against himself, nor be deprived of life, liberty, or property, without due process of law.

The Fifth Amendment term "infamous crimes" has been interpreted to be the equivalent of a modern felony (imprisonment for more than a year). As a result, all federal felonies must be charged by a grand

16. *Nix v. Williams*, 467 U.S. 431 (1984)
17. *Murray v. United States*, 487 U.S. 533 (1988)

jury indictment. A "grand jury" is a panel of between 16 and 23 citizens who review the evidence presented to them by a prosecutor. The grand jury does not rule on the guilt or innocence of a defendant. Instead, the grand jury decides by majority vote whether there is sufficient evidence to constitute probable cause to charge the defendant with a crime. The grand jury formally issues a "bill of indictment" (also called a "true bill"). In the states, unlike at the federal level, there are two ways criminal charges can be issued. Currently about twenty-two states require that a grand jury decide on charges for all felonies. In most of the remaining states, a prosecutor has the discretion whether to charge the defendant based on probable cause that the defendant committed a crime. Formally, the prosecutor issues an "information" that charges the defendant. The document is called an "information" because it informs the defendant of the charge. A few states allow a defendant to be charged either by indictment or by information.

The Fifth Amendment also states "nor shall any person be subject for the same offence to be twice put in jeopardy of life or limb." An attempt to try a person twice for the same crime after a valid acquittal is called "double jeopardy," and is prohibited. That is, if you are tried for a crime but the jury acquits you, you can not be re-charged and re-tried for the same offense. Without such a limitation, overzealous prosecutors could abuse the process by repeatedly and endlessly charging a defendant until some particular judge or jury finally convicts the defendant.

In addition, the Fifth Amendment declares that no person "shall be compelled in any criminal case to be a witness against himself." This means you have a right to refuse to testify against yourself during criminal interrogation or during a criminal trial. This is commonly known as "taking the Fifth" or "pleading the Fifth." This right was placed in the Constitution to prevent confessions—and very possibly *false* confessions—being gained through torture or other types of coercion, as has often happened throughout human history. Also under this rule, for it to be effective, judges must instruct juries that exercising one's right not to testify should in no way be taken as an admission or indication of guilt by that criminal defendant.

To be able to exercise your right not to be a witness against yourself you must be aware of such a right. You must similarly be aware that if you do decide to testify the police might use whatever you say against you. In the landmark Supreme Court case of *Miranda v. Arizona* (1966),[18] the Court announced that if you are arrested or even under custody and questioned based on suspicion, police must warn you of your right to not speak. The police must also let you know that if you do speak, they can use whatever you say in a court of law to convict you. Because of the case

18. *Miranda v. Arizona*, 384 U.S. 436 (1966)

name where this ruling came from, this information police need to give defendants came to be known as "Miranda rights," and the words the police say in this regard came to be called the "Miranda warning." Miranda warnings have become so famous they are often seen in TV shows and movies, and are so common that police say they "Mirandize" a suspect when the warnings are given. Specifically, under the ruling of the Court in *Miranda*, criminal defendants who are in custody or under arrest must be warned:

> You have the right to remain silent. Anything you say can and will be used against you in a court of law. You have the right to have an attorney. If you cannot afford one, one will be appointed to you by the court. Do you understand these rights?

The exact language can vary slightly, but each of the rights described in this example must be clear and present in the warning.

The Supreme Court has limited the situations, though, when Miranda warnings must be given. The need for such warnings does not apply to "noncustodial interrogation" such as stop-and-ask situations, ordinary questioning during vehicle stops, when consent is expressly or impliedly given for questioning at one's home, or voluntary appearance for questioning in a police station. However, as soon as you are placed in *custody* (defined as when you are not free to leave) or you are arrested, then you must be given Miranda warnings. As the Supreme Court has declared in *Miranda*, the rule applies "when the individual is first subjected to police interrogation while in custody at the station or otherwise deprived of his freedom of action in any significant way" but not to "general on-the-scene questioning as to facts surrounding a crime or other general questioning of citizens in the fact-finding process." Also, a defendant can waive receiving the Miranda warning, but police and prosecutors must show the defendant gave a "knowing and intelligent" waiver. That is, the defendant must be aware of his rights and the consequences of waiving his rights.[19]

*Sixth Amendment Protections* The Sixth Amendment states:

> In all criminal prosecutions, the accused shall enjoy the right to a speedy and public trial, by an impartial jury of the State and district wherein the crime shall have been committed, which district shall have been previously ascertained by law, and to be informed of the nature and cause of the accusation; to be confronted with the witnesses against him; to have compulsory process for ob-

19. *Patterson v. Illinois*, 487 U.S. 285 (1988)

taining witnesses in his favor, and to have the assistance of counsel for his defense.

The Sixth Amendment includes several important rights, including the right to be told of the charges against you, the right to cross-examine your accusers, the right to a jury trial, and the right to an attorney. This latter right was expanded by the Supreme Court in the landmark case *Gideon v. Wainwright* (1963)[20] to include a right to have the government provide you with a free lawyer not only in a federal trial, but also in a state trial. A book entitled *Gideon's Trumpet* and a film based on the book are frequently read and viewed by students, lawyers, and members of the public interested in legal history. The Supreme Court has also said your appointed lawyer must provide *effective* assistance of counsel for the right to assistance of counsel to be meaningful.[21] For example, imagine you are on trial for a crime, especially where the evidence is slim, but your appointed lawyer keeps falling asleep during the trial. If you are found guilty, you would be able to sue for a retrial on the grounds of ineffective assistance of counsel. Once a defendant has requested a lawyer, the police must avoid further interrogation until a lawyer is present.[22] Regardless whether the defendant has an attorney present, any confession must be voluntary.[23]

A criminal defendant's first or initial appearance in court is called a "preliminary hearing." This is where the defendant is formally informed of the charges, and the prosecution must establish probable cause to the judge in order to hold the defendant for further proceedings. If there is sufficient evidence to continue the criminal process, the judge will set "bail." This is a dollar amount temporarily paid by the defendant to the court as a condition of temporary release from custody. In cases in which the suspect poses a flight risk or a danger to the community, the judge might decide to keep the suspect in custody by denying bail.

The next appearance in court by the defendant is called the "arraignment." Here the defendant is again formally notified of the charges, but now the defendant formally responds with a "plea"—a statement by the defendant whether he admits to the charges. The defendant may enter with the court a plea of "guilty," or "not guilty." In about half the states and in federal court, defendants may also enter a plea of "*nolo contendre*" ("no contest"), which does not admit guilt, but also does not fight the charges. Depending on the jurisdiction, the de-

20. *Gideon v. Wainwright*, 372 U.S. 335 (1963)
21. *Strickland v. Washington*, 466 US. 668 (1984)
22. *Massiah v. U.S.*, 377 U.S. 201 (1964).
23. *Colorado v. Conelly*, 479 U.S. 157 (1986)

fendant also has the option of entering a plea of "not guilty by reason of insanity," or "guilty but insane." If the defendant pleads guilty, the court must determine if the defendant understands the plea and is doing so voluntarily.

In the large majority of all criminal cases—more than 90%—a "plea bargain" is usually entered. This is an agreement between the prosecutor and the defendant in which the defendant admits guilt to a charge in exchange for (a) a less serious charge, (b) the dropping of one or more other charges, or (c) a promise by the prosecutor to recommend the judge impose a lenient sentence. Judges have no control over prosecutorial discretion to grant (a) or (b), but judges can ignore the recommendation in (c) due to their own judicial discretion. Plea bargains are so common because they are administratively convenient for the judicial system. Prosecutors, public defenders, judges, and the criminal courts as a whole are already severely overburdened and backlogged with cases. For better or worse, plea bargains have become almost, if not entirely, essential for the criminal justice system to work. The money and resources simply do not exist to begin conducting 20 times the number of trials than the U.S. criminal justice system currently conducts.

## Trial, Judge, and the Jury System

In a criminal trial (as in civil trials), there are two possible entities who will determine guilt or innocence. In a "bench trial," the judge is the fact finder and thus decides guilt or innocence. Otherwise, in a "jury trial," a group of citizens called a jury decides the facts and declares the defendant either guilty or not guilty. In the Anglo-Saxon common law system, jury trials began in England around the year 1200. The function of the jury system is to serve as a check by ordinary citizens against potentially overzealous prosecutors and judges.[24]

We saw earlier in this chapter that grand juries of between 12 and 23 jurors sit in secret session and decide whether to issue indictments. The juries that rule in trials, however, are called "trial juries" or "petit juries." The word *petit* is French for "small," since trial juries have fewer jurors than grand juries. At the federal level, all trial juries are comprised of 12 adults who must reach a unanimous verdict in order to find a criminal defendant "guilty" of the charges. At the state level, jury unanimity in criminal cases was, until recently, more complicated. Two states, Louisiana and Oregon, have for many years allowed juries to convict defendants in criminal cases by a vote of 10-2 instead of a 12-0 unan-

24. *Duncan v. Louisiana*, 391 U.S. 145 (1968)

imous vote, except in death penalty cases. A 1972 Supreme Court ruling even upheld Louisiana and Oregon's position. However, a Supreme Court ruling decided in 2020, *Ramos v. Louisiana,* overturned the 1972 decision stating that, under the Sixth Amendment, juries in *all* states must now be unanimous in criminal cases.[25]

State criminal juries are selected from a "master jury list." Depending on the state, this master jury list is also sometimes called a "jury wheel" or "master jury wheel." This term comes from the Old West, where a roulette wheel was sometimes used to pick jurors. The master jury list comprises all potential jurors within a judicial district, which could be a federal, state, regional, or local district depending on the state. Voter registration lists are commonly used to generate master jury lists, but this process has been criticized because it disproportionately excludes young, minority, poor, and less educated voters. To reduce this potential bias, many cities or states use telephone directories, utility customer lists, or driver's license lists. Yet many towns in about one third of states, especially in the New England and Southern states, use a "keyman" system whereby political and civic leaders are asked for suggestions regarding who should be prospective jurors.

When a criminal trial is scheduled, a list called a "jury pool" or "venire" is created of potential petite jurors selected from the master jury list. This jury pool is then called to the courthouse where the potential jurors are asked a series of questions to determine whether any of the jury pool might have a possible bias in the case. For example, maybe a prospective juror is best friends with the prosecutor or the defendant, or has business dealings with one of the lawyers in the case, or admits to having some racial or religious bias, or simply believes that all criminal defendants must be guilty because "where there's smoke there's fire." This process of selecting the final jurors from among the jury pool is called "*voir dire.*" This is a French term meaning "to see to say." *Voir dire* is also called the process of "empaneling" the jury. For a dramatic thriller based on a fictional jury empaneling, see the film *Runaway Jury.*

During *voir dire*, if a juror admits to possible bias, then that juror is automatically excused from that jury. Not every trivial bias will automatically disqualify a potential juror, though, especially if a juror indicates he or she can disregard his or her bias and decide the case based on the law and facts alone. If it is later discovered that a juror lied or was mistaken about their ability to be fair, the defendant must show that bias actually came into play—that is, that the juror was not able to set aside bias when deciding guilt.

25. See *Ramos v. Louisiana* 590 U.S. ___ (2020) and *Apodaca v. Oregon* 406 U.S. 404 (1972) and its companion case *Johnson v. Louisiana* 406 U.S. 356 (1972).

The formal term for the prosecution or defense objecting to a potential juror is called a "challenge." There are two types of challenges; "for-cause challenges" and "peremptory challenges." For-cause challenges are exactly that: there is an admission or evidence of bias on the part of a juror. Both the prosecution and defense have an unlimited number of for-cause challenges during *voir dire*, but the judge must approve the for-cause challenge by agreeing that bias has been shown. A peremptory challenge occurs when either the prosecution or defense dismisses a juror without stating a reason. Both the prosecution and defense have a limited number of peremptory challenges during *voir dire* depending on the jurisdiction and the party exercising them. For example, in federal capital (i.e. death penalty) trials, each side gets twenty peremptory challenges. In federal felony cases, the defendant gets ten peremptory challenges, but the prosecution gets only six. In federal misdemeanor cases, each side gets only three peremptory challenges. Yet the Supreme Court has declared that using peremptory challenges to remove people from the jury based on race or sex violates the Equal Protection Clause of the Fourteenth Amendment.[26] This is difficult to prove absent an admission, so it depends on aggregate use of peremptory challenges combined with a lack of plausible alternative explanations.

In all criminal trials in the United States, defendants are innocent until proven guilty. The burden of proof for a finding of "guilty" in either a bench trial or jury trial is that the evidence must show the defendant's guilt "beyond a reasonable doubt."[27] From a philosophical perspective, nothing in life, not even scientific "facts" are ever perfectly 100% certain. "Certainty" or "beyond any doubt" are therefore not workable standards. For example, there can always be some extremely remote possibility that the crime was committed not by the defendant, but let's say, by a secretly long-lost twin double with identical DNA to the defendant. Some doubts, however, are not *reasonable* doubts. At the same time, we do not want to convict a defendant when there is strong evidence that calls into question the guilt of a defendant. For example, imagine that the victim of a mugging claims to identify the attacker based on the victim's appearance alone. Yet the victim has poor (20/400) vision and was not wearing glasses at the time of the mugging, which occurred in a park with no lights and on a night with no moon. In such a case, there would be reasonable (and more than reasonable) doubt about the defendant's guilt. Any standard that allows a guilty verdict in the face of such slim evidence would be too unfairly biased against criminal defendants. Thus, the middle ground is a standard that requires

26. *J.E.B. v. Alabama*, 511 U.S. 127 (1994)
27. *In re Winship*, 397 U.S. 358 (1970)

guilt be found to exist "beyond a *reasonable* doubt" but not "beyond all doubt."

The "beyond a reasonable doubt standard" is admittedly vague. When is a doubt "reasonable" versus "unreasonable"? Juries often ask judges to clarify the meaning of this phrase, yet further specification risks changing the legal standard. Thus, judges must be very careful about offering any clarification of the standard.[28] As a rough practical matter, though, "beyond a reasonable doubt" means that somewhere between 95–98% of the trial evidence indicates the defendant is guilty, but even here judges are not allowed to say this to juries. Or, put differently, there is at least roughly a 95–98% likelihood that the defendant is guilty. This crude percentage estimate should make clear that a verdict of "not guilty" is *not* a verdict of "innocent." A judge or jury might have found the evidence showed the defendant was completely innocent (zero percent), or most likely innocent (less than 50 percent). Yet a judge or jury might also have found the evidence showed the defendant was more likely guilty than not (greater than 50 percent) or even very likely guilty, such as a 70, 80, or even 90 percent likelihood of guilt. Yet this still leaves at least a 10% doubt of guilt, which is a "reasonable" doubt. In short, when a judge or jury issues a finding of "not guilty," it does not necessarily mean the judge or jury believed the defendant was innocent, but merely that the evidence was not strong enough to dispel any "reasonable" doubt of the defendant's guilt.

Juries have absolute discretion to acquit a defendant. Yet if a jury convicts a defendant, the judge has authority to review the jury's decision to see if they appropriately applied the law and property weighed the evidence. In other words, a judge can never overturn a jury's decision to acquit a defendant, but a judge can overturn a jury's decision to convict a defendant. The jury must decide unanimously whether the defendant is "guilty" or "not guilty." If the jury can not decide either way due to a deadlock among the jurors, the jury is called a "hung jury." In this case, the judge can declare a *mistrial.* If a mistrial is declared, then the Fifth Amendment's rule against double jeopardy does not prevent a retrial of the defendant. Whether a retrial occurs is up to the discretion of the prosecutor.

## Criminal Sentencing

If the judge or jury convicts a criminal defendant, then the sentencing options depend on the jurisdiction. In the federal government, as well as in many states, there are mandatory minimum sentences required by

28. See, e.g., *Victor v. Nebraska,* 511 U.S. 1 (1994)

statute for specified crimes. Regardless whether sentences are mandatory or discretionary, there are several sentencing options for a judge. At a minimum, the judge can sentence a defendant to pay a fine, make restitution, pay court costs, or perform community service (such as required volunteer time for a local charity). The judge might sentence a defendant to "time served," meaning whatever time the defendant has already spent in jail or prison before and during trial is sufficient punishment. The court can also order the defendant be sentenced to a probationary period. This means the defendant must undergo a period of monitoring and supervision (sometimes called "intensive supervision") by the court. This usually includes regular testing to make sure the defendant remains free of alcohol and other drugs and monitoring to make sure the defendant stays out of any other criminal trouble during the probationary period.

For serious crimes, the judge might sentence a defendant to a term of imprisonment (also called "incarceration") or even the death penalty (also called "capital punishment)." Regardless of the particular sentence, there are several theories or justifications for criminal sentences. Punishment is intended to deter and prevent not just future lawbreaking by the convicted defendant, but that of all other potential criminal defendants by sending a public message: "Don't do what this defendant did, or you'll get the same punishment." A sentence of confinement to a jail or prison is also intended to provide education and/or treatment to the offender so as to "cure" them and thus rehabilitate them of their lawbreaking ways. In addition, imprisonment is intended to isolate a defendant, thereby incapacitating them from further injuring members of the public. "Three-strike" laws, whereby a third felony receives an automatic life term in prison, attempts to implement this particular policy behind criminal sentences. Finally, punishment provides retribution or revenge on behalf of the victim(s) against the lawbreaker. This is a natural law idea of justice, compared to the more practical explanations for criminal sentences such as deterrence, incapacitance, and rehabilitation.

A more ancient concept, yet an idea that is relatively new to the U.S. criminal justice system, is that of "restorative justice." This theory of criminal justice argues that when an offender hurts a victim, the offender's actions have injured or broken the relationship not just between the offender and the victim, but between the offender and the community as a whole. To heal and restore this relationship requires not just a sincere apology by the defendant, but the active making of amends by the offender to do what is needed to restore the relationship between the defendant and the victim, the victim's family, and the community in general to wholeness again.

If a criminal defendant has been sentenced to imprisonment in a jail or prison, there are two general types of sentences. One type of sentence is called "determinate" or "fixed" sentencing. This assigns the defendant a specific amount of time of imprisonment, although usually the sentencing judge is given the discretion to choose from a narrow range of allowable sentences with specified minimum sentences. Fixed or determinate sentencing occurs in about half the states and in the federal court system. The other half the states, however, have "indeterminate" sentences. In these states, the judge is given wide discretion to assign a sentence. In jurisdictions that have indeterminate sentences, one common approach to sentencing is to impose a sentence, but with the possibility of early "parole." In such jurisdictions, a "parole board" reviews the files of criminal defendants after a minimum time of imprisonment. Depending on the age and prison behavior of the defendant (including education, work training, and religious involvement), the parole board can grant an early release of the defendant from prison. The granting of this early release is called "granting parole."

Also, under the laws of most states, the governor has authority to grant either a "pardon" or "reprieve" of a state criminal defendant. A pardon excuses the crime such that the legal effect of a pardon pretends that the criminal conduct never occurred. A pardon prevents any future criminal charges for the conduct pardoned, and erases any past convictions for crimes based on the conduct pardoned. Similar to a pardon, a "reprieve" does not remove the conviction from the defendant's criminal record, but commutes (excuses or waives) either the rest of the defendant's sentence or the type of sentence (such as death or life imprisonment).

*Eighth Amendment Protections* When it comes to sentencing, the Eighth Amendment of the U.S. Constitution is relatively brief, and states in its entirely: "Excessive bail shall not be required, nor excessive fines imposed, nor cruel and unusual punishments inflicted." The practical effect of the Eighth Amendment is that it prohibits the government from inflicting torture or other humiliating, degrading, inhumane, or excessive punishments. What constitutes "cruel and unusual punishment," however, is often disputed.[29]

The ultimate form of punishment in the U.S. criminal justice system, however, is the death penalty, more formally known as "capital punishment." Although the Eighth Amendment prohibits "cruel and unusual" punishment, the Supreme Court has so far said that the death penalty by itself is not cruel and unusual. The manner in which the death penalty is applied, however, can be cruel and unusual depending on the particular circumstances. For example, relatively "painless"

29. See, e.g., *Graham v. Florida,* 560 U.S. 48 (2010)

death by lethal injection is arguably different than death by hanging, electrocution, or firing squad.[30] Also, the age and mental capacity of the defendant both play a role in whether the death penalty is appropriate in a case. Under current law, and depending on the particular facts of a case, the death penalty is an option in federal court and in about three-fourths of the states.

The law regulating capital punishment is a highly technical, complex, and specialized area of law. In short, though, the death penalty can be imposed only for murder, and especially in the murder of a child or a law enforcement officer, or where the act of killing included torture. This is simply a more specific application of the general criminal law concept that appropriate criminal sentences should consider both the "aggravating factors" or "aggravating circumstances" of the case weighed against the "mitigating factors" or "mitigating circumstances" of the case. These factors are typically provided to the sentencing judge or jury in a pre-sentence report that looks at the characteristics of the offender (such as past criminal record, age, mental capacity, and so on), and the characteristics of the victim (such as age, occupational status, manner of death, and so on).

## The Future of Criminal Law and Procedure

Over the course of U.S. history, legal developments have always been slow to catch up with the latest in technological developments. For example, planes and automobiles went largely unregulated for many years after their invention. The telephone was around for almost a hundred years before the Supreme Court finally declared that the public has a reasonable expectation that their electronic communications are private.[31] Even though it was widely known since the mid-1900s that each person has a unique DNA sequence, it was not until 2013 that the Supreme Court decided that a DNA sample can be taken of arrestees along with their fingerprints and a photograph as a standard part of police booking.[32] More recently, with the rise of computers and the internet, legislation can barely keep up with rapid developments in digital technology, especially electronic communication. Cell phones existed commercially for three-and-a-half decades before the Supreme Court decided police needed a warrant to track the location of the cell towers to which one's cell phone is digitally connected.[33] Let's look at merely some

30. *Bucklew v. Precythe*, 587 U.S. ___ (2019)
31. *Katz v. United States*, 389 U.S. 347 (1967)
32. *Maryland v. King*, 569 U.S. ___ (2013)
33. *Carpenter v. U.S.*, 585 U.S. ___ (2018)

of the numerous recent issues that are confronting lawmakers and law enforcement when it comes to electronic communication.

"Cybercrime" is a rapidly growing area of law enforcement, yet the criminal justice system is behind on dealing with cybercrime. As one example, online harassment occurs when people use social media to target an individual for embarrassment. This might be done merely out of personal revenge or in an attempt to publicly shame the victim for their moral or political opinions or behavior. Such online harassment often includes the practice of "doxing" (from "docs," short for documents). Doxing is the public release of private information about an individual such as their home or business phone number or address, in the hope (often expressed) that other people will target the victim for further harassment. Doxing is often coupled with "revenge porn." This occurs when a jilted former romantic partner posts images online showing their ex-lover naked or engaged in sexual activity. Often the videos had been made without the victim knowing that filming was occurring during such activity. Many countries and a majority of U.S. states have recently outlawed such behavior after several high-profile instances of victims of revenge porn committing suicide due to the public humiliation.

As another example of cybercrime, cyberextortion is a growing issue. In this practice, remote hackers use "ransomware" to electronically seize computers, and threaten to destroy a person's or business's digital files unless the victim pays the hacker money. Or, a business website might be blocked through a "denial of service" attack, potentially causing a business to lose a great deal of money in online revenue unless the business pays the hackers to restore their service. If done for a political motive by private parties, such disruption of computer services is called "cyberterrorism." Even state actors (i.e. governments themselves) are increasingly using computer viruses, worms, and other methods as a means of attacking critical infrastructure of opposing nations. This "cyberwarfare" could attempt to disable a water distribution facility, an electrical or nuclear power plant, or even a key government or political institution. For example, during the 2016 U.S. Presidential election, Russia and other foreign entities tried but failed to hack into voting machines, but they did succeed to a degree in influencing many Americans to follow fake social media postings about U.S. political candidates. Because all these types of cyber attacks against computer systems in the U.S typically come from distant overseas countries, it is extremely difficult for U.S. investigative agencies to track and catch such hackers.

Identity theft is increasingly a concern as well. Despite intense efforts to stop the activity, online hackers are regularly able to break into government and business computer systems that contain confidential digital information about citizens and consumers. Such files can include information about employees, bank accounts, insurance and medical profiles, online store accounts, and so on. Through such files, hackers can gain victims' names, birthdates, credit card numbers, bank account information, or social security numbers. Hackers can then either use this information on their own or sell it to a third party. With a fake identity, the perpetrators can now receive fraudulent drivers' licenses, credit card accounts, mortgages, car loans, insurance claims, or tax refunds using the stolen identity. Law enforcement agencies at all levels are increasingly trying to coordinate with businesses and government institutions to improve internet security to prevent and punish such data breaches.

Perhaps the main challenge in stopping cyberterrorism, cyberwarfare, cyberextortion, identify theft, and other cybercrimes is the current lack of ability to catch and prosecute perpetrators of such illegal activity. Although the field of "computer forensics" can uncover digital evidence on a physical computer hard drive, clever hackers know how to avoid their online electronic activity from being digitally tracked. For example, cybercriminals typically use the "dark web," a part of the internet that is not accessible to ordinary web browsers and requires specialized software to access. Such dark web traffic is almost always encrypted—that is, such electronic communication is transmitted using secret, nearly unbreakable digital codes. These digital signals are also purposefully routed through numerous web servers before reaching their final destination so that the original location of the hackers is nearly impossible to trace. Besides using the dark web to conduct cyberterrorism, cyberwarfare, cyberextortion, and identity theft, cybercriminals also use the dark web to traffic in illegal drugs, weapons, and pornography. Law enforcement investigators such as the FBI's Cyber Division are in a digital arms race, so-to-speak, to keep up with the sophisticated methods that cybercriminals invent to avoid detection. In coming years, even as legislatures, courts, and law enforcement agencies eventually improve the legal frameworks and investigatory methods to handle these issues, other technological developments will undoubtedly create new unforeseen issues of criminal law and procedure.

---

*Questions for Review and Discussion*

1. Compare and provide examples of the authority that police officers have to stop and search individuals while:
    a. walking out in public,
    b. driving a vehicle,

   c. sitting in their home.
2. Describe the exclusionary rule and its exceptions and offer examples.
3. Describe the rights of criminal suspects granted by the Fifth and Sixth Amendments to the Constitution.
4. Susan failed to use her turn signal when she made a right turn out of her home driveway. As a result, a police officer pulled her over. When he got to Susan's car, he thought he smelled something like marijuana coming from inside the car. He asked Susan for permission to search the inside of the car. She declined permission, but the officer decided to search the interior of the car anyway. He found an unregistered handgun in the back seat. Susan told the officer it must have been put there by her husband because she had never seen the gun before. Not believing her, he then arrested her for possessing an unregistered firearm. How would a judge rule on the legality of the officer's stopping, searching, and arresting Susan? Be clear in explaining the specific legal doctrines that apply.
5. Responding to calls from neighbors, police went to Bob's apartment to investigate noxious odors coming from his apartment. No one answered the door. The officers called in a request for a search warrant. While they were waiting for the warrant to arrive, they saw Bob walking down the street coming towards his apartment. Rather than hide from Bob, they quickly knocked on the door and said "Police, open up!" This time, a woman answered the door who said she was a cleaning woman who was just there for the morning. The police asked her if they could search and she said yes. They found chemicals used in making explosives, and arrested Bob. In court, Bob asserted the chemicals were inadmissible as evidence because of the exclusionary rule, due to the fact the officers did not have a warrant or valid consent to search the apartment. How would a judge rule on the admissibility of the chemicals? Specify, define and apply three doctrines involving the exclusionary rule in support of your answer.

---

*Suggested Readings*


*Miranda v. Arizona* (1966) (right to warnings about rights)
*Gideon v. Wainwright* (1963) (right to an attorney)
*Mapp v. Ohio,* 367 U.S. 643 (1961) (exclusionary rule)
*Terry v. Ohio,* 392 U.S. 1 (1968) (in-person stops)
*Katz v. United States,* 389 U.S. 347 (1967) (telephone call searches)
*California v. Carney,* 471 U.S. 386 (1985) (automobile searches)
*Florida v. Riley* 488 U.S. 445 (1989) (helicopter searches)
*Kyllo v. U.S.,* 533 U.S. 27 (2001) (infra-red vision searches)
*Weeks v. U.S.,* 232 U.S. 383 (1914) (exclusionary rule)
*U.S. v. Leon,* 468 U.S. 897 (1984) (exclusionary rule good faith exception)
*Maryland v. King,* 569 U.S. ___ (2013) (DNA searches)
*Duncan v. Louisiana,* 391 U.S. 145(1968) (jury trials)
*Carpenter v. U.S.,* 585 U.S. ___ (2018) (cell phone tower data searches)

*Advanced Readings*

*Federal Rules of Criminal Procedure*

*Federal Rules of Evidence*

Wayne Lafave, Jerold Israel, Nancy King, and Orin Kerr, *Criminal Procedure, 5th Ed.* (2016)

Part Three

# THE SKILLS OF LEGAL REASONING

CHAPTER 9

# LEGAL REASONING

---

*Chapter Objectives*
*After reading this chapter, you should be able to:*

- Describe the concept of legal reasoning
- Describe deductive reasoning and identify examples of it
- Describe and identify major and minor premises in logical syllogisms
- Describe polysyllogism and how it is used in legal reasoning.
- Apply a legal rule to a hypothetical factual situation.

---

In the first chapter, we talked about law, its origins, the difference between positive law and natural law, the rule of law, the social contract, and the difference between common law and civil code law. As we saw, law is the collection of official rules that govern the ethical or moral behavior of a society. Law also simply prevents chaos: we legislate arbitrary decisions like requiring automobile drivers to drive on the right side of the road rather than the left, and using the color red rather than some other color to indicate that automobile traffic should come to a stop. In this chapter we move from philosophical or abstract legal ideas to more concrete legal applications and examples. The field of law that incorporates this is called *legal reasoning.*

## The Skill of Legal Reasoning

In essence, legal reasoning is the *application of an abstract definition to a concrete example.* The intellectual skill of legal reasoning can be likened to applying a dictionary definition. For example, what is a "dog"? We can take the definition of a dog, and then apply it to various animals to determine whether each animal is or is not a "dog." Some examples will be easy to place in the category of "dog" or "not-dog," such as a whale, eagle, or giraffe, or even a rock, boat, or pencil. These are obviously all "not-dog," whereas a terrier, poodle, and collie are all clearly "dogs." Other possible objects, however, will be a closer call: What about a fox, hyena, coyote, or wolf? Are each of these more "dog" or more "not-dog"?

Moving beyond physical objects, we can look at verbs, such the action word "run." We can watch various people engaged in various types of movement and decide whether any of these actions are "running." So what about crawling, walking, hopping, skipping, jumping, trotting, or dancing? And what about jogging? What about a slow jog? A fast jog? At what precise point does fast "jogging" become "running"? Different people might conclude differently depending on their perspective.

Examples using definitions of objects (like "dog") or physical actions (like "run") are relatively simple and easy. But the law usually deals with more abstract concepts which are much harder to define and apply. Take for example everyday concepts like the words "good" or "beauty" or "love. Philosophers have spent thousands of years trying to define these concepts and figuring out when they do or do not apply to everyday examples. Ordinary people use the word "love" every day. Does "friendship" or "family" always include love? If not, at what point does "friendship" or "family" become "love"? At what point does "liking" become "loving"? Is "infatuation" love? Is "obsession" love? Is "lust" love? Does "loving" someone mean you remain loyal to them even if what they are doing is wrong? Is love earned, or is it unconditional? How do these types of loves differ: "love" of a child, a parent, a friend, a lover, your fellow humanity, a god, a delicious meal, your pet, your favorite hobby, nature, life itself? It turns out that figuring out precisely what is or is not "love" is extremely complex and often difficult to apply in specific situations. As merely one example, does "loving" someone mean you always help them avoid suffering, or does it mean you let them suffer the consequences of their choices so that they learn from those consequences (i.e. "tough love")? So, if my adult son becomes a drug addict, do I continue to pay for his rent and food so that he does not become homeless and starving even though this enables him to continue his drug habit? Or do I let my adult son become homeless and starving even if that means risking that he hit "rock bottom" and realize he must turn himself around and learn to take responsibility?

Sometimes, there are no easy answers in life. The same is true in the law. When is a police search "unreasonable?" In constitutional law, when does the government's reason for passing a law become "rational" versus "important" versus "compelling"? What is "the freedom of speech" or "the free exercise of religion" or "an establishment of religion" or "equal protection of the laws"? When is punishment for a crime "cruel or unusual"? In civil liability, when does one's behavior become "negligent" or "reckless" or "extreme and outrageous"? When does a risk of harm become "foreseeable"? In contract law, when do your words or actions become an "offer" for a contract, or an "acceptance" of that offer? Almost every single line in every law has some vagueness about it. This leads ordinary people, lawyers, and judges to disagree about the meaning of the words contained in laws. As a result, one must be able to *think critically* to *reason* these questions and answers out, and reasonable people can disagree about those answers.

Legal reasoning is a critical thinking *skill*; it is *not* knowledge. Although the law itself can be memorized, legal reasoning must be *done or performed*—that is, legal reasoning must be *practiced.* Learning to practice law is like learning to ride a bicycle or learning to fly a plane. You might read every book ever written about how to ride a bicycle. Yet when you get on a bicycle for the first time you will probably fall over because you have not yet developed the *skill* of balancing a bicycle while pedaling with both feet off the ground. Similarly, let's suppose a flight school has their students read thousands of pages of instructional manuals about how to fly airplanes, but never has their students actually practice flying any planes. Upon graduating from this flight school, would you trust any of these students to be the pilot of a plane you are on? Of course not, because they haven't learned the *skill* of physically manipulating all the numerous flight controls simultaneously.

In short, it is one thing to *read* the *knowledge* of how to perform a skill, but another thing to learn the *skill* of *actually doing* it. Similarly, one could read a thousand law books, but still not necessarily be able to apply the law using legal reasoning. Legal reasoning can only be mastered through practice.

## Deductive Reasoning: Syllogisms

There are several different but related types of analytic reasoning skills that are involved in legal reasoning. These include deductive reasoning (going from the general to the particular), inductive reasoning (going from the particular to the general), and reasoning by analogy (going from the particular to the particular). Some of this we'll put off for future chapters. This chapter will look at the most basic, foundational building block in the skill of legal reasoning: deductive reasoning.

Recall from an earlier chapter the concept of legal formalism. According to legal formalism, judges use logic to apply abstract laws to concrete situations. There is a "legally correct" answer to every possible legal question. Without getting into the nuances of the accuracy of legal formalism, this basic concept is how lawyers and judges generally approach the law: given law X and facts Y, the outcome is Z. Or is it always?

Deductive logic is a particular manner of logical reasoning. The famous fictional English detective Sherlock Holmes uses deduction to reach his logical conclusions. Deduction involves taking one or more statements called *premises* to derive a conclusion. A premise can also be called a *proposition,* but in our discussions we'll stay with the term "premise." A deductive *syllogism* is the most simple form of deduction. A syllogism takes two premises, called a major premise and minor premise, to reach a logically necessary conclusion. Here is a famous syllogism that is probably the most commonly used example to illustrate the concept of a syllogism:

> *Major premise:* All men are mortal.
> *Minor premise:* Socrates is a man.
> *Conclusion:* Socrates is mortal.

The conclusion that "Socrates is mortal" necessarily follows logically from the major and minor premise. Negative conclusions can be reached as well:

> *Major premise:* All sunflowers are yellow.
> *Minor premise:* This flower is purple.
> *Conclusion*: This flower is not a sunflower.

This type of logical deduction is also sometimes called top-down logic, because one starts from a broad principle but applies it down to a very narrow example. The most common type of legal reasoning uses top-down deductive syllogisms to reach either positive or negative conclusions. Legal reasoning involves a broad, abstract legal principle/rule as the major premise and a fact pattern as the minor premise. The conclusion is the result of how the law applies, or the holding of the case. Here is a syllogism from the law:

> *Major premise:* The common law crime of murder requires the victim to die as a result of the injury within one year and one day of the injury.
>
> *Minor premise:* The victim X died from complications of a gun wound one year and two days after being shot by the defendant Y.
>
> *Conclusion:* The defendant Y is not guilty of the common law crime of murder of X.

Here is another, more complex deductive syllogism from U.S. constitutional law under the First Amendment:

*Major premise:* "Fighting words" are words that people of common intelligence would understand would be likely to provoke an average addressee to retaliate by fighting.

*Minor premise:* When Bob told Sue "I don't like your shirt," Sue slapped Bob.

*Conclusion:* Although Sue slapped Bob, ordinary people would not think the words "I don't like your shirt' would be likely to provoke average people to respond violently. Bob's words did not meet the legal definition of fighting words.

Given millions of laws and trillions of possible fact patterns, there is practically an infinite array of possible syllogisms in the law. Outside of the study and practice of law, the field of study that most often uses this type of logical-analytical reasoning is philosophy. This is why the study of philosophy also helps prepare one to practice law and legal reasoning.

## Complex Major Premises

Recall again that the core type of legal reasoning is applying an abstract definition to a concrete example. Since laws can be seen either as definitions or rules, we can also say that legal reasoning is the application of abstract rules to concrete examples. A major premise, however, can be complex and have numerous parts to it.

Let's take one simple example: What is a "chair"? According to *the Cambridge International Dictionary of English,* the word "chair" and its accompanying terms are defined as follows:

*Chair:* "a movable seat for one person which has a back, usually four legs, and sometimes two arms."

*Seat:* "an item of furniture that has been designed for someone to sit on."

*Sit:* "to be in a position in which the lower part of the body is resting on a seat or other type of support, with the upper part of the body vertical."

*Furniture:* "items such as chairs, tables, beds, cupboards, etc. which are put into a house or other building to make it more suitable for living or working in."

Thus, from these various definitions, we can refine the definition of a chair as follows. A "chair" is:

(1) an item put in a house or building;
and (2) which makes the building more suitable for living or working in;
and (3) which is movable;
and (4) is designed for one person;
and (5) which supports the lower part of the body
and (6) which keeps the upper body vertical;
and (7) usually has four legs;
and (8) sometimes has two arms.

An object need not meet every one of these elements, nor necessarily meet every one of these elements fully, to be considered a "chair." Yet clearly the more elements of the definition that an object meets, the more "chairlike" the object becomes. Similarly, in the law, most legal rules have multiple elements, and some legal rules have *many* elements. For example, the legal tort of defamation—falsely injuring someone's reputation—has numerous complex elements in the full legal definition. In the case of defamation, though, as with most torts, *all* of the many elements of the definition must be met, or else the defendant is not liable to the plaintiff. Thus, to win a defamation lawsuit, a plaintiff must prove that all of the elements of defamation are met. Depending on the specific facts of a defamation case, this can require extensive and detailed legal argument.

Importantly, when applying a complex syllogism, one cannot merely restate the minor premise and presume all the elements are met. For example, suppose you come across this *alleged* syllogism using the definition of a chair:

*Major Premise:* A chair is:
(1) an item put in a house or building;
and (2) which makes the building more suitable for living or working in;
and (3) which is movable;
and (4) is designed for one person;
and (5) which supports the lower part of the body
and (6) which keeps the upper body vertical;
and (7) usually has four legs;
and (8) sometimes has two arms.

*Minor Premise:* The object I see looks like a chair to me.

*Conclusion:* The object I see is a chair.

The conclusion of this syllogism may be technically correct from a logical standpoint. However, if it were a legal syllogism, the minor premise lacks adequate specificity and evidence to prove the conclusion. To sufficiently convince a judge or jury that the object in question is a chair, the legal argument would need to provide a complex minor premise as well:

*Major Premise:* A chair is:
(1) an item put in a house or building;
and (2) which makes the building more suitable for living or working in;
and (3) which is movable;
and (4) is designed for one person;
and (5) which supports the lower part of the body
and (6) which keeps the upper body vertical;
and (7) usually has four legs;
and (8) sometimes has two arms.

*Minor Premise:* The object I see:
(1+2) is an item in my house that makes my house more comfortable;
and (3) I can move it around and use it in any room of my house if I want;
and (4+5) only one person can fit on it, and my butt rests on it;
and (6+7+8) it has four legs with a wheel on the bottom of each leg, two soft cushioned arms, and it keeps my back upright, although the backrest can tilt slightly backwards if I desire.

*Conclusion:* The object I see is a chair (it is in fact a desk chair).

A lawyer arguing *against* an object being a chair would need to make similarly specific arguments on each element of the definition of a chair. In this circumstance, though, the lawyer would explain why the concrete particulars of the object do *not* meet all the elements of the definition of a chair:

*Major Premise:* A chair is:
(1) an item put in a house or building;
and (2) which makes the building more suitable for living or working in;
and (3) which is movable;
and (4) is designed for one person;
and (5) which supports the lower part of the body
and (6) which keeps the upper body vertical;
and (7) usually has four legs;
and (8) sometimes has two arms.

*Minor Premise:* The object I see:

(1+2) is an item in my house that makes my house more comfortable;

and (3) I can move it around from room to room of my house;

but (4) several people can and usually do fit around it but not on it;

nor (5) it doesn't support any of the body except maybe hands or arms; in fact all it usually supports is plates and cups filled with food and beverage, and maybe a decoration or two, and sometimes it stores mail until I've opened it;

nor (6) it has no way to keep the upper part of our bodies vertical;

also (7) it does have four legs;

but (8) it has no arms.

*Conclusion:* The object I see is a not a chair (but is instead a table).

Notice that whether one is arguing the legal rule is met or not met, each element of the rule is applied in a clear step-by-step process. No element is discussed out of order, and no element is missing. Each separate element is also analyzed in a logic-tight compartment. Indeed, perhaps the most common mistakes beginning law students make when engaging in legal reasoning are (1) leaving out elements of the legal rule, (2) analyzing the elements out of order, (3) confusing two or more elements of the rule by combining them or by applying one element to facts relevant to a different element, or (4) being vague and abstract when applying an element, thereby leaving out concrete, relevant, and important factual details in the application of that element. No step in the chain of logic should be left out or merely assumed.

Usually court cases involve both a complex major premise (a legal rule with several elements) and a complex minor premise (a detailed set of case facts). As both the major and minor premises—both the law and the facts—become more complex, there becomes more "wiggle room" for each party in a lawsuit to argue what the appropriate conclusion to the legal syllogism should be. This requires the lawyers to create nuanced arguments as to how the specific elements of the rule might apply to very particular aspects of the facts in the case.

Indeed, legal arguments should typically be made with as much specificity as possible. As a general guideline, the more particular the argument can be made, the more likely a judge or jury is to be persuaded by the argument. For example, let's say an imaginary legal rule exists that requires that a law outlawing alcohol sales will be upheld by the courts only if the government can prove a "compelling" reason for the regulation. Notice how the possible reasons listed below that a government attorney might offer as justification for the law increase in specificity and concreteness:

- promoting health
- preventing disease
- preventing serious disease
- preventing serious liver disease
- preventing deaths from serious liver disease
- preventing widespread deaths from liver disease
- preventing widespread deaths from liver disease due to alcohol consumption
- preventing widespread deaths from liver disease due to chronic alcohol consumption

From this example, you should be able to see how vague phrases sound weak, but concrete terms are forceful. The more you can avoid abstract terms and instead concretize your arguments, the more powerful your legal arguments will be.

*Legal Reasoning Example: "Motor Vehicle"* Let's look at a real-world example of an application of a dictionary definition of a word in a legal setting. When automobiles were first invented, the law had to be adapted to take their existence into account. These legal developments, however, were sometimes slow to come. Even though Henry Ford's Model T became the first mass-produced car in 1913, it took until 1919 for Congress to pass the Motor Vehicle Theft Act (MVTA). The MVTA outlawed transportation of stolen "motor vehicles" across state lines or causing such transportation. The MVTA also stated: "the term 'motor vehicle' shall include an automobile, automobile truck, automobile wagon, motor cycle, or any other self-propelled vehicle not designed for running on rails."

In 1926, William McBoyle operated a small airport in Galena, Illinois. He convinced a pilot named A.J. Lacey to steal an airplane from a nearby airplane manufacturing facility and fly it back to Galena. McBoyle changed the serial number on the plane and painted over it to hide the alteration. McBoyle then paid Lacey $150 to fly the stolen plane to Amarillo, Texas and told Lacey to telegraphically communicate with him using a fake name, Pat Sullivan. Lacey made it as far as Guymon, Oklahoma when apparently police began investigating McBoyle. McBoyle then telegraphed Lacey to either sell or store the stolen plan in Oklahoma and come back to Galena. To throw off investigators, McBoyle then paid Lacey $250 to fly to Oklahoma in a plane that belonged to McBoyle and was of the same make and model as the stolen plane. On the flight to Oklahoma, though, Lacey crashed in Kansas, but he was unharmed enough to return to Illinois.

Investigators eventually charged McBoyle with causing the transport of a stolen motor vehicle in violation of the MVTA. At the trial in Federal District Court for the Western District of Oklahoma (where the stolen plane had been found), the evidence hinted that McBoyle was also involved in other crimes including auto theft, theft of another plane, and illegal liquor transactions. Regardless, he was convicted of violating the MVTA and sentenced to three year's imprisonment and a fine of $2,000.

On appeal to the Tenth Circuit Court of Appeals, McBoyle argued that he did not violate the MVTA because an "airplane" is not a "motor vehicle." The question was whether an airplane is covered by the phrase "any other self-propelled vehicle not designed for running on rails"?

The U.S. Court of Appeals, in *McBoyles v. U.S.* (1930), looked at formal dictionary definitions of "vehicle" and concluded an airplane is a "vehicle":

> A 'motor vehicle' is a vehicle operated by a power developed within itself and used for the purpose of carrying passengers or materials. . . the definition of the word "vehicle" indicates that it is sufficiently broad to include any means or device by which persons or things are carried or transported, and it is not limited to instrumentalities used for traveling on land. . . An airplane is self-propelled, by means of a gasoline motor. It is designed to carry passengers and freight from place to place. It runs partly on the ground but principally in the air. It furnishes a rapid means for transportation of persons and comparatively light articles of freight and express. It therefore serves the same general purpose as an automobile, automobile truck, or motorcycle.

The U.S. Supreme Court, however, overruled the Court of Appeals' holding, disagreeing about the meaning of the word "vehicle":

> In everyday speech 'vehicle' calls up the picture of a thing moving on land. . . . [A]fter including automobile truck, automobile wagon and motor cycle, the words 'any other self-propelled vehicle not designed for running on rails' still indicate that a vehi-

cle in the popular sense—that is, a vehicle running on land—is the theme . . . it is reasonable that a fair warning should be given to the world, in language that the common world will understand, of what the law intends to do if a certain line is passed. To make the warning fair, so far as possible, the line should be clear. When a rule of conduct is laid down in words that evoke in the common mind only the picture of vehicles moving on land, the statute should not be extended to aircraft simply because it may seem to us that a similar policy applies, or upon the speculation that, if the legislature had thought of it, very likely broader words would have been used.

The Circuit Court and Supreme Court in *McBoyle* both applied a basic legal syllogism: In each case, the major premise was a definition of "motor vehicle," and the minor premise was an "airplane." Yet the two courts reached opposite conclusions about whether the minor premise was contained within the major premise. In this instance, the minor premise on its surface seemed relatively simple: "an airplane." In reality, though, the courts had to consider in detail the definition of an "airplane": Is it self-propelled? Does it carry passengers or cargo? Does it run on land? Depending on the definition used, there is not necessarily any definite answer, nor the same answer. The legal result in this case therefore depended on how the major premise was framed.

The Tenth Circuit's major premise was a *dictionary* definition of "motor vehicle," and *not* the particular legal definition provided by the MVTA:

*Major premise:* A 'motor vehicle' is a vehicle operated by a power developed within itself and used for the purpose of carrying passengers or materials.

*Minor premise 1:* An airplane is self-propelled by a gasoline motor.

*Minor premise 2:* An airplane is designed to carry passengers or freight.

*Conclusion:* Therefore, an airplane is a motor vehicle.

The U.S. Supreme Court, on the other hand, used the MVTA's *legal* definition of motor vehicle combined with *ordinary usage* of the term as the major premise:

*Major premise:* A 'motor vehicle' is any self-propelled vehicle and that is not designed for running on rails *and that runs on land.*

*Minor premise 1:* An airplane is self-propelled by a gasoline motor.

*Minor premise 2:* An airplane is not designed to run on rails.

*Minor premise 3:* An airplane does *not* run on land.

*Conclusion*: Therefore (because part of the definition of "motor vehicle" is *not* met), an airplane is *not* motor vehicle.

Indeed, even on this relatively simple issue of the definition of "motor vehicle," many state courts have had to grapple with similar questions regarding what constitutes a "vehicle" or "motor vehicle" under state law. Besides the question of airplanes, what about boats? Snowmobiles? Motorcycles? Mopeds? Bicycles? Horses? What about driving an airboat illegally on a highway while the driver is drunk? Does this action allow the driver to be charged with "operating a motor vehicle while intoxicated"? Does this action allow forfeiture of either the driver's license or the driver's vehicle? (See the first case in the list of suggested readings at the end of this chapter). There are plausible arguments either way, which is what lawyers provide, and why courts are needed to settle such disputes.

## Polysyllogisms

Understanding the basic two-premise syllogism is merely one small but critical foundation in understanding the larger system of logical reasoning. Usually however, logical reasoning is comprised not of a single, simple syllogism. Instead, multiple premises combine together to result in a logical conclusion. Recall that in a syllogism, there are two premises and a conclusion. Here is a simple syllogism:

*Premise 1*: All dogs are animals.
*Premise 2*: Fido is a dog.
*Conclusion*: Fido is an animal.

We can create a longer chain of logic, though:

*Premise 1*: All dogs are carnivores.
*Premise 2*: All carnivores are animals.
*Premise 3*: Fido is a dog.
*Conclusion*: Fido is an animal.

The chain of logic can be made even longer:

*Premise 1*: All poodles are dogs.
*Premise 2*: All dogs are carnivores.
*Premise 3*: All carnivores are animals.
*Premise 4*: Fido is a poodle.
*Conclusion*: Fido is an animal.

As you can imagine, the chain of logic could be extended indefinitely depending on the complexity of the argument one was trying to make, and in many court cases such is required.

What is happening in the example above is that multiple implied syllogisms are being formed. Let's analyze the example in detail by making clear the multiple pairs of syllogisms that are implicit in the chain of logic:

*Premise 1*: All poodles are dogs.
*Premise 2*: All dogs are carnivores.
*Conclusion*: All poodles are carnivores.

*Premise 3*: All poodles are carnivores
*Premise 4*: All carnivores are animals.
*Conclusion*: All poodles are animals.

*Premise 5*: All poodles are animals.
*Premise 6*: Fido is a poodle.
*Conclusion*: Fido is an animal.

A longer chain of logic that uses more than one syllogism as part of the chain is called a *polysyllogism*. "Poly" means "many." Just as most logical reasoning uses polysyllogisms rather than single syllogisms, the same is true in law. One classic example of a polysyllogism is the U.S. Supreme Court's explanation of judicial review, described in Chapter 2. Recall that judicial review is the power of the courts to review actions by other branches of government and if need be to declare those actions to be unconstitutional. Let's look at the Court's chain of logic in the case of *Marbury v. Madison* (1803), in which the Court first expressly announced that it had the power of judicial review. Notice the polysyllogism that is being applied:

*Premise 1*: Higher law always overrides contradictory lower law.

*Premise 2*: The Constitution is the highest law in the United States.

*Conclusion*: The Constitution overrides any other contradictory U.S. law, including laws by Congress or state governments, or executive orders by the President.

*Premise 3*: The Constitution overrides any other contradictory U.S. law, including laws by the Congress or state governments, or executive orders by the President.

*Premise 4*: The Supreme Court has the inherent power to interpret laws, including when there is a conflict between laws.

*Conclusion*: The Supreme Court has the inherent power to interpret when the Constitution overrides laws by the Congress or state governments, or executive orders by the President.

Here's a more recent example of a legal polysyllogism, but one that involves the Free Speech Clause of the First Amendment to the U.S. Constitution. The International Society for Krishna Consciousness (ISKCON) is a worldwide religious organization that practices a variant of Hinduism. Its members are more commonly known as *Hare Krishnas* due to the mantra they commonly repeat which consists of three of the names for their god: "Hare," "Krishna" and "Rama." One of ISKCON's primary methods of evangelism is to go out in public, sing or chant the Hare Krishna mantra, and ask people to donate money in exchange for pamphlets or books about their religion. During these activities, men typically wear white or orange outfits in a style traditionally common to India, while women typically wear white or colored saris, a dress common to India. Hare Krishnas call their form of evangelization the ritual of *sankirtan*.

The Port Authority of New York and New Jersey owns and operates the public airports in that region, including JFK and LaGuardia. Walter Lee was the official responsible for enforcing a regulation the Port Authority had adopted that banned all solicitation within the airports. This regulation effectively banned sankirtan. As a result, ISKCON filed a federal lawsuit against Lee in the U.S. District Court for the Southern District of New York claiming their free speech rights were being violated. The District Court ruled in favor of ISKCON. Lee appealed to the Twelfth Circuit Court of Appeals, which reversed the District Court decision and ruled in favor of Lee. After losing in the Twelfth Circuit, ISKCON appealed to the U.S. Supreme Court.

In *International Society of Krishna Consciousness* (ISKCON) *v. Lee* (1992), the Supreme Court had to interpret how the First Amendment protects speech that occurs on government property. Here is the logical reasoning of the Court, but put in polysyllogism form so you can see the Court's chain of logic more clearly (and note the Court's more detailed reasoning is oversimplified here for purposes of illustration!):

*Premise 1*: Traditional public forums are government property that have a long human history and a principal purpose of being used for open public discussion and discourse.

*Premise 2*: Public airports are relatively recent inventions and their principal purpose is to facilitate air travel, not to promote open public discussion.

*Conclusion*: Public airports are not traditional public forums.

*Premise 3*: Designated public forums have been intentionally opened up by the government for use by the public as a place for public discussion.

*Premise 4*: The public airports in New York have not been intentionally opened up by the government for use by the public as a place for public discussion.

*Conclusion*: The public airports in New York are not designated public forums.

*Premise 5*: Government regulation of speech that occurs on government property that is not a public forum need only be reasonable.

*Premise 6*: The New York public airports are not public forums.

*Conclusion*: Government regulations of speech in New York public airports need only be reasonable.

*Premise 7*: Government regulations of speech in New York public airports need only be reasonable.

*Premise 8*: Solicitation for money in an airport terminal obstructs pedestrian traffic flow, and risks both coercion and fraud.

*Conclusion*: The ban on solicitation in the New York public airports is reasonable.

As you can see, the U.S. Supreme Court had to proceed through multiple steps in logical deduction in order to reach the legal conclusion it did. Yet it's extremely rare that courts in their written rulings ever lay out the chain of logic so expressly as shown here by listing numbered premises. It's critical, then, to be able to spot on your own *every* step in the logical reasoning of the court even when the court isn't clear about it. Without being able to identify all the steps in logical reasoning used by a court in its written opinion, it will difficult or perhaps impossible for you the reader to understand how the court reached its ruling.

## Deductive Legal Reasoning Practice Cases

*What is a "chair"?* Recall our definition earlier that we created for "chair." Let's assume this is a legal rule, which declares:

A chair is:

(1) an item put in a house or building;

and (2) which makes the building more suitable for living or working in;

and (3) which is movable;

and (4) is designed for one person;
and (5) which supports the lower part of the body;
and (6) which keeps the upper body vertical;
and (7) usually has four legs;
and (8) sometimes has two arms.

Let's imagine you meet an intelligent extraterrestrial alien being that comes from a gaseous planet without any solid surface. The alien has no concept of "furniture" because their species is a hollow spherical air-filled blob that simply floats around. You give the alien the above definition of "chair." Then to see if it has learned the human concept of "chair," you ask it to apply the definition to various objects here on Earth. What would the alien (and you) say about whether each of the following items is a "chair," given the definition of chair listed above?

A 2-foot tall rock with a relatively flat top?
A footrest?
A big floor pillow?
A "beanbag chair"?
A chaise lounge chair?
An exercise ball one is supposed to sit on to improve posture?
A four-foot-tall three-legged bar stool?
A six-foot-long, two-foot-high bench with no backrest?
A seat with 10 legs and a one-inch-high back?
A box you climb into and sit in a seat enclosed by a windowed door?
A modern art sculpture comprised of a seat with one helix leg, 6 curving arms, and a 10-foot high curved back?
A seat nailed against a wall?
A swing on a playground?
A pad that rests on the floor but with a firm upright back?
A padded piece of furniture without legs that looks merely like a pair of camel humps, with one hump higher than the other?
What would otherwise be a typical chair, but it has needles coming up from the seat?
What would otherwise be a typical chair, but its legs are 8 feet tall?
What would otherwise be a typical chair, but its seat is angled at 30 degrees?
What would otherwise be a typical chair, but a hood comes down over the top so a person in the seat cannot see in any direction except downward?
A bathtub turned on end and fixed in an upright position to sit in?

In each of these instances, you and the alien would need to discuss why or why not each object does or does not meet each of the separate elements of the definition of "chair." You and the alien might end up agreeing on whether each item is a chair. Lawyers, however, either choose or are assigned only one side to argue, and must stick to that side. Legal ethics requires that they vigorously represent their client's position even if they personally disagree with it. The ability to see and argue either side (that is, *both* sides) of an issue is called "thinking like a lawyer." This legal skill takes practice as well as discipline.

As a small start in thinking like a lawyer, first look again at the list of possible "chairs" above. Next, go through the following questions in order and follow the instructions for each question fully. A good lawyer (or good future lawyer) will be able to answer each question with confidence, vigor, and passion:

> 1a. Pick the one item you believe *is* a chair more than any of the other items on the list. Legally argue *why* it is a chair, clearly and thoroughly analyzing and applying each and every element of the legal rule (the definition of chair above).
>
> 1b. Pick the one item you believe is *not* a chair more than any of the other items on the list. Legally argue *why* it is not a chair, clearly and thoroughly analyzing and applying each and every element of the legal rule.
>
> 2a. With the item you picked in 1a above that you thought was most a "chair," now make the best plausible legal arguments you can why it is *not* a chair, clearly and thoroughly analyzing and applying each and every element of the legal rule.
>
> 2b. Finally, with the item you picked in 1b above that you thought was most not a chair, now make the best plausible legal arguments you can why it *is* a chair, clearly and thoroughly analyzing and applying each and every element of the legal rule.

What you have just done by answering these pairs of questions is practice how to "think like a lawyer." If you can learn to argue convincingly for a position with which you disagree—even a position with which you strongly disagree—you're one step closer to becoming a successful attorney. Moreover, a significant side benefit of learning this technique is that even if you never go on to practice law, the ability to see both sides of an argument will serve you well in life in many contexts.

*Planet Earth v. Planet Zagor* Before we practice legal reasoning using actual law, let's start with an imaginary example. Pretend that outer-space aliens from the planet Zagor have just landed in your back yard! Luckily for you they speak fluent English. Since you're the first human they have encountered, they demand you give them a "bokmurfle" as a token of friendship. When you explain to them that you don't know what a bokmurfle is, they tell you that it is universally accepted as the standard, customary way of greeting a new species with a token of friendship. They remind you that failure to give them a bokmurfle is such an outrageous insult, it is considered a declaration of intergalactic war. Therefore, if you don't give them the gift of a bokmurfle within 10 minutes, they will destroy the Earth. Since you are now Earth's sole hope of survival, you ask them to define "bokmurfle." They define "bokmurfle" under intergalactic law as follows:

> *Bokmurfle*: A non-living object that is:
> (1) designed primarily to please the visual senses;
> and
> (2) is capable of changing appearance or orientation in a relatively fluid motion but without electrical power

The Zagorians allow you to phone a friend to help you brainstorm a list of objects that might meet this definition. You and your friend come up with the following tentative list:

A television
A weather vane
Computer screen savers
A hanging mobile
Wind chimes
Holographic photos
A Rubik's cube
A slinky
A gas fireplace
A water sculpture
A Zen sand garden
An analog clock
Silly Putty
A lava lamp
A disco ball
Laser lights
Soap bubbles
A Kaleidoscope
A CD, DVD, or Blu-ray disk

Which of the items listed above do you think are *definitely* bokmurfles? Why? Which of the items listed above do you think are definitely *not* bokmurfles? Why not? Which of the items listed above might or might not be bokmurfles as it is unclear to you whether they meet the definition? That is, you can see how someone might make the argument either way whether the object is or is not a bokmurfle. Explain the possible arguments on either side. Indeed, pick the item you thought was most likely a bokmurfle and argue that it is *not* a bokmurfle. Then similarly, pick the item you thought was most likely *not* a bokmurfle and argue that it *is*. If you can answer all these questions in thorough detail, you are well on your way to performing legal reasoning. And again, if you can appear confident and convincing when you argue either opposing positions, you are well on your way to being a successful lawyer.

*Snyder v. Phelps* Now let's practice a real-world example of a law-based complex major premise coupled with some complex minor premises. In other words, put in basic, commonly-used legal terminology, let's practice applying actual law. For purposes here, however, although the law is real, we will still apply the law only to hypothetical facts. We'll use the tort (a civil wrong) of *intentional infliction of emotional distress (also often referred to by the acronym IIED)* as our example. According to the Louisiana Supreme Court case of *White v. Monsanto* (1991):

> In order to recover for intentional infliction of emotional distress, a plaintiff must establish:
>
> (1) that the conduct of the defendant was extreme and outrageous;
>
> (2) that the emotional distress suffered by the plaintiff was severe;
>
> and
>
> (3) that the defendant desired to inflict severe emotional distress or knew that severe emotional distress would be certain or substantially certain to result from his conduct.

One can see that in this legal definition, within the formally numbered elements, there exists additional sub-elements as well, as indicated by the words "and" and "or." Regardless how many specific elements there are to this tort, there are actions that easily meet this definition, and actions that clearly do not. Calling someone merely a "stupid jerk," especially when the victim of the insult doesn't care, clearly doesn't meet this definition. On the other hand, imagine Chris throws poisoned dog treats into neighbor Pat's yard to kill Pat's two new puppies because Chris doesn't like Pat. If Chis knows Pat is a sensitive animal lover, and Pat needs to get grief counseling as a result of the puppies' deaths, Chris's actions would likely meet this definition in a court of law.

The problem is that often in life, factual circumstances result in "cases on the edge" which are a close call. These are more difficult situations where it is hard to apply the law to the facts. As a result, the case could easily go either way depending on which party can convince the judge or jury that the legal rule has been met or not met. Indeed, the reason every legal case exists is because of a basic disagreement over how a legal rule applies to the facts of the case. The plaintiff and defendant, or prosecution and defendant, disagree on whether the defendant's actions meet the definition of the conduct that the law either requires or prohibits. If everyone agreed, no judge or jury would be needed to decide how the law applies in any given factual situation. The job of lawyers, then, is to fully and vigorously argue on behalf of their clients that the law applies one way or the other, depending on which parties the attorneys represent.

Let's look at a situation where arguments could be made on both sides—that is, both the plaintiff and the defendant can make plausible, reasonable arguments as to how the case should come out. This isn't to say that equally good arguments can necessarily be made on both sides, but at least *plausible* arguments could be made on both sides. In other words, there is at least a reasonable possibility that either side could win the case depending on the judge or jury deciding the case.

For this exercise, apply the definition of intentional infliction of emotional distress to the hypothetical below which is based almost directly on a facts contained in an actual U.S. Supreme Court case from 2011. What would the plaintiff argue, and what would the defendant argue? Again, it's important that regardless which side you believe *should* win in the hypothetical below, you *can* argue for both sides. It's important to repeatedly emphasize that being able to separate your personal views from the law is a critical skill for an attorney. Without this ability, an attorney who disagreed with their clients' position would not give their clients vigorous advocacy. This failure would violate the attorney's ethical obligations to the client, possibly resulting in reprimand, suspension, or disbarment by the attorney discipline committee of the relevant jurisdiction.

After carefully weighing the best creative but plausible legal arguments on both sides, then you may consider how you would rule if you were the judge. In other words, do you believe on balance the legal definition (that is, the legal rule) of intentional infliction of emotion distress is met under these facts? Why or why not? Step through each element of the rule carefully and thoroughly.

> *Snyder v. Phelps.* The Westboro Baptist Church is led by the Reverend Fred Phelps. Phelps believes that gays and lesbians are so sinful they are going to hell and should all be executed on this Earth. This makes the U.S. sinfully evil for allowing gays and lesbians to continue to live. Any soldier fighting to defend the U.S. is therefore also sinfully evil and is going to hell as well. To bring publicity to their views, Phelps and his church picket burials of members of the U.S. military who die while serving in uniform. Michael Snyder is a U.S. marine who died in Iraq in 2006. At Sny-

> der's Catholic burial, Phelps and members of his church picketed on the public sidewalks outside the cemetery. They shouted and held up large signs that read (among other hateful things) "America is Doomed," "God Hates You," "God Hates Fags," "Fag Troops," "Thank God for Dead Soldiers," "Thank God for 9/11," "You're Going to Hell," "Pope in Hell," and "Priests Rape Boys." A large group of counter-protesters stood close to Phelps and his fellow protesters, and positioned themselves between Phelps and the Snyder family so that the family could not see the protesters. The counter-protesters also sang patriotic songs so that the Snyder family could not hear Phelps and his congregation yelling their hateful messages. The day after the funeral, Michael's father, Albert Snyder, saw the protest on the news. He became angry, tearful, and nauseated. After a week of still feeling depressed by what Phelps had done, Snyder filed a federal lawsuit in the U.S. District Court for the District of Maryland (due to diversity jurisdiction) against Phelps for intentional infliction of emotional distress under Maryland law.

Try your best to come up with the arguments on both sides for how each element of the legal rule for intentional infliction of emotional distress would apply to this case. This type of analysis—reading a factual situation, figuring out what the best legal arguments would be on both sides, and deciding how the law applies—is commonly called IRAC. IRAC stands for Issue, Rule, Application (or Analysis) and Conclusion. We'll look at IRAC more formally and in more depth in Chapter 12. For now, just understand that the essence of legal reasoning is the application of abstract definitions (legal rules) to concrete factual examples. This type of legal reasoning is therefore a particular example of deductive logic. Other types of logic are sometimes used in legal reasoning, but deductive logic is the most common and most fundamental. Regardless, legal reasoning is a particular intellectual skill that some people naturally have the talent for, some people can develop with effort, and some are never able to master. This is why not everyone can be (nor is allowed to be) a lawyer.

In the actual case of *Snyder v. Phelps*, a federal jury found Westboro Baptist Church liable for intentional infliction of emotional distress, and awarded Phelps $2.9 million in compensatory damages and $8 million in punitive damages. Both the Fourth Circuit Court of Appeals and the U.S. Supreme Court (in 2011), however, ruled that the First Amendment protected such speech on public issues. The Supreme Court did not analyze whether Phelps' actions would have otherwise met the legal elements of IIED. Instead, applying First amendment law, by an 8-1 vote the Court declared that although the speech was hateful, it involved public commentary in a public location:

> The 'content' of Westboro's signs plainly relates to broad issues of interest to society at large, rather than matters of 'purely private concern.' . . . While these messages may fall short of refined social or political commentary, the issues they highlight—the political and moral conduct of the United States and its citizens, the fate of our Nation, homosexuality in the military, and scandals involving the Catholic clergy—are matters of public import.

We can look at the reasoning of the majority and dissent in *Phelps v. Snyder* using legal syllogisms. Somewhat oversimplified, the majority's reasoning went as follows:

> Major Premise: Speech that involves public issues is protected from civil lawsuits by the First Amendment.
>
> Minor Premise: Phelps' verbal attack involved matters of public concern.
>
> Conclusion: Phelps' speech is protected from civil lawsuits.

Thus, the majority opinion in *Snyder v. Phelps* believed the application of IIED was barred given the particular facts of the case, but left the tort of IIED available to future plaintiffs who are victimized by outrageous conduct that does not involve matters of public concern.

On the other hand, the reasoning of Justice Samuel Alito in dissent went as follows:

> Major Premise: Speech that involves public issues is protected from civil lawsuits by the First Amendment.
>
> Minor Premise: Phelps' verbal attack against Matthew Snyder's private conduct (serving in the military and being Catholic) did not involve matters of public concern.
>
> Conclusion: Phelps' speech is not protected from civil lawsuits.

In short, both the majority and minority in *Snyder v. Phelps* agreed on the major premise (the law) but disagreed on the minor premise (the proper characterization of the facts). This was somewhat opposite to the situation in *McBoyle v. United* States, discussed earlier in this chapter. In that case, the Supreme Court and the Circuit Court agreed on the minor premise (the facts of an airplane) but disagreed on the major premise (the definition of "motor vehicle.") One can see, then, that individuals, lawyers, and judges can disagree on either the law or the facts of a case, and sometimes they disagree on both.

---

*Questions for Review and Discussion*

For each of the following major and minor premises, what are the possible arguments (if any) for the different conclusions? Try to take turns arguing for different conclusions so that you can see if there are any plausible argument for alternative conclusions.

1. *Major Premise:* Battery is an unwanted physical touching of either a person's body or an object intimately touching a person's body.
   *Minor Premise 1:* Greg angrily dared Eddie to knock Greg's baseball cap off his head.
   *Minor Premise 2:* Eddie knocked Greg's hat off his head by touching only the very edge of the brim of the hat and not any part of Greg's head.
   *Conclusion:* Battery or no battery?

2. *Major Premise:* Burglary is entering a building with intent to commit a crime therein.
   *Minor Premise 1:* Alicia smashed in a window of Carlos' home with a hammer.
   *Minor Premise 2:* Alicia planned to enter through the window and vandalize Carlos' house.
   *Minor Premise 3:* The end of Alicia's hammer entered the house through the window but Alicia then left before entering any party of her body through the window.
   Conclusion: Burglary or no burglary?

3. *Major Premise:* A 'motor vehicle' is a vehicle operated by a power developed within itself and used for the purpose of carrying passengers or materials.
   *Minor Premise:* A recreational helium balloon whose basket carries a small circus dog.
   *Conclusion:* A motor vehicle or not?

4. *Major Premise:* Intentional infliction of emotional distress occurs when one intentionally or recklessly causes severe emotional distress to another person using extreme and outrageous conduct.
   *Minor Premise 1:* Maria knows Dwayne has a mild allergy to peanuts such that he sneezes badly when he eats them.
   *Minor Premise 2:* Maria gave Dwayne cookies secretly containing peanuts in them late in the evening as a joke.
   *Minor Premise 3:* Dwayne ate the cookies and then sneezed so badly for the next few hours he lost some sleep.
   *Conclusion:* Intentional infliction of emotional distress or not?

5. *Major Premise:* A bokmurfle is a non-living object that is designed primarily to please the visual senses and is capable of changing appearance or orientation in a relatively fluid motion but without electrical power.

*Minor Premise:* Christmas tree lights.
*Conclusion:* Bokmurfle or not a bokmurfle?

---

*Suggested Readings*

*State v. Stagno*, 739 P.2d 198 (Alaska Crt. App. 1987) (driving an airboat on a highway while intoxicated)
*Pillars v. R.J. Reynolds Tobacco Co.*, 78 So. 365, 366 (Miss. 1918) (product liability: toe in tobacco)
*Christy Brothers Circus v. Turnage*, 144 S.E. 680 (Ga. Ct. App. 1928) (negligence: horse defecation)
*Seals v. Morris*, 410 So. 2d 715 (La. 1982) (negligence: snake in car accident)
*State v. Bryant*, 101 So. 3d 429 (La. 2012) (burglary: lack of entry)
*Terry v. Lock*, 37 S.W.3d 202 (Ark. 2001) (mislaid property: found cash)
*Wright v. Newman*, 467 S.E.2d 533, (Ga. 1996) (promissory estoppel: child support)
*Marles v. Texas*, 919 S.W.2d 669 (Tex. Ct. App. 1996) (evidence relevance: self-defecation)
*England v. S & M Foods, Inc.*, 511 So.2d 1313 (La. Ct. App. 1987) (battery: thrown hamburger)
*Kirkham v. Will*, 724 N.E.2d 1062 (Ill. App. Ct. 2000) (negligence: reasonable dog)
*Bass v. Aetna Insurance*, 370 So. 2d 511 (La. 1979) (negligence: running in church)

---

*Advanced Readings*

Edward Levi, *An Introduction to Legal Reasoning*, 2d ed. (2013)
Frederick Schauer, *Thinking Like a Lawyer*, Reprint Edition (2012)

CHAPTER *10*

# CASE LAW ELEMENTS

---

*Chapter Objectives*

*After reading this chapter, you should be able to:*

- Describe case law
- Define and identify the basic elements of court cases
- Describe the concept of case precedents and distinguish different types of precedents
- Explain how to brief court cases
- Identify numerous signaling words courts use to identify case elements

---

Although constitutions are themselves laws and legislatures make statutory law, courts also make laws. The law made by courts is called simply *case law*. Case law can be created based on one of two legal foundations.

## What is Case Law?

The most common type of case law is when a court interprets a written law made by one of the other branches of government. This other written law could be a constitution, statute, ordinance, treaty, administrative regulation, executive order, and so on. The court's interpretation of that law then itself then becomes law—*case law*. For example, the First Amendment to the U.S. Constitution says, among other things, that "Congress shall make no law . . . abridging the freedom of speech . . ." This is a law, but how is the phrase "the freedom of speech" to be interpreted? That is, what do the words "freedom of speech" *mean*? The Supreme Court has for a century, in hundreds of cases, created an elaborate framework to explain the meaning of "the freedom of speech." According to the Court, some types of speech, essentially political and religious speech, receive nearly absolute constitutional protection.

Other types of speech, however, receive a lesser degree of protection, such as commercial speech or conduct that happens to communicate a message. Still other types of speech, including threats, defamation, and the advocacy of immediate violence receive little or no constitutional protection. Each of these sub-types of speech comes with its own legal definition, also created entirely by the Court. Thus, federal constitutional law defining "the freedom of speech" is created by the Supreme Court (and other federal courts) in federal case law.

The other legal foundation of case law is when courts make up law entirely on their own. In the constitution, the principle of separation of powers formally says that only legislatures make laws. Yet this division of powers has never been technically accurate since all three branches (legislative, executive, and judicial) make law to some degree. Let's look at how courts make law entirely on their own.

The U.S. system of law is based on the English system of law which began to develop between the years 1100–1300. This is when annual court records started to be kept. From that point courts began to look to past court decisions—*precedents*—for guidance on deciding legal issues. Since English written codified law was still in its infancy, many areas of the law had little or no legislative statutes covering the law. It thus was left entirely to the courts to rule on many types of legal disputes. Over time, an elaborate system of laws eventually developed based on thousands upon thousands of judicial decisions. The courts followed precedents to maintain stability and uniformity in the law. This system of court-made law came to be known as the *common law*. Originally, entire fields of law such as torts, contracts, and property were almost exclusively defined by court-made common law. In modern times, most areas of law have been extensively codified by statute. Tort law, however, is one of the few remaining areas of law that has not been completely codified in legislative statute. That is, in common law jurisdictions, courts are still free to define the law of torts, as well as other areas of common law, if the legislature in that jurisdiction has still not fully codified the common law.

Whenever a court interprets a constitution, statute, ordinance, regulation, or treaty, or when a court issues a common law ruling, that decision becomes *case law*. Regardless the legal foundation for case law, each individual court decision that is part of case law becomes a legal *precedent*. Each decided case is called a precedent because that judicial decision *precedes* all future court decisions that will look back to that precedent for guidance. The practice of following precedents helps maintain stability, consistency, and uniformity in the law. Instead of having to haphazardly create new law in every case, courts tend to follow the precedent established by their brethren in justice.

Whenever a court looks back to the ruling in a prior case—that is, precedent—as support for the decision it is currently making, the court will in its ruling provide a citation to that precedent. Concurring and dissenting judges will do the same for precedents they believe should govern the outcome of the case. This is commonly and consistently done any time a general legal principle or rule from a prior case is being applied.

For example, in the 2006 Supreme Court case *Hamdan v. Rumsfeld*,[1] the Court was faced with the task of deciding whether President George W. Bush had constitutional authority to order military detainees in the war on terror to be tried by military tribunals specially ordered by President Bush rather than by pre-existing military or civilian courts. The Court disallowed the special tribunals, but splintered into a majority opinion along with several concurring and dissenting opinions. All of the many opinions written in the case heavily cited precedents in support of their respective positions. The majority cited numerous precedents, including some going back to the Civil War and World War II, in ruling that the Constitution did not give the President authority to create military tribunals without Congressional authorization:

> Exigency alone, of course, will not justify the establishment and use of penal tribunals not contemplated by Article I, §8 and Article III, §1 of the Constitution unless some other part of that document authorizes a response to the felt need. See *Ex parte Milligan*, 4 Wall. 2, 121 (1866) (Certainly no part of the judicial power of the country was conferred on [military commissions]); *Ex parte Vallandigham*, 1 Wall. 243, 251 (1864); see also *Quirin*, 327 U.S. 1, 11 (1946).[2]

Concurring with the Court's majority, Justice Kennedy, joined by three other justices, looked to, among many other cases, precedent decided by the Court during the Korean War that set out a broad general framework for evaluating presidential authority under the Constitution:

> The proper framework for assessing whether Executive actions are authorized is the three-part scheme used by Justice Jackson in his opinion in *Youngstown Sheet & Tube Co. v. Sawyer*, 343 U. S. 579 (1952) "When the President acts pursuant to an express or implied authorization of Congress, his authority is at its maximum, for it includes all that he possesses in his own right plus all that Congress can delegate." *Id.*, at 635. "When the President acts in absence of either a congressional grant or denial of authority, he

1. Hamdan v. Rumsfeld, 548 U.S. 557 (2006)
2. Hamden v. Rumsfeld, 458 U.S. 557, 591 (2006)

> can only rely upon his own independent powers, but there is a zone of twilight in which he and Congress may have concurrent authority, or in which its distribution is uncertain." *Id.*, at 637. And "[w]hen the President takes measures incompatible with the expressed or implied will of Congress, his power is at its lowest ebb." *Ibid.*[3]

Writing in dissent, Justice Thomas, joined by two other justices, used many of the same precedents cited by the majority and concurring judges to argue instead that the President did possess constitutional authority to create the military tribunals in question:

> [I]n the very context that we address today, this Court has concluded that "the detention and trial of petitioners—ordered by the President in the declared exercise of his powers as Commander in Chief of the Army in time of war and of grave public danger—are not to be set aside by the courts without the clear conviction that they are in conflict with the Constitution or laws of Congress constitutionally enacted. *Ex parte Quirin,* 317 U. S. 1, 25 (1942).[4]

In their opinions, judges often cite multiple precedents in reaching their legal conclusions, and occasionally the majority and minority opinions might cite the *same* precedents.

If the information a court is using came from a specific page of a precedent, that page number is included as well. For example:

> To prove negligence, a plaintiff must prove by a preponderance of evidence that the defendant (a) owed plaintiff a duty, (b) breached that duty, (c) the breach of duty caused plaintiff's damages, and (d) the plaintiff suffered damages as a result. *Smith v. Jones*, 999 U.S. 123, 127 (1902).

## The Legal Elements of Court Decisions

Now that you have some background about the judicial system and some of the more common procedural concepts and terms you might encounter, we can look more in depth at understanding court cases. There can sometimes be many different elements to a judicial opinion. At their core, however, all court decisions almost always have at least four basic legal elements:

3. *Id.* at 639 (Kennedy, J., concurring)
4. *Id.* at 680 (Thomas, J., dissenting)

1. The critical, key *facts* of the case;

2. The precise legal *question(s)* involved in the case that the court is to resolve;

3. The court's specific *answer(s)* to the legal question(s) involved; and

4. A detailed *explanation* of the court's reason(s) how and why it reached its answer(s).

In short, in every substantive court case, there are facts, a question, an answer, and an explanation for the answer. In more formal legal terms, the question is sometimes called the *question presented,* but is most often simply called the *issue.* The answer is called the *holding.* The explanation is called the *reasoning* of the court or the *rationale* of the court. This reasoning includes a discussion of both the relevant law and the application of that relevant law to the facts of the case. The relevant law is called the *rule,* as in "the legal rule" or "rule of law." The application of that rule to the specific facts of the case is most commonly called the *application.*

To put our list of essential case elements into more proper legal terms, almost all court cases have four legal elements:

1. facts

2. issue (a.k.a. question)

3. holding (a.k.a. decision)

4. reasoning (a.k.a. rationale) = rule + application

Unfortunately, judges rarely label the legal elements of cases clearly, if at all, in their written judicial opinions. It thus takes careful reading and re-reading (and often re-re-reading!) to spot these elements in a case and to understand them. Generally, this skill improves over time with practice. Indeed, mere memorization of this information is almost worthless because the ability to distinguish these case elements is not a knowledge, but a *skill.* Because differentiating these legal elements in court cases is a skill, it can only be learned through *practice* in *doing* it.

There's another bit of bad news in trying to spot the legal elements of cases. Besides often not labeling the elements of a case, different courts and judges often put the elements in different orders. Not only is there no set order for the elements, often the elements are intermixed and/or repeated. Nevertheless, here is a template that shows the most common orders of legal elements of cases:

[Issue or Holding]

[Issue]

[Holding]

Facts

[Issue]

[Holding]

Reasoning (Rule + Application)

[Issue]

[Holding]

The facts always come before the reasoning, although often courts bring in new facts in the application that were not mentioned during the initial discussion of the facts. The rule must necessarily come before the application, because an application by definition requires a rule to be applied. The issue and holding, however, often appear in different places. Sometimes the issue will be stated first, but sometimes the holding will be first. Sometimes the issue is stated after the facts. The holding usually is stated initially and then again at the end of the opinion. Many judges or courts, however, often do not provide the holding until the very end of the opinion, as if they are writing a suspense novel. The point is that once again, critical reading and re-reading (and often re-re-reading or even re-re-re-reading) is required to correctly identify each of the separate elements of a court case.

In attempting to determine the role and meaning of each and every sentence in a court opinion, you may—and sooner or later will—encounter many legal terms that you have not seen before. The study and field of law has its own extensive vocabulary. Even experienced lawyers sometimes discover a judge or an opposing lawyer using a legal term that the attorney has not heard before. Therefore, one of the standard references any law student or lawyer will want to have is a legal dictionary. By far the most popular legal dictionary in the United States is *Black's Law Dictionary*. When you read through court cases, you will want to have a copy of this or some other legal dictionary handy, either in print or online, to help you understand everything you read. Indeed, lawyers and judges are often accused of speaking and writing in unnecessarily complex ways, such as when drafting contracts. This needlessly complicated language is even referred to as "legalese." You sometimes may need to wade through legalese in understanding parts of court cases. This is why a legal dictionary, as well as a regular dictionary, are standard reference tools for anyone who is studying or practicing law.

## Case Briefs

The most common way law students, attorneys, judges, and judicial clerks differentiate the legal elements of a case is by creating a technical summary of the case. This technical summary is called a *case brief*, or often simply *brief*. A case brief is a short summary of a court ruling that highlights the key legal elements of the case. Case briefs are generally used for more efficient study of a ruling as many rulings can be quite long. It's not uncommon, for example, that U.S. Supreme Court opinions are over 100 pages in length. It's far easier and simpler for law students, lawyers, judges and law clerks to read a one-page case brief than to read or re-read a 100-page case every time one wants to refresh one's memory about the case. In short, a case brief boils down and distills the key legal elements of a court opinion into their essence.

*Case briefs* should not be confused with *court briefs*. A "brief" filed with a court is a summary by an attorney on behalf of a client that contains legal argument and legal citations supporting the client's position. There are different types of court briefs. For example, an "appellate brief" is a detailed legal argument on behalf of a client and filed with an appellate court. Case briefs, though, are simply summaries of decided court cases, and do not constitute legal argument on behalf of any client who will be appearing in court. When a lawyer says they will "brief a case" they are referring to creating a case brief, but if a lawyer says they will "file a brief" then they are referring to a court brief.

Case briefs are written mostly in the writer's own words. That is, a case brief should mostly summarize and paraphrase a court case. The only exception is when the legal rule is cited. Here, the legal rule must always be quoted in its entirety. Beyond that, only a few choice or critical words, phrases, or sentences should be quoted. Even then, quotations should be used only sparingly, or the case brief may end up being too long to be useful. Paraphrasing the court's opinion *in one's own words* also forces the writer to understand the court's opinion. Simply cutting and pasting sentences or paragraphs of the court's opinion does not indicate that the writer of the case brief understands any of what's happening in the court opinion. For example, anyone could look at a case in a foreign language one doesn't understand, cut and paste a few sentences and paragraphs, and then claim it's a summary of that case. Those sentences might be some of the key elements of the case, but merely by random guessing, not because of any actual comprehension of the case. Only if the case is mostly summarized in the writer's own words do both the writer and any readers of the case brief then know that it is likely that the writer grasps the legal elements of the case.

Anyone reading a case brief should be able to understand all the basic legal elements of the case merely from the information contained in the case brief. We just noted the four key elements of any case: facts, issue, holding, and reasoning (including both the legal rule and its application). Any accurate summary of a court case will and must include these key legal elements. A person trained in the law should be able to read a case brief and understand the case enough to be able to argue legal points from it in court.

Only by summarizing and paraphrasing a court's legal reasoning in your own words can you demonstrate a thorough grasp of what the court is doing. In any case brief, the rule must be directly quoted, but the application should be mostly in the case brief writer's own summarizing and paraphrasing.

One common mistake beginner case brief writers often make is leaving out parts of the court's application. A legal rule might have several elements, and so the application might have several corresponding elements as well. Each link in the chain of logic must be included. For example, if the court's application part of its reasoning follows the logical steps "A to B to C to D," then all those steps must be summarized. A case brief that states only "A to D" is leaving out two key parts of the court's explanation for its decision. Such a case brief is not accurately summarizing the case, and so someone reading the case brief cannot understand the court's ruling based on the case brief. In short, always make sure that the reasoning section of a case brief—both the rule and the application—are well organized, and that you summarize *all* the key steps in the court's reasoning.

Generally, as a rough rule of thumb, case briefs should be approximately no more than one single-spaced typed page maximum. More than one page can be used, but only if the case is unusually long and complex. This might occur if the case has complex facts, multiple issues, or many points of reasoning, such as a legal rule with many sub-elements that need to be applied, or an application of a rule where the court discusses many factors in support of its application. If a case brief is too long, however, it is no longer a "brief" summary of the case, and becomes not a "case brief," but a "case long"—which no longer is useful. Also remember again that unfortunately, judges rarely label the elements in their written judicial opinions. It therefore takes careful reading to correctly identify each of the elements in a written judicial opinion. Let's next look at each of those elements in detail.

## Case Elements: Name, Facts, Issue, Holding

Every law professor, college teacher, judge, or senior partner who asks for a case brief from a student, law clerk, or junior partner has their own format regarding how they want case briefs presented. There are numerous variations of possible elements, and how those elements are named, that might appear in a case brief. Here, though, we'll describe only the basic elements we just summarized, but with possible case brief variations noted.

*Case Name* Technically the name of the case is not one of the elements of the court opinion itself, but it is necessary to reference the court's opinion. The name of the case is given, often followed by a full legal citation to the case, or at least the year the case was decided. For example:

> *Smith v. Jones* (La. 1966)
>
> *Swanson v. Frost* (2015)
>
> *Smith v. Jones,* 227 So.2d 509 (La. 1966)
>
> *Swanson v. Frost,* 123 U.S. 456 (2027)

Because of these variations, sometimes you'll be asked to give the name, or name and year, or name, citation, and year. Again, always simply put the case brief in the format requested.

*Facts* Who is suing whom, and why, and on what alleged legal grounds? Only the facts necessary to understand the case should be included here. *Who* are the parties to the lawsuit, and *what* is their dispute? *In your own words,* only include the few *important,* relevant, critical facts necessary to understand the case. For example, the date or time of day a defendant was arrested is usually not important, but the crime a defendant committed very important. Or, in an auto accident, the make of the car is usually irrelevant. It all depends, though, on what facts the court relies on as part of its later reasoning.

At the appellate court level, the legal procedure regarding who won or lost at the lower court level is part of the facts of the case. That is, you must provide a simple description of how the case procedurally got to the appellate court. Note that often you'll be asked to summarize the legal procedure separately from the facts in a case brief. Indeed, this practice of separating the facts from the procedural history of the case is extremely common. This element of your case brief could be labeled "Procedure," "Procedural History," "Procedural Posture" or some similar label. Again, there are numerous variations of case brief formats, so always simply provide the case brief in whatever format you are asked to provide it. Regardless what format is used, however, it is important to include the procedural background of the case somewhere in the case brief, either in the facts or in a separately labeled "procedure" section.

*Issue* What is the precise legal *question* the court has to decide? Courts exist not to answer political questions, policy questions, or moral questions, but *legal* questions. So, what is the basic *legal* question? This requires including in the statement of the issue the specific provision of law that is involved in the case. In other words, the reason the case is in court is because there is a legal dispute—that is, there is a disagreement about the meaning or application of a law or laws. The court thus is being asked to interpret and apply that law. So what legal question exactly is the court being asked to decide? Is the court interpreting the meaning of a specific section of the U.S. Constitution? A particular subsection of a statute? A common law principal derived from one or more common law case precedents? A particular administrative regulation? An international treaty? A city ordinance? And so on.

Because courts do not always label the issue part of their opinion as "issue," other words or phrases might be used to indicate the issue. For example, a court might say "The question before us today is . . ." or "We must decide whether . . ." Or, the court might simply state the issue as a question: "Does the President have constitutional authority to suspend a national presidential election on the claim of wartime necessity?"

Regardless the particular type of law being evaluated, or the term used by the court to label its issue, in a case brief the legal issue should be stated in a one-sentence yes-or-no question. For example:

*Issue*: Is yelling "Fire!" in a crowded theatre protected as free speech by the Free Speech Clause of the First Amendment to the U.S. Constitution?

*Issue*: Is a tenant's refusal to pay rent to the landlord due to a collapsed bedroom ceiling a material breach of contract under common law contract principles?

*Issue*: Does using a non-working rifle as a walking cane during a robbery constitute "using a firearm during the commission of a felony" under 32 U.S. Code Section 42(a), thereby automatically requiring a mandatory minimum sentence of 30 years in prison?

If there is more than one legal issue in the case, then you would say "Issue 1," "Issue 2," and so on. For example:

*Issue 1*: Is a public airport terminal considered a public forum under the Public Forum Doctrine of the Free Speech Clause of the First Amendment to the U.S. Constitution?

*Issue 2*: Does a public airport terminal ban on in-person solicitation violate the Free Speech Clause of the First Amendment to the U.S. Constitution?

*Holding* What is the majority of the court's conclusion as to the question it was asked? That is, what is the court's specific legal *answer* to the particular legal question it was asked to decide? In answering this question, the court will necessarily decide who (which litigant) wins the case. The holding should be a one-sentence answer to the issue, and can be simple or complex depending on the complexity of the legal issue involved. The holding is also often called the *decision* in the case, as in "The court decided that . . ." For appellate court cases, you will often be asked to provide in your case brief the vote count regarding the number of justices who joined the majority, plurality, concurring, and/or dissenting opinions.

Here are examples of just a few of the practically infinite number of possible legal holdings depending on the particular legal issues in the case, some showing the appellate court vote count and some not:

*Holding*: No, yelling fire in a crowded theatre is not protected as free speech by the Free Speech Clause of the First Amendment to the U.S. Constitution.

*Holding:* (5-0) No, a tenant's refusal to pay rent to the landlord due to a collapsed bedroom ceiling does not constitute a material breach of contract under common law contract principles.

*Holding*: (7-2-1) Yes, sending an e-mail acceptance in response to an e-mailed offer is valid even if the other person calls to revoke the offer before receiving the acceptance.

*Holding*: Yes, using a non-working rifle as a walking cane during a robbery constitutes "using a firearm during the commission of a felony" under 32 U.S. Code Section 42(a), thereby automatically requiring a mandatory minimum sentence of 30 years in prison.

If there are multiple legal issues in the case, each issue receives a holding. For example:

*Holding 1*: (5-4) No, a public airport terminal is not considered a public forum under the Public Forum Doctrine of the Free Speech Clause of the First Amendment to the U.S. Constitution.

*Holding 2*: (6-3) No, a public airport terminal ban on in-person solicitation does not violate the Free Speech Clause of the First Amendment to the U.S. Constitution.

Since courts rarely label their "holding" specifically as such, you may have to look for other phrases signaling the court's holding. Among other possible terms used, a court might state that it is "declaring," "deciding," or "announcing" its "ruling," "decision," "judgment," or "opinion." Or, a court might simply state the holding as its answer to the legal question being considered: "After a consideration of relevant precedents, we conclude that absent express authorization by Congress, the President lacks constitutional authority to suspend a national presidential election on the mere claim of wartime necessity."

## Case Elements: Reasoning (Rule + Application)

Merely answering the legal question is not enough for a court. Critical is the majority opinion's *explanation* as to *why* it reached the decision it did. That is, what is the court's justification for its holding (its decision)? This explanation is called the *reasoning* part of the case, also often called the *rationale.* The reasoning always consists of two sub-parts: one, the legal rule involved and two, how that particular legal rule applies to the given facts of the case. The court's reasoning is usually the most important and usually longest portion of a court opinion, and hence, of a case brief. Often you will be asked in the reasoning section of a case brief to clearly and separately label the rule and application parts of the reasoning.

Let's now look at the two sub-parts of the court's reasoning: the *rule* and the *application.*

*Rule.* What is the precise legal *rule* (the particular rule of law) the court is quoting or creating that applies to the case? The rule could be a section of a statute, constitution, ordinance, treaty, administrative regulation, common law principles, and so on. The actual precisely quoted wording of the rule itself is also known as the "*black letter law.*" This is because legal treatises and other expert summaries of law have traditionally highlighted the legal rules in boldface text. This is so that the reader is clear as to what is law versus what is merely the writer's analysis or commentary on the law.

Very often the legal rule being applied is not the written law itself, but the court's interpretation of that law. So, for example, a court might be using a previous court's interpretation of the meaning of a statute, or a court might be creating its own new interpretation of the meaning of a statute. In either situation, the key rule the court is applying is not the statute itself, but how the court is defining the meaning of the statute. The same is true, for example, when the Supreme Court has to decide the meaning of a vague provision of the Constitution. What is the meaning of "the freedom of speech"? or "equal protection of the laws"? The rule in any given case applying these concepts is not "the freedom of speech" or "equal protection," but how the court ends up more particularly defining "free speech" or "equal protection."

When creating a particular rule, courts often include an explanation why the court is creating or following that particular rule rather than some other rule that might be applied. The alternative is usually some other possible legal interpretation that was argued by the losing party. This reasoning might be based on past case precedents, as well as the intent behind the law, public policy arguments, or other factors. Although the policy behind a legal rule is important, the policy or rationale behind the adoption of a rule is *not* the legal rule itself. For example, in cases involving the free exercise of religion, individuals whose religious practices have been prohibited by law have often argued that the Free Exercise Clause of the First Amendment ought to be interpreted to mean that religious believers have a right to religious exemptions to laws. Attorneys for the government have usually argued that the Free Exercise Clause prohibits only laws that intentionally discriminate on the basis of religion. Currently the Court has adopted the latter interpretation. The Court has explained that if anyone could claim a religious exemption to any law, then anarchy and chaos would result. The rule the Court therefore has adopted is that religiously neutral laws do not violate the free exercise of religion. The policy behind that rule is that a dangerous slippery slope would result if religious exemptions must automatically be given whenever someone violates the law. This reason the rule exists, however, is not the rule itself.

The rule the court announces is critical because it is the abstract, general legal principle that will be applied to all future cases involving this issue using this case as a precedent. Because of this, the *rule must always be quoted.* As we saw in previous chapters, the particular words a law uses can enormously change the meaning of the law. *Every* word matters. For example, there is a *huge* difference between "a" and "the," or between "may" and "must," or between a singular verus plural noun, and so forth. However, a case brief need *not* quote any explanation for how the court decided on that rule being the rule nor any explanation why the court rejected any proposed alternative rules. The justification and explanation for why a rule is being adopted and any alternative rules are being rejected (if these discussions occur) should be primarily summarized in a case brief in the writer's own words. For example:

*Rule:* To determine whether a law is permissible under the Establishment Clause of the First Amendment, "First, the statute must have a secular legislative purpose; second, its principal or primary effect must be one that neither advances nor inhibits religion; finally, the statute must not foster an excessive government entanglement with religion."

*Rule:* The Court announced that "all racial classifications imposed by government must be analyzed by a reviewing court under strict scrutiny. This means that such classifications are constitutional only if they are narrowly tailored to further compelling governmental interests."

At the same time, not every legal rule and not every part of every rule that a court states in its opinion need be included in the rule section of a case brief. As a common practice, appellate-level courts often list in their opinions the background procedural rules involving burdens of proof or standards of appellate review. This will usually occur regardless of the substantive legal issues involved. Unless these procedural rules or their application are themselves one of the primary disputes in the case, they typically need not be included in the reasoning section of a case brief even if the court quotes and applies them.

Moreover, even with the substantive rule that is the key issue in the case, only the parts of the rule that are at issue and applied by the court need be quoted and discussed in the rule and application parts of a case brief. Often a court will extensively quote all the elements of a lengthy legal rule even when only a single element is in dispute. This is done to provide a context for the court's discussion, but those other parts of the rule are not relevant to the court's reasoning in reaching its outcome in the case. As a result, only the relevant part or parts of the legal rule that are disputed and applied by the court need be quoted in the rule section of the brief.

Given that courts rarely label the "rule" they are using by that term, one must look for other words or phrases signaling that the court is quoting or summarizing a legal rule. Among other possible terms a court might use, a court might refer to the rule as a "test," "proposition," "standard," "framework," "doctrine," "inquiry," "approach," "scheme," "principle," or "analysis." Often, though, a court will simply begin quoting or summarizing the law without using any signaling word(s) of transition.

*Application* After the court figures out what specific legal rule (i.e., law) applies, the Court will then discuss its *application* of that rule of law to the concrete facts of the particular case it is deciding. Sometimes a court will spend a lot of time figuring out the law, and spend very little time applying that law to the facts if the facts are simple and clear-cut. Other times, a court will quickly determine the law to be applied, but spend a lot of time applying the law to a complex set of facts. Or, both the rule and application could be lengthy, or both could be short. Each case is different. This variation, along with the ability to distinguish the legal rule versus the application, is why critical thinking and critical reading skills are essential in understanding the reasoning part of a court case. Since identifying these differences is a skill, practice is needed. The more one practices, the better one becomes at this skill.

In the application part of the reasoning, the court explains how the rule of law specifically applies to the given set of facts in the case under consideration. In other words, given the rule of law that the court just decided should apply, which party should win when that rule is applied to the facts of the case being heard? Here courts consider not only the facts of the case before them, but frequently courts analogize or distinguish the facts of the current case to the facts of earlier similar or related case precedents (we'll look at the concept of "arguing from precedent" in more detail in Chapter 11).

Courts use numerous words and phrases to signal that they are in the application part of their opinion. Often, simply using the introductory word "Here," to open a sentence indicates the court is about to start applying the rule (or a sub-part of it) to the facts of the case. Other similar phrases can include "In the present case," "In the instant case," "In the case at hand," "In the case before us," "In the case at bar" or "To begin our analysis . . ." Longer introductory phrases can be used as well, such as "Considering the circumstances of this case under the framework of these principles . . ." A court might also indicate the application is occurring by noting that one of the parties is "asserting," "contending," "proposing," "arguing," "replying" or "responding." Also, if the court is moving through points of discussion indicated by words such as "first," "second," "next," "moreover," "also," "furthermore," "in addition," or "finally," this typically indicates the court is stepping through the application.

By definition, no facts of any *particular* case are or can be a part of a broad, abstract legal rule that would apply to numerous potential factual situations. Therefore, in the reasoning section of a court opinion, the moment a court starts to discuss any of the facts of the particular case being decided, it indicates the court has moved past the rule itself and is now beginning to apply the rule to the facts. Note, though, that some professors, mostly at the undergraduate level, will not necessarily require that the rule and application be clearly distinguished and labeled as such in a case brief. If this distinction is not required to be made, the "reasoning" section of the case brief need simply include a sufficient mixture of the rule and application so as to clearly summarize the court's overall reasoning in reaching its holding in the case.

When writing a case brief, the application should be largely in *the writer's own words,* using only occasional quotes of choice words, phrases, or sentences where it's helpful or important to use the exact language of the court rather than a summary or paraphrase. For example, in the context of free speech cases, different Supreme Court cases have provided many memorable quotes, such as Justice Potter Stewart's explanation that although he could not legally define "obscene" material with any clarity, "I know it when I see it."[5] Or, Justice Oliver Wendell Holmes once famously said "The most stringent protection of free speech would not protect a man in falsely shouting fire in a theatre and causing a panic."[6] The point is that if summarizing or paraphrasing a key word or phrase would not fully convey the meaning of what the court says, or if there is no better way to say it, then go ahead and quote it (And remember that anytime you quote, you must use quotation marks!)

## Other Case Brief Elements

Given the variety of case brief formats, it's helpful to be aware of some of the more common variations. We already discussed how the facts and procedural history of the case are often combined into the facts, but often divided up into a separate "facts" and "procedure" element. Let's now look at some other elements that often occur in court cases and which you might be asked to note in a case brief.

Often, as briefly noted earlier in this chapter when we discussed the holding of a case, depending on whom you are writing the brief for (such as a professor, senior partner, or judge), you might be asked to include the vote of the court in the holding. The number of justices in the majority or plurality would be listed first, followed by the number of judges in each separate concurrence and dissents. If only two votes are listed, this indicates there were no concurrences, only a majority vote and dissenting vote. For example, assuming all nine justices on the Supreme Court vote in a case but none concur, the vote could be 9-0, 8-1, 7-2, 6-3, or 5-4. If three vote counts are listed then this indicates majority or plurality, followed by votes for each concurrence and dissent. Again as an example, assuming all nine justices on the Supreme Court vote in a case, it could be 7-1-1, 4-3-2, 5-1-1-1, 4-2-2-1, or many other possible combinations. If it were a different appellate-level, the total number of justices could be fewer or greater. If you list the vote in the holding, it might appear like this:

*Holding:* (7-2) No, yelling fire in a crowded theatre is not protected as free speech by the Free Speech Clause of the First Amendment to the U.S. Constitution.

Also, whenever an appellate court decides a case, it must decide what to do with the lower court opinion that was being appealed. Recall from the chapter discussing appellate procedure that this is called the *disposition* of the lower court opinion. Also recall that there are many possible dispositions, the most common of which are "affirmed," "re-

5. *Jacobellis v. Ohio*, 78 U.S. 184, 197 (1964); (Stewart, J., concurring)
6. *Schenck v. United States*, 249 U.S. 47, 52 (1919)

versed," and "reversed and remanded" (where the issue is sent back for reconsideration by the trial court). Sometimes if there are multiple issues, a lower court opinion might be "affirmed in part and reversed in part" or "affirmed in part and reversed and remanded in part." There are other possible dispositions as well, such as "vacated," which means the lower court decision is made void. The disposition is also often called the *judgment* in the case, or sometimes the *result* of the case. There might be other terms as well. Regardless of the name used for this element of an appellate court opinion, however, this element is often requested to be placed in a case brief.

*Holding* (7-2): No, yelling fire in a crowded theatre is not protected as free speech by the Free Speech Clause of the First Amendment to the U.S. Constitution.

*Disposition*: The lower court decision convicting the defendant was affirmed.

Or, the disposition could perhaps simply be included in the holding. This could look something like:

*Holding* (7-2): No, yelling fire in a crowded theatre is not protected as free speech by the Free Speech Clause of the First Amendment to the U.S. Constitution. The lower court decision convicting the defendant was affirmed.

The disposition is also often simply placed in the application part of the case brief, especially at the very end of the application.

In addition, as we noted earlier in this chapter, when discussing the rule part of a case, courts often not only quote the rule, but also discuss the policy behind the rule. That is, courts will sometimes explain why the rule exists as opposed to some other possible alternative rule or rules. This discussion commonly occurs when the litigants disagree about which rule should be applied. Another similar situation is when two litigants agree which rule applies but disagree about the meaning of the rule. In either circumstance, the court will usually look at the history of the rule and why it was enacted. As a result, case briefs sometimes include a "policy" section. This "policy" might be listed as its own section, or could be included in the "rule" part of the case brief.

Case briefs also commonly note and briefly summarize concurrences and dissents. Recall that a concurring opinion is one that agrees with the holding of the court's majority but disagrees with the reasoning. A dissenting opinion disagrees with both the holding and the reasoning of the court's majority. Also recall that only the majority opinion in a court case creates the legal precedent in the case. Except in rare cases, the concurring opinion does not create the law in the case, and dissenting opinions never do. Therefore, given the relative lack of importance of concurring and dissenting opinions, when one or more concurrences or dissents exist in a case, the case brief will typically include only the briefest summary—perhaps a sentence or two—of each concurring and dissenting opinion. Just note the essence of the disagreement each concurrence and dissent has with the majority opinion. For example, maybe a concurring judge agrees with the holding but believes a different legal rule should have been applied. A dissenting judge might disagree with the majority opinion's application of the rule, or perhaps believe the majority opinion applied the wrong rule. This concise summary of disagreement can usually be done in just a couple or few sentences at most. Sometimes, though, if a concurring or dissenting opinion has major legal or historical significance, it can take up a larger part of the brief than a concurrence or dissent normally would.

Regardless of the case element you are trying to identify, remember that courts often use other signaling words or phrases than the ones indicated in this chapter. Also remember that courts often use *no* signaling words or phrases at all for different elements of their written opinions. This is why identifying the different legal components of court cases is a critical thinking and critical reading skill that takes practice.

## Well-written versus Poorly-written Case Brief Comparison

For comparison sake, let's look at some poorly written briefs of an imaginary case, followed by a well-written brief of the same case. Each of the elements of these poorly-written briefs—the facts, issue, holding, and reasoning (both rule and application)—is inadequate. The bracketed and italicized notes at the end of each section of the poorly-written briefs offer explanation as to the deficiency of that part of the case brief.

*Poorly written case brief Example 1:* *Case: Smith v. Jones*
*Facts*: It was 3:05 p.m. on the afternoon of Tuesday, September 6, 2013. It was sunny with a few clouds (about 23% cloudy) and a light breeze that was variable between 5 and 15 m.p.h. Humidity was about 67%. Smith was driving a 2005 Toyota Corolla, light navy blue color, four-door, with power seats and power windows standard, optional cruise control and leather seats, brown interior. Also Smith had an AM/FM radio with CD player installed. Jones was driving a 2009 Ford Focus, champagne with a hint of yellow, two-door, with power windows and cruise control standard, cloth seats, gray interior. Smith was driving to his visit his mother because he had just spoken to her a couple hours earlier. She missed him and wanted to see him. It had been 8 days since he last visited, and they had spaghetti for dinner that time. So Smith was driving on Main Street going Westbound in the right-hand lane, and was approaching the intersection of First Street where there is a four-way stoplight that was installed in 1978. He was driving about 33 miles per hour. Jones was

driving on First Street going Southbound. Jones had just run out of bread, and wanted to make a ham sandwich. Jones had enough mayo and mustard and ham, but needed bread. Jones could have waited but was hungry because he hadn't eaten in 5 hours. This is because he had been busy mowing the lawn before the heat of the day got too hot, and he might then risk getting overheated. This might complicate his medical condition of high blood pressure. So Jones was driving to the Albertson's grocery store that was 7 blocks away (that store had been a Kroger's but Albertson's bought out the local Kroger's). Jones was looking at his grocery list as he approached the intersection of Main and First. Jones also had toothpaste and toilet paper on this grocery list. Because he was reading, he didn't see the light was red. He drove through the red light and hit Smith's car in the side as Smith was going through the intersection. Smith was not injured, but his car sustained damage to the right side. The side doors were indented and the side windows broken. The damages cost $4,700 to fix. Smith filed a lawsuit on December 10, 2013 against Jones. Jones filed a reply denying negligence, saying the light had just turned green as he entered the intersection. [*excessive, unnecessary detail that is mostly tangential or irrelevant to the issue, reasoning, or outcome of the case*]

*Issue*: Is Smith liable to Jones? [*imprecise and incomplete*]

*Holding*: Smith wins the lawsuit. [*imprecise and incomplete*]

*Reasoning*: There was a witness who took Smith's side. [*grossly incomplete*]

*Poorly written case brief Example 2: Case: Smith v. Jones*

*Facts*: Smith is suing Jones for negligence. [*incomplete*]

*Issue*: Negligence. [*imprecise and incomplete*]

*Holding*. Yes there was negligence. [*imprecise and incomplete*]

*Reasoning*: "Within our state of Swansonia, the common law of the physical tort of negligence has been evolving for a century. It seeks to balance the interests of justice with efficiency and the interests of both the victim and the tortfeasor. *Black v. White*, 303 S.E.2d 205 (2007). We have not been presented with a situation or opportunity at this time to reconsider these longstanding rules of negligence. Thus, we follow well-established law. For a plaintiff to show negligence by a defendant, the plaintiff must establish four elements that have been met to the satisfaction of the trier of fact. As we stated recently in *Washington v. Lincoln*, 305 S.E.2d 144, 147 (2009) "First, there must be a duty of care owed by the defendant to the plaintiff. Second, the defendant must breach that duty, and in an unreasonable manner. Third, the plaintiff must have suffered damages. Fourth, the defendant's unreasonable breach of duty must be the cause of the plaintiff's damages." We turn now to the application of these legal elements to the case at hand."

"We have ruled that all drivers of motor vehicles owe a duty to fellow drivers to operate their vehicles in obedience to all traffic regulations and with a reasonable amount of care. *Roosevelt v. Taft*, 305 S.E. 2d 665 (2007). "Thus, Jones owed Smith a duty to operate his vehicle with a reasonable amount of care and obey all traffic regulations. Jones did neither, thereby breaching this duty. He proceeded through a red light in violation of Swansonia Civil Code Section 432, and he admitted to reading while driving rather than paying attention to the road, surroundings, and traffic signals. The witness confirmed this as she was standing on the sidewalk and saw directly into Jones' vehicle as he entered the intersection."

"Jones claims, however, that the light had just turned green as he entered the intersection, and therefore he neither violated state traffic law nor the duty of care he owed other drivers. Both Smith and the witness testified contrary to Jones. The trial court found Jones testimony was not credible, as Jones was belligerent and evasive on the witness stand. Regardless, even if we disregard the trial court's finding (which we may not do unless such a finding is clearly erroneous), when faced with witnesses who otherwise seem equally credible, the general rule is that if one side presents more witnesses providing testimony of equal weight and credibility than the other side presents, the side with more witnesses establishes their side of the case by a preponderance of the evidence. *Madison v. Hamilton*, 287 S.E.2d 509 (1988). Smith has therefore established the fact of breach of care by Jones by a preponderance of evidence.

"As to the final elements, Smith's vehicle was damaged, and it was damaged by Jones's vehicle. Both the fact of damages, and the cause of the damages, are uncontested by Jones. Smith has therefore met all four required elements of negligence in this case, and so we affirm the trial court ruling in Smith's favor for $4,700 in damages. Judgment affirmed." [*This reasoning section of the case brief merely extensively quotes the court and neither summarizes nor paraphrases the court's decision. This reasoning section thus defeats the purpose of a case brief, and also gives no indication to the reader whether the writer of the case brief understands any of the case. That is, anyone could have simply quoted the court without even being able to read English, hoping they guessed correctly as to some of the important sentences in the court's opinion. This poorly constructed brief also fails to distinguish the different elements of the reasoning (the rule versus the application) by not using subsection headings for the rule and application*].

*Well-Written Case Brief Example* Now let's take a look below at a well-written case brief of the same imaginary case. Notice the italicized and bracketed brief commentary at the end of each section.

*Case*: *Smith v. Jones* 123 U.S. 456 (2076)
*Facts*: Smith was traveling through an intersection with a stoplight and

was hit in the side of his car by Jones's car which also was entering the intersection from the cross-street. Both claimed the light was green for them. Smith sued Jones for damages to his car. At trial, Jones admitted he was reading when he entered the intersection, and this was confirmed by a witness who also said the light was green for Smith but red for Jones. The trial court ruled in favor of Smith. Jones now appeals to the state appellate court. *[This briefly summarizes only the relevant facts by explaining who is suing whom, why, and how the case has now reached the court that is deciding the matter].*

*Issue*: Was Jones negligent and thus liable to Smith for damage to Smith's vehicle? [*complete and accurate*].

*Holding*: Yes, Jones was negligent and thus is liable to Smith for damage to Smith's vehicle. [*complete and accurate*].

*Reasoning (Rule + Application)*

*Rule:* The court begins by noting negligence requires four elements: "First, there must be a duty of care owed by the defendant to the plaintiff. Second, the defendant must breach that duty, and in an unreasonable manner. Third, the plaintiff must have suffered damages. Fourth, the defendant's unreasonable breach of duty must be the cause of the plaintiff's damages." [*Complete and accurate, clearly identifies the legal rule, and quotes it.*]

*Application:* Applying the rule to the facts, the court says Jones owed Smith two duties: to obey the traffic signal and to drive carefully. The court says Jones was "evasive and belligerent" on the stand so that his testimony that the light was green was "not credible." Either way, though, the court notes the combined testimony of Smith and the eyewitness outweighs Jones' claim that the light was green. Also, Jones admitted (and the eyewitness corroborated) that Jones was reading at the time he entered the intersection. Thus, Jones violated both his duty to obey the red light and his duty to pay attention to the fact the light was red. Damages to Smith and the cause of damages were unchallenged by Jones. Therefore, Smith met all four elements of negligence, and so the appellate court affirmed the trial court ruling in Smith's favor. [*This completely and accurately summarizes and paraphrases every key logical step in the court's application of the rule of law to the facts, while appropriately quoting only a few key words or phrases used by the court while condensing and summarizing the rest of the application.*]

## Sample Cases with Case Briefs

Here are two actual appellate cases, a criminal case from Texas and a civil case from Louisiana. The text of each case is presented first. Bracketed labels have been added within each case to indicate the start of primary case elements: the facts, issue, holding, and reasoning, including both the rule and the application. To further aid in following the cases, parenthetical information inside the brackets indicates more particular detail of that portion of the court's opinion. Notice how sometimes some of the signaling words listed earlier are used, but often none are. Then, after the text of each case, a sample "model" case brief is provided for each case. Once again, however, keep in mind that the formats here provide only the most essential elements of a case brief. Different professors, senior partners, or supervising judges might require different additional elements be included.

*Marles v. Texas (With Case Elements Labeled)*
919 S.W.2d 669 (Tex Ct. App. 1996)
Opinion by Justice Phil Harderberger.

[ISSUE] This case decides the heretofore undecided question of whether the act of defecating in one's pants upon being informed of a pending criminal charge is a relevant fact for the jury. . . . [FACTS (arguments by the parties)] The state claims the act of defecating in one's pants is an "excited utterance" and therefore is admissible as nonverbal conduct. The defendant says that the mere mention of this social faux pas is so devastating that no amount of curative jury instruction can be effective in removing the stink from the jury box. . . .

[FACTS (and procedural history)] This unprecedented, or at least unreported, state of affairs grows out of a charge against James Marles, appellant, of four counts of aggravated sexual assault of a child. He plead not guilty, was tried by a jury who found him guilty and assessed punishment of 16 years confinement in the penitentiary, the various convictions running concurrently. Marles appeals the convictions . . .

Before his arrest Marles was, apparently, a well-liked teacher's aide. He was arrested at his place of employment. The prosecution's witness, present at the time of the arrest, was Detective Lana Kirkhum. In the pertinent part of the testimony, the State was questioning Kirkhum on direct:

Q: What, if anything, happened when you arrested him?

A: Well, it was at a school. We called him into the office of the principal, informed him that I had a warrant for aggravated sexual assault of a child and he defecated in his pants.

Defense counsel objected and there was an out-of-court hearing in which defense counsel argued that the comment was extremely prejudicial. After hearing both sides the court sustained the objection on the grounds of relevancy. Upon request by defense counsel, she also instructed the jury to disregard the comment. She refused to grant a mistrial though and the defendant complains. . . .

The relevance of this memorable evidence can be debated. The question itself was not improper. The objection really went to the last part of the witnesses answer. [REASONING: RULE] Many nonverbal actions of a defendant at the time of arrest are relevant and admissible. Tex. R. Crim. Pro. 104. If a defendant flees when the officer announces the arrest this evidence is admissible. Evidence of flight is admissible as a circumstance from which an inference of guilt may be drawn. Flight is not less relevant if it is only flight from custody or to avoid an arrest. Thus, if appellant here had fled out the window or run out the principal's door, that nonverbal act would have been admissible. If a defendant cries upon announcement of arrest is that not relevant under any circumstances? [REASONING: RULE (this is the central legal rule being applied in this case)] Rule 401 provides that "relevant evidence" means evidence having any tendency to make the existence of any fact that is of consequence to the determination of the action more probable or less probable than it would be without the evidence. Since almost any relevant evidence offered by one side is going to be prejudicial to the opposing party only unfair prejudice provides the basis for excluding evidence.

[REASONING: APPLICATION] In the instant case, Marles defecated when told that he was under arrest for sexual assault and he defecated at that very time and in response to the announcement of arrest if we are to believe the state's witness. Therefore, we cannot agree that there is no relevance.

On the other hand, defecation in one's pants upon arrest does not necessarily indicate guilt. Such an act could be evidence of the innocence of a man accused of a heinous crime he didn't do. It would be analogous to fainting upon being arrested for a crime. Granted, it could also be the act of a guilty person being found out. Or it could simply be the act of a man sick at his stomach. It is an act without clear meaning other than it happens in defiance of social custom.

In any event, the trial court sustained Marles' relevancy objection and instructed the jury to disregard. This instruction cured any possible error.

*[NOTE that the HOLDING in this case is directly implied rather than expressly stated: although the fact that Marles defecated in his pants may be slightly relevant, the error was slight in admitting the evidence, and the jury was instructed to disregard the fact, so the conviction is upheld.]*

[HOLDING (DISPOSITION)] We affirm the judgments of convictions.

*Model Case Brief of Marles v. Texas*

*Marles v. Texas* (Tex. 1996)

*Facts:* Defendant Marles was arrested for sexual assault. At the moment of his arrest, he defecated his pants. This fact came out during testimony at trial. The defense objected to the relevance of this fact, and moved for a mistrial. The judge denied the motion for mistrial but granted the relevancy objection and instructed the jury to disregard the fact. Marles was convicted, and now appeals the denial of mistrial.

*Issue*: Is the act of defecating in one's pants upon being informed of a criminal charge a relevant fact for the jury?

*Holding*: No, the act of defecating in one's pants upon being informed of a criminal charge has such slight relevance that the jury should not be told about it, but this error is not greatly prejudicial and can be cured by an instruction to disregard the fact.

*Reasoning (Rule):* "'Relevant evidence' means evidence having any tendency to make the existence of any fact that is of consequence to the determination of the action more probable or less probable than it would be without the evidence. Since almost any relevant evidence offered by one side is going to be prejudicial to the opposing party only unfair prejudice provides the basis for excluding evidence." Tex. R. Crim. Pro. 401

*Reasoning (Application):* The defendant's self-defecation has slight relevance, but is not necessarily any indication of guilt; it could simply have been caused by sickness or anxiety upon learning of the criminal charge. Despite his defecation being mostly irrelevant, the fact is only slightly prejudicial to Marles, and so does not warrant a new trial, especially since the trial judge instructed the jury to disregard the fact. The Defendant's conviction is upheld.

*England v. S & M Foods, Inc. and Garley (With Case Elements Labeled)*
511 So.2d 1313 (La. Ct. App. 1987)
Opinion by Justice Jones.

[FACTS (with appellate procedure)] The plaintiff, Betty England, instituted this action against defendants, S & M Foods, Inc. and Larry Garley, to recover damages for a battery which allegedly occurred in a work related argument. Defendants appeal the trial court judgment which awarded plaintiff $1,000.00 for humiliation and embarrassment as a result of the battery.

[HOLDING (disposition)] We affirm.

[FACTS] Plaintiff was employed by S & M Foods, Inc. at its Dairy Queen restaurant in Tallulah, Louisiana when the incident occurred. Larry Garley was the manager of this restaurant. Garley became upset when several hamburgers were incorrectly prepared resulting in them being returned by the customer who had ordered them. Garley allegedly expressed his dissatisfaction by using profane language and throwing a hamburger which hit plaintiff on the leg.

[ISSUE] The sole issue on appeal is whether the trial court erred in concluding a battery was committed.

[FACTS (arguments by the defendants)] Defendants contend no battery was committed because Garley did not intend to inflict bodily harm upon plaintiff. They argue Garley was disgusted about the returned hamburgers and he threw one hamburger toward a trash can and it inadvertently splattered on plaintiff. Defendants contend Garley did not intend to physically touch or injure plaintiff and her embarrassment was caused as much by her overreaction to the situation as by Garley's conduct.

[FACTS (arguments by the plaintiff)] Plaintiff contends a battery may consist of forcible touching in an angry, revengeful, rude or insolent manner and damages are recoverable for humiliation and mental distress. She asserts Garley admitted he may have struck her with the hamburger, he did not deny using profanity, he was looking at her when he threw the hamburger and several customers observed the incident. Plaintiff contends the incident caused her to cry and become emotionally upset. For these reasons, plaintiff contends the judgment should be affirmed.

[REASONING: RULE (legal rule of battery)] A battery is any intentional and unpermitted contact with the plaintiff's person or anything attached to it or practically identified with it. Prosser: Law of Torts, (4th Ed). In the area of intentional torts, intent means the defendant either desired to bring about the physical results of his act or believed they were substantially certain to follow from what he did. In order to recover for a battery, the plaintiff must prove by a preponderance of the evidence that his damages resulted from an unprovoked attack by the defendant. Mental distress and humiliation in connection with a battery are compensable items of damage.

[REASONING: RULE (procedural rule of appellate review)] The trial judge is in a better position to evaluate the credibility of witnesses and the weight of evidence than an appellate court which does not see or hear the witnesses. For this reason, a reviewing court should adopt the trial court's finding as its own in the absence of clear error, even if other conclusions from the same evidence are equally reasonable.

[FACTS (trial outcome)] The trial judge found that Garley committed a battery by throwing a hamburger which hit plaintiff on the leg. The trial judge further found the incident occurred in front of patrons and other employees of Dairy Queen and caused plaintiff humiliation and embarrassment.

[HOLDING] For the reasons which follow, we find no clear error in these findings of the trial judge.

[FACTS (plaintiff's testimony)] Plaintiff testified Garley used profane language when he told her to prepare the hamburgers correctly. She stated Garley, while looking straight at her, then threw the hamburger which hit her on the leg. Plaintiff testified she argued with Garley about the matter and several patrons observed the incident which caused her to cry and become emotionally upset.

[FACTS (defendant's testimony)] Garley testified he threw the hamburger toward a trash can because he was disgusted with the way the hamburgers were being prepared. He stated he did not see where the hamburger hit, but noticed some of it splattered on plaintiff and Alice Rash, another employee. Garley testified he did not intend to hit anyone with the hamburger. He stated he and plaintiff argued about the matter and he told the plaintiff to go home.

[FACTS (witness testimony)] Ms. Rash testified she did not see Garley throw the hamburger, but observed a hamburger hit the floor and it splattered mayonnaise and mustard on her and plaintiff.

[FACTS (witness testimony)] Two other employees who were working on the day of the incident heard Garley's complaints about the hamburgers going out wrong and saw a hamburger hit the floor, but did not see Garley throw it.

[REASONING: APPLICATION] The totality of the evidence provided a substantial basis for the trial judge to conclude Garley must have been substantially certain the hamburger would hit plaintiff or splatter on plaintiff when he threw it toward her after becoming disgusted over the manner in which the hamburgers were being prepared. His contact with plaintiff was, therefore, intentional and unpermitted and constituted a battery. The incident occurred in front of several patrons and other employees of Dairy Queen and caused plaintiff embarrassment and humiliation, although she suffered no physical injuries.

[HOLDING] The trial judge had the opportunity to see and hear the witnesses as they testified. The record shows no clear error in the trial judge's finding that a battery was committed.

[DISPOSITION] The judgment appealed is affirmed at defendants' costs.

*Model Case Brief of England v. S & M Foods, Inc. and Garley*

*Facts*: Defendant Garley, manager of a Dairy Queen owned by defendant S&M Foods, became angry at plaintiff employee England and threw a hamburger in her direction. The hamburger hit the floor and some of it splattered on England's leg. England sued for battery and won in the trial court. The defendants now appeal to the state appellate court.

*Issue*: Did the trial court err in concluding a battery was committed against the plaintiff?

*Holding*: No, the trial court did not err in concluding a battery was committed against the plaintiff.

*Reasoning (Rule):* "A battery is any intentional and unpermitted contact with the plaintiff's person or anything attached to it or practically identified with it. In the area of intentional torts, intent means the defendant either desired to bring about the physical results of his act or believed they were substantially certain to follow from what he did. In order to recover for a battery, the plaintiff must prove by a preponderance of the evidence that his damages resulted from an unprovoked attack by the defendant. Mental distress and humiliation in connection with a battery are compensable items of damage."

*Reasoning (Application):* The testimony of eyewitnesses confirmed that Garley angrily threw the hamburger in plaintiff's direction either intending to hit her or being substantially certain some of it would splatter and hit her. Also, even though no physical harm occurred, plaintiff was embarrassed and humiliated in front of other employees. The totality of the evidence thus supported plaintiff's claim as well as the trial court's ruling in her favor that a battery occurred.

---

*Questions for Review and Discussion:*

1. List and describe the main elements of most court cases.
2. When constructing a case brief, what facts should and should not be included?
3. When constructing a case brief, how should the issue and the holding be stated?
4. When constructing a case brief, how should the court's reasoning (both the rule and the application) be quoted versus summarized?
5. How does one spot/identify the key elements of a court case when reading a written court opinion?

---

*Suggested Readings*

*State v. Stagno*, 739 P.2d 198 (Alaska Crt. App. 1987) (driving an airboat on a highway while intoxicated)

*Pillars v. R.J. Reynolds Tobacco Co.*, 78 So. 365, 366 (Miss. 1918) (product liability: toe in tobacco)

*Christy Brothers Circus v. Turnage*, 144 S.E. 680 (Ga. Ct. App. 1928) (negligence: horse defecation)

*Seals v. Morris*, 410 So. 2d 715 (La. 1982) (negligence: snake car accident)

*State v. Bryant*, 101 So. 3d 429 (La. 2012) (burglary: lack of entry)

*Terry v. Lock*, 37 S.W.3d 202 (Ark. 2001) (mislaid property: found cash)

*Wright v. Newman*, 467 S.E.2d 533, (Ga. 1996) (promissory estoppel: child support)

*Marles v. Texas*, 919 S.W.2d 669 (Tex. Ct. App. 1996) (evidence relevance: self-defecation)

*England v. S & M Foods, Inc.*, 511 So.2d 1313 (La. Ct. App. 1987) (battery: thrown hamburger)
*Kirkham v. Will*, 724 N.E.2d 1062 (Ill. App. Ct. 2000) (negligence: reasonable dog)
*Bass v. Aetna Insurance*, 370 So. 2d 511 (La. 1979) (negligence: running in church)

---

*Advanced Readings*

Richard C. Wydick, *Plain English for Lawyers, 5th ed.*, Carolina Academic Press (2005)
Bryan A. Garner, *Black's Law Dictionary, 10th ed.*, Thomson West (2014)

CHAPTER 11

# ARGUMENT FROM PRECEDENT

---

*Chapter Objectives*
*After reading this chapter, you should be able to:*

- Explain how different types of precedents have different legal weight
- Explain how case precedents are treated differently in Louisiana
- Describe arguing from precedent and apply the concept to examples
- Identify and describe the difference between *ratio decidendi* and *obiter dicta*

---

As we saw in the previous chapter, court rulings—the outcome of court cases—are law, case law. Whether a court is creating new common law on its own, or interpreting a statute, constitution, treaty, or administrative regulation, the court's interpretation of that law becomes law, too.

## Common Law Precedents and the Courts

Any court case that has been decided is now called a *precedent* because that case outcome *precedes* all future cases. Lower courts must *follow* the *precedents* (past cases) set by higher courts—that is, lower courts must obey the decisions made by courts that exist above the lower court in the administrative hierarchy. Another way this is commonly worded is that these case precedents *control* the outcome of future court cases. Controlling precedent is also called *binding* precedent. For example, in 1973 the U.S. Supreme Court case *Roe v. Wade* ruled that the U.S. Constitution protects the right of a woman to terminate a pregnancy. As a result, in any later state or federal cases involving the question of abortion, state and federal judges have been legally required to follow the outcome of *Roe v. Wade* in their own rulings even if those judges were strongly opposed to abortion. As another example, in 2008 the Supreme Court case of *District of Columbia v. Heller* ruled that the U.S. Constitution protects a right of individuals to own a firearm. Since that case, all state and federal judges must follow that precedent in their rulings on questions of gun rights even if the judges are deeply opposed to the non-military ownership or use of guns. Although these are major high-profile cases, the principle of precedent applies regardless how controversial or mundane the legal issue is. In short, the legal authority of precedents helps constrain judges to follow the law rather than use their own personal opinions when ruling on cases.

Which courts must follow which precedents? Let's use the diagram below of a simple court structure to illustrate all this:

```
Supreme Court:                A
                            /   \
Appellate Courts:       B           C
                      /   \       /   \
Trial Courts:        D     E     F     G
```

According to this diagram, all decisions by trial courts D and E are heard by appellate court B; all decisions by trial courts F and G are head by appellate court C, and all decisions by appellate courts B and C are heard by supreme court A. As we saw in an earlier chapter describing the U.S. court system, this is a standard type of organization for both state and federal court systems in the United States although the number of courts at each level varies depending on the system.

Given this type of hierarchical court organization, all precedents by court A are controlling on all the other courts in this judicial system. That is, courts B, C, D, E, F, and G all must follow the decisions by court A. Courts B and C, however, need not follow each other's decisions because neither is hierarchically above the other in the chain of judicial authority. Neither must courts D, E, F, or G follow each other's decisions. Courts D and E must follow the precedents from court B but not necessarily from court C. Even though court C is a higher-level court, it is not *directly* above courts D and E in the hierarchical chain. Court C's decisions are not binding on courts D and E. In law, court cases that are not binding/controlling on a court are called *persuasive* precedent. In other words, all precedents are either controlling or persuasive. Non-binding precedents are called *persuasive* on the theory that all judges are experienced legal experts and so their opinions should be entitled to at least some respectful consideration.

Put in more straightforward terms, if a precedent came from a court that is not directly above the current court in the judicial hierarchy, then the current court need *not* follow that precedent; it may choose to either follow it or ignore it. Precedent that a court need not follow is variously called *persuasive, noncontrolling*, or *nonbinding* precedent. These terms are used interchangeably. Again, the term "persuasive" simply means that the legal argument contained in the precedent is somewhat influential merely by the fact that a court has formally adopted those arguments. Yet, the lower court is not required to agree with those arguments, and might find competing and contrary arguments *more* persuasive.

For example, even if all the state supreme courts in the United States other than the Illinois Supreme Court have ruled one way on an issue, none of those precedents is controlling on any Illinois court. Thus, if they choose to do so, all Illinois courts are free to ignore the decisions of other state courts, even neighboring states like Wisconsin, Indiana, and Missouri. Illinois Courts may instead rule for the opposite outcome on the same legal questions. Illinois courts are free to voluntarily follow those decisions of other states if they so choose, but Illinois courts are equally free to rule opposite to the persuasive authority from other states. The same principles apply across all state courts in the United States.

Similarly, and as another example, all federal District Courts in Alaska, Arizona, California, Hawaii, Idaho, Montana, Nevada, Oregon, and Washington must follow the decisions of the federal Ninth Circuit Court of Appeals, based in San Francisco. All federal District and Circuit courts outside the Ninth Circuit, however, are free to either follow or disregard precedents from the Ninth Circuit. The same concept is true across all the U.S. Circuits. If the Supreme Court rules on an issue of federal law, however, then all courts in the U.S.—both state and federal courts—must follow the Supreme Court's decision as controlling precedent.

*Stare Decisis* What about precedents that come from the *same* court? A court can ignore its *own* precedents in limited situations. As part of the common law tradition, all U.S. courts other than courts in Louisiana follow the principle of *stare decisis*. This is the doctrine that a court should follow its *own* prior cases as law whenever possible, but it can *overrule* those prior cases in exceptional cases. *Overruling* is also called *overturning*. Overruling a precedent might occur, for example, if the majority of a court believes the prior decision (the precedent) was very mistaken, or the precedent has caused significant legal problems with interpretation, implementation, or enforcement. The U.S. Supreme Court has many times explained that it follows the principle of *stare decisis*, yet at the same time, the Court has decided to overrule many of its precedents. One of the most famous, if not the most famous, instances of the Supreme Court overruling one of its own precedents was the 1956 case *Brown v. Board of Education*. In that case, the Court overruled *Plessy v. Ferguson*, one of its own rulings decided in 1896. *Plessy v. Ferguson* had ruled that racial segregation was constitutionally permissible, but over a half century later *Brown v. Board of Education* ruled that racial segregation violated the Equal Protection Clause of the Fourteenth Amendment to the U.S. Constitution.

In the U.S., the only jurisdictional exception to *stare decisis* is the state of Louisiana. As a hybrid civil law/common law jurisdiction, Louisiana does not follow the principle of *stare decisis*. Instead, it applies a somewhat similar principle that goes by the name *jurisprudence constante*, French for "constant (i.e. stable) jurisprudence." Under the common law principle of *stare decisis*, even a single case must be given deference. Under the French civil law concept of *jurisprudence constante*, however, a *series* of consistent court rulings by a court can result in that same court owing those cases some measure of deference. Imagine, for example, that the Louisiana Supreme Court applies Louisiana law a certain way in one of its cases and then consistently follows that particular legal interpretation in a series of Louisiana Supreme Court cases over a decade or more—perhaps even several decades. If yet another case involving the same legal issue comes before the Louisiana Supreme Court, although the court is not required to follow its own precedents, the court will give that chain of cases a significant measure of deference under the principle of *jurisprudence constante*. Only if the court is strongly convinced that the series of cases was initially wrong or has become problematic will the court overrule those cases.

## Argument from Precedent

We just saw how courts must follow controlling precedents. Even if a court is lower in the judicial hierarchy, however, a lower court is free to ignore a controlling precedent that comes from a court higher in the judicial hierarchy if that otherwise controlling precedent is somehow different in an important way. Then, the lower court *distinguishes* the controlling precedent by showing how the facts in the current case are somehow different from the facts in the controlling precedent. If the facts are so different, then the lower court need not follow that otherwise controlling precedent.

For example, assume in a case in Court A, facts a + b lead to outcome d. Case 1 has now become Precedent 1:

Court A: Precedent 1: facts a + b → outcome d

Now let's say that lower court B is faced with deciding the outcome of a new case that has facts a, b, and also c. Since fact c did not occur in Precedent 1, lower court B might be able to distinguish the case from

Precedent 1 based on the important additional fact c. The lower court is then free to reach outcome e instead, creating a new precedent:

Court B: Precedent 2: facts a + b + c → outcome e

Courts frequently distinguish both controlling precedents and persuasive precedents. Indeed, at least 99.99% of case law discusses prior case law precedents. In other words, regardless of the underlying law at issue—a constitution, a statute, a regulation, or so on—the court interpreting that law will *also* look to case law for guidance.

Let's look in more detail at how precedents are analogized or distinguished in this way. Recall from the chapter on the basic skill of legal reasoning that the essence of legal reasoning is the application of an abstract rule/definition/principle to a concrete example:

*Major Premise:* Abstract legal rule: ABC
*Minor Premise:* Concrete example: XYZ
*Conclusion:* Outcome: for the plaintiff or defendant

We can now take this type of reasoning one step further. So far we have only looked at the application of a legal principle to a single factual example. Yet this is almost never how the law works. Each law will eventually be applied numerous times to widely different factual situations. If the law is "ABC" then over time that legal principle will be applied to many different set of facts, not just XYZ. For example, the rule "ABC" might be applied to each of the following set of facts separately, each in a different case: X, Y, Z, XY, XZ, YZ, QRS, TUV, WXYZ, QRSX, QRSY, QRSZ, QRSXY, QRSZYZ, and so on. In the real world, given a nearly infinite number of possible different facts, the number of *combinations* of facts that might exist in any individual case approaches infinity. Each time the principle ABC is applied to a particular set of facts in an individual case, that case has now become precedent. That precedent has legal weight going forward into the future. Thus, in a case with a new set of facts such as JKL, the problem is not merely how the principle ABC applies to JKL, but how does ABC apply to JKL given all the precedents (prior cases) that have interpreted how ABC applies to *other* various combinations of facts. This particular type of analysis is often called *arguing from precedent.* Some writers might also use the terms arguing by analogy, argument from analogy, reasoning by analogy, reasoning from precedent, or some similar term. Regardless of the specific term used, they are all referring to the same concept.

A law needs to be applied only once by a court for a precedent to now exist in the interpretation of that law. Every subsequent case applying that law will then have one or more precedents to look back to for guidance. If a unique set of facts appears before a court for the first time, the case is said to be a *case of first impression.* Even then, however, courts will seek guidance from precedents with the closest approximate situations. As a result, almost all if not all legal arguments can and typically will use some degree of argument from precedent. That is, legal argumentation in a legal memo, legal brief, or orally in court almost always involves the use of case precedents as legal authority. You as a lawyer want to argue that your case is just like case precedents that seem to support your position, but that your case is different from case precedents that seem to go against your position. In other words, you want to analogize to case precedents that support you by showing how those precedents are similar to the current case you're arguing. Equally important, you want to distinguish the case precedents that don't support your position by showing how those precedents are different from the current case you are arguing.

Lawyers *analogize* to past case law (that is, precedents) similar to the current case. The current case is also called the present case, instant case, case at hand, or some other similar term. Lawyers and judges might also simply say "here" in reference to the current case and "there" in reference to the precedent. In analogizing the current case to a case precedent, one simply argues that the same rule applies given the issue involved, and that the facts in the current case are so similar to the facts in the precedent, that the same outcome as the precedent should be followed in the present case. In this situation, the current case and the precedent are *analogous* cases. Thus, the same or very similar legal conclusion (holding/judgment) should occur in the present case. Sometimes courts call these similar cases "apposite" (*not* opposite); and cases that are dissimilar are thus labelled "inapposite."

On the other hand, lawyers will want to *distinguish* any prior case precedent that seems arguably similar but which has an outcome that goes against the lawyer's own desired outcome in the case at hand. In distinguishing a case precedent, one simply points out how the facts in the precedent are *distinguishable* from the facts in the present case. It is correct legal terminology to say either that "the facts are distinguishable" or "the cases are distinguishable." Regardless of the exact phrase used, a lawyer will argue that the outcome in the present case should be—or at least can be or might be—different than the result (holding/judgment) of the precedent.

Analogizing and distinguishing precedents requires clever and creative critical thinking. Analogizing cases that look different on the surface requires emphasizing the similarities and de-emphasizing, minimizing, or trivializing the differences. Distinguishing cases that look similar on the surface, on the other hand, requires just the opposite: emphasizing the differences, and de-emphasizing, minimizing, or trivializing the similarities. In advanced legal argument, one might even try to argue that the court should create a new exception to the legal rule because the facts are so substantially different that an unjust outcome would be the result if a new exception to the rule were not created.

Sometimes a court lower in the judicial hierarchy might wish to ignore what otherwise looks like controlling precedent from a court higher in the judicial hierarchy. If that otherwise controlling precedent is somehow different in an important way, the lower court can *distinguish* the controlling precedent by showing how the facts in the current case are different from the facts in the controlling precedent. If the facts are different in an important way, then the lower court has leeway to not follow that otherwise controlling precedent.

For example, assume in Case 1 from the U.S. Supreme Court, the facts a + b lead to outcome d. Case 1 has become this precedent:

> U.S. Supreme Court: Precedent 1: facts a + b = outcome for plaintiff.

Now let's say that a lower federal District Court is faced with deciding the outcome of a new case that has facts a, b, and also c. Since fact c did not occur in Precedent 1, a lawyer for the defense might be able to convince the District Court that the current case is distinguishable from Precedent 1 based on the important additional fact c. The lower District Court is then free not to follow Precedent 1, even though all precedents from the U.S. Supreme Court are controlling on all U.S. courts. To reach a judgment in favor of the defense instead, the lower court distinguishes Precedent 1 and then creates a new precedent:

> District Court: Precedent 2: facts a + b + c = outcome for the defense.

As you can see, the ability to distinguish cases gives a great deal of flexibility to lawyers and judges to choose to either follow or distinguish a precedent.

In short, legal reasoning based on the application of a prior case precedent to a current case involves two basic situations:

First, Take the prior case precedent and the current case, and explain how they are similar. In other words, analogize how the current case is similar to the precedent. If the current case is similar to the precedent, then the precedent is controlling precedent, and it must be followed.

Second, Take the prior case precedent and the current case, and explain how they are different. In other words, distinguish the current case from the precedent. If the current case is different than the precedent, then the precedent is inapplicable, and it need not be followed even if the case is otherwise controlling precedent due to the judicial hierarchy of the court that issued the case.

Let's assume there are two precedents involving the same legal issue, and thus both apply the legal rule QQQ. The two precedents have the facts and outcomes as shown:

| Precedent | Facts: | Judgment: |
|---|---|---|
| Precedent 1 | ABC | plaintiff |
| Precedent 2 | DEF | defendant |

Let's consider the likely effect these two precedents would have on the outcome of several possible new cases, all which involve the same issue and hence the same legal rule QQQ.

| New case | Facts | Judgment |
|---|---|---|
| New case 1: | ABCG | plaintiff (controlling precedent favors plaintiff) |
| New case 2: | DEFG | defendant (controlling precedent favors defendant) |
| New case 3: | ACDF | ? (depends whether AC or DF are more critical facts) |
| New case 4: | JK | ? (depends whether ABC or DEF is more similar) |
| New case 5: | ABLM | plaintiff, unless defense lawyer can show that LM is more like DEF *and* that LM is more important than AB. |
| New case 6: | DFNP | defendant, unless plaintiff lawyer can show that NP is more like ABC *and* that NP is more important than DF. |

The question in any case is whether the current case is "more similar" or "more different" to the relevant case precedents. The lawyers will obviously disagree, and this is why lawyers are needed to argue for the two different possible outcomes. Just as the lawyers in a case will disagree, so too can the judges on a panel of an appellate court. For example, the majority opinion might believe a precedent is distinguishable and decide against it. The dissent, however, looking at the same precedent, might believe the precedent is nearly identical and must be followed. If a lawyer or judge distinguishes a precedent that looks similar, an opposing lawyer or other judge often ridicules the alleged distinction as "a distinction without a difference."

This kind of argument from precedent is really just a particular type of reasoning using deductive syllogisms, including polysyllogisms. Take a look at a couple simple examples of the logical flow in argument from precedent. In the first legal reasoning polysyllogism example below, the prior precedent is followed:

*Major Premise*: Case 1 has key facts ABC and Case 2 has key facts ABD.

*Minor Premise:* The key facts in Case 2 are more similar to, than different from, the key facts in Case 1.

*Conclusion:* The outcome in case 2 should be the same as the outcome in case 1.

*Major Premise:* The outcome in Case 2 should be the same as the outcome in Case 1.

*Minor Premise:* The outcome in Case 1 was a ruling in favor of the plaintiff.

*Conclusion*: The outcome in Case 2 should be a ruling in favor of the plaintiff.

Now, in this second legal reasoning polysyllogism example below, the prior precedent is distinguished and so is not followed:

*Major Premise:* Case 1 has key facts ABC and Case 3 has key facts CDE.

*Minor Premise:* The key facts in Case 3 are more different from, than similar to, the key facts in Case 1.

*Conclusion:* The outcome in Case 3 should be different from the outcome in Case 1.

*Major Premise:* The outcome in Case 3 should be different from the outcome in Case 1.

*Minor Premise:* The outcome in Case 1 was a ruling in favor of the plaintiff.

*Conclusion*: The outcome in Case 2 should be a ruling in favor of the defendant.

## Argument from Precedent: Motor Vehicle Cases

Let's look at some real-world examples of argument from analogy based on cases from the U.S. Supreme Court. The Fourth Amendment to the Constitution declares:

> The right of the people to be secure in their persons, houses, papers, and effects, against unreasonable searches and seizures. and no warrants shall issue, but upon probable cause, supported by oath or affirmation, and particularly describing the place to be searched, and the persons or things to be seized.[1]

The Fourth Amendment ordinarily requires a judge to issue a warrant before police can search a residence or other owned items, with exceptions. In the 1925 Supreme Court case of *Carroll v. United States*,[2] the Court created the "automobile exception" to the Fourth Amendment's warrant requirement. In *Carroll*, the Court announced that because cars are easily movable compared to homes or businesses, and because society has a lower expectation of privacy in cars compared to homes, no warrant is needed to search or seize cars. As the Court said, "It is not practicable to secure a warrant because the vehicle can be quickly moved out of the locality or jurisdiction in which the warrant must be sought."[3]

Decades later in *California v. Carney* in 1985,[4] the U.S. Supreme Court was faced with the question whether a warrant was needed for police to search a motor home. Carney was inside his motor home in a parking lot in San Diego, California. Police suspected Carney of paying for sex with drugs and searched Carney's mobile home without a warrant. The police found marijuana and Carney was charged with possession of marijuana. Carney moved to suppress the evidence on the ground that the police lacked a search warrant for his residence as required by the Fourth Amendment to the U.S. Constitution. The California Supreme Court ruled that Carney's vehicle fell within the automobile exception to the requirement for a search warrant, and Carney appealed to the U.S. Supreme Court.

The Supreme Court had to consider whether Carney's "motor home" was more like an automobile or more like a residence. The Court analogized the characteristics of Carney's mobile home to the characteristics of an automobile:

> While it is true that respondent's vehicle possessed some, if not many of the attributes of a home, it is equally clear that the vehicle falls clearly within the scope of the exception laid down in *Carroll* and applied in succeeding cases. Like the automobile in *Carroll* respondent's motor home was readily mobile. Absent the

1. U.S. Constitution, Fourth Amendment
2. *Carroll v. United States*, 267 U.S. 132 (1925)
3. *Id.* at 153
4. *California v. Carney*, 471 U.S. 386 (1985)

> prompt search and seizure, it could readily have been moved beyond the reach of the police. Furthermore, the vehicle was licensed to "operate on public streets; [was] serviced in public places; . . . and [was] subject to extensive regulation and inspection." And the vehicle was so situated that an objective observer would conclude that it was being used not as a residence, but as a vehicle.[5]

As a result of this reasoning analogizing Carney's motor home to other types of automobiles, the Court upheld the warrantless police search of Carney's motor home.

The Court was careful to note, however, that they were not declaring all motor homes to be automobiles, but merely Carney's particular motor home. The Court expressly left open the possibility that in future cases some "motor homes" could be deemed to be a fixed residence rather than an automobile, thereby requiring a warrant to be searched. The Court specifically listed some of the facts that should be considered on a case-by-case basis as to whether any particular "motor home" is more like an automobile or more like a residence:

> We need not pass on the application of the vehicle exception to a motor home that is situated in a way or place that objectively indicates that it is being used as a residence. Among the factors that might be relevant in determining whether a warrant would be required in such a circumstance is its location, whether the vehicle is readily mobile or instead, for instance, elevated on blocks, whether the vehicle is licensed, whether it is connected to utilities, and whether it has convenient access to a public road.[6]

Another way to look at this passage is that the court provided lawyers and judges with guidance as to how future similar cases might be distinguished from the precedent set by *Carney*.

*Carney* is a straightforward example of the U.S. Supreme Court applying argument from precedent. The motor vehicle definition and example in *Carney* was then in turn later applied to a houseboat by the Tenth Circuit Court of Appeals. In *U.S. v. Hill*,[7] police searched a houseboat owned by Hill while it was on Lake Texoma in Oklahoma. They found him on the boat along with an amphetamine laboratory and so arrested and charged him with drug offenses. Hill asked the court to declare his arrest invalid and the evidence inadmissible on the ground

5. *Id.* At 393 (quoting *Rakas v. Illinois*, 439 U.S. 128, 154, n. 2 (1978) (Powell, J., concurring)
6. Id. At 394, footnote 3.
7. *U.S. v. Hill*, 855 F.2d 664 (10th Cir. 1988)

that the police should have obtained a warrant because Hill's houseboat was a residence. The Tenth Circuit looked to *Carney* as precedent and analogized the facts of the two cases:

> Although *Carney* involved a motor home and we deal here with a houseboat, the two vehicles are similar. Both are of the "hybrid character" that place them "at the crossroads between the privacy interests that generally forbid warrantless invasions of the home and the law enforcement interests that support the exception for warrantless searches of automobiles based on probable cause." Both a houseboat and a motor home are readily capable of functioning as both vehicle and home. The Supreme Court has considered the tension created by this dual nature, and we are bound by its determination. We hold that *Carney* controls the disposition of this case.[8]

The Tenth Circuit in *Hill* believed that because a houseboat was analogous to a motor home, the motor vehicle rule from *Carney* should apply. Accordingly, the court then applied the rule from *Carney*:

> The houseboat here was obviously readily mobile and therefore satisfies the first *Carney* requirement. Indeed, the officers had observed it traveling up and down the lake during much of the night. Furthermore, Lake Texoma is a large lake, and the boat's occupants could have easily eluded the officers. The second *Carney* requirement is also satisfied. Given the Supreme Court's determination in *Carney*, we cannot say that the boat in this case was present in a setting that objectively indicated it was being used as a residence. We are persuaded that an objective observer would conclude that a moving boat navigating the waters of a large lake on a cold winter night was not being used as a residence. We therefore hold that the houseboat falls within the vehicle exception.[9]

A decade later, in *U.S. v. Albers* in 1998,[10] the Ninth Circuit Court of Appeals looked to both *Carney* and *Hill* as precedents. In this case, Albers was staying on a houseboat on Lake Powell, Arizona, part of Glen Canyon National Recreation Area. National Park Service rangers suspected Albers of parachuting off the top of cliffs within the park, a violation of the park rules. The rangers searched Albers' houseboat without a warrant and found parachutes, helmets, and other related equipment,

8. Id. At 668
9. Id.
10. *U.S. v. Albers*, 136 F.3d 670 (9th Circuit 1998)

along with film of his actions. Albers was charged in federal District Court with violating federal regulations, but Albers moved that the evidence be suppressed. Albers argued that the houseboat was a residence, not a vehicle, and so a warrant had been needed. The federal District Court agreed with Albers and so granted his motion to suppress the evidence. The U.S. government then appealed the ruling on the motion to the Ninth Circuit Court of Appeals. The Ninth Circuit turned to *Carney* as controlling precedent and *Hill* as persuasive precedent:

> Whether Albers' houseboat falls within the vehicle exception depends on whether, for purposes of *Carney*, houseboats are the same as motor homes. This is a question of first impression in our circuit but one the Tenth Circuit has resolved without much difficulty. See *U.S. v. Hill* (10th Cir. 1988). In *Hill*, defendants sought to suppress evidence obtained during the warrantless search of their houseboat. Noting that no case dealt with houseboat searches, *Hill* looked to cases involving motor vehicle searches, focusing particularly on *Carney*. Because houseboats, like motor homes, are readily capable of functioning as both vehicles and homes, and the Supreme Court considered and resolved the tension created by this dual nature, *Hill* concluded that *Carney* controls. We agree with the Tenth Circuit and hold that the vehicle exception applies to houseboats so long as *Carney*'s requirements are met.[11]

Notice the precise language the Ninth Circuit used: the court did not "follow" *Hill*, but instead "agreed with" *Hill*. Recall from earlier in this chapter that controlling precedent must be followed, but courts are free to either agree or disagree with precedent that is merely persuasive. Because the Ninth and Tenth Circuits are parallel to each other in the federal judicial hierarchy, neither court is required to follow each other's rulings. Instead, U.S. Circuit Courts of Appeal precedents are merely persuasive on other U.S. Circuit Courts of Appeal. This means U.S. Circuit Courts may choose to either agree or disagree with rulings from other federal circuits. All U.S. Circuit Courts of Appeal, however, are below the U.S. Supreme Court in the federal judicial hierarchy so they all must follow U.S. Supreme Court rulings such as *Carney*. This is why the Ninth Circuit in *Albers* said it chose to "agree with" *Hill* but it necessarily had to "follow" *Carney*. Accordingly, the Ninth Circuit applied the definitional rule of "motor vehicle" that the Supreme Court announced in *Carney*, and the Ninth Circuit's reasoning in applying that rule matched the reasoning of the court in *Hill*:

11. Id. at 673 (most citations omitted)

> *Carney* first asks whether the vehicle was "obviously readily mobile by the turn of an ignition key, if not actually moving." Albers' houseboat was found in open public waters, obviously mobile. *Carney* also asks whether there was "a reduced expectation of privacy stemming from its use as a licensed motor vehicle subject to a range of police regulation inapplicable to a fixed dwelling[.]" Albers had such a reduced expectation of privacy because at any time an authorized person could have stopped and boarded his boat "to determine compliance with regulations pertaining to safety equipment and operation." Indeed, the government's traditional power to board a vessel is far greater than its power to enter a motor home or a car. Finally, *Carney* asks whether "the vehicle was so situated that an objective observer would conclude that it was being used not as a residence, but as a vehicle." We recognize that in many situations it will be objectively apparent that a houseboat is being used as a home and not a vehicle. . . . [S]ince Albers had moved his houseboat to open waters on a large lake, an objective observer would conclude that he was using the houseboat as a vehicle. *Carney*'s requirements were satisfied and Albers' houseboat could be searched without a warrant.[12]

Both the cases, *U.S. v. Hill* and *U.S. v. Albers*, show how the analytic techniques of legal syllogisms and argument from precedent commonly work together. Indeed, as we saw in the previous section of this chapter, the way argument from precedent works is by comparing how rule "X" should apply to facts DEF given the prior way rule "X" was applied to facts ABC, depending on how similar or different facts DEF are to facts ABC. In short, legal syllogisms are used in arguing that facts DEF are either similar to or different than facts ABC.

## Argument from Precedent: "Chair"

Now that we looked at an example of argument from precedent using some actual court cases, let's turn to some practice exercises. In a previous chapter we saw what happens when we use deductive legal reasoning to apply an abstract definition to a concrete factual situation. Argument from precedent is almost always tied to the application of a particular legal rule. For learning purposes here, however, let's try to isolate argument from precedent apart from deductive legal reasoning. For this learning exercise, let's assume there are no legal or dictionary definitions, so judges must apply mostly reasoning from precedent as opposed

12. Id at 673 (citations omitted)

to deductive legal reasoning. Indeed, hundreds of years ago before statutory codes or literacy became widespread, the English common law arose from judges deciding cases based purely on the factual similarities or differences between each current case and prior case precedents.

Assume for the sake of this exercise that there is *no* definition or legal rule as to what comprises a "chair." There is, however, a single prior precedent involving whether an object is a "chair." This precedent therefore is the leading and only precedent on whether an object can be called a "chair." This case occurred as follows:

> *Simpson v. Burns* Lisa Simpson wanted a chair for her bedroom desk. She went on the Internet and found a cheap five dollar "chair" for sale by Montgomery Burns, but there was no picture attached to the advertisement. Lisa decided to purchase the "chair." When the object arrived, it was entirely made of wood with a couple foam pads as follows. The object had four straight legs, each 2 inches wide by 18 inches high. The legs were attached to the bottom of the four corners of a flat square area with one inch of foam padding affixed to the top of the square. On one side of the flat square a piece of wood 24 inches high was attached along the edge of the square and extended upward. One inch of foam padding was affixed to the upright board facing towards the flat square area. Wendy tried to return the object because it did not have wheels that allowed the object to roll around the room while being sat upon. Montgomery refused to give a refund. Lisa then sued Montgomery. The case made it all the way to the Supreme Court of the State of Swansonia. There, the Court ruled the object was a "chair," and so Lisa was not entitled to a refund.

Now imagine the following cases come before an intermediate appellate court within the state of Swansonia after *Simpson v. Burns.* The prior precedent of *Simpson v. Burns* is otherwise controlling authority on all courts in the state of Swansonia since it came from the state high court. However, a lower court need not follow *Simpson v. Burns* if the case facts are distinguishable. Therefore, the lawyers on both sides of each of the following cases will each argue whether the facts of *Simpson v. Burns* are more similar to or more different from, the case under consideration.

> *Testaburger v. Cartman* Wendy Testaburger needed a chair for her living room. She went on the Internet and found a cheap five dollar "chair" for sale by Eric Cartman, but there was no picture attached to the advertisement. Wendy decided to purchase the "chair." When the object arrived, it was a highly stylized modern art

sculpture comprised of a 45-degree angled five-foot-wide wavy seat, with a single, conical helix leg, 6 arms that curved outwards and upwards in a radiating fan shape, and a 10-foot high curved back that twisted into a partial spiral. Wendy tried to return the chair but Eric refused to give a refund. Wendy then sued Eric.

*Question*: How would the attorneys for Wendy and Eric each try to analogize or distinguish the object in question in *Testaburger v. Cartman* to the object that was ruled a "chair" in *Simpson v. Burns*? Keep in mind as you construct the possible arguments from precedent that Eric would want the same outcome as in *Testaburger v. Cartman.* That is, if the object Eric sold is also a "chair," then his lawsuit also will receive the same outcome in *Simpson v. Burns*: the defendant (Eric) would win the case. Wendy, on the other hand, would try to argue that the object at issue in her case was *not* like the object that was ruled a chair in *Simpson v. Burns.* If her argument was convincing, then the court in *Testaburger v. Cartman* need not follow the ruling and outcome in *Simpson v. Burns.* In other words, by distinguishing the facts in her case from the facts of *Simpson v. Burns,* Wendy can get the court to rule in the opposite direction from *Simpson.* If so, then the plaintiff (Wendy) would win.

Now let's assume that the following case comes up for decision in a different district of the Swansonia appellate court at the same time as *Testaburger v. Cartman.* This means the only precedent available to the current court as legal authority is the Swansonia Supreme Court case of *Simpson v. Burns.*

> *Johnson v. LePetomane* Gabby Johnson needed a chair for her office. She went on the Internet and found a cheap five dollar "chair" for sale by Bill LePetomane, but there was no picture attached to the advertisement. Gabby decided to purchase the "chair." When the object arrived, it was a three-foot round spherical ball labeled "Gel Floor Chair." The exterior shell was made of soft, smooth, polished pliable leather. This outer shell encased a thin rubber liner. The rubber liner was in turn filled with a thick, squishy silicon gel allowing the ball's shape to be highly manipulated. Gabby tried to return the chair but Bill refused to give a refund. Gabby then sued Bill.

*Question*: How would the attorneys for Gabby and Bill each try to analogize or distinguish the object in question in *Johnson v. LePetomane* to the object that was ruled a "chair" in *Simpson v. Burns*? Again, the defendant Bill would try to argue that the object he sold is similar to the object in *Simpson v. Burns.* If so, then the outcome of *Simpson v. Burns* should be followed, and Bill would win. The plaintiff Gabby, however, would try to argue that the object Bill sold is different than the object sold in *Simpson v. Burns.* If so, then the outcome should be different as well, meaning the plaintiff (Gabby) should win.

## Argument from Precedent: "Bokmurfle"

Recall from the chapter on legal reasoning that one example we used was an imaginary case involving contact between the people of Earth and aliens from the planet Zagor. The aliens demanded they be given the intergalactic symbol of peace, a "bokmurfle," and failure to do so would be an act of war. To prevent the Earth's destruction, you had to come up with an object that met the definition of "bokmurfle" given to you by the aliens. For the exercise here, however, let's assume that the aliens did not give you a definition, but merely gave you an example of a bokmurfle.

Imagine the aliens from Zagor look through the stores and shopping malls of Earth, and find a lava lamp. You have probably seen these before: two layers of a thick liquid are a contained in a glass cone. At the bottom of the cone the liquid is brightly-colored neon red, yellow, orange, green, or purple. The liquid at the top of the cone is clear. The base of the glass cone contains a light bulb that shines up into the liquid. When the lamp is plugged into an electrical outlet, the bulb grows hot. The colored liquid begins to rise into the clear liquid in pieces, forming spheres and blobs as it does so. Once the colored blobs get to the top of the clear liquid, however, they cool and slowly begin to sink to the bottom of the cone. There they heat up again creating an endless slow-motion up-and-down pattern of shifting blobs of colored liquid moving through the clear liquid. The aliens from Zagor plug in an 18-inch-tall lava lamp and wait for a few minutes until bright red blobs to start moving around in it. The aliens then point at the now-flowing lava lamp and tell you "*This* is definitely a bokmurfle. Now bring us something that matches the key characteristics of this object or your failure to do so will be an act of war. You have five minutes before we destroy your planet Earth due to your grave offense!"

You quickly look through your house and from among the objects you own you pick what you think are the best possible contenders:

1. An 8-inch long, 3-inch diameter hand-held children's toy made of lightweight plastic and cardboard with a single half-inch eyehole to view into the center of the tube as the opposite transparent end is pointed toward a light source. This allows the viewer to see the internal random symmetrical designs created by turning the tube, thereby causing several

small and loose multi-colored transparent items within the tube to jumble together while allowing light to pass through the, all while also reflected on mirrors inside the tube.

2. A 3-by-3-by-3 inch multicolored plastic cube-shaped twisty puzzle that allows a person to use manual physical manipulation to either scramble the colors or place a solid color on each side of the cube.

3. A set of yellow, blue, green, red, white, and black 4-inch long by 1/2-by-1/2 rectangular sticks of soft modeling clay capable of being easily molded by hand.

4. A set of six 3-foot long shiny silver-colored metal tubes all loosely hanging by one end from a circular base that itself is then hung from a metal outdoor bracket on the side of house, thereby creating deeply-resonating wind chimes when a breeze blows.

5. A 20-foot long single string of 40 small blue-colored Christmas tree lights that when plugged into an electrical socket, can be switched to either be always on, or placed in a constant mode of regular blinking or a pattern of blinking.

6. A one-foot-diameter many-faceted mirrored sphere that hangs from the ceiling and slowly twists from the natural air movement in the room and which reflects light at numerous different angles as it turns.

7. A battery-powered mobile with small multi-colored smiling animal faces hanging from it that gently spins and has blinking lights with soft bell-like music playing, and is designed to hang over a baby crib.

8. A three-inch-diameter, three-inch-tall, rainbow-colored plastic spring that can be manipulated by hand and that can "walk down stairs" on its own if given initial energy by lifting the top part of it up while it is resting on a stair and then pushing that upper part of the spring down onto the next-lower stair step.

9. A rocket that is launched from the ground by igniting it, causing it to shoot up a hundred or more feet in the air, where it then explodes in a bright multi-colored pattern.

Remember that in this exercise the aliens haven't given you a definition of a bokmurfle, they've only shown you an object (a lava lamp) as a model sample of a bokmurfle. Now, with each of the examples listed above, imagine you pick that item and offer it to the Zagorians as a bokmurlfe, yet the aliens reject it. You then get a chance in the Intergalactic High Court to argue why the key characteristics of the object you selected are more similar to the key characteristics of the lava lamp than different from them. What would you argue? How would the Zagorians argue that the key characteristics of the object you selected are more different from the key characteristics of a lava lamp than similar to them? Then, in each case, acting as a neutral judge in the case, who is more correct, and why?

This exercise can be expanded by imagining the Zagorians now give you some examples of what *are* bokmurfles along with several examples of what are *not* bokmurfles. Suppose the Zagorians give you the following list:

> Bokmurfles: lava lamp, kaleidoscope, disco ball, strobe light, fireworks
>
> Not bokmurfles: a paper bag filled with air, a pot of soil, a cup of water, a mouse, a blade of grass.

Using argument from precedent, which of the following items are or are not bokmurfles based on the list of precedents you were just given? Try arguing against a partner who takes the opposite position.

1. a candle in a glass jar
2. a flashlight
3. The tail of a Peacock
4. a brightly lit outdoor artistic water fountain
5. a Maple tree in Autumn that has yellow, orange, red, and brown leaves while all the leaves are quivering from the wind
6. a large outdoor brightly-colored hot-air balloon floating across a blue sky
7. a cluster of large Amethyst quartz crystals
8. a stained-glass window decoration

9. a rainbow

10. Niagara Falls lit up at night

## Argument from Precedent: "No Vehicles in the Park" Cases

In real life, only in rare situations will there be merely a single case precedent that exists discussing a legal issue. Usually there will be numerous relevant legal precedents. We'll expand on this point in an entire later chapter. For now, though, let's expand from arguing from one precedent to two precedents.

Here is a hypothetical example of argument from precedent that is directly based on an imaginary example discussed by two of the leading legal philosophers of the 20th century, H.L.A. Hart and Lon Fuller. Imagine a city ordinance that states "No vehicles in the park." The law itself does not state the policy behind the law, nor did the city council issue any written or spoken statements explaining the policy. What, then, is the unstated policy that law was intended to achieve? Promoting the safety of park users? Preventing damage to the lawn? Avoiding noise in the park? Keeping up the aesthetics of the park? Preventing vehicles from blocking pedestrian access? Some of these? All of these? None of these, but something else? A court's interpretation of the meaning of that law might differ depending on how the court views the purpose(s) of the law. Hart and Fuller imagine a war memorial comprised of an actual army tank that is driven into place and then parked permanently. Does locating this war memorial in the park violate the ordinance?

Hart and Fuller's discussion looks only at the legal reasoning of applying the ordinance to a single factual example—a parked army tank serving as a war monument and memorial. But let's expand on their example. Instead of a single army tank case, let's imagine instead the following two precedents are the only cases ever to have interpreted and applied the ordinance.

*No Vehicles in Park: Precedent 1*
*People v. Norton* (1996) State of Swansonia Supreme Court.
Opinion by Justice Fisher

The City of Ricksville was having a large amplified public music festival on the great lawn of the Ricksville City Park. Many vehicles were on the lawn, including equipment vans and safety vehicles. Ed Norton owns a large, diesel-operated food truck called The Insomnia Grill. At the festival, he parked his food truck on the great lawn so he could serve food at the festival. City police officer Marla Singer came by and ticketed

Ed for violating Ricksville City Ordinance 66, which states simply "No vehicles in the city park. Violation punishable by $20 fine." Ed appealed the ticket through the lower courts, which all upheld the ticket in favor of the City of Ricksville. Ed now appeals to this court.

Because human legislators are imperfect at foreseeing all possible unintended consequences of a law, the language of the law does not always match the purpose of the law. If the literal application of a law is contrary to the clear purpose of the law, justice requires that we must follow the spirit of the law and the not the letter of the law.

In the case at hand, we believe a food truck on the grass in the city park, serving food to the attendees at a large amplified public music festival, and operated while other types of vehicles are on the grass as well in conjunction with the festival, does not violate the spirit of the ordinance. Clearly the legislative purpose was not meant to apply in such an instance. We therefore disagree with the arguments by the City of Ricksville and as a result we overturn the lower court rulings. Mr. Norton's ticket is dismissed.

Judgment reversed.

*No Vehicles in Park: Precedent 2*
*People v. Pitt* (1999) State of Swansonia Supreme Court
Opinion by Justice Anderson

We once again decide the meaning of "No vehicles in the park." Brad Pitt is the owner of an electric golf cart that is capable of going 5 m.p.h. maximum. Using the cart, he operates a passenger transportation service called "Mayhem Rides." He picked up a passenger and was shuttling her from a retirement home to a nearby grocery store. He cut through the great lawn in the Ricksville City Park, which was the shortest route. City police officer Marla Singer stopped him and ticketed him for violating Ricksville City Ordinance 66, which states simply "No vehicles in the city park. Violation punishable by $20 fine." Ed appealed the ticket through the lower courts, which all upheld the ticket in favor of the City of Ricksville. Ed now appeals to this court.

It is not the job of judges or courts to impose their own conception of justice, but merely to apply the law. When the text of a law is clear and unambiguous, the law will be applied as it is worded. We will not attempt to divine some other intent that the legislators might have had.

In the present case, given the clear wording of the law, Brad obviously violated the ordinance. Moreover, even if we were to speculate as to the legislative purpose behind the law, we believe driving a motorized transportation vehicle through a city park disrupts the safety and enjoyment of pedestrians attempting to use the park for quiet individual recreation. As such, this case is clearly distinguishable from *People v. Norton.*

We therefore uphold the lower court rulings in favor of the City of Ricksville. Mr. Pitt's ticket stands.

Judgment affirmed.

*No Vehicles in Park: Current Case*

*Ricksville v. Durden* Case on docket awaiting oral argument in the present day before the State of Swansonia Supreme Court.

*Facts and Procedural Background*: In the grassy area of Ricksville City Park, Tyler Durden was operating a one-foot long, remote-controlled, gas-powered toy racing car that accelerates up to 20 m.p.h. top speed. A local police officer ticketed Tyler for violating Ricksville City Ordinance 66. Tyler appealed the ticket, and the lower courts all upheld the ticket. Tyler now appeals the ticket to the State of Swansonia Supreme Court.

*Question 1:* Using only *People v. Norton* (1996) and *People v. Pitt* (1999) as legal precedents, how would both Tyler and the City of Ricksville each try to argue the two precedents should apply and should be distinguished from the present case?

*Question 2:* Same hypothetical question, except Tyler was using a skateboard instead a remote-controlled toy car.

Assume both *People v. Norton* and *People v. Pitt* are controlling precedents. The legal outcome of *Ricksville v. Durden* thus hinges on whether the case is more like *People v. Norton* or *People v. Pitt.* How is *Ricksville v. Durden* similar and different from *People v. Norton*? From *People v. Pitt*? In short, which precedent should be followed and which precedent should distinguished? Different judges could very well reach different rulings, so the lawyers for both the prosecution and defense will make their best arguments. The local prosecutor for the City of Ricksvlle will argue that *People v. Pitt* is analogous to the present case, but that *People v. Norton* is distinguishable from the present case. The defense attorney for Durden will argue that his case is like *People v. Norton,* and is distinguishable from *People v. Pitt.* Who would be more correct, the prosecution or defense, about how similar or different the two precedents are to Durden's case? *Why*? The beauty (or bane, depending on one's view) of the law is that *there is no "correct" legal answer here.* It is whatever the judge or jury decides! What lawyers are paid to do is to convince judges or juries of the "right" legal answer.

One helpful method to be thorough in this kind of analysis is to create a table of precedents noting the similarities and differences that each party might try to argue. Separate columns list how the two parties will attempt to argue to their advantage the analogous and distinguishing factors between the precedents and the current case. In the table below are some of the arguments the parties in *Ricksville v. Durden* might make regarding the two relevant precedents. Notice how creative thinking skill is needed to find plausible relevant similarities and differences. You might think of other arguments regarding the precedents that could be made by the parties as well.

Precedent Analysis Table

| Precedent | Prosecution (Ricksville) will argue: | Defendant (Durden) will argue: |
|---|---|---|
| *People v. Norton*: Parked Diesel Food Truck | The food truck was permitted; it benefitted other park visitors; was not moving and large and visible so was easily avoidable by park-goers; whereas RC toy was not permitted, served only Durden's pleasure, and was moving fast and not easily seen so could hit someone or be tripped over if unseen. | Both vehicles were gas powered, emitting exhaust and noise; the toy racing car is much smaller than large food truck so causes even less damage to air, noise, and grass, and even less risk of injury than large truck. Also, like *Norton* said, the purpose of the statute must be looked at: it was not intended to apply to "toy" vehicles. |
| *People v. Pitt*: Moving Electric Golf Cart | Like the golf cart, the RC car was not permitted, was moving much faster than golf cart, could hit people and injure them. In *Pitt*, the statute must be applied as written. *Pitt* is newer law, so it overrides anything inconsistent in *Norton*. | Golf cart was large and carried people; RC car was tiny and could not carry people; so it was not a "vehicle"; also much less likely to injure park goers since it's so small compared to moving golf cart weighing hundreds of pounds |

To practice arguing from precedent, we can look at several other examples of possible "vehicles" in the park. For each example in the list below, how might the prosecution and defense lawyers argue controlling precedents *People v. Norton* and *People v. Pitt* would be analogous or distinguishable? With each example, you can create a precedent analysis table to help you reason out how the parties would try to analogize and distinguish the precedents. Then, how would you rule as a judge in each of these cases given the two controlling precedents *People v. Norton* and *People v. Pitt*? Why?

*Possible "vehicles" in the park:*

1. A remote-controlled model plane
2. A remote-controlled model boat on the park pond
3. A police car, ambulance, or fire truck
4. A trash, utility, sanitation, or tree-trimmer truck
5. A sit-in toy car pushed by a child's feet
6. A motorized electric sit-in kid's toy car
7. A skateboard
8. A bicycle
9. A non-motorized scooter
10. A motorized scooter
11. A baby stroller
12. A wheelchair
13. A motorized wheelchair
14. A parked but drivable army tank used as a war memorial monument
15. A parked and undrivable army tank used as a war memorial monument

All these are very simple examples using an extremely simple law with two extremely simple precedents. Yet they all illustrate and allow one to practice the concept of arguing from precedent. In the real world, there are usually far more than two precedents that must be analogized to or distinguished from. In some situations, there might be many dozens or even hundreds of precedents to sift through. Thus, good legal research skills are important in first sorting through numerous precedents to find the ones most directly on point. Then each party will analogize and distinguish those precedents most directly on point depending on which technique works to the greatest legal advantage of each party with each precedent.

In legal terms, lawyers and judges often say a case is "apposite" or "directly on point" or simply "on point" when a present case is similar to (analogous to) a precedent. There are various degrees of similarity, so that one case might be "directly on point," whereas another case might be "almost directly on point," or "somewhat on point." If the current case is different (distinguishable) from a precedent, lawyers and judges say the precedent is "inapposite" or "not directly on point" or "not on point."

## Ratio Decidendi versus Obiter Dicta

As was discussed in this chapter, the task of distinguishing cases is done by highlighting factual differences between the current case and the relevant precedent in question. There are a couple terms courts sometimes use in doing this. The core reasoning of a judicial opinion is called the *ratio decidendi.* The Latin term *ratio* means "reason", and is also the origin of the English words "rational" (the adjective) and "rationale" (the noun). The word "rationale" is also a synonym for the reasoning of a court decision, as in "The court's rationale was . . ." The Latin word *decidendi* means "decision." Thus, the phrase "ratio decidendi" means "the reason for the decision." In other words, the essence of the "reasoning" part of any court case comprises that case's ratio decidendi. Obviously, any ratio decidendi will discuss what the court believes are the most critical facts central to the court's reasoning.

Sometimes, though, a judge writing a majority opinion decides to offer some personal thoughts that are not necessary to the resolution of the case. These side comments offer some type of commentary on the case, but are not part of the court's ratio decidendi. The term for these extraneous statements is *obiter dicta.* The word "dicta" is Latin for "remark." *Dicta* is plural for the singular form, *dictum.* The English words "dictate" (the verb) and "dictation" (the noun) also come from the Latin word *dicta.* The Latin word *obiter* means "on the side" or "by the way," such that the remark is said only "in passing." Thus, the phrase obiter dicta means "side remark"—that is, an unnecessary off-hand comment. Obiter dicta are often simply referred to as either "dicta" or "obiter" for short. Obiter dicta contained in a majority opinion are by definition *not* part of the ratio decidendi. One relatively common example of obiter dicta is when a court criticizes the legislature for poor drafting of a vague, ambiguous, inconsistent, or gap-filled statute. Often the court will then suggest, recommend, or request that the legislature rewrite the statute to fix the problem. Another example of obiter dicta is where the court comments on the behavior of a party or lawyer involved in the lawsuit.

We now come to the significance of the difference between ratio decidendi and obiter dicta. Let's say in Precedent A, a majority opinion has added some obiter dicta in its written opinion in addition to the ratio decidendi. The court's ratio decidendi applied law X, but the obiter dicta expressed the court's desire that the law actually be Y. Now, in current case B, the majority wants to ignore the ratio decidendi of precedent A. To do this, the majority in B can claim the obiter dicta in A was actually the ratio decidendi of A, and the ratio decidendi in case A was actually nothing but obiter dicta! This allows the court in case B to distinguish case A even though case A looks on its surface to be controlling authority that is directly on-point. The court in case B then applies law Y rather than law X.

Another situation would be if controlling precedent A contains only ratio decidendi and no obiter dicta. For example, let's say the court in A justifies its holding on three reasons: Reason 1, Reason 2, and Reason 3. Yet in current case B, the court majority wants to ignore Reason 3 in precedent A. The court in case B can simply say Reason 3 was merely obiter dicta! The court in B is able to ignore part of the legal reasoning in a precedent that would otherwise be fully controlling on the current court's decision.

One famous example of this tactic occurred in the U.S. Supreme Court case of *Planned Parenthood of Pennsylvania v. Casey (1992)*[13]. There, a majority of the Court threw out *Roe v. Wade's*[14] (1973) trimester framework for analyzing abortion regulations. The Court in *Roe* had said the legal standard that applies to abortion regulations must vary depending on whether the restriction will affect the first, second, or third trimester of pregnancy. In *Planned Parenthood v. Casey,* however, the Court said the trimester framework was not part of the *ratio decidendi* for *Roe v. Wade (1973)* but was mere *obiter dicta.* The Court's decision in *Casey* still declared there is a constitutional right to abortion, but the decision applied a single looser standard throughout pregnancy which gave legislatures much more leeway in regulating and restricting abortion.

The vast majority of the distinguishing of precedents, however, is done by courts without resorting to differentiating between *ratio decidendi* and *obiter dicta.* Yet judicial references to these terms occur with

13. *Planned Parenthood of Pennsylvania v. Casey,* 505 U.S. 833 (1992).

14. *Roe v. Wade,* 410 U.S. 113 (1973)

enough frequency to make it necessary to be aware of these terms and their use.

---

*Questions for Review and Discussion*

1. What is argument from precedent and how is it important to legal reasoning? Give an example.
2. What is the difference between *ratio decidendi* and *obiter dicta*? How do these concepts relate to the concept of *stare decisis*?
3. In each of the following sets of concepts, select the two concepts you believe are the *most similar,* then list and describe all the ways the two concepts are similar. Next, in each of the following sets of concepts, select the two concepts you believe are *most different,* then list and describe all the ways the two concepts are different
   a. chair, stool, bench
   b. chair, stool, bench, couch, bed.
   c. pants, shirt, shoes
   d. pants, shirt, shoes, hat, gloves
   e. apple, orange, banana
   f. apple, orange, banana, grape, cherry
   g. earth, wind, fire
   h. earth, wind, fire, water, ice
   i. hop, skip, jump
   j. hop, skip, jump, run, dance
   k. sight, hearing, taste
   l. sight, hearing, taste, smell, touch
   m. eat, work, play
   n. eat, work, play, relax, sleep
   o. plan, organize, manage
   p. plan, organize, manage, invent, improve
   q. kindness, gratitude, generosity
   r. kindness, gratitude, generosity, honesty, friendship
   s. strength, beauty, intelligence
   t. strength, beauty, intelligence, courage, loyalty
   u. knowledge, creativity, curiosity
   v. knowledge, creativity, curiosity, truth, wisdom
   w. faith, hope, love
   x. faith, hope, love, joy, laughter
   y. happiness, pleasure, contentment
   z. happiness, pleasure, contentment, health, success
4. Now you'll be challenged to "think like a lawyer."
   a. Pick a pair of concepts from question 3 above that you believed and argued were highly *similar* in the exercise in question 3 above. Now argue that those two concepts are highly *different.*

b. Pick a pair of concepts from question 3 above that you believed and argued were highly *different* in question 3 above. Now argue that those two concepts are highly *similar.*

5. Pair up with another student who disagrees with you about the similarity or difference of any two concepts listed in question 3 above. Each of you should take turns presenting your arguments to the rest of the class and have the class vote on who presented the better, more convincing argument overall.

---

*Suggested Readings*

*The Cetacean Community v. Bush,* 386 F. 3d 1169 (9th Cir. 2004) (animal standing and obiter dicta)
*Planned Parenthood of Pennsylvania v. Casey,* 505 U.S. 833 (1992) (abortion and ratio decidendi)
*California v. Carney,* 471 U.S. 386 (1985) (motor vehicle v. mobile home)
*U.S. v. Hill,* 855 F.2d 664 (10th Cir. 1988) (vehicle v. houseboat)
*U.S. v. Albers,* 136 F.3d 670 (9th Cir. 1998) (vehicle v. houseboat)

---

*Advanced Readings*

Edward Levi, *An Introduction to Legal Reasoning,* 2d ed. (2013)
Frederick Schauer, *Thinking Like a Lawyer* (2012)

CHAPTER 12

# IRAC

*Chapter Objectives*
*After reading this chapter, you should be able to:*

Define Issue-Rule-Application-Conclusion (IRAC) analysis
Explain the role and importance of IRAC analysis
Compare and contrast high-quality and low quality IRAC analyses
Apply IRAC to hypothetical factual scenarios

In the earlier chapter on legal syllogisms we discussed how the essence of legal reasoning is the application of an abstract rule (like a definition) to concrete facts. Although this skill defines legal reasoning, this skill is not what lawyers (or law professors talking to their students) mean when they use the phrase "thinking like a lawyer." To "think like a lawyer" means you are able to see both sides (or all possible sides) in an argument. That is, you are able to imagine all the possible arguments that *could be* or *might be* used on all sides of an issue.

In the study and practice of law, a lawyer will often want an objective legal analysis, rather than a biased, partisan argument on behalf of a client. This neutral legal analysis needs to foresee and examine what the best legal arguments are for *all* parties involved in the lawsuit. There are many instances where one might want to do this. For example, assume you are a law clerk working for a judge. The judge has an upcoming case and wants you to first summarize the case so that the judge can understand the issue, the rule, and the arguments on *both* sides. Then, the judge also wants you to evaluate the relative strength of the arguments on both sides, and make a recommendation as to which side has the *best* legal arguments on balance. Indeed, this is what law clerks do. This requires that you maintain your objectivity and set aside personal feelings about the case.

Another situation where a neutral analysis is needed is when a senior partner in a law firm asks a junior partner to decide if a client has a valid case. The junior partner needs to write an objective, unbiased recommendation to the senior partner whether a potential client is worth taking on as a client. After all, the law firm doesn't want to take on losing cases, especially if the firm is being paid on a contingency basis where they only make money if they win the case. Therefore, they want an unbiased legal analysis regarding the strength of evidence and arguments on both sides.

Indeed, *any* good lawyer will want to first go through this type of analysis in their head to decide whether to take a case. Then even after taking a case, the only way any lawyer can offer high quality representation of a client is to make the best legal arguments on behalf of that client. This requires, though, foreseeing and preparing to respond to the best legal arguments that one's opponent can possibly make. That is, to properly prepare strong *rebuttal* arguments in advance, one must foresee the arguments that one will need to rebut. Just as a good military leader knows what the enemy might do or is capable of doing, a well prepared lawyer must predict what one's legal opponent can or will do.

An attorney's need to see all sides of an argument is why law schools require law students to engage in neutral, unbiased, nonpartisan analysis of legal questions on exams in law school classes. Indeed, even as an ordinary citizen, one cannot accurately understand one's legal rights unless one is able to *objectively* look at the law. A person needs to *neutrally* evaluate whether one *actually* has a winning legal argument, or if instead one is merely *hoping* that one has a winning argument. Otherwise, a litigant might waste much time, energy, and money in the courts based on nothing more than unrealistic wishful thinking. It is much more helpful to accurately know the law, rather than go to court based on an irrational fantasy or sheer optimism about what the law "should be" rather than what the law actually *is*.

## What is IRAC?

The field of law has a term for the neutral analysis of law: IRAC. This acronym stands for Issue-Rule-Application-Conclusion. Sometimes the "A" in IRAC is also said to stand for "Analysis" or "Argument," but here, these terms all mean the same thing. In an IRAC analysis, the person doing the analysis first briefly states the precise legal issue in the case ("I"). The writer then quotes *verbatim* the legal rule of law ("R") that applies to that particular legal issue. Then comes the most important and extensive part of IRAC: The writer must analyze how *both* parties to the lawsuit would present their best, strongest, and most plausible legal arguments on each side of the case. This realistically assumes each side will apply ("A") the legal rule in their own biased, partisan manner. The best IRAC analysis, then, looks at the best potential partisan legal arguments on both side of the case.

One way to think of the function of IRAC is to analogize to other areas of life where disputes occur. Good political commentators, military analysts, and sports announcers all must be able to provide neutral commentary about what each side needs to do to win, and which side is likely to win based on the strengths and weaknesses of the sides involved. IRAC similarly describes how both sides in a legal dispute will likely employ their best legal arguments against each other. IRAC thus allows lawyers, judges, and members of the public to make fully informed legal judgments. This is because IRAC provides an objective understanding of legal issues, thereby providing realistic expectations of the probable legal outcomes in each given case.

The reason for belaboring this point is that a common problem for students who first begin legal reasoning is that they have difficulty separating their own personal views from the law. At first, students often only see the arguments on the side they favor so students overlook the arguments that support the other side. Students also will make ethical, moral, or policy arguments to support the outcome they want, rather than providing *legal* arguments. Remember from an earlier chapter that law is not the same thing as morality. In the law, it doesn't matter if one believes "x" is morally right or wrong. When making a legal argument, all that matters is what the *law* says about "x."

In court, judges sometimes have to bluntly tell beginning attorneys "I don't care what you believe is right or wrong here. What *you* think is irrelevant. Just tell me what the *law* says." As a result, the most successful attorneys are those who can put aside their personal feelings and beliefs when evaluating a legal issue and instead look at the case from an objective *legal* standpoint. Only by foreseeing an opponent's best possible legal arguments can an attorney be fully prepared to rebut those arguments. Indeed, one of the biggest and most common mistakes lawyers make is underestimating the strength of their opponent's potential legal arguments. Moreover, a failure to tell a client the realistic odds of losing their case will set the client up for failure. This not only risks a lawsuit for malpractice, it violates the attorney's ethical duty to provide competent representation to their client. This failure in turn risks the attorney being suspended or even disbarred from the practice of law. The ability to engage in neutral, objective legal analysis is therefore not only more likely to provide winning arguments in court, it is ethically required and is career-saving.

## IRAC Format

The following outline describes a typical, model IRAC analysis. The facts are *not* restated, as they are assumed as already given to the reader. In other words, an IRAC is based on a set of facts that have already been provided, such as by a client, law firm partner, judge, lower court, or law professor on a law school exam. Notice how the issue and rule are the same as in a case brief. Indeed, you should be able to see that IRAC directly parallels what judges do in their written court opinions. That is, IRAC closely relates to the elements of a case brief, except now the writer must creatively foresee the *potential* legal arguments (the reasoning) on *both* sides of the case.

*Issue* The legal issue is given in one sentence precisely stating the specific, concrete legal question involved. This will reference the particular facts of the case and a clear statement of the precise law in question, just as the issue is stated in a court opinion or case brief.

*Rule* In just a few sentences the appropriate rule of law is quoted *verbatim.* The generally accepted legal rule—such as a statute or common law principle—is also often called the "black letter" law. This goes back to an old publishing practice in England when books summarizing legal principles printed those principles in boldface print, as opposed to italics, underline, or merely in quotation marks. Even today many legal books published in Anglo-Saxon legal jurisdictions like the United States still put precise statements of the law in bold "black letter" print. One common example is a type of legal education book known as a "hornbook" that summarizes an area of law for law school students. When it comes an IRAC analysis, the "black letter" rule should not be summarized or paraphrased, because then it is *not* the law. Again, the "rule" in an IRAC analysis should be identical to how a court opinion or case brief quotes the rule of law.

*Application/Analysis/Argument* This is the heart and most important part of the IRAC analysis. The Application should consist of several short and concise paragraphs. Each paragraph will apply *each* separate element of the rule of law to the facts of the case, describing how *both* sides of the case would try to argue that element. For example, if there are three necessary elements to the rule of law, then the application would contain a short paragraph for *each* the three elements of the rule. Within each paragraph, or perhaps further split into separate paragraphs, the possible legal arguments of *both* parties on that element of the rule are explained. In other words, each separate brief paragraph would present what would most likely be each side's best, *plausible* legal argument on each element of the rule. In this application, each element of the rule must be discretely applied step-by-step in appropriate order. The facts of the case must be expressly connected to each relevant element of the rule of law under analysis. No step in the logical sequence can be left out or assumed. Moreover, the analysis must be more than a mere conclusion that an element of a rule has been met or not met. Instead, it is essential that the discussion *explain why* and *how* each party would argue each element of the rule is met or not met. Otherwise, it's a mere conclusion, and not an analysis.

At each step of this analysis, critical thinking skills are required to imagine the strongest plausible legal arguments each of the parties might present in court. Imagining these arguments requires creativity, and this is what every lawyer must do every day. Clients do not come to an attorney's office with legal arguments in hand. Instead, the attorney's paid responsibility is to craft those legal arguments for the client. This requires carefully researching all facets of how the law might apply to the facts of the case. The job in IRAC is to describe the best arguments on both sides with equal clarity and vigor. This is the essence of being able to "think like a lawyer."

Sometimes, though, the facts are so clearly one-sided on an element of a legal rule that one party must concede that point. In performing a neutral IRAC analysis, it is okay to note that there is no realistic *plausible* argument on one side or the other if there isn't one. If this is the situation, then simply explain why applying the particular element of the rule in question to the facts clearly comes out better for one party than the other. Then move on to your neutral analysis of the next element of the rule. Using a tort example, if a defendant clearly punched a plaintiff on purpose, the defendant is liable for battery and there is no plausible argument that such an intentional touching does not constitute battery. The only possible issue would be if the defendant alleges a defense for committing the battery, such as self-defense. Or, to use another tort example, if A crashes her car into B's car and injures B, there would be no plausible argument than A's actions are not the proximate cause of B's injuries.

Nevertheless, good lawyers almost never concede a point unless there is no reasonable counter argument. Making an argument that has no merit is called a *frivolous* argument. Filing a frivolous lawsuit can actually get a plaintiff and/or the plaintiff's attorney sanctioned by the court. In such a case, the court could order the plaintiff to pay for the defendant's legal fees. In extreme cases, a plaintiff who repeatedly files frivolous lawsuits can even be barred from filing further lawsuits within a jurisdiction.

Although *legal* arguments need to be creative within reason, no *facts* can be added or assumed in IRAC analysis other than the facts that are given in the case. Indeed, in the real world, "creating" facts that change the outcome of a case would constitute a fraud upon the court, and can get the client and/or the client's attorney disciplined or perhaps even criminally punished for perjury. The only exception of facts that can be added to an IRAC analysis are facts that are a matter of common public knowledge. There is a technical legal term for when courts use commonly known facts. Courts may take *judicial notice* of matters of public knowledge without the need for any expert testimony. For example, in a negligence case involving a car accident, it is common knowledge that it is light outside when the sun is shining, that water makes roads more slippery, and that a car traveling 30 m.p.h. causes more damage and injury in a collision than a car traveling 5 m.p.h. On the other hand, a common mistake made by students is to add in facts that were not given in the case they are analyzing, such as adding in new parties or different actions of the existing parties. This changes the case, however, and would thereby change the analysis. Just as lawyers may not invent facts for their client without committing fraud, an IRAC writer must not invent new facts.

*Conclusion* Finally, after the extensive analysis of what both sides would probably present as their best, plausible legal arguments, the IRAC analysis ends with a brief conclusion. In a few sentences at most, the writer evaluates which party on balance has the better overall winning legal argument and why. There should be *no* new arguments presented in the conclusion that did not already appear in the application section of the IRAC analysis. Instead, the writer should simply refer back to the arguments made in the application section of the IRAC essay. For example, an IRAC conclusion in a car accident negligence case might state something like:

> *Conclusion*: The defendant would likely win here on the causation element of negligence. Even though the defendant had a duty not to run the red light and the defendant breached that duty, based on all the eyewitness testimony, it was the water on the road and the plaintiff's bald tires that caused the plaintiff's car to spin out, not the defendant's running of the red light.

Although there are many variations of IRAC, these four elements—issue, rule, application, and conclusion—comprise the most common and basic elements of an IRAC-type analysis. Lawyers, judges, and law clerks working for judges will all typically engage in more detailed IRAC analysis than would be expected of a student. Indeed, the *bench memo*s which law clerks craft for their judges and which summarize the cases for the judges are simply detailed IRAC analyses that include additional statements of the facts. The bench memo usually becomes the basis of the judge's written opinion, especially if the judge agrees with the recommended conclusion provided by the judge's law clerk. Even if the judge disagrees with the recommended conclusion of the law clerk's IRAC analysis, the judge usually need only modify the conclusion along with a few sentences in the analysis. Either way, most written judicial opinions began as IRAC analyses. This can be seen if one looks closely at court decisions.

An extremely simple IRAC using a short legal rule with only a couple basic facts (e.g. Bob knocked Christine's hat off her head after she asked him not to do it) and where the only plausible arguments occur on one side might look something like this:

> *Issue* Does knocking someone's hat off their head without their consent constitute battery?
>
> *Rule* Battery is an intentional physical act that results in harmful or offensive contact with another person, directly or indirectly, without that person's consent.
>
> *Application* Here, Bob intentionally knocked Christine's hat off her head after she asked him not to do so. She therefore did not consent to Bob's action. Moreover, by contacting Christine's hat Bob indirectly contacted Christine's head.
>
> *Conclusion* Bob committed battery against Christine when he knocked her hat off her head against her wishes.

Sometimes law school exams or real-world situations comprise such simple fact patterns. Lower-level trial courts often encounter such straightforward cases. Often, though, the facts of a case are more complex and allow room for both sides to make plausible arguments in their favor. Indeed, if the legal outcomes of cases were always so clear and certain, then lawyers would not be needed as judges would have an easy time deciding every case and no appeals would ever have a chance of winning. The more difficult situation, then, is where the fact pattern is complex enough that there are plausible legal arguments on both sides. These are especially the types of cases that reach higher-level courts like state high courts and the U.S. Supreme Court. Because these more disputable types of cases truly test a lawyer's ability to engage in legal reasoning, we will look at several more elaborate fact patterns in the rest of this chapter as we help you learn and develop the skill of IRAC.

## Sample IRAC: Incorporation Doctrine

Now let's consider a hypothetical example of an IRAC analysis where the factual background of a case is provided, along with the final, full text of the corresponding IRAC analysis. Don't worry if you're not familiar with the "incorporation doctrine" of the 14th Amendment. The point here is to see how an IRAC analysis considers the plausible legal arguments on both sides of an issue by attempting to foresee how each party would try to apply the relevant legal rule.

*State of Swansonia v. White* Imagine you are working as a law clerk to Justice Socrates on the Supreme Court. The following case with the following facts comes to the Court. In the state of Swansonia, grand juries are bodies of 12-to-24 citizens who examine the evidence of possible criminal guilt of a defendant, and decide whether to indict (charge) that criminal defendant with a crime. The standard these juries apply is to decide whether there is "probable cause that a crime has been committed by the accused." State costs for grand juries have been increasing due to the cost of having to pay the jurors higher hourly fees for their time. To save money, Swansonia enacted a law eliminating grand juries and instead allowing individual state prosecuting attorneys to indict criminal defendants. Prosecuting attorneys must use the same standard that the grand juries had used—that there is "probable cause that a crime has been committed by the accused." The probable cause standard is the same standard that has been used in most other states for many decades or more. Chris White, a resident of Swansonia, was indicted for murder by a state prosecutor. Chris demanded a grand jury under the 5th Amendment to the Constitution, which states: "No person shall be held to answer for a capital, or otherwise infamous crime, unless on . . . indictment of a Grand Jury." The state trial court judge rejected Chris's argument because the Supreme Court had never applied (incorporated) that provision in the Bill of Rights to the states through the 14th Amendment. This means that this part of the 5th Amendment has so far applied only to the federal government. Chris was convicted, and filed a lawsuit in Federal District Court, arguing the 5th Amendment right to a grand jury should be applied (incorporated) to the states through the 14th Amendment. He lost his federal district court case, but then won his appeal to the federal Court of Appeals. The State of Swansonia has now appealed that decision to the Supreme Court.

Your job as a law clerk to Supreme Court Justice Socrates is to provide a neutral IRAC analysis of this case so that Justice Swanson can make a fully informed decision in the case. In accordance with this responsibility, you provide the following IRAC analysis of the case.

*State of Swansonia v. White*

*Issue*: Is the federal 5th Amendment right to a grand jury in federal criminal cases incorporated by the 14th Amendment and thus applicable to the states as well?

*Rule*: Not all of the protective guarantees in the Bill of Rights apply to state laws. The Supreme Court has adopted the theory of "selective incorporation" when the question is whether a right in the Bill of Rights applies to the states. This analysis is performed for each separate right found in the Bill of Rights. The Supreme Court has declared that "a right in the Bill of Rights will apply to the states via the 14th Amendment only if that right is of the very essence of the scheme of ordered liberty" and is "a principle of justice so rooted in the traditions and conscience of our people as to be ranked as fundamental" such that "neither liberty nor justice would exist if it were sacrificed." *Palko v. Connecticut.* A right in a criminal proceeding must also be "essential to a fair trial" for it to be incorporated by the 14th Amendment. *Duncan v. Louisiana.*

*Application*: In the case here, Chris would argue that, just as *Duncan* held there is right to a jury trial in criminal cases because it is a long-standing procedural right to ensure fairness in criminal trials, a grand jury is a historical tradition and a basic part of our criminal justice system since before the Constitution. It is basic to our jurisprudence, and hence is "rooted in the traditions and conscience of our people." Also, just as *Duncan* said jury trials guard against an overzealous prosecutor, so too do grand jury trials guard against an overzealous prosecutor who might want to indict a person out of personal revenge or political ambition. That is, just as a jury can refuse to convict, a grand jury can refuse to indict. Thus, the protections from a grand jury are a necessary part of a "scheme of ordered liberty" such that "neither liberty nor justice would exist" if the grand jury would eliminated. As a necessary check against improper prosecution, a grand jury is "essential to a fair trial," so *Duncan* is controlling authority and should be followed directly here.

The State of Swansonia, however, would respond that *Duncan* is distinguishable. Unlike the situation with jury trials, many states have not used grand juries for many decades. Yet the criminal justice systems in those states have carried on with reasonable efficiency and fairness. Clearly grand juries are not "so rooted in the traditions and conscious of our people as to be ranked as fundamental." Also, in *Duncan*, a trial jury seemed to be the only safeguard against an overzealous prosecutor. Here, however, even if grand juries are eliminated, the trial jury itself still can refuse to convict. The trial jury therefore acts as a fundamental check against an overzealous prosecutor, and a grand jury is a redundant check. Thus, grand juries, although helpful to protect liberty of criminal defendants, are not *necessary* to a "scheme of ordered liberty."

In other words, liberty and justice for criminal defendants would still exist without grand juries, and so a grand jury is not "essential to a fair trial." Thus, although the rule in Duncan applies here, its specific holding does not directly control this case.

*Conclusion*: On balance, I think Swansonia has the winning legal argument because trial juries already protect against overzealous prosecutors, so the additional procedural safeguard of grand juries is not necessary to ensure either liberty or justice. Therefore, the 5th Amendment right to a grand jury trial should not be applied to the states via incorporation by the 14th Amendment.

If the example above was a sample exam question and student essay answer in IRAC format, the analysis could serve as a model IRAC answer to the hypothetical posed. Even though the analysis is not necessarily perfect, and there are many better or worse ways to word the analysis, overall it is a strong IRAC analysis. The IRAC analysis is concise, accurate, thorough, and creatively applies plausible and strong legal arguments on both sides. The essay is written using full sentences with paragraphs and headings, it uses proper academic or professional English, and avoids slang and hyperbole. It does not invent any facts that were not in the hypothetical factual situation or that were not a matter of common, general knowledge about basic aspects of the criminal justice system. It correctly follows the IRAC format in every way.

## Sample IRAC: Free Exercise Clause

Now let's compare a poor IRAC analysis with an excellent IRAC analysis in a different area of law, the Free Exercise Clause of the First Amendment to the U.S. Constitution. We will use the following hypothetical case and assignment to conduct an IRAC of the case. Again, don't worry if you are not familiar with the Free Exercise Clause rule. Just pay attention to how the excellent sample IRAC essay thoroughly applies each element of the rule on both sides of the case in a neutral way. Also notice how the excellent IRAC essay is much clearer, accurate, and complete compared to the poorly written sample IRAC essay.

*Swanson City v. Our Lady of Zagorsky Church* Swanson City, Kentucky, has a population of 2,000 people. The City Council, believing alcohol is highly addictive and medically harmful in most instances, adopted an ordinance outlawing the possession, consumption, or use of alcohol "unless prescribed by a licensed medical doctor as necessary to treat a medical condition." The "Our Lady of Zagorsky" Church, a church within Swanson City, uses wine during Communion, a religious ceremony central to their faith. They believe the wine actually becomes the blood of their savior, Jesus Christ, who commanded his followers to forever partake in such a ritual in his remembrance. The Church is the only church in town that uses alcohol as part of a religious ceremony. It refused to obey the ordinance and was given a citation with an accompanying fine for violating of the ordinance. The Church is appealing the citation.

Legally analyze the case, putting your answer in IRAC format: Issue, Rule, Application (by both parties) and Conclusion.

*Extremely Poor Free Exercise IRAC*
*Swanson City v. Our Lady of Zagorsky Church*

*Issue*: Is this wrong?

*Rule*: Religious discrimination is unfair and wrong.

*Analysis*: There is no neutrality of this law. The law isn't fair. The Church has a sincere religious belief, and its religion will be destroyed if it can't engage in religious practice. All it wants is a religious exemption. The Church would argue that there is a violation of its Free Exercise rights. It should get a religious exemption. This wouldn't harm the state's interests. The state has not shown the non-validity of the lack of argument of the non-neutrality of the law.

The state would argue that they are treating The Church fairly. They are doing the best they can. If they don't pass this law then horrible things will happen. The state has shown the validity of the importance of the necessity of the interest of the law.

*Conclusion*: The state was wrong.

*Excellent Free Exercise IRAC Pattern template*
*Swanson City v. Our Lady of Zagorsky Church*

*Issue*: Are [the facts here] a violation of the Free Exercise Clause of the First Amendment to the U.S. Constitution?

*Rule*: [quoted *verbatim* rule from *Church of Lukumi Babalu Aye v. City of Hialeah* (1993)]

*Analysis*: The Church would first argue that the law is not religiously neutral. It would argue that the text of the law is not neutral on its face because . . . [concrete facts] . . . The Church would also argue that the record shows the law is not neutral because . . . [concrete facts] . . . The Church would also argue that the effect of the law is not neutral because . . . [concrete facts] . . .

The Church would next argue that because the law is not neutral, the state must show a compelling government interest and that the law is narrowly tailored to further that government interest. The Church would argue that the law is not justified by a compelling government interested because . . . [concrete facts] . . . The Church would then argue that the law is not narrowly tailored because . . . [concrete alternative(s) proposed].

The City would first argue that the law is religiously neutral and thus valid. It would argue that the text of the law is neutral on its face because . . . [concrete facts] . . . The City would also argue that the record shows the law is neutral because . . . [concrete facts] . . The City would also argue that the effect of the law is neutral because . . . [concrete facts] . . .

The City would next argue that even if the law is not neutral, the law is justified by a compelling government interest, and the law is narrowly tailored to further that government interest. The City would first argue that the law is justified by a compelling government interested because . . . [concrete facts] . . . The City would next argue that the law is narrowly tailored because . . . [explanation why the Church's concrete alternative proposal(s) will not further the state interests at stake].

*Conclusion*: (one or two sentences) [name of winning party] would probably win because [the winning argument(s)].

*Excellent Free Exercise IRAC*

*Swanson City v. Our Lady of Zagorsky Church*

*Issue*: Does a city ordinance that outlaws the possession of alcohol, including wine during Catholic Communion, violate the Free Exercise Clause of the First Amendment to the U.S. Constitution?

*Rule*: "The right of free exercise does not relieve an individual of the obligation to comply with a valid and neutral law of general applicability on the ground that the law proscribes (or prescribes) conduct that his religion prescribes (or proscribes)." *Employment Division v. Smith* (1990). "A law failing to satisfy these requirements must be justified by a compelling government interests and must be narrowly tailored to advance that interest." A law is neutral and generally applicable if its wording is religiously neutral on its face. *Church of Lukumi v. Hialeah* (1992). "To determine the object of a law, we must begin with its text, for the minimum requirement of neutrality is that a law not discriminate on its face" (*Lukumi*). The Court also said the historical record in the case, as well as the effect of the law, can possibly indicate the intent behind the law.

*Application*: The Church would argue that the law is not religiously neutral. A non-religious exception is provided in the law—medical necessity—but there is no corresponding religious exception. Thus, religious use of alcohol is prohibited while non-religious use is allowed. By definition this makes the text of the law not religiously neutral. Although there is nothing in the record of the case that suggests an intent to discriminate, the effect of this law negatively impacts only this one church in town. This is evidence that the law might have been targeted to discriminate against the Church.

Because the law is not religiously neutral, the Church would then argue the city does not have a compelling interest in outlawing wine. Wine is legal in most places, so the health risks must not be that severe. In fact, it takes wine years to damage a person's liver or other parts of their body, so it is not nearly as dangerous as, for example, poison or other, far more dangerous drugs. Although the City might have a "legitimate" or perhaps even "important" interest in preventing harm from wine, the city's interest is hardly "compelling." Also, if the city's interest were so compelling in preventing alcohol going into people's bodies, they would not have given an exemption for medical reasons. People can still get addicted to medicinal alcohol, have allergic reactions to medicinal alcohol, drive under the influence of medicinal alcohol, or commit crimes under the influence of medicinal alcohol. People can also suffer long-term permanent liver damage, kidney damage, and other negative health effects merely from medicinal alcohol. All this shows that any interest behind this law is not compelling.

Further, even if the City had a compelling interest in the health and lives of its citizens, the law is not narrowly tailored to further that interest. There is a way to rewrite the law in a way that could further the government interest, but without a complete ban on alcohol. For example, the law could simply require that any alcohol consumed have a very low alcohol content, which then would not only be safe for consumption, but in fact medical studies have shown that it would be medically beneficial. The law could also limit the amount purchased by each individual per week or month. The possibility of these more narrowly tailored laws shows that the law as written is not narrowly tailored.

The City, on the other hand, argues that the law is religiously neutral on its face. The prohibition on alcohol applies to all religions, or even people who drink alcohol for non-religious reasons. The medical exception also applies to all people, regardless of their religion, and regardless whether they are religious are not-religious. The text of the law is therefore religiously neutral. There also is nothing in the record of the case that indicates any expressly stated intent by the city council or mayor to discriminate against the Church. Moreover, although the Church is currently the only religious entity negatively impacted by the ban, no other denomination or religion that wants to start a congregation in town may use alcohol as part of its religious ceremony, either. Nor may any nonreligious groups use alcohol, such as secular or atheist groups. The ban is therefore religiously neutral.

Because the law is neutral and generally applicable, the law is valid. However even if the law is not neutral, the city has a compelling interest and the law is narrowly tailored. The City has a compelling interesting in preserving human life. Banning all alcohol will prevent alcohol addiction, which leads to deaths from alcoholism. The ban will also prevent deaths from drunk driving and violent fighting, or crimes committed by persons under the influence of alcohol.

The law is narrowly tailored, because only a total ban will serve these purposes. In other words, none of the suggested alternatives by the plaintiff Church will achieve the government's compelling interest. If low alcohol content is allowed, then people can still become addicted to it. They will want more, consume large portions and become drunk. This will cause long-term negative health effects such as liver failure; it will lead to drunk driving; and it will cause more violence and other crimes if individuals are under the influence. The only way to guarantee the preservation of public health and safety is a total ban on alcohol. Because none of the plaintiff's suggested alternatives will achieve the government's interest, this shows the law is already as narrowly tailored as possible as it is currently written.

*Conclusion:* Because both the ban and its exemption apply to all religions and non-religious people as well, the law is religiously neutral and thus valid according to the rule in *Smith.*

## IRAC Practice: Intentional Infliction of Emotional Distress

Now you will have a chance to practice engaging in IRAC analysis using a legal rule you are familiar with from the chapter on torts. For the exercises here, you will analyze cases involving the issue of intentional infliction of emotional distress (IIED). Since you already know this legal rule, you should be able to apply the rule to hypothetical factual scenarios. To refresh your memory, here again is the rule but in slightly more detail:

> One who by extreme and outrageous conduct intentionally or recklessly causes severe emotional distress to another is subject to liability for such emotional distress, and if bodily harm to the other results from it, for such bodily harm. Restatement (Second) of Torts. Section 46(1).
>
> Thus, in order to recover for intentional infliction of emotional distress, a plaintiff must establish (1) that the conduct of the defendant was extreme and outrageous; (2) that the emotional distress suffered by the plaintiff was severe; and (3) that the defendant desired to inflict severe emotional distress or knew that severe emotional distress would be certain or substantially certain to result from his conduct. The distress suffered must be such that no reasonable person could be expected to endure it. *White v Monsanto,* 585 So.2d 1205, 1210 (La.1991)

> The conduct must be so outrageous in character, and so extreme in degree, as to go beyond all possible bounds of decency, and to be regarded as atrocious and utterly intolerable in a civilized community. Liability does not extend to mere insults, indignities, threats, annoyances, petty oppressions, or other trivialities. Restatement (Second) of Torts, Section 46 Comment d.

Now let's apply this rule to a sample hypothetical question. To maximize your learning, do not read through the sample model answer to the first hypothetical until you have first tried to answer the practice hypothetical yourself. Then, after seeing a sample model answer for the first hypothetical, try writing IRAC answers for the remaining hypotheticals as well. Look at the sample IRAC's from this chapter and the model IRAC below to help guide you. Also remember that it is especially helpful to always practice IRAC with a study group. Indeed, many hypotheticals are provided here because it takes a great deal of practice to become skilled at IRAC. These hypotheticals will take you only on the first few steps on the long journey of developing your legal analysis skills.

*IRAC Practice 1: Olson v. Svenson*

John Olson is an entry-level employee who works at the assembly line at Svensen Space Sprockets in Lafayette, Louisiana. The owner Arn Svensen is a die-hard fan of the local university football team, the University of Louisiana at Lafayette Ragin' Cajuns. Arn's new employee John is a fan of the Louisiana State Tigers, a main regional rival to UL-Lafayette. Arn always calls John "Loser" instead of his real name. Arn will only give John a nametag that reads "Loser" and he tells his other employees to refer to John only as "Loser." Usually once every day, Arn comes into the assembly area and yells in front of the other employees "How's the Loser doing today?" or "I see the Loser is hard at work!" or "Keep up the good job, Loser!" or some such similar thing. Throughout several weeks of this, John just ignores Arn and the other employees, and is afraid to speak out against the ridicule for fear of losing his job. One day Arn comes into the assembly area and leads the employees in a chant: "Lo-ser! Lo-ser! Lo-ser!" John is finally fed up enough with the abuse to quit and file a lawsuit against Arn for the intentional infliction of emotional distress (IIED). Is Arn liable for the tort? Prepare your own IRAC, and do *not* read through the model answer below until you have first worked out a detailed IRAC analysis of *Olson v. Svenson.*

*Sample Model IRAC for Olson v. Svenson*

*Olson v. Svenson*

*Issue*: Is Arn liable to John for the intentional infliction of emotional distress (IIED) due to Arn's repeatedly calling his employee John a "loser" in public at his workplace?

*Rule*: "One who by extreme and outrageous conduct intentionally or recklessly causes severe emotional distress to another is subject to liability for such emotional distress, and if bodily harm to the other results from it, for such bodily harm." Restatement (second) of Torts. Section 46(1).

"Thus, in order to recover for intentional infliction of emotional distress, a plaintiff must establish (1) that the conduct of the defendant was extreme and outrageous; (2) that the emotional distress suffered by the plaintiff was severe; and (3) that the defendant desired to inflict severe emotional distress or knew that severe emotional distress would be certain or substantially certain to result from his conduct. The distress suffered must be such that no reasonable person could be expected to endure it." *White v Monsanto*, 585 So.2d 1205, 1210 (La.1991)

"The conduct must be so outrageous in character, and so extreme in degree, as to go beyond all possible bounds of decency, and to be regarded as atrocious and utterly intolerable in a civilized community. Liability does not extend to mere insults, indignities, threats, annoyances, petty oppressions, or other trivialities." Restatement (Second) of Torts, Section 46 Comment d.

*Application*:

*Plaintiff's arguments:* John would first argue that the first element of IIED was because met Arn's conduct was extreme and outrageous such that it went beyond all bounds of decency in a civilized community. Arn made John wear a nametag the said "Loser." Arn calls John "loser" to his face. To make matters worse, John does this in front of other employees, making the humiliation pubic rather than doing this in private in his office. Almost every day for a period of several weeks he did this. Thus, the conduct was not isolated but was a systematic pattern over a long period of time. Finally, Arn had the other employees chant "loser' to John. Group harassment is worse than solo harassment, and had the effect of ostracizing John from the workplace team. Arn also was in a position of power over John, which made the conduct worse. Arn was in fact the owner of the business, the highest level of authority. John therefore had no recourse to complain to a manager or the personnel director or human resources to file a complaint.

John would next argue that the second element of IIED was met because the distress he suffered was severe. He had to endure public humiliation on almost a daily basis. He had no recourse to other managers to protect him, meaning he was completely defenseless. His nametag meant that any visitors to the work area would see his humiliation as well. His withdrawal from speaking to his coworkers shows his distress. He finally had to quit his job because he could not take the emotional pain and humiliation anymore.

John would finally argue the third element of IIED was met because Arn either desired to inflict severe emotional distress or knew that it would occur or was substantially likely to occur. Arn is a UL fan, whereas John is an LSU fan, and Arn knows that John is an LSU fan, which Arn hates. This shows that Arn intentionally singled out John for the ridicule. Even if Arn didn't *intend* to cause severe emotional harm, Arn *knew* that ridiculing John in the way he did would cause such severe distress, or would be substantially likely to cause several emotional distress. Arn's ridicule was consistent rather than isolated; it was over a long duration rather than a short period; it was public rather than private; it was done through abuse of authority rather than by a coworker; and rather than being done solo, it forced many people to join in the harassment. All these factors made the public humiliation about the worst it could be, such than Arn must have either intended or known it would cause John severe emotional distress, or at least was extremely likely to cause it.

*Defendant's arguments:* Arn would first argue that the first element of IIED was not met because his conduct was not extreme and outrageous such that it was beyond the bounds of decency in a civilized society. Arn did not call John a racial or religious insult, or anything vulgar. "Loser" is a fairly tame insult, something that kids call each other. Arn did not refer to John as "loser" every day, and even on the days he did, it was only once per day. He did so only for a few weeks during the peak of the sports season, not months or years. Also, he provided compliments or concern to John as part of his greetings, such as asking John how his day is going or praising his work. Arn's dislike is only of John's fandom of LSU, not John personally. Also, male friends and coworkers regularly tease and even insult each other when they are fans of rival sports teams. And, John was a new employee and hazing of new employees frequently takes place in employment contexts.

Arn would next argue that the second element of IIED was not met because there is no evidence that John suffered emotional distress. John never asked the teasing to stop when it occurred. He never complained to Arn in private, either. John never displayed any symptoms of distress, such as shaking, crying, vomiting, or taking sick days off work. Although he avoided interaction with coworkers, that is common among shy people so there was nothing to indicate he was distressed rather than merely being introverted. He didn't even give any reasons as to his quitting. The lawsuit itself is the first and only fact that even suggests he experienced emotional distress. Thus, he has not proven any emotional distress, let alone that it was severe.

Arn would finally argue that the third element of IIED was not met because there is no evidence that he intended to cause distress to John, or that he knew such distress would occur or was substantially certain to occur. As already discussed, the term "loser" is mild, it occurred only once a day, and not even all days, and it occurred only for a period of a few weeks rather than months or years. Also, it was merely sports trash-talking and/or hazing. There is no evidence that Arn intended to cause severe distress. Moreover, people understand that sports trash-talking is merely joking, as even friends do it to each other. Also, as was discussed, John showed no outward signs that he was under any distress other than quietness, which is not itself necessarily a sign of stress. Therefore, Arn had no reason to know that John would experience severe emotional distress or that such distress was substantially certain to occur.

*Conclusion*: [Here, you may conclude either way regarding which party you believe has, on balance, the winning arguments. Just provide a sentence or two of brief explanation regarding why that party should win. Here are two sample alternatives.]

[Alternative 1]. I believe John would win. With so many aggravating factors to the harassment, it was extreme and outrageous, and Arn must have known this would cause severe emotional distress in John.

[Alternative 2]. I think Arn has the winning argument. "Loser" is a relatively mild insult, and it gives all the appearance of friendly sports trash-talking here, especially since John initially showed no visible signs of distress.

*IRAC Practice 2: Johnson v. Smith*

Matt Johnson is a male underwear and swimwear model. He has worked for Cole Smith at the Smith Modeling Agency for three years. Matt is normally shy and introverted, but Matt and Cole have become close friends during that time. One day, Cole promoted Matt to Top Model at the agency. Cole decided to throw a congratulatory pool party for Matt. Cole thought it would be funny to pull a prank on Matt. Cole ordered a "dissolving swimsuit" from the internet. He gave it to Matt to model at the pool party but without telling Matt that it was a dissolving swimsuit. At the party, Matt wore the swimsuit, and then dove into the pool. Within a couple minutes, his swimsuit had dissolved. He came out of the pool covering the front of his private parts with his hands, and ran naked to the house to find his clothes and get dressed. Matt was silent, was not smiling, and his face appeared very red. Most of the guests at the party roared with laughter. Being a private person, he never told anyone what he was feeling. He simply refused to speak to Cole, and then he sued Cole for intentional infliction of emotional distress. Is Cole liable to Matt for intentional infliction of emotional distress? Write a detailed IRAC analysis.

*IRAC Practice 3: Austin v. Rossi*

Jane Austin was in a heated argument with her friend Susan Rossi in Susan's home. Susan's deceased mother had always been extremely judgmental and confrontational, and had always called Jane a "slut" and a "whore" to her face for having a child out of wedlock. Susan began defending her deceased mother, who Susan loved despite having a difficult relationship with her. Jane became so angry at Susan for defending Susan's mother, Jane grabbed the urn off of Susan's shelf where Susan kept her dead mother's ashes. Jane ran to the bathroom, quickly locked the door before Susan could catch her, and flushed the toilet. Jane yelled to Susan "That's what I think of your mother!" Believing that Jane had just flushed her mother's ashes down the toilet, Susan screamed in horror, and fell to the ground sobbing. After a half-minute or so, Jane came out of the bathroom with the urn, which still had the ashes in it. Jane said "I'm sorry. I didn't put your mother's ashes in the toilet; I was just kidding. I just wanted you to understand how angry and hurt I still am by your mother and your defense of her." Dumbstruck, Susan asked Jane to leave, which Jane did. Susan could barely eat or sleep for the next two days because she was so upset by the incident. Susan then decided to sue Jane for the intentional infliction of emotional distress. Is Jane liable for the tort?

*IRAC Practice 4: Garcia v. Carlson*

Fred Carlson's daughter was named Gail. Gail had been high school sweethearts with Jose Garcia since their freshman year in high school. Jose was one year older than Gail. Their senior year, Jose turned 18. Gail then became pregnant. Fred never liked Jose, and now hated the fact that Jose had "ruined his daughter's reputation." Fred reported Jose to the police, and Jose was convicted of statutory rape of his 17-year-old girlfriend Gail, since he was an adult and she was still a minor. Given the relatively innocent circumstances, the court sentenced Jose only to probation. Fred was angry that Jose had received such a lenient sentence. Over Gail's strong angry objections, Fred paid for a single billboard along one of the major streets in town. It had a large photo of Jose under which was written: "Watch out! This man is a convicted rapist!" The billboard stayed up for one week. Even though Jose was qualified for five different jobs he applied for in the area, he was turned down for all of them before he finally found one locally. Also, three of his rental applications were declined before he was able to find an apartment complex willing to rent to him. Jose told Gail "I'm absolutely furious with your father for what he's done!" Criminal convictions are a matter of public record, so Jose could not sue for public disclosure of private facts. Since the billboard statement was true, Jose could not sue for defamation. Jose decided to sue Fred for intentional infliction of emotional distress. Analyze the claim using IRAC to determine whether Fred is liable to Jose.

*IRAC Practice 5: Yee v. Anderson*

Jesse Yee had a phobia of spiders, called arachnophobia. He also had a fear of enclosed spaces, called claustrophobia. He wanted to join

Zeta Zeta Zeta (ZZZ) fraternity at Swanson State University (SSU). SSU rules officially prohibit "hazing" of new members. However, the fraternity culture at SSU is such that hazing often occurs, and new fraternity pledges expect that hazing is possible or even likely to happen at some point. Nate Anderson was president of ZZZ, and so was responsible for designing and running the hazing activities. One night, Nate arranged to have several senior fraternity members stuff and lock Jesse into a small closet filled with fake plastic spiders. Neither Nate nor any of the fraternity members knew that Jesse had either arachnophobia or claustrophobia. After Jesse was locked in the closet, he began kicking, banging, and screaming to be let out. He yelled that he was afraid of both spiders and enclosed spaces. At first Nate thought Jesse was joking to avoid being hazed. However, after Jesse's kicking and screaming got worse over the course of a minute, Nate realized Jesse wasn't kidding. Nate then let Jesse out of the closet. Jesse was shaken up emotionally for the rest of the night, and had trouble going to sleep. He even had a nightmare about the incident. After that night, though, Jesse was fine. The next week, Jesse filed a lawsuit against Nate for the intentional infliction of emotional distress. Analyze the claim using IRAC to determine whether Nate is liable to Jesse.

The examples provided here are just a few examples of the limitless different legal rules that might be applied in IRAC analyses. Each IRAC analysis will be unique given the specific legal issue and the particular facts of each individual case. You should have noticed by now that IRAC is simply a more formalized and detailed method of legal reasoning. That is, IRAC is merely the application of an abstract rule to a concrete example. You should also have noticed that IRAC is essentially a written court opinion, where the "conclusion" part of IRAC would be the judge's ruling in the case. Note, though, that judges are free to be both less neutral and less structured in their written analyses.

As explained before, legal reasoning is a skill, so the ability to engage in IRAC is a skill as well. Although the *format* of IRAC (Issue-Rule-Application-Conclusion) can be memorized, the *skill* in performing the logical reasoning essential for legal analysis requires *actual practice.* Toward this goal, multiple IRAC analyses typically comprise the entirety of most exams in most courses in law school. To prepare for these exams, law students form study groups and practice engaging in IRAC together on as many sample hypothetical cases they can find prior to taking the actual exams. By the end of law school, law school students should be well prepared to extensively engage in IRAC in the future as lawyers, law clerks, and judges. If you are fortunate enough to learn and develop the skill of IRAC while you are an undergraduate student in college, then you are a big step ahead of the curve when you enter law school. Even if you never go to law school or become a lawyer, knowing how to engage in IRAC analysis will significantly empower you to better understand and assert your legal rights throughout your lifetime.

---

*Question for Review and Discussion*

1. Here is one more practice IRAC hypothetical but this time involving the issue of vicarious employer liability for tortious employee conduct. Apply the following legal rule to the facts below.

    An employer is liable for its employee's torts committed if, at the time, the employee was acting within the course and scope of his employment. An employee is acting within the course and scope of his employment when the employee's action is of the kind that he is employed to perform, occurs substantially within the authorized limits of time and space, and is activated at least in part by a purpose to serve the employer. [See *Timmons v. Silman*, 761 So. 2d 507 (La. 2000)].

    Sam Lowery, a clerical worker working for a company called InfoMinistry was sent on a weekday worktime errand by his supervisor Mr. Kurtzman. Sam drove an hour's distance from the office to hand deliver an important legal document to Veronica Buttle, a client of InfoMinistry. Sam delivered the document to Veronica, and it was by then about 30 minutes to noon lunchtime. By coincidence, Veronica lived only a few blocks away from Sam's romantic interest, Jill Layton. Sam called up Jill and the two agreed to meet for an early lunch at a nearby restaurant. Sam planned that besides their regular conversation, he would also spend a minute trying to convince Jill to become a client of InfoMinistry. On the way to the restaurant, though, Sam, lost in thought about Jill and rushing to meet her, failed to notice a red light. Driving through the light, Sam collided into a car driven by Jack Lint, causing injury to Jack. Jack then sued both Sam and Sam's employer, InfoMinistry. Use IRAC to analyze whether InfoMinistry is vicariously liable for their employee Sam's negligence.

---

*Advanced Readings*

Tracy Turner, "Flexible IRAC: A Best Practices Guide," 20 *Legal Writing* 233 (2015)

Laura P. Graham, "Why-Rac? Revisiting the Traditional Paradigm for Writing about Legal Analysis," 63 *U. Kan. L. Rev.* 681 (2015)

CHAPTER *13*

# ISSUE SPOTTING

---

*Chapter Objectives*
*After reading this chapter, you should be able to:*

- Describe the concept of Issue-spotting
- Apply the concept of issue-spotting to a contract law factual hypothetical
- Apply the concept of issue-spotting to a tort law factual hypothetical

---

In the previous chapter we examined several cases and learned how to apply Issue-Rule-Application-Conclusion (IRAC) legal analysis. In effect, we looked at the issue, searched for the most relevant rule, applied that rule, and came do a conclusion: do we have a solid case. But the cases examined involved only one issue. Most of the time with most cases, several issues are involved for which separate IRAC analyses must be performed. Thus, another central skill to learn as an attorney is identifying the legal issues involved in the case. This skill is called *issue spotting*.

## What is Issue Spotting?

Just as doctors diagnose medical problems and automobile technicians diagnose mechanical problems, lawyers diagnose legal problems. It is true that sometimes people are able to correctly self-diagnose their medical, mechanical, or legal problems, but most people don't know medicine, mechanics, or the law *extensively*. This is why most people eventually seek out the advice of doctors, mechanics, and attorneys. In the case of legal problems, most people know or have a strong suspicion when some type of legal wrong has been committed against them, but the precise legal nature and language of the wrong is not common knowledge.

One legal example that is sadly all too common is domestic abuse cases. For example, client Jane is not likely to walk into her attorney's office and say "My ex-boyfriend Bob just committed trespass to chattel with my apartment door and then committed defamation against me!" Instead, Jane will simply say "Bob just kicked a hole in my apartment door and then called me a slut in public!" Jane knows, or at least believes, that Bob probably did *something* legally wrong. Jane doesn't know, however, the technical legal terms for what Bob did. Jane might not even be aware of the concept of defamation, and would then have no idea that there is a possible legal issue regarding Bob's allegation of Jane being a "slut."

A lawsuit is also called a *legal action*. Each separate ground for a lawsuit is called a *cause of action*. A client will come to an attorney with a long story where multiple causes of action exist, but the client is often unaware of some of those causes of actions. Indeed, this is why one seeks legal advice from a legal expert. An attorney will examine the client's story and literally segment it into separate issues each of which could be grounds for a lawsuit. Having worked through this process called issue spotting, the attorney will then proceed to engage in IRAC analysis for each issue in the hope of answering these questions: Was a legal wrong done to the client? What legal rights does the client have in this situation? Does the client have any legal duties in return? May the client sue? Will the client likely win? Can there be a countersuit against the client? Would the opponent likely win if the opponent counter-sues? Even if your client wins, what are the potential damages? Is filing a lawsuit even worth it for your client?

## Issue Spotting Example: Tort

Let's look at an extended example of the Jane-and-Bob story from a moment ago. Assume you are a lawyer and potential client Jane comes into your office. Jane tells you the following story of domestic violence that was committed against her by a recent former boyfriend:

> I broke up with my boyfriend Bob a week ago because he was controlling, obsessively jealous, and verbally abusive. He couldn't let go of the fact that I had a relationship in the past with this guy Dave who still lives in one of the condos next-door to me. Late last night around 2 a.m. in the morning, Bob showed up outside my condo honking his car nonstop with the car lights pointed at my building. All the noise he was making woke me and several neighbors up. He was screaming toward my front window "You're a slut and a whore for sleeping with Dave!" He got out of the car and started walking straight toward my window where the drapes were

> open. He looked right into my condo and saw me and started yelling "I'll teach you what happens when someone betrays me!" Then he went to my door. First he looked through my mailbox, which is always open at the top, to see if I had any mail and who it was from. Then he tried to kick in the door. I was scared! He dented the door, but luckily the door was too strong for him to kick it in. He gave up but then saw my favorite flowerpot on my patio. When my mom died, she left me that painted clay flowerpot that she made when she was a child. It was extremely sentimental to me. Bob knew how much it meant to me. He picked up the flowerpot and threw it down on the patio and smashed it all to pieces! I started crying. Bob then got back in his car and drove off. Several of my neighbors say they would gladly be willing to testify for me against Bob if need be!

As a lawyer, you need to spot all the potential legal issues—the potential "causes of action"—in Jane's story. Obviously Bob committed several crimes, and the police and prosecutors will handle those offenses in *criminal* court. Jane also might be able to get a restraining order against Bob, but let's leave that issue aside as well. Here, let's assume we want to know whether Jane also has any private *tort* causes of action here. That is, in addition to Bob's crimes, what private torts did Bob commit for which Jane could sue him in civil court? Jane's attorney would engage in issue spotting, and come up with this list of torts Bob committed, or at least arguably committed, given the facts as stated:

- Waking up Jane (and her neighbors): private nuisance
- Yelling that Jane is a slut and whore: defamation
- Yelling that Jane has slept with Dave: public disclosure of private facts
- Looking into mailbox and into apartment window: intrusion upon seclusion
- Coming on the private apartment complex property uninvited: trespass
- Trying to kick in door while threatening Jane: assault
- Damaging apartment door: trespass to chattel
- Smashing sentimental heirloom: conversion, intentional infliction of emotional distress

*IRAC Revisited* After spotting all the possible legal issues in Jane's story of what happened to her, you would next need to analyze each of these torts in detail. As a lawyer giving Jane advice, you would need to inform Jane whether any of the torts Bob arguably committed is supported enough by the facts that she would likely have a winning case on those issues. This means you have to go through IRAC either on paper or at least in your head *for each and every one* of the many possible causes of action that you spotted. Only then can you decide which of the causes of action are likely winnable by Jane, and if so, what the damages might be. Jane, in turn, needs the information regarding the probability and degree of success of a lawsuit against Bob before she can make an informed choice on whether she should file any lawsuit.

Each "issue" part of the many IRACs in the above example would be stated precisely. In the field of torts, each possible cause of action should be specifically stated following a pattern: Who is potentially liable to whom, for what, and why? Applying this pattern, the torts that Bob possibly committed in the above hypothetical could be stated as follows.

- Is Bob liable to Jane for private nuisance caused by his loud yelling which woke her up?
- Is Bob liable to Jane's neighbors for private nuisance caused by his loud yelling which woke them up?
- Is Bob liable to Jane for defamation for publicly yelling that she is a slut and a whore?
- Is Bob liable to Jane for public disclosure of private facts for his yelling that she slept with Dave?
- Is Bob liable to Dave for public disclosure of private facts for his yelling that Dave and Jane slept together?
- Is Bob liable to Jane for intrusion upon seclusion because of his looking through her mailbox and into her apartment window?
- Is Bob liable to Jane for assault when he tried to kick in her door while threatening her?
- Is Bob liable to Jane for trespass to chattel for damaging her apartment door?
- Is Bob liable for trespass to the apartment building owner when Bob came onto the property uninvited?

- Is Bob liable to the apartment building owner for trespass to chattel for damaging the apartment door?

- Is Bob liable to Jane for conversion or the intentional infliction of emotional distress for his smashing her sentimental heirloom?

In a real-world situation, Jane's lawyer is only representing Jane. As a result, her lawyer need only discuss the issues with Jane that involve Jane seeking what *her* rights are. In other words, when advising Jane, the attorney need not advise Jane regarding rights Jane's neighbors or apartment owner have. Notice that in some instances, the exact same conduct may meet the definition of more than one tort cause of action. For example, in this case, smashing the sentimental heirloom may be both conversion and the intentional infliction of emotional distress. A separate IRAC must be performed for both those separate possible causes of action.

This extended issue-spotting example above is what exams in law schools are like. Students are presented with a long factual hypothetical. Then the students are asked to spot all the possible legal issues and then analyze all those issues using IRAC. If a student overlooks some of the potential causes of action—that is, if a student fails to spot some of the issues—then significant points are lost on the exam. Indeed, often the main difference, and sometimes the only difference, between different law school exam grades is that the students scoring better grades have spotted more possible legal issues. Indeed, spotting the issue is half the battle. Think about it: an issue can not be analyzed if it has not been spotted. And, if an issue can not be analyzed, then it can not be argued. If it can not be argued, then it can not be won. Not spotting an issue guarantees your client will lose on that issue. In short, issue spotting is a critically necessary first step in real-world legal analysis and argument.

In the real world, or on a law school exam, a full legal analysis of a factual hypothetical would look something like this:

- Issue 1 IRAC

- Issue 2 IRAC

- Issue 3 IRAC

- Etc.

Using the above hypothetical of Jane-and-Bob, a full IRAC analysis would therefore look something like this:

- Issue 1: Is Bob liable to Jane for private nuisance caused by his loud yelling which woke her up?
    - Rule: [legal definition of nuisance]
    - Application: [application of the legal rule of nuisance to these particular case facts]
    - Conclusion: [statement whether Bob is or is not probably liable to Jane for nuisance, given the application]

- Issue 2: Is Bob liable to Jane for defamation for publicly yelling that she is a slut and whore?
    - Rule: [legal definition of defamation]
    - Application: [application of the legal rule of defamation to these particular case facts]
    - Conclusion: [statement whether Bob is or is not probably liable to Jane for defamation, given the application]

- Issue 3: Is Bob liable to Jane for public disclosure of private facts for his yelling that she slept with Dave?
    - Rule: [legal definition of public disclosure of private facts]
    - Application: [application of the legal rule of public disclosure of private facts to these particular case facts]
    - Conclusion: [statement whether Bob is or is not probably liable to Jane for public disclosure of private facts, given the application]

- Issue 4 . . .

  Etc.

*Importance of Issue Spotting* As a lawyer, you are expected to, and *required* to, spot *all* the legal issues in a client's statement of facts. This ethical standard of competence is the same whether you are the world's most-famous legal expert, or whether you failed some of your classes in law school. If you overlook any of your client's issues, you are committing a breach of legal ethics by not giving your client proper legal advice and representation. This is why law schools require issue spotting as an element of most law school exams.

On a law school exam, a failure to spot all the issues merely results in a lower grade. In the real world, however, the failure to spot all the legal issues in a case means a lawyer has failed to properly represent the client. A lawyer is in a position of trust and power in relation to a client. Therefore, the lawyer has an ethical obligation to give a client complete and accurate legal information. For example, in the extended hypothetical earlier involving Jane and Bob, imagine that Jane's attorney only knows about physical torts. As a result, the attorney believes that Jane can sue only for any physical damage Bob caused. The lawyer simply tells Jane "All you can get is a few dollars for the door and the flower pot, so it's not worth the trouble of a lawsuit as it would cost more than you'd get." In reality, Jane can potentially get much more money in total for all the nonphysical torts Bob committed against her: private nuisance, intrusion upon seclusion, public disclosure of private facts, defamation, and intentional infliction of emotional distress. This kind of failure to give proper legal advice could result in a malpractice lawsuit later by Jane against her attorney. Or again, if Jane were to find out later how bad the attorney's advice was, Jane could report her attorney to the attorney discipline board within that state. The lawyer then could be disciplined with a reprimand, a suspension of the attorney's license to practice law, or perhaps even permanent disbarment. To continue to be an attorney, then, attorneys need to protect not just their professional reputation, but also to preserve their ability to legally continue in the profession of law. This is why issue spotting is a critical skill that lawyers need to develop well even *before* they start practicing law as a licensed attorney.

At the same time, part of accurately spotting legal issues means the attorney must not see legal issues where there are none. Doing so would mean the attorney ends up charging the client for doing legal work that is not just unnecessary, but that has no chance of succeeding in court. This, too, violates the rule of professional ethics that an attorney should provide competent representation of clients. If an attorney were to bring what turned out to be frivolous legal claims that have no grounding in the law, he or she could incur financial penalties (legal fees and court costs) levied by the court against the client. If an attorney were to *knowingly* file fraudulent legal claims, he or she could be subject to suspension or disbarment. Thus, the two sides of issue spotting in any given case are spotting all the legal issues that *do* exist, and *not* spotting any legal issues that do *not* exist.

Besides being good at issue spotting, good attorneys also use good communications skills with their clients. A client who believes his or her attorney listens and cares will be more trusted. As a result, the client will be more likely to open up to the attorney and provide more relevant and detailed facts which can aid the attorney in helping the client. Asking the right questions in the right way will bring out the right information, not to mention it is polite and courteous to treat clients with respect. Moreover, because civil lawsuits and criminal prosecutions are often extremely stressful for clients, good attorneys must know how to assure the client that they are in good hands. Indeed, as the domestic abuse example just showed, the type of conflict a client is involved in can even be traumatic for a client. Just as the best doctors also have the best "bedside manner," the best lawyers are able to treat a client with respect and compassion, showing understanding and empathy for the client's situation. Having a good "deskside manner" is partly a natural skill, but even people who lack good communication skills can learn to improve them. Any improvement in this regard will help a lawyer be a better attorney, as well as be more successful in human relationships generally. Thus, if you are an undergraduate student, consider taking courses in communication that teach or help develop interviewing skills and other interpersonal skills. In law school, try to take a course such as "Client Interviewing" if one is offered.

Hearing about personal tragedies of clients can also be traumatic for lawyers. Just as is the case with doctors, nurses, mental health counselors, social workers, and other "caretaker" professions, "caretaker syndrome" can occur when lawyers become burned out emotionally. Thus, lawyers just as all caretakers need to learn to have a healthy degree of emotional detachment from their clients and their situations. This detachment is both for the personal mental and physical health of the lawyer as well as for the benefit of the client. Just as doctors need to maintain a calm strength for their patients, so too do lawyers need to maintain a confident relaxed presence for their clients. A stressed or overly reactionary attorney will not exude confidence to the client and thus will merely add to the client's anxiety. This in turn will hurt the client's physical and emotional well-being and can lead to the client making rash decisions against his or her best interest or against their attorney's advice. Moreover, getting involved in cases on too personal a level can lead attorneys themselves to make decisions based on emotions rather than objective analyses of the law. This is a recipe for disaster, and can lead to ethical compromises or breaches, in turn leading to suspension or disbarment. Law school thus is a training ground for students to maintain a calm rational approach when dealing with cases with troubling facts. Undergraduate pre-law courses likewise offer the groundwork for these important professional psychological skills.

## Contracts Issue Spotting Checklist

On a law school exam where you are asked to spot issues, one common and helpful technique is to first list all the common possible issues in that area of law that might appear in a factual hypothetical. This list should be written down even before the question is read, before any issues are spotted, or before any IRAC is performed. This checklist then serves as a tool to jog one's memory regarding all the most common potential issues that might occur in this area of the law as one reads over the facts of the case. Indeed, just as good pilots go through a checklist before taking off on plane flight, good lawyers will go through a checklist of possible legal issues, either printed or at least in their head. This checklist doesn't mean that every type of issue in an area of law will exist within every factual hypothetical involving that legal area. Nor does this list mean that these are the only possible issues within this area of law. Nevertheless, a lawyer confronted with a client's case or the reader of a factual hypothetical knows to look carefully through the facts at least to see if the facts might involve many types of *common* issues within that area of law.

As an example, let's assume that a contract law exam asks the reader to identify all possible legal issues and then perform IRAC on those issues. A student taking the contracts exam might first quickly jot down the following contract law issue-spotting checklist in the exam booklet, or perhaps on a sheet of scratch paper:

1. Offer
   a. Revocation/Rescission/Termination
   b. Lapse

2. Acceptance
   a. Express
   b. Implied by Performance
   c. Mailbox Rule

3. Consideration
   a. Action
   b. Forbearance
   c. Promise
   d. Promissory Estoppel
   e. Quasi-Contract (Contract at Law)
   f. Third Party Assignment

4. Enforceability
   a. Statute of Frauds
   b. Unconscionability
   c. Contrary to Public Policy
   d. Misunderstanding
   e. Mutual Mistake
   f. Unilateral Mistake
   g. Legal Incapacity
   h. Undue Influence
   i. Duress
   j. Fraud/Misrepresentation

k. Impossibility/Impracticability
l. Frustration of Purpose

5. Contract Terms
   a. Express Terms
   b. Parol Evidence
   c. Implied Terms

6. Breach
   a. Material Breach
   b. Substantial Performance
   c. Repudiation

7. Damages
   a. Expectation/Direct and Indirect
   b. Consequential/Special
   c. Restitution
   d. Reliance
   e. Liquidated/Stipulated
   f. Specific Performance

This contract law issue-spotting checklist could include many other contract law issues and/or sub-issues as well. Indeed, there is no generally agreed-upon "correct" or "complete" list of possible issues within contract law nor within any other area of law. The point is merely that the writer lists most of the main, common issues within an area of law so as to provide guidance in sifting through the facts of a factual scenario involving that legal area. Indeed, until beginning lawyers become better experts in their field of law, they will sometimes use an extended issue-spotting checklist in various areas of the law to help them avoid overlooking any possible issues in the factual stories their clients bring to them. An issue-spotting checklist can be created for any area of law.

## Contracts Issue Spotting Example

To practice issue-spotting, we can look at a few examples. We'll begin with a contract law hypothetical. In the factual hypothetical below, list all the possible legal issues involved. Here, though, you do *not* need to perform IRAC on the issues. Then examine some examples of poor-quality versus high-quality issue-spotting answers. After doing so, compare your issue-spotting with the high-quality set. To complete this exercise, make sure you have thoroughly reviewed the chapter on contracts. If not, either go back and review it, or skip ahead to the torts issue spotting examples.

*The Case of the Extra Football Ticket* Bob called up Jane early one Sunday morning and said "Hey, I have an extra $10 ticket to the University of Swansonia football game next Saturday afternoon. Would you like it? Just say you'll go to dinner with me and it's yours!" Jane replied "Hmmm . . . Most likely. I'll think about it and get back to you to confirm either way." On Tuesday morning, Bob sent Jane an e-mail saying "I can't find where I put the ticket, so it looks like I can't give it to you." On Wednesday evening, Bob found the ticket again, but still hadn't heard from Jane, so he gave the ticket to a co-worker instead. Thursday morning, Jane sent Bob an email that said "Hey, I'll take you up on that free ticket and then we can go to dinner after the game if I feel like it. I'll take off work on Saturday and get the ticket from you at the tailgate party before the game." Bob was too busy to check his e-mail until Saturday morning. He then replied to Jane's email late Saturday morning by stating "Sorry, I already gave the ticket to someone else." Jane was too busy to check her e-mail on Saturday so she never got the email from Bob stating that he had given the tickets to someone else. Jane works on Saturdays, and she used a sick day to take off work to go to the game. When Jane arrived at the tailgate party early Saturday afternoon, she found Bob and asked "Have you got the ticket?" Bob explained that he had given the ticket away. Bob's friend Bill, though, was with Bob. Bill had an extra ticket, but he told Jane he was willing to sell it to her for $10. Jane just turned and walked away. She left the tailgate party, and then sued Bob for $100 for her lost wages on Saturday.

*Question*: Identify all possible legal issues involving contract law. In each instance, be specific in stating the precise possible contract law issue involved. (Again, for purposes of this issue-spotting practice example, you don't need to analyze each of the issues using IRAC, even though IRAC for every issue would be done on a law school exam).

*Poor-Quality Issue Spotting Answer*

1. Did Bob make an offer to Jane?

2. Did Jane accept the offer?

3. Did Bill make an offer to Jane?

4. Did Jane reject the offer?

*High-Quality Issue Spotting Answer*

1. Did Bob make an offer of a football ticket to Jane?

2. Did Jane accept the offer of a football ticket by saying "Most likely"?

3. Did Bob revoke the offer of a ticket in his Tuesday email saying he lost the ticket?

4. Did Bob repudiate the contract in his Tuesday e-mail saying he lost the ticket?

5. Did Bob's offer of a football ticket to Jane lapse by Wednesday?

6. Did Bob revoke the offer of football ticket to Jane by giving the ticket to a co-worker instead?

7. Was Bob in material breach of contract by giving the ticket to a co-worker?

8. Did Jane accept the ticket offer in her Thursday email?

9. Was Jane's promise to go to dinner if she felt like it consideration for the ticket?

10. Did Bob revoke the ticket offer in his Saturday email?

11. Did Jane accept the ticket offer when she showed up at the tailgate party?

12. Did Bob revoke the ticket offer in his in-person conversation at the tailgate party?

13. Did Bill make an offer of a ticket to Jane?

14. Did Jane reject the offer of a ticket from Bill by saying nothing and walking away?

15. Did Jane fail to mitigate damages by not accepting the offer of a $10 ticket from Bill?

16. Is Bob liable for $10 in expectation damages to Jane?

17. Is Bob liable for $100 in reliance damages to Jane?

## Torts Issue Spotting Checklist

Now let's return to issue-spotting in the area of tort law. First, here's one of many possible ways a tort law issue-spotting checklist could be constructed. Just as was the case with the simplified contracts checklist listed above, this tort checklist would be only a simplified tort checklist that would cover just some of the most common tort issues. It can be very helpful, but is by no means a complete list of all possible torts or their defenses.

1. Intentional Torts
    a. Physical Torts to Persons
        i. Assault
        ii. Battery
        iii. False imprisonment
        iv. Transferred intent
    b. Nonphysical Torts to Persons
        i. Intentional infliction of emotional distress
        ii. Defamation
        iii. Intrusion upon seclusion
        iv. Public disclosure of private facts
    c. Physical Torts to Property
        i. Trespass to land
        ii. Trespass to chattel
        iii. Conversion

2. Reckless Misconduct

3. Defenses to Intentional Torts and Reckless Misconduct
    a. Self-defense
    b. Defense of others
    c. Defense of property
    d. Defense of private necessity
    e. Consent

4. Negligence

5. Strict Liability
    a. Strict product liability
    b. Abnormally dangerous activities

6. Defenses to Negligence and Strict Liability
    a. Contributory/comparative negligence of plaintiff
    b. Legal/proximate cause

7. Vicarious Liability of Employers

8. Defenses to Vicarious Liability
   a. Intentional tort or reckless misconduct by employee
   b. Employee acting outside the course and scope of employment
   c. Independent contractor rather than employee

9. Common Special Situations
   a. Medical malpractice (generalist v. specialist)
   b. Legal malpractice
   c. Alcohol providers (commercial v. social host)
   d. Recreational land users
   e. Good Samaritans
   f. Sovereign immunity
   g. Wrongful death
   h. Right of survivorship

## Torts Issue Spotting Example

Remember that to be able to spot the issues in any area of law, it first requires that one have a solid background understanding of that area of law. Thus, to compete the detailed issue-spotting practice exercises in the rest of the chapter, you need to have thoroughly familiarized yourself with the material in the torts chapter earlier in this textbook. This first practice exercise will walk you through a hypothetical in-depth, then the later practice exercises ask you to spot the issues on your own (with help and guidance from your instructor).

*Question*: Identify all possible private *tort* causes of actions and defenses plausibly indicated by the facts as stated below. In each instance, be specific in stating who would have which cause(s) of action(s) and/or defense(s) against whom, and for what reason(s). For example, "Is Ed liable to Jane for defamation for telling Bob that Jane had been cheating on Bob?"

*The Case of the Angry Ex.* Bob worked for Eris Delivery Services. Bob was driving a company truck making deliveries, but he decided to drive a few blocks off his route to stop by his favorite bar, the Drunken Gator Tavern for a few shots of whiskey. The bartender Ed kept serving Bob despite the fact that Bob was increasingly slurring his speech and having trouble sitting up on his stool. Ed happened to live in the apartment next to Bob's ex-girlfriend Jane, who had broken up with Bob two months ago due to Bob's anger management problem. Ed told Bob that Jane had cheated on Bob while he was dating Jane. Ed had no idea if that had happened, but he wanted revenge on Jane because she had recently rejected his dating advances. Ed hoped that Bob would go yell at Jane. Bob immediately carried his beer mug with him on the way out of the tavern and could barely drive. He headed toward his next delivery, but was swerving so badly as he pulled out of the parking lot that he ran another driver, Monica, off the road. Bob continued towards his next delivery, but his route took him only two blocks from Jane's apartment. Bob decided to swing by Jane's apartment before making his delivery. When he arrived, he left the engine running with the keys in the ignition and got out to look through the bedroom window of the ground-floor apartment. Peering in the crack between the drawn drapes, Bob saw Jane. Bob immediately yelled through the window "I'll show you!" He went around to the front door, kicked in the door and walked angrily toward the bedroom." Luckily Jane was able to quickly jump out the bedroom window and run away. Bob grabbed a small figurine from one of Jane's shelves, went to the window, and threw the figurine in Jane's direction. The figurine missed Jane, but hit a nearby pedestrian, Susan, in the upper arm. Bob then went to get back in his truck to leave, but saw Jane speeding away in his delivery truck.

*Torts Issue Spotting Table* There is a table diagramming technique that is sometimes helpful when analyzing tort law hypotheticals. This technique will not necessarily work (or not work as well) in other areas of law. Nor is the table diagram the analysis itself, but merely a way to help the writer avoid overlooking potential tort issues implicated by a complex set of facts involving many different possible plaintiffs and defendants. The list of plausible plaintiffs can be listed in the far left column, with one row per plaintiff. Then, the list of plausible possible defendants can be listed across the top row, with one column per plaintiff. In each cell where each possible plaintiff intersects with each defendant, list any possible torts the defendant might have committed against that plaintiff. Also list any plausible possible tort defenses the defendant might use to escape liability to that plaintiff for that tort. On the next page, we can see a full tort liability and defense table for the possible plaintiffs and defendants in *The Case of the Angry Ex.*

Regardless whether you have constructed a tort liability and defense table to help you identify plausible possible torts and plausible possible defenses, the legal issues must be clearly identified. Here is a list of clearly identified plausible tort issues as indicated by the hypothetical factual scenario called *The Case of the Angry Ex.*

Tort Factual Hypothetical Issue-Spotting Liability and Defense Table (The Case of the Angry Ex)

| | Plausible Possible Defendants | | | | |
|---|---|---|---|---|---|
| Plausible Possible Plaintiffs | Bob | Eris Delivery | Ed | Tavern | Jane |
| Bob | | | Intentional infliction of emotional distress | | |
| Tavern | Conversion | | | | |
| Monica | Negligence, reckless misconduct | Vicarious liability<br>*Defense*: employee acting beyond scope and course | Negligence, reckless misconduct | Vicarious liability<br>*Defense*: employee acting beyond scope and course | |
| Apartment Owner | Trespass to land, Trespass to Chattel | | | | |
| Jane | Intrusion upon seclusion, trespass to land, Assault, intentional infliction of emotional distress | Vicarious liability.<br>*Defense*: intentional tort by employee | Defamation, intentional infliction of emotional distress, reckless misconduct | Vicarious liability<br>*Defense*: employee was acting outside the course and scope of employment | |
| Susan | Battery (transferred intent) | Vicarious liability.<br>*Defense*: employee acting beyond scope and course | Negligence, reckless misconduct.<br>*Defense*: legal/proximate cause | Vicarious liability<br>*Defense*: employee was acting outside the course and scope of employment; legal/proximate cause | |
| Eris Delivery | Negligence | | | | Trespass to chattel or Conversion.<br>*Defense*: private necessity |

*Issue Spotting Answer:* Plausible Legal Issues (in chronological order):

- Is Ed liable to Bob for intentional infliction of emotional distress for telling Bob that Jane had cheated on him?

- Is Bob liable to the Tavern for conversion of the beer mug by taking it off the tavern premises without permission?

- Is Bob liable to Monica for either negligence or reckless misconduct for running her off the road while drunk?

- Is Eris Delivery vicariously liable to Monica for negligence due to their employee Bob running her off the road, or was Bob acting outside the scope and course of his employment?

- Is Ed liable to Monica for negligence or reckless misconduct for selling Bob alcohol when Bob displayed visible signs of drunkenness?

- Is the Tavern vicariously liable to Monica for negligence due to their employee Ed serving Bob liquor, or was Ed acting outside the scope and course of his employment?

- Is Bob liable to the Apartment Owner for trespass to land or trespass to chattel for kicking down the apartment door and then going into the apartment uninvited?

- Is Bob liable to Jane for intrusion upon seclusion for peering into her apartment windows?

- Is Bob liable to Jane for trespass to land for forcing his way into her apartment uninvited?

- Is Bob liable to Jane for assault or intentional infliction of emotional distress for yelling he would "show her," chasing her, and throwing a figurine at her?

- Is Eris Delivery vicariously liable to Jane for its employee Bob's actions against Jane, or was Bob acting outside the course and scope of employment?

- Is Ed liable to Jane for defamation because of his accusation that she had cheating on Bob?

- Is Ed liable to Jane for intentional infliction of emotional distress or reckless misconduct for his telling Bob about Jane cheating on Bob, given Ed probably knew about Bob's anger management problem and knew that Bob had been drinking?

- Is Bob liable to Susan for battery even though he did not intend to hit her with the figurine?

- Is Eris Delivery vicariously liable to Susan for battery due to its employee Bob hitting her with the figurine, or was Bob acting outside the course and scope of employment?

- Is Ed liable to Susan for reckless misconduct, given he gave Bob alcohol and got him angry by lying to Bob about Jane, or was Ed's giving alcohol to Bob and lying to him about Jane not a proximate cause of Susan's injuries?

- Is the Tavern vicariously liable to Susan for the reckless misconduct of its employee Ed, since he served Bob liquor and got him angry, or was Bob acting outside the course and scope of employment?

- Is Bob liable to Eris Delivery for negligence for leaving the keys in their truck while it was running, which led to the truck getting stolen?

- Is Jane liable to Eris Delivery for trespass to chattel or conversion for taking Acme's truck, or may Jane use the defense of private necessity since she arguably escaped in the truck to protect herself?

As you can see, there are many possible torts and tort defenses contained in the factual hypothetical above. There may be other more unusual or obscure tort issues as well in this hypothetical that were not covered by the introductory tort law chapter in this textbook. For purposes of this chapter, though, we're simply focusing on developing the skill of issue-spotting. Thus, being able to spot the common tort issues you have been taught to identify so far is sufficient for you to begin to develop the skill of issue-spotting. Again keep in mind, however, that on a law school exam or in actual legal practice the skill of IRAC would need to be conducted on each of the potential issues you spot. We'll now provide several more examples of tort law hypotheticals where you can practice issue-spotting—and IRAC as well if you wanted to take the next step.

## Torts Issue Spotting Practice 1

*Question*: Identify all possible private *tort* causes of actions and defenses plausibly indicated by the facts as stated below. In each instance, be specific in stating who would have which cause(s) of action(s) and/or defense(s) against whom, and for what reason(s).

*The Case of the Faulty Computer* Banana Computers designs and manufactures computers. Despite rigorous testing of the design and manufacturing process, there is an overlooked flaw in the design of the power converter in their X500 model. If left plugged in for over 5 hours, the power converter can on occasion overheat and perhaps even spontaneously combust. Banana Computers sells their X500 models exclusively to Best Deals Computer Warehouse. Best Deals then sold an X500 to Miranda, who lives in the small isolated rural town of Swansonville. Miranda left her X500 computer plugged in at home while she went to work for the day. Miranda is also a hoarder. Her apartment is filled from wall-to-wall, floor to ceiling, with boxes of papers (books, magazines, newspapers, and so on). She also hoards numerous different types of household cleaners. Although Miranda's landlord Cathy knows that this hoarding violates the local safety code and the apartment lease, Cathy has chosen not to enforce the rules so as to not lose a paying tenant. Several hours into Miranda's work day her X500 overheated and spontaneously combusted. The X500 was sitting alone on a metal table and ordinarily might not have caught her apartment on fire even if did start burning itself. Unfortunately, that day a construction explosives crew, Acme Bridge Construction, was doing blasting as part of building a new bridge on the small river immediately next to the apartment building. A team of safety experts was there and made sure exceptional safety measures were taken. However, one of the blasts shook Miranda's apartment building just slightly enough so that a box became dislodged off the top of a stack of boxes next to the table where the computer sat. The box slid onto the table where the computer was burning. The box caught fire, fell off the table, and the fire then spread to the rest of the apartment. Miranda's next-door-apartment neighbor, Scott, was an alcoholic and had drank himself to sleep. Because he was passed out, he did not wake up until flames were burning him. He ran outside and called an ambulance. When Scott was taken to Swansonville Emergency Care, the local general physician who is not a burn specialist put the wrong salve on Scott's burns, making the burns need much more time to heal. This left Scott with much more pain than he otherwise would have had if the correct treatment had been given. Indeed, because of the improper treatment, after a few weeks Scott's burn wounds became infected and he died as a result. Scott's only living relative is his mother, Wilma.

## Torts Issue Spotting Practice 2

*Question*: Identify all possible private *tort* causes of actions and defenses plausibly indicated by the facts as stated below. In each instance, be specific in stating who would have which cause(s) of action(s) and/or defense(s) against whom, and for what reason(s).

*The Case of the Hurricane Damage* Bob Lane owned a small bar, Bob's Suds, located right next to a home improvement store, Lucky Lumber. Both are located in a small town on the Gulf Coast. A sudden hurricane arose, and was forecast to do a great deal of damage. Bob went to his store to board it up. He realized he was out of plywood to cover the large windows on his bar, so he went next door to Lucky Lumber to buy some plywood. However, Lucky Lumber had already boarded itself up. Bob tore off the wood covering one of the doors, and pried open the door, damaging the lock. He grabbed some plywood, took it next door to his bar, and boarded up most of the windows on his bar. He realized he needed some more lumber so returned to Lucky Lumbers. Just after he walked through the door, a ceiling tile fell from the ceiling and knocked him unconscious, putting a serious gash in his head. He lay there bleeding as the hurricane went through the town. Bob had not put enough nails in the plywood to hold it. The hurricane ripped off and smashed to pieces much of the wood he used to board up the windows on his bar. After the hurricane past, Sue, the manager of Lucky Lumber went to the store to investigate the damage. She found Bob lying unconscious bleeding. She knew he was the owner of Bob's Suds, but thought he had been trying to burglarize the store. She took a photo of his unconscious, bloody body and posted it on the Internet, with his face clearly visible. She laughed out loud as she captioned the photo "Look at this moron Bob Lane who tried to steal from us; he got what he deserved!" Bob started to wake up from Sue's laughter so she quickly ran outside and locked the door so he couldn't escape. She then called the police. Before the police arrived, Bob took a sledgehammer from inside the store and knocked down the door so he could leave. When he saw Sue, he started walking towards her quickly with his hands clenched into fists. Just then the police arrived to sort everything out.

## Torts Issue Spotting Practice 3

*Question*: Identify all possible private *tort* causes of actions and defenses plausibly indicated by the facts as stated below. In each instance, be specific in stating who would have which cause(s) of action(s) and/or defense(s) against whom, and for what reason(s).

*The Case of the Backyard Disaster* DiHydrogen MonOxide (DHMO) is a fertilizer. Sam decided he needed the chemical for use on his corn farm, so he built a covered storage tank and filled it with DHMO. It is also highly flammable. The tank sat about a hundred yards behind his house at the edge of his cornfield, but was only about 50 yards from his neighbor Uma's house. Sam had the tank regularly inspected for safety, and it passed all safety inspections.

Sam has a five-year-old daughter named Tonya. Uma also has a five-year-old daughter named Vicki. Vicki came over to play with Tonya in the backyard and toast marshmallows on their outdoor fire pit. Sam started a fire and he used a pocketknife to make pointed marshmallow sticks out of some twigs. Sam went inside to go to the bathroom, but he left a pocket knife lying by the fire. Vicki grabbed the knife, opened it, and started "swooshing" it around Tonya as if she was sword fighting. Vicki took her marshmallow stick that was glowing with fire at the end of it, and started playfully "swooshing" back. The stick poked Tonya in the eye and Tonya screamed and started crying. Tonya angrily took her knife and slashed at Vicki, cutting her hand. Just at this point, Sam was returning to the campfire and saw Tonya cut Vicki. He ran to Tonya and forcefully grabbed her arm away that was using the knife. Tonya then yelled and tried to hit Sam with her other hand, but he ducked to avoid it. Sam grabbed the knife out of her hand and ran inside to get a bandage for Vicki. Tonya followed them inside. Sam then called Uma, who came over.

As Sam and Uma were inside Sam's house dealing with the physical and emotional aftermath of the conflict, a particularly large spark from the campfire slowly rose up, drifted through the air, and gently came to rest on the DHMO tank. After about 15 seconds of the ember still glowing, the tank violently exploded from the heat of the lit ember that landed on it. The explosion blew in all the windows on the nearest side of Uma's house.

## Torts Issue Spotting Practice 4

*Question*: Ignoring crimes, identify all possible private *tort* causes of actions and defenses plausibly indicated by the facts as stated below. In each instance, be specific in stating who would have which cause(s) of action(s) and/or defense(s) against whom, and for what reason(s).

*The Case of the Drunken Scuffle* Eddie and Greg visited New Orleans in the summer. They visited Rick's Tavern where Lisa was bartending. Eddie and Greg each ordered a strong mixed drink called a "Hurricane" that came in a tall glass. After three Hurricanes, Greg became rude to Lisa and began yelling at Lisa "give me something extra special!" Lisa replied "I'll give you a little something extra, all right!" She secretly poured a chemical cleaner into Greg's drink. Greg was too drunk to notice the difference in flavor, and he chugged the entire drink as he walked out of the bar without Lisa noticing that he was still carrying the glass. After Greg and Eddie left the bar, Greg then decided he would play a prank on Eddie by pulling down Eddie's shorts in public. He grabbed Eddie's shorts but was too drunk to pull them down as Eddie smacked Greg's hands away. Greg did notice, though, that Eddie was wearing what looked like women's lingerie beneath his shorts. Greg began yelling "This guy's wearing women's underpants!" Eddie told Greg to shut up. Greg said "Go ahead, I dare you to hit me!" Eddie then kicked Greg extremely hard in the groin. Dale, a bystander, saw what Eddie did and thought he would come to Greg's rescue. Dale swung his fist to hit Eddie, but Eddie ducked just in time. Dale missed Eddie but his fist swung around and knocked Greg's hat off. Just then Greg became ill from the chemicals he had consumed that Lisa had put in his drink. He vomited profusely for fifteen minutes, and then collapsed into unconsciousness as an ambulance arrived. The specialist in toxicology at the local hospital gave Greg the only antidote the hospital had on stock, but not the one that was actually needed, as only hospitals in a handful of the biggest cities in the country carried that particular rare, expensive, antidote on hand. Greg died later that night. Greg's wife Nicole was heartbroken.

This chapter focused on issue spotting and offered several opportunities to practice it on a substantive area of law. Recall, though, that on law school exams, just as when a client comes to you as a lawyer, spotting the legal issues involved in the situation is only the first step. The next critical step is to apply IRAC to each and every one of the legal issues present. As the next advanced step in learning and practicing legal reasoning, then, you can take the issue spotting examples in this chapter and perform a full IRAC analysis on the entire set of issues within each sample hypothetical scenario. If you do so, you will have practiced what you will do on a law school exam, bar exams, and in the real world as an attorney. In effect, you have gone a long way in learning how to construct a thorough and solid case for a client.

CHAPTER 14

# LEGAL BRIEFS

---

*Chapter Objectives*

*After reading this chapter, you should be able to:*

- Describe the concept of a legal brief
- Apply advanced argument from precedent using multiple case precedents applied to a factual hypothetical

---

In a previous chapter, we learned and practiced writing a *case* brief: a short summary of a judicial opinion in a court case used to help one study and review the law. There are other types of *legal briefs* in the law, however, that are filed in courts. These legal briefs can involve any type of law and will employ some of the legal skills we learned in other prior chapters, especially legal reasoning using deductive legal syllogisms as well as argument from precedent. The documents known as legal briefs which are filed with a court are called "briefs" because they are supposed to be (and are often required to be) limited in page length. Yet unlike a case brief, these other types of briefs apply detailed legal argument on behalf of a client. These arguments might involve ordinances, statutes, administrative regulations, a constitution, the common law, or other legal sources. Whenever case law is used, that prior case law will be analogized or distinguished depending on whether the lawyer finds the case precedent to be helpful or hurtful to the client's case. In a previous chapter, we also learned about argument from precedent. Since case law is almost always used in legal briefs, arguments from precedent are extremely common in legal briefs.

There are different kinds of legal briefs. At the trial court level, motions and other arguments made to the trial judge are often accompanied by written legal briefs. For example, imagine a plaintiff goes to court and files a complaint against a defendant. The defendant then files a "Motion to Dismiss the Plaintiff's Complaint" with the trial court judge assigned to the case. The defendant's motion will either include, or be accompanied by, a brief in support of the motion to dismiss. The defendant's legal brief will provide legal arguments and legal citations in support, explaining the legal rationale for why the motion to dismiss should be granted. The plaintiff, of course, will respond to the defendant's motion and brief by filing their own legal brief with the court. This document might have a title such as "Brief in Opposition to the Defendant's Motion to Dismiss Plaintiff's Complaint" or "Motion to Dismiss Defendant's Motion to Dismiss Plaintiff's Complaint" which includes or is accompanied by a brief supporting the plaintiff's position. As motions respond to opposing motions, the formal names of motions can sometimes become long and cumbersome. Legal briefs themselves can become quite long if the facts or legal arguments are complex or if multiple legal issues are involved.

## The Legal Brief

There are different types of briefs. The most complex form of legal brief has its own name: an *appellate brief.* Despite the fact that its name includes the word "brief" in it, an appellate brief is a lengthy legal memorandum that is filed with an appellate court arguing in behalf of one of the litigants involved in an appeal to that court. For example, if Smith sues Jones in a trial court but loses, then Smith could file an appeal in the court of appeals by arguing that the trial court made some legal mistake. The lengthy, detailed written document that would legally argue Smith's side is called an appellate brief. Jones would also then file an appellate brief in response, where Jones would argue that no mistakes were made during the trial court and that the trial court ruling should stand.

To write a legal or appellate brief one typically distills perhaps thousands of pages of law from hundreds of cases over a period of decades or more down to a relatively few dozen pages. It is similar in structure to a case brief, a court opinion, or an IRAC essay in that the appellate brief (as well as any legal brief) organizationally sets out (1) the facts of the case, (2) the precise legal issue(s) in question, (3) an argument and analysis section, and finally (4) a brief conclusion.

The lengthy argument section of a legal brief or appellate brief comprises most of the brief. This is where extensive legal analysis and reasoning is presented using deductive legal reasoning, argument from precedent using controlling and persuasive legal authority while distinguishing opposing precedents, policy arguments, and any other relevant legal arguments. Collectively, in the argument section of the brief, the attorney writing the brief tries to persuade the court to rule in favor of the lawyer's client. The legal or appellate brief is therefore unlike case briefs or IRAC because the legal or appellate brief is intended to be used in court and therefore it will present a biased argument that argues vigorously on behalf of the client's position.

There are two equally important aspects to any such legal analysis that argues on behalf of a client: (a) presenting your own best legal arguments, while at the same time (b) fully countering your opponent's best arguments. As a lawyer, if you only do (a) without equally doing (b), the court will think you are unable to respond to your opponent's best arguments. In that situation, your opponent must have the better, winning arguments! Both (a) and (b) can be blended together, but both must be included or you are effectively conceding to your opponent. In the real world, if you fail to make what would have been a valid rebuttal to a legal argument by an opposing party, you have breached your ethical duty to represent your client vigorously. In that situation, your client could perhaps sue you for malpractice or report you to the attorney discipline committee in your jurisdiction for reprimand, temporary suspension of your license, or perhaps even disbarment.

Given the serious consequences for such failure, all law schools require law students to learn to write legal and appellate briefs and to present such arguments orally as if standing before a judge. These classes can go by various names, such as "Legal Writing," "Legal Advocacy," "Oral Advocacy," "Legal Argumentation," "Moot Court," or other various similar names. Often the courses are divided into separate written and oral advocacy courses. In one course, for example, the student will learn to write legal and appellate briefs, then in a concurrent or later course the student will learn how to present and defend those legal arguments verbally in court.

The practice of presenting oral arguments before a court is most commonly referred to as "moot court." There are many different national moot court competitions in which moot court teams from law schools compete. There is even a national moot court competition at the undergraduate level as well. In a moot court competition, the student competitors are given detailed facts of a hypothetical appellate court case involving multiple legal issues. The student competitors act as mock attorneys and typically construct a detailed written appellate brief arguing for their imaginary client. Regardless whether a written brief is submitted, the teams of student competitors then compete in live head-to-head oral argument against each other before a panel of judges. The panel of judges might be composed of actual judges, as well as attorneys, professors, or perhaps even other law students. Plaintiff and defense arguments are presented by two-person teams with each student attorney arguing a share of the issues before a panel of judges. Judges ask probing questions requiring the students on both sides to defend their position. Just as in a real appellate court, the panel will discuss the merits of each side in chamber, and then will come out and deliver a ruling in court. Teams and individual competitors are given awards based on the substance of their arguments and the quality of their overall presentation.

## Constructing Legal and Appellate Briefs

In constructing arguments in a legal or appellate brief, you must present your legal arguments under the assumption that the judge(s) reviewing the case know *absolutely nothing* about the law relevant to the case. Perhaps it is a new judge, or maybe the judge is experienced but has never encountered this particular issue before. You can rightfully assume, however, that the judge is thoroughly experienced in understanding and engaging in legal reasoning. Even if a judge is familiar with a legal area, though, it's the responsibility of the attorney to lay out the legal argument clearly, thoroughly, persuasively, and with the proper legal citations in support. It is not the judge's job to make the argument for the attorneys. Thus, if you do not provide all the argument needed for your client to win, the judge will treat your argument as if it is the only argument on your client's behalf. Countless clients have lost their cases because the client's attorney mistakenly assumed the judge (or the judge's law clerk) would do the legal research necessary or would write the arguments necessary for the client to win.

Given the need for thoroughness in any legal brief or appellate brief, you must explain with exacting precision what legal rules apply and why they apply. For example:

> In *Fisher v. Anderson*, 123 N.W.2d 456 (1997), the Supreme Court of Alaska explained that whenever a plaintiff is suing merely for alleged psychological harm caused by hurtful words said to the plaintiff by a defendant, the applicable cause of action is the tort of intentional infliction of emotional distress. According to the Restatement (2nd) of Torts, section 46, "One who by extreme and outrageous conduct intentionally or recklessly causes severe emotional distress to another is subject to liability for such emotional distress . . ."

In any legal or appellate brief, any deductive legal reasoning must clearly explain how any applicable legal rule(s) apply to the facts. For example, a lawyer representing a plaintiff might state:

> According to the Restatement (2nd) of Torts, section 46, "One who by extreme and outrageous conduct intentionally or recklessly

causes severe emotional distress to another is subject to liability for such emotional distress . . ." The plaintiff was yelled at by the defendant who used a loud tone of voice to intentionally call the plaintiff a "no-good knee-biter." This was extreme and outrageous, as everyone knows there is no worse name one person can call another person than the abominable term "knee-biter," implying the plaintiff is a crawling zombie. The plaintiff went home, cried for days, could not sleep or eat, and finally had to get extended counseling to help them overcome the fear they might be a zombie. The documentation of this counseling demonstrates the plaintiff's emotional distress was severe.

When arguing that particular case precedents are relevant to your argument, you must briefly describe the basic nature (facts, issue, reasoning, and holding) of any relevant precedents. You must also clearly explain how those precedents relate to your case by either analogizing to them or distinguishing them. For example, if the case precedent of *Smith v. Jones* is relevant to a defendant, and you want to analogize to it as the defendant's lawyer, you might say something like:

> In *Smith v. Jones*, 123 U.S. 456 (1997), the plaintiff Smith sued the defendant Jones for the tort of intentional infliction of emotional distress. The Supreme Court ruled that merely calling a plaintiff an uncommon, silly name like "mouth-breather" did not rise to the level of "extreme and outrageous" conduct necessary to constitute the tort. *Smith* is just like the present case because here the defendant merely stated "You're a no-good knee-biter" to the plaintiff. This is an uncommon and silly term which no ordinary, reasonable person would take to be a seriously offensive term, and certainly not a term rising to the level of 'extreme and outrageous conduct.'

As was just seen in the several examples above, a citation must be provided whenever a case precedent or any other legal authority is referenced. Any quote, statement, or idea in your argument section that you derive from a legal source must provide a citation to that source. Here is an example which uses correct full legal citation format, and even cites more than one precedent in support:

> The U.S. Supreme Court has declared that the Free Speech Clause of the First Amendment to the U.S. Constitution prohibits government from enacting speech regulations that discriminate on the basis of viewpoint. *R.A.V. v. City of St. Paul*, 505 U.S. 377 (1992); *Texas v. Johnson*, 491 U.S. 397 (1989).

By far the most important element of any legal or appellate brief, however, is the quality of the arguments. You need to be clear, precise, accurate, logical, and thorough, offering creative legal analysis in applying the controlling and persuasive legal authority you have found. Controlling authority must always have primary importance in your arguments over persuasive authority, and you always must explain how and why the rules apply rather than make mere legal conclusions without supporting analysis. Every logical step in your reasoning must be clear; nothing can be left to implication or assumption. No steps in your logical reasoning can be overlooked or left out.

## Appellate Brief Organization

Because appellate briefs are the most lengthy, detailed, and complex type of legal briefs, law school courses on legal writing or moot court focus on the writing of appellate briefs. If a student can master the complexities of writing an appellate brief, they can master writing any other type of legal brief. This chapter as well will therefore focus on writing appellate briefs. Below is a simplified version of the key organizational structure of most appellate briefs:

*Question Presented* A short but precise statement of the primary legal issue (one sentence)

*Statement of the Case* A concise summary of the facts and procedure of the case (half-page)

*Summary of Argument* A concise summary of the main arguments you will make (half-page)

*Argument* Your legal arguments and analysis constitutes the bulk of your appellate brief

*Table of Authorities* A list of all the legal authority cited in your brief (one page)

Again, the key part of the appellate brief is the argument section, in which you make your best legal arguments and pre-emptively rebut your opponent's best legal arguments. Below is a sample outline to show how your argument should proceed logically; your own argument section will *not* match this outline but should instead contain as many rules/elements/arguments/points/subpoints you believe are appropriate. You will want to look at numerous examples of appellate briefs so you can see the nearly infinite ways legal arguments can be structured depending on the particular legal rules being applied. So again, here is only one of the numerous different ways an appellate brief might be structured.

I. Rule of Law I, with full quote and case citation, explaining why this rule applies
   A. Element/Argument A of Rule of Law I
      1. Your arguments, with analagous controlling and persuasive cases
      2. Rebuttal to opponent arguments, by distinguishing cases
   B. Element/Argument B of Rule of Law I [assuming there is a second element to the rule, or other major argument you have, etc.]
      1. Your arguments, with analagous controlling and persuasive cases
      2. Rebuttal to opponent arguments, by distinguishing cases
   C. Element/Argument C, etc. . . . [assuming you have such element/argument, etc.]

II. Rule of Law II, with full quote and case citation, explaining why this rule applies [assuming you have a second major legal argument, etc.]
   A. Element/Argument A of Rule of Law I
      1. Your arguments, with analogous controlling and persuasive cases
      2. Rebuttal to opponent arguments, by distinguishing cases
   B. Element B, etc. [assuming there are additional elements/arguments to the rule, etc.]

III. Rule of Law III, etc. [assuming you wish to argue another major rule or legal issue, etc.]

IV. Conclusion: a single short paragraph summarizing/concluding your position.

When addressing what you know will be your opponent's best arguments, you should only summarize or state in the briefest of manner your opposing arguments. Much more time should be spent explaining why your opponent's arguments are legally mistaken. For example, imagine a law in the state of Swansonia requires childhood immunization against Ebola, and a parent, Michelle Williams, files a lawsuit claiming the law infringes on her parental rights to raise her child as she wants. One part of the government's appellate brief in *Williams v. Swansonia* might look as follows:

II. The mandatory Ebola vaccination law passes strict scrutiny.

A. The mandatory Ebola vaccination law has a compelling government interest in preventing childhood deaths from Ebola.

[Detailed arguments as to the deadly dangers of Ebola and why its so overwhelmingly important for the government to require childhood vaccinations to prevent Ebola, with citations and discussions of several other cases where courts ruled there was a compelling government interest in preventing childhood illness and death]

The plaintiffs might attempt to argue that the case of *Johnson v. United States*, 38 U.S. 798 (1966) controls the outcome here. In *Johnson*, a United States veteran's hospital wanted to require a dying cancer patient to have a feeding tube inserted. The Court ruled mentally competent adults have a constitutional right to refuse unwanted medical treatment, including unwanted food and hydration. The holding and rationale of *Johnson* case do not apply in this instance. *Johnson* is easily distinguishable because . . . [Detailed explanation why the situation in *Johnson v. United States* is distinguishable from the facts in *Williams v. Swansonia.*]

## Legal Brief Template Example: Public Forum Doctrine

Here is an example of a template for an appellate brief of an imaginary case, *Durden v. U.S. Navy.* Assume Durden was an environmental protester on a remote U.S. military base in part of Antarctica who tried to hand out flyers to military personnel to convince them to leave Antarctica. He was arrested for violating a military regulation prohibiting distributing unauthorized information on the Antarctica base. Durden is arguing that his Free Speech rights were violated under the public forum doctrine. Durden lost in the trial court and in the 13th Circuit Court of Appeals, so he is now appealing his case to the U.S. Supreme Court. This makes him the "appellant" because he is the one bringing the appeal. Durden is also called "petitioner" because he is petitioning the Supreme Court to reverse the lower court ruling against him. Since the U.S. Navy is responding to Durden's appeal, this makes the U.S. Navy the "appellee" or "respondent." Note, of course, that the U.S. Navy will argue exactly the opposite legal points in its appellate brief. You don't need to know the law regarding the public forum doctrine. The example here is merely used to illustrate (a) how the brief is organized around each rule, element, and sub-element of the rules, (b) how the section headings and subheadings make affirmative legal statements, (c) how case precedents are analogized and distinguished regarding their relevance to each particular legal sub-element of the rule, and (d) how each relevant precedent is briefly summarized in one or two sentences.

Argument on behalf of plaintiff Durden in *Durden v. U.S. Navy:*

I. ANTARCTICA IS A PUBLIC FORUM

A. *Antarctica is a traditional public forum.*

According to *ISCKON v. Lee* (1992), there are several features of government property that indicate the property is a traditional public forum. These features are . . . [explanation of those criteria with full quoting of the rule].

1. *Antarctica has a long history of being used for free public discourse.*

[Detailed discussion applying this element of the rule to the facts.]

Indeed, Antarctica is very similar to the Alaskan tundra that the Supreme Court ruled was a traditional public forum in *Snowman v. Alaska* (1966). The historical use of Antarctica is like the historical use of the Alaskan tundra because . . . [Explanation how the facts in *Snowman v. Alaska* are similar to the facts in *Durden v. U.S. Navy* on this sub-element of the rule regarding the historical, traditional use of the property in question.]

2. *A principal purpose of Antarctica is for use as a public meeting space.*

[Detailed discussion applying this element of the rule to the facts.]

Opposing counsel for the U.S. Navy may try to argue that Antarctica is like the moon, which the Supreme Court ruled was not a traditional public forum in *Svensen v. United States* (1978), given that the moon cannot sustain life. That case does not apply here, however, given that the case here is easily distinguishable from *Svensen* because . . . [detailed discussion how Antarctica is different from the characteristics of the moon that *Svenson v. U.S.* said indicated the moon is not a traditional public forum]

B. *Antarctica is a designated public forum.*

Even if Antarctica is not a traditional public forum, it is a designated public forum. *ISKCON v. Lee* (1992) also set out several criteria that indicate public property is a designated public forum. [explanation of those criteria.]

1. The U.S. Navy has [explanation of conduct by the Navy]
The U.S. Navy may try to argue that Antarctica is like Death Valley National Park, which the Supreme Court ruled is not a designated public forum in *Johnson v. National Park Service* (1984). However, Antarctica is unlike Death Valley, due to the fact that . . . [detailed discussion how the facts of this case differ from the *Johnson v. NPS* on this point whether the government has declared its intent regarding the use of public property.]

II. THE NAVY'S PROHIBITION ON LEAFLETTING IN ANTARCTICA FAILS TO MEET STRICT SCRUTINY
The Supreme Court in *ISKCON v. Lee* (1992) explained that regulations in either traditional public forums or designated public forums must pass strict scrutiny—that is, the regulation must be narrowly tailored to further a compelling government interest. The Navy's ban on leafleting fails to meet pass either element of strict scrutiny.
A. The Navy's ban on leafleting in Antarctica lacks a compelling government interest.
[argument with citations]

. . . B. The Navy's ban on leafleting in Antarctica is not narrowly tailored.
[argument with citations]

III. Even if Antarctica is not a public forum, the Navy's ban on leafleting in Antarctica is not reasonable.
[argument with citations]

## Common Legal Brief Mistakes

In preparing a legal or appellate brief, one could make any number of mistakes. Here are the most common mistakes that might weaken your arguments:

*Failure to use frequent organizational headings and subheadings* Without such, judges will have difficulty trying to determine what the writer's main points are. Headings and subheadings should be clear, prominent, and affirmatively state the main legal claim expressed by that section of the brief. For example, if one of the elements of a rule regarding murder looks at an alleged defendant's intent, the section heading in an appellate brief should *not* be merely a brief label like "The Defendant's

Intent." Instead, that part of the brief should affirmatively be labeled using a phrase stating the argument that will be made in that section of the brief. This heading could therefore be something like "Defendant Smith Intended to Murder Jones" or "The Prosecution failed to Prove Intent" or "Defendant Smith's Intent to Murder Jones was Established by his Personal Diary" or "The Evidence at Trial Failed to Show Any Intent by the Defendant to Murder Jones."

*Mistakenly organizing the brief around individual case precedents rather than the rules and elements of applicable laws* Remember that the larger, overall structure of the brief should be organized around the elements of whatever rule(s) apply, and then the sub-structure within each element will analogize to or distinguish facts from individual cases dealing with related issues and fact patterns. Also keep in mind that *following* an organizational outline is not the same as *being* an outline. Your appellate brief, just like any good written work, should follow a clear organizational outline with headings and subheadings, but only outlines themselves will be written in outline form such as further indenting at each sub-level of the outline.

*Incorrectly summarizing a case when analogizing or distinguishing it* When referring to cases, you want to always summarize them briefly and clearly. An attorney can not assume the reader knows the case. In fact, the judge reading the brief might know absolutely nothing about this area of the law and its cases. Thus, you must assume the reader knows nothing, and so must be fully educated about every case that is discussed. When discussing a case for the first time, first say something like:

> In *U.S. v. Smith*, 123 U.S. 456 (1990) the Court considered the issue whether a defendant's personal diary stating "I'd like to see Jones dead" was sufficient evidence of intent to kill. The Court reaffirmed the rule that "any substantial evidence of intent is sufficient for a jury finding of intent." Applying that rule, the Court declared a diary entry directly stating a desire to murder the victim was "substantial evidence" that was sufficient for a jury finding of intent. Therefore, the defendant's conviction was upheld.

Once that summary is provided, you can analogize or distinguish the case, such as "*U.S. v. Smith* is analogous to the case here because . . ." or "*U.S. v. Smith* is distinguishable from the case at hand because. . . ." The reader won't understand why the case at hand is analogous or different to the other case without first knowing what happened in the other case.

*Mistakenly arguing for your opponent* In pre-emptively rebutting one's opponent's best arguments, the lawyer writing the brief mistakenly makes such lengthy, extensive arguments in the opponent's favor that it is unclear which party the lawyer is actually representing! Instead, just briefly explain in a couple sentences what your opponent's strongest arguments would be. For example, in the case of *U.S. v. Smith*, the brief for the government might state:

> Defendant Smith may assert that case *X v. Y* should apply here because [the rule is relevant][the facts are analogous][the case is controlling][etc.] However, Smith would be mistaken in arguing case *X v. Y* controls of the outcome here, because [the rule does not apply ] [the facts can be distinguished][*X v. Y* is a persuasive precedent only] [*X v. Y* has been superseded by more/better/subsequent cases][etc.]"

Once the case of *X v. Y* is briefly summarized in a couple or few sentences for the reader, then the rest of the arguments by the U.S. government would be spent clearly stating why Smith's argument is mistaken. In short, only briefly explain the essence of one's opponent's argument, but then extensively explain and elaborate on your rebuttal argument.

*Writing in the first person pronoun* Beginning legal writers often incorrectly write in the first person, saying things like "I think" "I feel," "I believe" or "I would argue," and so on. For example, look at how weak the following statements sound:

> "I think the case of *X v. Y* would control here."
>
> "I believe the facts of this case are distinguishable from the facts of *Z v. QQQ.*"
>
> "I feel the government's action here violates the 3rd Amendment."

There are several problems with these statements. First, one "feels" emotions like happiness or sadness or anger; one does not "feel" a thought such as legal argument. Even if one could "feel" a legal argument, it is irrelevant. It's also legally irrelevant what *you* think or believe. The only thing that matters legally is what the *law* says. Therefore, just affirmatively state how the law applies:

> "The case of *X v. Y* controls here."
>
> "The facts of this case are distinguishable from the facts of *Z v. QQQ*"
>
> "The government's action here violates the 3rd Amendment."

*Not addressing cases or rules relevant to your opponent* Sometimes highly relevant cases are not cited or they are merely cited but left out of the actual discussion and analysis. Legal thinking and arguments requires creativity. An attorney for one side often leaves out discussion of cases the attorney thinks are not helpful to his or her argument, but the very reason those cases seem unhelpful is because they are helpful to an opponent! This means those seemingly unhelpful cases *must* be addressed and discussed so as to undercut one's opponent's arguments, or else one has effectively admitted legal defeat.

On a similar note, sometimes a highly relevant rule or rules are either not mentioned or are left out of the detailed discussion and analysis. Again, creative critical thinking is required. If there is a way a legal rule might help you, use it. If you don't, your opponent will. Sometimes legal authority can be applied that at first look doesn't seem like it applies, but the issue can be analogized. For example, in 2002 a judge in San Francisco had to decide which of two fans had rightfully caught a home-run baseball at a Major League Baseball game. The baseball was part of an all-time home-run record, and so the baseball was estimated to be worth roughly a million dollars. Since there was no caselaw regarding such a legal issue, the lawyers and the judge looked to cases that involved competing claims over the capture of wild animals and competing claims over the discovery of hidden or lost treasure troves.

*Not having fallback arguments* It is essential to have a strong leading argument, but if it is somehow shredded by the opposing attorney, you will want some solid fallback arguments to support your appeal.

*Other common errors* In addition to the errors described above, there are many other errors legal writers frequently make in preparing appellate briefs, legal memos, oral arguments, IRAC analysis, and so on.

> Arguments are highly summary or conclusory in nature and not explanatory and analytical.
>
> Arguments skip key steps in logic.
>
> An incorrect or irrelevant rule is applied that is not at issue in the case.
>
> An analysis is used that actually applies to a different part of a rule.
>
> Points are argued that are actually irrelevant under the legal rule.

The rules are quoted but then not all the elements are discussed, analyzed, or applied.

Important or critical facts of the case are ignored, which significantly alter the correct legal analysis.

Irrelevant or even made-up facts are added to the case, thus incorrectly altering the legal analysis.

Non-academic language is used: slang, colloquial expressions, rhetorical questions, etc.

Poor English grammar and punctuation, incorrect spelling, awkward phrasing or word choice, etc. is used.

## Argument from Precedent Example: Capture of Wild Animals

To get a better idea of arguing from precedent, let's look at a more extended example, complete with a sample written argument. One famous example commonly used to teach the concept of argument from analogy is the early common law regarding the capture of wild animals. In a series of cases from the early 1700's through the early 1900's, courts in England and the United States established common law rules regarding legal possession of wild animals. Each subsequent case built upon prior precedents, sometimes following them, sometimes distinguishing them, and often doing both. In the process, the courts also created exceptions to the capture rule. The essence of the basic rule, but with exceptions, is that a hunter does not possess a wild animal until either it is physically possessed in hand, or it is controlled by the hunter to a degree by which capture is "practically inevitable." This latter type of capture typically would be capture in a net, trap, cage, or pen, or if the animal were mortally wounded and being closely tracked.

The following cases are classic first-year law school readings. They not only show the common law rules regarding possession of wild animals, but they are used to show how courts reason from precedent. In the cases you can see the judges analogize to and distinguish from prior case precedents to reach their decisions. At the end of this group of readings, you will practice how lawyers would try to analogize or distinguish the precedents in a hypothetical case that is inspired loosely on an actual case. Then you'll see a sample of what a written argument from precedent would look like using the cases.

*Keeble v. Hickeringill, 11 East 574 (England 1707)* Action upon the case. Plaintiff [Keeble] declares that he was, 8th November in the second year of the Queen, lawfully possessed of a close of land called Minott's Meadow, containing a decoy pond, to which divers waterfowl used to resort and come: and the plaintiff has at his own costs and charges prepared and procured divers decoy ducks, nets, machines and other engines for the decoying and taking of the wildfowl, and enjoyed the benefit in taking them: the defendant [Hickeringill], knowing which and intending to damnify the plaintiff in his vivary, and to fright and drive away the wildfowl used to resort thither, and deprive him of his profit, did, on the 8th of November, resort to the head of the said pond and vivary, and did discharge six guns laden with gunpowder, and with the noise and stink of the gunpowder did drive away the wildfowl then being in the pond: and on the 11th and 12th days of November the defendant, with design to damnify the plaintiff, and fright away the wildfowl, did place himself with a gun near the vivary, and there did discharge the said gun several times that was then charged with the gunpowder against the said decoy pond, whereby the wildfowl were frighted away, and did forsake the said pond. Upon not guilty pleaded, a verdict was found for the plaintiff and 20£ damages. [The defendant now appeals.]

Chief Justice Holt: I am of opinion that this action doth lie. It seems to be new in this instance, but is not new in the reason or principle of it. For, 1st, this using or making a decoy is lawful. 2dly, this employment of his ground to that use is profitable to the plaintiff, as is the skill and management of that employment. As to the first, every man hath a property may employ it for his pleasure and profit, as for alluring and procuring decoy ducks to come to his pond. To learn the trade of seducing other ducks to come there in order to be taken is not prohibited either by the law of the land or the moral law; but it is lawful to use art to seduce them, to catch them, and destroy them for the use of mankind, as to kill and destroy wildfowl or tame cattle. Then when a man useth his art or his skill to take them, to sell and dispose of for his profit; this is his trade, and he that hinders another in his trade or livelihood is liable to an action for so hindering him . . .

[W]here a violent or malicious act is done to a man's occupation, profession, or way of getting a livelihood, there an action lies in all cases. But if a man doth him damage by using the same employment; as if Mr. Hickeringill had set up another decoy on his own ground near the plaintiff's, and that had spoiled the custom of the plaintiff, no action would lie, because he had as much liberty to make and use a decoy as the plaintiff. This is like the case of 11 Hen. IV p. 47. One schoolmaster sets up a new school to the damage of an ancient school, and thereby the scholars are allured from the old school to come to his new. (The action there was held not to lie.) But suppose Mr. Hickeringill should lie in the way with his guns and frighten the boys from going to school and their parents would not let them go thither sure that schoolmaster might have an action for the loss of his scholars. A man hath a market, to which he hath toll for horses sold: a man is bringing his horse to market to sell: a stranger hinders and obstructs him from going thither to the market: an action lies because it imports damage. Action upon the case lies against one that shall by threats frighten away his tenants at will. 9 Hen. VII pp. 7-8, 21 Hen. VI p. 31, 14 Edw. IV p. 7. [Judgment for the plaintiff.]

*Pierson v. Post, 3 Caines 175, 2 Am. Dec. 264 (N.Y. 1805)*

Justice Tompkins delivered the opinion of the court.

The question submitted by the counsel in this cause for our determination is, whether Lodowick Post, by the pursuit with his hounds in the manner alleged in his declaration, acquired such a right to, or property in, the fox, as will sustain an action against [Jesse] Pierson for killing and taking him away?

The cause was argued with much ability by the counsel on both sides, and presents for our decision a novel and nice question. It is admitted that a fox is an animal *feræ naturæ* [wild animal], and that property in such animals is acquired by occupancy only. These admissions narrow the discussion to the simple question of what acts amount to occupancy, applied to acquiring right to wild animals?

If we have recourse to the ancient writers upon general principles of law, the judgment below is obviously erroneous. Justinian's Institutes adopt the principle, that pursuit alone vests no property or right in the huntsman; and that even pursuit, accompanied with wounding, is equally ineffectual for that purpose, unless the animal be actually taken. The same principle is recognised by Bracton.

Puffendorf defines occupancy of beasts *feræ naturæ,* to be the actual corporal possession of them, and Bynkershoek is cited as coinciding in this definition. . . . The foregoing authorities are decisive to show that mere pursuit gave Post no legal right to the fox, but that he became the property of Pierson, who intercepted and killed him.

It therefore only remains to inquire whether there are any contrary principles, or authorities, to be found in other books, which ought to induce a different decision. Most of the cases which have occurred in *England,* relating to property in wild animals, have either been discussed and decided upon the principles of their positive statute regulations, or have arisen between the huntsman and the owner of the land upon which beasts *feræ naturæ* have been apprehended; the former claiming them by title of occupancy, and the latter *ratione soli* [by reason of the ownership of the soil]. Little satisfactory aid can, therefore, be derived from the *English* reporters.

Barbeyrac, in his notes on Puffendorf, does not accede to the definition of occupancy by the latter, but, on the contrary, affirms, that actual bodily seizure is not, in all cases, necessary to constitute possession of wild animals. . . . That is to say, that actual bodily seizure is not indispensable to acquire right to, or possession of, wild beasts; but that, on the contrary, the mortal wounding of such beasts, by one not abandoning his pursuit, may, with the utmost propriety, be deemed possession of him; since, thereby, the pursuer manifests an unequivocal intention of appropriating the animal to his individual use, has deprived him of his natural liberty, and brought him within his certain control. So also, encompassing and securing such animals with nets and toils, or otherwise intercepting them in such a manner as to deprive them of their natural liberty, and render escape impossible, may justly be deemed to give possession of them to those persons who, by their industry and labour, have used such means of apprehending them. . . . The case now under consideration is one of mere pursuit, and presents no circumstances or acts which can bring it within the definition of occupancy by Puffendorf . . . or the ideas of Barbeyrac upon that subject.

The case cited from *Keeble v. Hickeringill*, I think clearly distinguishable from the present; inasmuch as there the action was for maliciously hindering and disturbing the plaintiff in the exercise and enjoyment of a private franchise; and in the report of the same case, Holt, Chief Justice, states, that the ducks were in the plaintiff's decoy pond, and *so in his possession,* from which it is obvious the court laid much stress in their opinion upon the plaintiff's possession of the ducks . . .

However uncourteous or unkind the conduct of Pierson towards Post, in this instance, may have been, yet his act was productive of no injury or damage for which a legal remedy can be applied. We are of opinion the judgment below was erroneous, and ought to be reversed. Judgment of reversal.

*Young v. Hichens, 6 QB 606, 115 ER 228 (England 1844)*

[Young, a commercial fisherman, was fishing off the coast of Cornwall, England and had partially enclosed a shoal of fish within his fishing net, but still had a gap in the net of about 7 fathoms (42 feet) to finish closing. He was in the process of blocking the opening in the net with another net while his boats were stationed at the gap in the net. His boats were splashing the water in the gap to scare the partially enclosed fish away from the gap in the net, thus hopefully preventing the fish from escaping before the gap in the net was closed. Hichens, another commercial fisherman on his own boat, saw what Young was doing. Hichens then rowed up to the opening of the net and deliberately disrupted the attempt to close the gap in the net. This damaged Young's net, and allowed most of the fish to escape out of Young's net. Hichens then caught most of the fish in his own net as the fish were fleeing Young's net. Young brought an action in trespass, suing for the damage to the net, and the loss of the value of the fish. The trail court awarded £568 total in damages for loss of the fish and damage done to the net. Hichens appealed, arguing that since the fish were not yet in Young's possession, he did not yet own the fish, so he could not sue for loss of property in the fish.]

Chief Justice Lord Denman: . . . It does appear almost certain that the plaintiff would have had possession of the fish but for the act of the defendant: but it is quite certain that he had not possession. Whatever interpretation may be put upon such terms as "custody" and "possession", the question will be whether any custody or possession has been obtained here. I think it is impossible to say it had, until the party had actual power over the fish. It may be that the defendant acted unjustifiably in preventing the plaintiff from obtaining such power; but that would only show a wrongful act, for which he might be liable in a proper form of action [such as perhaps common law tortious interference with business, or a violation of some statute.]

Justice Patteson [concurring]: I do not see how we can support [Young's claim] upon the present evidence, unless we were prepared to hold that all but reducing into possession is the same as reducing into possession. . . .

Justice Wrightman [concurring]: I am of the same opinion. If the property in the fish was vested in the plaintiff by his partially enclosing them but leaving an opening in the nets, he would be entitled to maintain trover [a lawsuit for wrongful taking of personal property] for fish which escaped through that very opening.

[The Court of Queen's Bench thus agreed with Hichens, reversing the trial court award of damages for the value of the fish, and thereby reduced the overall damage award to only 20 shillings (£1), representing the damage to the net.]

*Ghen v. Rich, 8 F. 159 (Mass. 1881)*

District Judge Nelson: This is a libel to recover the value of a fin-back whale. The libellant lives in Provincetown and the respondent in Wellfleet. The facts, as they appeared at the hearing, are as follows:

In the early spring months the easterly part of Massachusetts bay is frequented by the species of whale known as the fin-back whale. Fishermen from Provincetown pursue them in open boats from the shore, and shoot them with bomb-lances fired from guns made expressly for the purpose. When killed they sink at once to the bottom, but in the course of from one to three days they rise and float on the surface. Some of them are picked up by vessels and towed into Provincetown. Some float ashore at high water and are left stranded on the beach as the tide recedes. Others float out to sea and are never recovered. The person who happens to find them on the beach usually sends word to Provincetown, and the owner comes to the spot and removes the blubber. The finder usually receives a small salvage for his services. Try-works are established in Provincetown for trying out the oil. The business is of considerable extent, but, since it requires skill and experience, as well as some outlay of capital, and is attended with great exposure and hardship, few persons engage in it. The average yield of oil is about 20 barrels to a whale. It swims with great swiftness, and for that reason cannot be taken by the harpoon and line. Each boat's crew engaged in the business has its peculiar mark or device on its lances, and in this way it is known by whom a whale is killed.

The usage on Cape Cod, for many years, has been that the person who kills a whale in the manner and under the circumstances described, owns it, and this right has never been disputed until this case. The libellant [Ghen] has been engaged in this business for ten years past. On the morning of April 9, 1880, in Massachusetts bay, near the end of Cape Cod, he shot and instantly killed with a bomb-lance the whale in question. It sunk immediately, and on the morning of the 12th was found stranded on the beach in Brewster, within the ebb and flow of the tide, by one Ellis, 17 miles from the spot where it was killed. Instead of sending word to Provincetown, as is customary, Ellis advertised the whale for sale at auction, and sold it to the respondent [Rich], who shipped off the blubber and tried out the oil. The libellant heard of the finding of the whale on the morning of the 15th, and immediately sent one of his boat's crew to the place and claimed it. Neither the respondent nor Ellis knew the whale had been killed by the libellant, but they knew or might have known, if they had wished, that it had been shot and killed with a bomblance, by some person engaged in this species of business.

The libellant claims title to the whale under this usage. The respondent insists that this usage is invalid. It was decided by Judge Sprague, in *Taber v. Jenny*, 1 Sprague, 315, that when a whale has been killed, and is anchored and left with marks of appropriation, it is the property of the captors; and if it is afterwards found, still anchored, by another ship, there is no usage or principle of law by which the property of the original captors is diverted, even though the whale may have dragged from its anchorage. The learned judge says:

"When the whale had been killed and taken possession of by the boat of the Hillman, (the first taker,) it became the property of the owners of that ship, and all was done which was then practicable in order to secure it. They left it anchored, with unequivocal marks of appropriation."

In *Bartlett v. Budd*, 1 Low. 223, the facts were these: The first officer of the libellant's ship killed a whale in the Okhotsk sea, anchored it, attached a waif to the body, and then left it and went ashore at some distance for the night. The next morning the boats of the respondent's ship found the whale adrift, the anchor not holding, the cable coiled round the body, and no waif or irons attached to it. Judge Lowell held that, as the libellants had killed and taken actual possession of the whale, the ownership vested in them. In his opinion the learned judge says:

"A whale, being feroe naturoe, does not become property until a firm possession has been established by the taker. But when such possession has become firm and complete, the right of property is clear, and has all the characteristics of property."

He doubted whether a usage set up but not proved by the respondents, that a whale found adrift in the ocean is the property of the finder, unless the first taker should appear and claim it before it is cut in, would be valid, and remarked that "there would be great difficulty in upholding a custom that should take the property of A. and give it to B., under so very short and uncertain a substitute for the statute of limitations, and one so open to fraud and deceit." Both the cases cited were decided without reference to usage, upon the ground that the property had been acquired by the first taker by actual possession and appropriation.

In *Swift v. Gifford*, Judge Lowell decided that a custom among whalemen in the Arctic seas, that the iron holds the whale, was reasonable and valid. In that case a boat's crew from the respondent's ship pursued and struck a whale in the Arctic ocean, and the harpoon and the line attached to it remained in the whale, but did not remain fast to the boat. A boat's crew from the libellant's ship continued the pursuit and captured the whale, and the master of the respondent's ship claimed it on the spot. It was held by the learned judge that the whale belonged to the respondents. It was said by Judge Sprague, in *Bourne v. Ashley*, an unprinted case referred to by Judge Lowell in *Swift v. Gifford*, that the usage for the first iron, whether attached to the boat or not, to hold the whale was fully established; and he added that, although local usages of a particular port ought not to be allowed to set aside the general maritime law, this objection did not apply to a custom which embraced an entire business, and had been concurred in for a long time by every one engaged in the trade.

In *Swift v. Gifford*, Judge Lowell also said:

"The rule of law invoked in this case is one of very limited application. The whale fishery is the only branch of industry of any importance in which it is likely to be much used, and if a usage is found to prevail generally in that business, it will not be open to the objection that it is likely to disturb the general understanding of mankind by the interposition of an arbitrary exception."

I see no reason why the usage proved in this case is not as reasonable as that sustained in the cases cited. Its application must necessarily be extremely limited, and can affect but a few persons. It has been recognized and acquiesced in for many years. It requires in the first taker the only act of appropriation that is possible in the nature of the case. Unless it is sustained, this branch of industry must necessarily cease, for no person would engage in it if the fruits of his labor could be appropriated by any chance finder. It gives reasonable salvage for securing or reporting the property. That the rule works well in practice is shown by the extent of the industry which has grown up under it, and the general acquiescence of a whole community interested to dispute it. It is by no means clear that without regard to usage the common law would not reach the same result. That seems to be the effect of the decisions in *Taber v. Jenny* and *Bartlett v. Budd.* If the fisherman does all that it is possible to do to make the animal his own, that would seem to be sufficient. . . . I hold the usage to be valid, and that the property in the whale was in the libellant. . . .

Decree for libellant for $71.05, without costs.

*State v. Shaw, 65 N.E. 877 (Ohio 1902)*

The defendants in error were indicted in Lake county for the crime of grand larceny. The indictment is as follows: "In the court of common pleas of Lake county, Ohio, of the term of May, in the year of our Lord one thousand nine hundred and one. The jurors of the grand jury of the state of Ohio, within and for the body of the county of Lake, duly impaneled, sworn and charged to inquire of crimes and offenses committed within the said county of Lake, in the name and by the authority of the state of Ohio, upon their oaths do find and present, that Henry Shaw, John Thomas and James Postine, late of said county, on the fifteenth day of May, in the year of our Lord one thousand nine hundred and one, with force and arms, in said county of Lake and state of Ohio, unlawfully and feloniously did steal, take and carry away seven hundred and thirty pounds of fish, of the value of forty-one dollars, of the personal property of Morris E. Grow and John Hough, partners as Grow and Hough, contrary to the form of the statute in such case made and provided, and against the peace and dignity of the state of Ohio."

One of the defendants, John Thomas, was tried separately. [At] the trial, no evidence was offered by the defendant. The evidence offered by the state disclosed that on the morning of May 15, 1901, about 5 or 6 o'clock, a small sail-boat was discovered two or three miles off Fairport harbor; a tug ran out and overhauled this boat and discovered they had fish on board. In reply to an inquiry where they had got the fish, they said near Cleveland out of a trap net. They were asked to come to the harbor with the tug, and refused; two other tugs came to the assistance of the one already there, and brought in the defendants, with their boat, and they were arrested. It is in evidence that on the way in, the defendant, John Thomas, said that "they lifted two pound nets west of the pier and got the fish." The testimony further tended to show that the two pound nets belonged to Grow and Hough, the parties named in the indictment, and that the defendants had taken from these two nets somewhere from 100 to 150 pounds of fish, each. It also appears that the construction of these pound nets is such that the entrance to the net was about thirty-five feet deep, eight rods long, and terminated in an aperture leading into the net which was two feet and ten inches in diameter. This tunnel, as it is called, extended into the net, or pot, some five or six feet, and the pot was about twenty-eight feet square, reaching, perhaps, four feet above the water. The evidence shows that the opening of the tunnel into the pot was the place where the fish entered, and that it was at all times left open. There is no evidence as to the quantity of fish escaping from the nets; it simply appears that it was possible for the fish to go out in the same way they got in. It was also in evidence that these nets were frequently disturbed by wind and storm, and at such times so disordered that fish escaped over the top. When the state had rested its case the defendant, Thomas, moved the court to arrest the testimony from the jury and direct a verdict of not guilty. The court overruled this motion, but after argument did direct a verdict of not guilty, which was returned by the jury, and to which the state excepted. . . .

Justice Davis: Fish are ferae naturae; yet, where the animals or other creatures are not domestic, but are *ferae naturae*, larceny may, notwithstanding, be committed of them, if they are fit for food of man and dead, reclaimed (and known to be so) or confined. Thus . . . fish in a tank or net, or as it seems in any other enclosed place which is private property, and where they may be taken at any time at the pleasure of the owner . . . the taking of them with felonious intent will be larceny. 2 Russ. Cr. 83. "Fish confined in a tank or net are sufficiently secured." 2 Bishop Cr. Law section 775.

The trial judge seems to have directed the jury to return a verdict of "not guilty" on the theory that the fish must have been confined so that there was absolutely no possibility of escape. We think that this doctrine is both unnecessarily technical and erroneous. For example, bees in a hive may be the subject of larceny, yet it is possible for the bees to leave the hive by the same place at which they entered. To acquire a property right in animals *ferae naturae,* the pursuer must bring them into his power and control, and so maintain his control as to show that he does not intend to abandon them again to the world at large. When he has confined them within his own private enclosure where he may subject them to his own use at his pleasure, and maintains reasonable precautions to prevent escape, they are so impressed with his proprietorship that a felonious taking of them from his enclosure, whether trap, cage, park, net, or whatever it may be, will be larceny. For such cases, as is clearly shown by the authorities above quoted, the law does not require absolute security against the possibility of escape. . . . *Young v. Hichens,* 6 Q.B. 606 is not applicable to this case. That was an action for the conversion of fish which were never in the plaintiff's net, but had been frightened away from entering into the plaintiff's net by the defendant and caught in his own net.

In the present case the fish were not at large in Lake Erie. They were confined in nets, from which it was not absolutely impossible for them to escape, yet it was practically so impossible; for it seems that under ordinary circumstances few, if any, of the fish escape. The fish that were taken had not escaped, and it does not appear that they would have escaped, or even that they probably would have escaped. They were so safely secured that the owners of the nets could have taken them out of the water at will as readily as the defendants did. The possession of the owners of the nets was so complete and certain that the defendants went to the nets and raised them with absolute assurance that they could get the fish that were in them. We think, therefore, that the owners of the nets, having captured and confined the fish, had acquired such a property in them that the taking of them was larceny.

## Wild Capture Hypothetical: *Stephens v. Albers*

You have just read several rulings from common cases over the centuries regarding the capture of wild animals. You have also seen how the judges in the cases both followed and distinguished case precedents to reach their decisions. Now consider the following hypothetical case, based loosely on an actual historical case, *Stephens v Albers.*

Andy Albers was hunting on his own wooded property during deer season in the State of Swansonia within the United States. Suddenly he saw a remarkable sight: an African red-and-green-striped gazelle appeared. Albers shot the gazelle and did not find any brand or tag on the animal. He took it to a local taxidermist to have it stuffed and mounted for display in his home. The local TV news reported the unusual story. Scott Stephens, a nearby local rancher, saw the news story, and thereby learned what had happened to the African red-and-green-striped gazelle that he had been raising on his ranch, but had escaped from its fencing a week earlier. Stephens contacted Albers and explained how the gazelle was his but had escaped. Stephens asked Albers to compensate Stephens for the lost value of his gazelle. Albers refused, stating the gazelle was a wild unmarked animal on his Albers' own property. Stephens filed a lawsuit in state court against Albers for the value of the gazelle. Assuming all the facts are true as given, and considering the five cases you read involving the law regarding capture of wild animals, how would Stephens and Albers each make legal arguments in support of their respective positions using the relevant precedents? In other words, how would Stephens and Albers each try to analogize their situation to the case precedents they would like the court to follow? Equally important, how would Stephens and Albers each try to distinguish their situation from the case precedents that go against their respective positions so that the trial court does not follow those cases? Do not look at the possible arguments below until you have thoroughly tried to come up with the arguments yourself.

*Precedent Analysis Table of Stephens v. Albers* Again, do *not* look at the solution below until you have thoroughly tried to come up with your own answers first. The table on the next page shows how both Stephens and Albers each might try to argue which certain aspects of the relevant precedents should either be followed or distinguished. There might be other arguments they each could make, but the points listed would be some of the main points they would argue.

*Written Argument in Stephens v. Albers* In legal writing, just as in any type of writing, creating an outline first is always highly recommended because it helps organize the writer's thoughts. Here is one possible outline of what Alber's arguments might look like:

I. Albers' introductory summary overview of argument
II. Argument
 A. The Rule of Possession should be followed here
  1. *Pierson v. Post* should be followed: gazelle was running wild and capture on Albers' own private land
  2. *Young v. Hichens* should be followed: gazelle was not in any enclosure
 B. No exceptions to the rule of possession apply to Albers or to the gazelle
  1. Distinguish *Keeble v. Hickeringill*: Albers was not trespassing on anyone's land nor intentionally interfering with anyone's ownership
  2. Distinguish *State v. Shaw*: the gazelle was not stolen from any enclosure
  3. Distinguish *Ghen v. Rich*: the gazelle had no tags or other man-made markings to indicate prior ownership
III. Conclusion re-summarizing the argument

Precedent Analysis

| Precedent Cases | Plaintiff STEPHENS will argue: | Defendant ALBERS will argue: |
|---|---|---|
| *Keeble v. Hickeringill* (1707) | STEPHENS will argue *Keeble v. Hickeringill* should be followed: just like Keeble exerted effort at ownership of the ducks through creation of his private pond and duck decoys, Stephens exerted personal effort at possessing the gazelle by enclosing it in a fence, and just like Hickeringill interfered with Keeble's duck hunting, Albers interfered with Stephen's ownership of the gazelle by shooting it, | ALBERS will argue *Keeble v. Hickeringill* should be distinguished: Unlike Hickeringill, who acted maliciously to disturb ownership of wild animals on someone else's (Keeble's) property, Albers acted in good faith, and was on Alber's own property, not that of Stephens. |
| *Pierson v. Post* (1805) | STEPHENS will argue *Pierson v. Post* should be distinguished: Although possession is the rule, unlike the fox in *Pierson v. Post,* which had never been possessed, here Stephens already had prior possession of the gazelle | ALBERS will argue *Pierson v. Post* should be followed: Just like the fox in the wild in *Pierson v. Post* was not owned until it was shot, here the gazelle was in the wild, and so it was not owned until Albers shot it. |
| *Young v. Hichens* (1844) | STEPHENS will argue *Young v. Hichens* should be distinguished: Unlike the fish in *Young v. Hichens,* which were never fully possessed, Stephens was in full possession of the gazelle before it escaped. | ALBERS will argue *Young v. Hichens* should be followed: Just like the fish escaped from Young and then became owned by Hichens, the gazelle here escaped from Stephens and so became owned by Albers. |
| *Ghen v. Rich* (1881) | STEPHENS will argue *Ghen v. Rich* should be followed: Just like a marked harpoon in a whale gives public notice of ownership, an African red-and-green-striped gazelle so far from its native habitat is public notice to others that it is already owned | ALBERS will argue *Ghen v. Rich* should be distinguished: Unlike the whale in *Ghen v. Rich,* which had a harpoon stuck in it marked with the identity of the whalers, there was nothing on the gazelle branding it, tagging it, or other man-made marks indicating prior ownership |
| *State v. Shaw* (1902) | STEPHENS will argue *State v. Shaw* should be followed: Just like a carefully crafted fish net creates possession even though fish might possibly escape, a fence creates possession even though the enclosed animals (like the gazelle here) might possibly escape. | ALBERS will argue *State v. Shaw* should be distinguished: Shaw criminally stole the fish from someone else's net, but the gazelle here escaped on its own, so Albers did not steal the gazelle or commit any other crime or act to help the gazelle escape enclosure. |

Now, here is what the detailed written argument by Albers might look like:

*I. Summary of Argument:*

Ownership of a wild animal is determined by possession. Albers was hunting on his own land when he shot the gazelle in the wild and immediately took possession of its body. Albers was not trespassing on anyone's land; Albers did not steal the gazelle from any fence, net, or trap; and there were no markings on the gazelle to show prior ownership or possession. Thus, Albers owns the dead gazelle and is not liable to Stevens for damages.

*II. Argument*

*A. Albers took possession of the gazelle, thus he owns it and has title to the gazelle.*

In the landmark case *Pierson v. Post*, 3 Caines 175 (1805), the court set up the rule of possession that applies when a wild animal becomes owned by a hunter. In the case, Post was pursuing a fox with his hounds when Post shot the fox and took possession of the body. Pierson sued Post, claiming pursuit was enough to make the fox his. The court ruled that "pursuit alone vests no property or right in the huntsman; and that even pursuit, accompanied with wounding, is equally ineffectual for that purpose, unless the animal be actually taken."

A similar holding resulted in *Young v. Hichens*, 6 QB 606, 115 ER 228 (1844). In *Young*, fisherman Young had almost but not quite finished enclosing a net around a shoal of fish, when Hichens came along and captured the fish. The court ruled that no matter how close Young was to capturing the fish, "all but reducing to possession" still is not "reducing to possession" and thus Hichens obtained ownership of the fish by actually, fully possessing them. In the case here, like Post in *Pierson v Post* and like Hichens in *Young v. Hichens,* Albers took full, complete possession of the gazelle in its natural state in the wild. Thus, Albers owns the gazelle and is not liable to plaintiff Stevens for any value of the gazelle.

*B. Albers owns the gazelle because no exception to the possession rule applies here.*

The Plaintiff, opponent Stevens, might try to argue several cases that held possession of a wild animal is not enough for ownership in some instances. None of those cases, however, applies here because each case can be easily distinguished from the present case.

1. *Albers was not trespassing on anyone's land and was instead on his own land*

Opponent Stevens first might try to argue *Keeble v. Hickeringill*, 11 East 574, (1707). In *Keeble*, the court ruled that the defendant Hickeringill was liable to the plaintiff Keeble for the cost of wild ducks on Keeble's land, even though the ducks were not yet possessed by Keeble. That case, though involved trespass by the defendant on the plaintiff's land. In the case at hand, Albers was on his own land when he shot the gazelle. Thus, *Keeble v. Hickeringill* does not apply here.

2. *Albers took no action to steal the gazelle or free it from enclosure*

Opponent Stevens might similarly try to argue *State v. Shaw*, 67 Ohio St. 157, 65 N.E. 877 (1902). In that case, Shaw stole fish that were at the time of the theft already fully enclosed in someone else's fish net with very little chance of escape, although it was possible they might escape on their own. The court upheld prosecution of Shaw for theft. Here, however, the gazelle broke free from Steven's fence on its own and was shot in the wild on Alber's land. Albers did not trespass on Steven's land, nor did Albers steal the gazelle. Thus, Stevens was no longer in possession of the gazelle, as the gazelle escaped on its own from a less-than-perfectly secure fence. The gazelle was then not in any fence, net, or other trap, but was roaming freely in the wild. The gazelle wandered onto Albers own land where he shot it and thus took possession and ownership of the gazelle at that point.

3. *There were no man-made markings on the gazelle indicating ownership*

Finally, opponent Stevens might try to argue that this court should follow the case of *Ghen v. Rich*, 8 F. 159 (Mass. 1881). There, the court ruled that whales were a unique type of wild creature such that ordinary methods of capture did not work. Thus, the court said whales could be possessed by mere killing rather than capture, and ownership would be determined later by the markings on the harpoon stuck in the whale when the whale washed up dead on a beach. In the present case, a gazelle is at issue, not a whale, so the unique exception to the rule of possession in the case of killing and capture of wild animals does not apply. Regardless, even if it were to apply, there were no brands, tags, or other markings on the gazelle that would indicate any prior ownership. Thus, Albers was in the legal right to kill and capture the gazelle on his own property, and thereby acquiring ownership of the gazelle through such possession.

*III. Conclusion*

For all the foregoing reasons, defendant Albers asks this court to rule for the defendant by following the rule of possession of wild animals and thus holding that Albers owns the gazelle by killing and capturing the gazelle in the wild on Albers own land. None of the exceptions to the rule of possession applies, as all those cases are completely distinguishable from the present case and thus do not apply here. Thus, defendant Albers asks this court to hold that Albers is not liable to the defendant for any damages.

In a real life Colorado supreme court case (1927), a rare, expensive silver fox bred in captivity, escaped, and was shot by a rancher and sold to a pelt dealer. The original owner found out and sued for value of fox. The court did not look to precedents, but made a ruling similar to *Ghen v. Rich.*

> Having then neither statute nor applicable common law rule governing the case we must so apply general principles in the light of custom, existing facts, and common knowledge, that justice will be done.
>
> This defendant in fact had, or is charged with, knowledge that the pelt . . .was from an animal taken in a locality where its kind *ferae naturae* was unknown and in a state where large numbers were kept in captivity.
>
> We are loath to believe that a man may capture a grizzly bear in the environs of New York or Chicago, or a seal in a mill pond in Massachusetts, or an elephant in a corn field in Iowa, or a silver fox on a ranch in Morgan County, Colorado, and snap his fingers in the face of its former owner whose title had been acquired by a considerable expenditure of time, labor and money; or that the rule which requires that where one of two persons must suffer the loss falls upon him whose carelessness caused it, has any application here. If the owner was negligent in permitting the escape the dealer was even more reckless in making the purchase.
>
> Under all the circumstances of this case we feel obliged to hold that the defendant obtained no title which it can maintain against the plaintiff. *Stephens v. Albers*, 256 P. 15, 18 (Colo. 1927)

*Popov v. Hayashi* These old common law cases involving wild animal capture still have legal relevance today. Some of the wild capture cases discussed above were used as precedents in *Popov v. Hayashi*, a trial court case out of California in 2002. In *Popov*, two men each claimed to have rightful legal possession of a record-setting home run baseball worth an estimated one-million dollars. Popov claimed possession of the ball because he caught it first, even though he held onto it only briefly as he was immediately knocked to the ground by a packed crowd of spectators all struggling to catch and grab the valuable baseball. Video and eyewitnesses corroborated that the baseball did hit Popov's baseball glove. Neither the video evidence nor eyewitness testimony, however, could corroborate that Popov at any time had firm control and possession of the baseball. As the large crowd was still struggling on top of each other on the ground trying to find and grab the baseball, Hayashi stood up and smiled at one of the video cameras as he clearly held the ball up firmly in his hand. Both Popov and Hayashi claimed rightful ownership of the baseball. Popov sued Hayashi for the value of the baseball.

Among other legal principles the trial judge considered, the judge discussed the common law rule regarding capture of wild animals to help decide who had rightful lawful possession of the baseball. In the court's written opinion, the judge noted that although the wild animal capture cases were somewhat analogous, none of the situations was directly identical to catching a baseball. The trial court judge distinguished the wild animal precedents from the case at hand, noting specifically how the situation was different between animals and baseballs: "It is impossible to wrap one's arms around a whale or fleeing fox . . . the opposite is true of a baseball hit into the stands of a stadium."

In *Popov. v. Hayashi*, the trial court judge concluded that none of the precedents from various areas of law were directly on point, although they were all somewhat on point. The court then fashioned a new common law rule to define possession of a baseball caught under the narrow circumstances of the case, and then applied that rule to the facts of the case.

In the end, the judge equally divided the value of the baseball between Popov and Hayashi. The ball then sold for $450,000. Unfortunately for Popov and Hayashi, they both had spent so much on legal fees fighting each other's claims that each of them netted only a small proportion of the sale compared to what they might have received if they had just agreed to split the value of the baseball in the first place. See the 2004 comedic documentary film about the case, *Up for Grabs*.

In this chapter, we have shown how more complex argument from precedent is used by lawyers when they make arguments in legal briefs submitted to both trial and appellate courts. You can use your handling of the concepts and exercises in the current and past several chapters to gauge your own interest and ability toward a legal career. If you found yourself performing the skills of legal reasoning taught in the past several chapters correctly, and were interested or even excited to engage in these legal analyses, then you are already well on your way to success as a law student and a practicing attorney.

---

*Questions: for Review and Discussion*

1. What is a legal brief and how does it use argument from precedent?
2. You saw a short sample brief in this chapter arguing for Albers in the hypothetical case of *Stephens v. Albers.* Now write a similar brief arguing for Stephens.
3. Choose a side in the hypothetical version of *Stephens v. Albers,* presented earlier.
   a. Using argument only from the precedents provided in this chapter, write a legal argument in behalf of your chosen client that will take three minutes to present verbally.
   b. Orally present your three-minute legal argument to a panel of three other students acting as judges, but without interrupting questions by the judges being allowed.
   c. Orally present your three-minute legal argument a panel of three other students acting as judges, while allowing the panel of student judges to ask interrupting questions about your legal arguments.
4. Switch sides: Write a three-minute legal argument in behalf of the party you did *not* choose as your client in question 2 above. That is, now write the argument for your *opponent.* Then go through steps b and c from question 2 above, continuing to argue for the opposite side.
5. Pair up with another student. One of you will orally argue the side of Stephens for three minutes and one of you will orally argue the side of Albers for three minutes. Each of you then has one minute to rebut your opponent's arguments. You can do this with or without a panel of student judges asking questions as you present your oral arguments.

---

*Suggested Readings*

*Keeble v. Hickeringill,* 11 East 574, 103 ER 1127 (England 1707) (animal capture)

*Pierson v. Post,* 3 Caines 175, 2 Am. Dec. 264 (N.Y. 1805) (animal capture)

*Young v. Hichens,* 6 QB 606, 115 ER 228 (England 1844) (animal capture)

*Ghen v. Rich,* 8 F. 159 (D. Mass. 1881) (animal capture)

*State v. Shaw* 65 N.E. 875 (Ohio 1902) (animal capture)

*Popov v. Hayashi,* WL 31833731 (Ca. Sup. Ct. 2002) (caught baseball)

*Advanced Readings*

Bryan A. Garner, *The Winning Brief: 100 Tips for Persuasive Briefing in Trial and Appellate Courts* (2014)

Bryan A. Garner and Antonin Scalia, *Making Your Case: The Art of Persuading Judges* (2008)

Brian K. Keller, "Whittling: Drafting Concise and Effective Appellate Briefs," 14 *J. App. Prac. & Process* 285 (2013)

Part Four

# PHILOSOPHY OF LAW

CHAPTER 15

# ADVANCED JURISPRUDENCE

---

*Chapter Objectives*

*After reading this chapter, you should be able to:*

- Identify and describe ways in which U.S. positive law attempts to incorporate natural law.
- Identify and describe examples that legal realists would use to argue the law is simply the exertion of power.
- Identify and describe examples that critical legal studies would use to argue the law has oppressed economically disadvantaged people through utilitarian reasoning.
- Identify and describe examples that feminist legal thinkers would use to argue the law has oppressed women.
- Identify and describe examples that critical race theorists would use to argue the law has oppressed racial minorities.

---

In the earlier chapter on jurisprudence, we introduced the concepts of positive law, natural law, legal realism, critical legal studies, feminist jurisprudence, and critical race theory. In this chapter, we will explore each of these concepts in a little more detail, using examples.

Earlier, we learned about the distinction and tension between positive law and natural law. Natural law is the moral law inherent in the nature of the universe, whereas positive law is human-made law. If the positive law is something other than natural law, then where does the moral duty come from to obey the positive law? Although positivists can easily explain why it's *helpful* or *wise* to obey the law, they have a hard time explaining why it's *morally required* to obey the law. Back in the introductory chapter on jurisprudence, we saw how positivists use social contract theory to argue that people have agreed to obey the positive law by accepting or joining the social contract. We also saw how there are several philosophical problems with this position, such as the fact that most people have never expressly or impliedly agreed to any social contract. But perhaps there are other solutions for the "weak" positivist who wishes to incorporate at least some of the natural law into the positive law.

## Positive Law Mandates Obedience to Natural Law

Of course, the positive law can and does outlaw individual harmful negative actions like murder, rape, robbery, arson, and so on that natural law theorists believe violate the natural law. Even most ordinary people believe such actions are objectively "wrong." Indeed, Anglo-Saxon law has always included criminal prohibitions on behavior that is also prohibited by the moral commandments (especially the "Ten Commandments") of the predominant Western religion, Christianity. But beyond such narrow legal requirements of outlawing a handful of particular crimes, what if a lawmaker wants the positive law to include broad categories of what they conceive to be the natural law? For example, what if the positive law somehow directly references and includes the natural law? Wouldn't there now be a moral duty to obey the positive law, or at least part of it? The question then arises how the positive law might be written to incorporate major portions of the natural law. There are actually at least several different ways this might occur. Indeed, throughout the history of Anglo-Saxon law, there have been numerous practical attempts at reconciling positive law and natural law. Some of these efforts are still currently applied in U.S. law.

There are several circumstances in which courts or legislatures have decided that persons have a general *legal* duty to act consistently with *moral* duty to take affirmative, positive actions. The primary situation where this occurs in the law is where legislatures have declared that persons have a legal duty to protect another person. This includes coming to the rescue of that other person if he or she is in physical danger. This legal duty of care especially occurs in situations where one stands in a special status over another person, such that one is responsible for the care of another person. This category of special relationship includes parents and their children while the parent and child are physically together, employers and their employees while the employee is working, teachers and their students while the students are at school or on an official school field trip, police and criminal defendants while the defendant is in custody, or prison officials and their incarcerated inmates.

A second type of relationship where one owes a special legal duty of care is where one has assumed a contractual duty to care for another. This includes relationships such as as doctor and patient, babysitter and children, nursing homes and their residents, or private security guards and their clients. In these situations, the contract itself creates a legal agreement whereby one party to the contract agrees to care for another person or persons. In this way, an ethical promise thereby becomes a legally binding promise.

A third such situation is where one has spontaneously and voluntarily assumed the care of another person, even though there was no other pre-existing duty to care for the other person. This could be, for example, a rescuer who is not a "first responder" (that is, a fire fighter, ambulance personnel, or law enforcement officer), yet who chooses to spontaneously help an accident victim or crime victim. In other words, when an ordinary citizen decides to help out an injured person, that rescuer takes on an added legal responsibility to provide appropriate care to the victim he or she is helping. The reason for this increased legal liability is because the act of rescue itself might possibly prevent or foreclose the likelihood that others might come to the rescue of the victim. Yet some other bystander with more medical expertise might have performed the rescue more safely or successfully.

For example, imagine a highly trained trauma doctor happens to witness a serious car accident. Before the doctor even has time to attend to the victims, several other bystanders begin helping the victims. The doctor might presume that the other bystanders have some medical expertise themselves since they were so quick to offer medical assistance. The doctor therefore decides to leave the scene, even though as it later turns out the bystanders offering assistance have no medical training whatsoever. The victims might even die as a result of improper medical care given by the bystanders who lack any medical expertise. This would subject the rescuers to heightened legal liability since they voluntarily of their own initiative took on the responsibility of providing medical treatment. The imposition of legal liability in such situations, however, might deter would-be bystander rescuers from making such rescue attempts. This would mean victims of accidents and crimes might unnecessarily die because people refuse to help them for fear of potential liability in such circumstances. As a result of this exact possibility—that is, out of a concern that people might not come to the aid of victims out of fear of lawsuits—most states have enacted statutes that limit the liability of rescuers for injuries caused to the people they are attempting to rescue. Usually these laws protect against lawsuits for *negligently* mishandling a rescue, but not for *grossly reckless* misconduct during the rescue. For example, if a rescuer fails to revive a victim through the use of CPR, the rescuer would not be legally liable if it turns out the rescuer was mistaken about the number of chest compressions to apply per breath. On the other hand, if a rescuer carelessly tosses around a victim with a broken back, and the victim ends up permanently paralyzed as a result, the rescuer could be liable. These statutes that protect people who rescue strangers are typically referred to as "Good Samaritan" laws. This is because such laws protect people who come to the aid of strangers in trouble, such as occurred in the parable of the "Good Samaritan" in the Christian New Testament.

In the previous three types of situations just described, the person who owes a legal duty of care has in some way voluntarily assumed such a duty by choosing to enter into either a broad relationship (like becoming a parent), or particular employment (like becoming a doctor), or a particular situation (like the becoming the rescuer of an accident victim). There is yet a fourth such situation, however, that comes closest to incorporating a general natural law duty to care for others into the positive law. In many European countries, as well as in several U.S. states, there is an additional legal requirement that *requires* regular, ordinary people to come to the aid of complete strangers if the rescue can be performed at relatively minimal risk to the rescuer. For example, here is Vermont's statute:

> Duty to Aid the Endangered Act
> Emergency Medical Care
>
> (a) A person who knows another is exposed to grave physical harm shall, to the extent that the same can be rendered without danger or peril to himself or without interference with important duties owed to others, give reasonable assistance to the exposed person unless that assistance or care is being provided by others.
>
> (b) A person who provides reasonable assistance in compliance with subsection (a) of this section shall not be liable in civil damages unless his actions constitute gross negligence or unless he will receive or expects to receive remuneration. Nothing contained in this subsection shall alter existing law with respect to tort liability of a practitioner of the healing arts for acts committed in the ordinary course of his practice.
>
> (c) A person who willfully violates subsection (a) of this section shall be fined not more than $100.00[1]

These statutes that require rescue by bystanders are referred to as "Good Samaritan" laws even though laws that protect rescuers from lawsuits are also called "Good Samaritan" laws.

For example, in Florida in 2017 five teenagers watched, ridiculed, insulted, laughed at, and filmed on one of their cellphones 31-year-old Jamel Dunn as he was drowning in a public pond. They made no effort

1. Vermont Statutes 12:23:519 (1967, No. 309 (Adj. Sess.), §§ 2-4, eff. March 22, 1968.)

to help him despite his cries. After about ten minutes of struggling against drowning, of which about two minutes was filmed, he died. When the cell phone recording was leaked, public outcry demanded that the teenagers be charged with a crime. Law enforcement officials then issued a public statement that Florida law did not require bystanders to rescue strangers, so the teenagers had committed no legal violation by not helping the man. The teenagers were, however, eventually charged with failure to report a dead body, which was a crime under Florida law.

## Positive Law Criminalizes Violating Natural Law

Besides the concept of the justice of *individual* laws, there is an important concept that applies to the justice of *systems* of laws. On an international basis, under generally agreed-upon principles of international law, the *rule of law* requires transparent, consistent, fair, and impartial application of laws. For example, Article I, Section 1 of The Treaty of Lisbon, which updated the Constitution of the European Union in 2007, sets forth the "universal values" of the European Union: "the inviolable and inalienable rights of the human person, freedom, democracy, equality and the rule of law."[2] In the United States, after the terror attacks of 9/11, the U.S. government declared that its new official policy would be that it would not recognize any nation's government as legitimate unless that government respects the rule of law.

To examine this idea of the rule of law, let us consider merely one aspect of it. Suppose the government of a nation passes a law that states the following: "Any violation of Natural Law is subject to a sentence of one year in prison." Or, "All morally unjust acts are prohibited by punishment of one year in prison." As one can imagine, these laws are so vague that there is no way for the public to know what is prohibited or allowed under these laws. Either of these wordings of the law would essentially be the same thing as saying the following:

> Any violation of the following three Natural Laws is subject to a sentence of one year in prison:
> 1. ______________________
> 2. ______________________
> 3. ______________________

Yes, those are empty blanks in that quote. The point is that it is laughable that this law could be considered anything even approaching being fair.

2. Treaty of Lisbon, Article 1, Section 1, (2007).

More precisely, this type of vague law basically criminalizes behavior after the fact. That is, the prohibited behavior is not clearly defined as a crime at the time the person commits the act, and the law is then applied retroactively. Basically the prosecutor or judge would be saying "Well, we simply don't like what you did, so now you're going to prison." This kind of law is called an *ex post facto* law, Latin for "after the fact." Article I, Section 9, Clause 3 of the U.S. Constitution expressly prohibits ex post facto laws: "no . . . ex post facto law shall be passed." Indeed, under U.S. Supreme Court interpretation of the U.S. Constitution, any vague criminal law violates the Due Process Clause of the Fifth Amendment to the U.S. Constitution. The "process" that is "due" you is, in simple terms, the fair procedure you are owed. Due process requires that the public receives clear advance warning about what conduct is expected of them. Only by having such clear advance notice can people know how to avoid violating the law. The basic list of rights of most, if not all, democratic nations and organizations, including the European Union, prohibit *ex post facto* laws.

More generally, the Fifth Amendment's Due Process Clause requires that under all federal law, "No person shall . . . be deprived of life, liberty, or property, without due process of law. " The Fourteenth Amendment's Due Process Clause applies the same restriction to state law: "nor shall any state deprive any person of life, liberty, or property, without due process of law." The term "due process" generally means "fair procedure." That is, the "process" that is "due" you means the fair procedure that you are owed by the government. Among several basic requirements of due process, the concept requires at a minimum that members of the public get advance warning about what conduct is expected of them. Only by having advance notice can people know how to avoid violating the law. This is a basic requirement of fairness. Given that a vague law is subject to widely different interpretations, it does not give the public clear notice as to what behavior is prohibited or required. Thus, a vague criminal law violates the Due Process Clauses of the Fifth and Fourteenth Amendments. The Supreme Court has declared that the Due Process Clause requires fair procedure not just in criminal trials, but in other important questions involving individual rights. Such issues include termination of parental rights, institutionalization of mentally ill persons, denial of government benefits such as social security disability payments, and school disciplinary hearings.

The concept of due process is at the heart of the rule of law. Legal thinker Lon Fuller put forth several criteria for law to be legitimate that are widely accepted today.[3] Some of these factors are that all laws must

3. Fuller, Lon L. *The Morality of Law, Revised Edition.* New Haven: Yale University Press, 1964.

be made following a regular, publicly known process; all laws must be announced to the public or be easily discoverable by the public; and all individuals in that society, both ordinary citizens and political rulers alike, must all be equally subject to those laws. In other words, the rule of law means that *law* itself is what governs the actions of all individuals in that society, and not the mere whims of individuals—either ordinary citizens or leaders—of that society. If a president, prime minister, or king is able to violate law without punishment, then that ruler is "above the law," and the rule of law therefore does not exist in that nation. Any nation controlled by a dictatorial ruler or regime is an example where the rule of law does not exist.

Not only does the rule of law promote fairness for all individuals in a society, the rule of law also promotes economic development for the benefit of everyone. For example, without the rule of law in operation in a territory, people are unlikely to build schools, or hospitals, or banks, or other businesses. If at any moment the government may without warning or reason simply confiscate your buildings or wealth after the fact, people won't spend time, energy, and money on creating such helpful enterprises.

Even though there is a near-universal consensus among international legal scholars about the procedural aspects of the rule of law, there are still instances where application of the procedural components of the rule of law have come into serious dispute. For example, there are cases in Western law where new (or arguably new) law was applied retroactively by nations that claimed to be model examples of the rule of law. Most famously, at the end of World War II the victorious Allied Powers (the U.S., Soviet Union, Great Britain, and France) created new crimes under international law. These international crimes were named "crimes against peace," "war crimes," and "crimes against humanity." The Allied Powers then prosecuted and punished key Nazi leaders for committing those crimes. The trials were held in the German city of Nuremburg; hence the prosecutions are known as the Nuremburg Trials. Legal philosophers still debate whether the Nuremburg Trials violated the international standard against *ex post facto* laws, and hence whether the trials themselves violated the rule of law.

In 1989, the German Democratic Republic (East Germany) and the Federal Republic of Germany (West Germany) reunified simply as Germany. Essentially the democratic West German government peacefully took over the formerly communist East Germany. It had been official policy in East Germany to shoot anyone attempting to leave East Germany by crossing the border into West Germany without authorization. After German reunification, the new combined Germany then prosecuted some former East German border guards for the murder of individuals attempting to flee East Germany. Yet at the time of the murders, the soldiers were under direct orders to shoot, and doing so in that situation was not an East German crime. The prosecutions and resulting convictions were controversial. Throughout the lengthy course of the trials and appeals, even some of the judges involved in the cases believed the prosecutions violated the defendants' rights against *ex post facto* laws. Yet the majority of judges on the court believed that it should have been clear to the defendants that murder was both immoral and illegal. As a result, the appellate courts ultimately upheld the convictions of the defendants.

Although the examples of the Nuremburg Trials and the East German border guards involve only the *ex post facto* component of the rule of law, they illustrate that the rule of law is an important value yet subject to interpretation. In short, the rule of law is expected to govern modern society for the benefit of everyone, yet people disagree about the application of the concepts of the rule of law in particular circumstances.

## Positive Law Expressly Includes Natural Law Rights

Instead of the positive law *punishing* people based on natural law, perhaps it could *protect* people based on natural law. There are several ways this could occur.

*The positive law declares natural law is the foundation of positive law rights* Interestingly, one of the key founding documents of the United States does this. The U.S. Declaration of Independence (1776) attempts to ground the entirety of positive law rights on the natural law. It does this by declaring: "We hold these truths to be self-evident, that all men are created equal, that they are endowed by their Creator with certain unalienable rights; that among these are life, liberty, and the pursuit of happiness." By declaring all people have the same rights, the Declaration of Independence is saying that according to the natural law we are *political* equals. That is, we're not necessarily equals in other ways, such as intelligence, physical strength, talents and skills, moral virtue, or so on. We simply have an equal right to rule and a right to be ruled equally. This notion of political equality is an express rejection of the theory of divine right of kings, which says that some people have more political rights than others because some particular people (especially men) are created by god to rule over others. If no one is created to rule over others, however, then all people have an equal right to rule. That is, all have an equal right to share in political rule by an equal vote, and an equal chance to run for office and get elected. These principles underlie democracy. This foundational principle about equality is why Abraham Lincoln repeatedly argued not that slavery violated the U.S. Constitution, but that slavery violated the U.S. Declaration of Independence. Lincoln saw the Declaration of Independence as even more important than the Constitution in this regard. The Declaration of Independence establishes the moral foundation for the existence of the United States as a separate, independent nation; whereas the Constitution merely creates the structure of government supporting that foundation. The Constitution could be amended at any time, but because of the Declaration of Independence, the United States would continue to exist as a nation founded on the core principle of political equality.

Despite the express statement in the Declaration of Independence regarding natural law rights, however, the Supreme Court has never found any particular substantive rights to be protected by the Declaration of Independence. Instead, according to the Court, rights must be protected by the Constitution and its amendments for the Court to legally uphold asserted rights.

*The positive law expressly protects natural law rights* Many members of Congress involved in the drafting of the Bill of Rights were concerned that an enumeration (listing) of specific rights would be misunderstood in the future as listing the *only* rights citizens have. Alexander Hamilton had made this very argument against having a Bill of Rights in *Federalist Paper No. 84*.[4] After the ratification of the Constitution without a Bill of Rights, James Madison, then a member of the U.S. House of Representatives, responded to this concern by suggesting that when a Bill of Rights is added to the Constitution that lists particular rights, that list should contain an additional open-ended clause declaring that the people still have many other unwritten rights. Speaking in the House of Representatives on June 8, 1789, Madison read an early draft he wrote of what became the Ninth Amendment to the U.S. constitution. He explained:

> It has been objected also against a bill of rights, that by enumerating particular exceptions to the grant of power, it would disparage those rights which were not placed in that enumeration; and it might follow by implication, that those rights which were not singled out, were intended to be assigned into the hands of the General Government, and were consequently insecure. This is one of the most plausible arguments I have ever heard urged against the admission of a bill of rights into this system; but, I conceive, that it may be guarded against. I have attempted it, as gentlemen may see by turning to the last clause of the fourth resolution.[5]

4. Hamilton, Alexander, et al. *The Federalist Papers*. Dover Publications, 2014.
5. Madison, James. *Speech Introducing Bill of Rights in the U.S. House of Representatives*, June 8, 1789.

That fourth resolution became the Ninth Amendment, and Congress passed Madison's proposal in 1791. It states simply: "The enumeration in the Constitution, of certain rights, shall not be construed to deny or disparage others retained by the people."[6]

The Ninth Amendment basically says the people have other natural law rights not listed in the Bill of Rights. But what are the "other rights" protected by the Ninth Amendment? The problem is that nowhere did the author of the Bill of Rights, James Madison, ever list the "other" rights the Ninth Amendment references. Nor did any other writers, historians, or legal scholars of that time explain what "other rights" the Ninth Amendment protects. One constitutional scholar, Judge Robert Bork, writing in the 1980's, famously compared the problem to a hypothetical situation. Imagine the Ninth Amendment did list some specific rights, but ink was spilled on the only original copy of the Ninth Amendment just after it was written, and no one at the time corrected the problem or ever explained what was under the spilled ink. If even the best of modern technology is unable to determine what text is under the inkblot, then the Ninth Amendment today would say "The other rights are ________." Absent a list provided by some authoritative figure from that time period, there seems to be no principled way to determine what "other rights" the Ninth Amendment refers to. Instead, the creation of such a list would simply be the whim of a majority of justices on the Supreme Court as to how to fill in the blank. The most reasonable and fair solution, then, is to conclude that unfortunately, the Ninth Amendment as it appears is meaningless and unenforceable. The consequence of this interpretation would be that the only enforceable rights people have are those that are *expressly* listed in the Constitution. Although an individual justice on the Supreme Court occasionally has cited the Ninth Amendment in support of his or her individual opinion, no Supreme Court majority has ever declared a "right" is protected specifically by the Ninth Amendment.

## Positive Law Impliedly Protects Natural Law Rights

As we just saw, the Supreme Court has refused to read any specific rights into the Ninth Amendment. It would seem, then, that only those rights that are expressly listed by the Constitution will be protected. Yet such is not the case today. Starting in the mid-to-late 1900's, the Court began to declare that a handful of rights are protected by the Constitution even though these rights are nowhere listed in the Constitution. Rather

6. U.S. Constitution, Ninth Amendment

than applying the Ninth Amendment, however, the Court said these unlisted, or *unenumerated,* rights come from the Fourteenth Amendment, which was ratified in 1868.

The Fourteenth Amendment contains many provisions, but there are two particular parts of the Fourteenth Amendment in which the Supreme Court has protected unenumerated rights. The Privileges and Immunities Clause of the Fourteenth Amendment states: "No state shall make or enforce any law which shall abridge the privileges or immunities of citizens of the United States." This clause does not specify what the particular "privileges" or "immunities" of citizens are. In the late 1900's, however, the Supreme Court declared that the right to travel is a basic right and is impliedly protected by this clause.[7]

More significantly, the Fourteenth Amendment's Due Process Clause states "nor shall any state deprive any person of life, liberty, or property, without due process of law." The term "due process" generally means "fair procedure." The Supreme Court has declared that the Due Process Clause requires fair procedure not just in criminal trials, but in questions such as termination of parental rights, institutionalization of mentally ill persons, denial of government benefits such as social security disability payments, or school disciplinary hearings.

In the late 1800's and early 1900's, the Supreme Court declared that individuals had a "liberty of contract" derived from the Due Process Clause. The Court said there were some rights that were so important that they could not be interfered with by government no matter how fair the procedure. This concept became known as *substantive due process.* This term was used because the concept protected the *substance* of rights, rather than the *procedure* by which rights can be regulated. Procedural rights, such as a right to be told of criminal charges against you, are now referred to as *procedural due process.* The substantive due process right of liberty of contract meant that state governments could not regulate business-labor relations or contracts. This included such things as wages, work hours, or other conditions of employment.

The high point of liberty of contract was the Supreme Court case of *Lochner v. New York* in 1905.[8] In that case, the Court said the State of New York could not restrict bakers to ten hours of work per day, nor to 60 hours of work per week, because doing so would interfere with the right of the bakers to contract to work however many hours they wished to work per week. The Court dissent criticized the majority for simply imposing its own economic beliefs in disregard of the effort of the New York legislature to apply a general health and safety regulation. Once

7. *Saenz v. Roe,* 526 U.S. 489 (1999)
8. *Lochner v. New York,* 198 U.S. 45 (1905)

the Great Depression hit, however, the public, President Roosevelt, and a majority in Congress demanded that legislatures be allowed to regulate businesses. In the late 1930's the Court overruled *Lochner* and all the other cases that had upheld any rights under the concept of "liberty of contract.[9] Since the mid-1930's, the Court has never again upheld any economic substantive due process rights.

Despite the disappearance of liberty of contract, the Supreme Court, in the latter part of the 20th century, began to resurrect the concept that the Constitution protects certain rights that are implied in the Constitution. The Court ruled that there are particular *non-economic* rights inherent in the concept of "liberty." As such, these rights cannot be taken away from individuals by the government no matter how fair the procedure used. That is, the *substance* of some types of personal moral choices will be protected regardless of *any* procedure the government might try to use to restrict those decisions. Specifically, the Supreme Court declared that the word "liberty" in the Due Process Clause of the Fourteenth Amendment protects a cluster of related rights. This group of rights is sometimes, though confusingly, called the "right of privacy." A more accurate term for this cluster of rights is *familial privacy* because the rights all involve decisions that intimately involve one's family. The concept of privacy in the context here does not refer to keeping information confidential or secret, but instead to private *decisions* that should be made only by one's family and not by the government. Familial privacy thus means you should have the right to make some kinds of family-related decisions without the government interfering with that decision. This right of familiar privacy is therefore also sometimes called a right of personal autonomy. Regardless how these rights are labelled, the concept essentially is the application of rights perceived by the Supreme Court as part of the natural law, despite the absence of any concrete positive law protecting such rights.

This right of familial privacy or personal autonomy includes decisions involving sex, procreation, childrearing, marriage, and the right to refuse unwanted medical treatment, including life-sustaining nutrition and hydration. Put simply, between consenting adults you can choose whether to have a romantic or sexual relationship with someone, and you can choose whom to have that relationship with.[10] You can then choose whether to get married or not, which includes the right to marry someone of the same sex.[11] Whether you decide to get married or remain unmarried, you can choose whether to have one child, multiple children, or no children. This includes a right to use contraception, in-

9. *Nebbia v. New York*, 291 U.S. 502 (1934)
10. *Lawrence v. Texas*, 539 U.S. 558 (2003)
11. *Obergefell v. Hodges*, 576 U.S. ___ (2015)

cluding abortion, as a means of birth control.[12] If you have children, you can choose how to raise those children. You can send them to private school or teach them yourself, and you can teach them any language, or given them any religious or political views.[13] And, if you become ill, you have a right to refuse medicine, food, and water.[14] This is technically not a "right to die" because under current U.S. law there is no right to accelerate death by suicide or doctor-assisted suicide.[15] Instead, you may only refuse measures that prolong dying. All these rights allow us to make these personal (non-economic) choices mostly free from government interference.

The Court has at times tried to define the right of familial privacy based on what personal rights the original writers and ratifiers of the Fourteenth Amendment's Due Process Clause thought were rights at the time. In more recent cases, however, the Court has abandoned that legal test, and has merely talked vaguely about modern conceptions of "dignity" and "autonomy" providing these privacy rights. By all appearances, then, the Court looks as if it is simply applying its own conception of what it—a majority of the Court—believes the natural law is (or should be) in any given case. Indeed, the dissent in *Obergefell v. Hodges*, the 2015 same-sex marriage case, criticized the majority as disregarding the law and instead merely imposing its own conception of morality. The dissent argued the majority was merely returning to the now-repudiated substantive due process doctrine of *Lochner v. New York*.[16]

## Positive Law Expressly Allows Natural Law as a Legal Defense

For centuries, the Anglo-Saxon common law has included the legal defense of *necessity*. That is, you can legally break the law if doing so is a necessity. But when is breaking the law a necessity? Isn't this simply an attempt to apply natural law without expressly saying so? Basically, yes: the necessity defense is a concession to the fact that the natural law sometimes excuses violating the positive law. U.S. law still today includes the necessity defense. For example, as we saw in a prior chapter, the Model Penal Code is written by a team of legal experts known as the American Law Institute (ALI). The Model Penal Code defines the necessity defense as follows:

12. *Roe v. Wade*, 410 U.S. 113 (1973)
13. *Pierce v. Society of Sister*, 268 U.S. 510 (1925)
14. *Cruzan v. Director, Missouri Department of Health*, 497 U.S. 261 (1990)
15. *Washington v. Glucksberg*, 521 U.S. 702 (1997)
16. *Lochner v. New York*, 198 U.S. 45 (1905)

> Conduct that the actor believes to be necessary to avoid harm or evil to himself or to another is justifiable, provided that: . . . the harm or evil sought to be avoided by such conduct is greater than that sought to be prevented by the law defining the offense charged.[17]

Notice the use of the vague, undefined term "evil": positive law may be broken if doing so prevents a greater "evil."

All state laws in the United States allow some version of the necessity defense. This always includes self-defense, usually includes defense of others, and often includes the defense of property as well. Federal case law also recognizes the existence of a necessity defense to violations of federal law. Modern examples of the necessity defense include anti-abortion activists and animal rights activists who have tried to assert the necessity defense in prosecutions for attacks on abortion clinics or animal labs. So far, these political activists have not won those arguments in court.

There are limits to the necessity defense, however. For example, the most well-defined and widely-recognized and applied instance of the necessity defense is self-defense. Yet even under self-defense, the law-breaking conduct must be proportional to the need for the conduct, and the law-breaking conduct must have a reasonable chance of succeeding in preventing the harm in question. If a five-year child hits a large grown adult, for example, the adult can't shoot the child and then claim self-defense.

There are famous historical attempts to use the necessity defense. One such famous example was *U.S. v. Holmes* in 1842.[18] A ship carrying emigrants to the U.S. struck an iceberg in the North Atlantic. One lifeboat became so overloaded with people that it threatened to capsize, in which case everyone would have quickly died in the icy water. The nine crewmembers in the lifeboat threw overboard 14 of the 32 passengers in the boat. These 14 people were all but 3 of the male passengers in the lifeboat, based on the principle of saving "women and children first." Upon reaching the U.S., crewmember Holmes was charged with murder. Holmes argued the necessity defense. A jury, however, convicted him based on his duty as a sailor to put the passengers' lives ahead of the crew. That is, the jury believed the crew should have gone overboard before the passengers.

Holmes was sentenced to six months in prison and a $20 fine. U.S. President Tyler refused to grant a pardon despite much public outcry for him to do so. Holmes appealed, arguing that the judge should have

17. Model Penal Code, Section 3.02
18. *U.S. v. Holmes*, 26 F.Cas. 360 (1842)

instructed the jury that in such a life-and-death situation, the laws of nature put all people—both crew and passengers—on an equal level. The federal appellate court upheld his conviction on the basis that the necessity defense as already stated in the positive law was all that the defendant was entitled to have the jury be told. The court explained:

> It is true . . . as is known by everyone, that we do find in the text writers, and sometimes in judicial opinions, the phrases "the law of nature," "the principles of natural right," and other expression of a like signification; but, as applied to civilized men, nothing more can be meant by those expressions than that there are certain great and fundamental principles of justice which, in the constitution of nature, lie at the foundation and make part of all civil law, independently of express adoption or enactment. And to give the expressions any other signification, to claim them as showing an independent code . . . would be to make the writers who use the expressions lay down as rules of action, principles which, in their nature, admit of no practical ascertainment or application. The law of nature forms part of the municipal law; and, in a proper case (as of self-defense), homicide is justifiable, not because the municipal law is subverted by the law of nature, but because no rule of the municipal law makes homicide in such cases criminal.

In other words, the court said the positive law already sufficiently includes the natural law in the necessity defense, and so the defendant was not entitled to tell the jury about other alleged natural law rules.

Lest the reader think that such a case would be unique, a similar famous case occurred in England just a few decades later, in *Queen v. Dudley and Stephens* in 1884.[19] In that case, four crewmen were stranded in a lifeboat after the English-chartered ship they were on was destroyed in a storm at sea off the coast of South Africa. The Captain was Tom Dudley, with crewmen Edwin Stephens, Thomas Brooks, and Richard Parker. After a while at sea, and with the four men at risk of dying from starvation and thirst, Captiain Dudley argued that the four men should draw straws to see who should commit suicide and allow the other three crew members to feast on the dead crewmember. Brooks refused to take part. After almost 3 weeks at sea, with extremely little to eat or dink in the meantime, Parker was unconscious due to weakness. Beliving Parker was dying, Dudley killed Paker by stabbing a pen-knife in his neck while Stephens stood by to hold Parker down if he struggled. A few days later the men were rescued by a passing ship. Upon returning to England, Dudley and Stephens were charged with murder. Although the defen-

19. *Queen v. Dudley and Stephens*, 14 QBD 273 DC (1884)

dants tried to assert the necessity defense, the Lord Chief Justice of England rejected the argument that necessity could ever be a justification to a charge of murder. Although Dudley and Stephens were both convicted of murder and sentenced to death, their sentence was later commuted to six months' imprisonment.

One important distinction to make here is the difference between the necessity defense and civil disobedience. When engaging in civil disobedience, protestors think the law *itself* is immoral in *all* circumstances. In the case of the necessity defense, one believes the law itself is moral in general, but its application in a particular circumstance would be immoral. For example, to return to the example of the U.S. Civil Rights Movement, protesters did not think that racial segregation was okay in some circumstances but not others. Instead, they believed racial segregation was itself unjust, in every situation. Thus, when the protesters sat in legally segregated areas of restaurants, they did not assert a necessity defense to violating the segregation laws only in those instances. Instead, they were practicing civil disobedience to protest the immorality of segregation laws as a whole. In the 1970's and 1980's, some political protesters have avoided prosecutions in state courts for trespassing or other crimes committed while protesting nuclear weapons, nuclear power, U.S. foreign policy, or the policy of foreign nations. More recently, however, federal courts have been stricter in applying the necessity defense, rarely allowing it.

Moral/ethical/legal philosophers like to create bizarre hypotheticals to test the boundaries of what might be "necessary" to save lives. Here are three fairly well-known hypothetical examples of this question.

A trolley driver suddenly realizes the breaks have gone out. Five people are standing on the track ahead, but have their backs turned, and seem to be unable to hear the oncoming trolley. The track splits into two just before the group of people. On the other track is a single person with his back turned, who also seems to be unable to hear the oncoming trolley. The trolley driver has a choice: do nothing, and let the trolley continue to go straight and run over the five people, or intentionally steer the trolley off onto the other track. If the trolley driver chooses to intentionally veer the trolley to kill the one person rather than allow the trolley to kill the other five people, can the trolley driver use the necessity defense against a murder charge?

A doctor has five patients who need immediate organ transplants to live. Two of them need a lung; two need a kidney; the fifth needs a heart. A healthy man walks into the doctor's office for an annual check-up. The doctor kills the man, gives his lungs to the first two patients, his kidneys to the other two, and his heart to the fifth, thus saving five lives at the price of one. May the doctor use the necessity defense against a murder charge?

A person is hiking deep in a jungle and accidentally comes across a drug lord about to shoot six innocent villagers. The drug lord hands the hiker a gun with one bullet. There are dozens of armed men standing around so it would be impossible to fight or run. The drug lord says the hiker is free to leave, but if the hiker shoots one villager, then the drug lord will let the other five villagers live. If the hiker does not shoot a villager, then all six will die. The hiker decides to shoot a villager but just at that moment the police arrive and arrest the hiker for murder. May the hiker use the necessity defense against a charge of murder?

In considering these three hypotheticals, do you believe the outcome of the necessity defense should differ between these three situations? If so, why?

## Positive Law Impliedly Allows Natural Law as a Legal Defense

The necessity defense is found expressly in the positive law, either in case law or in statutes depending on the jurisdiction. Yet there is another way defendants can escape a positive law conviction by invoking the natural law. In jury trials, the judge *instructs* jurors regarding the law in the case. These jury instructions tell the jury to apply the law given by the judge to the facts in the case. That is, *judges* decide questions of *law*, but *juries* ordinarily are supposed to decide questions of *fact*. Examples of such factual decisions would be whether a criminally accused defendant was guilty of a crime, or whether a civil defendant is liable to a plaintiff. In criminal cases, the judge instructs the jury of what the law is regarding murder, or robbery, or aggravated assault, or other criminal law. In a civil lawsuit, the judge instructs the jury as to the relevant tort law, or contract law, or other civil law. The jury then applies the laws that the judge gives them to the facts of the case. Did the defendant violate the law? Did the defendant cause harm to the plaintiff? These questions of fact are decided by the jury.

Yet within the criminal law, there is a long history of a power by juries to refuse to apply the law even when the facts clearly indicate the law was violated. That is, juries have the power to acquit criminal defendants even when the defendant admits violating the law. This power of juries to ignore the positive law is called *jury nullification*. The jury can declare that the facts show a defendant is not guilty even when the facts prove the defendant is guilty—including when the defendant admits guilt. In such a case, jurors officially declare that they are ruling on a question of fact, but in reality they are ruling on a question of law. Essentially, the jury is deciding that either the substance of the law itself, or the application of the substantive law in the particular case, is unjust.

In other words, the jury has decided to follow what it believes is the natural law rather than the positive criminal law in that particular case. Juries are "nullifying" the positive law and hence are nullifying any subsequent criminal charges for violating what, to them, is unjust positive law.

The power of jury nullification was first established in 1670 during the trial in England of Quaker leader William Penn. At the time, Quakerism was an illegal religion, and Penn was on trial for preaching Quakerism. Penn had clearly broken the law, and he admitted doing so. Four of the twelve members of the jury, however, ignored both the statute and the judge who instructed the jury to convict Penn. Since the jury verdict needed to be unanimous, Penn was going to be acquitted. The judged then ordered the four dissenting jurors to be put in jail without food until they changed their votes from "not guilty" to "guilty." After the jurors starved for four days but still refused to change their votes, the highest court in England set the jurors free. England's high court declared that jurors could not be punished for their verdicts even if the jurors deliberately ignored the positive law in their decision. Ever since that precedent, this immunity from prosecution means jurors are free not just to decide the *facts* in cases, but they also have the power to decide if the *law* is unjust.

Jury nullification helped to establish the principle of free speech in America. In 1735 newspaper publisher John Peter Zenger was charged with the crime of seditious libel—that is, criticism of government. Zenger had criticized the colonial governor of New York with true facts in print. A young lawyer, Andrew Hamilton (no relation to Alexander Hamilton), represented Zenger. Hamilton argued to the jury that they should vote to protect free speech. Zenger had clearly violated the law, but the jury set Zenger free nonetheless. This set a precedent of jury nullification in U.S. law. Within the next couple centuries, jurors similarly refused to convict violations of the Alien and Sedition Act in the 1790s, the Fugitive Slave Act during the 1800's, and the prohibition on alcohol in the early 1900's. Jury nullification was also occasionally used to acquit civil rights protesters and Vietnam War protesters. However, jury nullification was also infamously used by Southern all-white juries before and during the civil rights movement during the 1950's and 1960's. The all-white juries acquitted whites charged with violence—including lynching or other forms of murder—committed against blacks or white civil rights activists. Hence, jury nullification is a double-edged sword. That is, it is merely a tool that can be used to achieve widely different political goals depending on the jury exercising the power.

Jury nullification is still an issue today. Libertarians often urge the use of jury nullification in civil liberty cases. In some instances, juries have refused to convict doctors or family members in assisted suicide cases even where the facts are admitted. In drug cases, juries are increasingly refusing to convict medical marijuana use or even possession of small amounts of non-medical marijuana and other petty drugs. Some juries have refused to apply the death penalty even when the law dictates that it should be applied. The U.S. Supreme Court has declared, however, that criminal defendants have no right to demand that the jury be told of the jury's power of nullification.[20] Judges' refusals to inform the jury about jury nullification were re-affirmed by more recent U.S. Courts of Appeals cases: *U.S. v. Dougherty* (1972)[21] and *U.S. v. Thomas* (1997).[22]

As one might expect, the vast majority of prosecutors and judges oppose jury nullification because it removes control from prosecutors and judges over the law. Indeed, judges now often allow prosecutors to dismiss *for cause* any potential juror who admits they might follow their conscience instead of the law. For example, in death penalty cases, prosecutors are allowed an unlimited number of dismissals against any potential jurors who say they will not be able to set aside their personal views against the death penalty. A jury where all its members have been selected based on their willingness to impose the death penalty is called a "death qualified" jury. On rare occasions, individuals who have distributed leaflets outside of courthouses informing potential jurors of their right to jury nullification have even been criminally charged with jury tampering. These charges have eventually been dismissed due to the free speech rights of the protestors, but such tactics reveal how strongly some prosecutors hate the concept of jury nullification.

## Legal Realism, Critical Legal Studies, and Utilitarianism

In the introductory chapter on jurisprudence, we discussed how legal realism argues that law is merely the application of power. We also considered how its more modern variant, critical legal studies, argues that the power differential in law is systematically skewed in favor of the politically powerful over those with less political power. One way this power differential manifests itself is through application of the philosophy of utilitarianism. Recall also from the introductory chapter on jurisprudence that utilitarianism is the moral and legal philosophy founded by thinkers like Jeremy Bentham[23] and John Stuart Mill.[24] They believed that the most moral choice in any given situation is whatever decision

20. *Sparf v. U.S.*, 156 U.S. 51 (1895).
21. *U.S. v. Dougherty*, 473 F. 2d 1113 (D.C. Cir. 1972)
22. *U.S. v. Thomas*, 116 F.3d 606 (2d Cir. 1997).
23. Bentham, Jeremy. "An Introduction to the Principles of Morals and Legislation," in *The Collected Works of Jeremy Bentham*. Clarendon Press, 1996.
24. Mill, John Stuart. *Utilitarianism*. Hackett Publishing Company, 2002.

eventually results in the greatest happiness for the greatest number of people. This decision-making guideline is also called the "Greatest Happiness Principle."

Regardless whether the terminology of utilitarianism is expressly used, the philosophy of utilitarianism has highly influenced law and public policy in the United States and throughout the world. There are many products and activities that cause much harm, but that legislatures have decided they will not outlaw because of the net positive contribution that such products or activities contribute to society. This includes products like stairs, swimming pools, ladders, bathtubs, lawnmowers, or even playground equipment. Between 30,000 and 40,000 people are killed each year in the United States from automobiles alone, plus deaths due to planes, trains, and boats. People even die from falling out of beds. Similarly, tobacco, alcohol and firearms remain legal despite the serious negative health consequences of such products. Potentially dangerous activities include all forms of sport and recreation, such as youth sports like soccer, baseball, softball, swimming, and football, as well as more adult activities like skydiving, hang gliding, scuba diving, and rock climbing. Yet all these products and activities remain legal because society deems that the net benefits from them outweigh any harm caused by them. Cases involving the above are relatively apolitical. Sometimes, however, political power does come into play.

There are several famous cases in U.S. law where courts upheld actions that intentionally destroyed entire neighborhoods that lacked enough political clout to stop those actions from happening. The reasoning of the courts in each case used utilitarian justifications in upholding their actions. In 1904, several residents in rural Tennessee sued a copper company for nuisance because smoke from its nearby copper mine was destroying the ability of their land to be used for agricultural purposes. In *Madison v. Ducktown Sulphur*, the Tennessee Supreme Court agreed that the copper plant was creating a nuisance, but refused to grant the plaintiffs' request for an injunction to shut down the mine. The court explained:

> In order to protect by injunction several small tracts of land, aggregating in value less than $1,000, we are asked to destroy other property worth nearly $2,000,000, and wreck two great mining and manufacturing enterprises, that are engaged in work of very great importance, not only to their owners, but to the State, and to the whole country as well, to depopulate a large town, and deprive thousands of working people of their homes and livelihood, and scatter them broadcast.[25]

25. *Madison v. Ducktown Sulphur*, 83 S.W. 658, 666–67 (Tenn. 1904)

Decades later, in *Poletown Neighborhood Council v. City of Detroit*, the Michigan Supreme Court upheld the city of Detroit's seizure through eminent domain of an entire working class neighborhood in Detroit so that the homes and businesses could be destroyed to make way for a new General Motors automobile manufacturing plant.[26] A similar action in the state of Connecticut was more recently upheld by the U.S. Supreme Court in 2005 in *Kelo v. City of New London*.[27] The Court held that a middle-class neighborhood could be destroyed to make way for a high-end riverfront development project because the project would bring increased jobs and tax revenues. According to a majority of the Court, these broader benefits constituted a "public purpose" for a "public use" that allowed the city to use *eminent domain* to seize the property. The decision was extremely controversial and in response many state legislatures enacted laws making it more difficult to seize private property through the use of eminent domain.

We can look at one final but very different example of legal realism using utilitarian thinking. Recall from earlier in this chapter the agonizing that some legal philosophers go through trying to justify the legality of the Nuremburg trials. As we discussed, the potential problem for the Nuremburg trials is that the trials arguably violated the rule of law by creating and applying *ex post facto* war crimes to captured Nazi leaders. This is no problem at all, however, for legal realists. The Allied Powers had won the war; they were going to execute some of the Nazi leaders anyway; those leaders deserved to be executed; the worldwide public demanded it; and doing so would send a message to other would-be tyrants. Having trials also allowed the evidence of war crimes to be gathered, documented, and publicized to demonstrate just how horrendous the crimes were. On balance, then, the justifications for creating and applying *ex post facto* war crimes far outweighed any concerns that might have been caused by the fact such crimes might have been *ex post facto.* That is, arguably violating the rule of law in this instance served a much greater purpose of promoting the rule of law in general. Put in more direct utilitarian terms, trying and sentencing the Nazi leaders created far more happiness for far more people, both in the short term and the long term, than if no such trials had happened.

## Feminist Jurisprudence

Recall from our chapter that introduced jurisprudence that one common critique of law is that it discriminates against women. This view is

26. *Poletown Neighborhood Council v. City of Detroit*, 304 N.W.2d 455 (Mich. 1981).
27. *Kelo v. New London*, 545 U.S. 469 (2005).

broadly called feminist jurisprudence. A few examples commonly given for how public policy oppresses women are:

- laws prohibiting sexual harassment in the workplace prohibit only "severe" or "pervasive" harassment, thereby still allowing other forms of harassment
- restrictive abortion regulations limit women's freedom of choice and imposes unequal economic burdens on women since society still places most childrearing responsibility on the mother and not the father
- the failure of police, prosecutors, and judges to take allegations of rape or domestic violence against women seriously and to prosecute such cases fully
- the lack of a requirement for paid maternity leave sets back women's careers and financial situations more than men
- lax enforcement of anti-prostitution laws contributes to the ongoing victimization of women
- legalized pornography hypersexualizes women thereby fostering a social climate where women are viewed primarily as sexual objects

On this last point, in 1984, feminist legal scholars Andrea Dworkin and Catharine MacKinnon helped the city of Indianapolis write a new city ordinance outlawing pornography. The ordinance first listed a legislative finding that:

> Pornography is a discriminatory practice based on sex which denies women equal opportunities in society. Pornography is central in creating and maintaining sex as a basis for discrimination. Pornography is a systematic practice of exploitation and subordination based on sex which differentially harms women. The bigotry and contempt it promotes, with the acts of aggression it fosters, harm women's opportunities for equality of rights in employment, education, access to and use of public accommodations, and acquisition of real property; promote rape, battery, child abuse, kidnapping and prostitution and inhibit just enforcement of laws against such acts; and contribute significantly to restricting women in particular from full exercise of citizenship and participation in public life, including in neighborhoods.[28]

28. *American Booksellers Association v. Hudnut*, 598 1316 (S.D. Ind. 1984).

The ordinance then defined "pornography" as:

> Pornography shall mean the graphic sexually explicit subordination of women, whether in pictures or in words, that also includes one or more of the following:
>
> 1. Women are presented as sexual objects who enjoy pain or humiliation; or
> 2. Women are presented as sexual objects who experience sexual pleasure in being raped; or
> 3. Women are presented as sexual objects tied up or cut up or mutilated or bruised or physically hurt, or as dismembered or truncated or fragmented or severed into body parts; or
> 4. Women are presented as being penetrated by objects or animals; or
> 5. Women are presented in scenarios of degradation, injury, abasement, torture, shown as filthy or inferior, bleeding, bruised, or hurt in a context that makes these conditions sexual; or
> 6. Women are presented as sexual objects for domination, conquest, violation, exploitation, possession, or use, or through postures or positions of servility or submission or display."
>
> The use of men, children, or transsexuals in the place of women in paragraphs (1) through (6) above shall also constitute pornography under this section.[29]

The American Booksellers Association legally challenged the ordinance on the grounds that the ordinance would outlaw much film and literature that is constitutionally protected free speech. Both the U.S. District Court and the Seventh Circuit Court of Appeals agreed and ruled the ordinance unconstitutional as a violation of the Free Speech Clause of the First Amendment to the U.S. Constitution. The Seventh Circuit explained that the U.S. Supreme Court has allowed only narrowly defined categories of pornography to be outlawed as "obscene," but not if the sexual material also has serious literary, artistic, political, or scientific value. The Seventh Circuit then declared:

> We do not try to balance the arguments for and against an ordinance such as this. The ordinance discriminates on the ground of the content of the speech. Speech treating women in the approved way—in sexual encounters "premised on equality" is lawful no matter how sexually explicit. Speech treating women in the disapproved way—as submissive in matters sexual or as enjoying humiliation—is unlawful no matter how significant the literary, artis-

29. *American Booksellers Assocation v. Hudnut*, 771 F. 2d 323 (7th Cir. 1985)

> tic, or political qualities of the work taken as a whole. The state may not ordain preferred viewpoints in this way. The Constitution forbids the state to declare one perspective right and silence opponents.[30]

The Supreme Court summarily affirmed the Seventh Circuit decision in a brief memorandum opinion,[31] effectively ending the attempt by some feminist legal scholars to redefine pornography in the law. Other feminist thinkers, however, have strongly opposed the effort to restrict pornography, as well as the enforcement of anti-prostitution laws, on the grounds that such laws impose mandatory views on what constitutes "appropriate" sexual desires and behavior for women. In the views of these competing feminist legal writers, this type of thinking reinforces patriarchal attitudes of femininity and perpetuates the sexual repression of women through the denial of women's sexual autonomy.[32]

## Critical Race Theory

Just as feminist legal theory argues the law oppresses women, critical race theory argues the law oppresses racial minorities. This argument is perhaps most prominent in the United States when it comes to African Americans. Even if the face of the law no longer discriminates on the basis of race (as it did during the "Jim Crow" era),[33] the collective biases built into the system result in "institutional racism." Some examples commonly given of this racism in U.S. public policy are:

- The failure of legislatures to adequately fund predominately minority public schools or to provide for sufficiently subsidized college tuition results in significant racial disparities in educational achievement

- The lack of affordable housing provided to low-income residents disproportionately impacts minorities

- The government at all levels refuses to provide sufficient job training or other employment and business opportunities for minorities, resulting in higher poverty levels for minorities

30. *American Booksellers Assocation v. Hudnut*, 771 F. 2d 323 (7th Cir. 1985)
31. *American Booksellers Ass'n, Inc. v. Hudnut*, 771 F.2d 323 (7th Cir. 1985), aff'd mem., 475 U.S. 1001 (1986).
32. Ellen Willis. *The Essential Ellen Willis*. University of Minnesota Press, 2014.
33. Blackman, Douglas A. *Slavery by Another Name: The Re-Enslavement of Black Americans from the Civil War to World War II*. Anchor, 2009

- The "war on drugs" imposes much harsher sentences for using the primary drugs of choice in minority communities compared to sentences imposed for using the primary drugs of choice in non-minority communities

- The criminal justice system arrests, convicts, sentences, incarcerates, and imposes the death penalty on defendants who are members of racial minorities at significantly higher rates than defendants who are not members of racial minorities

On this latter point, a famous (or infamous) Supreme Court case is often used by proponents of critical race theory to illustrate institutional racism in the U.S. legal system. In 1978 in Georgia, Warren McCleskey, a Black man, was convicted of killing a white police officer and received the death penalty as a result. On appeal, McCleskey argued that evidence of systematic racial bias in the application of the death penalty in Georgia violated the Eight Amemdment's prohibition on cruel and unusual punishment, as well as the Fourteenth Amendment's mandate that people receive equal protection of the laws. In a 1987 decision, *McCleskey v. Kemp,* the U.S. Supreme Court admitted that a detailed study (the "Baldus" study) of the death penalty in Georgia documented clear evidence of racial bias in imposing capital punishment:

> The Baldus study is actually two sophisticated statistical studies that examine over 2,000 murder cases that occurred in Georgia during the 1970's. . . . Baldus also divided the cases according to the combination of the race of the defendant and the race of the victim. He found that the death penalty was assessed in 22% of the cases involving black defendants and white victims; 8% of the cases involving white defendants and white victims; 1% of the cases involving black defendants and black victims; and 3% of the cases involving white defendants and black victims. Similarly, Baldus found that prosecutors sought the death penalty in 70% of the cases involving black defendants and white victims; 32% of the cases involving white defendants and white victims; 15% of the cases involving black defendants and black victims; and 19% of the cases involving white defendants and black victims. Baldus subjected his data to an extensive analysis, taking account of 230 variables that could have explained the disparities on nonracial grounds. One of his models concludes that, even after taking account of 39 nonracial variables, defendants charged with killing white victims were 4.3 times as likely to receive a death sentence as defendants charged with killing blacks. . . . Thus, the Baldus study indicates that black

> defendants, such as McCleskey, who kill white victims have the greatest likelihood of receiving the death penalty."[34]

Despite these facts which the Court accepted as valid evidence of *systematic* racial bias, the Court concluded that based on prior Supreme Court rulings, McCleskey could claim unconstitutional discrimination only if he could prove *intentional* discrimination *in his particular case.* Since McCleskey had not provided any such evidence—and such evidence is usually extremely difficult to obtain even when such particular bias occurs—, the Court upheld McCleskey's death sentence. McCleskey was eventually executed in 1991. The case of *McCleskey v. Kemp* has been widely criticized as legally immunizing the U.S. criminal justice system against strong evidence of systematic patterns of racial bias.[35]

The discussions in this chapter barely scratch the surface in covering the ideas and debates within the field of jurisprudence. Many universities, for example, have entire courses that cover only CLS thought, or just feminist jurisprudence, or only critical race theory, and so on. There are also many other approaches to evaluating and critiquing the law that have not even been mentioned here. This chapter and Chapter 1 on jurisprudence merely touch on a few of the more common topics considered in the study of jurisprudence. If one desired, one could make an entire academic career out of contemplating questions and possible answers regarding the content and impact of law.

---

*Questions for Review and Discussion*

1. Considering the cases of *Madison v. Ducktown Sulfur* and *Poletown Neighborhood Council v. Detroit,* both discussed in this chapter, how would a legal realist, a CLS theorist, and a utilitarian each analyze what happened in these cases?
2. How would a legal realist, a utilitarian, a CLS theorist, and competing feminist thinkers each analyze the issue whether prostitution should be legal?
3. Considering the case of *Queen v. Dudley and Stephens,* how would a natural law theorist, a positive law theorist, a legal realist, and a utilitarian theorist each evaluate what happened in the case?
4. Considering the case of *Brown v. City of Oneonta* (found in the reading list below), how would a legal realist, a CLS theorist, a Critical Race Theorist, and a utilitarian theorist all analyze the case?

34. *McCleskey v. Kemp,* 481 U.S. 279, 286-7 (1987)
35. Keys, David P. and R.J. Maratea, editors. *Race and the Death Penalty: The Legacy of McCleskey v. Kemp.* Lynne Rienner Publishers, 2016.

---

*Suggested Readings*

*U.S. v. Holmes*, 26 F.Cas. 360 (1842) (necessity defense)
*Queen v. Dudley and Stephens*, 14 QBD 273 DC (1884) (necessity defense)
*U.S. v. Dorrell*, 758 F.2d 427 (9th Cir. 1985) (necessity defense)
*U.S. v. Dougherty*, 473 F.2d 1113 (D.C. Cir. 1972) (jury nullification) *The Nuremburg Trials* (ex post facto)
*K.-H. W. v. Germany*, ECtHR 22 March 2001, no. 37201/97, 49 ILM 773 (2001) (ex post facto)
*Madison v. Ducktown Sulphur*, 83 S.W. 658 (Tenn. 1904) (nuisance)
*Poletown Neighborhood Council v. City of Detroit*, 304 N.W.2d 455, (Mich. 1981) (eminent domain)
*Kelo v. New London*, 545 U.S. 469 (2005) (eminent domain)
American Booksellers Assocation v. Hudnut, 771 F. 2d 323 (7th Cir. 1985) (definition of pornography)
*McCleskey v. Kemp*, 481 U.S. 279 (1987) (racial bias in death penalty)

---

*Advanced Readings*

Oliver Wendell Holmes, *The Path of the Law*
John Austin, *The Province of Jurisprudence Determined (1832)*
Lon Fuller, "The Case of the Speluncean Explorers" in *Harvard Law Review*, (1949)
H.L.A. Hart, *The Concept of Law* (1961)

APPENDIX

# LEGAL EDUCATION, LICENSING, AND RESEARCH

---

*Chapter Objectives*

*After reading this chapter, you should be able to:*

- Describe basic aspects of law school education and study
- Describe the qualifications for being a lawyer
- Describe the basics of legal research and legal citation format

---

In today's world, all jobs are affected by the law. Workers are subject to numerous labor laws and must comply with all health and safety laws that regulate their work, such as in schools, hospitals, nursing homes, restaurants, factories, construction sites, and oil fields. Business owners and managers must comply with tax laws, environmental laws, and labor laws, among many others. For this reason, an understanding of law will help you advance in any career.

Yet there are many different types of careers that focus more exclusively on law. The primary legal career is being a *lawyer*, also called being an *attorney*. Lawyers exclusively study the law and represent clients who have legal problems or concerns. Lawyers are assisted by *paralegal* help. Paralegals often help interview clients and perform investigations, conduct legal research, and sometimes even help write legal memos. In court, *judges* decide legal cases, and are assisted by their staff. Judges usually have *law clerks* (also called *judicial clerks*) who have law degrees themselves and help the judge with legal research and in writing the judge's opinions. *Court reporters* transcribe what happens in court. *Legal journalists* are members of the media who cover what happens in court for the public. Legal publishers provide books or journals discussing law for the benefit of lawyers and judges. Also, *legal educators* provide education and training to students in law school or to students in undergraduate programs who hope to go to law school. Other educators such as political scientists and sociologists also study and teach the politics of law and courts. In the criminal justice system, *prosecutors* bring charges against criminal defendants, and *public defenders* represent those defendants in court. Prosecutors and public defenders are all attorneys, but there are also many jobs in the criminal justice system usually filled by non-lawyers. Such careers include police officers and investigators who perform law enforcement, and jail and prison personnel who manage the correctional systems that house inmates. Also, parole officers, mental health counselors, and social workers all help criminal defendants improve their lives so as to avoid returning to the criminal justice system.

Because the largest and most basic law-related career is that of being a lawyer, we'll discuss attorney education and training in detail. In the United States, there are many national associations of lawyers, but the leading and most influential professional organization that represents lawyers is the American Bar Association (ABA). The ABA provides the rules governing legal education in the United States, such as accreditation of law schools. There are just over 200 accredited law schools in the U.S., with about a dozen unaccredited ones, mostly in California.

## Law School

To get into a U.S. law school, an applicant must first complete a four-year undergraduate degree from an accredited college or university. Almost all law schools require that applicants take the Law School Admission Test (LSAT). The LSAT is a several-hour exam that tests one's reading comprehension and logical reasoning skills. The Law School Admission Council (LSAC) runs the LSAT and helps students apply to law school. Law schools also require a one-to-two-page essay called a "personal statement," and several letters of recommendation. These letters typically come from current or past teachers and employers of the applicant. Each letter writer should be able to testify both as to the applicant's intellectual ability and their work ethic. Altogether, the application process is lengthy and has many components. As a result, students wishing to go to law school should start the process early in their junior year of college. The LSAT especially takes numerous hours of study, preparation, and practice.

All law schools require three years of full-time coursework. Full-time in law school is five three-credit-hour courses, or fifteen credits total, per semester (or the equivalent). The law school curriculum is heavily restricted the first two years of law school. Law school students take standard required courses in torts, contracts, property law, constitutional law, criminal law and criminal procedure, civil procedure, legal research and writing, legal argumentation, and legal ethics. Many of these topics are extended over multiple courses, typically including civil procedure, criminal procedure, constitutional law, property, contracts, and torts. Only at the end of the second year or perhaps not until the third year of law school will students have a chance to take electives. A student who graduates most commonly earns a J.D. (juris doctorate) or sometimes an LL.B. (Bachelor of Laws). In the U.S., the two degrees are equivalent. U.S. law schools do not offer specialized degrees. That is, a J.D. is a generalized degree. Students who earn a J.D. and wish to earn an advanced one-year specialized degree in law can pursue an LL.M. (Master of Laws). Areas in which a person can earn an LL.M. include bankruptcy law, patent law, and tax law, among others.

The standard way of teaching law school topics is called the "Socratic method," based on how the ancient Greek philosopher Socrates taught by only asking his listeners questions. In law school classes, the professor will typically call on students to present case summaries in class. These written one-page summaries of court cases are called "case briefs" (see Chapter 10). Then the professor will ask students numerous questions about the case and other hypothetical factual situations that might relate to the law or facts of the case. Another common practice in law school teaching is that the entire grade for a course rests on a single several-hour-long essay exam at the end of the semester. In these exams, students are expected to have the legal rules for each course memorized and, more importantly, must then apply the law to detailed hypothetical factual situations involving each course topic. In recent years, however, many law schools have increasingly offered multiple exams throughout the semester rather than have only a single all-inclusive exam at the end of the semester. Besides coursework, law school students also have opportunities to write for the school's law journal, compete on a moot court team, get legal practice training in the school's legal clinic, or work at legal internships in the region.

The purpose of law school is to teach students the skills needed to practice law successfully. Substantive courses provide background knowledge in basic areas of law. The primary goal of these courses, however, is to use these areas of the law as a means of teaching the *skills* of legal reading, writing, and argumentation. In all courses, students will summarize the law in case briefs and perform legal analysis on exams. Other law school courses will focus specifically on other legal skills, such as conducting legal research and citation, creating lengthy written arguments and engaging in detailed oral legal argumentation (e.g. "Appellate Advocacy"), and practicing the conduct of legal trials (e.g. "Trial Advocacy.") The lead, overall goal of law school is that by the end of law school, a student will have all the skills to learn about, and competently practice in, new areas of law that were not covered during the student's time in law school. Competitive moot court teams, law reviews sponsored and managed by law students, and law student organizations all offer additional opportunities to develop such skills beyond law school courses themselves.

Because legal analysis is a skill, it must be *practiced*. As a result, law school exams involve lengthy written legal analyses. In these lengthy essays, the student must provide in-depth legal analysis of hypothetical factual situations. The legal analysis students must apply on these exams is called IRAC [Issue-Rule-Application (or Analysis) and Conclusion] which we took up in Chapter 12. Given the need to practice IRAC, it is common custom for law schools to keep old exams given by their school's law professors on file in the law school library so that students can practice IRAC in each of their courses.

Law school is so demanding that there are many methods of study that are unique and extremely helpful or even essential for succeeding in law school. The workload is so overwhelming that most law school students rely on study groups to survive. Since 100% of a course grade is often determined by a single semester-end exam, study groups are critical in helping students prepare for the exams. When it comes time for exams, study groups allow students to practice IRAC by giving each other invented factual hypotheticals. The students then practice answering those hypotheticals with each other using IRAC, and then correct each other on their analyses.

Law school exams also usually do not explain what the legal issues are, leaving it to law students to spot the legal issues involved prior to performing IRAC analysis. Study groups therefore allow students to help each other learn to identify hidden legal issues in factual scenarios. Spotting the legal issues in a legal problem is half the battle (see Chapter 13). One cannot analyze a legal problem if one is not aware that a legal problem exists. Hence, success in law school and in the practice of law requires that one be able to identify what legal issues exist within any given factual situation.

Also, because there is a large amount of material that must be memorized in a law school course, study groups usually work together to create "outlines" of each course. An outline is a summary of the law within a given legal area, along with leading cases in each area of the law. As a result, instead of memorizing a 500-page book for each course, students need only memorize a roughly 50-page outline for each course. To further help with understanding the law, students can also read legal "treatises" and "hornbooks" written by expert scholars that summarize each area of law.

## The License to Practice

Upon graduating with a degree from an accredited law school, one then applies to become a member of the "bar." This term comes from medieval England and refers to the wooden bar used in courtrooms to separate the public from the area in the front of the courtroom where the judge, jury, the litigants, and their attorneys sit. The application process to become a lawyer involves several components. First, students must pass a lengthy exam called the *bar exam*, which tests the applicant's knowledge of law in the state or other jurisdiction where the applicant wishes to practice. The exam will cover many different areas of law, and will last a full eight-hour workday or two. The scores for passing the bar differ from year-to-year and from state-to-state depending on how many students are taking the exam, how those students do overall on the exam, and the current need within that jurisdiction for more lawyers. The bar exam can be taken more than once if need be. There are books and commercial courses to help those taking the bar to prepare for the exam.

One other critical part of law school education is familiarizing law students with the ethical rules that apply to lawyers. The American Bar Association has issued recommended nationwide guidelines called the *Model Rules of Professional Conduct*, often simply referred to as the "Model Rules." The Model Rules cover such issues as attorney competence, communication, confidentiality, and conflict of interest. Every state has enacted its own set of legal ethics guidelines typically by adopting the ABA's Model Rules in whole or with slight modifications. All states require applicants to the bar to pass a test on legal ethics. Almost all states use the Multi-state Professional Responsibility Exam (MPRE) which measures knowledge of the Model Rules. In law school, required courses on legal ethics will teach students the Model Rules and any relevant variations their state has adopted.

Before one can be licensed to practice law, each state also requires that an extensive background check be conducted on the bar applicant. This investigation is called the "moral character and fitness" report. Law students typically submit their character and fitness application around the end of their final year in law school. This report evaluates one's record of criminal charges and convictions, academic misconduct, financial record (such as whether debts have been avoided), driving record, mental health status, and history of civil lawsuits. Other items might be asked about and evaluated as well depending on the state. The committee looking over the character and fitness application looks for a pattern of conduct that displays "moral turpitude" (dishonest or irresponsible conduct) that would disqualify someone from practicing law. Crimes such as embezzlement, fraud, forgery, perjury, or identify theft would count toward disqualification, as would academic violations like plagiarism or even lying on a law school application or the character and fitness application itself. Applicants to the bar have even been denied a license to practice law due to mishandling debt, collecting numerous parking tickets, and driving while drunk or without a driver's license and insurance. All these types of behavior show a disregard for rules and/or the law. In each state, the highest court in that state is responsible for overseeing attorney ethics within that state. This includes approving the "character and fitness" of potential and all current lawyers. Applicants who fail to meet this standard will be denied a license to practice law. Also, practicing attorneys who violate legal ethics can be reprimanded, suspended, or even disbarred.

Once one becomes an attorney, many states require lawyers to maintain professional competence by keeping regularly updated on developments in the law through what is called continuing legal education (CLE). Typically, lawyers can take courses or workshops periodically that provide CLE credits. As long as an attorney earns the required minimum CLE credits within the required time frame, the attorney can keep their bar license. The annual renewal of the bar license also can cost several hundred dollars. States typically charge higher bar license renewal rates the longer the attorney has been practicing law on the theory that the longer one practices law, the more money one earns.

## Legal Research

Both law school students and practicing lawyers must be able to research the law using specialized research skills. For example, knowledge of the Dewey Decimal System or the Library of Congress system will not help you very much in doing legal research. First we'll look at how different types of laws are recorded, and then we'll look at how those different types of laws are cited.

*Case Law* Recall from the chapter on caselaw that regardless what a constitution or a legislative statute says, courts have the power to review those laws, and interpret what those laws actually mean. This case law (court opinions) can be found in published "reporters." This term is used because a reporter "reports" the court rulings, meaning the reporter records and publishes the full text of the cases. Since there are hundreds of thousands of case decisions each year in the United States, a "reporter" is one of several multi-volume sets each comprised of as many as 1,000 volumes or more. If the reporter passes the 1,000 volume mark (technically once it passes the 999th volume), then a new "series" is issued which starts the volume numbering over at 1. Most reporters in the U.S. have multiple series which means each reporter will have well over 1,000 volumes in total.

The U.S. federal Court system contains the U.S. Supreme Court, 13 Circuit Courts of Appeal, and 94 Federal District Courts. Each level of court has its own separately titled reporters. There are several reporters for each level of the federal courts which include private publishers as well. Most importantly, though, there are "official" reporters meaning these reporters are authorized by the U.S. government. Even though the official reporters are published by private publishers, they do so under contract from the U.S. government. As a result, the official reporters, the case law they contain, and the citations to the case law they contain, are all in the public domain as pubic documents. This makes the official reports by far the most commonly read and cited reporters of federal (and state) case law. Here are the primary official federal reporters:

- *United States Reports* contains U.S. Supreme Court Cases, and is abbreviated as "U.S." All Supreme Court opinions are published.

- *Federal Reports* contains U.S. Circuit Courts of Appeal cases, and is abbreviated as "F.", "F.2d", or "F.3d" depending on the series. Only opinions that the Circuit Courts declare have precedential value are published in the printed reporter.

- *Federal Supplement* contains U.S. Federal District Court cases, and is abbreviated as "F. Supp." Only opinions that the District Courts declare have precedential value are published in the printed reporter.

Note that not all Circuit Courts of Appeal or District Court cases are published in printed form. Many of the opinions of these courts that are available in electronic form should not be cited if the issuing court indicates that the case does not have precedential value. To have value as a "precedent" means the case is worthwhile for future court decisions to look back to for guidance.

Reporters that contain state case law are often referred to as the "regional reporters" since each reporter contains case law from several states within the same region. Under the regional reporter system, the U.S. is divided into seven regions. The regional reporters contain most state supreme court opinions and sometimes state intermediate appellate court decisions, but not state trial court decisions. All the regional reporters are past their first series. The list below shows how the more recent second series of each regional reporter would be abbreviated, along with the states covered by each regional reporter.

*Atlantic Reports*, abbreviated as "A.2d": ME, NH, VT, CT, RI, DE, PA, MD, NJ
*Northeast Reports*, abbreviated as "N.E.2d": NY, MA, OH, IN, IL
*Northwest Reports*, abbreviated as "N.W.2d": MI, WI, MN, ND, SD, IA, NE
*Pacific Reports*, abbreviated as "P.2d": KS, OK, CO, WY, MT, NM, AZ, UT, ID, WA, OR, CA, NV, AK, HI
*Southeast Reports*, abbreviated as "S.E.2d": WV, VA, NC, SC, GA
*Southwest Reports*, abbreviated as "S.W.2d": TX, AR, MO, KY, TN
*Southern Reports*, abbreviated as "So.2d": LA, MS, AL, FL

Together, the official federal and regional reporters make up the "National Reporter System." The National Reporter System is currently published by Thomson/West legal publishers under contract by the federal and state governments.

*Statutes* Statutes (laws enacted by Congress or state legislatures) are found in "codes." Each code from the federal or state governments is found in multi-volume sets, usually containing several dozen volumes. Because codes are continually revised, these multi-volume sets are updated regularly. This is done either by issuing an entirely new set of volumes or by "supplements" added either as additional volumes to the set or as pamphlet-style inserts within the already published individual volumes. For example, the laws of the United States are found in the "U.S. Code," abbreviated as "U.S.C." If the multi-volume set also contains case law interpreting each statute, the code is said to be "annotated." Hence, the multi-volume set containing U.S. statutes along with federal court decisions interpreting those statutes is called "U.S. Code Annotated," abbreviated as "U.S.C.A." Regulations issued by all federal administrative agencies, such as the Environmental Protection Agency (EPA) or Occupational Safety and Health Administration (OSHA), are found in the Code of Federal Regulations, abbreviated "C.F.R."

At the state level, each state similarly publishes its own state code. These legislatively created statutes might be called a "code," or "statutes" or "revised statutes." The abbreviation will vary depending on what each state calls its legislative code. Note that city ordinances are usually published only by and within the city enacting the ordinances.

*Legal Literature* Legal academic and scholarly literature analyzes cases, statutes, constitutions, other types of laws, and legal issues in general. This legal literature is found in law journals and law reviews published primarily (but not exclusively) by law schools. Every law school runs at least one legal journal or law review (these terms are often used interchangeably). Most legal journals are available in on-line databases, such as as Lexis/Nexis, Westlaw, or "Legaltrac," a division of Infotrac academic database, published by Thomson-Gale.

*Updating Caselaw* Another legal research aid, and one that is often used by lawyers, is "Shephard's Citations." Shephard's Citations is a private publication that tracks which later court cases have cited earlier cases. The ability to find the most current, up-to-date case law is an essential skill for a lawyer. Indeed, this technique is so common and important, it has its own label: the act of finding which subsequent cases have cited a prior case is called "Shephardizing" the earlier case. If you go to law school, you will learn how to Shephardize, often in your first year of law school during your first legal research course.

*Other Legal References* There are many other types of legal documents that are available in print and/or electronic form. These other types of legal references include constitutions, administrative regulations, treaties, attorney general opinions, and appellate briefs, among other types of legal documents. Consult a reference librarian to determine whether and where to obtain the relevant legal document(s) you seek. There are also many legal research aids, both printed and in electronic form, to help you locate legal materials. One such aid is called a legal "digest." This is basically a legal encyclopedia that summarizes the law in a particular jurisdiction or in a substantive area of the law (such as torts, property, or contracts). One of the most well-known legal digests is called *American Jurisprudence.* It attempts to comprehensively summarize the entirety of U.S. law in its numerous volumes.

The most influential scholarly treatise, however, is called the *Restatement.* It is a summary of different areas of law and is produced by a team of top legal scholars and judges with the American Law Institute (ALI). The ALI produces Restatements in most areas of law, such as contracts, property, torts, and many others. Some of the Restatements are now in their second or third edition. These are often referred to in more than one way. For example, the second edition of the Restatement of Contracts was published in 1981. It is often variously referred to in text either as the *Restatement (Second) of Contracts* or *Restatement of Contracts (Second)* or *Second Restatement of Contracts.*

One other common legal reference is *Black's Law Dictionary* (11th ed. 2019). *Black's Law Dictionary* is a standard reference tool used by lawyers and law students. It is also frequently cited by courts, especially in statutory construction cases. No legal library is complete without one.

*Legal References Online* Case law from the National Reporter System, statutes and codes, constitutions, administrative regulations, many other types of legal documents, and legal literature such as law journal articles are all available via online electronic legal databases. The two most extensive and commonly used legal databases are LexisNexis and Westlaw. Both databases are available either by paid individual subscription or are free to individual users via paid library subscriptions or corporate subscriptions. FindLaw is currently a free privately owned online legal database that is extensive yet not as thorough or easily searchable as paid services. Many other websites, especially academic and university websites, also have extensive collections of legal resources. These too, however, are not as thorough or as easily searchable as the paid services provided by Westlaw or LexisNexis.

## Legal Citations

Legal writing generally does not use APA (American Psychological Association) style, MLA (Modern Languages Association) style, nor Chicago Manual Style rules of citations, all of which are commonly used citation styles in the social sciences and humanities. Instead, legal writing uses the citation form found in *The Bluebook: A Uniform System of Citation*, 20th ed. 2015. There are other competing legal citation forms, but *Bluebook* citation is still the most common standard, and variations across the different alternative legal citation standards are relatively minor. The U.S. Supreme Court and the entire federal court system, for example, follow *Bluebook* citation style. The *Bluebook* is so commonly used that lawyers often refer to it simply as "*Bluebook* style" or even just simply as "*Bluebook*." For example, a senior partner in a law firm who assigns a new junior partner to write a legal memo might remind the junior partner "Make sure you follow *Bluebook*!" Be aware, however, that there are legal citation variations sometimes required by particular state or local courts when filing legal documents with those courts. For purposes here, though, we will look at some of the most common *Bluebook* legal citation types. Also keep in mind that the *Bluebook* is several hundred pages long and covers hundreds of rules! To make matters more complicated, the *Bluebook* keeps revising many of its citation rules every so often. Citations in older legal documents therefore might not match the newer citation format. Be careful, then, not to be confused if you see a citation that doesn't match the currently approved citation format. Since *Bluebook* rules are so detailed, this section provides only a very brief introduction to a few of the most commonly cited types of legal sources.

*Case Law* Case citations follow a general format of the following pieces of information listed in the following order:

- Case name (almost always the lead parties in the case, e.g., *Johnson v. Smith*)
- Volume of the reporter in which the case is published
- Abbreviated reporter title in which the case is published (and series if applicable)
- Page at which the case begins
- Jurisdiction if other than U.S. Supreme Court
- Year the case was decided.

For example, a citation of a case decided by the U.S. Supreme Court, which is found in U.S. Reports, would look like:

*Swanson v. Frost*, 23 U.S. 456 (1998)

A citation for a case out of the 7th Circuit Court of Appeals, which is found in the third series of the Federal Reports, would look like:

*Laughlin v. Blanchard*, 24 F.3d 1009 (7th Cir. 2004)

A citation for a case out of the U.S. District Court for the Eastern District of the state of New York, which is found in the Federal Supplement, would look like:

*Jones v. Smith*, 200 F. Supp. 111 (E.D.N.Y. 1970)

According to the *Bluebook*, each state has a required abbreviation—or no abbreviation—that varies between two and six letters depending on the state. For example, Louisiana is "La.", California is "Cal.", Connecticut is "Conn.", and Alaska, Idaho, Iowa, Ohio, and Utah are all spelled out fully. Do note that postal codes, NE, MA, TN, et cetera, are not used. A citation for a case from the Massachusetts Supreme Court, found in the second series of Northeast Reports, would look like:

*ACLU v. National Right-to-Life Coalition*, 43 N.E.2d 6 (Mass. 1984)

A citation for a case from the intermediate appellate court of Tennessee, found in Southeast Reports, would look like:

*Lee v. Grant*, 8 S.E. 20 (Tenn. Ct. App. 1925)

Note that by *Bluebook* convention, case names are either *italicized* (*Johnson v. Smith*) or underlined (Johnson v. Smith). Underlining of case names began back when typewriters could only underline and not print italics. Today, with computer-based word processors, italics are mostly used, but underlining is still allowed as an alternative. Regardless which format, italics or underlining, is used, the writer must be consistent throughout any legal document such as legal memorandums or appellate briefs. In modern writing such as legal journals or legal textbooks, italics will always be used and not underlining.

Also note that full case names are often much longer, but citations use shortened case names for convenience. These official shorthand methods include the use of acronyms, using only the first party listed on each side, and using only last names. For example, here is a case name fully written out as it might appear on a legal document:

> *American Civil Liberties Union and Rick Swanson, Governor of the State of Swansonia, versus Bryan Frost, President of the Board of Commissioners of Swansonia State University, and Nathan McCune, President of the Higher Education Teachers' Association*

In a legal citation, however, this case would be referred to simply as:

> *ACLU v. Frost*

The *Bluebook* has extensive lists of the proper abbreviations to be used in case names.

A citation to a particular page of a case is done as follows, with the cited page number appearing immediately after the page of the reporter where the case begins:

> Negligence requires proof of four elements: duty, breach, causation, and damages. *Smith v. Jones*, 123 U.S. 456, 462 (1998)

If the full case name is used in the text of a sentence, then only the numerical parts of the citation are needed:

> In *Smith v. Jones*, the court declared that negligence requires proof of four elements: duty, breach, causation, and damages. 123 U.S. 456, 462 (1998)

Once a case has been fully cited in a text, the text may later refer to the case by a shorthand name. This shorthand is usually only the plaintiff or petitioner in the case unless doing so would be unclear. If an abbreviated citation is used, it will list the shorthand name, the volume, reporter, and the particular page cited. For example, assume the case of *Smith v. Jones*, 123 U.S. 456 (1998), has already been cited in a text. If *Smith* is cited again in the text, it might be cited later as follows:

> In *Smith*, the Supreme Court ruled that blah blah. *Smith*, 123 U.S. at 471.
>
> In the *Smith* case, the Court declared that yada yada. *Smith*, 123 U.S. at 488.
>
> *Smith* held that blah blah yada yada. *Smith*, 123 U.S. at 460.

If a quote taken from a source was itself already a quote in the source cited, then the source of the original is indicated in the citation by parenthetical information as follows:

> *Smith* held that "blah blah yada yada." *Smith*, 123 U.S. at 460 (quoting *Red v. Green*, 155 U.S. 777 (1865)).

Similarly, if a cited source was itself citing a previous source, then that previous source is noted via parenthetical information as well:

> *Smith* held that "blah blah yada yada." *Smith*, 123 U.S. at 460 (citing *Red v. Green*, 155 U.S. 777 (1865)).

*Other Legal Sources* In a citation to a constitution, first cite the name of the Constitution, followed by the article, section, and clause, depending on how precise the citation needs to be given the context. Applying *Bluebook* style, "Article" is abbreviated "art.", "amendment" is abbreviated "amend.", "clause" is abbreviated "cl.", and "section" is abbreviated using either "s." or by the section symbol, "§". For example:

> U.S. Const. art. III, § 2, cl. 2.
> U.S. Const. amend. XIII, s. 2.
> La. Const. art. I.

Citations to statutes will similarly vary the specificity of the citation depending on the need for exactness given the context. When citing statutes using *Bluebook* form, "Statutes" is abbreviated "Stat.", "Revised" is abbreviated "Rev.", and "Annotated" is abbreviated "Ann." The term "annotated" means the volume containing the statute also includes brief summaries of court cases interpreting the statute. The word "code" is generally not abbreviated, but it is at the federal level. "Civil" is abbreviated "Civ.", "Criminal" is abbreviated "Crim.", and "Procedure" is abbreviated "Proc." If there are multiple volumes of the code, the volume comes first, unless the state follows a different format, such as [volume:section]. Just a few of the many different examples of statutory citations therefore might look as follows:

42 U.S.C. § 405(a)(2).
La. Rev. Stat. Ann. 10:1-101.
6 Minn. Code Crim. Proc. s. 55(c)(3)(B)(iv).

Federal administrative regulations created by either Cabinet departments or independent agencies are found in the *Code of Federal Regulations* (CFR). A citation example would be:

20 C.F.R. § 404.260.

Book titles have the author's name, followed by book title in italics, followed by the section or page number if relevant. If the book consists of multiple volumes, the volume number comes first. Book citations examples might look like:

Rick A. Swanson, *A Brief Guide to the Universe*, 351-56, (3rd ed. 2044).
3 Rick A. Swanson, *The Answers to All Life's Question,* § 12.3 (2032)

Articles in journals have the author's name, followed by the title of the article in italics. This is followed by the journal volume, journal title, journal page, and year. Journal titles must also use any abbreviations required by the *Bluebook*. The Bluebook provides a list of approved title abbreviations for hundreds of legal journals. For example:

Rick A. Swanson, *The Meaning of Life*, 52 J. Existential Phil. 35 (2042)
Rick A. Swanson, *Justice Clearly Defined*, 87 Harvard L. Rev. 542 (2045)

Also according to the *Bluebook*, a reference that is found only online and not in printed form can be cited using the "most stable electronic location available." For example:

Rick A. Swanson and Griff Blakewood, *Readings in Love and Friendship*, July 16, 2063, http://internetsource.com/swanson/lovereadings.htm

Regardless of the type of legal source involved (e.g. case, statute, constitution, administrative regulation, book or journal article, etc.)

there are some common legal citation conventions that Bluebook applies to all citations. If a citation refers to the *exact* same source *and* page as the *immediately preceding* citation, then the italicized Latin abbreviation "*Ibid.*" is used. For example:

> In *Smith,* the Supreme Court ruled that blah blah blah. *Smith,* 123 U.S. at 471. The Court went on to declare "yada yada yada." *Ibid.*
>
> Federal liability of state government officials for violations of federal constitutional civil rights are found in a Congressional statute enacted back in 1871. 42 U.S.C. Sec. 1983. The person or persons committing the violation must be acting "under color of" state law. *Ibid.*

If a citation refers to the *exact* same source as the *immediately preceding* citation, but comes from a *different* page, then the italicized Latin abbreviation "*Id.*" is used, along with the page number. For example:

> In *Smith,* the Supreme Court ruled that blah blah blah. *Smith,* 123 U.S. at 471. The Court went on to declare "yada yada yada." *Id.* at 475.
>
> According to some authors, the meaning of life must be determined by each individual for themselves. Eldred Griffin Blakewood, *All Things in Life Explained* (8th ed. 2057). As Blakewood put it, "Meaning is created, not given." *Id.* at 55.

Combining these citation rules into an extended example, a section of case law that is discussing the constitutional rules of the First Amendment's Free Speech Clause might read as follows:

> In *Texas v. Johnson,* the U.S. Supreme Court considered whether the Free Speech Clause of the First Amendment protected the physical act of burning the U.S. flag in public. 491 U.S. 397 (1989). The Court declared "If there is a bedrock principle underlying the First Amendment, it is that the government may not prohibit the expression of an idea simply because society finds the idea itself offensive or disagreeable." *Id.* at 414. There is no exception to this principle even when desecration of the U.S. flag is involved. *Ibid.* The same Court also then ruled that government regulations of the content of speech (including viewpoint) are subject to "the most exacting scrutiny." *Texas,* 491 U.S. at 412 (quoting *Boos v. Barry,* 485 U.S. 312 (1988)).

Once again, though, keep in mind that the relatively few common types of citations provided here as examples merely scratch the surface of the numerous and detailed other *Bluebook* rules. If you end up being an attorney or going into legal writing of any kind, you will want and need a *Bluebook* within arm's reach on your reference shelf.

---

*Questions for Review and Discussion*

1. Describe what legal education is like in law school
2. Describe the requirements to be licensed to practice law
3. Give examples of proper *Bluebook* citations of a case, a statute, and a section of a Constitution.

---

*Suggested Readings*

*The Bluebook: A Uniform System of Citation,* 20th ed. 2015.
American Bar Association, *Model Rules of Professional Conduct*
*In re Griffin,* 943 N.E.2d 1008 (Ohio 2011) (unpaid debt)
*In re DeBartolo,* 111 Ill.2d 1 (1986) (numerous parking tickets)
*In re Kunz,* 122 Ill.2d 547 (1988) (DUI and driving without license)

---

*Advanced Reading*

Scott Turow, *One-L: The Turbulent True Story of a First Year at Harvard Law School* (2010)
Robert H. Miller, *Law School Confidential: A Complete Guide to the Law School Experience* (2011)

# INDEX